INTERMEDIATE MICROECONOMICS

INTERMEDIATE MICROECONOMICS

Neoclassical and Factually-Oriented Models

LESTER O. BUMAS

M.E.Sharpe
Armonk, New York
London, England

Copyright © 1999 by M. E. Sharpe, Inc.

Library of Congress Cataloging-in-Publication Data

Bumas, Lester O., 1928–
   Intermediate microeconomics : neoclassical and factually-oriented
models / Lester O. Bumas.
      p. cm.
   Includes bibliographical references and index.
   ISBN 0-7656-0520-1 (alk. paper)
   1. Microeconomics. 2. Neoclassical school of economics.
I. Title.
HB172.B867 2000   99-41505
338.5—dc21   CIP

Printed in the United States of America

For

Janet Marie Shaskan

CONTENTS IN BRIEF

CHAPTERS

CONTENTS

Chapter Two *(continued)*

Chapter Three *(continued)*

Chapter Four: **Models of Consumer Behavior**   83

Chapter Four *(continued)*

Chapter 5 *(continued)*

Chapter Six: **Cost Functions**   **160**

Chapter Six *(continued)*

Chapter Nine *(continued)*

Chapter Eleven *(continued)*

Chapter Twelve *(continued)*

Chapter Thirteen *(continued)*

Chapter Fifteen *(continued)*

Preface

Scores of textbooks have been written on intermediate microeconomics. The problem is that those in print are all variations on the theme of the neoclassical paradigm, a paradigm full of imperfections—of contentions not exactly in accord with reality. Some examples follow:

1. The subject matter is the allocation of *scarce* resources. **But** surpluses are common. Plant and equipment generally lie idle two-thirds of the hours in the week; millions of workers are unemployed and underemployed; and the worldwide overcapacity of major industries is a serious international economic problem.

2. Production functions show the rate of production as increasing as the employment of labor alone is increased. **But** you cannot increase the production of cars without more parts, or shirts without more material, or books without more paper. The production function of our popular texts is mythic. They are actually value-added functions which cannot yield valid factor demand functions.

3. Labor is paid its marginal revenue product. **But** the product of about half of those employed, largely white-collar or information workers, is not marketed. Their marginal revenue product is zero and that should be their pay under the neoclassical paradigm.

4. Marginal cost is postulated as "U"-shaped. As the output rate increases it should become equal to and then greater than average cost. As a result, marginal cost pricing, efficient allocation pricing, can be profitable. **But** a half-century of empirical work shows that marginal cost is generally constant over normal rates of production. Marginal cost and average variable cost are then equal. Marginal cost pricing, a fundamental neoclassical goal, would then cover variable costs but no fixed costs at all, making allocative efficient pricing suicidal to the firm.

5. Price is the only economic variable decision-makers need know to properly allocate resources. **But** on the average price tends to be changed only once a year, a period during which most allocative decisions are made. The allocative workhorse of the economic system is the quantity not the price system. As the quantity of cars demanded increases, the auto manufacturer employs more resources to increase production. Moreover, only in scarcely found competitive markets is market price also the firm's product demand function. In all other markets producers require price-quantity information to properly allocate resources.

6. Economic decision-makers are rational maximizers. **But** Daniel Kahneman and Amos Tversky have shown that consumers lack the logical tools required to maximize their satisfaction (1986, pp. 67–94). And Daniel Suits shows that hog prices follow the oscillations of the cobweb model, a model of producer irrationality (1982, p. 20).

7. The firm is a profit-maximizing institution. **But** executives and their teams are often paid far more than their opportunity cost; takeovers, profitable to shareholders, are resisted until golden parachutes are provided those at the top; members of boards of directors are often overpaid and underinformed; and the firm's buildings and grounds are frequently far from the least cost requisite of profit maximization.

8. Unemployment can be resolved by a reduction in the real wage. **But** the demand for labor is highly inelastic. A large reduction in the real wage would yield a relatively small increase in employment and a relatively large decrease in earned income—decreasing spending and employment. The net effect of a reduction in the real wage would probably be an increase in unemployment.

Nobel Laureate Herbert A. Simon put his negative evaluation of our neoclassical textbooks this way:

> I think the textbooks are a scandal. I think to expose young impressionable minds to this scholastic exercise as though it said something about the real world, is a scandal.... I don't know any other science that purports to be talking about real world phenomena, where statements are regularly made that are blatantly contrary to fact (1986, p. 23).

This sets the mission of this text: to move away from the neoclassical paradigm in the direction of factually oriented models.

Lester O. Bumas
Polytechnic University

Acknowledgments

I should like to acknowledge the patience and assistance of the staff of M. E. Sharpe, particularly, economics editor Sean Culhane and his administrative assistant Esther L. Clark, and production editors Angela Piliouras and Christine Florie.

I should also like to thank colleagues at the Polytechnic University who stimulated and broadened the views of an ex-communicant electrical engineer: Shane Mage, David Mermelstein, and the late Murray N. Rothbard.

Acknowledgments are also due the following authors, periodicals, and publishers:

Katherine G. Abraham. 1983. "Structural/Frictional vs. Deficient Demand Unemployment," *American Economic Review*, vol. 73, no. 4, September, pp. 708–724.

Baumol, William J. 1967. "Macroeconomics of Unbalanced Growth," *American Economic Review*, vol. 57, no. 3, June, pp. 415–426.

Blinder, Alan S., Elie R. Canneti, David E. Lebow, and Jeremy B. Rudd. 1998. *Asking About Prices: A New Approach to Understanding Price Stickiness,* New York: Russell Sage Foundation.

Ernest R. Breech. 1953. "The American Method of Pricing," in Jules Backman, ed. *Pricing Practices and Policies,* New York: The Conference Board, pp. 81–82.

Chandler, Alfred. 1977. *The Visible Hand,* Cambridge: Harvard University Press.

Coase, Ronald 1937. "The Nature of the Firm," *Economica*, 4, November, pp. 386–405.

———. 1960. "The Problem of Social Cost," *Journal of Law and Economics,* no. 3, October, pp. 1–44, copyright 1960 by the University of Chicago.

Gordon, Robert Aaron. 1976. "Rigor and Relevance in a Changing Institutional Setting," *American Economic Review,* vol. 66, no. 1, March, pp. 1–14.

Hagerty, Michael, James Carmen, and Gary Russell. 1988. "Estimating Elasticities with PIMS Data," *Journal of Marketing Research*, pp. 1–9.

Robert E. Hall. 1986. "Market Structure and Macroeconomic Fluctuations," *Brookings Papers on Economic Activity*, no. 2, pp. 285–322.

Hirsh, Fred. 1976. *The Social Limits to Growth,* Cambridge: Harvard University Press.

Houthakker, H. S. and Lester D. Taylor. 1970. *Consumer Demand in the United States,* 2d ed., Cambridge: Harvard University Press.

Kahn, Alfred E. 1970. *Economics of Regulation,* New York: John Wiley & Sons.

Marx, Karl, and Friedrich Engels. 1957 [1848]. *The Communist Manifesto* in Max Eastman, ed., *Capital and Other Writings by Karl Marx*, New York: Modern Library, pp. 315–353.

Pechman, Joseph A., and Benjamin A. Okner. 1974 *Who Bears the Tax Burden?* Washington: The Brookings Institution.

Skinner, Wyckham. 1986. "The Productivity Paradox," *Harvard Business Review*, vol. 64, no. 4, July–August, pp. 55–59.

CHAPTER ONE

Some Economic Perspectives

Economics is a fascinating, dynamic discipline. This is essentially so because the economy continually changes, and economists are continually trying to understand why these changes have come about. But the ruling economic theory has not readily changed. The current paradigm is roughly a century old—and may be in need of some serious updating.

Adam Smith is generally credited as the founder of economic analysis. The paradigm of Smith and his followers is called "classical economics." That system of ideas, ideology if you will, dominated economic thinking from 1776 to roughly a century later. Smith stressed the role of productivity growth in advancing a nation's living standards. David Ricardo combined Smith's analysis with Malthus's theory of population to attain long-run predictions regarding the distribution of income among workers, capitalists, and landowners.

The production-supply-side approach of Smith and his followers was countered by the demand-side stress of William Stanley Jevons, Leon Walras, and Carl Menger. In the 1870s they independently discovered or rediscovered marginal utility-demand analysis. They emphasized it to such an extent that virtually no recognition was given to the supply side. Shortly thereafter Alfred Marshall developed a new paradigm which is still in vogue today, "neoclassical" economic analysis. It combined the supply- and the demand-side approaches. The main concern of the neoclassical paradigm became efficient resource allocation in a static economy, quite at odds with the classical school's focus on the dynamics of growth and the distribution of income.

Adam Smith's Emphasis on Increasing Productivity

The title of Adam Smith's 1776 masterpiece, *An Inquiry into the Nature and Causes of the Wealth of Nations,* implies that Smith felt that the primary concerns of economics were the material well-being of people and the way in which it could be increased. Smith saw the "division of labor," specialization in narrow areas of work, as the key to increasing productivity and production. The effects were direct and indirect. Narrow specialization could directly increase the expertise and productivity of workers and save time in moving from one part of

Table 1.1. **Malthus's Theory in Numerical Form**

	Generation				
	1	2	3	4	5
Unchecked population	2	4	8	16	32
Food supply	2	4	6	8	10

the process of production to another. Then, with production broken down into numerous small tasks, machinery could be designed more readily to augment productivity further and more dramatically. Smith's famous growth example is that of a pin factory in which labor productivity was greatly increased by the division of labor and mechanization:

> These ten persons [with the division of labor and mechanization] ... could make among them upwards of forty-eight thousand pins a day. Each person might be considered as making four thousand eight hundred pins in a day. But if they had all wrought separately and independently ... they certainly could not have made twenty; perhaps not one pin in a day (1937 [1776], p. 5).

Productivity growth remains a major contemporary concern. Substantial productivity growth was experienced in our post–World War II economy. But starting about 1973, productivity growth declined and has yet to regain the rate experienced in the earlier period. The significance of the decline is indicated by the fact that had we maintained the growth rate of the 1948–1965 period, our 1990 national output would have been roughly 50 percent greater than that actually experienced.

Ricardo's Stress on the Future Distribution of Income

The classical model, created by David Ricardo, combined a polished version of the analytical content of Smith's work and the population theory of Thomas Robert Malthus. The Reverend Malthus, by the way, wrote his famous essay on population as a polemic against the proposal of English Prime Minister William Pitt to liberalize the dole, the scant welfare payments doled out to the poor. The Malthusian theory of population is really a model of population and food supply growth. Unchecked, Malthus had the population growing as a geometric series: two begets four; four begets eight; eight begets sixteen; and so on. At best, Malthus guessed, the food supply could be increased as an arithmetic series, a series with equal increments, here over each generation. Appropriate numbers for the growth of population and food appear in Table 1.1.

The numbers imply that for the first and second generations, population and food supply growth are in accord. Starting with the third generation, however, there is an increasing shortfall of food per person. Growth in the population is then checked by malnutrition and starvation. Malthus contended that any rise in the standard of living above the subsistence level, coming from a good harvest or a more generous dole, would result in an increase in population growth until living standards were again driven down to or below the subsistence level. The only thing that would help the poor, according to Malthus, was their abstinence from procreation—not far from an important argument in the debate of recent years on welfare reform.

Ricardo's dynamic model is primarily concerned with the prospective returns to the owners of labor, capital, and land. As Ricardo saw it, the standard of living of the masses would tend toward the subsistence level. Were the standard of living higher, population would increase driving living standards back to the subsistence level. As investment in plant and equipment increased over time, new investment opportunities would disappear and the rate of profit would tend to fall toward zero. Only landowners would prosper as a result of the fixed supply of land and an increasing demand for it by a growing population.

Ricardo's analysis and forecasts were developed in the 1815–1819 period. Fortunately, the English economy paid no heed to them. Statistical evidence available in the 1830s and 1840s falsified every one of these Ricardian predictions according to Mark Blaug. Nonetheless, Ricardo's classical paradigm dominated economics for another half-century.

Marginal Utility Analysis: Transformation of the Focus of Economics

During the 1870s William Stanley Jevons, Leon Walras, and Carl Menger independently discovered or rediscovered marginal utility analysis. Their work displaced the then existing focus of economic analysis in several fundamental ways:

- It replaced the classical focus on dynamic change with one concerned with the operation of the economy at a moment in time.
- It changed the basic focus of economic analysis from productivity, the standard of living, and the distribution of income to the efficient use of resources for the benefit of consumers.
- It replaced the stress of the classical model on the supply side, the side of production, with stress on the demand side, particularly consumer demand.
- It broadened and stressed maximizing behavior. Consumers were theorized as maximizing their satisfaction, workers as determining the hours per week they would work to maximize their satisfaction, and producers theorized as maximizing profits.

This fundamental change is sometimes called the marginal revolution.

Jevons's opinion concerning what economics should be about is summed up in the last chapter of his 1871 work, *The Theory of Political Economy.* In it he essentially defined the neoclassical perspective decades before its arrival:

> The problem of economics may, as it seems to me, be stated thus: *Given, a certain population, with various needs and powers of production in possession of certain lands and other sources of material: required, the mode of employing their labour which will maximize the utility of the produce* (1970 [1871], p. 254).

Jevons's slighting of the supply side went so far as to make the costs of production irrelevant with respect to price setting. What was relevant to him was the willingness of the holder of a good to sell from his inventory at a price acceptable to buyers. There is no explicit or conscious recognition of the firm, the institution of production, and its need for revenues to cover its costs.

Alfred Marshall and Neoclassical Economics

Alfred Marshall created what is now called "neoclassical economics" toward the end of the nineteenth century. The first edition of his *Principles of Economics* was published in 1890. His text is far richer in cultural and institutional matters than are modern economic tracts as indicated by his definition of economics:

> Political Economy or Economics is the study of mankind in the ordinary business of life; it examines that part of individual and social action which is most closely connected with the attainment and with the use of the material requisites of wellbeing.
> Thus it is on the one side a study of wealth; and on the other and the more important side, a part of the study of man. For man's character has been molded by his every-day work, and the material resources which he thereby procures, more than by any other influence unless it be that of his religious ideals (1961 [1890], p. 1).

Particularly interesting is Marshall's contention that our character is strongly affected by economic and religious institutions, those stressed a half-century earlier by a famous follower of Ricardo, Karl Marx. "The more important side," the study of man, has been obviated by the construction of "Economic Man," a maximizing robot.

Popular Perspectives Defining Economic Activity

Two of the most popular approaches to defining the realm of economics are those associated with Frank Knight, a founder of the Chicago school of economics, and Lord Lionel Robbins. Knight's approach can be viewed as institutional. It stresses the role of the social organizations required to respond to what are deemed the basic questions of economics. Robbins's approach is highly abstract or analytical and yields a perspective from which we can identify those human actions that are economic.

The Social Organization of Economic Activity

There is embedded in humankind, as in all species, the instincts of self-preservation and the survival of the species. From the Garden of Eden to the present, we all need food and water and protection from environmental hazards. The social institutions developed to provide these biological necessities to members of a primitive society are the same institutions that today, in advanced industrial societies, provide products well beyond those that are biologically required.

In his 1933 monograph, *The Economic Organization,* Knight raises the question as to why we have social institutions to perform the economic activities of a society and answers it with one word: *efficiency.* Knight points out that efficiency is related to ever-increasing specialization and this leads to the need for social institutions to serve as "mechanism[s] of coordination and control." Without that coordination starvation rather than high living standards would be our common lot.

Knight specifies five functions that all economies must perform—in effect, defining the economic matters requiring social organization. Modern textbooks frequently reduce this to three and generally pose them in terms of questions all economies must confront:

- *WHAT* is to be produced and in what quantities during some specified period of time?

- *HOW* are these goods and services to be produced?

- *TO WHOM* will these products be distributed?

These questions are highly interdependent. *What* is to be produced is limited, for example, by the resources that a society can command and the state of its technology—by the *how* of production. *What* to produce is also related to the recipients *to whom* it goes. There is not much point in producing wonderful books on economics if recipients are disinterested in the subject.

The other two function of economic organization specified by Knight are quite important. The first is the adjustment of demand or consumption to production in the short run. In 1973 an oil boycott was organized by the Oil Producing Export Countries. With a serious loss in supply the government had to face the problem of maintaining the rationing by price, as is normal, or by some other technique. All economies must confront the problem of such short-run shortages. The second social function is long run involving the maintenance and progress of the economy. Under *progress* Knight includes making provisions for population growth, changes in its composition and education, the accumulation of plant and equipment, and advancement of the processes of production. He clearly recognized the dynamic character of economic systems.

Adjusting demand to short-term shortages can be considered to fall under the question of *to whom* does the production go. And economic maintenance and progress can be considered to fall under the question of *what* to produce. But in integrating these two functions into the three basic questions and functions, we fail to highlight the problem of short-term shortages and the enduring goal of growth.

Knight discusses five types of social organization capable of responding to the economic functions of a society: (1) an economy based on status and tradition; (2) one based on an autocratic or military approach; (3) an anarchic system, one where there is no ruling authority; (4) democracy or democratic socialism; (5) and an exchange economy. Knight categorizes our economy organization as an exchange system "in which the whole system is worked out and controlled through exchange in an impersonal competitive market." Thus to Knight *the* social institution of concern is the impersonal competitive market.

What is excluded from the purview of economics is also of interest. Economics is not concerned with the concrete processes of producing or distributing goods. We need not know how a refinery produces 87 octane gasoline and the technology used to transport it from the refinery to our local gas station in order to understand the market for petroleum. Knight also specified that economics has nothing to do with the use of goods and services to satisfy wants. The purview of economics is limited to the exchange taking place in markets. Economists virtually never study what actually goes on within producing or consuming units. They are assumed to be, for the sake of expediency, black boxes that maximize profits and satisfaction, respectively.

The Firm: The Institution of Production

The firm is a generic term that covers a host of organizations engaged in production. They go by different names: factories, mills, mines, offices, schools, hospitals, farms, stores, government agencies, etc. The firm has as inputs the factors of production. It organizes them in such a way as to create the desired set of outputs or products. In doing this it determines the *how* of production.

Economic Resources: The Factors of Production

Economic resources are those inputs to the process of production that have an opportunity cost:

> *The opportunity cost* of an economic resource is its value in its best foregone alternative use.

The opportunity cost of the time of a college student who forgoes a $20,000-a - year job, the best she can obtain, is $20,000 a year.

> *Free resources* are those that have no opportunity cost. No production is foregone by virtue of the productive use of a free resource.

Salt water used to make potable water has no opportunity cost since it does not cause any other productive use of salt water to be foregone. The employment of an unemployed worker has no opportunity cost since no production or earnings are foregone by such an employment.

Economic resources are generally broken down into three categories: land, labor, and capital.

> *Land* encompasses all natural resources in their original or natural state. It includes the surface of the earth and whatever is under and above it.

Under the surface are the nutrients of the earth useful for agriculture and forestry, metallic ores, minerals, fossil fuels, and bodies of water. Above the earth are air and the electromagnetic spectrum used by radio, TV, cellular phones, and microwave transmitters. Ricardo characterized land as "the fixed and indestructible powers of the soil." But soil does not have fixed and indestructible powers. The use of land for mining, forestry, agriculture, structures, manufacturing, and transportation erodes its powers and pollutes it and the air above.

> *Labor* is the factor of production that is human. It includes people performing all kinds of work related to the process of production.

Of special interest from the perspective of economic change are workers who invent or discover new products, production processes, and markets and those who exploit these discoveries (entrepreneurs). These inventive, risk-taking, and sometimes unscrupulous people are those responsible for economic progress.

Johann Gutenberg, a German printer, invented the movable type press in the fifteenth century, an invention central to our development of widespread literacy and education. Thomas Alva Edison, probably the greatest of American inventors and a top-ranked entrepreneur, had virtually no formal schooling but the number and extent of the inventions made by him and those who served under him is mind boggling. Today, however, much of our technological progress comes from research and development groups staffed with highly educated scientists and engineers. They tend to be the source leading to radical changes in products and production processes. Essential to the process are entrepreneurs who support the research and development and then attempt to exploit the discoveries There is additionally the substantial amount of research and development supported by what can be called entrepreneurial agencies of the government.

> *Capital* is, as Marx put it, the produced means of production. It includes all tools, equipment, structures, and goods-in-process that are produced for use in the process of production.

The use, improvement, and new discovery of capital equipments and processes of production help in maintaining and advancing the productivity of labor and the standard of living of members of the society.

It is noteworthy that as soon as something is done to a natural resource, land in one form or another, it becomes a capital good. Crude oil in its original setting is a natural resource; bring it to the surface and it becomes a capital good. A tree in a virgin forest is a natural resource. Cutting it down transforms it into a capital good. Because natural resources taken for production are capital goods, production is generally specified to be a function of the employment of labor and capital.

Note the omission of money as a factor of production. Aristotle characterized money as barren. It makes no direct connection to the process of production. But it is of significance indirectly: through its ability to bring land, labor, and capital into the productive process. This should not be taken lightly. New firms often lack the funds required to obtain the resources needed to become profitable.

The production of a firm can be for its own use, the use of other producers, or that of consumers. A computer manufacturer, for example, can produce computers for itself, for other firms, for consumers, or some or all of the above. And those computers can be found in a vast variety of places and uses. Those for consumers can be located on wrists, as in watches; in cars, as a control unit; and on desks, as a personal computer.

The Household: The Institution of Consumption

Another major economic institution is the household. Economists consider everyone in a society to be a member of a household. The household encompasses families (two or more related people living together), unrelated people living together, and those living alone.

The demand for consumer goods and services come from households and their individual members. And, in a sense, to the extent that we have private ownership of the means of production, the factors of production come from the household and its members. The qualifying words, in a sense, arise from the institutional reality that corporations, particularly large ones, may be privately owned but their financial and physical capital are not controlled by absentee owner-householders but by their managers.

The Market: The Institution for Buying and Selling

The market plays a crucial role in answering the basic questions, *what, how,* and *to whom.* It is in markets that consumers, business, and government manifest their demands and sellers offer, in exchange, their supplies of goods and services. Thus the *what* of production is worked out in product markets. In like manner the supply of and derived demand for the factors of production manifest themselves in a multiplicity of factor markets. The state of technology and factor costs established in markets play an important role in the firm's determination of the *how* of production. At the same time factor markets determine the income levels of the owners of the factors of production, their effective demand, and *to whom* the production goes.

A major role of markets is that of eradicating surpluses and shortages.

> *Surpluses* are the excess of the quantity supplied as compared to the quantity demanded at a particular price.

Surpluses are irrational in the sense that they represent a waste of the resources used in producing products in excess of the demand for them. Surpluses in labor markets (unemployment) represent a serious social problem and a wasted resource. The employment of the unemployed would result in the creation of useful products. Perhaps more important than this is the deprivation and depression caused by unemployment. People adjust to all sorts of problems and calamities but not all adjustments to unemployment are socially desirable.

That product market surpluses and labor market surpluses have some connection should be readily apparent. The auto manufacturer with a surplus inventory of cars will first of all curtail overtime work and, if a surplus of production persists, lays off surplus workers.

> *Shortages* are the amount by which the quantity supplied falls short of the quantity demanded at a particular price.

Shortages are also troublesome, and their eradication is, as has been indicated, a responsibility of the market. Some shortages are rather trivial but others can be monumental in social cost. If there is a shortage of your favorite brand of beer or other beverage, you can substitute another brand. A shortage of milk or food in general is another thing. Infants may be badly affected by the former, the poor by the latter. Shortages are also anathema to the process of production. A supercomputer normally worth tens of millions of dollars might be rendered worthless by the shortage of a single part. Nations are blockaded to create shortages and hardship in the targeted country.

Economics Defined from an Analytical Perspective

The most popular analytical definition of economics is that of Lionel Robbins:

> *Economics* is the science which studies human behavior as a relationship between ends and scarce means which have alternative uses (1935, p. 16).

Here indeed is a wonderfully abstract definition that requires many words of explanation. The words "studies human behavior" may be misleading. Economics is not a behavioral science, and I am unaware of any part of the neoclassical paradigm based upon such study. To avoid the study of human behavior, economists have created Economic Man, a robot programmed to maximize.

Figure 1.1.   **The Production Possibilities Frontier**

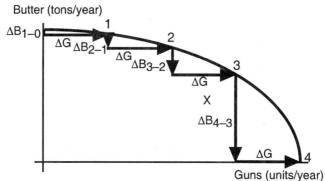

Butter (tons/year)

Scarce Means and Alternative Ends

Scarce means refers to economic resources, resources that have an opportunity cost. Alternative uses or ends refer to that opportunity cost with the cost of a resource used in the production of X, the value of its best foregone alternative use, the production of Y. Scarcity also implies that we want more than we can have. Societies tend to want more of X and Y than it is possible to produce—but cannot because of the scarcity of resources.

The concept of the production possibilities frontier allows the problem of scarcity and the concept of opportunity cost to be shown graphically. In Figure 1.1 all resources are assumed to be fully employed in the production of either "butter" or "guns." Butter is symbolic of consumer products-in-general; guns serves that function for all others. I have divided the gun axis into four equal segments. Assume that we start out with only butter being produced. That puts us at point *0* on the frontier. Then a decision is made to produce guns moving the economy to point *1* on the frontier. The increase in gun production is ΔG and the decrease in butter production is ΔB_{1-0}. Resources had to be taken from the production of butter in order to increase the production of guns. The value of the first ΔG of guns is the foregone production of butter, ΔB_{1-0}, the opportunity cost of the given increase in the production of guns.

As the production of guns increases, its opportunity cost increases. The second increase in the production of guns has an opportunity cost of ΔB_{2-1} which is larger than ΔB_{1-0}. This is because we increasingly have to draw on resources that are more productive in making butter and less productive in producing guns. It gives the function its concave-to-the-origin shape.

Problems with the Concept of Scarcity: Unemployment and Social Norms

The production possibility frontier helps in illustrating the character of the scarcity of resources problem. If the production of some item is increased, a decrease in production of one or more other items is required. But that may not be true for two reasons. First, the production possibilities frontier is based on the assumption of full employment and that is frequently not the case. Were the economy at some point within the frontier, at point X, for example, more butter could be produced without foregoing the production of guns or more guns could produced without foregoing the production of butter or more of both could be produced without foregoing any production. Production within the frontier is troublesome to theory because the unemployment of labor and capital means that they have no opportunity cost. This undermines their status as scarce or economic resources. Scarce resources must be fully employed.

The second problem relates to the vagueness of the concept of the "full employment of resources." Does it imply workers laboring 60, or 48, or 40, or 35 hours a week? And how many of the 168 hours in a week must capital goods be in use for them to be fully employed? Resources must be fully employed to qualify as economic resources—but how do we define fully employed?

Scarcity, Economizing, and Efficiency

Microeconomists commonly state that scarcity is *the* economic problem. This logically leads to a concern for economizing, using these scarce resources sparingly, getting the most possible out of these resources, using them efficiently. Bound together in the neoclassical perspective are the concepts of scarcity, economizing, and efficiency.

The Breadth and Narrowness of Robbins's Definition

Robbins's definition of economics is magnificently broad. Alternative allocations of the scarce resource labor includes working, eating, sleeping, dancing, cooking, playing, praying, and so on. The extent to which all these non-marketed allocations of labor should fall within the purview of economics is debatable.

The narrowness of Robbins's approach is his failure to recognize the major institutions of the economy. All of Robbins's examples are concerned with the action of an individual and never with an organized group or institution such as the household, firm, or market. Nonetheless, he asserts that "the generalizations of the theory of value [microeconomic analysis] are as applicable to the behavior of isolated man or the executive authority of a communist society, as to the behavior of man in an exchange economy" (1935, p.20).

Robbins's Opposition to Macroeconomics

Robbins's essay on the nature of economics was initially published in 1932 with a second edition in 1935. In 1936 John Maynard Keynes's *General Theory of Employment, Interest, and Money* was published. It led to the creation of macroeconomics. But Robbins was opposed to aggregate measurements and the analysis of aggregate phenomena:

The idea of changes in the total volume of production has no precise content. We may ... attach certain conventional values to certain indices and say that we *define* a change in production as a change in this index. But there is no analytical justification for this procedure (1935, p. 66). Instead of regarding the economic system as a great machine for turning out an aggregate product and proceeding to enquire what makes this product greater or less ... we regard it as a series of interdependent relationships between men and economic goods (1935, p. 69).

Robbins, thus, opposes both classical and Keynesian economics.

The Great Depression and the Accomplishments of Microeconomics

Consider Robbins's magnificent commercial for neoclassical microeconomics made in the midst of the Great Depression of the 1930s,

The efforts of economists during the last hundred and fifty years have resulted in the establishment of a body of generalizations whose substantial accuracy and importance are open to question only by the ignorant or the perverse (1935, p. 1).

According to that grand body of generalizations the Great Depression could not have occurred. The surplus of labor would merely cause wages to decrease, thereby bringing quantities supplied and demanded into equilibrium. The substantial inaccuracy and worthlessness of the application of neoclassical microeconomics in the Great Depression led to Keynes development of aggregate economic analysis in his *General Theory.*

Recall that in his *Essay* Robbins claimed that the generalizations of microeconomics are applicable to all economic actors in economies ranging from communist to free exchange. But Robbins blamed the Great Depression on the power of monopolies, unions, and government controls. The resulting rigid wages and prices prevented prices from falling low enough to stimulate demand and demeaned the value of the neoclassical paradigm. In fact, it would appear that from the perspective of the macroeconomy, the body of neoclassical generalizations are appropriate to nothing more than the mythic neoclassical economy. But even then, relevant data seems to make dubious the hypothesis that flexible wages and prices would increase employment. (See "Would Employment Increase if the Real Wage Decreased?" in Chapter 13.)

Maximization of Self-Interest: An Expository Device—Not a Fact

Robbins recognized that students of economics might be led astray–led to believe that economics assumes that real economic decision-makers are maximizers. He characterizes the assumption as "an expository device of pure analysis"

(1935, p. 94). He points out that economic subjects can be egoists, altruists, as-
cetics, sensualists, or some combination of all of the above. Robbins subsequently states that he purchases bread from a baker at a higher price than those
of other bakers, because of ties to the baker and concern for his well-being. He
is, of course quite right in calling maximization an expository device.

The Stress on Scarcity: The Non-Recognition of Surpluses

A major limitation of the neoclassical view is its tight focus on scarcity. This
blinds it to the existence of surpluses. But surpluses are a major worldwide
problem as exemplified by surplus production capacity in agriculture, steel,
auto, textiles, and electronics. Labor is frequently in surplus, and capital equipment, continuous flow industries aside, tends to lie idle two-thirds of the time.
All these surpluses imply far greater inefficiency than that which is the concern
of neoclassical analysis.

Some Challenges Facing Microeconomic Analysis

There are many challenges confronting economic analysis. Some of those which
would help bridge the gap between microeconomic analysis and reality follow:

Models Versus Theory

According to Andreas Papandreou, the late prime minister of Greece:

> A model is a logically correct set of abstract relationships and it becomes a
> theory when it has been subjected to and survived empirical test (1958, p.
> 10).

In common economic usage, the words *model* and *theory* are interchangeable.
But it would advance the cause of economics as a positive science if Papandreou's differentiation were accepted. It should stimulate the process of testing
whether or not models presented as truth are actually supported by fact and
create a competitive rush to replace those which fail appropriate tests.

The Ordinality of Theory: A Woeful Weakness

Economic theory is ordinal but decision-makers generally require cardinal information. *Ordinal information* is about the place of an item in a set. Theory tells
us, for example, that if the price of Car X is increased by 5 percent, the quantity
demanded will decrease. The place of the quantity of cars demanded will be
lowered. *Cardinal information* answers the question of "how many or how
much?" It gives a numerical estimate, a cardinal number, to answer the question
"how many fewer cars are expected to be sold if the price is increased by 5 percent?

Consider a few more examples indicating the need for cardinal estimates.

1. The administration of your university is contemplating increasing tuition by 10 percent. The leading economic theorist on the faculty is called upon and asked: What does she expect will happen if tuition is increased by 10 percent? Her response is that the quantity demanding admission will probably decline, more or less. The vice president of finance, an accountant by training says, "Look, our costs are pretty much fixed so the problem is on the revenue side. If tuition is increased by 10 percent and enrollments drop by 1 percent, revenue will go up by about 9 percent; if the drop in enrollments is 10 percent, revenue will stay constant; and if it drops by more than 10 percent revenue will decrease. Professor Theorist, what is your estimate of the percent of enrollments we can expect to lose as a result of a 10 percent tuition increase?" But Professor Theorist, armed with only a negative-sloping demand function, can add nothing to the initial answer—which is of no value to the administration.

2. Congress is contemplating increasing the minimum wage by a certain amount. A Member of Congress asks a college chum, a brilliant student of economic theory, to advise him about the unemployment that this will create. His answer can be no more specific than that employment will probably decrease, particularly if the wage increase results in a product price increase. This information is valueless to the member of Congress who intends to base his vote on an informed estimate of the number of jobs the minimum wage increase is expected to destroy.

3. A good Marxist colleague, knowing my adventurous spirit (in theory), tells me that capitalists are expropriating income from me—implying I should do something about it. I ask him "*How much* of my income is being expropriated?" I have no intention of joining a revolution for nickels and dimes.

It is hard for me to imagine an economic problem worth talking about which is not essentially quantitative in character. Nonetheless, an important group of economists is radically opposed to empirical measurement—the Austrian school. One of its principal leaders, Ludwig von Mises, put the matter this way:

> What assigns economics its peculiar and unique position in the orbit of pure knowledge and of the practical utilization of knowledge is the fact that its particular theorems are not open to any verification or falsification on the grounds of experience.... The ultimate yardstick of an economic theorem's correctness is solely reason unaided by experience (1949, p. 858).

But I am uncomfortable with theorems that appear to be contrary to fact.

Econometrics: Estimating the Relationship Between Economic Variables

Econometrics involves the application of statistical techniques to economic problems to obtain estimates of the quantitative relationship between economic variables. The subject is handled in three ways in this text. First, the superficial presentation in this section is intended to crudely show the relationship of the variables of a demand function and how the quantitative relationship between the variables might be estimated graphically. Second, a more technical presentation is given in Appendix 2, at the end of this text. It is a brief primer on descriptive statistics and regression analysis. They are lumped together because

Table 1.2.　**Quantity of Cars Demanded as a Function of Price**

Price ($thousands/car)	Quantity Demanded (millions of cars per year)
5	3.75
10	3.50
15	1.50
20	2.50
25	0.50
30	1.25
35	0.50

you know some descriptive statics and basic concepts such as the mean and the standard deviation are close cousins of the regression line, or estimating equation, and its standard error. Finally, you will find me testing a number of neo-classical models using regression analysis in the body of this text. It is hoped that the sum of these will give readers a feel for quantitative economics.

Assume that the model we want to quantify is that of the basic demand function: the quantity of cars demanded per year, Q^D, is a function of its price, P: $Q^D = f(P)$. Empirical economists frequently assume that the relationship is linear (or linear in logarithms of the data). The linear model in equation form is:

$$(1) \qquad Q^D = A - BP + \mu$$

where Q^D is the quantity demanded, A and B are the parameters we would like to estimate, P is the price of the product, and μ is a stochastic disturbance term. It stands for all the variables that cause the quantity demanded to vary and are not included in the model. Assume that a and b are estimates of A and B. We then have the estimating equation:

$$(2) \qquad Q^{D'} = a - bP$$

where, $Q^{D'}$ is the estimated quantity demanded.

With estimates of the parameters a and b, we can calculate the estimated quantity demanded, $Q^{D'}$, at various prices. Let us crudely develop these estimates graphically.

The hypothetical data available are as shown in Table 1.2. Our model has quantity demanded as a function of price. The normal graphing convention is that the *dependent variable*, quantity which depends on price, is plotted in the vertical direction and the *independent variable,* price, is plotted in the horizontal direction. That plot of the data consists of the points found in Figure 1.2.

To crudely estimate the magnitudes of a and b in our model an "eyeballed" line has been drawn through what I have judged to be the *central tendency* of the data. The intercept of that line with the vertical axis, 4, is a, the estimate of A.

Figure 1.2.   **Quantity of Cars Demanded as a Function of Price**

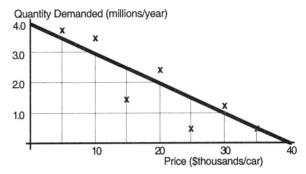

The slope of the line is its vertical distance, –4, divided by its horizontal distance, 40. As a result, *b,* the estimate of *B,* is –0.1 (–4/40). This yields the estimating equation:

(3) $Q^{D'} = 4 - 0.1P$

If someone asks how many cars per year will be sold at a particular price, just put the price in the estimating equation, multiply it by 0.1, add 4 to it and you have the answer, in the form of an empirical estimate.

Econometrics is not a panacea in quantifying the relationship between economic variables. It is a valuable method. The most obvious limitation of the technique is that problems can be modeled in a number of different ways. Variables which can be added to the above model of the demand for cars include income, last year's sales, and the price of complements such as gasoline and car insurance. The addition of each variable results in a different quantitative estimate of the parameters already in the model, such as those above relating price.to quantity demanded. Are models with more explanatory variables better models? Sometimes they are and sometimes not. How the best can be chosen is shown in Chapter 14 in a section towards the end on "investment spending models."

Blending Fact-Supported Microeconomic Theory with Macroeconomics

It makes no particular sense to me that unemployment is a key problem in macroeconomics but non-existent in microeconomics. Both areas of economic analysis should recognize the same realities and there should be substantially increased complementarity between the two fields. Analysis of unemployment can be found in Chapter 13. Another important market in macroeconomics is that concerned with investment spending, spending on plant and equipment. Such spending is conventionally hypothesized as varying inversely with the interest rate by both micro and macroeconomists. That market is examined in Chapter 14. There are other micro-markets which are important to the macroeconomy including the markets for cars and trucks, steel, petroleum, banking, computers, and so forth. They warrant the microanalysis which will allow their proper inclusion in studies of the macroeconomy. The more this blending is done , the greater will be the understanding and integration of both major economic fields.

Changing the Preference for Unsupported Theory over Fact

In the physical sciences when a model is found to be unsupported by the data, it is junked; the data are maintained. In economics, it is frequently the other way around. Recall that Malthus's dismal classical model in which population growth tended to drive wages to the subsistence level. This model was maintained by classical economists decades after rising standards of living, became obvious. The model was maintained while the facts were in effect junked.

Allow three examples in which models are maintained while contrary facts are essentially junked. First, the university which has the most faculty Nobel Laureates in Economic Science rejects research findings which do not support the neoclassical paradigm. Rent control, for example, is modeled as discouraging new residential construction and research findings to the contrary have been rejected. Second, a half century ago and since then empirical studies have indicated that total cost curves tend to be linear or, what is the same, that marginal cost tends to remain constant over the normal range of production. Nonetheless, virtually all textbooks maintain the myth of the "U" shaped marginal cost function and disregard the contrary empirical findings. (See Chapter 6 on cost functions.) Microtexts show full employment, as the demand for and the supply of labor equilibrate, despite the fact that substantial unemployment may exist for years of time. Perhaps the most outrageous or interesting view reject the existence of of involuntary unemployment contend that those conventionally categorized as unemployed have merely chosen leisure in preference to work. What we should then study is why, at various times, large numbers of workers opt for leisure in preference to work—as in the Great Depression. The challenge is to respect facts and to develop models that accord with them.

Making Microeconomics a Positive Science

Economists talk about two different kinds of economics: positive and normative.

> *Positive economics* describes *what is*. It covers economic statements that are true, statements which conform to actuality.

The neoclassical paradigm contends, for example, that workers determine the number of hours they will work, for example, per week. Part of the contention is that employers demand hours of labor services per week and are indifferent to the number of workers employed to reach that number. If the facts support this hypothesis, this model should become accepted theory, an example of positive science. If not, alternatives in accord with the facts should be developed.

Normative economics involves statements about what should be.

"We should have less unemployment" is a normative statement. "In the range of actual output rates, marginal cost should increase" is also a normative statement. Changing the wording to—marginal cost increases with the rate of production—does not transform what should be to what is. The statement is still normative since empirical studies show that marginal cost tends to be constant over the operating range of production.

Consider the case of the neoclassical production function in which the rate of production is increased by the application of increasing units of labor, all other factors held constant. How is it possible to produce more cars, or more computers, or more CDs without more material to fashion into these products? It is no more possible to do this than it was for the alchemists to convert base metals into gold. This form of the production function is at best normative.

The challenge is simple. Drop models that do not conform to reality and replace them with those that do.

Assumptions and Their Relevance

Nobel Laureate Milton Friedman argues that the accuracy of assumptions is irrelevant in a positive science. This can be found in his 1953 *Essays in Positive Economics.* He actually extols the virtues of invalid assumptions in positive economics:

> Truly important and significant hypotheses will be found to have "assumptions" that are wildly inaccurate descriptive representations of reality, and, in general, the more significant the theory, the more unrealistic the assumptions (1953, p.14).

A major problem is the common failure to state what the assumptions in a problem or analysis are. Take the case of "U"-shaped cost curves. At best they are extremely scarce. Is their profusion in textbooks an assumption? If so, that should be so stated. But why assume that the average and marginal cost curves are "U"-shaped when there is substantial empirical evidence indicating that they are not?

In the interest of positive science, all analyses should make clear what is assumed and what is based on empirical evidence.

Fixed Price and the Allocation of Resources via the Quantity System

Microeconomics is frequently called *price theory.* This is so because in theory price is the only *economic variable* which need be known to make rational (i.e., maximizing) decisions. But Ronald Coase has pointed out that while the price incentive determines the allocation of resources in the sphere of markets, within firms resources are allocated by command. Moreover, the allocation of goods within a family is not determined by the price bids of family members. Alternative rationing techniques are used.

But the limited role price has on the allocation of resources goes well beyond the firm's command structure and the families' non-price-based rationing of the goods and services it possesses. Product prices change, on the average, once a year or less frequently. But during that fixed-price year firms frequently change the allocation of resources, especially if the demand for its product(s) vary. The workhorse allocation variable to the firm is not price; it is quantity demanded.

We have an economic system, *not* a price system. In that system it is sometimes variations in price and more often variations in quantity demanded that brings about changes in the allocation of resources. The immediate challenge is to make it understood that shifts in demand tend to be more common than variations in price in changing resource allocations.

The Grants Economy

Exchange is usually described as buyers paying sellers to acquire goods or services. But many transactions are unidirectional. They are manifest in the giving and receiving of grants. Grant recipients receive money or goods and services at no cost or below market cost. Grants involve voluntary and involuntary transfers. Voluntary or charitable grants tend to be from the rich to the middle class or poor and from the middle class to the poor. Involuntary or government transfers tend to be more complex in terms of which class or classes are being supported by the tax dollars of rich and poor. Welfare tends to involve grants from the better-off to less-well-off. But other grants include subsidies to farmers, people in flood-plain areas, students at public colleges and universities, firms which mine, log, and graze animals on public lands. Finally, there is the grant of sections of the electromagnetic spectrum to radio and television networks. Much of these grants involve the transfer of income from poorer to richer taxpayers.

Analysis of this major allocative area deserves more study by the profession.

Some Other Challenges

There are numerous other challenges that, when faced, can enrich microeconomic analysis. Among them are the following: One, decision-making in the neoclassical paradigm is by Economic Man who is capable of making any and all rational calculations. But economic decisions are actually made by people who are neither logicians nor mathematicians. The profession would be enriched by knowing how people really tend to make their decisions. We should work with behavioral scientists to learn more about the decision-making of consumers, workers, producers, inventors, and entrepreneurs. Second, we live in a dynamic economy but our analysis tends to be static. This badly limits the social value of economic analysis. A start to dynamic analysis may be in order. It might be aided by knowing more about the actual behavior of people who seem most responsible for change—inventors and entrepreneurs.

A Proposed Definition and Methodology

The perspective drawn from the presentation of this chapter leads to a proposed definition of economics and the methodology to be followed.

The following definition of economics is essentially based on the perspectives of economists of the past:

> *Economics* is an incipient positive social science, a science whose theory should reflect actual activity in the economy. The main goal is to understand economic phenomena, phenomena involving the processes of exchange, grants, and command in the operation of a changing and usually growing economy. Basic concerns are unemployment, growth in the standard of living, inflation, the distribution of income and wealth, the allocation of resources and products, and the interactions or tradeoffs involving these matters.

In the main, *macroeconomics* should commence from analyses of the broad aggregates of the economy, with emphasis on the issues of unemployment, inflation, and growth. *Microeconomics* should start from study of the economic role and behavior of the key institutions of the economy—the firm, the government, families and households, education, discovery, entrepreneurship, and markets. A major goal should be to develop factually oriented microanalysis that would help in understanding the operation of the macroeconomy. Both fields should be concerned with the standard of living and the distribution of income.

The methodology should be that of the conventional scientific method. Hypotheses or models developed to explain economic phenomena should be subject to empirical test, to the extent possible. Those supported by a preponderance of evidence should comprise the theory of the discipline. And a strong respect for the facts should be substituted for a strong respect for logic-based theory whether or not they accord with the facts.

Summary

In the beginning, there was Adam, Adam Smith. He was a moral philosopher who in lecturing on the subject of expediency became engrossed with the discovery of the determinants of national income and the standard of living. He believed that high income implied the growth of productivity arising from the advance of what we today call "technology." His followers, particularly David Ricardo, integrated Malthus's theory of population into his work. Pursuing hard-headed logic Ricardo concluded that the living standards of workers would stay at or near the subsistence level, the rate of return on capital would move toward zero, and landowners would prosper. His predictions were badly off the mark because he failed to foresee the great advances that were to take place in technology. Productivity substantially increased in agriculture and industry and, as a result, the standard of living increased and the growth of population moderated.

The marginalists turned the Smithian perspective on its head. Primary concern was switched from the supply side and dynamic growth process to the demand side and static efficiency. Alfred Marshall brought together the demand and the supply side in a process in which the functions came into price-quantity equilibrium, a static situation. Shifts of supply and demand, *comparative statics,* yielded new equilibria and today's microeconomics. Marshall's neoclassical system is much more manageable than the classical model of Smith-Ricardo-Malthus because its focus is more limited and sharper.

The neoclassical paradigm is more or less 100 years old. It would be hard to envision a field of science that has the same focus and basic analysis that the field had a century ago. A less scholastic or axiomatic discipline and one more attuned to reality should be in the offing.

Questions on Chapter 1

1. In Adam Smith's analysis, how can the standard of living be increased both directly and indirectly? Please be clear in explaining just *how* these two matters increase the standard of living.

2. The emphasis on scarcity obscures the problem surplus. Discuss. Draw a supply-demand diagram showing what a surplus is as part of your answer.

3. According to William Stanley Jevons, what was the goal of economics? Why can that goal be considered as somewhat trivial?

4. The neoclassical model is "ordinal." Explain what this means with the help of an example. Why is this a substantial weakness?

5. Explain the idea of the opportunity cost of a factor of production. Illustrate the idea with the help of a production possibility frontier.

6. What is the weakness of explaining the opportunity cost of a factor through the use of the production possibility frontier? What are some unstated norms embedded in the concept of production possibilities?

7. What are the basic economic questions according to Frank Knight and how do they fit together?

8. What is Lionel Robbins definition of economics and what is meant by scarce resources and alternative ends?

9. Briefly compare Jevons and Robbins definitions of economics.

CHAPTER TWO

Fundamentals of Supply and Demand

There is an old aphorism, "Teach a parrot the words supply and demand and it becomes an economist." There is much truth in this statement since work in economics often involves analysis of supply or demand or both.

In this chapter, the rationale of the breakdown into supply and demand is discussed first. This is followed by a presentation of demand-related and then supply-related matters. A reasonable degree of understanding will allow readers to rise to heights above parrots—at least in the eyes of economists. The interaction of supply and demand can be found in Chapter 3.

The Breakdown into Supply and Demand

Adam Smith noted that economic transactions are between buyers and sellers "whose interests are by no means the same." Buyers prefer lower and sellers higher prices. The reactions of buyers and sellers to price increases and decreases also differ. At a higher price buyers tend to purchase less while firms have the incentive to produce more.

Some economic variables affect buyers and others affect producers. An increase in income allows buyers to purchase more and better products—but has no direct effect on the costs of their production and supply. Technological progress may dramatically change the way a product is made and its cost of production and supply, but that will not change the demand for it. A related matter is that demand and supply are generally, but not always, independent of each other. This creates the need to analyze each separately and in isolation from the other. There are few things as disheartening to instructors than finding students asked to confront demand-side issues slipping their analysis into the realm of supply and vice versa.

Demand

The demand function is defined as:

> *Demand* is the quantity of a product per unit of time, Q^D, willingly purchased at various prices, P, all other variables held constant.

Note that the D in Q^D is a superscript which identifies the quantity variable as associated with demand. Superscripts are used to identify variables particularly if subscripts are set aside for time tags, as P_{96} for the price in 1996. If time tags are not used, subscripts are usually used for identification purposes.

Standard Specifications of Demand and Supply Functions

Several matters specified with regard to demand and supply functions warrant attention. (1) The variable "quantity" is generally shorthand for quantity *per unit of time*. Saying that 60,000 bushels of wheat will be purchased at a price of $4 per bushel just makes no sense. Will this quantity be purchased per hour, day, week, month, or year? The unit of time must be specified. (2) Demand and supply must refer to a standardized or homogeneous product or factor of production. The same supply function, for example, cannot refer to both the most rudimentary Chevy and the most sophisticated Cadillac. (3) In its basic form the quantities supplied and demanded are functions of price alone. This is because all other relevant variables are held constant—making them *shift parameters.* (4) Basic demand and supply functions are static. They only hold true during short durations of time; time periods during which shift parameters do not vary. (5) Supply and demand functions are really expectational. They cannot tell us how many cars will be bought per month, at various prices, but how many *are expected* to be bought per month at various prices. We are actually dealing with probabilistic matters—not certainties. (6) Finally, for market functions, the boundaries of the market or the population of buyers and sellers should be given. Markets for residential housing are usually specified as covering a particular locale; those for grains and precious metals can be worldwide. Monopoly markets have one seller with the number of buyers dependent on the particular market. Your demand is that of an individual.

The Individual Consumer Demand Function

Economists view the individual demand for consumer goods in two different ways: as the demand of a single person or as that of a household. We smoothly slip from one to the other, but in some ways they are quite different. It is assumed in this chapter that the demand of an individual consumer is the same as that of the household to which she belongs. In Chapter 4 the difference between the two is examined. Of course, for individuals who live alone there is no difference.

Three Forms of the Demand Function

The demand function, as other functions, can be shown in three different forms: graphical, tabular, and mathematical. Consider the graphical approach first.

Figure 2.1.   **Arthur's Demand for Brand X Bread**

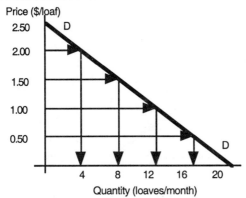

Table 2.1.   **Arthur's Demand for Brand X Bread**

Price ($/loaf)	Quantity Demanded (loaves/month)
0.00	20
0.50	16
1.00	12
1.50	8
2.00	4
2.50	0

Arthur is an old friend of mine and his demand for Brand X bread is illustrated in Figure 2.1. It shows the number of loaves per month he would willingly buy at various prices—with all other variables held constant. At $1.50 per loaf, for example, Arthur is expected to buy 8 loaves a month. It also shows the effect of a price change on his bread consumption. Were the price to increase by $0.50 per loaf, Arthur would buy 4 fewer loaves per month.

Arthur's demand for bread implies the existence of a table of data used to draw the graph. These data appear in Table 2.1. The table yields the same information as the graph. How many loaves will be bought at a price of $1.50 per loaf? The answer is again 8 per month. How much less will be bought per month if the price increases by 50 cents? The table, as the graph, shows that each time that occurs, the quantity demanded decreases by 4.

How do we convert the information on demand into an equation, the third form of the linear demand function? The answer is *not* to find a friend to do it. The answer involves four straightforward steps: (1) Observe a plot of the data and judge whether it approximates a straight line. If not, go no further. (2) If the relationship seems linear, draw a straight line through what appears to be the central tendency of the data. (3) Recall or learn the *slope-intercept* form of the equation of a straight line: $P = P_0 + m\,Q$, where P_0 is the intercept of the curve

Figure 2.2.   **Converting Arthur's Demand Function into an Equation**

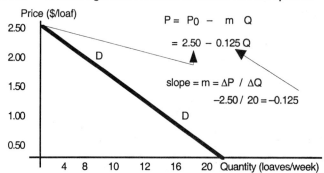

with the vertical *P or price* axis and *m* is the slope of the line relative to the horizontal *Q* axis. (4) Determine the values of P_0 and *m* and plug them into the above equation of a straight line.

Figure 2.2, Figure 2.1 with the grid removed, is intended to help in transforming the graph of Arthur's demand into an equation. The intercept of the demand function with the price axis is at $2.50 per loaf. The slope of the function, $\Delta P / \Delta Q$, is its vertical distance,–$2.50 per loaf, divided by the horizontal distance of 20 loaves per month. That equals –0.125. The units of the slope are dollar – months/loaf^2. Ugh! But that is okay since when multiplied by the quantity units of loaves per month, the result is what we want, dollars per loaf. The equation form of Arthur's demand for bread is:

(1) $P = 2.50 - 0.125Q$

Substituting any and all of the quantities in Table 2.1 into the above equation and solving for price should yield the price data of that table. If that is not so I am in big trouble.

An equation consistent with the definition of demand would have the quantity demanded as a function of price. That can be obtained by solving the above equation for Q^D:

(2) $Q^D = (2.50 - P)/0.125$

                 $= 20 - 8P$

This equation says, among other things, that for each dollar increase in price, the quantity demanded decreases by 8 loaves per month—consistent with our table and the previous equation. By the way, the above equation can also be obtained by the slope-intercept approach. For this quantity-demanded equation, the intercept is that with the *Q* axis, namely *20*, and the slope of the line is relative to the price axis: $\Delta Q/\Delta P = 20/-2.50 = -8$. The more elegant way of developing

an equation from a set of data involves the use of *Regression Analysis.*
In sum, there are three different forms of the demand function—graphical, tabular, and mathematical and they all have the same informational content.

Why Demand is Negatively Sloped: The Substitution Effect and Perhaps the Income Effect

In the above demand function, a negative relationship between price and quantity has been assumed: The higher the price, the lower the quantity demanded. This relationship is sometimes called the law of negative-sloping demand. The usual cause is the substitution effect.

> The substitution effect is the change in the quantity of a product demanded which arises exclusively from a change in its price relative to that of substitutes.

If the relative price of Brand X bread increases, the quantity demanded decreases and the demand for the substitutes, Brand Y and Z bread, increases. This substitution leads to a negative-sloping demand for Brand X bread. If margarine is judged a substitute for butter, a rise in the relative price of butter will be accompanied by a decrease in its consumption and an increase in the demand for margarine.

If there are no substitutes according to the tastes of a consumer, a price increase does not create a decrease in the quantity demanded. There is no substitution effect and the demand function is vertical. There are a number of substitutes for coffee but not to coffee addicts. The same is true for many other products habitually consumed. There are no substitutes for broad categories of goods—such as food. There are no substitutes for consumption dictated by others. You cannot substitute a blue shirt for the white shirt required by an employer—or the khaki shirt required by another employer. There may be no substitute for a prescription drug that is both vital to your health and low in creating unwanted side effects.

The great majority of individual price changes have a negligible effect on the purchasing power of our income. But there are some that do—college tuition, the cost of rental housing, the price of a new car. Nonetheless, economists consider the effect on real income of the price changes of all goods:

> The income effect is the change in the quantity of a product demanded which arises exclusively from the effect of a change in the price of the product on real income. For normal goods, an increase in income increases the quantity demanded; for inferior goods it decreases the quantity demanded.

Most goods are normal goods—a greater quantity of them is demanded as in-

Figure 2.3.   **A Change in Price Leading to a Movement on the Demand Curve**

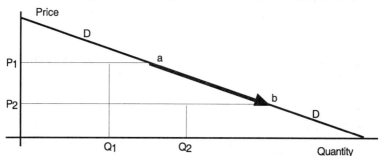

come rises. Some are inferior goods—the quantity demanded decreases as income increases. A price decrease that measurably increases real income allows the purchase of more of that or other goods. If your income is $30,000 and your rent drops from $10,000 to $9,000 a year, your remaining income in- creases from $20,000 to $21,000. The income effect should allow you to get better housing and/or something else that will give you greater enjoyment per dollar of spending.

Movements Along the Demand Function

Consider the demand function shown in Figure 2.3, a function so abstract that no specification is made regarding whose demand it is or the product to which it refers. Assume that the price of the product is initially P_1 and that at that price Q_1 is demanded. The price then drops to P_2 and more is demanded, namely, Q_2. What we have as a result of the price change is a movement along the demand function as is shown by the darkened portion of the demand function. Beware—this is *not* an increase in demand. Demand is the entire function or curve, and it has not changed at all. As a result of the price change the *quantity* demanded changed on the original and only demand function.

Market Demand

The market demand function is generally portrayed as additive: as the horizontal sum of the quantities demanded by individual buyers at each relevant price. But the addition will be different if one or more of the shift parameters vary. And market demand may be "non-additive." This occurs when individual demand is affected by the buying propensities of others.

Additive Demand

Assume that there are *n* buyers in the market for wheat and that each of their demand functions is known. In Figure 2.4, three of these individual demand func-

Figure 2.4.   **The Sum of Individual Demand Curves Yield the Market Demand Curve**

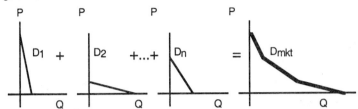

tions are shown with the others implied by the ellipsis. At each price the quantity demanded on the market is the horizontal sum of the quantities demanded by each of the n buyers at that price.

Non-Additive Demand

A source of non-additive demand arises from "keeping up with the Joneses" or the *bandwagon effect*. Other kids on the block are getting bicycles and those who do not have them develop an intense desire to have one. High school seniors find classmates given cars in anticipation of graduation, and it becomes "essential" to have one. Students and their parents realize that others in their peer groups have digital computers, and they want them, too. A salesperson tells the boss that she just sold her system X to his leading competitor, and the boss becomes actively interested in buying that system. In all these cases market demand is greater than the addition of the individual demand functions by virtue of the bandwagon effect.

 People can also react to the purchases of others in a negative way. Finding that others are purchasing a product, they decide not to—transferring their demand to substitutes. A co-worker buys a suit you had your eyes on and you become no longer interested in one of that style, color, and fabric. People on the block are buying Hondas and not wanting to be lost in the crowd, you drop your interest in this brand and look for another. This *snob effect* tends to make demand less than the addition of individual demand functions.

Unlocking the Demand Shift Parameters

The stipulation appended to functions, that all other variables are held constant, is the *ceteris paribus* condition: essentially that the other things are held at their par or current values. A variable held constant is called a *parameter,* and those associated with economic functions are called *shift parameters*. When shift parameters are allowed to vary, functions either increase or decrease. They *shift.*

> An increase in demand occurs when, at various prices higher quantities are demanded.

Figure 2.5.   **Shifts in Demand**

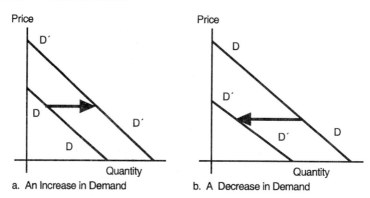

a. An Increase in Demand   b. A Decrease in Demand

A decrease in demand is the opposite condition: At various prices the quantities demanded are lower.

An increase in demand is shown in frame *a* of Figure 2.5, a decrease in frame *b*.

The common shift parameters follow:

The Number of Buyers. An increase in the number of buyers, increases market demand. If the number of buyers changes from 1,000 to 2,000, the quantities demanded on the market at various prices will be substantially greater. But even if the increase is only from 1,000 to 1,001, the quantity demand at various prices should increase.

The Income of Potential Buyers. An increase in the income of buyers increases the demand for "normal goods and services." These are products people enjoy consuming, and greater income allows the increased consumption of them. An increase in income might give an individual a chance to buy a car, a stereo system, a good steak, more or better clothing, and the like.

An increase in income will decrease our demand for inferior goods and services. It might, for example, decrease an individual's demand for canned pork and beans assuming that its consumption was predicated on it being affordable rather than desirable.

Tastes or Preferences. If tastes or preferences for a product increase, the demand for that product is increased. As mammals, at birth and for some weaning period, our desire is for mother's milk, adequate warmth, and the absence of irritants. Subsequent tastes are socially derived by experience. Some producers attempt to increase the tastes for their products by advertising and marketing.

The Price of Substitutes. If the price of a substitute increases, the demand for the product increases. An increase in the price of butter, for example, tends to increase the demand for margarine.

The Price of Complements. If the price of a complement decreases, the demand for the product will increase. Complements of the automobile include insurance, gasoline, maintenance, parking fees, registration, and the cost of a driver's license. A decrease in the price of one or more of these complements tends to increase the demand for automobiles.

The Expected Price. If a future increase in the price of a product is expected, demand for the product tends to increase in the current period. An expected increase in the price of cars should increase demand in the current period—and decrease it in one or more subsequent periods.

These are the shift parameters most relevant to the consumer demand function. Those associated with the demand for the factors of production are examined in Chapter 12.

The Demand for Public Goods

A public good is one that cannot be profitably produced because it has the following two characteristics: Consumption of a public good is not mutually exclusive, and exclusion from the consumption of the product is not possible. Take the case of national defense. My consumption of it does not exclude my neighbors from consuming it. In addition, if I and others do not pay for it, it is not possible to exclude us from the benefit. These characteristics make national defense and other public goods poor candidates for their production and sale by private profit-making firms.

 How is the market demand of a public good formed? Assume that one fire company is protecting the homes of 1,000 families and that, on the average, each family would be willing to pay $10 per month for the protection of the fire company. The market demand is obtained from the vertical addition of the 1,000 individual demand functions. The market value, or demand price for one fire company, is accordingly $10,000 a month.

Price Is Variable; Other Variables Are Constant. Why?

Assume that we have an economic model in which the quantity of widgets demanded is a function of half a dozen variables: its price, the real income of widget buyers, the amount their income has increased from one year to another, the amount of spending on ads and commercials for widgets, the number of widgets bought last year, and the price of substitutes and of complements.

The basic form is that the quantity demanded is a decreasing function of the price of widgets while all the other variables are held constant. Why? The essential justification for specifying price as *the* economic variable is that it tends to change with greater frequency than the variables classified as parameters. Some prices do vary from moment to moment, but others are constant for years on end. Product prices, on the average, are changed once a year. Real income is far more variable, changing as the price of consumer goods in general changes. Thus, the use of price as the basic variable is subject to question.

The Demand Function Viewed Two Different Ways

Those who know some mathematics may feel uncomfortable with the fact that economists, following Alfred Marshall, put price on the vertical and quantity on the horizontal axis. Under the norms of mathematics, the dependent variable, quantity, should be on the vertical axis, and the independent variable, price, should be on the horizontal axis. Marshall was in fact quite expert in mathematics, but he viewed the demand function in a different way. Instead of looking at it as the quantities that would be purchased at various prices, Marshall thought of demand as the prices that would have to be charged to clear the market of various quantities of the product.

The two different ways of portraying the idea of a demand—quantity demanded as a function of price and price as a function of quantity demanded—are shown schematically in Figure 2.6. The approach corresponding to our conventional definition is in frame *a*. The arrows show that we start with an independent value of price, which goes on to determine the dependent quantity demanded, an approach associated with Leon Walras. In frame *b* the independent variable is quantity supplied to the market; the dependent variable is the demand price that will clear the market.

The difference in the approaches matters in the case of equilibrating with negative-sloping supply functions. This is shown toward the end of Chapter 3.

Price Elasticity of Demand

Much of economic analysis has to do with the responsiveness of one economic variable to changes in another. Such information is readily available in the slope or inverse slope of empirical supply and demand functions. From them you can determine, for example, the extent to which the quantity supplied or demanded is expected to change in response to a specified change in price. But using the slope or the inverse of the slope poses a problem because its numerical value is different when different units are used for the price or the quantity or both variables. The responsiveness of quantity demanded per year to a given price change

Figure 2.6.   **Walras's and Marshall's Views of Demand**

a. Walras's Approach: Quantities
   Demanded at Various Prices

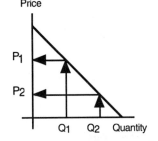

b. Marshall's Approach: Demand Prices
   Required to Buy Various Quantities

might be 365 times greater than if quantity were specified as per day—although the effect of one variable on the other is essentially the same in both cases.

Elasticity: A Unitless Measure of Responsiveness

The way out of the dilemma of multiple magnitudes describing the same responsiveness is to make responsiveness unitless. This is embedded in the concept of elasticity. Consider the case of the price elasticity of demand:

> *The price elasticity of demand, E,* is the ratio of the percentage change in the quantity demanded to the percentage change in price that brought it about.

(3) $E = (\Delta Q/Q) \div (\Delta P/P)$

By dividing change in quantity by quantity, the units of quantity are done away with. The same is accomplished by dividing the change in price by price. Rearranging the variables, elasticity can also be written as:

(4) $E = (\Delta Q/\Delta P) \cdot (P/Q)$

Note that elasticity at a point on the demand function is the inverse of the slope of the demand function, $\Delta Q/\Delta P$, multiplied by the ratio of price to quantity, both at a given point or region on the demand function.

Calculating Elasticity: Arc, Geometric, Point, and Logarithmic Approaches

There are four common ways of calculating elasticity. They are found in sections on the arc, geometric, point, and logarithmic approaches. All techniques, using the same data, should yield essentially the same results.

Table 2.2.   **Demand for Seats for the Football Game Against Maximumity University**

Price ($/seat)	Quantity (seats)	Price ($/seat)	Quantity (seats)
0	16,000	8	8,000
2	14,000	10	6,000
4	12,000	12	4,000
6	10,000	14	2,000
		16	-0-

The Arc Elasticity of Demand

The formula for the arc elasticity of demand is:

(5) $$E = (\Delta Q / \Delta P) \cdot (P/Q)$$

It is the average elasticity over the range of the demand curve covered by the arc ΔQ or ΔP. The values of price and quantity used are their averages in the intervals ΔP and ΔQ. The magnitude of the elasticity obtained best approximates the elasticity at the midpoint of the arc.

Take the case of the demand for seats to the game against Maximumity University. Data on the demand function are found in Table 2.2 . Note that although quantities demanded are usually per unit of time, this one is not. It is timeless, just the demand for a quantity of seats for a particular event.

> Given: $P = \$5$ a seat; $Q = 11,000$
> Find: An estimate of the price elasticity of demand at the current price. (If it is inelastic, the administration will raise the ticket price.)
>
> Use data in the $4 to $6 price range where the quantity demanded drops from 12,000 to 10,000 seats—the midpoint of which is $5 per seat and 11,000 seats.
>
> $E = \Delta Q / Q \div \Delta P / P$
>
> $= (12,000 - 10,000)/11,000 \div (4-6)/5 = -5/11 = -0.4545$
>
> A price increase would increase total revenue, as can be seen in Table 2.2.

The Point Elasticity of Demand

The point elasticity of demand uses information pertaining to a single point on the demand function, namely, the inverse of its slope and the ratio of price to quantity at that point:

(6) $$E = dQ/Q \div dP/P$$

Rearranging terms yields:

(7) $E = (dQ/dP) \cdot (P/Q)$

Note that this formula is the same as the formula for the arc elasticity of demand except that the far smaller dQ has been substituted for ΔQ and and the far smaller dP has been substituted for ΔP. As a result we have the (inverse) slope of the demand function at a point rather than over an arc of the function.

Again, refer to the demand function of Table 2.2. Note that the demand function is linear—for each $2 change in price, quantity demand changes by 2,000. The slope is then $-1/1000$ and the inverse of the slope is $-1,000$. This is true for all points on the linear function. And at a price of $5 a seat, it is expected that 11,000 tickets will be sold. Inserting these numbers into equation (7) yields:

(8) $E = -1,000 \cdot 5/11,000 = -5/11 == -0.4545$

Thus, we get the same estimate of the price elasticity of demand using the arc elasticity and point elasticity—for a linear range on a demand function.

The Range of Elasticities on a Linear Demand Function. Allow the use of the formula for the point elasticity of demand, $E = (dQ/dP) \cdot (P/Q)$, to determine the price elasticity of demand at the extremes of a demand function. The first term in parentheses is the inverse of the slope of the demand function at a point; the second is the ratio of price to quantity at the same point on the demand function. At the intercept of the demand function with the price axis, Q equals zero. As a result the magnitude of the elasticity of demand at the intersection with the price axis is minus infinity. At the other end of the curve, where it intersects the quantity axis, P equals zero and this makes the elasticity zero. Then, over the range of a demand function drawn to contact both axes, can be found all elasticities in the range of zero to minus infinity.

The unreality of this range of elasticities is related to the unreality of a demand function which at one end has a product price of zero and at the other end, a price so high that it obviates all sales. A more realistic range of prices yields a more realistic range of elasticities.

The Geometric Determination of Elasticity

Elasticity can also be determined geometrically. If the demand function is linear, the elasticity at point X is the ratio of the distance along the function from the Q axis to X to the distance from X to price axis: $E = Q_0X / XP_0$. Why this is so is explained with the help of Figure 2.7.

The elasticity is the inverse of the slope of the function times the ratio of price to quantity. In geometric distances, this comes to:

(9) $E = -(QQ_0 / XQ) \cdot (XQ / 0Q)$

Cancel out the *XQs:*

(10)
$$= - (QQ_0) / (0Q)$$

Substitute *PX* for *OQ:*

(11) $= -(QQ_0) / (PX)$

Note that the numerator and denominator of the right-hand side of the above equation are the bases of two similar triangles, QXQ_0 and PP_0X. Substitute the ratio of their hypotenuses for the ratio of their bases:

(12) $E = - (Q_0X) / (XP_0)$

Thus, the price elasticity of demand at a point equals the ratio of the distance from the quantity axis to that point to the distance from that point to the price axis. This holds for linear demand functions and also those that can have tangents drawn to the point in question—with the tangent serving as the linear demand function.

Note that were X at Q_0, the numerator would be zero and the elasticity would be zero. If it were at the midpoint of the demand function, the numerator and denominator would be equal and the elasticity would be minus 1. And if X were at P_0 the denominator would be zero and the elasticity would equal minus infinity.

The Logarithmic Form of the Price Elasticity of Demand

Students of mathematics may recognize that the percentage change in quantity, dQ/Q, equals the differential of the natural logarithm of Q, $dlnQ$. In like fashion dP/P equals $dlnP$. Thus, the price elasticity of demand is written as:

(13) $E = dlnQ / dlnP$

What is the meaning of dP and then $dlnP$? The former, dP, is the difference between two values of P that are very close to each other; $dlnP$ is the difference in the logarithms of those values of P. The values of Q are those that correspond to the two close values of P on the demand function. And $dlnQ$ is the difference in the logarithms of those values of Q.

Calculation of the elasticity should make the above abstractions concrete and somewhat more intelligible. This can be done by resorting to the equation of the demand function used in prior calculations:

(14) $Q = 16,000 - 1000 \ P$

Figure 2.7 **Geometric Determination of the Price Elasticity of Demand**

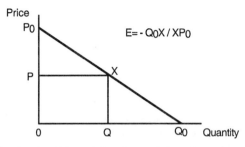

What we want is the elasticity of the demand function where the price is $5 a seat. Take a price very slightly less than $5 and very slightly more than $5 and then their logarithms. Subtracting the former from the latter yields an approximation of *dlnP*. Then, through the equation for the demand function find the values of Q at the slightly lower and higher values of P. Take the logarithms of these values of Q; subtract one from the other and you have *dlnQ*. Dividing it by *dlnP* gives us the desired point elasticity. All of this is shown below:

Given: (1) The demand function, Q = 16,000 – 10,000P; (2) P = 5
Find: The price elasticity of demand using E = dlnQ ÷ d lnP

P	ln P	Q	ln Q
5.0001	1.6094579	10,9999	9.3056415
4.9999	1.6094179	11,0001	9.3056596

Subtracting the bottom from the top numbers yields *dlnP* and *dlnQ*:
    dlnP = 0.0000400   dlnQ = –0.0000181
        E = –181/400 = – 0.45

All three approaches—arc, point, and logarithmic—yield the same price elasticity of demand.

The Demand and Total Revenue Functions

The demand for the product of the firm and its total revenue function are closely related so that if one of these functions is known, the other can be easily gotten. Assume that we have the demand function for widgets produced by a firm and that at a price of $5 per widget, 200 widgets per week are sold. Total revenue, *TR*, the price of the good times the quantity sold at that price, $TR = P \cdot Q$, would be $1,000 per week. For the case of the linear demand function, the total revenue function is parabolic, the curve traversed by a projectile, such as a baseball, in a vacuum. The linear demand function is of the form:

(15) $P = P_0 - mQ$

The total revenue function is that function multiplied by Q:

(16) $TR = PQ$

(17) $TR = P_0Q - mQ^2$

The relationship between demand and total revenue is shown in Table 2.3 and Figure 2.8 for the case in which the price intercept, P_0, is 20 and the magnitude of the negative slope of the demand function, m, is 0.1. Each value of total revenue is merely the price times the quantity in each row. In the third row, for example, price is $10 a shirt and expected sales amount to 100 shirts per day. This yields an expected total revenue of $1,000 per day.

With the data of Table 2.3, total revenue can be plotted as a function of price or as a function of quantity. The latter is more conventional and that has been done in Figure 2.8. The demand function from which it is derived is also shown.

Note that where quantity is zero, total revenue has to be zero and the price elasticity of demand is minus infinity. As price decreases, demand becomes less elastic. At the midpoint of the demand function the elasticity becomes unity. Thereafter, lower prices are accompanied by inelastic demand. Finally, at a price of zero, the elasticity of demand is zero–perfectly unresponsive to price changes.

The Effect of Price Changes on Total Revenue

There are three ranges for the price elasticity of demand. They are the elastic range, unitary elasticity, and the inelastic range. The are defined on the basis of the effects which price changes have on total revenue.

The elastic range covers elasticities with magnitudes in the interval from minus infinity to less than –1. In this range the percentage change in quantity exceeds the percentage change in price. If price is cut, total revenue increases. Conversely, if the price is increased, total revenue declines.

Given: (1) Price is at a point on the demand function at which the price elasticity of demand equals –2. (2) Price then decreases by 5 percent.
Find: The change in total revenue in percent.

Before the change in price, total revenue equals the initial price times the initial quantity sold at that price:

   $TR = P \cdot Q$

Then the price drops 5 percent to $0.95P$ and, with an elasticity of –2, the quantity increases by 10 percent to $1.1Q$. As a result, the new total revenue, TR', is:

   $TR' = 0.95P \cdot 1.1Q = 1.045PQ$

In the elastic range a price cut increases total revenue. Here a 5 percent cut increased total revenue by 4.5 percent.

Table 2.3.   Demand and Total Revenue

| Demand | | Total Revenue |
| Price | Quantity | Price • Quantity |
($/shirt)	(shirts/day)	($/day)
0	200	0
5	150	750
10	100	1000
15	50	750
20	0	0

Figure 2.8.   Demand, Elasticity, and Total Revenue

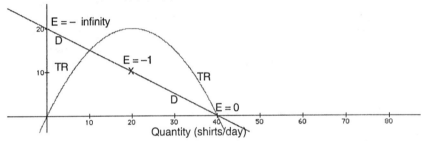

Price ($/shirt)
Total Revenue ($/day) (multiply scale by 50)

The inelastic range covers elasticities in the range of greater than –1 to zero. In this range the percentage change in quantity is less than the percentage change in price. Price cuts in this range are accompanied by total revenue decreases. Price setting producers, who know they are in this range and wish to increase profits, can do so by raising prices. This increases revenues. It also decreases costs since less will be bought and produced at the higher price. Both add to profits.

Assume that the price elasticity of demand is – 0.3 and that price is decreased by 5 percent. What is the effect of this on total revenue? The initial total revenue is:

$$TR = P \cdot Q$$

Price is then decreased by 5 percent and this results in an increase in purchases of 1.5 percent (– 0.05 • – 0.3 = 0.015). As a result:

$$TR' = 0.95P \cdot 1.015Q = 0.96425 \, TR$$

Thus, it is seen that in the inelastic range a decrease in price reduces total revenue. Here a 5 percent decrease caused revenue to decline by 3.575 percent.

The derived demand for steel is typically about –0.3. This indicates that steel-makers should increase their prices substantially in order to maximize their profits. But they face two problems in doing this: First, other steel producers might maintain their price and gladly acquire the customers of the price increasing firm. This makes the effective demand individual steel-makers face far more elastic. Second, were they all to increase the price of the steel they sell, their profits would be scandalously high creating the probability of government intervention.

Unitary elasticity occurs when the percentage change in quantity demanded equals the percentage change in price that brought it about. Total revenue remains constant as the percentage change in price is compensated for by the same percentage change in quantity.

Table 2.4 summarizes the effects of price changes on total revenue in the three ranges of elasticity. It should be clear that the linear demand curve and parabolic total revenue function of Figure 2.8 conform to the information in Table 2.5. Start at the price intercept at which no shirts are purchased. As price is lowered and quantity demanded increases by a greater percentage total revenue increases. This defines the elastic range. As price drops to that at which unitary elasticity occurs, the percentage of price decrease is equaled by the percentage of quantity increase and total revenue stays constant. We are at the maximum of total revenue. As the price is reduced further, quantity demanded increases by a smaller percentage than price and total revenue decreases—the hallmark of the inelastic range.

Constant Elasticity Functions and Total Revenue

Economists not infrequently assume that elasticity is constant in the relevant ranges of functions of concern, demand included. Moreover, elasticity is constant in all logarithmic functions. How do such constant elasticity of demand functions relate to total revenue? If the function is elastic, total revenue keeps increasing as price decreases and quantity demanded increases. If the elasticity is −1, total revenue is constant. This implies that the demand function is a rectangular hyperbola: $Q^D = constant/P$ where the constant equals total revenue. Finally, if the function is inelastic, total revenue decreases as price decreases. All of this conforms to the above analysis.

Other Elasticities of Demand

There are three other elasticities of demand of more or less importance: the income, the cross, and the derived elasticity of demand.

The Income Elasticity of Demand

The income elasticity of demand, E_y, is defined as follows:

> *The income elasticity demand* is the ratio of the percentage change in the quantity of a product demanded, per unit of time to the percentage change in real income, Y: $E_y = \Delta Q/Q \, \Delta Y/Y$.

Table 2.4   **The Effect of Price Changes on Total Revenue, by Price Elasticity**

Elasticity	Effect on Total Revenue	
	Price Increase	Price Decrease
Inelastic $(0 \geq E \geq -1)$	Increases	Decreases
Unitary $(E = -1)$	None	None
Elastic $(-1 \geq E \geq -\infty)$	Decrease	Increases

The income elasticity quantifies the shift in the demand function arising from a variation in real income. It is an important form of elasticity due to the fact that real income continually changes as a result of continual changes in the price level, particularly as indicated by the consumer price index. It also changes as an employee's money income changes, usually once a year.

For normal goods and services the income elasticity of demand is positive; for inferior goods and services it is negative. Most products are normal but there are some that are inferior. As a poor family's household income increases, for example, its members might eat more meat and less starchy vegetables.

The Cross Elasticity of Demand

The cross elasticity of demand is a measure of the responsiveness of the quantity demanded of Y to the variations in the price of X, a substitute or a complement.

> *The cross elasticity of demand* is the ratio of the percentage quantity of Y demanded to a percentage change in the price of X:
> $$E_{cross} = \Delta Y/Y \div \Delta P_X/P_X$$

An increase in the price of substitute X should yield an increase in the quantity of Y demanded and a positive value for the cross elasticity. But an increase in the price of a complement has the opposite effect. It causes the quantity of Y demanded to decrease and the cross elasticity is then negative.

It can be argued that highly skilled draftsmen (or drafters) are substitutes for engineers. It can also be argued that they are complements. Which of these is the more common relationship of draftsmen to engineers? Were the data available, a positive sign for the cross elasticity of demand would means that they tend to be substitutes; a negative sign that they tend to be complements.

The Elasticity of Derived Demand, E′

One producer rarely makes an entire final product. The loaf of bread is the product of farmers, millers, bakers, transporters, equipment manufacturers, and others. The demand for what they produce is derived from the demand for the final product, the loaf of bread. Each of the producers receives a fraction of the price of the final product, and to effect a given percentage change in the final price they must change their fractional share of the price by a larger percentage. As a result of this, the elasticity of demand these producers see, derived from the demand for the product, is more inelastic than the elasticity for the final product.

> *The derived elasticity of demand* for a factor of production including goods in process, E', is the ratio of the price received by the factor to the final price the good, P_{share}, times the elasticity of demand for that final good: $E' = P_{share} \cdot E$

To show that the derived elasticity of demand is less than the final product elasticity of demand, consider the following example:

Assume that apples sell for $1 a pound; the price elasticity of demand for apples is –2.0; apple growers receive $0.50 for a pound of apples; and the store marks up the price paid for apples by $.50.

If the price of apples decreases by 1 percent, the quantity demanded increases by 2 percent. By what percentage must the apple grower decrease his price for the final price to decrease by 1 percent or 1 cent per pound? The grower has to decrease his price 1 cent from 50 to 49 cents a pound, by 2 percent, to get the price to drop by 1 percent.

A 2 percent drop in the apple grower's price yields a 2 percent increase in the quantity of apples purchased. Thus, the derived demand experiences is –1, half the elasticity of demand at the produce store.

Consider another example: The cost of steel has been estimated to be on the average about 10 percent of the price of products using steel. Were the price elasticity of demand for the typical steel-using product –3, the elasticity of the demand for steel would typically be 10 percent of that or –0.3. The smaller the share of price of a factor or supplier, the less elastic and more inelastic is the derived demand.

What is implied here is of more than passing interest. If the derived demand is inelastic, less in absolute magnitude than –1, the addition to total revenue obtained from the sale of the marginal unit of production is negative. It makes no economic sense to operate in the inelastic range of the demand function.

The Effect of Time on Demand Functions

As time passes demand functions should become more horizontal or elastic. This is shown in Figure 2.9. The original demand function is the short-run curve, D_{SR1}; the function reached over time is the long-run curve, D_{LR}. The argument that elasticities increase over time goes along these lines: Assume that you are currently somewhat addicted to having orange juice for breakfast six days a week at a price of $1 per 6-ounce glass. (On the seventh day you rest and

Figure 2.9. **Short-Run Demand Shifting Along the Long-Run Demand Function**

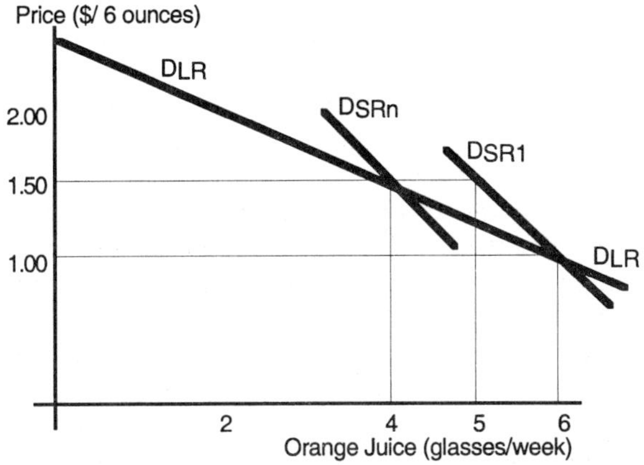

forego breakfast.) Then its price is increased to $1.50 a glass. According to Figure 2.9, your addiction will be partially broken by the large price increase as you quickly drop to 5 glasses per week on the short-run demand function D_{SR1}. But ultimately, or in the long-run, consumption drops to 4 glasses of orange juice a week as the short-run demand function decreases to D_{SR2}. Why? As time goes on there are more opportunities to try substitutes and they increasingly become more or less acceptable. The long-run demand function as a result includes the quantity-price points 6,$1 and 4,$1.50. It is more horizontal, more responsive to price changes, than the short-run functions.

The following equation covers both the short and long-run demand functions:

(18) $$Q_t = 5 + 0.5Q_{t-1} - 2P_t$$

where, Q_t is the quantity of orange juice demanded in week t, Q_{t-1} is the quantity of orange juice consumed in the previous week, and P is the price of a 6-ounce glass of the juice. Assume that Orlando, who eats breakfast at a neighborhood diner, consumes 6 glasses of orange juice a week when the price is $1 per 6-ounce glass. The short-run form of the above equation is then:

(19) $$Q_{SR} = 5 + 0.5 \cdot 6 - 2P = 8 - 2P$$

At a price of $1.00, 6 glasses are purchased per week. If the price goes up to $1.50 a glass, consumption drops to 5 in the short-run.

The long-run function represents the amount of consumption that will take place, after the process of substitution has come to an end. At that time, assuming that the price of $1.50 has been maintained, this manifests itself by this week's orange juice consumption being the same as last week's: $Q_t = Q_{t-1}$. As a result the original equation (18) becomes:

(20) $\qquad$ $Q = 5 + 0.5Q - 2P$ or $0.5Q = 5 - 2P$

Solving for Q yields the long-run function:

(21) $\qquad$ $Q_{LR} = 10 - 4P$

Under the long-run demand function, at a price of $1.50 a glass, Orlando will ultimately drop from consuming 5 to 4 glasses per week. In effect the short-run function, D_{SR1}, shifts along the long-run demand function until it reaches D_{SR2}. The functions shown mathematically are the same as those of Figure 2.9. The process described above is reversible. If, for example, the price drops from $1.50 to $1.00 a glass, the quantity demanded, *always determined by the short-run function,* here D_{SR2}, would quickly increase from 4 to 5 glasses a week. Over the course of time the short-run demand would shift along the long-run function, until equilibrium of $Q_t = Q_{t-1}$ is reached at D_{SR1}. Orlando would again consumes 6 glasses a week.

Supply

The approach to the supply side of the market is structured in the same way as that used in the analysis of demand. First, supply is defined. Its standard specifications were given with those for demand, above. Then, the supply function of an individual producer is presented along with the rationale for its having a positive slope. Movements along the supply function are differentiated from shifts. Individual supply functions are added together to yield the market supply function. The shift parameters are given. Finally, the concept of the price elasticity of supply is briefly presented.

Although supply functions are usually shown as positive sloped, the most common by far are zero-sloped functions. This is the shape of the supply of price setters who maintain the price they have set throughout the range of actual rates of production. Some price setters develop their prices or tuition levels from negative-sloped planning–supply functions and that is shown in Chapter 3.

The definition of supply is:

> *Supply* is the quantity per unit of time of a standardized product or resource, Q^s, which is willingly produced for sale at various prices, P, *ceteris paribus.*

The definition of supply is quite similar to that for demand except that the concern is with production and selling while that of demand is with buying.

Individual Supply

Hypothetical data on Farmer Brown's Supply of Wheat Function appear in Table 2.5. A supply curve corresponding to the data can be found in

Table 2.5.   **Farmer Brown's Supply of Wheat**

Price ($/bushel)	Expected Quantity Supplied (thousands bushels/month)
2	0
4	2
6	4

Figure 2.10.   **Farmer Brown's Supply of Wheat**

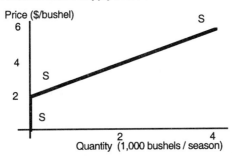

Figure 2.10. Using the slope-intercept form, Farmer Brown's supply curve is:

(22) $P = 2 + Q^S$ or $Q^S = -2 + P$

where P is in dollars per bushel and Q^S is in thousands of bushels per month (the annual estimate divided by 12). As can be seen in the above equation, table, and graph, each dollar increase in the expected price of wheat per bushel stimulates Farmer Brown to plan to produce 1,000 more bushels per season.

The Law of Diminishing Returns and Positive-Sloped Supply

The law of diminishing returns is generally cited as the reason for the positive slope of the supply function. John Stuart Mill, in his 1848 *Principles of Political Economy*, called this law "the most important proposition in political economy," and his formulation is used here:

> In any given state of agricultural skill and knowledge, by increasing the labour, the produce is not increased in an equal degree: doubling the labour does not double the produce; or, to express the same thing in other words, every increase in produce is obtained by a more than proportional increase in labour to the land (1961 [1848], p. 177).

This is shown in Figure 2.11 in what is called the production function. It gives the rate of production, Q, as a function of the employment of the factors of production—land, labor, and capital. In Mill's above approach only labor is varied; the other factors are held constant.

Figure 2.11.   **The Production Function with Diminishing Marginal Returns**

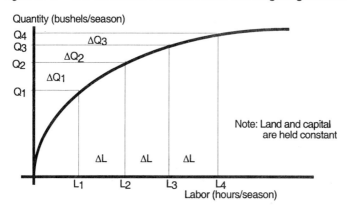

First note that the employment of L_1 units of labor yields an output of Q_1 and that the employment of twice as much labor, L_2 yields Q_2, far less than twice Q_1. The reason for this is the increasing scarcity of one or more factors of production as the rate of production increases. The fixed size of the farm, for example, makes the land of the farm increasingly scarce. Note also the ΔLs, increments of labor which are constant in amount, give rise to diminishing marginal returns, increments of output or product of diminishing size: $\Delta Q_3 < \Delta Q_2 < \Delta Q_1$. As a result, the law of diminishing returns can be called the law of diminishing *marginal* returns or the law of declining marginal productivity.

Consider the cost implications of the law of declining marginal productivity. Assume that there are unitary increases in the rate of production: $\Delta Q = 1$. Each unitary increase in the rate of production requires a greater increment in the employment of labor. As a result, incremental cost increases as the rate of production increases. To cover these increased costs, producers must receive higher prices; thus, the positive-sloped agricultural supply function. But if the same factor increments are required to produce the unitary increases in production, incremental cost is constant and the law of diminishing marginal productivity is an irrelevancy.

Neoclassical theorists have expanded the use of the law of diminishing returns beyond agriculture, a matter critically examined in Chapter 5.

Zero-Sloped Supply: The Most Common of All

Firms are usually price-setters which on the average change price once a year. (See Chapter 10 for the data and sticky price hypotheses.) This implies that during the course of the year the firm's supply function is horizontal at the price it has set. The *New York Times* will sell as many copies as people will buy at the price of 60 cents a copy—but never on Sundays when the newspaper and price

Figure 2.12.   **Movements Along Supply Functions**

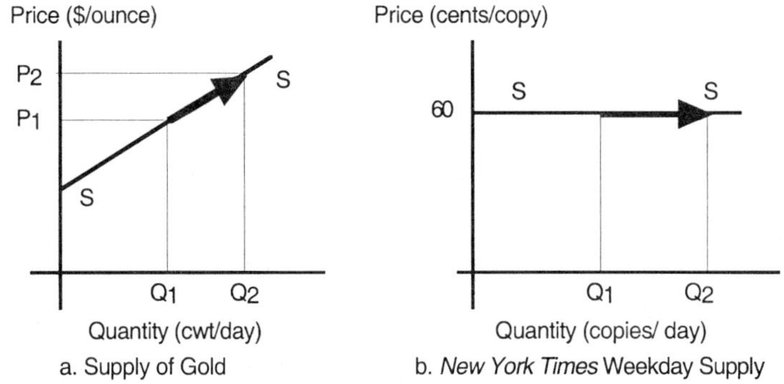

a. Supply of Gold

b. *New York Times* Weekday Supply

are more voluminous, the latter at $2.50 a copy. The non-Sunday supply function is horizontal at a price of 60 cents; the Sunday supply horizontal at $2.50.

Movements Along the Supply Function

Consider the positive-sloped supply function of frame *a* of Figure 2.12. Price increases from P_1 to P_2 is an incentive to increase the rate of production from Q_1 to Q_2. This represents a movement along the supply function as is shown by the darkened line and arrow—*not* an increase in supply. In frame *b* can be found a horizontal supply function which informs us that at a price of 60 cents, the *New York Times* will produce as many copies as people are willing to buy. Assume that Q_1 copies per day of the *Times* are initially sold and that there is a presidential scandal, and as it heats up demand increases such that Q_2 copies a day are sold. Note two matters: the movement along the supply function, and, that an increase in *quantity demanded* is the incentive to increase the rate of production—*not* to increase the price.

Market Supply

The market supply is the horizontal sum of the quantities individual suppliers are willing to provide, during a given interval of time, at various prices. Here we take the case of the market for wheat in which there are many, many producers. The quantity of wheat ready for harvesting is completely independent of the price Farmer Brown can get for it. Wheat is unaware that the higher the market price, the more should appear to be harvested. Nonetheless, the individual supply and the market supply are not vertical; they both tend to have some positive slope. At lower prices, less care is taken in harvesting and more of the crop is placed in storage in the hope that the price will increase in the future. At higher prices the current production tends to be marketed augmented by withdrawals from storage.

Figure 2.13.   **The Sum of the Individual Supply Curves Yields the Market Supply Curve**

Thus, the supply of wheat of individual farmers and the market supply have some positive slope as shown in Figure 2.13. Were the supply perishable, as that of fish, the supply function would be virtually vertical.

Shifting Supply: Unlocking the Shift Parameters

Variations in the magnitude of shift parameters are required to increase or decrease the product supply function.

> *An increase in supply* occurs when, at various prices, higher quantities are willingly sold.

> *A decrease in supply* occurs when, at various prices, lower quantities are willingly sold.

Changes in supply that shift the whole function are shown in Figure 2.14. In panel *a* increases in supply are shown for a positive-sloped and a horizontal supply function. Panel *b* does the same for decreases in supply.

In the left frame of panel *a*, the shift of the positive-sloped supply function from *SS* to *S′S′* represents an increase in supply. At all relevant prices, the quantity supplied is greater as a result of the shift. In the right panel of frame *a*, the supply function is horizontal. In this case, an increase in supply is represented by a downwards shift from *SS* to *S′S′*. With *SS* in force, nothing is supplied at a lower price than that at its intersection with the price axis. But with an increase in supply, the downward shift to *S′S′*, higher quantities are supplied at a lower price.

Frame *b* has decreases in supply. For both the positive-sloped and horizontal supply functions, a higher price is required to attain a given rate of production.

Product Supply Shift Parameters

Shift parameters increase and decrease supply. They are presented here in the way required to increase supply. Turn them around and decreases will occur.

Figure 2.14.   **Supply Shifts**

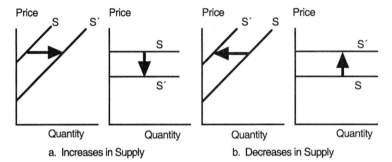

a. Increases in Supply   b. Decreases in Supply

The Number of Producers. An increase in the number of producers increases the market supply function.

Technology. Technology is knowledge of the process of production. An advance in technology implies better organization of the workforce or the provision of better tools to that workforce, or both. This should yield an increase in productivity, decrease in production costs, and increase in supply.

Capital per Worker. The provision of additional equipment per worker tends to increase productivity, decrease the cost of producing at various rates of production, and increase supply.

Factor Costs. A decrease in the cost of one or more of the factors of production will cause an increase in supply.

The Price of Substitute Products. Assume that a farmer can produce either wheat or corn. A decrease in the expected price of corn would increase the supply of wheat.

The Price of a Joint Product. The rancher who raises cattle for beef also produces the joint product hides. Were the price of hides expected to increase, the supply of hides and beef would tend to increase.

Note that there may be a delay between the change in a shift parameter and a shift in the supply function. In addition if the producer is a price setter and prices are normally changed each year on July 1, appropriate price changes tend to be delayed until that date is reached.

The Price Elasticity of Supply

The price elasticity of supply is the ratio of the percentage change in the quantity supplied per unit of time to the percentage change in price.

Figure 2.15. **Supply Functions in Different Elasticity Ranges**

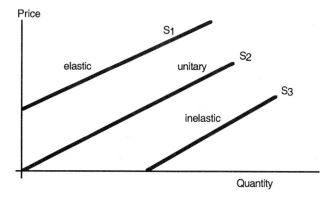

E^S = percent change in quantity supplied ÷ percent change in price

It is conceptually the same as the price elasticity of demand, except that the quantities in question are those supplied: It is a measure of the responsiveness of the rate of production to variations in price. It can be estimated at a point, over an arc, and through the use of logarithms.

Let us briefly scrutinize a set of linear supply functions to get a feel for their relationship to the magnitude of the price elasticity of supply. This is done by resort to the three supply functions shown in Figure 2.15. The first intersects the positive price axis and is elastic; the second intersects the origin of the axes and is of unitary elasticity; and the third intersects the quantity axis (and the price axis where it is negative) and is inelastic. Why this is so can be shown by putting the equation of the supply function into the definition of elasticity followed by modest manipulation. All three supply functions are shown as linear. In the slope-intersect form each can be described as:

(23) $P = P_0 + mQ$

The price elasticity of supply can be written as:

(24) $E^S = (dQ/dP) \cdot (P/Q)$

Since dQ/dP is the inverse of the slope of the supply curve, it equals $1/m$,

(25) $E^S = 1 / m \ (P/Q)$

Substitute for P the equation for the supply functions:

(26) $E^S = (1 / m) \ [(P_0 + mQ) / Q]$
    or,
(27) $E^S = [P_0 / (m \ Q)] + 1$

For S_1S_1, P_0 is positive. This makes the terms in the brackets positive and the elasticity greater than one: The function is elastic. In the case of S_2S_2, P_0 equals zero making the bracketed terms equal zero. As a result all linear supply functions passing through the origin have unitary elasticity. For S_3S_3, P_0 is negative. This could be shown by the projection of the supply function to the price axis. As a result, the bracketed terms in are negative and the elasticity of supply is less than one or inelastic. It is noteworthy that as Q increases the (P_0/mQ) becomes smaller causing the elasticity of supply, irrespective of its intercept, to increasingly approach unity.

Consider briefly the supply elasticity of horizontal and vertical supply functions. The slope, m, of horizontal functions is zero, and as a result, its elasticity approaches infinity. For the vertical function, the ratio of the percentage change in quantity to price is zero, as is its elasticity.

The Usual Independence of Supply and Demand Functions

Supply and demand are usually but not always independent of each other. Assuming independence, if the task at hand is the analysis of a demand relationship, one is well advised to stay away from the supply side, and vice versa. This is merely an example of the advantage of keeping one's eye on the ball. Were we interested in both the supply and demand functions of a particular market, they should still be analyzed separately.

There are a few important exceptions to the general rule that supply and demand are independent. First, in labor markets, the supply of workers to an activity is frequently an increasing function of the quantity of job vacancies in that activity. Job vacancies are the difference between the quantity demanded and supplied, and this makes supply a function of demand. Consider their importance. Engineers are usually paid more than school teachers. If there are no jobs available, however, that becomes an irrelevancy, and the lower-paying job of school teacher, with jobs available, may well become more attractive. Second, when credit card holders demand more credit, credit card companies tend to increase the supply of credit. Thus, the supply of credit may be a function of the demand for credit. Finally, according to Victor R. Fuchs and Marcia J. Kramer the demand for medical services is an increasing function of the supply of physicians and surgeons. The more physicians and surgeons there are, the greater is the number of referrals that they make.

Summary

Transactions are made between buyers and sellers whose interests are by no means the same. They both respond contrarily to price changes and also differently to other behavioral variables or parameters. This is why economic phenomena are frequently broken down into supply and demand. The same supply and demand functions can be represented by graphs, tabular data, or mathematical equations. Once played with, all will be found to be user friendly.

Quantity demanded is generally portrayed as a decreasing function of price. The reasons cited are the substitution and income effects. As price increases consideration is given to substitute products. We all have finite incomes, although some are quite a bit more finite than others. So the more price increases, particularly the price of "big-ticket" products, the more it consumes our income and the less we tend to purchase.

Market demand tends to be additive by quantity at various prices but there are exceptions. If many in a high school class have the latest computer games, others will want them as well—the bandwagon effect. In this case there is feedback from the market to individual buyers tending to augment demand. But the opposite may be observed, as well. Some may shy away from getting a Brand X car because of its extraordinary popularity—the snob effect. Here information from the market tends to diminish that demand.

Public goods, although uncommon, are often very important. They exist when consumption is not mutually exclusive and it is impractical to exclude users from consuming the good or service. The services of a fire department in a densely populated community affords a good example. Here the market demand is the sum of the prices individual consumers would be willing to pay for the fixed quantity of the good.

Economists, entrepreneurs, their agents, and others are frequently interested in the responsiveness of one economic variable to changes in another. To avoid the problem created by the multiplicity of units which can be affixed to economic variables, the measure of responsiveness commonly used is elasticity, a pure or unitless number.

Supply tends to be treated symmetrically with demand except that individual supply functions are generally shown as positive sloped. But by far the most common supply functions are horizontal, infinitely elastic if you prefer. This is because the price of a vast majority of the products we buy are set by sellers and these prices are sticky—they are not very responsive to changes in the quantity demanded and produced. Just about half of the prices in our economy change once a year or less often.

Why is price a variable, while other determinants of demand (or supply) are relegated to being parameters? The reason is that price is supposed to be more variable than the other determinants—but frequently and perhaps usually, that is not the case. Income, which varies with the price level and other factors, may very well be the most important determinant of quantities purchased. This will be seen in Chapter 4 on consumer behavior.

Shift variables play an important role in changing demand and changing supply, and they warrant more consideration than is normally awarded to them.

It is important, in general, to consider supply and demand to be independent of each other. When demand is being analyzed, care must be taken not to enter the realm of supply and vice versa. There are, however, important cases in which supply is a function of demand or demand a function of supply, and we should be aware of them and the need to determine whether or not such dependencies exist in a market that may concern us. An important example is the role of job vacancies, the difference between demand and supply, in drawing supplies of workers to occupations, industries, regions, and employers. This anticipates Chapter 12's discussion on aspects of the supply of labor.

Questions on Chapter 2

1. Explain the sense of the breakdown into supply and demand?

2. a. Define the price elasticity of demand.
   b. Explain why a firm that found its price to be in the inelastic range would like to raise its price. (Use a numerical example to help explain your answer.)

3. a. Show an elastic and an inelastic positive-sloped supply function. Explain why one is elastic and the other inelastic.
   b. As Q increases, the price elasticity of supply approaches unity. Show why this is so.

4. Supply functions tend to be horizontal for a period of a year, on the average. Explain why this is so. Give a few examples.

5. If price is constant for a substantial period of time, what signal is used by producers to make their rate of production decision.

6. Assume that people are wealthy enough to buy most habitual products irrespective of price. What variable, conventionally a shift parameter, might influence them to buy more of a product or more of higher-quality products? Comment.

7. There is an argument about whether or not drafters are substitutes or complements of engineers. Assuming that the required data are available, how would you determine which side is correct?

8. Assume that the price elasticity of the demand for milk is 0.5 and that dairy farmers' share of the price is 50 percent. What is the derived elasticity of demand seen by the dairy farmers? Explain with the help of a numerical example.

9. Assume that you have just been sworn in as president of a well-regarded but poor university. Assume that the cost of running the university is fixed. Under what demand condition would it make economic sense to (a) increase tuition or (b) decrease tuition. Explain with the help of numerical examples.

CHAPTER THREE

Equilibrium and Its Attainment

Microeconomics is frequently called price theory. Perceptive readers may be surprised at this since conventional definitions of the field omit use of the word *price* and seem to stress quantity. Frank Knight's formulation emphasized the quantity of the various products to be produced and their distribution. Lionel Robbins's approach stressed the quantities of resources allocated to the production of the various goods and services. The argument justifying the narrowness which can be associated with the words *price theory* arises from the assumption that quantities demanded and supplied are principally a function of price. This makes price a profoundly important variable in theory.

The idea that supply and demand set price came from the independent works of the great English philosopher John Locke and his countryman Sir Dudley North. Both published papers on this in 1691. Until that time the ruling price doctrine was the *theory of just price,* the work of the greatest of the scholastic writers, the thirteenth-century cleric St. Thomas Aquinas. According to St. Thomas, the just price of the necessities and other conventional goods is equal to the reasonable cost of their production. Locke and North, in successfully arguing that price is and should be set by the forces of supply and demand, came close to destroying the moral content of economic activity. This was advantageous to them. Locke's business activities were highly speculative; North was a wealthy trader skillful at buying cheap and selling dear.

In this chapter the roles of price are first considered. Then the price-setting institution, the market is examined. Two processes of attaining equilibrium are discussed. In Leon Walras's approach, discrepancies between quantities supplied and demanded at the existing price, bring about the price change required to equalize these quantities. This is followed by Alfred Marshall's analysis under which differences in the supply and demand price at the existing quantity brings about the quantity change required to equilibrate the supply and demand price. Both approaches tend to yield the same results except when supply functions are negatively sloped. Appropriate cases are presented to show this.

Thereafter will be found Marshall's model which has supply functions getting more elastic over the course of time as he goes from market, to short-run, to long-run functions. The market period and short-run supply functions are then used in a so-called "cobweb model," a model implying economic irrationality.

Lengthy disequilibria may be more common than is usually believed. Examples presented are in the markets for labor, commercial space, and manufacturing facilities and equipment.

The Role of Price in Theory

Price has several key functions in neoclassical theory:

- Price information is the only economic information required by decision-makers in *competitive markets.*

- The relative price of various scarce resources determines their potential employment by producers.

- Product price relative to factor cost creates *the* incentive to produce or not to produce.

- Increases in the relative price of a product creates the incentive to increase its rate of production of the product as well as the incentive to curtail its consumption.

- The higher the relative price of higher quality resources, the greater the incentive of improving the quality of resources, for example, by the increased education of labor.

All of this makes the institution which in theory creates price, the market, of fundamental importance.

The Great Efficiency of Money Prices

Money prices as compared to barter prices curtail the number of prices required in an economy in which a substantial number of products are exchanged. Were only three products—A, B, and C—exchanged, three money prices or three barter prices would be required. The barter prices would be that for A in units of B and C, and that for B in units of C. Note that if you have the price of A in units of B you also have the price of B in units of A and that this is true for all pairs of products. Were there four goods, four money or six barter prices would be required. But with 1,000 products exchanged, there would have to be 1,000 money prices or 499,500 barter prices. (For a small number of products, it is easy to count the number of barter prices required. As the number of products gets larger, prudence requires the use of the formula for combinations. For the problem at hand, the formula required is that for the number of combinations, C, of n objects taken two at a time: $C = (n)(n-1) \div 2$ or $C = (n^2-n) \div 2$.) The use of money prices makes exchange far more efficient.

The Market and the Law of One Price

While price is portrayed as the key variable of concern to decision-makers, the market is the institution of primary concern to economists. This is because the market is the price-quantity setting institution. In doing this the market system answers the basic questions, "What?" "How?" and "To whom?" Alternatively put, the market system determines the allocation of scarce resources.

The classic definition of the market is that promulgated in 1838 by the remarkable French economist A. A. Cournot:

> Economists understand by the term MARKET, not any particular market place in which things are bought and sold, but the whole of any region in which buyers and sellers are in such free intercourse with one another that the prices of the same goods tend to equality quickly and easily.

Cournot's definition of a market implies what is known as *the law of one price.* It should be quickly added that the market, in setting the price of a product, at one and the same time, determines the quantity bought and sold and, in effect, the quantity produced to the extent that production is variable.

Some markets are highly localized while others are close to worldwide. The market for construction tends to be local. A family wants or demands a house in community *X;* a corporation wants a plant in area *Y.* The market for blue-chip stocks and bonds, however, is virtually worldwide. They are sold in many countries. Moreover, were they any cheaper in Tokyo, London, or Frankfurt, than in New York, there would be a tendency to buy the stocks at the cheaper stock exchange. The implied increase in demand at the lower-priced market drives price up; as the decreased demand at the higher-priced market drives price down. Thus, the tendency is toward one price.

Equilibrium and Its Attainment

Our concern here is with how the market equilibrates the supply and demand price and the quantity demanded and supplied. There are two approaches to the attainment of equilibrium. One is that of Leon Walras; the other the creation of Alfred Marshall. Textbooks generally utilize a simplified version of Walras's model, which is presented first. Marshall's takes second place. The examples used by both Walras and Marshall involved commodities exchanged in auction markets.

Walras's Model

In Figure 3.1 can be found hypothetical market supply and demand functions. The product in question is wheat. The demand function is shown as negative-sloped, a manifestation of the income and substitution effects. The supply func-

Figure 3.1. Equilibrium via the Response of Price to Quantity Disequilibria

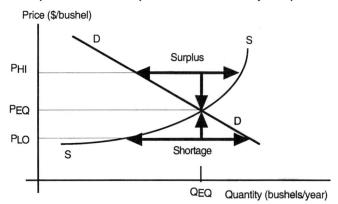

tion is shown as positive-sloped in keeping with the law of diminishing marginal returns or marginal productivity.

Assume, that at the start of the trading day the price of wheat is P_{HI}. At that price the quantity supplied exceeds the quantity demanded yielding the surplus shown. That surplus causes the price to be bid down until the quantity supplied equals that demanded. At that quantity equilibrium, the market-clearing or equilibrium price, P_{EQ}, would occur.

> *Equilibrium* is the condition in which the quantity supplied is equal to that demanded. The price at which this takes place is called the equilibrium or market-clearing price.

The *market-clearing price* is important because it is the price at which neither surpluses nor shortages exist. It is the price at which the market is cleared of its supply. Were trading to begin with a price lower than the equilibrium price, P_{LO}, a shortage of wheat would occur as shown. That shortage would tend to cause the price to be bid up to its equilibrium or market-clearing value.

Walras's approach was anticipated by Adam Smith who put the matter this way:

> When the quantity of any commodity brought to market falls short of the effectual demand ... a competition will begin ... and the market price will rise (1937[1776], p. 56).

Today, we would have the price rising to the *equilibrium level.*

The price-changing mechanisms of the Walrasian model are so important that they deserve keynoting:

> *Price increases* are caused by shortages and shortages alone.

> *Price decreases* are caused by surpluses and surpluses alone.

So whenever a market-set price changes, either a shortage or a surplus existed and was eradicated or at least diminished by the price change.

Price increases commonly occur without the benefit of some related shortage. To the extent this is true, these are examples of producer rather than market-set prices.

Marshall's Model

Marshall's scissors analogy regarding the roles of supply and demand in setting price is well known to economists:

> We might as reasonably dispute whether it is the upper or the lower blade of a pair of scissors that cuts a piece of paper, as whether value is governed by utility [consumer demand] or cost of production [producer supply] (1961 [1890], p. 348).

Walras would agree with this statement. Where he and Marshall differ is with respect to the method or process through which the market goes from disequilibrium to equilibrium.

Marshall reasoned this way: Consider the auctioning of wheat at a commodity exchange as illustrated in Figure 3.2. Assume that trading starts with the demand (or bid) price of buyers, P^D, exceeding the supply (or ask) price of sellers, P^S, which is unknown to buyers. At that demand price buyers would purchase Q_{LO} bushels of wheat. Sellers would gladly accept the bid price and increase the quantity supplied, as well. Buyers, sensing the greater availability of wheat on the market would lower their demand price while sellers increase their supply price. The more the prices move toward equality, the more the quantities supplied and demanded become equal and this process continues until the demand and supply prices are equal. At this equality, Q_{EQ}, the quantity supplied equals that demanded.

Had trading started with the supply price exceeding the demand price, as is the case at Q_{HI}, sellers would find that they are unable to sell the quantity of wheat brought to market. They would accordingly cut the quantity supplied and the supply price. Buyers, realizing the lower availability of wheat would increase the demand price. This process would continue until the supply and the demand price were equal.

According to Marshall's approach:

> *Quantity increases* are caused by the demand price being higher than the supply price.

> *Quantity decreases* are caused by the demand price being lower than the supply price.

Were supply fixed or vertical, sellers would accept the demand price and that would be the equilibrium price.

Figure 3.2.   **Equilibrium via Quantity Responding to Price Disequilibria**

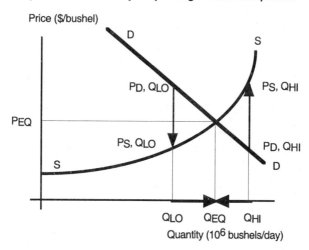

Both Walras and Marshall recognized the fact that whereas all trading, in theory, should be at the equilibrium price, much trading could have been consummated at higher or lower prices. Walras handled this by making all trades provisional with the actual price becoming the equilibrium price at the end of the trading day. Marshall argued that the equilibrium price attained is the "true equilibrium price: because if it were fixed at the beginning and adhered to throughout, it would exactly equate demand and supply" (1961, p. 333). Neither approach is persuasive. Prices are not adjusted at the end of a trading day. And if all of the day's trading takes place at equilibrium, there is no need for a price-quantity adjustment mechanism.

Which view of the process of equilibration conforms to reality? One has to examine the actual operation of a particular market to understand how it in fact responds to disequilibria. Auction and auction-like markets seem to conform to Marshall's model. Other markets appear to be Walrasian or Smithian.

The speed with which equilibrium is attained is more important than whether quantity or price differences are the signals which move a market toward equilibrium. Walras and Marshall had equilibrium attained in the course of a trading day. The equilibrating time of the labor market, as indicated by the long and deep depressions of the 1890s and 1930s, may at times be more like a decade.

Less Laudatory Characteristics of the Market

The market is the institution which rations the resources and production of market societies. In doing this it is heartless. Take the case of a society which has little food for its citizenry because of some national disaster. The market price of food would be driven out of the reach of the poor whose lot would be that of

Figure 3.3.   **Shifts Leading to Shortages and Price Increases**

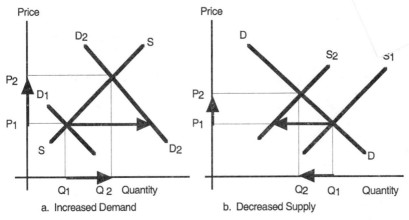

a. Increased Demand   b. Decreased Supply

malnutrition, starvation, and death. At the same time, the rich could eat to their belly's content.

The market also shields us from reality, an insight owed to Karl Polanyi. We tend to buy at the cheapest price known to us with no consideration of the reason for the existence of that price. Was the price cheapest because the producer paid unfairly low wages, exploited child labor, used prison labor at low or no cost, provided a filthy and dangerous workplace, and dumped toxic wastes into local waterways? The market shields us from such matters of social concern.

Shifts and the Resolution of Shortages and Surpluses:Comparative Statics

Were there no shifts in supply or demand, prices would remain eternally fixed, in theory. Alternatively put, variations in prices reflect shifts in supply and demand caused by variations in the shift parameters. We shall consider this under two headings: In one, shortages are created and prices increase; in the other surpluses are created and prices decrease. In both we are going from one static equilibrium to another. This commonplace method of analysis is formally called *comparative statics*.

Shifts Causing Shortages and Then Price Increases

Shortages at an existing price can be created by an increase in demand or a decrease in supply. The former can be seen in frame *a* of Figure 3.3, the latter in frame *b*. The initial functions in frame *a* are D_1 and SS and the initial equilibrium price and quantity are P_1 and Q_1. Then demand increases to D_2, and a shortage at P_1 is created. This leads to the price being bid up until it reaches P_2. At that price the quantity supplied and demanded are again equal. The case of decreased supply is shown in frame *b*. This also brings about a shortage at

Figure 3.4.   **Shifts Leading to Surpluses and Price Decreases**

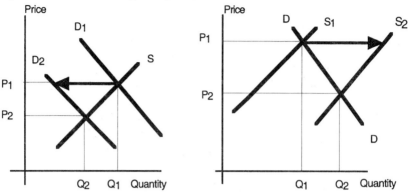

the initial price, that shortage causing the price to increase to P_2. Keep in mind that although price increases can occur as a result of an increase in demand or decrease in supply, the former increases the equilibrium quantity; the latter decreases it.

Shifts Causing Surpluses and Then Price Decreases

Figure 3.4 shows that surpluses at an existing price can be created by a decrease in demand or an increase in supply. In frame *a* demand and supply are initially D_1D_1 and SS and the resulting price and quantity are P_1 and Q_1. Demand then decreases to D_2D_2 and a surplus is created. This leads to the price decline from P_1 to P_2 and the quantity reduction from Q_1 to Q_2. In frame *b* the initial functions are DD and S_1S_1 yielding the price and quantity P_1 and Q_1. Then supply is increased to S_2S_2 creating a surplus at the original price. In response to the surplus, price decreases from P_1 to P_2 and the equilibrium quantity increases from Q_1 to Q_2.

Thus, both demand decreases and supply increases create surpluses and a reduction in price. But demand decreases tend to decrease the quantity bought, sold, and produced while supply increases tend to have the opposite effects.

Applying Comparative Statics to the Labor Market

The Korean War started in 1950 and ended in 1952, whereupon it was replaced by the Cold War between the United States and the Soviet Union and Soviet-bloc countries. An important aspect of this period was the substantial increase in military spending to advance military technology. As a result, there was a large increase in the demand for engineers and scientists, reflected in a substantial increase in the amount of advertising for engineers and scientists by defense contractors. During this period there was much talk and media coverage about "the shortage of engineers."

Figure 3.5.   **Growth in Relative Pay indicating a Relative Shortage**

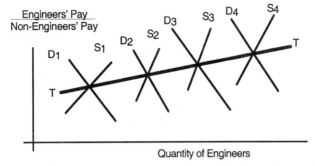

In order to have this national problem properly analyzed and to certify the existence of the shortage, the National Science Foundation awarded a grant to two prominent economists, David M. Blank and George J. Stigler. Blank and Stigler's methodology was that of the section above. They reasoned that since shortages cause price increases, a shortage of engineers should cause an increase their pay. Their focus was accordingly on the earnings of engineers over the course of time and particularly during the 1950–1955 period.

Blank and Stigler recognized that in reality wages in general tend to increase with time. They, therefore, used relative engineering earnings, the ratio of the earnings of engineers to the earnings of those in other occupations and professions, to evaluate whether or not a relative shortage existed. Figure 3.5 illustrates the comparative statics methodology used. It is constructed in a way indicating that the growth in demand each year exceeded the growth in supply. Relative shortages were created each year, shortages causing engineering pay relative to non-engineering pay to increase—as shown by the trend line, *TT*.

The failure to find an increase in relative engineering pay led Blank and Stigler to this conclusion:

> In the five years after 1950 the increases in engineering and scientific salaries have been essentially the same magnitude as those in other occupations, i.e., somewhat larger in the several years years following 1950 and somewhat smaller, in many cases, after 1952....We have found no evidence of any shortage of substantial magnitude (1957, p. 32).

The authors recognized that "our conclusion that there is no evidence of a shortage of engineers will strike many readers as surprising and some as "patently wrong" (p. 32).

Those who believe the findings of Blank and Stigler to be patently wrong are unable to understand their failure to use the direct data on the shortage as manifest in want ads for engineers. They contend that the substantial increase in the want ads for engineers, during the period of concern, was a measure of the increase in the shortage of engineers.

But critics of the Blank-Stigler methodology are on the defensive when they have to confront this question: Assuming that a substantial shortage existed, why did engineering salaries fail to increase by a greater percent than others? The answer goes along these lines. Engineering salaries largely reflect the salaries paid by the major employers of engineers: the federal government, major defense contractors, and other large corporations. These institutions tend to have formal salary structures specifying the pay relationships of almost all jobs and occupations in their employment. Such salary structures are difficult and costly to change so relative wages in comparable occupations tend to be constant. Moreover, there is a hierarchy of responses to a shortage of engineers: the first is to increase the amount of overtime worked by engineers; the last is to raise their pay. As a result, a relative shortage need not manifest itself in increasing relative pay.

Demand- and Supply-Side Economics: Demand- and Supply-Side Shifts

Macroeconomics and particularly demand-side macroeconomics was the invention of of John Maynard Keynes. Just as in an individual market, an increase in aggregate demand, with aggregate supply positively sloped, would increase production, employment, and price with the last an irrelevancy in 1936, the year of the publication of Keynes's masterpiece, *The General Theory of Employment, Interest, and Money.* The title of his text, particularly interest and money, implies emphasis on the use of an increase in the stock of money to drive the interest rate down thereby increasing spending on interest-sensitive products such as houses and factories, cars and assembly lines. Only at the end of *The General Theory* does Keynes discuss increasing aggregate demand through fiscal policy—either having the government spend more or taxing less and having consumers spend more, or both.

Supply-side macroeconomics is an invention of the 1970s, a period in which inflation and unemployment were relatively high and productivity growth low. Increased aggregate supply commanded the attention of many economists because an increase in supply tends to decrease price and increase output. The most important way to accomplish this would be to somehow or another increase investment spending. A lower interest rate should do the trick, in theory. That will not be looked into here but in some depth in Chapter 14.

Demand Shifts with Various Sloped Supply Functions

An increase in demand, with a positive-sloped supply function, leads to an increase in price and quantity. What, however, happens if the supply function is vertical, or horizontal, or negative-sloped?

Figure 3.6.   **Demand Increases with Vertical and Horizontal Supply**

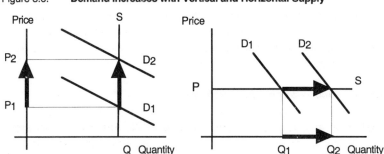

a. Vertical Supply   b. Horizontal Supply

The Vertical Supply Function

The case of the vertical supply function is shown in frame *a* of Figure 3.6. It is the supply function associated with land, the factor fixed in supply. It is also the supply function of Marshall's "market period"—a period during which there is inadequate time to change the quantity supplied. The vertical supply function also holds for the stock of items which can no longer be produced: pictures by Rembrandt and Van Gogh, Stradivarius violins, antiques, classic cars, and the like. When demand increases in a fixed supply market, the only effect is to increase price. Price, in this case, cannot be an incentive to increase the quantity supplied. It serves only as a pure rationing device.

The supply function of rental housing during the span of several years is essentially vertical. This is a basic reason for rental housing being the most popular candidate for price controls in many parts of the world. On the one hand increases in demand largely cause increases in rent with little increase in the quantity supplied for a considerable period of time. On the other hand, the negative effects of controlling rents on the production of housing are not felt for many years since annual residential housing construction tends to add a very small percent to the overall stock. "Rent control," by the way, does not generally mean that rents are fixed at a certain dollar value. It tends to mean that the increase in rent is limited by a rent control bureaucracy following a set of administrative guidelines.

The Horizontal Supply Function

The case of the horizontal supply function is shown in frame *b* of Figure 3.6, above. It is the supply function which is most familiar to buyers, the case of the sticker, posted, or catalog price with the seller holding to that price. With this supply function, an increase in demand brings forth an increase in the quantity supplied and vice versa. Price is unchanged and cannot serve as a signal or incentive to increase the rate of production. The signal which producers respond to is quantity demanded. Buy more bread and the grocer will see to it that more bread is available for sale.

The Negative-Sloping Supply Function

Two negative-sloping supply functions are shown in Figure 3.7. The supply function in frame a is more vertical than the demand function. The demand curve D_1D_1 and that of supply SS yield a price and quantity of P_1 and Q_1. If demand is increased from D_1D_1 to D_2D_2, following Walras, a shortage is created; the shortage drives the price up to P_2 and with the negative-sloped supply function, the equilibrium quantity decreases to Q_2.

Try Marshall's reasoning on this case. As he saw it, the increase in demand increased the demand price so that it was higher than the supply price at Q_1. This should stimulate an increase in the rate of production—but that would cause a movement down the negative-sloped demand function and away from equilibrium. Marshall's analysis does not work if the negative slope of the supply function is less than that of the demand function.

In frame b the negative-sloped supply function is less vertical than the demand function. Again, the initial functions yield price P_1 and quantity Q_1. If demand is increased from D_1D_1 to D_2D_2, according to our conventional Walrasian reasoning, the excess demand or shortage at P_1 should cause the price to increase—but that would drive it away from equilibrium. Try Marshall's approach. The increase in demand makes the demand price greater than the supply price—a signal to increase production. That leads the market to an equilibrium involving a decrease in price and an increase in quantity.

Should sleep be lost about he problem of equilibration posed by the negative-sloped supply function? Are there cases in which the market response to a shift in demand increasingly caused disequilibrium? Not to my knowledge. Moreover, the cases of negative-sloped supply functions are generally associated with firm-set rather than market-set prices, and once the price is set the supply function becomes horizontal, making the negative-sloped supply function a planning function.

Examples of Negative-Sloping Supply Functions

There are a number of common examples of negative-sloping supply functions. The overall supply of labor may be backward-bending. Instead of higher wages bringing forth more labor, it tends to bring forth less. The university at which I teach seems to have a negative-sloping supply function. As enrollments decline, tuition is raised to cover costs, which are largely fixed. Stockbrokers faced with

Figure 3.7. **Demand Shifts with Negative-Sloping Supply Functions**

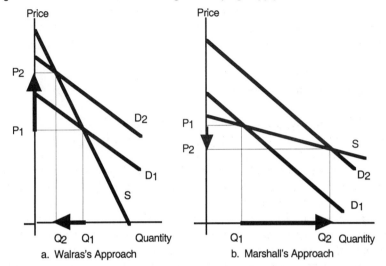

a. Walras's Approach   b. Marshall's Approach

declining sales, some years ago, attempted to increase their commission schedules. A local water company asked its customers to conserve water. They did. This decreased revenues, and the water company reacted by increasing its price schedule. Physicians and surgeons with fewer visits per day sometimes increase their fees or the procedures performed on a patient to maintain their income level. I suspect that there are numerous other examples of backward-bending supply functions. Note that the negative-sloped functions mentioned above tend to be based on costs or income.

Supply Functions and Time Horizons: Marshall's Schema

Alfred Marshall broke time into three conceptual periods: the market, the short-run, and the long-run period. The shapes of the associated supply functions are shown in Figure 3.8.

> *The market-period* is a period of time during which no additional production can be accomplished.

Whatever quantity has been brought to market is there irrespective of price. The market-period supply function is vertical, of zero elasticity. It is shown in frame *a*. Where prices are set by markets, the relevant supply function is the market supply function.

> *The short-run* is a period long enough to allow the rate of production to be varied but not long enough to change the current size of the producing unit, which is fixed.

Figure 3.8.   **Marshall's Time Periods: Market, Short Run, and Long Run**

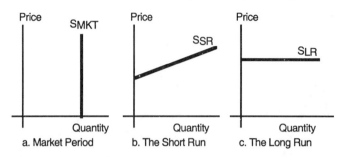

The short-run supply function is shown in frame *b*. The positive-slope may be due to the law of diminishing marginal returns. As more variable factors are employed to increase the rate of production, fixed factors of production become increasingly scarce. This drives down the marginal productivity of the variable factors increasing the cost of marginal units of production and the price required to cover such costs. For producers who are price takers, the short-run supply functions should be used to determine the rate of production.

> *The long-run* is a period of time sufficiently long to allow changes in all aspects of production.

New plants can be built and stocked with the latest state-of-the-art equipment. The organization of work can be altered to obtain the highest efficiency. People with the new required skills can be sought and employed.

The long-run supply is generally shown as horizontal at a price which just covers all the costs of production, including the opportunity cost of capital. It is generally assumed that the long-run function yields the lowest per unit or average cost of production possible. The long-run supply function is shown in frame *c*. It has no direct role in price determination nor in the determination of the rate of production.

Three matters are noteworthy: (1) Price is exclusively set in the market period. (2) Production is exclusively performed in the short-run period. (3) The long-run is the period in which planning for new plant and equipment takes place. Its supply function tends to be shown as infinitely elastic at a price equal to minimum average cost, the minimum price required for sustainable production. Were the price higher, economic profits would be experienced and the industry would expand until the minimum average cost price is attained. Were the price lower, the industry would contract until the long-run price is again attained. An implied assumption is that in the long-run all firms in a market have the same minimum average cost and, seemingly, cost-saving productivity advances are countered by factor price increases.

Figure 3.9.   **The Converging Cobweb**

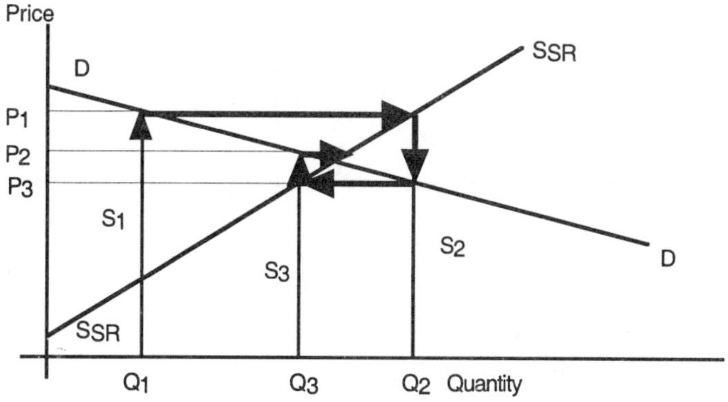

The Cobweb Model and Economic Irrationality

The cobweb model applies Marshall's vertical market-period supply function and positive-sloped short-run supply function to markets in which there is considerable time between the decision to produce a certain quantity of a product and the completion of its production. The model has been applied to the markets for hogs and engineers. It takes about three to four years to produce a market-ready hog and four or five to produce a market-ready engineer. Demand is assumed to be stable in this model.

Three kinds of cobwebs are presented: A converging cobweb, a non-converging cobweb, and a diverging cobweb.

A Converging Cobweb

In Figure 3.9 the initial market supply function is S_1. It and the demand function DD establish the price, P_1, which is the expected price for the next period. At that price, the short-run supply function, $S_{SR}S_{SR}$, specifies the quantity which should be produced. (Follow the arrow from the initial equilibrium point to the short-run function.) Some years later this manifests itself in the market supply of S_2, which, with the demand function, yields the lower price P_2. At that lower price, the short-run supply function specifies that the market supply be lowered to S_3. When that low supply is marketed, the price increases to P_3, again, some years later. If you follow the cobweb, you can see that over the course of years, the price comes closer to that of equilibrium between the demand function and the short-run supply function. This convergence occurs only because the absolute magnitude of the slope of the supply function in this figure is greater than that of the demand function.

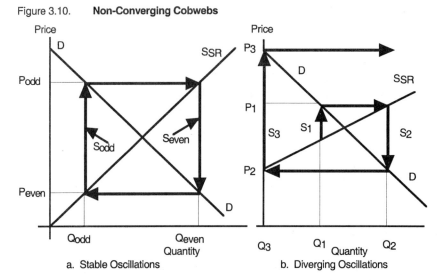

Figure 3.10. **Non-Converging Cobwebs**

a. Stable Oscillations

b. Diverging Oscillations

Non-Converging Cobwebs

Two non-converging cobweb models are shown in Figure 3.10. In frame *a* the absolute magnitudes of the slopes of the short-run supply function and the demand function are equal. In this case stable oscillations occur forever. The same high price, P_{odd}, and low quantity, Q_{odd}, arise from all odd-period supply functions, S_1, S_3, S_5, and so on. And the same low price, P_{even}, and high quantity, Q_{even}, accompany all even-period market supply functions, S_2, S_4, S_6, and so on. Compared to equilibrium the quantity supplied is either lower and the price higher or the quantity supplied is higher and price lower.

The case of the diverging cobweb is shown in frame *b*. It arises when the absolute magnitude of the slope of the supply function is less than that of the demand function. Initially the market-period supply function, S_1, interacts with the stable demand function to give price, P_1. Subsequent prices and quantities increasingly diverge from the equilibrium as the variation in price from period to period continues to increase.

The Issue of Rationality

The title of this section implies that there is some connection between the cobweb model and economic irrationality and that requires some explanation.

> *Rational economic decision-makers* use past experience and current information in making predictions about the future.

That is rather the opposite of the action of producers in the cobweb model. When the current price is relatively high, decision-makers continually predict that the future price will be high, despite the fact that experience shows that it will be just the opposite. Conversely, when the current price is low the continual prediction is for a low future price even though price always turns out to be high. The model is a wonderful example of *not* learning from past experience, and that is irrational.

The question then is, does actual market behavior conform to the cobweb model? Daniel B. Suits reports that it does in the case of the U.S. market for hogs:

> Eight price peaks can be shown in the nearly 30-year period shown.... This works out to an average of three to four years to cycle from high to low prices and back again. The relatively long period of this cobweb cycle reflects the time required for farmers to build up the herd of brood-sows ...and the additional time that must elapse after the sows are bred before mature hogs are ready for market (1982, p. 20).

Data on the market for hogs has been chosen with malice aforethought. John Muth who authored *the* famous article on rational expectations used the market for hogs to support his hypothesis that economic decision-makers act rationally. But the patternless price data he alludes to are from the United Kingdom rather than the United States. Ours conforms to the irrationality of the cobweb model.

Attaining Equilibrium Through Quantity Changes

Adam Smith observed that "in many places the money price of labour remains uniformly the same sometimes for half a century together" (1937 [1776], p. 78). Recent research shows that firms producing half of our gross domestic product vary their prices once a year or less. (See the findings of Alan S. Blinder on this in Chapter 10.) Price is of limited variability—it is sticky.

With price fixed much of the time, the product supply function is horizontal much of the time and the task of market-clearing equilibration is accomplished by varying the quantity supplied to conform to variations in the quantity demanded. Figure 3.11 shows the horizontal constant-price supply function and a few demand functions. As demand increases from low to medium to high, the quantities supplied increase from Q_{LO} to Q_M to Q_{HI}. The role of price in the case of the horizontal supply function is neutered. It does not serve as the signal to change the rate of production.

The most important signal and incentive to change the rate of production is the quantity demanded, the signal which largely determines the allocation of resources. The quantity system *rather than the* price system is the workhorse of the economy. The quantity system tends to be continually active while the price system only works sporadically.

Note that the equilibrium process associated with the horizontal supply function puts the entire stress of demand shifts on quantity produced and, indirectly, on employment. No cushioning is afforded by change in the product price.

Figure 3.11.   **Quantity Demanded as the Determinant of the Quantity Supplied**

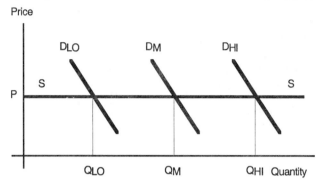

Shifts and the Feedback Process

Take the case of the markets for goods which are substitutes such as butter and margarine. Assume that the supply of milk and then that of butter increases. As a result of this the price of butter decreases, more butter is consumed, and the demand for its substitute, margarine, decreases. Carrying the analysis further, the decline in the demand for margarine lowers its price and that decreases the demand for butter, and so forth.

 Thus, the decrease in the price of butter feeds into the market for margarine and causes its price to decline; this feeds back into the market for butter causing its price to decline; and the process continues. Have no fear that such a process would drive the price of substitutes to zero. The feedback loop appears to be highly damped or attenuated so that, for example, a 10 percent decrease in the price of butter might experience subsequent decreases of one-tenth that of the previous decrease: 10, 1, 0.1, 0.01 percent and so forth. Adding up these numbers indicates that the feedback process would cause the initial 10 percent decrease in the price of butter to end up with a larger decrease, here conveniently of 11.1111 percent.

Equilibria with Buyers Paying and Sellers Receiving Different Sums

In all the examples thus far, at equilibrium the price paid by buyers equals that received by sellers. But that is frequently *not* the case. The two parties to an exchange respond to different prices where there is a tax or a tariff on a product anin cases in which there are transaction costs. These matters are handled in turn.

Figure 3.12.   **The Incidence of a Specific Tax**

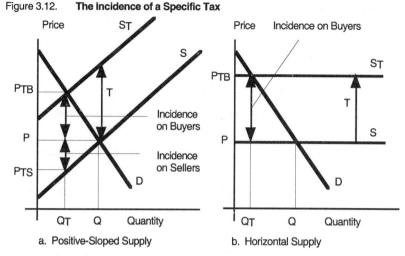

a. Positive-Sloped Supply   b. Horizontal Supply

Taxes or Tariffs on Goods and Services

The existence of taxes or tariffs implies that the buyer is paying a higher price than the seller is receiving with the government pocketing the difference. How this works out, particularly with respect to *incidence*, is shown for two common kinds of tax: a *specific* and an *ad valorem tax*.

> *A specific tax* is an involuntary payment to the government of a fixed amount per unit. A 20 cents tax on a pack of 20 cigarettes, irrespective of its price, exemplifies a specific or per-unit tax.

With a 10 percent tax on clothing the ad valorem tax on a $100 suit would be $10; on a $200 suit it would be $20.

> *An ad valorem tax* is an involuntary payment to government which is a designated percentage of the value (i.e., price) of a covered product.

Tariffs, taxes levied on imports, are also specific or ad valorem.

The Effects of a Specific Tax

The effects of a specific tax are presented for two cases shown in Figure 3.12. In frame *a* the supply function is positive and the demand function negative-sloped. Initially, the supply function is *SS* and the equilibrium price and quantity are P and Q. Then the government imposes a specific tax of T cents per bushel to be paid by the seller. This shifts the supply function upward by the amount of the per-unit tax, T, namely, from SS to $S_T S_T$. The shift is of this magnitude because after the firm pays the tax, it is right back on its original supply function.

Of special interest is the incidence of the tax.

> *The incidence of a tax on a buyer* is the amount the price increases to the buyer as a result of the tax.

> *The incidence of a tax to a seller* is the amount the price decreases to the seller after payment of the tax.

Note that under *incidence* no consideration is given to the decrease in the equilibrium quantity resulting from the tax.

Return to frame *a* of Figure 3.12 to examine the incidence of tax on a bushel of whatevers. As a result of the tax, the price to the buyer increases from P to P_{TB}. That, $P_{TB} - P$, is the tax incidence on them. For the seller the incidence is the price drop from P to P_{TS}, as shown.

In frame *b* can be found the incidence of the specific tax, T, for the case of a horizontal supply function. The before tax equilibrium is at price P and quantity Q. The imposition of the tax again shifts the supply function up by the amount of the tax. In this case the entire incidence falls upon the shoulders of buyers. That sellers pay none of the tax should come as no surprise since the horizontal supply function at P implies that nothing will be produced and sold at any price lower than P.

The bottom line on tax incidence is this: The greater the inelasticity of a function relative to the other function, the greater is its share of the burden of a specific tax.

The Effects of an Ad Valorem Tax

The effects of an ad valorem tax are similar to the case of the specific tax. This can be illustrated with the assistance of Figure 3.13. The case chosen is one in which there is a 50 percent tax on cigarettes with the tax paid by the seller. We first assume (unrealistically) that the price of cigarettes is set by the market supply and demand functions. The pre-tax functions, SS and DD yield a price of P and a rate of consumption, sales, and production of Q. Now impose the 50 percent ad valorem tax. At any given quantity, the price on the supply function inclusive of the tax, S_T, is 50 percent higher than on the pretax function, SS. Again the incidence on buyers is $P_T - P$ and $P - (P_T - T)$ or $T - (P_T - P)$ is the incidence on sellers.

Figure 3.13.   **The Incidence of an Ad Valorem Tax**

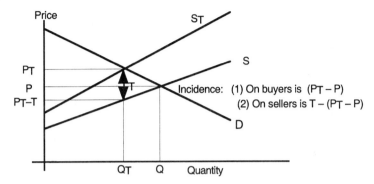

Transaction Costs

Transaction costs also cause buyers to pay and sellers to receive different prices at equilibrium:

> *Transaction costs* are costs incurred by the process of exchange in addition to the price paid for a product.

These costs, scrutinized in Chapter 6, are only mentioned in passing here. Typical of the transaction costs of buyers are the opportunity cost of their time and the transportation costs used in making a purchase. Common costs of sellers are shipping and handling costs. Transaction costs experienced by buyers shift their demand functions downward by the magnitude of the per-unit cost. Transaction costs realized by sellers shift their supply functions upward by the magnitude of the per-unit cost. The reasoning for the form of these shifts is the same as that found above in the case of specific taxes.

Note the ambiguity of the effect of transaction costs on price. They lower demand and by so-doing tend to *lower price* and quantity. They also lower supply and this tends to *increase price* and lower quantity. With one shift lowering price and the other increasing it, the effect of transaction costs on price is theoretically unknown. Estimates of the pre- and post-transaction costs supply and demand functions are required to estimate the sign and magnitude of the price change.

Attaining Equilibrium When a Fraction of Supply and Demand is Actively Marketed

In a number of important markets, a fraction, often a very small fraction, of the overall supply and demand is on the market at any given time. This is true, for example, in the case of the markets for stocks, bonds, real estate, and labor services. Assume that all buyers and sellers, whether active in the market or not, are

Figure 3.14.   **Supply and Demand: On the Market and Total**

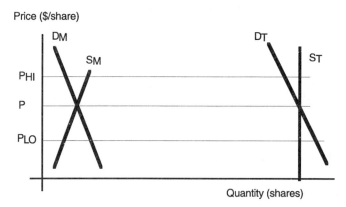

aware of the market price. Then the price set by the fraction of buyers and sellers on the market will be identical with that which would have been set by the equilibration of the demand and supply functions of all buyers and sellers.

The reason that both the on-the-market portion and total supply and demand functions yield the same equilibrium price can be explained with the help of Figure 3.14. At the left of this figure are the market supply and demand functions, S_MS_M and D_MD_M. At the right are the total functions, S_TS_T and D_TD_T.

Consider the overall functions first. We show the supply function to be vertical or of zero elasticity, a condition which accurately portrays the short-run supply of the stock of Apple Computer. If it and the overall demand function were on the market, they would establish a price of P. The portion of the total functions on the market are shown as yielding the same price as the total functions. Why is that? Assume that the price is P_{LO}, which is less than the equilibrium price. At that price the total functions shows that the quantity demanded exceeds that supplied. This excess demand goes to the market to buy shares of Apple at P_{LO}—a price they consider to be less than a share's true value. This tends to drive the price up until it reaches its equilibrium value, P. There is then no excess total demand to manifest itself in excess market demand.

Were the price P_{HI}, there would be an excess total supply as more shareholders than not believe that it is profitable to sell their shares. This is manifest as excess supply on the market, which would tend to drive the price of a share of Apple down until a common equilibrium is reached.

Dynamic Models of Equilibration

Under comparative statics we go from one equilibrium to another with no cognizance taken of the amount of time this process involves. This is fine for auction markets—markets in which price seems to be continually changing and going from one equilibrium to another. But in non-auction markets price tends to be slow to change despite changes in supply, demand, or both. This matter is confronted in dynamic models.

> *Dynamic economic models* are those in which time is an explicit part of the model.

The most common way of introducing the dynamic of time into a model is through the use of lagged variables.

> *A lagged variable* is one which refers to past circumstances. An occurrence in a given period may be modeled as a function of circumstances in a previous period or set of periods.

Here are some examples which could be modeled with lagged variables: (1) My consumption spending in this period is a function of my income in the previous period. If my income increases, in a subsequent period I will buy a new printer—if I have the courage to ask my wife and she agrees. (2) A change in the price of printers in this period reflects a change in demand in a previous period; Apple is now giving rebates. (3) The number of new engineers brought to market in this period is an increasing function of the job vacancies in engineering N periods ago.

Another way of modeling change over time is through the use of a time constant.

> *A time constant* is a measure of the amount of time it takes a variable to go from one state to another—as from one equilibrium to another.

My favorite example of the use of a time constant can be found in a RAND study of the engineering shortage of the 1950s. The model was developed by William Capron and Kenneth Arrow. Their Department of Defense–supported work argued that findings of Blank and Stigler could have been wrong because they did not recognize the time delay involved in the response of engineering salaries to the shortage of engineers. The Capron-Arrow model had the rate of change of the price of engineering services, dP/dt, as an increasing function of the size of the shortage, X, and a decreasing function of the time constant, T: $dP/dt = X/T$. The larger the time constant, T, the slower the rate of change of engineering salaries, P, and the longer the persistence of the shortage.

Disequilibrium

With a shortage of a given magnitude relative to the quantity supplied or demanded, equilibrium can be reached almost instantaneously or, alternatively, over the course of a number of years. Those disequilibria which are long lasting are problematic. They are considered briefly with respect to labor, manufacturing capacity, and commercial space.

Surpluses and Shortages of Labor

Disequilibrium in the labor market is far greater than appears on the surface. First of all, there are the unemployed. Add to these surplus workers, discouraged workers—workers who want jobs but have given up searching for them. In addition there are many part-time workers who want to work full time—adjuncts, for example, who passionately desire full-time faculty positions. Finally, many full-time workers are also in disequilibrium. Some of them would like to work more and others fewer hours per week. The percentage of workers in disequilibrium typically amounts to about 40 percent of the labor force—a matter detailed in Chapter 13.

Shortages of registered nurses were reported for roughly half a dozen years as growth in demand, fueled by an aging population, ran ahead of growth in supply. The pay of nurses never resolved the problem of the shortage. It was, however, "solved" by the stroke of a pen. A major advisory organization to health insurers recommended that hospital stay coverage be made a fraction of what it had been. Instead of five days in the hospital for the birth of a child, for example, mother and child were discharged after twenty-four hours. The new set of hospital-stay dictates turned the shortage of nurses into a significant surplus.

Surplus Manufacturing Facilities

Endemic surpluses of capital, of structures and equipment, exist in manufacturing—at least from the perspective of economic rationality. Factories tend to be in operation about 54 hours of the 168 hours of the week. They are unemployed or in surplus on the average 114 hours a week or 68 percent of the time.

My surplus capital contention fits in with a recent (1992) decision of the Ford Motor Company, which holds a historic place in the quest for productive efficiency. The company announced that by going from two to three shifts in their Lords-town, Ohio, plant, they would be able to close down another plant and, thereby, cut their costs of production. The plant being closed has all along represented surplus capital.

Surplus Commercial Space

David Dunlap's report on surplus commercial space amazed me:

> Some 56.7 million square feet of space are now available in Manhattan.... That is as much space as in the entire office market of San Francisco. And it represents an increase of 5.5 million square feet ... from this time last summer (1991, Sec. 10, p. 1).

This disequilibrium is not a Manhattan malady. Large amounts of surplus commercial space can be found in many metropolitan and suburban areas.

Seller-Set Prices

Much of the above standard fair gives the impression that we live in an economy in which the institution which brings many buyers and many sellers together is the market and that it yields a single price for all. Stocks and bonds aside, what products have you ever bought on such a market? A large majority of the product prices seen by consumer, business, and government buyers—by you and me—are set by producers or sellers. Just as the firm has triumphed over the market in the realm of production and the allocation of resources (see Chapter 9) it has also triumphed over the market in price-setting and bringing buyers and the seller together. The attenuated power of the market has been matched, to a large extent, by the reduction in the prevalence of the law of one price.

Sellers have acquired the market's price-setting role; buyers its quantity-setting role. In general, the floor on price-setting is cost. The ceiling is limited by the extent of competition and potential competition, the homogeneity of a product, the existence of substitutes,and to a lesser extent, by product demand. Occasionally the threat of government intervention dampens the price setting fevers of firms and industries. (See Chapter 10 for more on price setting and price behavior.)

Why are market set prices so uncommon in our economy? Allow me to hazard a guess. Organized markets are concentrated in the areas of what I call land-based products: agricultural products, forest products, minerals, and metals. The products of these industries are homogeneous or can be placed in homogeneous groupings. And homogeneity is a necessity for the conventional price-setting market. Over the years land-based industries' share of national production decreased sharply as the economy progressed from a focus on agriculture, to manufacturing, to services and now, perhaps, information systems. The rise has been in industries whose products cannot be sold in organized markets because they are substantially differentiated.

It is hard to specify what equilibrium is in a system in which firms set sticky prices. This means that the firm has a horizontal supply function which tends to stick where it is—typically for a year. Where on that supply function is the firm in equilibrium? Back off—where we have markets setting prices there is market equilibrium but is no such thing as "firm equilibrium." Nor is there when the firm is the price-setter. With the loss of the market as price-quantity setter, we have lost not only the the law of one price but an equilibrium of significance. No longer does a shortage drive the price up until there is no shortage; nor does a surplus drive the price down until there is no surplus. The equilibrium process is largely nonexistent in the microeconomy.

Summary

Price plays such a major role in the neoclassical paradigm that microeconomics is frequently called price theory. Price is the only variable economic decision-makers need know—at least in competitive markets. Price relative to cost affords the incentive or disincentive to engage in a particular activity. And the relative price of substitutable and complementary resources helps determine the extent of their employment.

The market is the basic institution since it establishes the magnitude of price and, along with it, the quantity bought and sold at that price: It determines the allocation of scarce resources. In other words, it is the institution which plays a central role in answer the basic questions of what to produce, how, and to whom the production goes. And market forces lead to equilibrium, the solution to the problems of shortages and surpluses. Note that shortages may be painful to a few or to many and surpluses imply the waste of scarce resources.

Markets also shield us from reality. In obtaining goods and services at the lowest price found, we may be buying the product of badly treated workers, including women and children.

Textbooks stress the equilibration process of Adam Smith and Leon Walras under which quantity differences, shortages and surpluses, lead to price changes and the equality between quantities demanded and supplied. Alfred Marshall saw it the other way around, the difference between the supply and demand price leading to quantity changes and the equality between the demand and supply price. Both conform to the law of one price. Marshall's model seems applicable to auction markets; Walras's to others.

Comparative statics is the "meat and potatoes" of microeconomic analysis. It involves starting from equilibrium, shifting supply, or demand, or both, and going to a new equilibrium. Comparisons are frequently made of price and quantity at the two or more equilibria. Price increases

Time is intrusive in all human action. Marshall recognized this in differentiating between the supply functions of the market, short-run, and long-run periods. Price is set in the market period and the rate of production in the short-run period. The basic horizontal long-run supply function can be considered to be a crude long-run price predictor. At higher prices industry expansion would drive the price down; at lower prices, exits from the industry would drive the price up. More importantly, the long-run is the period in which plans are made and carried out with respect to the modernization of plant, equipment, and methods of production.

The cobweb model applies Marshall's market and short-run supply functions, in conjunction with a fixed demand function, to markets with long production periods—hogs and engineers make good examples. The model has, for example, low market prices leading to the expectation of low future prices. That low expected price leads producers to provide a relatively small supply. But a small supply with fixed demand yields a high market price. The high price leads to the expectation of high future price. Supply, accordingly becomes high and the resulting price is low. Thus, when the expectation is for a low price, it ends up high, and when the expectation is for a high price it ends up low. No learning takes place as perverse guesses are perpetuated. The model poses a wonderful example of economic irrationality.

United States data on hog prices conforms with irrationality—but that is not necessarily so. It could be that when prices are low hog farmers are driven from the industry and those remaining find the previous rate of production unaffordable. One would have to examine the market more closely to determine the extent to which the alternative views describe the actual practice of hog farmers.

Prices set by sellers, administered prices, are far more common than prices set by markets. As long as a particular price is maintained, the supply function is horizontal. Moreover, seller-set prices change, on the average, only once a year. Equilibrium is attained by varying the quantity supplied to meet variations in the quantity demanded. During the period over which price-setters keep it constant, price plays no role in the process of equilibration and in that of allocating resources. It is generally a variable with more hype than substance.

Auction markets seem to continually seek equilibrium. The process is much, much slower in other markets such as those for labor and those involving long periods of production. Models of these markets must take cognizance of this. A popular way is to use lagged variables such that, for example, quantity produced in this period is a function of circumstances in some prior period or periods. The percentage of college students graduating with engineering majors this year, for example, is a function of the state of that market four and five years ago—at least in part.

Most prices are actually set by sellers with buyers determining the quantity demanded and, in effect, the quantities produced and supplied. With prices changing, on the average once a year or less, the quantity system serves as the workhorse of the economy. Moreover, the victory of firms over markets as the price-setting-institution implies both the loss of of the law of one price and price as a cushion responding to demand increases and decreases.

Finally, there is the extensive existence of disequilibrium. In labor markets its most troubling manifestation is unemployment. But capital facilities and equipments are also frequently in surplus. Capital is more unused than used in manufacturing. Amounts of surplus commercial space are sometimes so large that it takes years to fill them. And worldwide surplus capital is not uncommon. The facilities in some key industries can provide supplies far in excess of demand. This is true, for example, with respect to industries which produce automobiles and trucks, steel, semiconductors, a number of electronic products, textiles, and garments. All of this shows that the process of attaining equilibrium is often of substantial complexity.

Questions on Chapter 3

1. Explain the single source of market price increases according to Walras. According to Marshall. Draw two graphs of supply and demand indicating these alternative views of disequilibrium.

2. What are some examples of negative-sloping supply functions? Explain why the supply function of your college or university might be negative-sloping.

3. Why are shortages "a bad thing" and modest surpluses "a good thing"?

4. Draw the graphs of a converging cobweb model. Why can it be applied to the market for hogs and new engineers? Why does it imply economic irrationality? The model has a low future supply arising from a low current price. What alternative reason might cause low numbers of hogs to be raised when the price is relatively low?

5. Assume that a firm with 100 engineers would like to hire 5 more but cannot find people with the desired qualifications. Why is the firm nonetheless reluctant to raise the wage, for example by 5 percent, in order to obtain the additional personnel desired?

6. Write an equation in which the quantity of hogs brought to market in this period is a function of the price of hogs four years ago.

7. Assume that a state imposes a sales tax of T on automobiles. Show and explain the effect of this on the demand function.

CHAPTER FOUR

Models of Consumer Behavior

Neoclassical economists, consciously or not, tend to espouse utilitarian philosophy which contends that happiness is the primary goal of human existence. In line with this, the neoclassical paradigm postulates that the consumer is the economic sovereign: The economy exists to serve his or her hedonism. Jeremy Bentham, an outstanding utilitarian philosopher and contemporary of Adam Smith, started the development of a "felicific calculus," which requires the measurement of happiness as units of pleasure net those of pain. We have not as yet been able to perform this measurement—but attempts have been made along the way.

We all consume both goods and services and consideration of their relationship is first discussed. Both rich and poor are constrained by the amount of money available for spending during some period of time—we are all constrained by our budgets. Budget lines are a handy tool, and that is the next matter presented. This is followed by models of consumer behavior: revealed preference, marginal utility analysis, indifference curve analysis, and the expected utility model. The last comes closest to developing the cardinal measurements of utility required by the "felicific calculus." Subsequent to the presentation of each model and at the end some of their important imperfections are discussed.

Two important issues regarding models of consumer behavior should be kept in mind: To what extent does any given model explain the behavior of actual consumers—your behavior, for example? And to what extent does it make more profound your understanding of consumer demand?

The Connection Between Goods and Services

Are goods and services really that different? The late Kenneth Boulding, a wonderfully profound economist, has answered that question in the negative. Boulding points out that the pleasure drawn from goods is through the services which

Figure 4.1.   **Two Budget Lines**

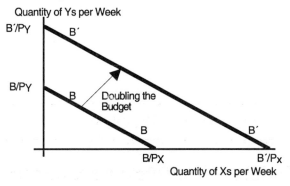

they render. Our car yields transportation services as does the bus ride to campus. Food yields nutritional services with various attached pleasures or displeasures. Records, tapes, CDs, video cassettes, films and the like yield a variety of services, entertainment and educational included. Goods are, in a sense, storage devices from which a flow of services can be drawn.

The Budget Line

The budget line or function is relevant to all models of consumer behavior and consequently warrants early consideration. It portrays the monetary limit to the spending of a consumer, rich or poor.

Assume that an individual has a budget equal to $\$B$ per week and that it is entirely spent on two goods, X and Y. That budget line is shown in Figure 4.1 and by the equation:

(1) $$B = P_XQ_X + P_YQ_Y$$

where P is the price and Q is the quantity purchased per week of the products subscripted. Solving the above equation for the quantity of Y, Q_y, yields the equation of a negatively-sloped straight budget line:

(2) $$Q_Y = (B/P_Y) - (P_X/P_Y)Q_X$$

Note that at the intercept with the Q_y axis, all of the budget is spent on product Y, and this allows the purchase of the number of units equal to the budget divided by the price of that product, P_y. A \$100-a-week budget and a price of \$5 per unit of Y would allow the purchase of 20 Ys per week. Note also that the mag-nitude of the slope of the budget line is the ratio of the price of X to the price of Y. Finally, the intercept of the budget line with the Q_x axis is the budget divided by the price of X, the number of Xs which could be bought with the entire budget.

Figure 4.2.   **Shift in the Budget Line via a Decrease in the Price of Y**

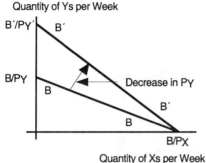

Quantity of Ys per Week

B'/PY'   B'

B/PY
   B

Decrease in PY

B'

B

B/PX

Quantity of Xs per Week

If by some stroke of fortune our weekly budget is doubled, the budget line would shift to $B'B'$ in Figure 4.1. This same shift would arise were the price of both of the two products halved. The shift resulting from the latter formulation is a manifestation of the income effect of a price decrease.

Were the price of only Y lowered, from Py to Py', more units of Y could be purchased with a given budget. And if the price of X remains constant, the budget line shifts clockwise as is shown in Figure 4.2.

There is, of course, a great deal of artificiality in specifying that a consumer expends her budget on just two products. That can be responded to in a number of ways: (1) One of the goods can be considered a specific good and the other a composite of all others. (2) Both goods can be composites with each having different characteristics covering all consumer products. One might be all consumer durables and the other all consumer non-durables or one could be all goods and the other all services. (3) We can forsake two dimensional graphs and go to multidimensional space with the dimensions of space equal to the number of different products demanded during a budget period. The budget line is then transformed into a budget plane in multidimensional space—a difficult-to-imagine construct. (4) The "budget" can be considered as a residual which allows only the purchase of some combination of a set of two additional goods such as beer and pretzels.

The Opportunity Cost of Consumption

Assume that an individual is considering an increase in the rate of consumption of hamburgers with the best alternative being hot dogs. The budget line is shown in Figure 4.3. Hamburgers are plotted on the X axis and hot dogs on the Y axis. The price of hamburgers is assumed to be twice that of hot dogs, so if all spending is on hamburgers, four a week can be consumed. If all is spent on hot dogs, deadly according to nutritionists, eight a week can be consumed. Initially four hot dogs and two hamburgers are consumed per week. Consider the

Figure 4.3.   **The Opportunity Cost of Hamburgers in Units of Hot Dogs**

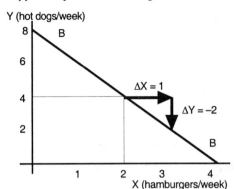

opportunity cost of increasing the rate of consumption of hamburgers by 1, $\Delta X=1$. This requires a decrease in the consumption of hot dogs by $\Delta Y=2$—the consumption foregone due to a unitary increase in the rate of consumption of hamburgers.

Revealed Preference and the Slope of the Demand Function

Nobel Laureate Paul A. Samuelson's revealed preference model shows that the individual's demand function, in the absence of an income effect, is either vertical or negative sloping. This is done through the use of the budget line. The graph of Figure 4.4 has the quantity of hot dogs per week on the vertical axis and the quantity of all other goods on the horizontal axis. The original budget line BB shows the various combinations of hot dogs and all other goods which can be purchased at the initial set of prices.

It is assumed here and in all other models that the individual's preference is to spend his entire budget to maximize consumption and satisfaction. This puts him at some point on the budget line. All combinations within the budget line, the cross-hatched area, are inferior. Assume that the set of goods chosen is that specified by point R on the budget line.

Wonder of wonders, the price of hot dogs falls and this yields the budget line $B'B'$. Samuelson then confines his interest to the substitution effect created by the hot dog price drop and *not* its effect on real income. This is realistic—for the great majority, a drop in the price of hot dogs will have no discernible income effect. The income effect caused by the decrease in the price of hot dogs is removed by the parallel downshift of the budget line $B'B'$ to $B''B''$ so that it goes through and includes the combination R. The final argument is that having revealed a preference for R as opposed to any point in the inferior cross-hatched region, a decision-maker will reject combinations of goods on the lower leg of $B''B''$. He will instead either choose the combination of goods defined by R or

Figure 4.4.   **Budget Lines and Revealed Preference**

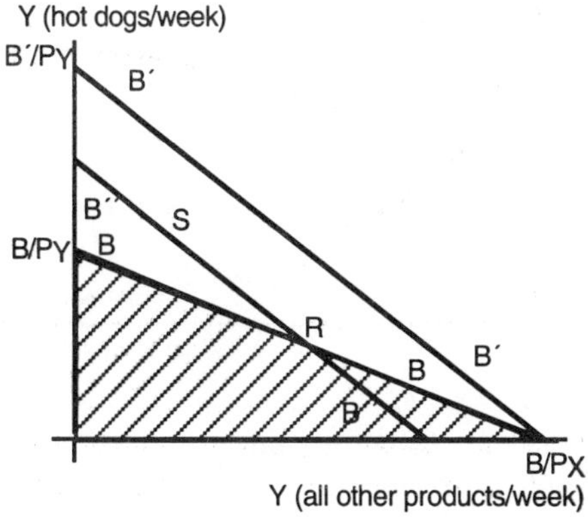

some other combination specified by a point on the upper leg of $B''B''$, for example, S.

If the choice, at the lower price of hot dogs, is for combination R, as before, then the individual's demand is of zero price elasticity—it is vertical over the specified price range. For all other choices, such as S, more hot dogs are bought at the lower price and a negative-sloped demand function is implied.

The Marginal Utility Model

The concept of marginal utility was discovered independently by three economists in the 1870s: Leon Walras in Switzerland, William Stanley Jevons in England, and Anton Menger in Austria. An understanding of the model requires knowing the concepts of utility or total utility, marginal utility, and the law of diminishing marginal utility.

Utility or Total Utility

The words *utility* and *total utility* are synonymous to economists, the former being the short form of the latter.

> *Utility* or *total utility, U or TU,* is the level of satisfaction obtained from a certain rate of consumption in a given social context.

Consider what you consumed last week. Included might be found the consumption of certain quantities of a variety of foods, beverages, clothing, residential housing services, educational services, medical services, recreational services, and so on. That consumption yielded a certain level of satisfaction or utility measured in units called "utiles." Were you able to consume more or better goods and services, your utility, satisfaction, or happiness would have been higher. Utility is an increasing function of the rate of consumption—in a static social context.

Figure 4.5. Total and Marginal Utility as a Function of the Rate of Consumption

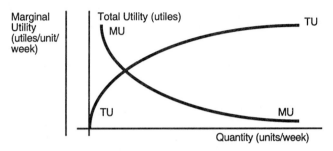

The generally assumed shape of the total utility function is shown in Figure 4.5. Several matters should be noted: (1) The curve represents the maximum utility attainable for the rates of consumption specified. (2) It shows the various *levels* of satisfaction obtainable from various *rates* of consumption. (3) The slope of the function declines with the rate of consumption. Equal increments in the rate of consumption yield decreasing increases in satisfaction. (4) Each individual has a unique utility function. (5) The total utility function never reaches a maximum. It is assumed that increases in the overall rate of consumption can always increase satisfaction, that wants are not satiable. (6) Finally, utility is a static function holding true in a given social context. A person categorized as "middle class" in woefully poor Bangladesh transported to a middle-class United States suburb, with the same consumption in both locales, would probably experience a substantial drop in satisfaction.

Marginal Utility

Marginal utility is important historically. It is *the* concept which started the so-called marginal revolution, the paradigm which succeeded classical economics. The revolution probably succeeded because, on the one hand, the dynamic classical system yielded long-run forecasts badly out of line with long-run facts. On the other hand, the marginal approach gave a central role to maximization and the ability to develop, logically and mathematically, an integrated economic system of great elegance, the neoclassical paradigm.

Jevons, whose presentation is followed here, presented two close concepts which relate to marginal utility. He called one of them the degree of utility or final degree of utility.

> *Degree of utility* or *final degree of utility* is the slope of the utility function, dTU/dQ, the ratio of the change in utility to the infinitely small change in consumption which brought it about. We call this *marginal utility*.

Jevons's related concept is incremental utility:

Incremental or *differential utility* is the change in utility, ΔTU or dTU, brought about by an incremental change in the rate of consumption. Incremental or differential utility is related to final or marginal utility as follows: $\Delta TU = MU \cdot \Delta Q$ or $dTU = MU \cdot dQ$.

Were it specified that the incremental change in the rate of consumption is unity, the numerical magnitude of marginal utility would equal that of incremental utility. The units of both would remain different as would their meaning. Assume that we are interested in the effect on utility of an increase in the rate of consumption of Ben and Jerry's vanilla ice cream by one pint per week. The slope of the utility function, marginal utility, might be six utiles per pint of ice cream per week. Incremental utility, which is that slope times the increment in quantity, here one pint of ice cream per week, is simply six utiles.

Economists tend to use the words *marginal utility* to cover both what is technically marginal utility and also what is technically incremental utility. This can be found, for example, in statements such as: "The increase in utility obtained from increasing the consumption of hot dogs from three to four a week is marginal utility." Although this is actually incremental utility, the meaning of the statement is not hard to understand.

The Law of Diminishing Marginal Utility

An important element in developing the logic of consumer satisfaction maximization is the law of diminishing marginal utility.

The law of diminishing marginal utility specifies that as the rate of consumption, Q, is increased, marginal utility decreases.

So the second pint of Ben and Jerry's ice cream per week will add less to satisfaction than the first. Note that my explanation is in terms of incremental rather than marginal utility. The technically correct wording in keeping with the law is that incremental increases in the consumption of ice cream tend to decrease the slope of the utility function, marginal utility.

Jevons explains declining marginal utility with a number of examples. One goes as follows:

> Let us imagine the whole quantity of food which a person consumes on an average during twenty-four hours to be divided into ten equal parts. If his food be reduced by the last part, he will suffer but little; if a second tenth be deficient, he will feel the want distinctly; ... with every subsequent subtraction of a tenth part his sufferings will be more and more serious, until at length he will be on the verge of starvation.... The meaning of these facts is that each increment of food is less necessary, or possesses less utility, than the previous one (1970[1871], pp. 105–6).

Then Jevons shows this graphically with marginal utility declining with the rate of consumption. And he points out that the area under the marginal utility curve is total utility: $\int MU\ dQ = \int (dU/dQ)\ dQ = U.$

The Budget Constraint

How much total utility an individual is able to attain is constrained by the money he has to spend during some specified period of time, by the individual's budget. That budget is the person's after-tax income which may be augmented by grants of money, borrowings, and past savings, and diminished by gifts, loans, and current savings. To equate budget and income assumes that inflows into income equal the outflows mentioned above.

Assuming that the individual's budget, B, is expended on n different goods and services during the budget period, the budget constraint is:

(3) $$B = P_1Q_1 + P_2Q_2 + ... + P_nQ_n$$

where P_i is the price of the ith good and Q_i is the quantity of it purchased during the budget period.

The Logic of the Condition-Defining Utility Maximization

How does the individual spend his budget so that total utility is maximized? The condition which must prevail is that for all goods and services the incremental utility per dollar is equal:

(4) $$\Delta TU_1/P_1 = \Delta TU_2/P_2 = ... = \Delta TU_n/P_n$$

At this equilibrium, no change in the combination of goods purchased can increase the satisfaction of the consumer.

Let us transform the utility maximization condition from the equation (4) form of incremental utility per dollar to the more common one of marginal utility per dollar. First, recall that marginal utility is the slope of the total utility curve: $MU = \Delta TU/\Delta Q.$ Solve for incremental utility and we have, $\Delta TU = MU \cdot \Delta Q.$ Now substitute for ΔTU in equation (4) $MU \cdot \Delta Q.$

(5) $$MU_1\Delta Q_1/P_1 = MU_2\Delta Q_2/P_2 = ... = MU_n\Delta Q_n/P_n$$

Set all ΔQs, all changes in the rate of consumption equal to one and we have:

(6) $$MU_1/P_1 = MU_2/P_2 = ... = MU_n/P_n$$

In this form it is seen that the utility maximizing consumer adjusts his purchases so that all items yield the same marginal utility per dollar.

The Mathematics of Utility Maximization

The logic of satisfaction being maximized when all marginal utilities per dollar are equal is handled mathematically here with the inclusion of the budget constraint. To simplify the problem it will be assumed that only two different goods are consumed and exhaust the individual's budget. The utility function is:

(7) $U = f(X, Y)$

where X and Y are the rates of consumption of the two goods. The budget constraint is:

(8) $B = P_X X + P_Y Y$

Most maximums in economic theory involve functions which increase, reach their peak or maximum, and then decline. At that peak the slope of the function is zero and the problem is essentially to find where that occurs, where the slope or the first derivative of the function equals zero. But in the case of consumption it is assumed that the individual's utility function never reaches a point beyond which it will start to decline. This complicates the mathematics of finding the condition at which utility is maximized.

There are two ways to handle this problem. Both involve, in effect, putting the budget equation/constraint into the utility function. This modification allows determination of the constrained maximum. The most straightforward way to confront this problem is to exploit what is called the *Lagrange multiplier*. Take the utility function, $U=f(X,Y)$, and subtract from it the Lagrange multiplier, μ, times the budget equation, with the budget equation arranged so that it equals zero:

(9) $Z = U = f(X, Y) - \mu[P_X X + PyY - B]$

where Z is the Lagrangean function and μ is the Lagrange multiplier. It can be shown that the slope of this function does reach zero where it is a maximum (or minimum). Accordingly, take the derivative of the Lagrangean with respect to the rate of consumption of X and then Y.

(10) $\partial Z/\partial X = \partial U/\partial X = \partial f/\partial X - \mu P_X$

(11) $\partial Z/\partial Y = \partial U/\partial Y = \partial f/\partial Y - \mu P_y$

Set the first of the two equations equal to zero:

(12) $\partial f/\partial X - \mu P_X = 0; \qquad \partial f/\partial Y - \mu P_y = 0$

But $\partial f/\partial X$ is the marginal utility of X and $\partial f/\partial Y$ is the marginal utility of Y. Solving for the Lagrange multiplier in both cases yield:

(13) $$\mu = MU_X/P_X = MU_Y/P_Y$$

Again it is found that a consumer maximizes utility when the combination of goods consumed during a given period is such that the marginal utility per dollar of one good equals that of all others.

Deriving the Negative-Sloped Demand Function

Demand functions, including those for individuals, are generally shown as negative-sloped. Such functions can be shown as an outgrowth of the marginal utility maximization condition and the law of diminishing returns.

Assume that the consumer had been in equilibrium and that subsequently the price of the first good, ice cream, is decreased. As a result:

(14) $$MU_1/P_1 > MU_2/P_2 = ... = MU_n/P_n$$

The reduction in the price of ice cream relative to all other prices brings about a two-step process. First, the *substitution effect* manifests itself in an increase in the consumption of the ice cream cones. This implies the existence of a negative-sloping demand for ice cream function: The price decreased and the rate of consumption increased. This takes place until equilibrium is again attained by means of the declining marginal utility of ice cream cones.

The second step confronts the *income effect*. If the demand for ice cream is inelastic, less money will be spent on ice cream at the lower price. To get back on the budget line a bit more consumption of all goods is required. If the demand is unity, no income effect is experienced and no second-step action is required. Finally, if the individual's demand for ice cream is in the elastic range, spending exceeds the budget and a decrease in the consumption of all goods is required.

While the income effect of a change in the price of ice cream cones would probably be negligible, it could be of substance for products consuming a substantial share of a consumer's budget.

Marginal Utility as a Demand Function

Were the marginal utility of money constant, the marginal utility function could serve as the individual's demand function. Assume this to be the case and consider how much ice cream someone would consume at the price of $2 for a double cone. Logically, the rate of ice cream consumption should be that at which the marginal utility of ice cream and the marginal utility of $2 were equal. And

Figure 4.6.   **From Marginal Utility to Consumer Surplus**

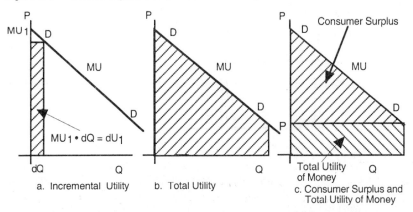

a. Incremental Utility   b. Total Utility   c. Consumer Surplus and
Total Utility of Money

if the price increased to $2.20 for that double cone, an individual bent on maxi-
mizing satisfaction would reduce the rate of consumption until the marginal
utility of the ice cream equaled the marginal utility of $2.20. The result of this
is that marginal utility could be denominated in dollars per cone and that this
function would then serve as the consumer's product demand function. The assumption that the marginal utility of money is constant is reasonable for goods
which comprise a very small part of the consumer's budget, but not for big-ticket items.

Consumer Surplus

Consumer surplus is a concept developed by Alfred Marshall to quantify the
difference between the satisfaction obtained from the consumption of a good and
the money paid for it:

> Consumer surplus is the excess of the total utility obtained from the con-
> sumption of a product over the total utility of the money used to pay for it
> (1961[1890], p. 830).

Marshall's concept assumes the constancy of the marginal utility of money—a
reasonable assumption if the spending involves a very small portion of the consumer's budget.
 Assume that the individual's demand for pizza is that shown in frame *b* of Figure 4.6 and that its price is *P*. At that price *Q* slices are consumed per week. The
utility gotten from this consumption is the area under the demand-marginal utility function–which is cross-hatched.
 Why does the area under the demand function equal the total utility obtained
from the consumption of pizza? This can be explained with the help of frame *a*.
Note the rectangular cross-hatched area which corresponds to the consumption of
one slice of pizza per week. The height of that rectangle is marginal utility,

Figure 4.7. The Binary Demand for Washing Machines

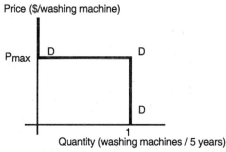

$MU_1 = dTU_1/dQ$, the rate of change of utility with respect to the consumption of pizza. The cross-hatched area, $MU_1 \cdot dQ$ is the increment of utility, dTU, obtained by consuming the first terribly small piece of pizza per week. Less incremental utility is obtained from each subsequent increment to consumption. In total they cover the area under the marginal utility function out to the consumption rate of Q slices per week, as can be seen in frame *b*. This cross-hatched area represents the total utility obtained from the consumption of pizza.

 In like manner the area under the price line going from *0* to Q represents the total utility of the money spent for pizza as is shown in frame *c*. Subtracting this loss of utility from the total utility obtained from eating pizza yields the consumer surplus shown.

Marginal Utility and the Binary Demand Function

We frequently demand either zero or one of a product: zero or one car, zero or one tuxedo, zero or one clothes washer, zero or one dryer, and so forth. This binary demand is shown in Figure 4.7 where the demand is for zero or one clothes washer. That function has been drawn in a peculiar way in that a portion of the function runs vertically along the price axis. That has been done to indicate that there is a maximum price the individual is willing to pay for the washing machine and that at any higher price no purchase will be made. At that maximum price and below it, one unit will be bought during the budget period. There is a sharp dichotomy in this common demand function.

 Assume that the maximum price, the marginal utility of the washing machine per dollar equals the marginal utility per dollar of all other goods purchased during the budget period. Assume further that the washing machine is bought at a sale for half the maximum price. As a consequence the consumer gets more marginal utility per dollar from the purchase of the washer than from all other products purchased. This disequilibrium signal can be thought of as causing the consumer to consider buying another washer but finding that it yields zero utility he returns to purchasing just one. This is the best that can be done with *lumpy* or indivisible products.

Figure 4.8.   **The Irrationality of a Fair Gamble**

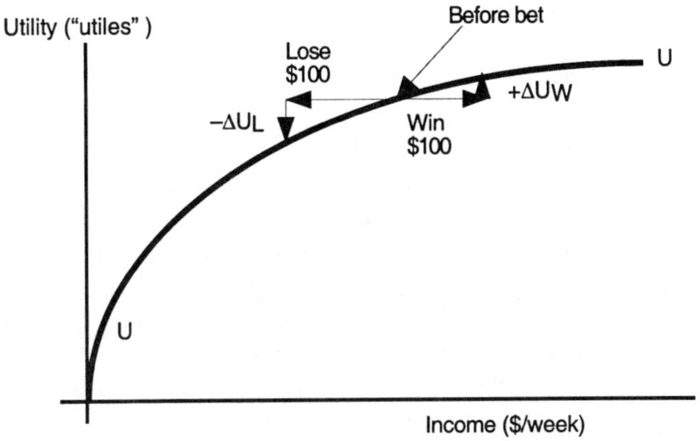

Is Gambling an Indication of Economic Irrationality?

If a person has a utility function which lives up to the law of diminishing marginal utility, gambling per se is an irrational activity. Figure 4.8 shows a utility function with declining slope—a function which corresponds to the law of diminishing marginal utility. It also illustrates the case of a fair gamble, here one in which winning or losing $100 is equally probable. As you should expect and can see, the incremental utility obtained from winning, ΔU_W, is less than that lost by losing, ΔU_L. With both events equally probable, an individual should expect that gambling will decrease his total utility. Formally put:

> *Expected value* is the average value of a set of events with each event weighted by the probability of its occurrence.

For the subject case the expected incremental utility, $E\{\Delta U\}$, equals $0.5\Delta U_W - 0.5\Delta U_L$. Since the expected loss of utility is greater than the expected gain in utility, the expected incremental utility is less than zero and betting is irrational.
 In addition, the great bulk of gambling is at unfair odds and this makes gamblers even more irrational. Typically, the house takes about 20 percent of a bet. As a result a gambler betting $100 would have an equal expectation of losing $100 or winning $80. The expected value of such a bet is –$10:

(15) $E\{V\} = 0.5\,(80) + 0.5\,(-100) = -10.$

This adds to the irrationality implicit in the declining-sloped utility function.
 There are two arguments defending the rationality of gamblers. First, there are people who just love to gamble. They are buying a service somewhat like the entertainment services bought by going to a horse race or basketball game. What they lose is the price they pay for the fun of gambling. Second, some distinguished neoclassical economists argue that the utility function of a gambler has

a range of increasing slope. Increasing marginal utility conveniently converts irrationality into rationality.

Is There a Diamond-Water Paradox?

We pay very little for water, a biological necessity, whereas relatively huge sums seem to be paid for diamonds, which are not. This paradox is unraveled by resorting to the concept of marginal utility. The argument is that the marginal utility of water is initially so high that it would be incalculable. But, if water is plentiful enough, more than the amount required for life is consumed and its marginal utility at the implied high rate of consumption becomes quite low. On the other hand, the great majority of us possess few, if any, diamonds and its marginal utility, the discounted sum of the marginal utility covering the period of ownership, can be very high.

Allow me to look at the diamond-water paradox in a somewhat different way. Assume that I drink eight glasses of water a day. Accordingly, a single glass of water hydrates me for three hours whereupon it yields no utility whatever. Allow the cost of the glass of water to be blank for a while. What is the cost of a $2,000 diamond during a three hour interval? If "diamonds are forever," its cost is the foregone interest on $2,000. At an annual interest rate of 6 percent, its opportunity cost is $120 a year. With 8,760 hours in a year (24 x 365), the hourly cost is $0.0137 and the cost for three hours is $0.0411. As a result, if the cost of a glass of water is in the neighborhood of $0.04, the budget-period cost of a $2,000 diamond and glass of water are comparable and there is no paradox. The larger issue is that care must be taken in comparing the price of perishables and durables.

Some Problems with the Marginal Utility Model of Consumer Behavior

Marginal utility analysis has a number of noteworthy problems, some of which are considered below.

The Problem of Complements

Recall that if the price of one product decreases relatively more of it and relatively less of *all other goods* are purchased. If the price of frankfurters decreases, more of them would be purchased and fewer hot dog buns, mustard, sauerkraut, catsup, and so on would be bought. That, of course, makes no sense.

A way around the problem posed by complements is to include them in a composite product, for example, a frankfurter, a roll, and the kind and amount of condiments used with them by a particular consumer. Then, if the price of a constituent of the composite good decreased, more of the composite good would be consumed.

The Problem of Durable Goods

Durable goods and services are here those which yield utilities beyond the current budget period. Alfred Marshall handled the durable-good problem by calculating the present value of the discounted flow of future differential utilities over the expected life of the good or service:

(16) $$PV(dU) = \int_{t=0}^{n} dU / (1+i)^t$$

where, dU is an increment in utility, $(1+i)^t$ is the discount rate for the future budget period t, and i is the rate of time preference—the interest rate used by an individual to discount the value of future benefits. Marshall assumes that a piano, the example he uses, would yield the same "element of happiness," dU, in each period. After getting the integral or summation of future discounted utilities, the consumer can divide it by the price of the piano to get marginal utility per dollar—for comparison with other marginal utilities per dollar.

For each durable good or service you have to (1) quantify the magnitude of the differential utilities for all the budget periods of its expected life; (2) decide what your time preference is; (3) discount the future utilities expected in each budget period; (4) add up these discounted utilities; and (5) divide the sum by price to obtain marginal utility per dollar for comparison with that of all other products. My guess is that even Nobel laureates in economic science gain utility by avoiding such calculations.

The Problem of Lumpiness

Assume that the marginal utility per dollar of a car, camera, stereo system, or piano is higher than that of all other goods. If it is, we should be buying more than one camera, or stereo, or piano. But the purchase of two yields a lower marginal utility per dollar than all other goods. You should buy an additional fraction of such goods—but you cannot.

The Quantification Problem

What we need to equate, based on the above profound discussion, is the marginal utility per dollar of a hot dog with the marginal utility per dollar of the piano. This means that the marginal utility of the hot dog and the piano have to be quantified to determine whether or not the ratio of their marginal utilities equals the ratio of their prices. But there is really no way to measure the future differential utility of a piano any more than you can measure the future differential utility of a marginal hot dog. Tastes, real income, products, health information,

Figure 4.9.   **An Indifference Curve and Its Declining Marginal Rate of Substitution**

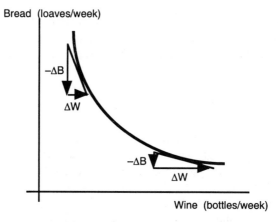

and the consumption of peers change over time, and all affect the satisfaction a product will yield in the future.

Indifference Curve Analysis

Indifference curve analysis is ordinal in character. In this model the consumer is only required to decide whether or not one set of goods is preferred to another set. With a given budget, the set preferred to all others is that which maximizes satisfaction. No cardinal measures are required—making this an easier task for consumers to perform than that required by marginal utility analysis.

The Indifference Curve

At the heart of the analysis is the indifference curve, an example of which appears in Figure 4.9.

> *The indifference curve* is the locus of points involving combinations of the rates of consumption of two products or sets of products, X and Y, with all points on the curve yielding the same level of satisfaction.

Since each point on the curve yields the same satisfaction as any other point, the individual consumer is indifferent to them and the various combinations of goods they represent. The indifference curve is generally postulated as being convex to the origin. The absolute magnitude of the slope of the indifference curve is declining. That slope is called the marginal rate of substitution.

> *The marginal rate of substitution* is the absolute value of the slope of the indifference curve at a point. It is the ratio of a change in the rate of consumption of Y, ΔY to a change in the consumption of X, ΔX.

Figure 4.10.   **An Indifference Map**

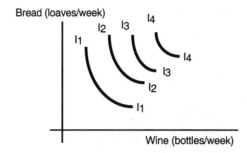

The reason for the declining absolute magnitude of the marginal rate of substitution is not hard to find. Consider this by starting at a point on the curve where the rate of consumption of bread is relatively high and that of wine relatively low. At such a point, the consumer would be willing to trade off a substantial amount of bread for an additional bottle of wine a week. As she moves southeast on the indifference curve, less and less bread and more and more wine is consumed, and the magnitude of the trade-off changes. The consumer is increasingly satiated with wine but misses her bread and is, therefore, willing to give up decreasing amounts of bread to get a unitary increase in the consumption of wine. Thus, the absolute magnitude of the slope of the indifference function, the marginal rate of substitution, declines as the rate of consumption of the product plotted on the horizontal axis increases.

The Indifference Map

The indifference map consists of a set of indifference curves with each curve representing a different level of satisfaction. Such a map is shown in Figure 4.10.The farther a curve is displaced from the origin, the higher is the individual's level of satisfaction. The highest satisfaction is obtained by consumption on indifference curve I_4I_4; the lowest on I_1I_1. How much more satisfaction is involved in going from one curve to another is irrelevant to the analysis.

Note that higher satisfaction arises from higher consumption. Thus, if the rate of consumption of wine is fixed, the higher the consumption of bread, the higher the level of satisfaction. While it is assumed that greater consumption in general adds to satisfaction, this is not the case with individual goods. If the consumption of bread keeps increasing marginal units will yield disutility and the more wine will be required to compensate for it. This describes a positive-sloped, irrational portion of the indifference function.

The Budget Constraint and Satisfaction Maximization

Few of us spend our budgets on just bread and wine these days. This is recognized by using the axes "bread" and "all other things" on the indifference map

Figure 4.11.   **Satisfaction Maximization**

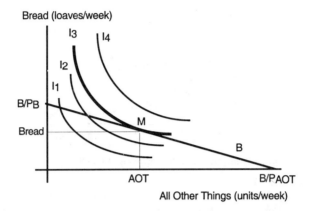

Bread (loaves/week)

All Other Things (units/week)

of Figure 4.11. The budget line has been added to this indifference map. As can be
seen, the highest level of satisfaction attainable occurs where the budget line is
tangent to the indifference curve I_3I_3 at point M. At this maximum satisfaction
the slope of the budget line, which is the ratio of the price of the good plotted
on the X axis to that plotted on the Y axis, $-P_x/P_y$, equals the slope of the indifference curve, the marginal rate of satisfaction. Accordingly, the maximization condition can be written as $MRS = -P_x/P_y$. If hot dogs are on the Y axis
and hamburgers on the X, and the latter costs twice as much as the former, the
right side of the above equation equals -2 and consumers at maximization will
be indifferent to the substitution of two hot dogs for one hamburger.

Maximization Conditions of Indifference Curve and Marginal Utility Analysis

It can be shown that the maximization conditions found using indifference curve
analysis equals that previously derived using marginal utility analysis. This is
done with the help of Figure 4.12. Assume that the individual is at maximum
satisfaction with her budget line tangent to the indifference curve I_3. Now increase the rate of consumption of X by an exceedingly small amount, dX, and
decrease that of Y by dY so that there is no change in satisfaction. Then the differential in utility obtained by the increased consumption of X, $(\partial U/\partial X)dX$, minus the differential of utility suffered by the decreased consumption of Y,
$(\partial U/\partial Y)dY$, equals zero:

(17) $(\partial U/\partial X)\, dX - (\partial U/\partial Y)\, dY = 0$

     or,

(18) $(\partial U/\partial X)\, dX = (\partial U/\partial Y)\, dY$

Figure 4.12.   **The Indifference Condition at Maximum Satisfaction**

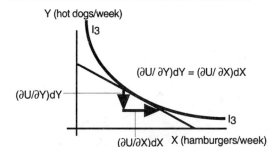

Figure 4.13.   **Quantity of Bread Demanded at Various Prices**

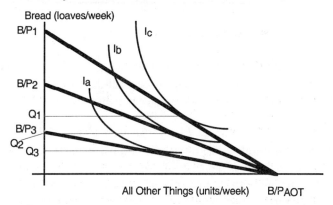

The terms in parentheses are the marginal utility of X and Y, respectively. Rearranging terms yields:

(19) $MU_x/MU_y = dY/dX$

(20) $MU_x/P_x = MU_y/P_y$

Thus it is seen that the indifference curve maximization condition is the same as that of marginal utility analysis.

Deriving a Consumer's Demand Function

An indifference map of bread and all other things is shown in Figure 4.13. Four bread prices are shown ranging from a high of P_{B3} to a low of P_{B1}. As can be seen from the satisfaction budget line–indifference curve maximization tangencies, as the price is lowered the quantity of bread demanded decreases from Q_1 to Q_2 to Q_3 loaves per week. Thus the indifference curve map yields the information required to draw a demand curve, here of negative slope.

Figure 4.14   **The Income and Substitution Effects**

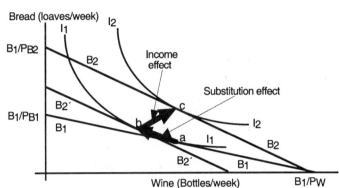

The Income and Substitution Effects

As the price of a product decreases it is consumed at a higher rate because people are better able to afford it; moreover, they substitute it for other products. The income and substitution effects, associated with a cut in the price of bread from P_{B1} to P_{B2}, are shown in Figure 4.14.

At the original price of bread of P_{B1}, the associated budget line is B_1B_1. A drop in the price of bread to P_{B2} causes the original budget line to rotate clockwise to B_2B_2. This allows the consumer to increase his satisfaction by going from point a on indifference curve I_1I_1 to point c on indifference curve I_2I_2. In order to separate the change in the rate of consumption caused by the price decrease into income and substitution effects, budget line $B_2'B_2'$ is included. It represents a down-shift in budget line B_2B_2 until it is tangent with indifference curve I_1I_1. This removes the income effect of the price decrease, as was done under *revealed preference*. The movement from a to b on indifference curve I_1I_1 is the substitution effect arising from the reduction in the price of bread. The increase in satisfaction obtained in going from point b on I_1I_1 to point c on I_2I_2 represents the income effect.

It should be noted that the substitution effect associated with a decrease in price always causes an increase in the rate of consumption of the good made relatively cheaper—as long as some substitutability exists between the sets of products being examined. But the income effect may cause the rate of consumption to increase or decrease.

Changing Income and the Engel Curve

The effect of increasing income on the set of goods chosen to maximize satisfaction is shown in Figure 4.15. Income increases are manifest in budget increases.

Figure 4.15.   **The Income-Consumption Curve**

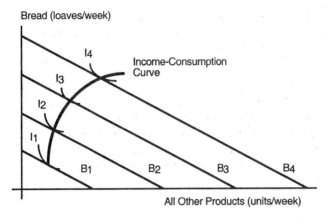

Figure 4.16.   **The Consumption of Bread as a Function of Income—An Engel Curve**

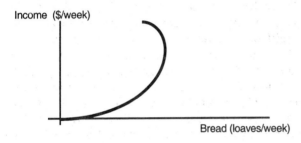

The higher the budget, the higher is its subscript in the figure. All the budget lines are parallel. They have the same slopes because the price of the products on the X and Y axes are constant. Connecting the maximum satisfaction points for the various income levels shown, yields the *income-consumption curve*. Ernst Engel, a nineteenth-century German statistician, proposed plotting the rate of consumption of a good as a function of income, and the resulting curve, bearing his name, is shown in Figure 4.16. Note that as income increases the consumption of bread increases and then decreases, indicating that to the hypothetical consumer, bread is a normal good at relatively low income levels and an inferior good at relatively high income levels.

Should quantity demanded be shown almost invariably as a function of price with other variables held constant? This seems to mean that price is the most important variable to consumers and that income and the other shift parameters are of secondary importance. But it may be the other way around. The empirical work of H. S. Houthakker and Lester D. Taylor implies that income variations are more important than price variations in changing rates of consumption:

> Clearly the most important factor explaining the pattern of consumption in the United States is total expenditure. PCE [private consumption expenditure] is excluded from only two of the 81 categories [of empirical demand equations].... Prices, on the other hand, are much less important than PCE in explaining United States consumption. Of the 81 equations, prices appear in only 44, and they barely border on significance in many of these (1970, p. 165).

It may very well be that the neoclassical stress on price reflects its importance in the neoclassical paradigm rather than its importance to consumers. If so, the more microeconomics becomes a positive science, the more the role of income variations will be stressed. Engel curves would then have a far more prominent role and microeconomics would be better integrated with macroeconomics which stresses the role of income variations.

Perfect Complements

Recall that marginal utility analysis had trouble dealing with complements. Indifference curve analysis handles them with relative ease. This is shown with the help of the right-angled indifference curves of the car and its complement gasoline, shown in Figure 4.17. The consumer is considering three options for the use of a car he intends to rent for the day. He can go to a movie he would like to see in the next town. Alternatively, he can drive still farther to attend a picnic set up by former classmates, and that would be even more pleasurable. He can drive still farther and spend some time at the beach, and that is preferred. Each option requires one car and specified amounts of gasoline. Neither additional cars nor additional gallons of gas would increase utility nor would a relative change in the price of the complements lead to the substitution of one for the other. If price declines have a measurable income effect it could allow the consumer, otherwise only able to afford to go to a movie, to go farther afield.

Perfect Substitutes and Corner Solutions

The consumer may view brand X and brand Y of a product to be perfect substitutes. They may be brands of milk or beer or aspirins and the like. Or one may be perfectly indifferent to butter as compared to margarine, sugar relative to other sweeteners, varnish and polyurethane. The result of this form of indifference yields the straight line indifference curves of Figure 4.18. With the prices given, maximum satisfaction is attained by purchasing butter alone, a *corner solution.* If the price of margarine were lowered, the budget line would shift counterclockwise and could become identical to the indifference curve I_3I_3. The consumer would be indifferent to combinations ranging from all butter to all margarine. At a still lower price of margarine, only margarine would be consumed, another corner solution.

Figure 4.17.   **An Indifference Map of Complements: A Car and the Required Gasoline**

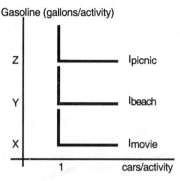

Figure 4.18.   **An Indifference Map of Perfect Substitutes**

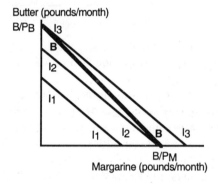

Indifference Curve Analysis and Some Public Policy Issues

Indifference curve analysis can be applied to numerous public policy issues, particularly those involving subsidies, taxes, and non-price rationing.

Subsidizing Price Versus Subsidizing Income

Consider the case of the subsidization of the price of milk for school children. Assume that the relevant indifference map is that given in Figure 4.19. The budget line without subsidization is B_1B_1, that with milk price subsidization $B_{ms}B_{ms}$. Initially, M_1 quarts of milk are consumed a week. With the subsidized price consumption increases to M_s quarts per week. There is also a small increase in the consumption of all other goods from Y_1 to Y_s. With the consumer buying milk at the subsidized price, the amount of the subsidy, measured in units of all other goods, is the vertical distance between the two budget lines, ΔY, at the subsidized rate of consumption.

If instead of subsidizing the price of milk, the government subsidized the in-

Figure 4.19.   **Subsidizing the Price of Milk Versus Subsidizing Income**

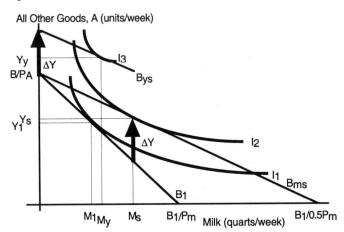

come of the consumer by ΔY, the budget line would be B_{ys}. The consumer could then reach a higher level of satisfaction than was possible with the subsidized price of milk.

From the perspective of the sovereign consumer, a subsidy to income is preferred. But policy-makers of the sovereign government, interested in improving the nutrition of children, might find the argument for an income subsidy wanting. As can be seen in Figure 4.19, subsidizing the price of milk to consumers leads to greater consumption, M_s, than is obtained from an income subsidy, M_y. Dairy farmers and the industry and its suppliers also prefer the subsidization of the price of milk, of course.

By the way, whose indifference map should be used here? The increase in the consumption of milk is that of the child. The budget and its allocation is that of a parent (or guardian). If we specify the indifference map as that of the parent, we are not dealing with the increase in satisfaction attained from the consumption of more milk but the increase in satisfaction obtained by the parent from the child's increased consumption of milk.

Taxing Products Versus a Lump-Sum Tax on Income

There are taxes on gasoline, cigarettes, booze, and a whole host of other products. The effect of a tax with respect to the budget line and the resultant rate of consumption is rather the opposite of that found in the above case of subsidization. This is shown in Figure 4.20 for the case of cigarettes.

Before the imposition of a tax, the cigarette-smoking consumer maximizes his satisfaction by choosing the bundle of goods which allows the tangency between the budget line BB and indifference curve I_1I_1. Consumption is C packs of cigarettes and Y units of other goods per week.

Figure 4.20.   **A Tax on Cigarettes Versus a Lump-Sum Tax on Income**

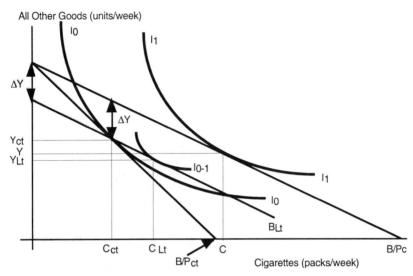

Assume then that the government imposes a specific tax on cigarettes and the price increases from P_c to P_{ct}. This causes the budget line to rotate from B to B_{ct}. With this budget line, utility maximization occurs at its tangency with indifference curve $I_0 I_0$, which not surprisingly yields lower satisfaction than the untaxed case. The consumption of cigarettes drops to C_{ct} and the consumption of other goods increases from Y to Y_{ct}. At this rate of consumption of cigarettes, the original budget line would allow the consumption of ΔY units more of all other goods, the cost of the tax to the individual measured in units of all other goods.

Were the specific tax on cigarettes replaced by a lump-sum tax on income, the original budget line would be shifted down by the magnitude ΔY to B_{Lt}, whereupon maximum satisfaction would be obtained by the tangency of that budget line and indifference curve I_{0-1}, a higher level of satisfaction than that obtained with a specific cigarette tax. But more cigarettes are consumed, namely $C_{Lt} - C_{ct}$, under the lump-sum tax.

An overall comparison of a lump-sum tax as opposed to a tax on cigarettes is like comparing apples and oranges. A lump-sum tax would affect all taxpayers; only smokers pay a tax on cigarettes. If the goal of the sovereign state is to reduce cigarette consumption, then tax cigarettes. If the purpose of the tax is merely to raise revenue then do not pick on the cigarette smoker.

Were the smoker addicted to cigarettes the set of indifference curves would be right angled with the vertical portion at the rate of the consumption of cigarettes. The tax would then cut the consumption of all other goods but not cigarettes.

Figure 4.21.   **Non-Price Rationing with the Price of a Good Held Constant**

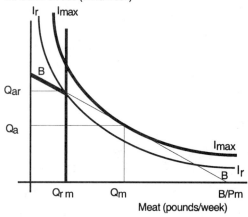

All Other Goods (units/week)

Meat (pounds/week)

Non-Price Rationing

The generally accepted method of rationing resources and products in our society is by price—laying aside the internal rationing of firms and households. Less common is rationing by the queue. Long lines are found for special entertainment events and sometimes for mundane matters, like getting on a bus during the rush hour. Rationing by government-issued rationing stamps is relatively rare but was successfully used during World War II.

World War II succeeded the Great Depression and full employment finally made an appearance. But civilian production was substantially limited as much of the nation's productive resources were used to fight the war. With the supply of consumer goods low and demand high, heavy inflation would probably have occurred and that was thought to be undesirable. As a consequence, price controls were put into place—essentially freezing prices at the level existing at the advent of controls. Price controls mean setting prices below market levels and thus the creation of shortages. Some were trivial; others of some importance. The supply of meat, for example, was less than the demand. The shortage was resolved by rationing. The government-issued rationing coupons which specified the maximum amount of meat that an individual could purchase each week. The effects of this can be seen in Figure 4.21.

Note first the budget line BB. The hypothetical consumer shown would maximize his satisfaction at the tangency between that budget line and indifference curve $I_{max}I_{max}$. This would involve consuming Q_m pounds of meat a week and Q_a units of all other goods. Assume, however, that due to the limited production of meat products the consumer is given ration coupons which allow the purchase of no more than Q_{rm} pounds a week. Were the price of meat and all other goods unaffected by the coupon rationing, the budget line would be would terminate at Q_{rm}. Maximum satisfaction would be achieved on the indifference curve, $I_r I_r$, which intersects the budget line at the rationed amount of meat. Thus, the rationing of meat yields a decrease in satisfaction.

Problems with Indifference Curve Model of Consumer Behavior

There are a number of problems associated with indifference curve analysis and several are considered below.

The Role of Habit

Recall that Houthakker and Taylor found that price variations were relatively unimportant as compared to income variations in determining rates of consumption. Their explanation is:

> The lack of a strong overall influence of prices [on consumption] is consistent with habit formation. Prices should be expected to exert less of an influence on consumption at high levels of income because income becomes less of a constraining factor and more commodities become subject to habit formation (1970, p. 165).

To the extent that the goods we consume are habitual, they have no substitutes over the normal range of price variations. And over that range of prices, the habitual demand function is vertical, of zero elasticity. Assume that the same rate of consumption takes place from a price of zero to a price double that of the normal price. This means that a large range of budget line slopes have to be tangent to the same indifference curve—implying a discontinuity in the curve at the habitual rate of consumption.

The Problem of Binary Demand

As indicated above, the demand for many products is binary in character. We either buy a new house, or apartment, or car, or washing machine, or dish washer—or we do not. What does such an indifference curve look like if, for example, one axis has one house or none and on it and the other axis all other things? What is the price of the house per budget period? (For a better appreciation of the way the price question should be answered see the section in Chapter 5 on the cost of capital goods.)

How Do All Other Things Substitute for a Hamburger?

It makes sense to consider the effect of price changes on substitutable products such as hot dogs and hamburgers, tea and coffee, and bread and wine—if you are not addicted to one in preference to the other. But it makes little sense to assume that an entire budget is spent on only two products. As a result we have used a single good and *all other things*. What is the price of a unit of all other things and what is the meaning of its substitutability, for example, with hamburgers? What is the meaning of the marginal rate of substitution between the hamburger and the thousand products in all other things when only a handful of them can be substituted for a hamburger? Assume that it is only substitutable for hot dogs. Is the substitution of hamburgers and all other things a mask for the substitution of hamburgers and hot dogs?

Indifference curve analysis makes sense when a budget is spent on two goods with unambiguous prices provided provided that the individual views the two goods as substitutes. But we buy many more than two goods during a budget period. And only small clusters of these goods are substitutes. What is the relevance of a change in the price of a product to the many products which are not substitutes? Problems with my mouse are driving me a bit berserk. What mouse substitutes can I buy to return some of my lost equilibrium?

The Expected Utility Model

Since Adam Smith's time utilitarian philosophers have attempted to quantify pleasure and pain. Jeremy Bentham's felicific calculus pointed to the value of such quantification. About a century-and-a-half after the publication of Bentham's work, expected utility analysis was developed by two brilliant men, John von Neuman and Oskar Morganstern. In their famous work of 1944, *Theory of Games and Economic Behavior*, they came close to solving the problem of quantifying utility. Paul J. H. Schoemaker, in an exhaustive survey article on their expected utility model, evaluates von Neuman and Morganstern's work this way:

> It is no exaggeration to consider expected utility theory the major paradigm in decision making since the Second World War (1982, p. 529).

Schoemaker is surely correct in this assessment. The model shows how utility might be quantified, although it turns out, not truly in a cardinal sense.

Calculating a von Neuman-Morganstern (N-M) Utility Index

Calculating the N-M utility index for any product requires an individual to do the following:

> 1. Arbitrarily specify a utility index for a very high-utility product and a very low-utility product. The high-utility product could be a new car and the index chosen might be 100. The low-utility product could be a can of sardines. Its utility index might be set at 1.

> 2. Then, calculate utility values for a set of lottery tickets on the basis of the probability, *p,* of winning the low-utility product and the recip-

rocal probability, *p-1*, of winning the high-utility product.

3. Finally, if the individual is indifferent to a given lottery ticket and the consumption of the marginal unit of product *X*, the expected utility of *X* is that of the indifferent lottery ticket.

The expected utility of a lottery ticket which has a 0.9 probability of winning a can of sardines and a 0.1 probability of winning a car is 10.9: $(0.9 \cdot 1) + (1 - 0.9) \cdot 100$. If an individual is indifferent between a new computer and that lottery ticket, the expected utility of the computer is 10.9.

A lottery ticket predicated on a .95 probability of winning a can of sardines and a 0.05 probability of winning a car has an expected utility of 5.95: $(.95 \cdot 1 + 0.05 \cdot 100)$. If an individual is indifferent between this lottery ticket and a television set, the expected utility of the television set is 5.95. In like fashion, the utility index of all products can be calculated. Assuming our quantifications are with respect to marginal additions to the rate of consumption, we have numerical measures of expected marginal utility.

The Maximization Condition

Armed with quantified measures of the expected marginal utility of all products, the condition for satisfaction maximization would of course be the equality of expected marginal utility per dollar of all goods and services consumed:

(21) $E\{MU_1\}/P_1 = E\{MU_2\}/P_2 = ... = E\{MU_n\}/P_n$

Were the expected marginal utility per dollar of one product higher than that of other products, to maximize satisfaction, the consumption would be increased relative to that of all other goods and vice versa.

The Problem of the Expected Utility Model

The supposed advance of the expected utility model is its ability to measure utility as a cardinal number—but the index is actually ordinal.

We have calculated expected utility on the arbitrarily set 1 to 100 scale and obtained 10.9 as the expected utility of a new computer and 5.95 as the index of a new television set. The ratio of their expected utilities is then 10.9/5.95 or 1.832. If these expected utilities are cardinal numbers, the same ratio must be obtained when any other scale is arbitrarily chosen. That this ratio must be maintained can be seen by considering the equilibrium condition between the two products:

(22) $E\{MU_{comp}\}/P_{comp} = E\{MU_{tv}\}/P_{tv}$

or

(23) $E\{MU_{comp}\}/E\{MU_{tv}) = P_{comp}/P_{tv}$

With the prices of the products fixed, equilibrium requires that the ratio of the expected marginal utilities be that of the ratio of their prices and, for this example, equal to 1.832.

Let us test this by arbitrarily setting another scale. Let the index of a can of sardines be 90 instead of 1 while we allow the index of a car to remain at 100. The individual is still indifferent between a new computer and a lottery ticket with a 0.9 probability of winning a can of sardines and a 0.1 probability of winning a car. The utility index for the computer is now 91 (0.9 • 90 + 0.1 • 100). And the utility index for the television set is now 90.5 (0.95 • 90 + 0.05 • 100). The ratio of expected marginal utilities is now 1.006 rather than the ratio required, 1.832. The von Neuman-Morganstern utility index is thus shown to be ordinal and not cardinal.

Some Other Problems with Models of Consumer Behavior

All of the models of consumer behavior can be handled with ease by Economic Man but not by other consumers. Laboratory tests show that many of us lack the logical skills which are required. In addition many purchases made by individuals are for the family or household with each member of the group having different tastes—clones aside. If the buyer maximizes satisfaction, no one else in the family or household can. A second best approach might be to develop the preference order of a household—by democratic vote. But Nobel Laureate Kenneth Arrow has shown that this is impossible. There are also the problems that increased consumption may not lead to increased happiness and that properly calculating the price of products is difficult.

The Logic Embedded in the Models

There are a number of assumptions embedded in the models of consumer behavior which Economic Man readily handles but you and I might have trouble with. Some of them follow: (1) It is assumed that all goods and services are comparable. But can the marginal wedding of a couple deeply in love really be compared to a marginal hot dog? Can a good meal be compared to a course in economics? Can necessary medical attention be compared to a loaf of bread? (2) The *principal of asymmetry* is assumed to exist: if you prefer *A*, which might be on a higher indifference curve, to *B*, you cannot prefer *B* to *A*. But laboratory tests show that many people frequently violate this assumption particularly when the relation involving *A* and *B* are "framed" differently in subsequent statements. An example of the framing problem is implicit in the following two questions asked of business people: Are all of your actions based on profit maximization? The answer is frequently "no." What actions have you recently taken which would have to be changed to increase profits? The answer is frequently "I

Table 4.1.   **The Preferences of Three People for Three Products**

	Individual		
	I	II	III
Preference	R	S	T
Order	S	T	R
	T	R	S

know of no such actions." The answers are contradictory indicating both non–profit maximizing and profit maximizing behavior. (3) People frequently violated the *logic of transitivity*: If A is preferred to B and B is preferred to C, then A is preferred to C. A might be a point on the highest of three indifference curves with B in the middle and C on the lowest curve. A substantial percentage of respondents, in laboratory tests, choose the wrong preference order, when asked to rank by value, three different hypothetical bets with given probabilities of winning. Economic Man is a logician but the great majority of consumers are not.

The Individual Versus the Multiperson Household

In 1991, George Bush announced that now that he was president of the United States, he would no longer eat broccoli. Apparently, through decades of married life, Mr. Bush had been unable to maximize his satisfaction having been leaned on to eat this estimable vegetable—which he found to be distasteful. The point is that purchases for a household, which maximize the satisfaction of one member will not maximize the satisfaction of others. We all have different tastes.

Arrow's Impossibility Theorem can be applied to the problem posed by the different tastes of each individual in a multiperson household or family. A compromise would be to vote on what is to be consumed with household preferences determined by majority vote. To avoid tie votes and unnecessary complexity, the household is assumed to consist of three people *I*, *II*, and *III*. They have different preference orderings with respect to three products or sets of products, *R*, *S*, and *T*. This is shown in Table 4.1.

Start with the preferences of *I* who prefers *R* to *S*. So does *III*. Consequently, a majority prefers *R* to *S*. Consider now the preference of *S* to *T*. Both *I* and *II* have that preference—again, a majority. Logical preference ordering requires transitivity so with *R* preferred to *S* and *S* preferred to *T*, *R* must be preferred to *T*. This is not the case, however. A majority, *II* and *III*, prefer *T* to *R*. The household cannot develop the preference ordering required to make rational consumption choices on the basis of a majority vote.

What this leaves us with is that individuals in multiperson households and multiperson households cannot maximize satisfaction.

The Assumption that Higher Consumption Yields Greater Happiness

All our models assume that higher rates of consumption yield higher levels of satisfaction or happiness. Is the assumption true? From the empirical work of Richard A. Easterlin we know that the answer to this question is "no" and "yes." Using survey data from nineteen countries, Easterlin found that, despite huge differences in standards of living, people in the richest countries tend to be little, if any, happier than those in the poorest. In this respect the answer is "no." However, those who are relatively rich tend to be somewhat happier than those who are relatively poor, in the same society. In this sense the answer is "yes."

The reality of social living is that we evaluate our circumstances relative to that of others in our society. A person could be happy as a lark with his current salary and rate of consumption but as more and more co-workers advance over him in salary and consumption, gloom and dissatisfaction would tend to prevail. Easterlin likens the quest for higher incomes and happiness to that of rats on a hedonic or pleasure-seeking treadmill. For the overall group no progress is made. But some in the pack do move ahead, and others fall behind. For them there is a change in relative standing and satisfaction.

Easterlin's analysis implies that consumer sovereignty is not that important in and of itself since increasing consumption does not yield more satisfaction. What is required is increasing consumption more than others. It requires moving higher in the income distribution. With the increased disparity of incomes experienced since the mid-1970s, it might be expected that the relatively poor had become even more disaffected and discouraged than they had been earlier on.

Easterlin's findings were well anticipated by Adam Smith who pointed out:

> The common complaint is that [when] luxury extends itself to the lowest ranks of the people ... the labouring poor will not now be content with the same food, cloathing, and lodging which satisfied them in former times (1937 [1776], p. 78).

The Problem of Determining the Proper Price of a Product

We have previously mentioned the complex problem of determining the price of a durable good. But even very ordinary perishables are difficult to price. Take former President Bush's broccoli. There is the price paid for the broccoli, and its transaction, its preparation, and consumption cost. Except for the price paid the seller, the other activities involve the opportunity cost of time. But what is the opportunity cost of a person's time? Is the time used in buying, preparing, and perhaps arguing about broccoli the foregone enjoyment of reading a book, or watching the French Open on television, or whatever? How is that converted into dollar terms so that we have a complete broccoli price? Otherwise we lack the denominator required to maximize our satisfaction under marginal utility analysis and the ability to position a budget line under indifference curve analysis.

The cost assigned to a consumer durable is even more complex. Is it the same analytically as the capital cost to a planner prior to purchase and the capital cost of the producer-user after the purchase has been made? I think so, but I have never seen this approach to consumer durables.

What is the Purpose of Models of Consumer Behavior?

Brilliant economists and others have invested a great deal of time and effort in inventing models of consumer behavior. The models are appropriate to Economic Man but not to me. They remind me of a wonderful story about a group of scholastic sages arguing about the number of teeth in a horse's mouth. The English philospher Thomas Carlyle suggested to them that they might profit by looking into a horse's mouth and counting them.

Why have such fantastic models been created? What is their purpose? Nobel Laureate Gary S. Becker, in effect, answers the question in this way:

> Since we have demonstrated that the market demand curves tend to be negatively inclined, ... and since this is usually considered the main implication of utility maximization, why bother with utility?... The reason has to do with the implication of utility theory that receives insufficient emphasis—namely, that consumers prefer more goods to less. This is an extremely powerful implication that can explain [a number of things] (1971, p. 25).

The number of things explained by the preference for more are, according to Becker: (1) "why consumers end up on the boundary of their opportunity sets;" (2) "why they buy at the lowest price known to them;" (3) why they in Adam Smith's words "truck, barter, and exchange;" (4) "the incentive to invest in education, on-the-job training, information about the quality and prices of goods, and other human capital" (1971, p. 25).

But Becker's fundamental claim, that consumers prefer more goods to less, is not an implication of consumer theory— it is an assumption of consumer theory. We assume, for example, that consumers prefer the indifference curve that is farther from the origin because it is developed on the basis of greater consumption.

A modest proposal is that consideration be given to substituting for our untested models which are dubiously related to consumer behavior, Becker's easily sustained hypothesis that people prefer more to less—a most efficient change.

Summary

Several popular models of consumer behavior, popular to economists, have been presented: revealed preference, marginal utility, indifference curve analysis, and expected utility. These models are intended to advance our understanding of consumer behavior and its relationship to demand. Whether or not they do so is an open question.

Revealed preference handles the substitution but not the income effect. It indicates that a decline in the price of a product should result in either the same amount or more of it being purchased. It thereby covers two cases of demand: demand which has zero elasticity and demand which is negative-sloped, demand particularly appropriate to the many products with negligible income effects.

The marginal utility model, the model which started the marginal revolution, assumes that all products are substitutable for each other. The maximum satisfaction condition occurs when the marginal utility of all products per dollar are equal. Under it, if the price of a can of soda increases, the quantity purchased of it should decrease and the consumption of all other products should increase. The former allows for an increase in the marginal utility per dollar of the chosen beverage; the latter decreases the marginal utility per dollar of all other purchases during the budget period. I suspect that neither of these things really occurs. Habit tends to maintain the consumption rate of beverages and the substitution of other products will not change perceptibly. But if the consumption rates of the beverage and all other things do not change, maximum satisfaction equilibrium cannot be attained!

Indifference curve analysis shows that under the substitution effect an increase in the price of a product always results in an decrease in the quantity demanded. It also shows that the income effect is ambiguous. If a great majority of price changes have a negligible effect on income, then less should be purchased of any item which experiences a price increase and more of its substitute, all other things. If this does not generally happen, indifference curves must generally be right angled. The same consumption then occurs as relative price changes—at least up to a point.

Assuming substitutability of the goods analyzed, the maximization condition of both the marginal utility and indifference curve models can be shown to be consistent.

The intent of the expected utility model is to create cardinal measures of the expected utility of products. This would be of great assistance to the marginal utility model which almost all believe requires quantification. Alas, the measures of expected utility are ordinal rather than cardinal so the problem of measuring the utility of goods remains.

Determining the proper price of goods is a problem. This is frequently because to obtain the relevant price requires adding to the price of a product its transaction, preparation, and consumption costs. And the most difficult assessment is the cost of the time involved in these processes. Vacations are time intensive and you may never take one if you put a high enough price on your time. Durable goods pose a special problem. Marshall handled it by calculating the present value of the discounted stream of (expected) marginal utilities obtained from the durable good. But not many consumers know how to do such a calculation and few, if any, of those who do would bother to make the calculation.

There is also the problem that much of consumption is based on habit—not logic. One can argue, however, that habit is an efficient form of logic—so efficient that no time need be spent on the logic of making a habitual purchase including the determination of its proper price.

Economics is not a behavioral science and our models of consumer behavior, unfortunately, reflect that reality. My own vote is that they all be "filed" and replaced with the simple assumption that people tend to prefer more to less goods.

Questions on Chapter 4

1. There are two time periods. In the first, you drink 5 ounces of orange juice each day as part of your breakfast. In the second, orange juice consumption is increased to 6 ounces a day.
   a. Explain the idea of marginal utility using the above example.
   b. What is the difference, if any, in the utility derived from drinking a glass of juice on Monday as compared to drinking it on Thursday?
   c. When you drink a glass of juice, is the utility you derive from it average or marginal?

2. Draw an indifference curve involving the consumption of orange juice and steak. Vary the price of steak. Does this yield the data for constructing a demand for steak function? If so, explain why.

3. Do you attempt to maximize the satisfaction you obtain from your spending? If not, what have you bought recently which did not tend to maximize your satisfaction? What should you have bought instead of the purchase you made? If you attempt to maximize satisfaction, how do you go about it? Is your approach close to that used under marginal utility analysis, indifference curve analysis? Explain your approach.

4. Explain how revealed preference yields the idea of the demand function considering only the substitution effect. Is it frequently realistic to neglect the income effect? Explain.

5. Explain how Morganstern and von Neuman go about developing the quantification of the expected marginal utility derived from the consumption of a marginal Coke or a Pepsi?

6. Assume that we know that demand functions tend to be vertical or negative sloped and that people prefer more to less consumption. Then what do we learn from marginal utility and indifference curve analysis? (Your answer need not be confined to economics.)

CHAPTER FIVE

The Production Function, Productivity, and Productivity Growth

The production function relates the rate of production to the state of technology and the employment of the factors of production. It is arguably the most important function in the neoclassical paradigm because: (1) It is the basis of the cost functions. (2) Its slope, the marginal productivity function, is the foundation of the factor demand functions. (3) And with factor supplies given, marginal productivity functions yield the distribution of income to the factors of production.

In a general sense, the production function represents very practical and well-known relationships implicit in all employment change decisions made by managers to vary the rate of production.

The analysis used in the area of production closely parallels that used in the basic neoclassical models of consumer behavior. Marginal productivity analysis, to be used here, is very much like marginal utility analysis previously covered. The same is true of the close relationship between the isoquant analysis of this chapter and the previously presented indifference curve analysis.

Finally, an increasing standard of living, a common aspiration in acquisitive societies, essentially requires advances in technology and productivity, which shifts the production function.

The Production Function

The production function is defined as follows:

> The *production function* relates the maximum rate of production possible, Q, to the employment of the factors of production—labor, L, and capital, K—at a given level of technology, T: $Q = f(T; L, K)$.

Why the omission of the third factor of production, land or natural resources? The answer rests on David Ricardo's definition of land as "the original and

Figure   5.1.   **Production Functions with Increasing, Constant, and Decreasing Marginal Productivity of Labor**

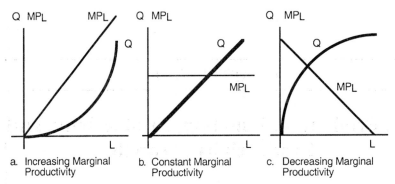

a. Increasing Marginal
   Productivity

b. Constant Marginal
   Productivity

c. Decreasing Marginal
   Productivity

indestructible powers of the soil." Once a unit of land is worked on by labor or capital, it is no longer in its original or natural state. This transforms land into capital, the produced means of production. There is, however, no law against breaking capital down into categories, one or more of which could be land or closely related to land. Thus, a not uncommon form of the production function has the rate of production as a function of the employment of labor, L; capital in the form of facilities and equipments, K; and materials purchased from other producers, M: $Q=f(T; L,K,M)$. The omission of the level of technology, T, implies its constancy. A crucial assumption in production function analysis is that the rate of production can be varied by varying the employment of a single factor, all others held constant. This is an assumption which deserves serious scrutiny.

Three production functions, Q, and their marginal productivity of labor functions, MP_L, are shown in Figure 5.1. The production functions illustrate the rate of production, Q, as a function of the employment of labor, L, with capital held constant. The marginal productivity of labor functions, MP_L, are, in each case, the slope of the production function. In frames a, b, and c can be seen increasing, constant, and decreasing marginal returns as manifest in the marginal productivity of labor.

Marginal Productivity

All factors have their own marginal productivities. That of labor is discussed here, but the same reasoning holds for capital or any subgroup of labor or capital. The marginal product of labor is defined as follows:

> The *marginal product of labor*, MP_L, is the slope of the production function, Q, with respect to the employment of labor, L. The slope at a point equals $\partial Q/\partial L$. Over a small range of the production function, MP_L equals $\Delta Q/\Delta L$.

The marginal product of labor is the rate of change of the rate of production with respect to the employment of labor.

Note that the marginal product of labor is the rate of change of production with respect to the employment of labor. It is *not* an increment of production although in oral discourse we talk as if it were. The incremental or differential product is the marginal product of labor times an increment in the employment of labor: $dQ = \partial Q/\partial L \cdot dL = MP_L \cdot dL$. The dichotomy between the marginal and the incremental product is the same analytically as the difference between marginal and differential utility.

The Law of Diminishing Marginal Returns or Marginal Productivity

What is known as the law of diminishing returns is generally thought to be the 1767 discovery of Anne-Robert-Jacques Turgot. It became well known to English intellectuals in 1815 when in a three-week period, four British economists—Edward West, Robert Torrens, Thomas Robert Malthus, and David Ricardo—independently used it in deriving the theory of differential rent.

The crucial reason for diminishing marginal returns or diminishing marginal productivity in agriculture is that the supply of land is fixed making it increasingly scarce as the employment of labor is increased. As a result, as West stated, "Each additional quantity of work bestowed on agriculture yields an actually diminished return." Economists point out that were diminishing marginal returns not a fact of life, food for the world could be grown in a single flower pot. But you just cannot add more and more seed to the flower pot and grow more and food.

The law of diminishing marginal productivity holds true for the employment of all variable inputs on a fixed amount of land—not just for labor. Eventually, diminishing marginal returns or marginal productivity would arise from the increased application of any single factor of production—seed, fertilizer, equipment, water, herbicides, pesticides, or insecticides—with all other inputs held constant. Moreover, to the extent that it is possible to vary the employment of inputs one at a time, the contribution to the rate of production of the marginal unit of each factor can be identified.

Marshall's Use of Doses of Fixed Amounts of Labor and Capital

Alfred Marshall proposed a different form of the law of diminishing returns than that presented above. In Marshall's version doses of capital *and* labor are varied with land held constant:

> The law of or *statement of tendency to Diminishing Return* may be provisionally worded thus: An increase in the capital and labour applied in the cultivation of land causes *in general* a less than proportionate increase in the amount of produce raised, unless it happens to coincide with an improvement in the arts of agriculture (1961, [1890] p. 150).

Figure 5.2.   **A Production Function and Its Marginal Productivity Function**

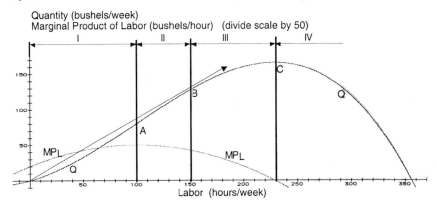

Here, the diminishing marginal product is not that of a single factor but that of a "dose" of the two factors, labor and capital. If, for example, additional units of labor are required to increase the application of seed, fertilizer, water, and the like to the land, the contribution to production of the individual factors cannot be identified.

The law of diminishing marginal productivity was applied only to agriculture until 1899 when John Bates Clark applied it to industry with a single sentence: "For a fixed area of land read, now, a fixed fund of permanent social capital" (1965 [1899], p. 197).

Regions of the Production Function

Assume that the rate of production is a function of a single variable factor, such as labor, with all other factors held fixed in supply. Assume in addition, that as the employment of labor increases, production first displays increasing and then diminishing marginal productivity with marginal productivity eventually becoming negative. The logic of this changing situation is as follows: Start with a plant with a substantial amount of capital equipment but no workers. As the first workers are employed their marginal productivity is low. There are too many different machines that each has to operate and time is wasted in going from one to another. As employment is increased, the organization of work is improved and marginal productivity rises. But beyond a certain point the employment of additional workers yields diminishing marginal productivity. The fixed amount of capital equipment is becoming scarce. Marginal productivity falls and reaches zero. as more and more people are put to work. Were even more workers employed in the plant, they would get in each other's way causing marginal productivity to be increasingly negative. This process would yield a marginal productivity function and a production function of the form shown in Figure 5.2.

Figure 5.3.   **The Marginal and Average Product of Labor**

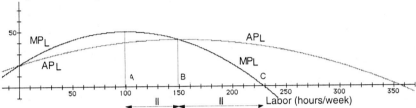

Marginal and Average Product of Labor (bushels/hour)

The production function is broken down into four regions: *I, II, III,* and *IV*. They are delineated by the maxima of the marginal, average, and total product functions. Region *I* ranges from the origin to the factor employment at which its marginal product is a maximum. In region *II*, the range is from that maximum of labor's average product. Region *III* covers the range of factor employments from average product maximum to that at which the rate of production is maximum. Finally, region *IV* goes from the maximum rate of production to lower rates.

The marginal product of labor, MP_L, as the slope of the production function at a point, reaches a peak at point *A*, becomes zero at point *C*, and is negative thereafter. In Figure 5.3 the marginal productivity function is again shown but along with the average productivity function. At the employment level at which the average product of labor is maximum, the average and marginal products are equal.

> The *average product of a factor, AP F*, equals the total product, *Q*, divided by the number of units of the factor, *F*, required to yield that product: $AP_F = Q/F$.

The average product of a factor equals it marginal product, $\partial Q/\partial F$, at the rate of production at which the average product is a maximum: $AP_{F\,max} = MP_F$.

Employment should take place only in regions *II* and *III* if the employer is a profit maximizer. Why this is so is shown in Chapter 12. In these regions the marginal product of a factor is decreasing rather like a demand function.

The Production Function and the Advance of Technology

Technology has been advancing throughout human history and particularly since the onset of the Industrial Revolution. More is known about the process of production today than was known yesterday, last year, and a century ago and this tends to make us more productive. As a result the production function tends to rotate counter-clockwise or, loosely put, "upward" over the course of time. Then, with a fixed stock of capital, fewer units of labor are required to produce a

Figure 5.4.   **Production Functions Increased by Technological Progress**

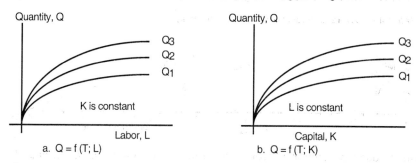

a. $Q = f(T; L)$

b. $Q = f(T; K)$

given output rate. That is shown in frame *a* of Figure 5.4. In similar fashion, as shown in frame *b,* as technology advances with a fixed stock of labor, fewer units of capital would be required to attain a given rate of production.

Planning Using Marginal Productivity Analysis

Two matters are covered in this section. The first is the optimal employment of the factors. The second is the close analytical tie between marginal utility and marginal productivity analysis. It is assumed here that we know the cost of the factors of interest. In the next section, the proper determination of those costs, particularly for capital goods, will be presented.

Optimal Factor Employment

The optimal employment of the factors of production is based on the following assumptions: (1) the factors can be substituted for each other; (2) their marginal products can be identified; (3) their costs or prices are known; (4) the producer is a cost minimizer; (5) and, the law of diminishing marginal productivity is in force.

> *Optimal Factor Employment* occurs when the marginal product per dollar of each of the *m* factors employed is equal:
> $$MP_1/P_1 = MP_2/P_2 = ... = MP_m/P_m$$

Optimal factor employment means that a given rate of production is attained at minimum cost (or that with a given budget, the maximum rate of production is attained). The above equation represents cost minimization for a given rate of production because no change in the employment of any factor will yield a greater marginal or differential product per dollar.

What if, at the desired output rate, the marginal product per dollar of one of the factors exceeded that of the others? As in the case of utility maximization, two steps are required to minimize the cost of producing a given output. First, more of the factor with the higher marginal productivity per dollar is employed until its marginal productivity per dollar equals that of the other factors. Second, since the rate of production has increased slightly above the desired rate, a modest negative adjustment of the employment of all factors is required to reattain the desired rate of production at the new equilibrium. The marginal product per dollar of a factor can increase if its marginal productivity increases or if its unit cost decreases. The increased employment of a factor as its price decreases is a manifestation of its negative-sloped demand function.

Why did I go from two factors of production to m of them? This was done because the abstractions "labor" and "capital" cover a multitude of non-homogeneous factors. A firm employs many different kinds of labor and forms of capital and the use of m factors is indicative of this. It allows creating groups in which labor and capital are homogeneous with a particular marginal productivity function associated with a particular group.

The Close Tie Between Marginal Utility and Marginal Productivity Analysis

The reasoning regarding the optimal employment of the factors is the same as that regarding maximizing satisfaction in marginal utility analysis. The set of "substitutions" are these: (1) The production function replaces the utility function; (2) the law of diminishing marginal productivity replaces the law of diminishing marginal utility; (3) the budget spent on factors and factor services replaces the budget spent on consumer goods and services; and (4) production maximization (or cost minimization) replaces satisfaction maximization. A basic difference between the two analyses is that marginal productivity should be measurable while marginal utility is measurable only to the extent that the marginal utility of money is constant.

The Cost of Capital Goods

Planners must be able to properly calculate the cost of capital goods in order to attain optimal factor employments. How that should be done is discussed first. *Producers* must also determine the cost of using the equipment under their command so that they can organize production in a least cost manner. But their view of costs should be different—as is subseququently explained.

The Cost to Planners

What is the cost or price which planners should assign to a capital good for its use during a particular budget period, such as a year? It is the *rental cost* of the capital good plus the expected operational costs.

The term *rental cost* gets its name from the fact that it is the cost which owners should charge for the rental of a capital good. It consists of three components:

(1) The foregone interest on the money paid for the capital good—its cost, C, times the annual rate of interest, i (Ci). (2) The depreciation in value, d, of a capital good due to its use expressed as a percent per year of the original cost. Thus far the cost is $C(i+d)$. (3) In addition, capital equipment usually lose value over time—largely because of the   development of new and more productive equipment. Last year's unused computer is of less dollar value today than it was a year ago and that loss in value, l, is a cost. The annual rental cost is $C(i+d+l)$. (If a capital good is expected to gain in value, the sign of the capital loss variable is negative. A structure on a piece of land, for example, may increase in value because of the inflation of land values.)

> The *rental cost of a capital good*, C_r, is the sum of the foregone interest arising from the cost of the good purchased, Ci, its depreciation from use, Cd, and the loss of its value due to the preference for new forms of capital goods, Cl: $C_r = C(i + d + l)$.

The cost of the capital good, C, is known to planners. Other costs are anticipated. The addition of operating costs yields the annual cost of a capital good.

> The *annual cost of a capital good to planners*, $C_{A.PL}$, is the sum of its annual rental cost, based on original cost, plus the expected annual operating costs— the costs of energy, repairs, and maintenance:
> $$C_{A.PL} = C(i+d+l)+ E + R + M.$$

The calculation of annual cost allows planners to assign the proper cost or price to each of the capital goods considered for use in production and to choose those having the highest ratio of marginal product to annual cost.

The Cost to Producers

The cost of a capital good is again the sum of its rental cost plus the expected operating costs. But the rental cost to producers should be quite different than it was to planners.

The rental cost of a capital good at the planning stage was a function of its original cost but that is not the case once a good has been purchased. Historic costs are irrelevant to decision-making; estimates of future costs are what is required. The original cost is replaced by the resale price, the price the producer could get from selling the capital good, P_{RS}. The future use of the capital good causes the interest on its resale value to be foregone, depreciation of that value arising from its use, and, age-related loss of its future resale value.

> The *Rental Cost to Producers* is the foregone interest on the resale value of the capital good, its depreciation from use, and its loss of value due to the preference for new forms of capital:
> $$C_{RP} = P_{RS}(i+d+l)$$

The resale price of a capital good tends to be less than its original cost and to decrease over the course of time. As a result, the rental cost in production tends to be less than it was in planning and sometimes much less.

> The *Annual Cost of a Capital Good to a Producer*, $C_{A.PR}$, is the sum of its annual rental cost, predicated on its resale price, plus its operating costs (the cost of energy, repairs, and maintenance),
>
> $$C_{A.PR} = P_{RS}(i+d+l) + E + R + M.$$

Sunk Costs

Consider the case in which a capital good has no resale value. Its original cost has been *sunk*—the market value of the good has disappeared. It then has no rental cost. There is no resale value foregone through its use. The costs which should be assigned to it are the anticipated costs of energy, repairs, and maintenance.

But sunk cost capital may pose an allocation problem. The capital which has sunk may be quite servicable and popular with the workforce. They like and are comfortable with the computer which has gone out of style. With very modest hourly job charges, its usage could be excessive. If so, producers may wish to consider placing a congestion toll or other charge on the use of the computer.

Dismantling Costs

Steel mills which have been unprofitable for a quarter-of-a-century are still in use to avoid the cost of dismantling them. As you can imagine, their dismantling cost, C_{DM}, is extremely high. By keeping a mill in operation for another year, interest is earned on the foregone spending on dismantling C_{DM}. Thus, the cost of using the mill another year is:

$$C_{A.PR} = -C_{DM}(i) + E + R + M$$

I suspect that their annual capital cost is sometimes negative, even with high maintenance and repair costs.

Optimization Using Isoquant Analysis

A number of matters are presented. First, the definition of an isoquant. Then, its derivation from a set of production functions is shown. Subsequently, an isoquant map is used to plan optimal factor employments. Next, the expansion path is presented, showing optimal combinations of factors as the budget and production are increased. Finally, consideration is given to the case of perfect substitutes and that of perfect complements.

An *isoquant* is the locus of points showing the combinations of two factors, usually labor and capital, which yield the same rate of production.

Isoquants, curves of constant rates of production, look like indifference curves, curves of constant satisfaction. Both tend to be convex to the origin. Just as the logic of marginal productivity analysis was rather the same as previously studied marginal utility analysis, the same logic previously used in indifference curve analysis is used in isoquant analysis.

Deriving Isoquants from Production Functions

A set of production functions which relates the production of wheat to the employment of labor appears in frame *a* of Figure 5.5. The original function is Q_1. The shifts arise from increasing the amount of capital by equal increments, ΔK. Note the line representing an output rate of 100 widgets a day. With the lowest amount of capital available L_1 units of labor are required to perform the specified production. Then capital is augmented in the amount of ΔK units, the amount of labor required is reduced substantially to L_2. But when the amount of capital is increased to $2\Delta K$, a smaller increment of labor employment is saved $(L_3 - L_2) < (L_4 - L_3)$. And the final substitution of ΔK units of capital for labor saves even less labor. This is because as the amount of capital is increased its marginal productivity declines so it can substitute for fewer units of labor. And as the employment of labor decreases, its marginal productivity increases, so a smaller decrease in employment implies a larger decrease in production.

 The labor-capital information in frame *a* is that required to construct a set or map of isoquants. This connection is shown for just one isoquant, that involving the production of 100 widgets per day. The four production functions yield four pairs of data on the labor and capital which can produce that rate of production, the information used to construct the isoquant of frame *b*.

 Note that the absolute magnitude of the slope of the isoquant declines with the increased use of L. On one hand, as more and more increments of L are employed, each adds less than the previous one to production—due to the increasing scarcity of K. On the other hand, the increasing amount of L available to K makes marginal units of K increasingly more productive. As a result, to maintain a constant rate of production, as L increases in fixed increments, smaller decreases in Y are required. This is why the derived function is convex to the origin.

Planning Optimal Factor Employments

An isoquant map and a budget line can be found in Figure 5.6. Maximum production with the given budget occurs at the tangency of the budget line and iso-

Figure 5.5.   **Derivation of an Isoquant from a Set of Production Functions**

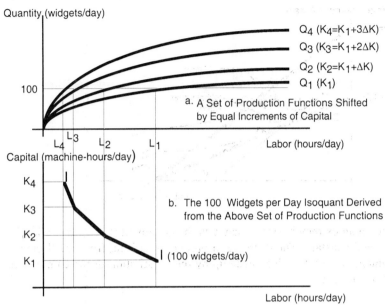

a. A Set of Production Functions Shifted by Equal Increments of Capital

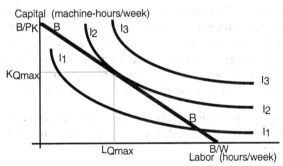

b. The 100 Widgets per Day Isoquant Derived from the Above Set of Production Functions

Figure 5.6.   **An Isoquant Map, Budget Line, and Employments for Maximum Production**

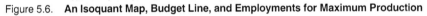

quant I_2. No higher rate of production is attainable with that budget. As can be seen, the amount of labor and capital which yield the maximum output rate are, L_{Qmax} and K_{Qmax}.

Note that at maximum production the slope of the isoquant, *the marginal rate of technical substitution,* equals the slope of the tangent budget line, here the wage rate divided by the price of capital, $-W/P$.

> The *marginal rate of technical substitution, MRTS,* is the slope of an isoquant at a point, dY/dX.

It represents the ratio of an extremely small change in the employment of factor

Figure 5.7.   **A Drop in the Price of Capital and the Substitution and Income Effects**

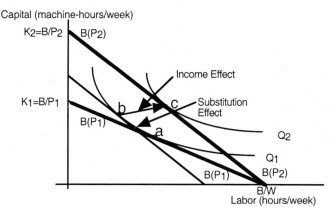

Y, dY, to an an extremely small change in the employment of X, dX, with production held constant. The decrease in production arising from the decreased employment, say of Y, is just made up by the substitution of the employment of X, at the margin.

Factor Price Variations and the Substitution and Income Effects

Figure 5.7 shows the effects of a decrease in the price of capital relative to that of labor on the employment of labor and capital. The initial prices of labor and capital, W and P_1, yield the slope of budget line $B(P_1)B(P_1)$. Maximum production is at a, the tangency between the budget line and isoquant Q_1. Then the price of capital drops from P_1 to P_2. The two effects arising from this change in relative factor prices are the substitution and the income effects.

> *The substitution effect* is the change in the employment of the factors arising from a change in their relative price, with the rate of production held constant.

The substitution of capital for labor commences from point a until point b is reached at the tangency of the isoquant, Q_1, with a budget line of slope $-W/P_2$, a budget line parallel to the new budget line but tangent to the original isoquant, Q_1 at point c. This substitution of capital for labor would be the only interest of a firm comitted to produce Q_1 units per week.

But the firm, producing on the basis of a given budget, is interested in determining the increase in the rate of production obtainable by virtue of the drop in the price of capital. It is concerned with the income effect.

Figure 5.8.   **Two Expansion Paths**

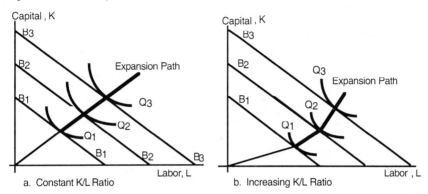

a. Constant K/L Ratio   b. Increasing K/L Ratio

> *The income effect* is the change in the rate of production arising from a
> change in the real value of the budget (or income) resulting from a
> change in the price of a factor of production.

The decrease in the price of capital rotates the budget line from $B(P_1)$ to $B(P_2)$.
The highest rate of production which can be obtained arises from the tangency of
the new budget line with isoquant Q_2 at point c. The income effect is, therefore,
the shift from b to c.

According to the substitution effect, a decrease in the price of capital leads to
more capital and less labor demanded. But the income effect is ambiguous regarding the change in the employment of the factors. In the case of Figure 5.7,
for example, the income effect leads to a small increase in the employment of
capital and a relatively large increase in the employment of labor.

The Expansion Path

A firm may wish to consider the combinations of factors it should employ either at different rates of production or with different budgets. This yields what is
called the expansion path. Two of them are shown in Figure 5.8. (The expansion path is akin to the income consumption curve found in indifference curve
analysis.) An expansion path in which the ratio of labor to capital is constant is
shown in frame a. All points of optimum factor employment are on a ray drawn
from the origin of the graph. This would tend to be the case if the same method
of production is used at relatively low and relatively high rates of production.

More pizza ovens are purchased and more workers are hired to stretch more
dough, add the other ingredients, put the uncooked pizza into the oven and re-

Figure 5.9.   **Perfect Substitutes in Planning; Perfect Complements in Production**

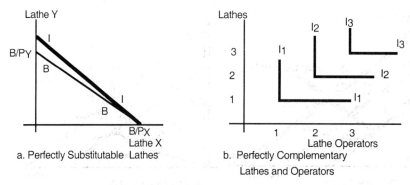

a. Perfectly Substitutable Lathes

b. Perfectly Complementary Lathes and Operators

move it when the pizza is done. In frame *b*, the production process is shown as becoming increasingly capital intensive as the rate of production increases. At low rates of production the use of existing equipment is exploited. At higher expected rates of production labor-saving devices are built or bought. And at still higher expected rates more specialized methods of production are developed to handle the production of a product. Thus, the increasing capital-labor ratio of frame *b*.

The Vagueness of the Magnitude of Capital Required

Assume that we produce turned pieces of metal under a contract for 120 of them per week, and that it is estimated that a lathe operator can turn one of these pieces in an hour or 40 per week. We, therefore, need three lathe operators to work on this contract. How many lathes are required? The answer is either three, two, or one. One lathe implies operating on three shifts; two, operating two shifts; and three, operating a single shift. Are all three alternatives examples of economic rationality?

Perfect Substitutes and Complements

Perfect substitutes can be found in the area of capital goods. Brands X and Y of cars, trucks, paper, and machine tools may be evaluated as equivalent in their productive roles. They are perfect substitutes. Then the cheaper of the set of perfect substitutes should be purchased. That is shown in frame *a* of Figure 5.9. Lathe X is chosen because it is cheaper than Y and of equal quality. The perfect substitutes of planning end up as perfect complements in production since each lathe requires the complement of a lathe operator, or a number of operators using it one at a time.

The Frequent Absence of Practical Substitutes—Even in Planning

First of all, it is important to recognize that there are no practical substitutes for many factors of production, even in planning. There is, for example, no practical substitute for copper in electrical transmission and devices. Any metal can conduct electricity but none but copper will receive a whit of consideration by informed designers. There is no practical substitute for tungsten carbide tools to cut steel on a lathe. There is no substitute for tungsten as the filament in an incandescent light bulb. There is no substitute for clay in making the ceramic materials used in high-temperature furnaces. There is no practical substitute for electricity as the energy source for illumination. Candles may be more romantic but if used in the kitchen take care that you are slicing the carrots and not a favorite finger.

Substitutes in Planning; Complements in Production

The use of marginal productivity analysis to determine the best allocation of resources rests on the assumption that the factors of production are substitutable.

Five centuries ago pundits might have sensibly forecast that the book would be substituted for the teacher in the schools of the future. In fact, however, they are used as complements—the norm for production in general.

I have claimed that, once put into use, the lathe, lathe operator, energy, and stock to be worked on are complementary. Some readers may be familiar with lathes; others not. Consider the processes of production you know and the extent to which the factors are substitutable, if at all. You probably know the method used in the production of pizza, hamburgers, transportation services such as a busing, the production of dental services, the technology of the car wash, and so on. To what extent can labor be substituted for capital or capital for labor in these processes once a method of production has been put into use? If the answer is virtually none, as it seems to me, the factors are complements and factor substitution to minimize cost in production is difficult and often impossible.

The Equality of the Maximum Conditions of Isoquant Analysis and Marginal Productivity Analysis

Assume that the producer faces the isoquant, budget line, and production maximum of Figure 5.10. Now, decrease the employment of Y a minute amount, dY, and increase the employment of X just enough to keep production constant.

Figure. 5.10.   **An Increase in Labor Substituted for a Decrease in Capital in the Region of Production Maximization**

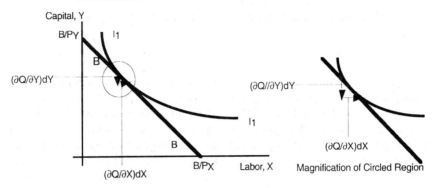

The condition described is:

(1) $\partial Q/\partial X \cdot dX - \partial Q/\partial Y \cdot dY = 0$, or

(2) $MP_X \cdot dX - (MP_y \cdot dY) = 0$

Put the expression in parentheses on the right side of the equation.

(3) $MP_X\, dX = MP_y\, dY$

Rearrange terms:

(4) $MP_X/MP_y = dY/dX$

The slope of the budget line and the isoquant at their tangency is dY/dX which equals P_X/P_Y. Thus:

(5) $MP_X/MP_y = P_X/P_y$ or $MP_X/P_X = MP_y/P_y$

At the maximum production attainable from a given budget, the isoquant equilibrium condition is the same as that of marginal productivity analysis.

The Cobb-Douglas Production Function

The most famous of all production functions is the one developed by Paul H. Douglas with the help of his mathematician friend Charles W. Cobb. Its fame arose because the empirical estimates of the function, properly manipulated as shown below, implied a distribution of income between labor and capital felt by many to be reasonably close to that which actually existed. This was seen as confirmation of the neoclassical theory of factor demand based on marginal productivity. A glance at Douglas's 1934 *Theory of Wages* (1957) shows the immense and excellent effort Douglas and his associates put into the quantifications of the Cobb-Douglas function.

The Cobb-Douglas production function is of the form:

(6) $$Q = T L^a K^b$$

where, Q is real production per year and L and K are the amounts of labor and capital employed in producing it. Douglas viewed T as a constant used to convert the units of the right side of the equation to those on the left. Nowadays it is viewed as an estimate of the level of technology and what is now called *total* or *multifactor productivity*. The exponents a and b are parameters assumed to be constant. They are, as shown below, the production elasticities of labor and capital, respectively. A production elasticity is the ratio of the percentage of change in output, $\Delta Q/Q$, to the percentage change in factor employment, $\Delta L/L$ or $\Delta K/K$, which brought it about. If, for example, $a = 0.7$, a 1 percent increase in the employment of labor would bring about a 0.7 percent increase in the rate of production.

Factor Shares According to Marginal Productivity Theory

The manipulations of the Cobb-Douglas production function to determine the distribution of the product between labor and capital follows:

(7) The production function: $Q = T L^a K^b$

(8) The wage rate, the marginal
product of labor: $W = MP_L = \partial Q/\partial L = aTL^{a-1}K^b = aQ/L$

(9) Labor's share of production: $WL = aQ$

(10) Return to a unit of capital,
the marginal product of capital: $R = MP_k = \partial Q/\partial K = bTL^aK^{b-1} = bQ/K$

(11) Capital's share of production: $RK = bQ$

(12) Return to both factors: $WL + RK = (a + b)Q$

(13) Exhaustion of the product: $WL + RK = Q$, if $a + b = 1$

Thus, you see the wonderful analytical coverage emanating from the production function and its marginal productivity functions.

Table 5.1.   **Estimates of the Production Elasticities of Labor and Capital**

| | Average Production Elasticities | | |
| | Labor | Capital | |
	a	b	a + b
Time series (4 runs)	0.74	0.23	0.97
Cross-section (6 runs)	0.63	0.34	0.97

Source: Table 1 of Douglas's December 29, 1947 presidential address to the American Economic Association "Are There Laws of Production?" Reprinted in Douglas (1957).

Estimates of the Parameters a and b

Douglas faced the following tasks: (1) to statistically estimate the magnitudes of *a* and *b*, (2) to test whether or not the sum of their values equaled one, and (3) to see whether or not labor's actual share of manufacturing income corresponded to aQ and capital's share to bQ, which would show that the data supported marginal productivity theory.

Douglas estimated the parameters of the production function by transforming his production function into logarithmic form:

(14) $\ln Q = \ln T + a\ln L + b\ln K$

From a computational perspective this meant that after taking the logarithm of his data on Q, L, and K, he had a conventional linear multiple regression model:

(15) $Q^* = T^* + aL^* + bK^*$

where, T^* is the intercept with the vertical axis, a is the slope of L^* relative to Q^*, and b is the slope of K^* with respect to Q^*.

Douglas made ten estimates of the parameters a and b using different sets of data. Four estimates were made by using annual data, "time-series" data on Q, L, and K covering the years 1899–1922: The four sets of data imply that each data set was somewhat different than the other. In one, for example, he used the hours of labor of production workers while in another he added the hours of work of clerical and salaried workers. And he calculated six estimates of the parameters using cross-sectional data. The average estimates are in Table 5.1.

Douglas's estimates show that he met the first two of the three challenges he faced: He estimated the magnitudes of the parameters a and b, and their sum came very close to one. What remained was determining whether or not the estimates of a and b came close to labor and capital's share of income in manufacturing.

The Test of Marginal Productivity Theory

Douglas's third and final challenge was to show that the actual distribution of income in manufacturing had aQ going to labor and bQ to capital. This can be considered as the test of marginal productivity since those shares came about through the assumption that the factors were paid their marginal products. Econ omists generally felt that the estimates of a and b were close to the actual shares of labor and capital and, therefore, evaluated Douglas's empirical work as supporting the marginal productivity theory of factor pricing.

In truth, though, the estimates based on time-series data were quite different from those based on cross-section data. Labor's share according to the former was 74 percent and according to the latter 63 percent. Capital's share was estimated as 23 percent using the former data set and 34 percent using the latter, 1.48 times as much. This led Douglas, a heroic Figure   to me in many respects, to present two sets of income distribution data in support of the two differing estimates.

He pointed out that the National Bureau of Economic Research "found wages and salaries [during the decade 1909–1918]formed on the average 74 percent of the total value-added by manufacturing," precisely the average figure implied in his time-series studies (1957, p. 173). To support his cross-sectional regressions, under which labor should have received 63 percent of total manufacturing income, Douglas uses the unweighted average of the shares of the *net* value product of labor in manufacturing industries which was 60.5 percent during the 1889–1919 period. I am personally uncomfortable with the use of *total* value-added in one instance and *net* value-added in the other. Net, by the way, is total value-added minus an allowance for the depreciation of capital.

The Elasticities of Production, a and b

The elasticity of production of a factor, $E_{Q/F}$, is the ratio of the percentage change in the rate production, $\Delta Q/Q$, to the percent change in the employment of the factor of production which brought it about, $\Delta F/F$: What is done here is to show that the exponents of the Cobb-Douglas function, a and b are estimates of the production elasticities of labor and capital, respectively.

(16) $E_{Q/F} = \Delta Q/Q \div \Delta F/F$

If the change in the employment of a factor is exceedingly small:

(17) $E_{Q/F} = \partial Q/Q \div \partial F/F$

And as was shown in Chapter 2, elasticity can also be put in logarithmic form:

(18) $E_{Q/F} = \partial \ln Q/\partial \ln F$

With the production function in logarithmic form:

(19) $\ln Q = \ln T + a \ln L + b \ln K$

Take the partial derivative of the logarithm of (value-added) production, $\ln Q$ with respect to the logarithm of the employment of labor. And do the the same for capital: Take the partial derivative of $\ln Q$ with respect to $\ln K$.

(20) $\partial \ln Q / \partial \ln L = a;$ $\partial \ln Q / \partial \ln K = b.$

thus we see that the parameters of the production function are the elasticities of production with respect to the employment of labor and capital, respectively. If a equals 0.75, a 1 percent increase in the employment of labor should yield a 0.75 percent increase in production. And if b equals 0.25, a 1 percent increase in the employment of capital should yield and increase in the rate of production of 0.25 percent—on the average.

Workers Are *Not* Paid a Real Wage Equal to Their Marginal Product

That workers are not paid the value of their marginal productivity is shown in two ways. In the first, I estimate the magnitude of the marginal product of labor over the 1948–1990 period. It is then shown why real compensation, the real wage, should change proportionate to the changes in marginal productivity. But it does not. In the second exercise, I redo Douglas's regression equation using the data corresponding to his best run. Then the twenty-four sets of data—on Q, L, and K—are examined. Two sets are obviously wrong in terms of the quantity of capital employed in manufacturing. Then, using over 90 percent of the Douglas data, results are found not in support of the hypothesis that workers are paid on the basis of their marginal products.

The Real Wage and the Marginal Product of Labor

Two problems are confronted here. First, I am unaware of the existence of any data on the marginal productivity of labor. But the marginal product is equal to the product of two other variables, shown forthwith. One of the variables is readily available, and a common proxy is used for the other. Second, workers are not paid in units of what they produce, but in dollars. The real wage in competitive industries equals the product price times the marginal product of labor: $W = P \cdot MP_L$. But those who work for firms that sell their products in monopolistic industries supposedly receive their marginal revenue product: $W = MR \cdot MP_L$. What is then shown is that in both sectors the change in wages should equal the change in marginal productivity. But it does not.

The Marginal Product as the Average Product Times Production Elasticity

Start with the definition of the production elasticity of labor:

(21) $\qquad E_{Q/L} = \partial Q/Q \div \partial L/L$

Rearrange terms:

(22) $\qquad E_{Q/L} = \partial Q/\partial L \div Q/L$

The numerator is the marginal, the denominator the average product of labor.

(23) $\qquad E_{Q/L} = MP_L \div AP_L$

Solve for the marginal product:

(24) $\qquad MP_L = AP_L \cdot E_{Q/L}$

Data on the average product of labor are readily available in the annual editions of the *Economic Report of the President* (EROP) as "real output per hour." Although data on the production elasticity of labor, are not common, it can be estimated as labor's share of national income, WL/NI. Therefore,

(25) $\qquad MP_L = (WL/NI) \cdot AP_L$

The Hypothesized Relationship Between the Real Wage and the Marginal Product of Labor

The neoclassical paradigm has two basis models which relate wages and marginal productivity. In the competitive product market, profit is maximized when the real wage equals the marginal productivity of labor, $W/P = MP_L$. In monopolistic product markets, profit is maximized when the money wage divided by marginal revenue equals labor's marginal productivity, $W/MR = MP_L$. The problem is to transform the two forms of the relationship between the real wage, here the same as real compensation, and marginal productivity into one.

To develop a common form of the two different wage–marginal productivity relationships, two expedient assumptions are made: (1) It is assumed that workers in competitive and monopolistic product markets receive the same money wage, W. (2) It is also assumed that the ratio of marginal revenue to price is constant. This allows the two wage equations to be manipulated into a common form as follows:

Product Market

| Competitive | Monopolistic |

(26) $W = P \cdot MPL_C$ $W = MR \cdot MPL_M$

where, the subscripts C and M refer to workers in competitive and monopolistic industries. Note that the words real wage and real compensation are used interchangeably.

Assume that the ratio of marginal revenue to price is constant: $MR = K \cdot P$ where K is a constant greater than zero and less than one.

(27) $W = P \cdot MPL_C$ $W = KP \cdot MPL_M$

Divide both sides by the price level:

(28) $W/P = MPL_C$ $W/P = K \cdot MPL_M$

Take the first difference of the terms in equation (27) and divide it by (25):

(29) $\Delta(W/P)/W/P = \Delta MPL_C/MPL_C$ $= K \, \Delta MPL_M / K \cdot MPL_M$

Thus, for both the competitive and monopolistic product markets the percentage change in real compensation should equal the percentage change in marginal productivity. This, by the way, should keep the real wage equal in both sectors

The Model Testing the Hypothesis

The linear in the logs regression model is:

(30) $lnRComp = A + BlnMPL + \mu$

where: $RComp$ is real compensation; MPL is the marginal product of labor, and μ is a stochastic disturbance term. Note that B equals the derivative of the logarithm of real compensation with respect to the marginal product of labor, $dlnRComp/dlnMPL$, the ratio of the percentage change in the real compensation to the percentage change in the marginal product of labor. Since both percentage changes should be equal, the marginal productivity model implies that B is unity and that is what has been tested.

The regression equation which follows was obtained by the least squares method using 1947–1990 data:

(31) $lnRComp = 1.0836 + 0.7637 lnMPL$ $R^2adj. = 0.99863$ $DW = 0.5$
                        $(t = 177.2)$

Thus, it is estimated that a 1 percent increase in marginal productivity, on the average, leads to a 0.76 percent increase in real compensation—far less than the 1 percent required by the neoclassical paradigm. Moreover, the standard error of the slope is 0.0043. Thus, the estimate of 0.7637 is 54.95 standard errors less than one. The probability that b, the estimate of B, equals one is accordingly minute.

The conclusion here, contrary to that of Douglas, is that the data do not support the hypothesis that workers are paid on the basis of the marginal productivity of labor.

A Correction of Douglas's Data Undermining Support of the Marginal Productivity Model

I have re-estimated the parameters of the run which came closest to the average of the time-series runs. The 1899–1922 annual data Douglas and I used can be found in Table 5.2. Note that the hours of labor per year include both clerical workers and wage earners. How clerical workers add to the rate of production in manufacturing is quite mysterious— but their inclusion leads to better statistical results.

The regression equation obtained from these data and a least squares statistical program follows:

(32) $\qquad \ln Q = -0.033 + 0.764 \ln L + 0.245 \ln K \qquad R^2 \text{adj} = 0.95065$
$\qquad\qquad\qquad\qquad (5.300) \qquad (3.818)$

Take the antilogs of equation (32) to get the results of (33):

(33) $\qquad\qquad Q = 1.033 L^{0.764} K^{0.245}$

Thus, the correctness of Douglas's regression is confirmed. But the regression is limited by the quality of the data used. Douglas knew that the data on the employment of capital in manufacturing was imperfect:

> No allowance is made for the capital which is allowed to be idle during periods of business depression or the greater than normal intensity of use in the form of second shifts, etc., which characterizes the periods of prosperity (1957, p. 122).

Consideration of this matter warrants some attention

Two substantial depressions occurred during the 1899–1922 period. As a result of the banking panic of 1907, manufacturing employment in 1908 was 11.9 percent less than it was in the previous year and value-added decreased by 16.6 percent. With a production elasticity of labor equal to 0.75, the reduced employment should have caused production to drop by 8.9 percent. In order to obtain

Table 5.2. **Value-Added, Employment of Labor, and Capital in Manufacturing, 1899–1922**
(1899 = 100)

Year	(1) VA	(2) L	(3) K	Year	(1′) VA	(2′) L	(3′) K
1899	100	100.0	100	1911	153	148.1	216
1900	101	104.8	107	1912	177	155.0	226
1901	112	110.0	114	1213	184	156.2	236
1902	122	117.2	122	1914	169	152.2	244
1903	124	121.9	131	1915	189	155.8	266
1904	123	115.6	138	1916	225	183.0	298
1905	143	125.0	149	1917	227	197.5	335
1906	152	134.2	163	1918	223	201.1	366
1907	151	139.9	176	1919	218	195.9	387
1908	126	123.2	185	1920	231	194.4	407
1909	155	142.7	198	1921	179	146.4	417
1910	159	147.0	208	1922	240	160.5	431

Source: Douglas, 1957.
Cols.1 and 1′ are from Table 14, col. 1, p. 134; cols. 2 and 2′ are from Table 9, col. 4, p. 126;
cols.3 and 3′ are from Table 6, col. 5, p. 121.
Note: Douglas's data on labor hours include both "wage earners and clerical workers."

the 16.6 percent drop in production experienced, I would anticipate a substantial drop in the employment of capital. But Douglas's data has capital increasing by a healthy 5 percent. The data for 1908 are wrong. A similar picture occurred in the post–World War I depression year 1921.

My partial and expedient correction is to drop the data for two of the twenty-four years. When data for 1908 and 1921 are dropped, the following regression equation is obtained:

(34) $\ln Q = 0.895 + 0.394 \ln L + 0.418 \ln K$. $R^2\text{adj} = 0.92291$
                    (2.220)   (5.076)

According to this regression equation, labor would receive 39.4 percent of manufacturing value-added, roughly half of the actual amount. This does not support the neoclassical marginal productivity wage model. In addition, whereas the sum of the production elasticities should equal one, they actually add up to only 0.812 (0.394 + 0.418).

How can empirical estimates change drastically when only two of twenty-four observations are dropped from a data set? When we have data on two variables, Y and X, a regression *line* is established such that the sum of the squares of the errors from that line is minimized. But for three variables $\ln Q$, $\ln L$, and $\ln K$—a reggression *plane* is positioned in three dimensional space such that the sum of the square of the errors from that plane in the lnQ direction is minimized. But if there is a linear relationship between the independent variables the data appear as a line in three dimensional space and there is no way to fit a plane to such data. All planes rotating around that line would fit the data, and each would give different estimates of the parameters. The independent variables used here are the logarithms of L and K, and their relationship is highly linear. What largely defined the plane in space was the erroneous out-of-line data of 1908 and 1921. When I removed the data of these two years, the least squares–defined plane rotated substantially around the almost linear remaining observations, yielding substantially different estimates of the parameters A and B.

Do the Production and Marginal Productivity Functions Really Exist?

The production function assumes that the rate of production can be increased by an increase in the employment of a single factor of production. But many economists believe that such a production function does not really exist. First, I attempt to show that the increased employment of a single factor cannot increase production in manufacturing and agriculture. Then the anti-production function views of three of the most distinguished economists of the twentieth century (John Hicks, Joseph A. Schumpeter, and Herbert A. Simon) are presented. Not included here is the analysis of John Bates Clark, the inventor of the marginal productivity based wage model. Clark believed that very little added production, if any, could be accomplished by the increased employment of labor with capital held constant! Highlights of Clark's work can be found in Chapter 12 where it is particularly germane.

Production in Manufacturing

The production function has the rate of production increased by the increased employment of a single factor of production, while all other inputs are held constant. This is important to neoclassical analysis because it allows the determination of the added product attributable to a marginal unit of the single factor varied. Consider the reality of this for the case of a factory which assembles automobiles.

The fixed capital used in production is, essentially, the plant and its assembly line. Assume that a factory employs 100 production workers (17,300 labor hours per month) and has an inflow of 1,000 "kits" per month. Each kit has the *variable capital* required to produce a single car: parts, assemblies, paint, welding rods, energy, replacement tools, lubricants, gasoline, and so on. How many cars can be produced if labor employment is increased to 101 production workers—with all other inputs held constant? With an inflow of 1,000 kits per month, no more than 1,000 cars per month can be produced. Labor cannot be sensibly substituted for the items, the capital, in a kit. Thus, no additional production arises from the employment of the 101st worker and the associated marginal product is zero (cars per worker month). Were we to keep employment at 100 workers and increase the inflow of kits to 1,001, the marginal product of capital would likewise be zero. The 100 workers can assemble 1,000 cars in a month and no more.

To increase production the additional employment of both labor and capital is required. A staff of 101 workers and 1,010 kits could allow the production of 1,010 cars per month assuming that adequate fixed capital is available.

The assembly of automobiles is a metaphor for the production of all goods in the economy. The increased employment of labor, capital held constant, will bring about no increase in the produce of cars, or shirts, or computers, or anything else. Along with the increased employment of labor must go additional capital—the essential "kit" required for the production of each additional unit.

Production in Agriculture

I would be quick to agree that the output of a crop, wheat as an example, varies with the application of seed, irrigation, fertilizer, herbicide, pesticide, insecticide, equipment, and labor. Disagreeableness arises when the question is raised: Are these resources independently employed? These inputs to agriculture do not fall from heaven upon the place beneath. Does not the planting of more seed require more labor services? Does not increased watering require an increase in labor and capital services to haul water or to pump it to its destination? Does not more frequent spraying of the various "-ides" require greater labor, energy, and equipment usage? And as for labor, how often is it applied to a wheat farm without being accompanied by capital goods—a seeder, a tractor, a water truck, spraying equipment (including airplanes), harvesting equipment, and so on? Rational production requires the contemporaneous application of two or more factors. As a result the contribution of a single factor cannot be identified.

Distinguished Voices Denying the Existence of a Short-Run Production Function

All production takes place in the short-run. None in the market period and none in the long run. The latter is a planning period—the period in which a hopefully superior system of production is designed and built. But once it is put into productive use we are in the short-run. So if we talk about actual production and the actual employment of the factors, we are referring to the short-run period.

Schumpeter's Denial of the Existence of the Production Function

Joseph A. Schumpeter put the matter of the production function this way in his encyclopedic and brilliant post-humous *History of Economic Analysis*:

It cannot be repeated too often that this production function is valid only at a high level of abstraction, for planned and not for existing plants, and for a limited region of the production surface at that (1954, p. 1038).

The absence of the production function in actual operations means the absence of its slope or first derivative, marginal productivity.

Hicks's Denial of the Existence of Marginal Productivity

John R. Hicks did much to popularize marginal productivity theory through his 1932 work, *Theory of Wages,* particularly its first chapter, "Marginal Productivity and the Demand for Labor." But in a revised edition, he renounced the theory: "I can no longer defer discussion of that terrible first chapter.... There are several things which are wrong; marginal productivity (used in the way I used it) is one of them"(1963, p. 321).

Hicks's renunciation of the marginal productivity model was based on its nonexistence in normal productive operations, "since the whole conception of marginal productivity depends on the variability of industrial methods" (1963, p. 20). Industrial methods are not varied during the short-run, the period of actual production, but in long-run, the period of planning new and better ways of production.

Simon and the Mistaken Distortion of the Value-Added Identity

In his article "On Parsimonious Explanations of Production Relations," (1979) Nobel Laureate Herbert A. Simon has brought together many of the criticisms of the legitimacy of the Cobb-Douglas function including the following: (1) Time series data do not yield a production function but points on a series of production functions shifted vertically with time as technology advances. (2) The parameters of a production function cannot be estimated because of the high collinearity of the logarithms of labor and capital. (This is why when I removed two years data, estimates of the parameters of the Cobb-Douglas function changed radically.) (3) Finally, there is the parsimonious approach which, in effect, confronts the question: What is the simplest function related to data on spending on the factors, Q, and the amounts of their employments, L and K? The answer is the accounting or value-added identity: Simon suggests that the data Douglas associated with his production really traced the linear value-added identity or equation (35).

(35) $$Q = WL + RK$$

where Q is value-added and the money paid to the factors during a period of a year, WL is the amount which goes to labor and RK is the amount received by capital. The payments to labor and capital must exhaust value-added, Q.

Recall that labor's share of value-added under the Cobb-Douglas production function is aQ, equation (9), and capital's share is bQ. Then,

(36) $Q = aQ + bQ$

In order for the the product to be exhausted the sum of a and b must equal one. But if the data trace out the value-added identity they have to equal one since value-added must manifest itself as payments to labor and capital.

Total or Multifactor Productivity and Its Growth

Until recently, the measure of productivity was that of labor productivity—the average product of labor, the output divided by the amount of labor used in bringing it about: $APL = Q/L$. The measure of productivity *growth* was growth in labor productivity in percent per year: $[(Q/L)_2 - (Q/L)_1)] / (Q/L)_1$. Assume that the average product of labor in year two was higher than in year one. Then, a given number of workers could create a greater output in the second year relative to the first. This seems to imply that credit for the advance should go to labor. In fact though, the increase in output could have been the result of an increase in the employment of capital or to an advance in the state of technology embodied in labor or capital or both. Total factor productivity was developed as a better measure of productivity growth.

Total Factor or Multifactor Productivity

Recall the Cobb-Douglas production function: $Q = TL^a K^b$. Solve it for T and you have the level of technology or *total factor productivity.*

> *Total factor productivity, T,* is a measure of the state of technology. It equals the ratio of the output of the process of production, Q, to the employment of labor, L, raised to the power of its elasticity of production, a, times the employment of capital, K, raised to the power of its elasticity of production, b:
> $$T = Q / (L^a K^b)$$

Recall the statement in the above section that one factor could get credit for a productivity advance when, in fact, the advance arose from the increased employment of another factor. In the case of total factor productivity, neither labor nor capital receives credit for an advance in productivity. The hero is the state of technology—usually the fruit of the brain-power of labor as manifest in more productive equipment.

Consider two examples to get a feel for the concept of total factor productivity.

The initial conditions in both examples are: Q = 100, L = 100, K=100, T=1 and a and b equal 0.7 and 0.3, respectively. In both cases the issue is how much did total factor productivity increase.

Example 1:
Given: K increases by 10 percent and Q increases by 3 percent.
Find: The magnitude of the advance in technology.

$T = 103 / (100^{0.7} \cdot 110^{0.3}) = 103 / (25.119 \cdot 4.0966) = 103 / 102.9 = 1.00$
According to the data technology did not advance.

Example 2:
Given: All Figures are the same as in the previous example except that production increased to 105.
Find: The magnitude of the advance in technology.

$T = 105 / 102.9 = 1.02$
The state of technology advanced by 2 percent.

Total Factor Productivity Growth

Total factor productivity attempts to measure the growth in technology over the course of time. It can be measured by subtracting a later calculation of total factor productivity from an earlier calculation. A somewhat more direct approach follows:

> Total factor productivity growth, dT/T or dlnT, is the growth in production due to the advance of technology in percent per year:
> $dT/T = dQ/Q - (a\ dL/L + b\ dK/K)$

The percentage growth in technology equals the percentage growth in output minus the percentage growth in output due to the increase in the employment of labor and capital, the terms in parentheses. An example is again used to make the concept concrete.

Given: (1) The annual growth in output, dQ/Q, equals 5 percent; (2) the production elasticities, a, equals 0.7 and b equals 0.3; (3) the growth in the use of capital, dK/K is 10 percent.
Find: The magnitude of the growth in technology.

$dT/T = 5-(0.7 \cdot 0.0 + 0.3 \cdot 10) = 2$ Technology advanced by 2 percent per year.

From 1948 through 1968, total factor productivity grew almost continually. The average rate of growth was 1.81 percent per annum. During the 1968–1990 period there were several years in which growth was negative and average total factor productivity growth dropped to a puny 0.41 percent a year.

Why Has Productivity Growth Declined?

There are many hypothesized causes of the decline in productivity growth: (1) The service sector, government included, has experienced relatively high growth and it tends to have less productivity growth potential than manufacturing and agriculture. (2) The percentage of jobs filled by new entrants to the labor force has increased and workers who are at the beginning of the job learning process are less productive than others. (3) The quality of the labor force has declined, as implied by standardized test scores, particularly in mathematics. (4) Corporations are increasingly led by executives with great expertise in legal and financial matters and less in the area of production. (5) Management has failed to exploit the productivity potential of new technology, particularly in the form of the ubiquitous digital computer. (6) Workers are increasingly concerned with personal and after-work projects and activities and less with work activities. (7) There has been a declining trend in the number of innovations developed each year. (8) Government regulation have drawn funds away from productivity-enhancing investments to those required to improve worker safety and the environment. (9) The potential of increasing productivity by moving workers from lower to higher-productivity industries, as exemplified by the movement from agriculture to manufacturing, has lessened. (10) We have experienced a slowdown in the growth of years of education completed. (11) Raw materials have become scarcer, causing more hours of labor to be required to produce a given amount of them. (12) The work ethic—as manifest in the effort, diligence, and thoughtfulness of workers—has declined. (13) The growth in employment in non-productive occupations has increased, as exemplified by security guards and matrimonial attorneys. (14) The capital-to-labor ratio has decreased. (15) And the average age or vintage of the capital stock has increased.

The general problem with these hypothesized causes of the decline in productivity growth is that almost all of them refer to matters occurring during periods of relatively high as well as low total productivity growth. But a recent work by Martin Neil Baily and Alok K. Chakrabarti indicates a fall in the rate of innovation after 1973 and that may be a key to determining what the problem is. There is also an anomaly in the area of investment. Gross nonresidential investment, investment in structures and durable equipment, tends to be a relatively fixed percentage of gross domestic product. The percentage actually increased slightly in the post-1973 period. This implies that net investment, gross minus depreciation, should have followed the same trend—but it did not. It declined as a portion of gross domestic product because of an increase in the outflow of capital , depreciation—due largely to the write off of plants made obsolete by new technology and the decline of certain industries.

Historic Attempts to Increase the Productivity of Workers

Adam Smith was the first to stress growth and the role of labor productivity. His approach is presented at the outset of this section. You will then find three different approaches to the reorganization of work as exemplified by the most influential innovators in this area during the twentieth century: Frederick Winslow Taylor, Elton Mayo, and W. Edwards Deming. (Recent approaches of economists, the "efficiency wage" included, are discussed in Chapter 13.)

Adam Smith and Labor Productivity Growth

The opening sentence of Book I, Chapter I of the ...Wealth of Nations is:

> The greatest improvement in the productive powers of labour, and the greater part of the skill, dexterity, and judgment with which it is anywhere directed, or applied, seem to have been the effects of the division labour (1937 [1776], p.3).

Smith's terse explanation of why this is so follows:

> This great increase in the quantity of work, which is a consequence of the division of labour ... is owing to three different circumstances; first, to the increase of dexterity in every particular workman; secondly, to the saving of the time which is commonly lost in passing from one species of work to another; and lastly, to the invention of a great number of machines which ...enable one man to do the work of many (1937 [1776], p.7).

The last advance has been by far the most powerful.

Frederick Winslow Taylor and Scientific Management

Frederick Winslow Taylor was a shop worker, shop foreman, and mechanical engineer whose abiding interest was in increasing labor productivity. His work is captured in two books: Shop Management and Principles of Scientific Management. Both were published in 1911. To a large extent Taylor's work follows that of Adam Smith. That is implied starting with the opening sentence of Scientific Management:

> The principal object of management should be to secure the maximum prosperity for the employer, coupled with the maximum prosperity for each employee (1911, p. 9).

That was done by increasing labor productivity with its value shared by workers and employers.

Based upon his experience as a shop worker and manager, Taylor states that "in a majority of the cases ... [a] man deliberately plans to do as little as he safely can...."(p. 13). Taylor recognizes that workers possess the mass of traditional knowledge relevant to their jobs as do supervisors who came from their ranks. He believed, however, that since workers prefer to loaf on the job, the task of increasing productivity was management's alone and that the most productive way a job could be done can be specified scientifically. This involved the determination of the qualities a worker should possess to do a particular job; the precise motions a worker should make to perform the job; the precise tools that should be used; the correct incentives to be given for productivity increases; monitoring each worker's daily performance, and the removal of those incapable of maintaining high levels of production. In a wonderful Smithian statement Taylor points out that "management ... invariably finds that work can be done better and more economically by a subdivision of the labor...."(p. 38).

Two of Taylor's examples of productivity improvement are illustrative of the work of the scientific management movement. The first involved the shoveling of materials in the steel plant in which Taylor worked. He first posed the question: How heavy a shovel load is optimum? He varied the load handled by the workers he considered the best at shoveling and found 21 pounds per load ideal. Moreover, since different materials varied in density, different-sized shovels were required to maintain the approximately 21-pound shovel load. Taylor had a shovel room built to store the different shovels as well as a similarly designed array of picks, crowbars, and the like.

Taylor had thousands of stop-watch measurements taken of workers shoveling different materials, from different parts of a pile, with piles on different bottom materials, with shovel throws of various distances and heights. Workers were then instructed regarding the precise way they should shovel the various materials of the steel yard.

Much labor time had been lost in moving workers from one part of the large steel yard to another in the course of the day. Under Taylor's approach the specific work, work time, and locational movement of each worker was planned in advance for the following day. At the outset of the workday, each worker found in his assigned box detailed instructions defining his work and work locations for the day. He also was informed how much he had earned for the work of the previous day.

The upshot of this "scientific" approach was a reduction in the number of yard laborers from about 500 to 140, a 63 percent increase in their average earnings, and a 54 percent decrease in the cost of handling a ton of material.

Taylor's report on bricklaying is indicative of the extent to which scientific managers involved themselves in the details of the work of skilled craftsmen. He pointed out that:

> Bricklaying is one of the oldest of our trades. For hundreds of years there has been little or no improvement made in the implements and materials used in this trade, nor in fact in the method of laying bricks (1911, p.77).

Here is indeed a case involving the absence of technological growth–although I suspect that many enjoy doing things in traditional ways. He then goes on to describe the work of Frank B. Gilbreth in increasing the productivity of masons. Gilbreth determined "the exact position which each of the feet of the bricklayer should occupy with respect to the wall, the mortar box, and the pile of bricks," and he designed the mortar box and scaffolding required to maintain the optimum relationship between these elements. He also found that bricklayers generally used 18 motions in laying brick and was able to reduce them to 5. This reduction is related to Gilbreth's observation that workers frequently use one hand in doing something such as picking up a brick while the other lies idle. He reorganized the motions workers used so that both hands were continually in productive use. As a result of the reorganization of work Gilbreth increased the productivity of bricklayers from 120 to 350 bricks per hour. Those unable to perform at this rate were fired; those who could receive substantial pay increases.

The limitation of these kinds of productivity increases is that they represent one-shot rather than continuing advances in productivity growth. You learn or are programmed to lay a brick precisely right every 10.3 seconds of a workday, but there is no advance from that point. But were profits actually maximized, all workers would have to labor under the yoke of scientific management.

Elton Mayo and the Hawthorne Experiments

Elton Mayo was an industrial sociologist who taught at the Harvard School of Business Administration. The Western Electric Company, for many decades the exclusive manufacturer of all the equipment used in the Bell Telephone System, was dissatisfied with the production of relays at its Hawthorne Works near Chicago. It called on Mayo for professional assistance. He started his Hawthorne experiments in the late 1920s and went on with them well into the 1930s.

Mayo understood the factory to be a social organism with many social subgroups. Productivity did not merely depend upon the skill of the workers and the equipment at their disposal. It was also a function of the norms set by the work group, norms determining the maximum production of a day. Mayo recognized that these quotas reflected the attitude of the work group toward the company. The challenge of management, to him and his followers, was to win the allegiance of workers thereby allowing the quality and quantity of production to be increased.

The Hawthorne experiments were mainly a set of changes in the workplace ambience intended to show the concern of the company for its workers. Almost without fail, a change in the work environment increased productivity temporarily. Mayo, for example, had the illumination in the relay assembly department increased and productivity increased—for a while. He had the illumination decreased and productivity increased—for a while. Apparently, the work group saw these changes as manifestations of the concern of the employer for them and responded positively to that perception.

Two aspects of Mayo's work are of continuing interest. The first is captured in the phrase "the Hawthorne effect." Its direct implication is that change will yield temporary but not permanent improvement. The second is a logical outgrowth of the first. Management's continuing display of concern for its employees will cause them to increase the quality and quantity of their production, the "human relations" approach.

W. Edwards Deming and Quality Circles

The World War II Japanese were no great favorite of Americans and this was particularly true of Japanese political leaders and their industrialist friends. Subsequent to our dropping atomic bombs on Hiroshima and Nagasaki, the Japanese surrendered, and we saw to it that their political and industrial activities were more congenial to us. One of the institutions brought to Japan was the *Quality Circle*, an invention of W. Edwards Deming. Deming was a New York University professor of statistics who specialized in quality control. The members of a work group or team are members of its Quality Circle. Its mission is to deal with the production problems experienced by the group from the perspective of improving the quality of what was produced. Common examples are decreases in the failure rate of products produced and the number of input errors punched into computers. Worker participation in Quality Circles is at their own initiative and during their own time. They have been effective in improving product quality and, along the way, work group productivity.

Quality circles are well suited to the culture of the Japanese corporation which, in some fundamental respects, is quite different than ours. The major Japanese employers have personnel practices which give workers lifetime job security, pay and promotion systems largely based on seniority, a far more egalitarian pay structures than ours, status based on rank rather than pay, and group decision-making. Japanese corporations tend to be paternalistic. Workers are part of the corporate family, and to a large degree, they are made to feel that the company is theirs. In this setting, Quality Circles have flourished.

The Limitation of Short Run-Programs

Wickham Skinner, of the Harvard School of Business, visited a company which had what seems to be a wonderful systematic approach to increase productivity:

> The program has included: appointing a corporate productivity manager; establishing departmental productivity committees; raising the number of industrial engineering professionals by 50%; carrying out operation-by-operation analyses to improve efficiency levels, avoid waste, and simplify jobs; retrain employees to work 'smarter not harder;' streamlining work flow and materials movement; replacing out-of-date equipment; retooling operations to cut operator time; tightening standards; training foremen in work simplification (1986, p. 55).

The painful irony is that with all of this systematic effort, productivity increased by only 7 percent after three years. The moral of the story is that fundamental changes in technology are required to substantially increase productivity. Nothing less can do the trick.

Other Aspects of Increasing Productivity

There are a number of elements which are required to increase productivity including invention or discovery, entrepreneurship, research and adequate development, and, frequently, government subsidies.

Invention or Discovery

The most common kinds of discoveries are those involving advances in the process of production and those which lead to the development of new products.

Mechanization of production tends to be labor saving, shifting the production function so that the average product of labor increases. Such advances are inherent in the ongoing industrial revolution. The pin factory described by Adam Smith represented a great increase in the productivity of labor. It came about by virtue of the better organization of the process of production, Smith's "division of labor," and the invention of machinery to perform simplified tasks. A somewhat more recent advance was that engineered by Henry Ford who worked assiduously on advancing productivity so that owning an automobile could fall within the grasp of a substantial portion of our population. In 1909, Ford sold 12,000 Model T Touring Cars at a price of $950; by 1925 the price of a Model T had dropped to $290 and 1,495,000 were sold. By today's norms Ford's use of standardization was extreme in that you could buy his Model T in any color you wanted—as long as it was black.

Thomas Alva Edison, who left school at the age of seven, was the most distinguished inventor of new products in American history. He was a telegraph operator and his early inventions were in that area: transmitters and receivers for automatic operation, a system for transmitting four simultaneous messages, and an improved stock-ticker system. Edison is probably most famous for his invention of the practical incandescent bulb in 1879. He is less famous for developing the complete electric power system, the Pearl Street Plant in the City of New York (1882), a system required for the widespread use of his bulbs. While Edison is famous for the invention of new products he should be as famous for developing the production processes and systems which allowed the products to be used by large numbers of people.

This is not the place to even list the many other inventions of this great inventor-entrepreneur. Edison's early inventions were largely his own. Over the course of time, however, the number of projects and complexity of the work required the involvement of teams of workers. This led to his establishing laboratories in

Menlo Park and West Orange, New Jersey, prototypes of the research-development laboratories of today—the locus of much of our era's discoveries for advancing productivity.

Certain firms and industries have cultures which give innovation a high priority. The chemical, drug, computer, and telephone industries afford examples of the continuing tendency to innovate and the need to continually innovate or perish. Investment in innovation involves two major interrelated decisions. The first requires choosing a small set of areas to pursue from a large set of possibilities. The second decision is the amount of investment to be made in each of the areas chosen. This has two dimensions: how large an effort, in staff and money, is required, and for how long a time it is to go on. These decisions are made in the context of the establishment of an overall budget. Some complexity is reduced by the expedient of a norm in which X percent of the budget is set aside for research and development.

Entrepreneurship

There have been numerous attempts to determine the essence of the entrepreneurial function and some of the best known are presented here.

Johann Heinrich von Thünen, in his 1850 work, *The Isolated State*, described the entrepreneur as a residual claimant of a risky unpredictable income. These risks were of a kind that no insurance company would cover because of their unpredictable character.

Following Frank Knight's *Risk, Uncertainty, and Profit* (1921), we now semantically differentiate between insurable and unpredictable ventures:

> *Risk* involves activities well enough known that they can be described by objective probability functions. As a result, the cost of a risk can be insured against.

The cost of this "insurance," as others, diminishes profit. Firms are generally, in effect, self-insured in this area. The most important of the entrepreneurial functions to Knight, as it was to Thünen, is the bearing of uncertainty:

> *Uncertainties* involve activities which cannot be described by an objective probability function. The activity is either completely unprecedented or sufficiently unprecedented that existing data are inadequate to define the activity's objective probability function.

Those entrepreneurs who by insight or luck are able to divine that a particular economic activity will be successful, in an unknown future, justify a return in excess of marginal productivity–based returns to the factors of production. This return to entrepreneurs for overcoming uncertainty is economic profit.

Joseph Schumpeter, more than any predecessor, stressed the importance of the entrepreneur to the economy and particularly to economic change. In his *The Theory of Economic Development* (1911). Schumpeter characterized *invention* as the discovery of new technology, products, and forms of productive organization. *Innovation* involves the introduction to the economy of inventions or discoveries. The innovator is the entrepreneur and his actions are the source of all dynamic change in the economic system. Schumpeter claimed that it was impossible to understand capitalism without understanding the socioeconomic conditions leading to entrepreneurship.

Non-Productive Innovations

Much entrepreneurship in recent decades has been non-productive in character. They have involved creating mergers and acquisitions and the development of innovative financial instruments as exemplified by "junk bonds," option futures, and derivatives. These activities and instruments have no connection to advancing productivity and the standard of living.

Marketability Requires Adequate Development

The words research and development are so often used together that we may be prone to forget their fundamental difference. Applied research involves the discovery of the basic concepts which make possible the development of new products, services, and methods of production. Development is concerned with transforming the applied research into products which are marketable. Development costs are frequently greater than research costs, and this has sometimes lead to the abandonment of the development of worthwhile projects.

The relatively recent development by the Japanese of electronic products based on our research has stimulated investigation into this problem. According to the work of Edwin Mansfield, the Japanese spend 44 percent of their investment in innovation on development while we spend roughly half as much— namely, 23 percent. This may be a reason for our failure to exploit some of our discoveries.

The Role of Government

Does government play a role in the inventive process? In this post-Edison age, it is hard to imagine major advances in technological products and processes which do not utilize the services of groups of scientists and engineers with advanced degrees. It is equally hard to find an appreciable number of them whose graduate-level tuition and research were not subsidized in one way or another by the government. The government has played an entrepreneurial role in the process which yields new products, technology, supplies, and markets.

The Bads of Technological Progress

Technological progress leads to greater strength of nations and the material well-being of their populations. For some workers and investors, however, technological progress means unemployment and loss of wealth. Technological progress also entails the depletion of resources and, at least until recently, increasing pollution of the environment. If a byproduct of technology is global warming, the cost of material progress may be incalculable.

The Rise and Fall of Firms and the Employment They Provide

New industries, making products destined to have widespread popular appeal, tend to follow this pattern: Innovations in the process of production take place. This leads to productivity growth lowering the cost of production and price. Sales grow substantially and employment grows at a somewhat lower pace. Rival firms are forced to use the new innovations in order to remain competitive. But some of the advances are very expensive and some firms find them to be either not affordable or not required. These firms, failing to keep up with the state of the productive arts, tend to fail. Their failures frequently involve substantial losses to investors, vendors, employees, and sometimes customers.

Over the course of time, households tend to own as much of the not-so-new product as they desire—cars, radios, television sets, and the like—and much of the demand is limited to newly formed households and the replacement of older with newer versions of the product. Growth in sales abate. Productivity increases then tend to imply employment decreases in the industry. In "mature" industries, workers rightfully fear productivity advances.

Pollution and Depletion

The more we produce, the more we tend to deplete nonrenewable resources and to pollute the environment. It would be wrong to believe that only good arises from the advance of technology and the increase of production. Automobile production involves production and pollution in the steel, plastics, chemical, textile, energy, paint, and petroleum industries. Then, consumers, users of motor vehicles, have their opportunity to pollute the environment largely through the exhaust system of the car but also in the disposal of tires, and batteries. High production also means high rates of depletion of the minerals in the crust of the earth, particularly metallic ores and energy sources. Petroleum affords a case in point. The United States used to export substantial amounts of gasoline and other petroleum products. Today, half of the petroleum we consume is imported. We can, of course substitute other sources of energy for petroleum—but if that is true, why have we failed to do so? Why is our economy so dependent on the petroleum of others?

Economists do not generally lose sleep about the depletion of resources. As supply dwindles, prices are forced up. This should discourage the use of the resource—in general, cause its use to be increasingly curtailed in applications of relatively low value, and spur the development and use of substitutes. All of this sounds fine—but is it? Like the losers in the "creative destruction" of economic progress, there will be losers here as well, particularly if substitutes are hard to discover and employ. And as was pointed out in Chapter 1, markets are a heartless rationing institution. Those who cannot afford to buy a resource as its price increases must do without it.

Summary

The per capita level of production is the principal determinant of the standard of living in a nation. And its growth relative to that of others determines the rise or fall of a nation's economic standing. Thus, the importance of production and its advance and of the production function and its shifts. In the analysis of production it is important to recognize the significance of Marshall's time frames: no production takes place in the market period; all production takes place in the short-run; and the long-run is the period for planning the use of new plant, equipment, and methods of production. A concern for production implies interest in the short-run; interest in growth requires a long-run focus.

In the planning stage, the long run, optimal factor employments can be determined for substitutable factors by the equality of their marginal productivities per dollar as constrained by a budget or budget line. More directly, more labor or more capital intensive methods of production can be advocated by planners to those who control the budget and the firm. The budget or budget line is fundamentally important because it defines the quality of the structure and equipments which can be specified by the planners in designing a system with a specified production capacity. It can be argued that at this level a production function exists—but its range is limited by the reality of best current practice. Nails can be forged by hand but planners would not, really could not, consider such an alternative. And planning is expensive so the range of practical considerations is limited and largely involves the substitution between capital equipment differing in price and expected durability.

A large majority of economists believe in the existence of a production function. It allows for increasing production by varying the employment of a single factor of production with all others held constant. This actually occurs only in trivial cases. Jewelers, working with gold, could employ someone to collect gold scraps. Such a person could have a marginal product without the employment of additional capital. And a member of "the world's oldest profession" could sell factor services with no additional capital required. But such activities comprise a negligible portion of overall production. In the overwhelming norm, additional production requires additional labor and (circulating) capital.

The Cobb-Douglas production function shows how important the production function is to current economic analysis. It defines the amount of value-added production which can be obtained as a function of the employment of labor and capital. It forms the basis of the factor demand functions, and it shows the distribution of income to the factors. There is good reason to oppose the contention that it and, more generally, the neoclassical production function is non-existent.

Once the method and tools of production are in place, not very much substitution can be found. One can then no longer contend with any generality that an increase in the relative price of a factor will decrease its employment and increase that of substitutes, and that the increased employment of a single factor will increase the rate of production. It generally will not. The factors tend to be complementary in production and production managers told to increase the rate of production will generally submit requisitions for labor and a "bill of materials" listing the many forms of capital required.

The conventional measure of productivity is the average product of labor or output per hour of work. An increase in labor productivity may mean that people are working harder or smarter. But it might also mean that they are more productive because they have more or better tools at their disposal. This has led to the development of the concept of total or multifactor productivity, which attempts to measure the growth of technology and productivity by subtracting from an increase in production the amount ascribable to the increased employment of the factors.

Minor or "one-shot" changes in productivity can be accomplished by a variety of means associated with "good management." Major changes require major changes in technology coming from investment in the latest state-of-the-art plants, equipment, and production processes. These advances are an outgrowth of invention and successful entrepreneurship.

The post-1973 decrease in productivity growth implied that this process is not performing as well in the second half of the post–World War II period as it did in the first half. Many hypotheses have been proposed as the key explanation of this situation—but none have received widespread acceptance.

The bads and potential bads of production require recognition. Pollution and the depletion of non-renewable resources may have a frightening effect on future generations. There are at this time major metropolitan areas in which the air is unfit for breathing, regions in which the water is unfit for human and animal consumption, and regions in which the sun represents a serious health hazard.

Questions on Chapter 5

1. a. Draw a production function in which the quantity produced is a function of the employment of labor during a specified period of time.
   b. What is the reason for the declining slope or marginal productivity of labor?

2. Define and show graphically, at some output rate, the average product of labor. Whatever you are producing, how can production be increased by increasing the employment of labor alone.

3. a. Why does the model of production vary one factor while keeping all other factors constant?
   b. Consider the production of pizzas or some other good whose production is familiar to you. Can additional production be accomplished by varying one factor alone? Explain.

4. a. Explain why the standard of living is based on productivity.
   b. Productivity growth has fallen substantially since 1973 or 1974. What are some of the hypotheses which attempt to explain the drop in productivity growth?

5. What groups are responsible for the advance of technology? Why do you think their current efforts are relatively ineffective in creating productivity growth?

6. The condition for cost minimization requires knowledge of the cost of all factors used and considered for use. How should the cost of a durable capital good be determined?

CHAPTER SIX

Cost Functions

The number of traditional cost functions is seven: three kinds of total cost (total, total variable, and total fixed), three related kinds of average cost (average, average variable, and average fixed), plus marginal cost. It is important to know the meaning of each of these costs, how the average and marginal and totals are related, and the ways in which each of the costs is of importance.

Cost functions fall into the time horizon established by Alfred Marshall: the market, short-run, and long-run periods. Emphasis at the outset is on short-run functions, the cost functions related to actual productive activities. Then long-run cost functions are considered. They are useful in planning new facilities, particularly the structure, equipment, and method of production expected to yield minimum cost per unit of production. Finally, some of the major aspects of transaction costs are discussed.

In common usage, cost functions unadorned with any designation are short-run in character—the functions associated with actual production. Cost functions pose a problem since those found in empirical studies are basically different from the logic-based functions of the neoclassical paradigm. Moreover, empirical cost functions tend to be inconsistent with the neoclassical production function.

Total Cost and Its Constituents

Two sets of cost functions are presented. The first is based on the total cost functions generally found in textbooks and probably in agriculture. This function starts out with a decreasing slope which becomes increasing as the rate of production increases. Such a total cost curve yields "U"-shaped average, average variable, and marginal cost curves. The marginal cost function equals the average variable and average cost functions at their minimum. This total cost function, in which *all factors* capable of being varied are, is consistent with production functions in which only *one factor* is varied leading to increasing, constant,

Figure 6.1.   **The Total Cost Functions of Textbooks and Agriculture**

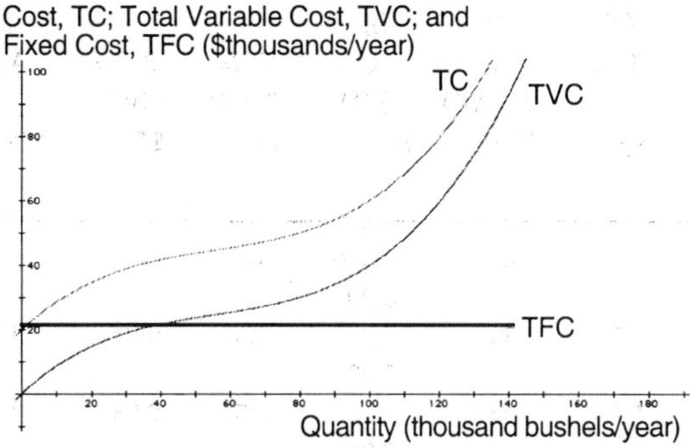

Total Cost, TC; Total Variable Cost, TVC; and
Total Fixed Cost, TFC ($thousands/year)

Quantity (thousand bushels/year)

and then decreasing marginal productivity.

The second total cost function is linear. It is the cost function virtually always found in empirical studies. It yields a marginal cost which is constant and equal to average variable cost. With a linear total cost function, average cost declines up to the full capacity rate of production. It is consistent with linear production functions which arise from production with the same dose of variable factors used for production in cost analysis.

The Textbook Agricultural Cost Functions

The logic-based textbook total cost function arises from these assumptions:
- All costs are current and not historic costs.
- Proper planning allows for total cost minimization over the range of expected rates of production.
- As relative factor prices change, the relative employments of the variable factors of production are modified to maintain least cost production.
- As the rate of production increases from zero, operational economies are experienced so that the cost of producing the marginal unit declines; but at higher rates the increasing scarcity of fixed factors results in an increase in the cost of producing marginal units.

A typical textbook total cost function is given in Figure 6.1. The hypothetical data upon which this and the related cost functions are based appears in Table 6.1. Figure 6.1 shows the three total cost functions: Total cost, TC, total variable cost, TVC, and total fixed cost, TFC—all as a function of the rate of production, Q.

The Total Cost Function

Total cost is the sum of all costs incurred by the firm as a function of the rate of production, Q. Total cost is the sum of total variable and total fixed costs:

Table 6.1.   **Wheat-Grower Brown's Costs**

(1) Q	(2) TFC	(3) TVC	(4) TC	(5) MC= Δ(3)/Δ(1)	(6) AFC= (2)/(1)	(7) AVC= (3)/(1)	(8) AC= (4)/(1)
bushels/yr b/yr	$/yr	$/yr	$/yr	$/b	$/b	$/b	$/b
0	20	0	20	slope 15/20	∞	slope	∞
20	20	15	35		1.0	0.75	1.75
				7/20			
40	20	22	42		0.5	0.55	1.05
				3/20			
60	20	25	45		0.33	0.42	0.75
				5/20			
80	20	30	50		0.25	0.38	0.63
				10/20			
100	20	40	60		0.20	0.40	0.60
				20/20			
120	20	60	80		0.17	0.50	0.67
				32/20			
140	20	92	112		0.14	0.66	0.80

Note: Columns (1), (2), (3), and (4) are in thousands.

$TC = TVC + TFC$. If two total costs are known the third can be calculated. For profit maximization, total cost should be as low as possible over the range of expected rates of production.

The Total Variable Cost Function

Total variable cost is the sum of all costs incurred by the firm which vary with the rate of production, Q. Typical variable costs are those of labor and variable capital. *Variable* capital implies capital instruments which can be purchased with time lags roughly commensurate with that required for the hiring of new employees. It consists of items such as the following: purchases of off-the-shelf equipment, tools, parts and materials, and lubricants and energy.

Total variable cost is usually described as composed of the variable costs directly associated with production. In actuality, however, the staff of non-production workers and the equipment and materials they use also increase with the rate of production and, therefore, warrant inclusion in total variable cost. Why is it that non-production costs tend to increase at approximately the same pace as production costs? My best guess follows: To a large extent variation in the employment of non-production workers appears to be related to the variation of the number of transactions effected, internal and external to the firm. The higher the rate of production, the higher is the employment of production workers, and the greater is the need for additional employment in departments such as human resources, receiving, shipping, inspection and quality control, and payroll. In addition, the greater is the number of employees, the greater is the number of managers employed to supervise their work and the more higher managers are required to supervise lower managers.

Total Variable Cost as the Sum of Total Labor and Total Variable Non-Labor Costs

Were labor the only variable cost of production, the total variable cost function would merely be a transformation of the production function. Two simple alterations would be needed: First, the employment of labor axis would be multiplied by the wage rate making it total variable cost—at least the total variable cost of labor, TLC. Second, the axes would be reversed so that quantity would be on the horizontal axis and the employment of labor times its wage on the vertical axis. Thus, the total labor cost function of Figure 6.2.

But while the neoclassical production function has producers increasing production by increasing the employment of a single factor at a time, the neoclassical cost function has producers increasing production by increasing the employment of all variable factors together, pursuant to cost minimization, I have therefore added the total variable non-labor cost function, $TVNLC$, to the total labor cost function. The function is shown as linear with the rate of production as one kit required per unit of output.

Note the effect of adding a linear total variable non-labor cost function to a substantially curved total labor cost function. The total variable cost function becomes quite linear. Furthermore, over a reasonable operating range of the total variable cost function—for example, from 80,000 to 120,000 bushels per year—the function is even more linear. Finally, the total cost function is total variable cost displaced vertically by the magnitude of total fixed cost.

The Total Fixed Cost Function

Total fixed cost is the sum of all fixed costs the firm is obligated to pay, per unit of time, irrespective of the rate of production. These are generally payments required by contract or by government: rent (for buildings and equipment), interest and principal payments on loans, payments to executives under contract, real estate taxes, license fees, and the like. Total fixed cost is $20,000 per week in Table 6.1 and Figure 6.1. Were production shut down, certain fees, such as license fees, need not be paid. Thus, fixed costs at shut down are somewhat less than those during normal operations.

Figure 6.2.   **Total Variable Cost as the Sum of Total Labor and Total Variable Non-Labor Costs**

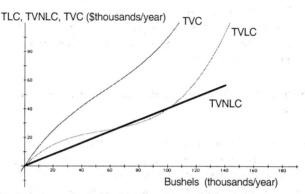

Average Cost, Average Fixed Cost, and Average Variable Cost

How can average cost be calculated? Take total cost and divide it by the number of units produced in attaining that cost. Thus, in Table 6.1, when the total cost is $60,000 per year and the rate of production is 100,000 bushels per year, the average cost is $0.60 per bushel The same approach yields average fixed and average variable cost except the former requires the use of total fixed cost, the latter total variable cost:

(1) $AC = TC/Q = AFC + AVC$

(2) $AFC = TFC/Q = AC - AVC$

(3) $AVC = TVC/Q = AC - AFC$

As with the three total cost functions, if two of the average costs are known, the third can be calculated.

Marginal Cost

Arguably, the most important of the cost functions in economic theory is marginal cost:

> *Marginal cost* is the ratio of change of total cost to the change in the output rate: $\Delta TC/\Delta Q$ or dTC/dQ.

It is the slope of the total cost and total variable cost functions at a given rate of production. In Table 6.1, the marginal cost data have been placed between the quantities traversed in arriving at the particular number. This is because the mar-

Figure 6.3.   **Average Fixed Cost as the Slope of the Vector from the Origin to the Total Fixed Cost Curve**

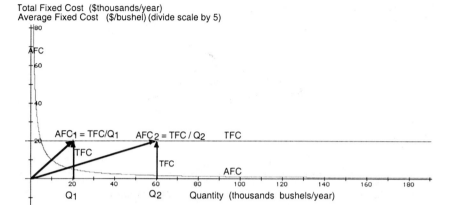

Total Fixed Cost ($thousands/year)
Average Fixed Cost ($/bushel) (divide scale by 5)

ginal cost of going from an output rate of 80 to 100 is the same as that involved in going from 100 to 80. And the estimate obtained from TVC(100) – TVC(80) divided by the quantity change, 100 – 80 best approximates the slope of the total variable cost curve at an output rate of 90—and that is where the marginal cost figure is placed.

Average and Marginal Cost as Slopes Related to Total Functions

Cost functions are frequently given in graphical form. It is, therefore, helpful to understand the geometric relationship of the marginal and average cost functions to the total functions to understand, for example, why marginal cost equals average variable and average cost at their minima and why it also equals average variable cost at an output rate of zero.

Average Fixed Cost

Average fixed cost is troublesome because it is not fixed; it is total fixed cost which is fixed in amount. Average fixed cost represents the allocation of a part of total fixed cost to each unit produced according to the formula $AFC = TFC/Q$. If the rate of production is one, all of total fixed cost is charged to that single unit; if it is one million, one millionth of total fixed cost is applied to each unit. From the perspective of average fixed cost, the higher the rate of production possible, the lower is this cost.

As is shown in Figure 6.3, average fixed cost at Q_1, AFC_1, is the slope of the vector from the origin to the total fixed cost function at Q_1. When the rate of production is zero, that vector is vertical. Its slope is infinite and so is average

Figure 6.4.   Marginal Cost as the Slope of the Total Cost Curve

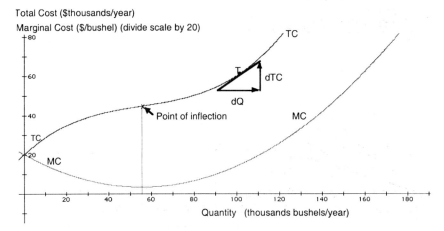

Total Cost ($thousands/year)

Marginal Cost ($/bushel) (divide scale by 20)

fixed cost. As the rate of production increases the slope of the vector decreases and, in the limit, approaches zero. Thus, while *total* fixed cost is constant, *average* fixed cost is variable. The average fixed cost curve is a rectangular hyperbola, a curve which has the property that the product of its variables, here $AFC \cdot Q$, equals a constant, TFC. Firms engaged in mass production tend to have very high fixed costs. But if they sell a million units, each unit will be burdened with one-millionth of total fixed cost.

Marginal Cost

Marginal cost is the rate of change of total cost with respect to the the rate of production: dTC/dQ. It is the slope of the total cost function at a given rate of production and, what is the same, the slope of the total variable cost function: $dTVC/dQ$, at the same rate of production.

  The total cost function and its associated marginal cost function are shown in Figure 6.4. Consider the tangent to the total cost function at point T. Its slope, dTC/dQ, is the magnitude of marginal cost at the rate of production which corresponds to T. Also note point x on the total cost function. It is a "point of inflection"—the point on the total cost curve at which its slope reaches a minimum and begins to increase. At the corresponding output rate, marginal cost is at its minimum. At higher output rates, the law of diminishing marginal productivity makes its appearance in the form of increasing marginal cost.

  In oral discourse we frequently describe marginal cost as the increase in total cost, dTC, caused by production of the marginal unit. In fact, that increase is in differential cost, $dTC = MC \cdot dQ = (dTC/dQ) \cdot dQ$.

Figure 6.5.   **Average Cost: The Slope of a Vector from the Origin to Total Cost Curve**

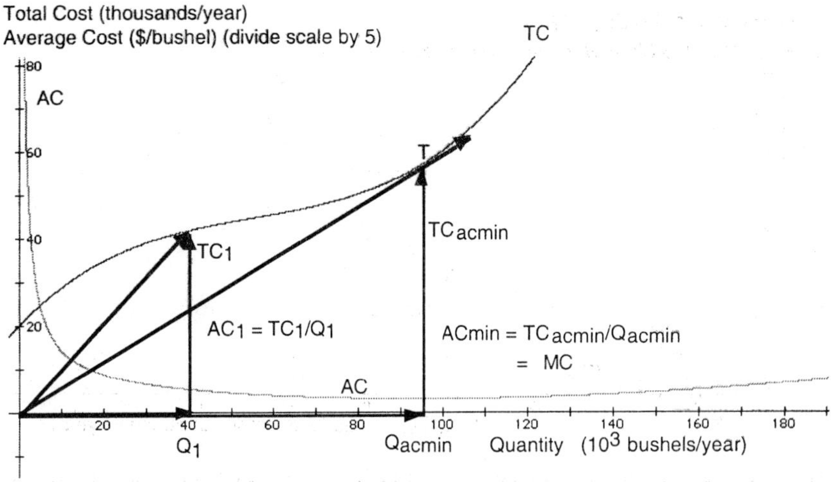

Total Cost (thousands/year)
Average Cost ($/bushel) (divide scale by 5)

Average Cost

Average cost equals total cost divided by the output rate corresponding to it: $AC=TC/Q$. Average cost at a given output rate is the slope of the vector from the origin to the total cost curve at that rate of production.

The difference between the selling price of a product and its average cost, $P-AC$, tells us whether or not economic profits are being realized. If, for example, the price is $11 and average cost is $10, one dollar of economic profit per unit of production is realized.

The geometry which yields average cost appears in Figure 6.5. The slope of the vector from the origin to the total cost curve at Q_1 is TC_1/Q_1. The slope of the vector at $Q = 0$ is infinite. The slope of the vector to the total cost curve and average cost decreases until the vector becomes tangent to the total cost function at Q_{acmin}. At this rate of production average cost is a minimum and equal to marginal cost—the former comes from the vector's minimum slope, the latter from its tangency with the total cost function.

Average Variable Cost

Average variable cost equals total variable cost divided by the associated rate of production:

> $AVC=TVC/Q$ AVC at a given rate of production is the slope of a vector from the origin of the TVC function to the total variable cost curve at that rate of production.

Figure 6.6.   **The Geometric Relationship Between Total and Average Variable Cost**

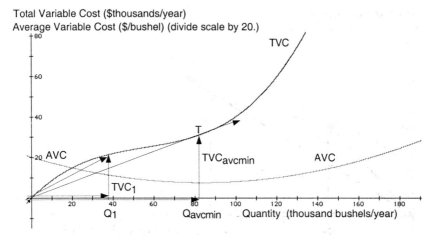

The geometric relationship defining the average variable cost function can be seen in Figure 6.6. At Q_1 average variable cost equals total variable cost by the rate of production: $AVC_1 = TVC_1/Q_1$—the slope of a vector from the origin of the total variable cost function to the function.

There are two rates of production at which average variable cost equals marginal cost. One is at a zero rate of production. At that point on the function the slope of the function and that of the vector to the function are equal. That can be seen by drawing vectors from the function's origin to the function for smaller and smaller rates of production. The other equality is at the minimum of the average variable cost function, AVC_{min}. This is because the minimum is where the slope of the vector is lowest—where it is tangent to the total variable cost function. And the slope of that tangent is also marginal cost. At output rates greater than zero and less than Q_{avcmin}, marginal cost is less than average variable cost. In this range the slope of the function is less than the slope of the vector to the function. Thereafter marginal cost is greater than average variable cost.

The Linear Total Cost and Related Functions

Of the nine empirical cost studies I am aware of, six estimate marginal cost to be constant, two estimate it to be declining, and one that it is increasing. Thus, only one of nine is consistent with the logic-based neoclassical cost functions. As a consequence of these studies I assume that the marginal cost function tends to be constant and that the total cost curve tends to be linear. Such a total cost curve and its related functions are illustrated in Figure 6.7 and Table 6.2.

Since the total cost function is linear, the total variable cost function is also linear—displaced downward by the total fixed cost of $500 per day. The result-ing marginal and average functions are interesting in that they are quite different

Figure 6.7.   **A Linear Total Cost Curve and Related Functions**

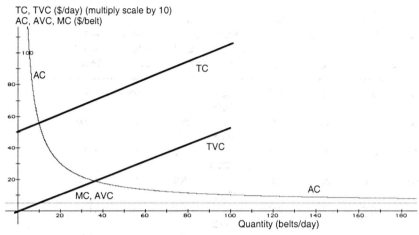

TC, TVC ($/day) (multiply scale by 10)
AC, AVC, MC ($/belt)

than the conventional textbook functions. With constant-sloped total cost and total variable cost functions, marginal and average variable cost are constant and equal to $5 per belt at all rates of production. The constancy of marginal cost controverts the law of diminishing marginal returns. Since this is common, it indicates that much and perhaps most of the economy is lawless.

With the mathematical form of the linear total cost function, $TC = TFC + mQ$, the average cost function is $AC = (TFC/Q) + m$, and average fixed cost, as always, is $AFC = TFC/Q$. The average cost and average fixed cost functions are rectangular hyperbolas, with the former displaced upward by $m = \$5$ as compared to the latter, which has not been graphed.

Note in Table 6.2 the numerical relationship between the average and marginal and total costs. In calculating marginal cost as the ratio of the difference in total variable cost, ΔTVC, to the difference in the rate of production, ΔQ, I have left the ΔQs denominated in 20s. This is done to help avoid the carelessness of assigning the number one to these quantity differences. Again, marginal cost calculations have been centered between the quantities used in its calculation. The change in total cost, for example, in going from quantities of 0 to 20 yields an estimate of the marginal cost at an output rate of 10 belts per day. If you want an estimate of marginal cost at 20 belts per day, try using cost data related to 0 and 40 belts per day.

Why the Failure to Recognize Constant Marginal Cost?

Almost half a century ago it was realized that the marginal cost actually tends to be horizontal and not "U"-shaped as is the logic-based function of neoclassical economics. In 1955, Richard B. Heflebower reported that "there is now significant evidence to the effect that, in manufacturing operations at least, marginal

Table 6.2.   **The Costs of Belt-Maker Braun**

(1) Q belts/day	(2) TFC $/day	(3) TVC $/day	(4) TC $/day	5) MC= Δ(3)/Δ(1) $/belt	(6) AFC= (2)/(1) $/belt	(7) AVC= (3)/(1) $/belt	(8) AC= (4)/(1) $/belt
0	500	0	500	slope 100/20	∞	slope	∞
20	500	100	600		25	5	30.00
				100/20			
40	500	200	700		12.5	5	17.5
				100/20			
60	500	300	800		8.3	5	13.33
				100/20			
80	500	400	900		6.25	5	11.25
				100/20			
100	500	500	1000		5	5	10.00
				100/20			
120	500	600	1100		4.17	5	9.17

costs do not vary for a fairly wide range of output rates" (1955 p. 370). Subsequent research confirms this in manufacturing, electrical power plants, and railroads.

Why has the neoclassical school failed to change its "U"-shaped marginal cost function to one which tends to be flat—one which tends to accord with what is? The reason is that accepting the constant marginal cost functions undermines major aspects of the neoclassical paradigm.

The Impossibility of Attaining Allocative Efficiency

Allocative or short-run efficiency requires price to be equal to marginal cost, $P=MC$. This represents the lowest price firms can rationally charge for their products—a price which just covers the additional costs incurred by the production of the marginal unit. With prices as low as is possible, sovereign consumers are able to buy as much as possible and to best maximize their consumption and satisfaction. But if the marginal cost function is horizontal it is equal to average variable cost as can be seen in Figure 6.7. This means that marginal cost pricing would leave total fixed cost totally uncovered, leading to the quick demise of the firms needed to serve consumers.

Constant marginal cost means that producers cannot allocate scarce resources efficiently. This undermines the very focus of the neoclassical paradigm, the efficient allocation of scarce resources.

Undermining the Law of Diminishing Marginal Productivity

Marginal cost is supposed to increase with the rate of production because marginal productivity is supposed to decrease with the rate of production due to the increasing scarcity of the factors which are fixed in supply. Looked at the other way, the constancy of marginal cost implies the constancy of marginal productivity in manufacturing, electrical power generation, and railroading. And without declining marginal productivity all the wonders related to marginal productivity analysis become somewhat suspect: the production function, the factor demand functions, and the distribution of income between labor and capital.

The Problem of Production Efficiency

In the neoclassical paradigm production efficiency is attained when, in the long-run, firms operate at the rate of production at which average cost is at its minimum. This is an efficient condition because it represents production of the output using the smallest amount of resources possible, as measured in monetary terms. Moreover, with "U"-shaped cost functions the attainment of production efficiency is accompanied the attainment of allocative efficiency. When average cost is minimum, it equals marginal cost.

How is this long-run minimum average cost rate of production attained? If price is greater than average cost, above normal profits are attained. This stimulates entry into the industry. The resulting increase in supply tends to drive the price down until it reaches a minimum average cost long-run equilibrium.

Allow a look at the operation of the firms in this process. With price greater than average cost, production was on the positive sloped portion of "U"-shaped average cost function—where marginal cost is greater than average cost. As price decreased, profit maximizing firms had to decrease the rate of production until minimum average cost was attained

But price signals are perverse in the case of firms with flat marginal cost and declining average cost functions. As described above, if price is greater than average cost, new firms enter the market, and the price and the rate of production of existing firms decline. But here, a lower rate of production means higher average cost and lower production efficiency.

Fixed Factor Proportions

The constancy of marginal cost implies that production is increased by adding fixed doses of labor and capital to the firm's employment. Constant marginal cost implies that no factor experienced an increase in cost per unit of production. There is, therefore, no reason to substitute for any factor in the dose. Thus, production tends to be accomplished with fixed factor proportions.

A Summary on Rejection of the Existence of Constant Marginal Cost

There are a number of important reasons why the neoclassical paradigm blinds itself to the fact that marginal cost tends to be constant over the range of common rates of production: (1) Marginal cost pricing is precluded. This rules out the efficient allocation of scarce resources, the central focus of the neoclassical paradigm. (2) Economic profits which should lead to production efficiency seem to have the opposits effect. (3) Constant marginal cost implies production by factors in fixed proportions. This brings into question the role of marginal productivity and isoquant analysis and their factor substitution stress. (4) If fixed factors sets are the norm in production, identification of the marginal productivity of individual factors is dubious. Lost by this is factor demand analysis.

Recognition of the constancy of marginal cost would undermine much of the neoclassical paradigm, the neoclassical system of ideas, the neoclassical ideology, if you will. And that is why almost all textbooks are inundated with "U"-shaped cost curves.

The Planning Function: Long-Run Average Cost

Recall the assumption that producing units were built so that total cost is minimum in the region of the expected rate of production. This suggests that prior to construction of a unit of production, planners choose the design expected to minimize total cost and, along with it, the average cost of production. In planning a new producing unit, all costs are considered to be variable. After production begins, the planning function essentially disappears and the short-run cost functions appear with some categorized as fixed and others as variable.

The Theoretical Shape of the Planning Function

In planning a new plant or office, how do we know that the structure and equipment chosen are expected to yield the lowest possible cost? Decision-makers could design or have designed for them a set of least cost producing units, each of which has its minimum average cost at a different rate of production. This is shown in Figure 6.8. The *envelope* which surrounds the four average cost curves is the long-run average cost curve. It envelopes the curves by being tangent to them.

The planning long-run average cost function, *LRAC*, has three ranges. At first, as the scale of production increases, larger producing units are shown to be capable of producing at lower unit or average cost—there are economies of scale due to the ability of larger plants to exploit more efficient forms of technology including the organization of production. Then, from c to r plants have the same minimum average cost. In this range constant returns to scale are found. Finally, larger sized units have higher minimum average cost. They suffer from disec-

Figure 6.8.   **The Planning Long-Run Average Cost Function**

Average Cost   ($/ton)

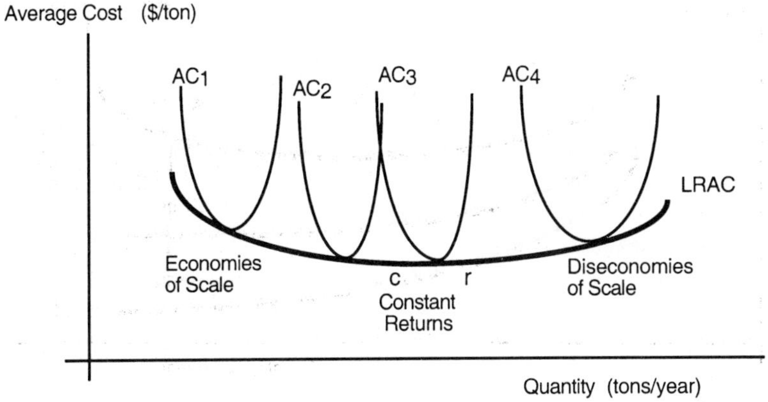

onomies of scale. Very large production units are difficult to manage. They are so large that it is hard for top management to know what the various levels of managers are doing, what problems exist, and which ones are not being solved.

The plant chosen would be the one which corresponds to minimum long-run average cost—at the anticipated demand.

The Shape of the Planning Function in Empirical Studies

What is the actual shape of the planning long-run cost function? Three methodologies have been used to answer this question. The first uses questionnaires. Producers are asked to estimate the average cost which would be incurred had their scale of production been specified percentages higher and lower than their actual operations. A second approach employs cross-sectional studies of industries. Observations are made of the actual size of the units of production being built in an industry. If they tend to be approximately the same size, the implication is that the planning function is "U"-shaped. If the units are of a variety of sizes, the planning function would seem to be "L"-shaped. And if they seem to be getting larger and larger, the implication is that the planning function is "declining L"-shaped. The third and last approach uses engineering studies of the minimum unit cost associated with production units of various scales.

The three shapes of the planning long-run average cost function found in empirical studies are shown in Figure 6.9. They indicate that small producing units tend to be inefficient. This conforms to all three variants of the planning functions. A minority of studies indicate that the planning function is "U"-shaped, a majority that it is "L"-shaped, and a small minority that it is "declining "L"-shaped. Technology determines the efficient size or range of sizes of plants in an industry. Competitive markets require that producers supply an insignificant portion of the market demand. But if the efficient scale of production covers a

Figure 6.9.   **Experiential Variants of the Planning Long-Run Average Cost Curve**

Average Cost ($/unit)

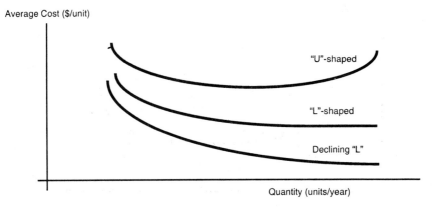

"U"-shaped

"L"-shaped

Declining "L"

Quantity (units/year)

substantial portion of market demand, the competitive market cannot exist.

The technology implied by the "U"-shaped function tends to be friendly to the competitive market—provided that one firm does not own too many small plants; the "L"-shaped function tends to be unfriendly, and the "declining L"-shaped function extremely unfriendly. The larger the efficient scale of production, the fewer are the number of plants required to produce a given output and to satisfy market demand.

The Reality of New Plant Design

Plant designer friends and former students tell me that the design of a single plant is quite expensive and that it is the client's responsibility to determine how large the production capacity of a plant should be. This is made easy by the fact that new plants are usually replacements for older ones, and the size chosen corresponds to sales experienced in past years. The responsibility of the designers is to develop the plans for a plant which will produce the specified output at minimum total cost. The alternatives are rarely a larger or smaller plant but alternative equipment to produce at the specified rate. The trade-off usually faced is between more expensive, efficient, and durable equipment as opposed to less expensive alternatives.

Transaction Costs

Recall that transaction costs are those involved in the process of exchange. They are experienced in both product and factor markets, external and internal to the firm. These costs involve searching for and communicating information (including misinformation) on the price and quality of products and factors, bringing buyers and sellers together, transporting goods and factors to the

Table 6.3.   **Expected Price as a Function of the Number of Canvasses**

Number of Canvasses	Probability Minimum Price of		Expected Transaction Price	Cost	E{P}+TrCost
	$2.00	$3.00	E{P}	TrC	
1	0.5	0.5	2.5	.10	2.60
2	0.75	0.25	2.25	.20	2.45
3	0.875	0.125	2.125	.30	2.425
4	0.9375	0.0625	2.0625	.40	2.4625
∞	1.0	0.0	2.0	∞	∞

location of their use, negotiating or dictating the terms of explicit and implicit "contracts," enforcing contracts, and handling the accounting problems associated with buying and selling. All of these are briefly discussed here.

The Search for Information

In price theory, a basic function of markets is to communicate price information about standardized products and factors. If buyers or sellers lack such information, the market has failed by not performing this basic task. Since a very small fraction of all transactions take place in organized markets, such as stock and commodity exchanges, this failure is widespread. To resolve the problem consumers and producers search for information–an idea popularized in economics by the late George J. Stigler in his article "The Economics of Information." He describes the problem as follows:

> Prices change with varying frequency in all markets, and, unless a market is completely centralized, no one will know all the prices which various sellers (or buyers) quote at any given time. A buyer (or seller) who wishes to ascertain the most favorable price must canvass various sellers (or buyers)—a phenomenon I shall call "search" (1961, p. 213).

Stigler set up a simple example to show the value of search. He specifies that half of the producers sell a product for $2 while the other half sell it for $3. In the first "canvass," it is equally probable that buyers will find the price to be $2 as it is to find it to be $3 and this yields an expected price of $2.50.

Two canvasses could result in four different price combinations: 2, 2; 3, 3; 2, 3; and 3, 2. So in three out of four cases, the searcher finds the lower price of $2 after making two canvasses. The expected price is then $2.25 (.75•$2+.25•$3). In similar fashion, three searches yields eight combinations of the two prices. In only one of them is there a failure to find the lower price. The resulting expected price becomes $2.125, (7/8•$2 + 1/8•$3).

Stigler's Table 2 (p. 214) on this example is reproduced as Table 6.3. To it I

Figure 6.10.   **Marginal Transaction Costs and Expected Marginal Benefits as a Function of Canvasses**

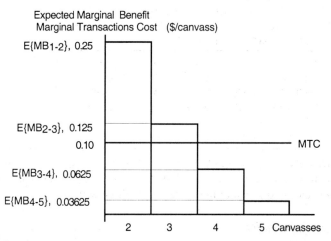

Expected Marginal Benefit
Marginal Transactions Cost   ($/canvass)

have added on the right two columns of data. The first is the transaction cost which I have arbitrarily set at 10 cents per canvass. The second is the sum of the expected price and the transaction cost. Without the inclusion of transaction costs, there is no rational limit to the number of canvasses which should be made. But with transaction costs, the incremental costs and benefits of another canvass can be recognized. Note that in going from the first to the second canvass, the incremental cost is 10 cents and the benefit, the decrease in expected price, is 25 cents. This yields an expected gain of 15 cents. In going from the second to the third canvass the incremental cost is again 10 cents and the expected benefit is 12.5 cents. The expected gain is 2.5 cents. In going from the third to the fourth canvass the incremental cost is 10 cents, but the expected benefit is only only 6.25 cents. Making the fourth canvass does not make sense. Three should be made here. A graph of the incremental approach can be found in Figure 6.10.

An alternative way of determining the optimum number of searches is to add the transaction cost to the expected price as is shown in the last column of Table 6.3. Three canvasses are optimal since they yield the lowest expected price, $2.425.

Search Should Wipe Out Price Differentials

The dynamic implication of Stigler's search model is that the average market price would quickly drop from $2.50 to $2.00. If all the decision-makers adopted a three-canvass rule, seven-eighths of them would have found the minimum price to be $2. While suppliers with this price originally commanded half the market, the $2 price would soon lead them to have a seven-eighths share of the market. The high-priced firms would find their half of the market reduced to one-eighth. They could either cut their price to $2 or go out of business. The search process should transform the $2 and $3 prices into a single $2 price charged by all sellers—obviating the rationale of search.

The actual continuing existence of price differentials indicates the existence of conditions such as the following: (1) Higher-priced sellers have transaction cost advantages, perhaps because of their convenient location to some buyers. (2) Higher-priced sellers offer what some buyers believe to be higher quality products. (3) The seller gives or is thought to give better service than others. (4) Buyers have over the course of time developed a personal relationship with the seller and are willing to pay for it. (5) Some are satisfied with the current supplier and see no reason to canvass others. (6) The cost of the product is viewed as being trivial and unworthy of search.

Intermediaries and Transaction Costs

The market is generally portrayed as the institution bringing buyers and sellers together. But even in organized markets intermediaries are required. Brokers of sellers and buyers must be paid. So, too, must exchange institution—directly or indirectly.This means that the cost of purchases are augmented by the transaction costs arising from the charges of intermediaries.

Whole industries serve as intermediaries in bringing buyers and sellers together. Security exchanges and brokerage houses bring the buyers and sellers of securities, of stocks and bonds, together. Banks and other financial intermediaries, bring borrowers and lenders together. Real estate brokerages bring the buyers and sellers of real estate together. Wholesale trade serves as the intermediary between producers and retailers; retail trade serves as the intermediary between wholesalers and consumers. And much of transportation is involved in the movement of factors and products from the location of their supply to that of their demand, thus also bringing buyers and sellers together.

Lawyers generally serve as intermediaries. They act as agents of clients in negotiations with adversaries, in hearings, and in the courts. Advertising agencies serve as intermediaries between the firm and the media. Government relations and public relations firms act as intermediaries between the principals who retain them and relevant governmental officials and agencies. Intermediaries are ubiquitous, as are the transaction costs they command.

Non-Production Workers and Transaction Costs

Within a firm, to a large extent workers and capital not directly engaged in production are employed in activities associated with transactions. Consider some areas of non-production employment. The personnel or human resources department is involved in the buying and selling of labor services. It searches for or helps search for qualified employees and plays a role in handling employee grievances against management and management's actions effecting employees, directly and indirectly. If some or all of the work units are unionized, it participates in the negotiations and the enforcement of labor agreements. And it is often responsible for the the administration of pension and insurance agreements covering employees. The payroll department is also involved in transactions between employees and the employer. Purchasing groups are responsible for the purchase of capital goods. Accounts payable is responsible for paying vendors for these goods. Accounts receivable sees that the firm is paid for the products it sells. Marketing is responsible for maintaining and increasing the sales, the transactions, of the firm.

What about the various levels of management? Managers engage in buying the labor services of new subordinates. To the extent that they oversee the activities of workers or other managers, they monitor transactions between the firm and its employees. This is more or less in the realm of obtaining "a fair day's work for a fair day's pay." They also hold responsibility for determining the capital equipment required for their use and that of underlings.

Thus, it is seen that within firms many employees are engaged in transaction-related activities. The costs of these workers and the capital they utilize falls within the purview of transaction costs. It is stylish to call all non-production workers "information workers." A substantial percentage of them might be better characterized as "transaction workers."

Transaction Costs and Profit Maximization

Recall that in Stigler's model on the search for information, the optimal number of canvasses could be determined by either price minimization or by a comparison of marginal transaction costs and marginal benefits. What about the cost minimizing employment in one of the firm's departments which operates in the region of transactions? Reckoning costs in such a department is straightforward but empirical quantification of benefits is not. The failure of the payroll department to issue one or more checks on pay day may cause "all hell to break loose"—but that defies normal quantification. It may be prudent to have some slack capacity to handle the breakdown of machinery or workers in payroll activities. This slack capacity is akin to the safety factor that engineers use in their design of structures and equipments.

A more complex and interesting area is that of accounts receivable. It may very well be possible to estimate the incremental revenues expected by the employment of another person in the department. And with the cost of such an employment known, action expected to be profitable can be taken. But what about the pursuit of delinquent accounts where the expected revenues are less than the expected costs? As a "matter of principle," many firms attempt such collections. But it is not clear whether such actions are unprofitable or are investments in ensuring that more bills are paid than otherwise would be the case.

Asymmetric Information

There are some transactions in which information regarding products and factors tends to be unequal for buyers and sellers—it is asymmetric. Generally, the seller knows more about a product than could be known by the buyer. A classic case is the market for used vehicles, where the seller frequently knows more than the buyer concerning the imperfections of a vehicle. George Akerlof, a brilliant microtheorist, divided cars into two categories: "lemons" and "cream puffs." He hypothesized that if buyers cannot tell the quality of a product until after its purchase, lemons will dominate the market. (This is a variant of Gresham's law under which bad money drives good money out of circulation.) People are, of course, more prone to want to unload lemons than cream puffs and buyers tend to guess that and tend to be willing to pay the price a lemon deserves—a discouragement to cream puff owners looking to sell at a higher price.

Logic, however, is a poor substitute for reality in the case of motor vehicles and in general. An empirical test of the eminently logical lemon hypothesis was not supportive of it. Erik W. Bond in his article "A Direct Test of the 'Lemons' Model": The Market for Used Pickup Trucks," found no significant difference in the maintenance costs for trucks of the same mileage irrespective of whether they had been bought new or used (1982, p. 839). This, of course, in no way diminishes the fact that information is frequently asymmetric, but questions its significance.

Advertising Costs

Firms in some industries engage in a substantial amount of advertising; those in other industries engage in virtually none at all. To some extent advertising is factual and informative and decreases the search costs of buyers. Where misinformation is involved the advertisement adds to the cost of buyers. Advertising costs increase the costs of firms which advertise and that investment tends, over the course of time, to be covered by an increase in the demand of buyers, which can manifest itself in higher quantity demanded or a higher price. The economics of advertising is covered in Chapter 11.

Problems with the Cost Functions and Costs

Recall the assumptions made at the outset of the presentation of the total cost function. They were that (1) a firm produces (or adds value) and sells a single product; (2) all costs used for decision-making are opportunity and not historical costs; (3) the plant and its equipment are such that total cost can be minimized in the expected range of operations; and (4) factor ratios are varied, as relative factor price changes, to maintain the minimum cost of production. There is also the problem that while economists categorize costs as variable and fixed, accountants and businesses present them as direct and overhead. Each of these matters is considered in turn.

The Production of Multiple Products

Some farmers do produce a single crop and many electrical utilities produce only electrical energy. Your supermarket, however, may sell thousands of different products, and Sears sells and sets the price on 50,000 of them. But even the production of only two products substantially complicates and compromises the quantification of costs. The biggest problem is the assignment of a share of overhead costs to each of the products. Overhead costs are the costs of labor and capital which are not directly involved in the production of products marketed. Some of overhead is fixed; some variable. The plant and its major equipments are fixed. Executives under contract are fixed costs. Beyond that overhead costs are variable. There is no completely objective way to allocate these costs to the various products and, therefore, no completely objective way to identify the cost of production of one product where more than one is produced.

The normal accounting practice is to develop an overhead rate: as the ratio of overhead spending to total cost. Assume that a university's overhead rate is 75 percent. Then for a job with direct costs of $1,000, the overhead cost assigned is $750 and the total cost is $1,750. The problem is that some jobs consume more overhead spending than others per dollar of direct cost: A new product may, for example, require substantially more effort from employees in design, development, and marketing than an established product. One product may require more physical space than others. To make a sale, the overhead rate on some products may be reduced making their cost artificially lower and, if total overhead cost is to be covered, the overhead rate and cost of other products artificially higher.

Without objective costs on products it is not possible to objectively know their profitability or lack thereof.

Accounting Costs Versus Economic Costs

While the method used by economists to determine costs is analytically correct, it is not the information economic actors tend to have at their disposal. What they usually are given and are controlled by are accounting costs. The purpose of accounting costs is to systematically account for the costs incurred by a firm. Economic costs are established to help decision-makers make rational decisions——to help in determining the optimal allocation of resources. The use of a $1 million computer system will be used to illustrate the difference.

Assume that the $1 million computer is bought for cash. It can be "written off" over a five-year period. Straight-line depreciation is used and the annual accounting cost is $200,000 for each of five years. The problem is then to assign the $200,000 annual cost to the various jobs or products for which the computer system is used. This requires the development of the "standard cost" of the computer—the hourly charge to jobs and products for its use. Cost accountants get this figure by dividing the annual cost, $200,000, by the expected hours of use of the computer. Assume that the expectation is that it will be used for 2,000 hours during the course of the fiscal or budget year. The standard cost is then $100 per hour ($200,000 per year/2,000 hours use per year). (The computer center at your university probably charges contracts and grants on the basis of such a standard cost calculation.) Decision-makers then know how much their budget will be charged for the use of the computer system and can determine the extent to which computer system services will be used.

Decisions, however, should not be based on accounting costs but on economic costs—here the rental cost of the computer system. That cost might be somewhat higher in the first year of the computer's economic life, and much lower as it ages and it resale value plummets downward. But decision-makers do not know the rental cost of the computer. Even if they did, they would be charged its accounting cost and would, therefore, have to make decisions on that basis. (Some of my colleagues found at one time that a neighboring university computer center charged less than ours and took their work there.)

Sunk Costs and Congestion Tolls

Assume that two years after its purchase, no one is willing to buy the firm's computer. Its use entails no opportunity cost because its value has "sunk." The rental cost drops to zero. Thus, while the accounting cost remains $100 an hour, the economic cost to decision-makers should be zero.

Had the cost of an hour's use of the computer system been set at zero, there may be more calls for its use than the hours of its availability. The theoretical solution is to set an internal *congestion toll* to users which equilibrates its supply with the demand for it.

Undercapitalization

It may well be that a firm should buy a zillion-dollar plant to minimize the average cost of production, but it may lack that sum and the credit-worthiness to obtain it from others. New firms frequently lack the funds required to succeed, and they, therefore, have a high mortality rate. But even large firms may shy away from making large investments. The most efficient steel mills are arguably the multibillion-dollar integrated mills of the Japanese. We do not have any comparable steel mills—seemingly because American producers fear that the substantial surplus of world steel-making capacity may make such a mill unprofitable.

Overcapitalization

A number of factors are hypothesized as the reason for overcapitalization: (1) overoptimistic forecasts of sales from products using the subject equipment; (2) keeping up with the Joneses, here buying capital goods because a prominent rival has done so; (3) taste for technology which exceeds its value to the firm; (4) bias in favor of capital equipment over labor due to the fact that equipment is easier to control than people. Equipment does not set job quotas, unionize, and engage in slowdowns and strikes. The other side of the ledger is that if demand is lower than expected, workers can be laid off but capital equipment cannot.

Intrafirm Inefficiencies

Firms are populated by humans who make decisions regarding what activities should be performed, with what amounts of labor and capital, how the factors are to be combined, who should perform the work, and its actual performance. Each of these steps can be efficiently performed by a properly programmed robot. But the decisions are made by humans and the work is performed by people of the same genus. To err is human, and the degree of perfection of decisions and performance at each stage should be viewed in that light.

There is a wonderful body of literature on "downsizing" and much of it indicates the employment of substantially more people than are required to perform the available work. An example is that of General Motors, which realized in 1987 that it was employing 40,000 more white-collar workers than it required. This inefficiency was estimated as costing $1.8 billion per year with an after-tax earnings loss of $1.4 billion per year. That amounts to a lot of inefficiency. In another auto industry example, the new president of Chrysler, near the outset of 1998, stated his belief that one-third of the cost of a car represented bureaucratic inefficiency.

The economist who has done the most to stress the importance of intrafirm inefficiency is Harvey Leibenstein who coined the terms *X-efficiency* and *X-inefficiency*. In Chapter 3 of his *Beyond Economic Man* (1976), Leibenstein surveys numerous studies which show substantial inefficiencies in production. The sources of inefficiency enumerated in one of the studies give some idea of the types of inefficiency found. Some had poor plant layouts; others had imperfections in their machine utilization and work flow. Some required simple technical alterations; others were poor at materials handling, waste control, work methods, method of pay, and worker training and supervision. Leibenstein claimed that management consultants tend to find cost savings in the range of 10–15 percent of total cost.

The isoquant and budget lines of Figure 6.11 should be useful in picturing the effects of allocative and technical inefficiencies. Efficiency requires the use of the

Figure 6.11.   **Production with Allocative and Technical Inefficiencies**

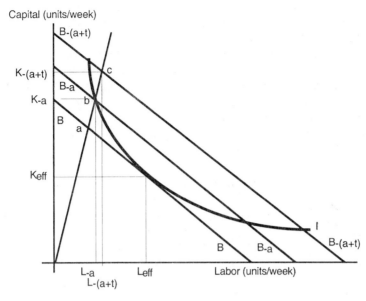

least cost set of factors. This can be found when isoquant I, involving the production of 100 widgets per week, is tangent to budget line BB, which represents
the least cost budget for this production. Efficient use of the factors is obtained
by employing L_{eff} units of labor and K_{eff} of capital per week.

  Assume, however that the producer employs more capital than the allocative efficient amount, namely, K_{-a} units of capital, corresponding to point b on the
isoquant. L_{-a} units of labor per week are consequently required to produce 100
widgets per week. This more capital intensive production process requires an increase in the budget from BB to $B_{-a}B_{-a}$, which goes through point b on the isoquant.

  Now draw a line from the origin of the graph, o, through point b. Label the in-
tersect with the original budget line with an a. Allocative efficiency, instead of
being 100 percent, becomes the ratio of spending with efficient allocation to that
of actual allocation, oa/ob. Alternatively put, allocative inefficiency is ab/oa,
the percentage of excess spending caused by misallocation.

  All points on the isoquant represent technical efficiency. For a given rate of
production, it is a plot of the minimum amount of labor required, given a specified employment of capital—and the minimum amount of capital required given
the employment of labor. While all points on an isoquant are technically efficient, all firms are not. Assume that the firm has the allocative inefficiency
shown above plus technical inefficiency. It then requires more of both labor and
capital than that of point b to produce the rate of production defined by the iso-

quant. The with both allocative and technical inefficiency $L_{-(a+t)}$ units of labor and $K_{-(a\&t)}$ units of capital are required. This puts the employment mix at point c. The budget required to pay for the factors is $B_{-(a+t)}B_{-(a+t)}$. Technical inefficiency is then the ratio bc/oa.

Leibenstein shows, rather persuasively I think, that the misallocation losses caused by government intervention and monopolistic powers are small as compared to intrafirm inefficiencies. He accordingly criticizes neoclassical brethren for their high interest in the relatively unimportant and low interest in the relatively important area of intrafirm inefficiency.

Executive Compensation and the Edifice Complex

There are numerous recent examples indicating that the pay of corporate executives is excessive. In early 1982 President George Bush went to Japan with twenty-four officials of some of our largest corporations to meet with a similar number of Japanese corporate leaders. The meeting was held because Japanese producers have been far more successful than ours and some redress was hoped for by having the Japanese buy more of our products. The average compensation of the Japanese executives was one-sixth of ours.

The feature story of the March 6, 1991 issue of *Business Week* was titled "Are CEO's Paid too Much?" Statistics covering 1980 to 1990 showed that over the decade the pay of workers increased by 53 percent; corporate profits increased by 78 percent, and the pay of chief executive officers increased by 212 percent. In 1960 the average CEO in a *Business Week* survey was paid 19.4 times the average engineer; in 1990 the ratio was 39.6 to 1. To the best of my knowledge, there has been no contention that the increase in the relative pay of executives reflected a relative shortage of such workers. It would be quixotic to contend that executive compensation is a manifestation of cost minimization.

My favorite example of the edifice complex is the PepsiCo headquarters in Purchase, New York, a very expensive suburb of New York City. The following quotation is from a four-page writeup available to visitors of "The Donald M. Kendall Sculpture Gardens at PepsiCo."

> The Gardens are conceived by Donald M. Kendall, chairman of the board and chief executive officer of PepsiCo, Inc. until 1986, as an environment that encourages creativity and reflects essential qualities of corporate success.... The sculpture collection ... now includes 40 [monumental] pieces by twentieth century artists. They are set in approximately 112 acres of carefully landscaped gardens.... The building, designed by Edward Durell Stone, ... was opened in 1970 on land that was formerly a polo field.... The original gardens comprised sweeping lawns, a large lake and a screen of trees to conceal the parking lot.

The corporate headquarters, sculpture, and gardens are first rate—but they are hardly examples of cost minimization. Similar examples are not hard to find.

The Divergence of Private and Social Costs

The production and use of gasoline-driven motor vehicles affects not only the buyer and seller of the device but also others external to the transaction—hence the expressions external effects or externalities.

> External effects or externalities are effects, costly or beneficial, which impinge on people or property not directly involved in a transaction.

If the effects are beneficial, the transaction yields positive externalities or benefits; if they are deleterious, the far more common case, we have negative externalities or costs. Positive externalities are found, for example, if a firm trains workers in skills which are applicable to the work of other employers or if the education of people benefits them and others as well. Negative externalities frequently are manifest in pollution of the land, water, and air (noise included) arising from production and consumption.

Virtually all production and much consumption creates negative externalities and this undermines the role of price as an efficient allocator of resources from a social perspective. The car affords a wonderful example. The production of the metals, plastics, rubber, glass, and other products used in the manufacture of a car pollute our air, water, and land. The social costs of these pollutants should be added to the cost of the car. The use or consumption of the car also pollutes the environment. The complementary good, petroleum, has a wondrous pollution record. The construction of oil pipelines destroys natural habitats. Leaking pipelines and barges have caused great ecological damage. And the pollution from the tail pipes of our cars, trucks, and buses has substantially worsened the quality of the air. The disposal of spent engine oil, tires, batteries, and junked cars are also manifestations of pollution. Highway noise has led to the construction of noise barriers the cost of which seems to rival that of the highway itself. All these bads are negative externalities. Their dollar value is a social cost.

> *Private Costs* are the costs borne by the parties to a transaction, sellers and buyers.
> *Social Costs* are private costs plus the costs and minus the benefits of externalities implied by a transaction.

Many social costs are easy to calculate. Some are not. It is particularly difficult to estimate the cost of a year of life shortened, for example, by air pollution. While our cars afford a dramatic representation of external costs, mundane pur-

Figure 6.12. **A Tax Internalizing the Negative Externalities of the Production of Cars**

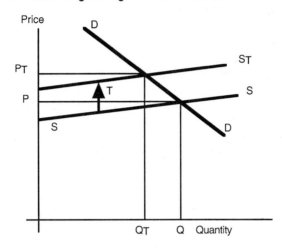

chases also pose serious externalities. The packaging used for our fast-food ham-burgers are often not biodegradable and degrade the land; gases used in our re-frigerators and air conditioners are destroying the ozone layer which helps pro-tect us from the deleterious effects of ultraviolet rays. Even the organic carrots brought home in a recycled paper bag have external costs. They come to the gro-cer in a truck which worsens the quality of the air and were washed with water from a reservoir created by the destruction of the natural environment.

Assume that with respect to the production of cars, it is possible to quantify the magnitude of the external cost of production and that it amounts to $T per year per car. In Figure 6.12 the original supply function is SS. It, with the origi-nal demand function, DD, yields an equilibrium price and quantity of P and Q, respectively. Then, the external cost is internalized by a tax of $T per car. This causes a vertical shift of the supply function equal to the magnitude of the tax. Then, at equilibrium buyers pay P_T and sellers receive that minus the tax. The equilibrium quantity then drops to Q_T which is less than the pre-tax equilibri-um, Q. This indicates that the failure to internalize external costs caused an ex-cessive amount of resources to be allocated to the production of cars. From a so-cial perspective, the tax converts an inefficient allocation of resources to one which is more efficient.

The external cost of the use of a car could be covered by a tax on gasoline. The analysis would be comparable to that of Figure 6.12. This would add to the price of complements and further discourage the purchase and use of cars. But there is a profoundly difficult problem involved with respect to external costs and that involves determination of the cost of a life.

Differential Productivity Growth and the Problems of the Cost of Education, Medical and Hospital Care, and the Performing Arts

Perhaps the most interesting model applicable to the problems of the rising relative costs of education, medical and hospital care, and the performing arts is that of William J. Baumol and William J. Bowen. Both were at Princeton at the time they developed the model which arose from a study of the performing arts. A succinct form of the analysis can be found in Baumol's article "Macroeconomics of Unbalanced Growth."

The model is based on differential productivity growth in an economy divided into two sectors. In one productivity grows steadily; in the other it remains constant. The output in the productivity growth sector in year t is Q_{pt} and that in the non-productivity growth sector is Q_{npt}. Output varies with the employment of labor, L. Assume that in the first sector productivity growth is exponential at the rate of r percent per year and non-existent in the second. Annual outputs are then:

$$(4) \qquad Q_{pt} = aL_{pt}e^{rt} ; \qquad Q_{npt} = bL_{npt}$$

It is assumed that wages in both sectors grow at the rate at which productivity grows in the productivity growth sector:

$$(5) \qquad W_t = We^{rt}$$

Assume in addition that the only cost is that of the labor employed. The average cost in a sector is then the total wage payment divided by the output in the sector.

$$(6) \qquad AC_{pt} = (We^{rt} \cdot L_{pt}) \div aL_{pt}e^{rt} = W/a$$

$$(7) \qquad AC_{npt} = (We^{rt} \cdot L_{npt}) \div bL_{npt} = We^{rt}/b$$

Thus, while unit cost in the productive sector is constant, it increases exponentially in the non-productive sector as does its relative cost and price.

The thrust of the model conforms to reality. Agriculture and manufacturing tend to have relatively high rates of productivity growth as compared to the service industries. But workers in the service industries believe they should receive gains as good as those of others and tend to experience comparable advances. What remains to be understood is why service workers frequently have low productivity growth.

Consider the effects of a 2 percent per year productivity increase for an elementary school teacher, general medical practitioner, and string quartet player. Assume that the productivity growth continued over the past thirty-five years making each subject twice as productive now as then. The elementary school teacher who initially had thirty students in a class would now have to have sixty in a class—but actually still has thirty. The medical practitioner who scheduled six patients per hour thirty-five years ago would have to see twelve an hour now—but still tries to see six an hour. The Mozart quartet played by four thirty-five years ago would now have to be played by two—literally impossible. Alternatively, the size of the audience would have to double every thirty-five years.

Without these unrealistic productivity increases, we have the problem of education, medical and health, and entertainment costs rising exponentially relative to others. And, if it makes sense to maintain the relative size of these sectors constant: (1) the ratio of the employment in the non-productive to productive sector would grow exponentially relative to the productive sector; (2) and, the ratio of national income spent in the non-productive to the productive sector would also increase exponentially.

Education, medical and hospital care, and the performing arts are important to our well-being and culture. In this context, the Baumol-Bowen model's accurate description of the escalating prices in these sectors should be a source of unease to many.

Summary

There are two principal time horizons for cost functions: the long-run and the short-run. The long-run average cost function is the planning function of economic theory. If there is no limit to prospective sales or the ability to buy the most efficient plant, the producing unit which should be chosen and built is the one which is expected to yield the lowest average cost of production. Once that unit has been built and put into production, the long-run planning function disappears and the historic costs of the plant and its equipment become irrelevant—in theory.

Empirical studies of costs in non-agricultural sectors indicate that the total cost function tends to be linear with respect to the rate of production— or what is the same, that average variable and marginal cost are constant and equal over the range of actual production. And average cost declines with the rate of production until full capacity is reached. This undermines the law of diminishing marginal productivity, the ability to achieve allocative efficiency, and the practicality of achieving production efficiency.

Applying cost findings to production, the expectation is a linear production function with the rate of production increasing with fixed doses of labor and capital.

It is far easier to assume c ost minimization than to find it in productive organizations which are complex institutions. And those who are at the top and seemingly responsible for overall costs allow their boards of directors to pay them, on the average, five times that received in other countries for running comparable organizations.

The proper reckoning of the price of durable goods is necessary for decision-making regarding the employment of all factors of production. But that computation is devilishly complex involving, for example, knowledge of the resale value of all the equipments and facilities of the firm. The information usually available is the standard cost established by accounting.

Production frequently involves external costs (and sometimes benefits). Negative externalities are common in almost all production and much consumption. Thus, social costs tend to be higher than private costs and far more difficult to capture. These external costs frequently involve the pollution of air, water, and land and the resulting damage to property and people. The failure to have external costs reflected in the price of products implies the failure to efficiently allocate scarce resources.

Finally, there is the Baumol-Bowen model under which services which are relatively immune to productivity growth tend to experience increasing relative costs. This is unsettling because some of these services represent basic parts of our culture and social fabric.

Questions on Chapter 6

1. a. Draw a conventional total cost function.
   b. Explain why its slope is at first decreasing and why, after a certain rate of production, its slope is increasing.
   c. Draw the following curves on the same figure as the total cost curve: average cost, average variable cost, average fixed cost, and marginal cost.

2. a. Why does marginal cost always equal average variable cost at a zero rate of production?
   b. Where is marginal cost equal to average variable and average cost? Why?

3. a. Draw a linear total cost function.
   b. Explain why it is linear up to full capacity.
   c. Draw the following curves on the same figure as the total cost function: average cost, average variable cost, average fixed cost, and marginal cost.
   d. Why are the average variable cost and marginal cost functions identical?

4. a. Define transaction costs and explain this through the use of an example.
   b. Define transaction costs and give an example of the matters covered.
   c. Take the case of an automobile. What is its private cost? Its social cost?

5. What is the significance of the constancy of marginal cost to marginal productivity?

6. Enumerate the social costs associated with the production and consumption of a MacDonald's hamburger.

7. Explain the concept of differential productivity growth and how it pertains to the relative cost and price of educational and medical services and tickets to the performing arts.

CHAPTER SEVEN

The Firm and the Competitive Product Market

In the "competitive market" there are many buyers and sellers of a homogeneous product. None of these buyers or sellers or groups of buyers and sellers have command over a significant amount of supply or demand. As a result of this they themselves have no influence over price. Price-setting power resides in the equilibration of inanimate market supply and demand functions.

The actors in the competitive market do not themselves engage in competitive activities. Farmer Brown does not attempt to win over the customers of other farmers by price cutting or non-price activities such as advertising. It is the market which sets the price and provides the competitive element. Like it or not, producers must supply their product at the price determined by the market, no matter how low they might view it to be.

The Firm and the Competitive Market

The crude relationship of the firm and the competitive market is shown in Figure 7.1. The market functions are in frame a; the functions associated with a firm in frame b. The market supply function, $S_m S_m$, is the horizontal sum of the supply functions of the firms in this market. The market demand function, $D_m D_m$ is the horizontal sum of the demand functions of all buyers in this market. The resulting equilibrium price, P^*, is that at which the quantity supplied equals that demanded and the supply price equals the demand price. This yields to the firm an infinitely elastic demand function at the market price, $D_f D_f$, as shown in frame b. This demand function indicates that the firm can supply as much as it wishes at the market price.

The Scarcity of Competitive Markets

Product markets in which price is determined by the force of market supply and demand involve forms of production which are closely related to land: markets

Figure 7.1.   **The Firm's and the Market's Supply and Demand Functions**

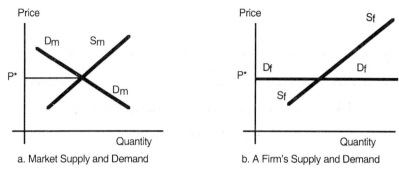

a. Market Supply and Demand   b. A Firm's Supply and Demand

for crude foods, feeds, fibers, grains and oil seeds, and some metals and minerals. These product markets cover a small portion of our overall production. If we subtract from this group those markets in which government plays some role in price or quantity setting, the competitive market's share of production becomes small indeed.

Major financial markets also tend to conform to the characteristics of the competitive market in that security prices and interest rates tend to be set by supply-demand forces. The prices of widely held stocks and bonds are set in markets. In setting the price of bonds, the market at one and the same time sets the interest rate that buyers receive. This is not to say, however, that you cannot walk down a street in a metropolis and find that different banks pay savers somewhat different interest rates and charge somewhat different rates to mortgage and other borrowers. The "law of one price" in financial markets seems to be "the law of a very narrow range of prices."

The Importance of the Competitive Model

Despite the fact that competitive markets are relatively uncommon, they are of great importance in the neoclassical paradigm. The basic reason for this is the contention that the behavior of prices, profits, and outputs in general corresponds to that described in the neoclassical model of the competitive market. Thus, for example, the contention is that an increase in demand for a product will increase its price, rate of production, and the profits of firms in the competitive and all other markets. Moreover, the same claim is made for factor markets such that an increase in the demand for a certain form of labor will increase its price and employment in competitive and all other factor markets.

The competitive market is also commonly used as the standard against which all other market forms are judged in terms of allocative and production efficiency —essentially producing at the lowest possible short- and long-run price. Agriculture is the economic sector generally considered to be the best example of a competitive product market.

Characteristics of the Competitive Model

The characteristics of the competitive model follow:

Standardized Products

The existence of a competitive market requires the products of all producers in the market to be the same—to be: standardized or homogeneous, if you prefer. Thus all products in a competitive market must be perfect substitute for each other. They should all then have the same price.

Were a producer able to differentiate his product from others in the industry, he could have some control over price thus escaping from total domination by the market. The producer of carrots who advertises and markets "The World's Best Organic Carrots" leaves the market for ordinary carrots by differentiating his.

A Large Number of Producers

The more producers there are, the lower is the portion of the market supply provided by an individual producer. The competitive market must have so many producers that even if the largest ones stopped production, no trace of the action could be found on the overall market supply and price.

The inability of farmers to control supply can be surmised by reference to the market for grains. The largest 2 percent of grain growers produce about half of all the grains supplied—but the number of farms in this group totals about 25,000. It would be profitable for all these farmers to curtail production by an agreed-to percentage. But it just is not possible to obtain such an agreement from this large number of producers. Even if an agreement could be reached, it would be unenforceable. The profitability of selling more than one's quota would be contagious and that would lead to the destruction of the agreement.

A Large Number of Buyers

The competitive market requires the existence of a large number of buyers. Then, no buyer purchases enough to measurably effect market demand and price.

Are there so many buyers in a market such as that for wheat that not one of them, nor group of them acting together, can affect price? It is hard to say "yes" because of the large size of some of the buyers of wheat. If you go down the cereal aisle in a supermarket you will find the dominant producers to be Kellogg and General Mills. Flour is mostly made by Pillsbury and Gold Medal, a division of General Mills. The great profusion of cookies and crackers frequently bear the logo of Nabisco, Sunshine, or Keebler. Domestic-made pastas are from Muellers and Prince. Then there are some large packaged bread bakers, pastry bakers, cattle feed sellers, and so on. The result seems to be that for each products which uses wheat, a relatively small number of large firms dominate the market. But there are many products which use wheat so that we have scores of major and hundreds of minor buyers. Seemingly, no single buyer controls enough of market demand to affect its price—to be able to dictate or negotiate a price lower than that set by the market.

Market-Set Prices

Price in competitive markets must be set by the unfettered forces of supply and demand.

Market-set prices are found in large organized auction type markets such as the Chicago Board of Trade and the New York Stock Exchange. At any given instant of time all buyers pay the same price and sellers receive the same price for a particular commodity, stock or bond. (The difference is a form of transaction cost.)

Easy Entry and Exit

Easy entry into an industry implies that there are many who have or can amass the expertise and financing required to start and operate a firm. The lure of entry is above-normal profits, profits which are also an incentive to expand to those already in the industry.

By and large, there is easy entry into agriculture, retail trade, household services, automotive services, local moving and storage, house painting and the like.

Easy exit implies that a firm can leave the market without effective government, community, or union power to stop this action. It also implies that the cost of leaving an industry is modest—that no major cleanup or dismantling costs are required.

Perfect Knowledge

Perfect knowledge means that buyers and sellers must know the price of the product is at a given instant of time. Perfect knowledge of product price is the foundation of the "Law of One Price." Were that price not know buyers might pay more than the market price and sellers might receive less than the market price.

Actual product sales are normally conducted through agents, cooperatives and brokers, who have access to the latest possible price information. But the "one price" (minus transaction costs) is frequently transient in organized markets making perfect knowledge now different than it was a short time ago.

While there is perfect knowledge in the product market, firms in the competitive market have to buy factors in markets that are far from competitive. Many factor inputs are not standardized and not produced in competitive markets. Ex-

Figure 7.2.   **Expected Price, Costs, and Profits**

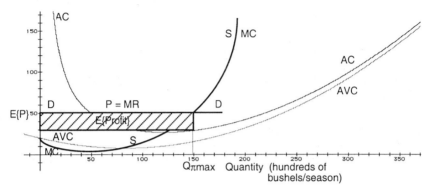

Price; Average, Average Variable, and Marginal Cost
($/bushel)(divide scale by 10)

pensive farm equipment, such as tractors and combines, are differentiated products made by just a few firms. This is also largely true with respect to the producers of seed, hormones, chemical fertilizers, pesticides, and the like.

Of special interest in the realm of knowledge is that required to rationally decide upon entry into a competitive industry. Entry is predicated on expected above normal profits. But farmers, retail store owners, and other small producers do not generally expose their profit and loss statements to public scrutiny—except when they are selling their farm or store. Otherwise potential entrants must use alternative information as proxies for the rate of return. One might, for example, find that farm equipment sales have been increasing and assume that farmers have been obtaining increasing rates of return. In addition, relevant information can be found in *the price system* except that it has to be *future* factor costs and product prices as shown in Figure 7.2.

How could a farmer, in effect, draw Figure 7.2? The economic information needed is exclusively on prices. The product price gives him the infinitely elastic demand function. Factor prices coupled with his expertise in farming allow him to develop the data for the total cost curve. That plus his calculation of total fixed cost allows calculating all the other curves. Thus Figure 7.2.

Developing data on the range of outputs from a zero rate of production to one approaching full capacity may not be the sensible thing to do. What is really required are the data and curves in the neighborhood of profit maximization.

Making the data expectational largely requires knowing where prices and technology have been going over recent years to the present, projecting this information into the future with due consideration given to special changes which are expected.

What information does the farmer glean from Figure 7.2? The difference between expected price and average cost at the planned operating rate yields economic profit per unit. That number times quantity gives expected profit, a crucial decision variable. The expected price is $5 per bushel, the profit-maximizing rate of production occurs where marginal cost equals the expected price and that is at about 15,000 bushels per season. The average cost at that output is $3 per bushel yielding an expected profit per bushel of $2 and $30,000 for the entire crop, the cross-hatched area in Figure 7.2.

Is there a simpler method that farmers can use to approximate the output rate at which maximum profits are expected? Yes there is. Note that average cost times the output rate equals total cost—the farmers budget for the production cycle. Farmers frequently develop budgets. Total revenue is merely the price times the quantity produced and sold at that price. The difference is profit. Do the calculation again for a higher output rate. If profit is higher try a still higher rate. If lower, try a lower rate. Four or so tries should yield a good approximation of the expected profit-maximizing rate of production. Do farmers perform profit calculations at several output rates? Not according to those who help them with their budgeting and accounting problems.

Although agriculture and retail trade are characterized by free entry, that entry may require substantial investments; in that sense it is not free. Those who desire entry into the industry, cannot if they lack the required funds.

The Equality of Price, Average and Marginal Revenue, and Demand

The demand for the firm's product in a competitive market is infinitely elastic at the market price. And if the price of soy beans for example, is $8 a bushel, a farmer can sell another bushel at that price and marginal revenue is also $8 per bushel: $P = Demand = AR = MR$.

Price and average revenue are equal in all markets in which a product are sold at a single price. But for firms in other markets price is greater than marginal revenue.

Elasticity of Demand

The elasticity of demand is infinite for the firm but lower and perhaps negative for the market.

For the firm the price elasticity of demand is infinite at the market price. In other words, the demand for its product is horizontal. At a price higher than that set by the market, nothing could be sold by the firm. It can sell all it wants at the market price. And selling below that price would be irrational.

The market demand function is another matter. It is frequently inelastic. This is because the demand for farm products tends to be inelastic and the demand for the product of farmers, a derived demand, makes the demand they see even more inelastic.

Using U.S Department of Agriculture estimates, the price elasticity of demand for oranges, –0.62, is the median for seventeen farm products. It is quite inelastic. If citrus fruit growers receive 40 percent of the final price of oranges, the derived demand elasticity is 40 percent of –0.62 or –0.248. If the elasticity is less than unity, marginal revenue is negative. Farmers would accordingly attain greater profits if they grew less. And they sometimes do this by destroying part of crop, spilling raw milk on the road, and the like.

A Theoretical Supply Function

Only in the competitive market can economists derive a theoretical supply function of the firm.

 Thus, only for firms producing a very small part of the gross domestic product can we construct theoretical supply functions. Ironically though, we can do better for firms in other markets. A large majority of them are price-setters and their actual supply functions are horizontal or infinitely elastic at the product price.

Profit Maximization—Variations on a Theme

The typical ways of determining the output rate at which profit is maximized are presented here. They involve the use of total functions, marginal functions, and mathematical functions which use both and a bit more.

Maximum Vertical Displacement Between the Total Revenue and Total Cost Curves

Profit, π, is the difference between total revenue and total cost: $\pi = TR - TC$. Maximum profit occurs at that rate of production, Q, at which total revenue is most vertically displaced relative to total cost. This can be seen in Figure 7.3. When the rate of production is zero, total fixed costs amount to $100,000 per year and profits are minus $100,000. Total cost equals total revenue at a rate of production of about 150 units per year. This is the "break-even" rate of production. At higher rates of production, profits increase, decrease, reach another break-even output rate and then become negative as total cost exceeds total revenue.

 How do producers know the profit-maximizing rate of production? If they have the tabular data the curves are based on, they can subtract total cost from total revenue in the region of YY. The rate of production yielding the highest difference should be chosen. Were the data lost, the graphs could be used. Profit maximization occurs where the slope of the total cost curve equals that of the total revenue curve. That is shown in Figure 7.3 by a line parallel to the total revenue curve and tangent to the total cost curve. Were a lower output rate chosen, the functions would be diverging and greater production would yield higher profits. Were a higher output rate chosen the functions would be converging and a lower rate of production would yield higher profits.

Figure 7.3.   **Total Revenue, Total Cost and the Profit-Maximizing Output Rate**

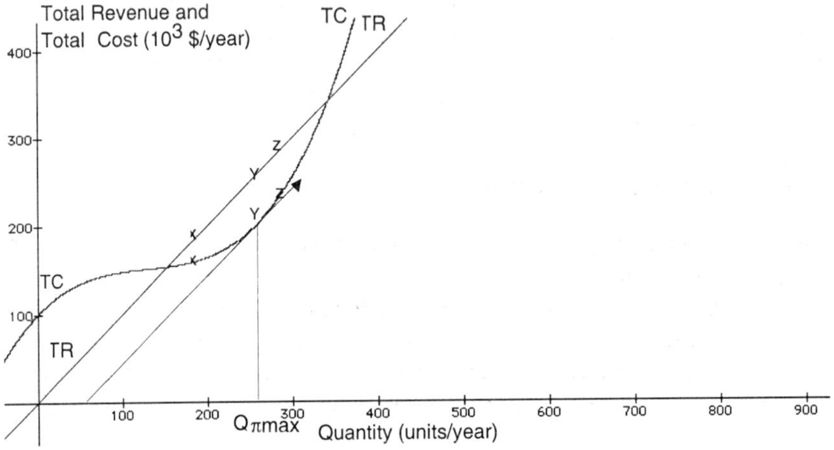

Stick with a rate of production at which the slope of the total revenue function, *MR*, equals the slope of the total cost function, *MC*.

The Equality of Marginal Revenue and Marginal Cost with Two Conditions

The use of the equality of marginal revenue and marginal cost has two problems. The first is that the equality takes place at the minimum as well as the maximum profit output rate. This problem is handled by requiring that the slope of the marginal cost function is greater than that of the marginal revenue function. The second is that even at profit maximization, profits may be so negative that it pays to shutdown. This is handled by limiting production to the condition that marginal cost is equal to or greater than average variable cost, limiting loss to total fixed cost.

Why does the equality of marginal revenue and marginal cost, with the slope of marginal cost greater than marginal revenue, define the profit-maximization rate of production? The answer is aided by the cost and revenue functions of Figure 7.4. Assume that the price is initially P_1, $30 per unit. This means that the competitive producer receives an additional $30, MR_1, for each additional unit sold. Starting from $Q = 0$, marginal cost is downward sloping and greater than marginal revenue. Production of the marginal unit involves a loss (added to the loss of total fixed cost). Loss increases until marginal cost equals marginal revenue, at an output rate of about 10 units per month. This equality of marginal revenue with declining marginal cost represents profit *minimization.* Every unit produced up to this point has a greater marginal cost than marginal revenue which adds to loss.

For subsequent additions to the rate of production, marginal revenue exceeds

Figure 7.4.   **Profit-Maximizing Output Rate: MC= MR, Slope MC > MR, MC ≥ AVC**

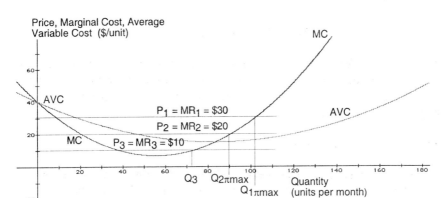

marginal cost and adds to profit (subtracts from loss). This is the case until $MR_1 = \$30$ is again equal to marginal cost—at an output rate of about 102 units per month. Thus, the profit-maximizing rate of production, at a price of $30 per unit is $Q_{1\pi max}$.

Note that the condition for profit maximization at $Q_{1\pi max}$, has three elements: (1) Marginal revenue equals marginal cost, $MR=MC$. (2) The slope of MC is greater than the slope of MR. (3) The price is equal to or greater than average variable cost making production more profitable than shutdown. At a price of $20, the three conditions are met at the profit-maximizing output rate of $Q_{2\pi max}$. But what about price and marginal revenue of $10 per unit? Here price is less than average variable cost. The loss is that of total fixed cost and some of total variable cost. It is less unprofitable to shut down production.

Doing Profit Maximization Mathematically

Profit equals the difference between total revenue and total cost:

(1) $\pi = TR - TC$

All variables are functions of the rate of production, Q. At maximum and minimum profit, the profit function has a slope of zero. It has gone as far as it can go. The slope of a function in calculus is its derivative, here, $d\pi/dQ$. (The basics of differential calculus can be found in Appendix A.1. near the end of this text.) Consistent with normal usage this slope and derivative could be called marginal profit. It equals the difference between marginal revenue and marginal cost:

(2) $d\pi/dQ = dTR/dQ - dTC/dQ = MR - MC$

At the profit-maximizing rate of production the slope of the profit function is zero. Therefore,

(3) $MR - MC = 0$ or $MR = MC$

Since this is the condition for both profit and loss maximization, there is a need for another requirement. As discussed above, for profit maximization the slope of the marginal revenue function must be less than that of the marginal revenue function.

(4) $dMR/dQ < dMC/dQ$ for profit maximization

While the mathematical manipulation identifies the profit-maximizing output rate, it does not tell us whether or not the price (and marginal revenue) is equal to or greater than average variable cost. Thus, we have to add the requirement that production requires price to be equal to or greater than average variable cost. Were price less than average variable cost, total variable cost would not be covered and shut down would maximize profits.

Firm and Market Supply Functions

Three sets of supply functions are presented: (1) The cost functions are "U"-shaped and firms are profit maximizers; (2) the cost functions are "U"-shaped and the firm's produce at full capacity; (3) marginal and average variable cost are constant until full capacity is reached. Each of the three sets of supply functions has two alternatives. In the first all firms have the same cost functions; in the second, there is a bell-shaped distribution of average variable cost—so each firm enters the market at a different price. In all cases it is assumed that there are 1,000 firms of the same size in the market.

It was shown above with the help of Figure 7.4 that at a market price of P_1, the rate of production at which profit maximization occurs is that at which positive-sloped marginal cost equals that price. This yields a point on the firm's supply function. More generally:

> The profit-maximizing firm's supply function is that part of the positive-sloped portion of the marginal cost function which is equal to or greater than average variable cost.

This is shown in Figure 7.5. Nothing is supplied until the price reaches the (minimum) average variable cost of $38 per unit. At this price the quantity supplied jumps to 90,000 units per year, on the marginal cost function. At higher prices the supply function is the marginal cost function and the quantity supplied increases with price.

Figure 7.5.   **The Firm's Supply Function in Competitive Markets**

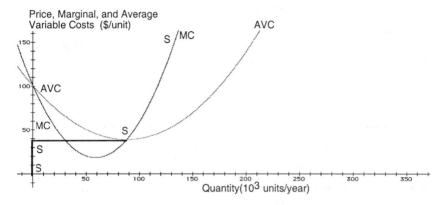

Profit-Maximizing Firms with the Same Cost Functions

Figure 7.6 shows the market supply function for the case in which the 1,000 firms have the same cost and supply functions. Until price equals the average variable cost of the firm, nothing is supplied. At average variable cost the quantity supplied jumps to 5,000 bushels per year, thereafter it increases with price along its marginal cost curve. The market supply function is the same shape as the firm's except that the quantity at all prices is 1,000 times the firm's.

Profit-Maximizing Firms with a Bell-Shaped Average Variable Cost Distribution

A crude version of firms with a bell-shaped distribution of average variable cost appears in Figure 7.7. In this distribution there are relatively few efficient firms with the low average variable cost implicit in supply function S_1. As a result while the price increases, quantity increases by a relatively small amount. As the price increases it reaches the mean or central tendency of the average variable cost distribution, as exemplified by supply functions S_{500} and S_{501}. There are many firms willing to supply to the market in the neighborhood of the mean and the quantity supplied increases substantially. Finally, a still higher price brings forth the supply of a relatively small number of inefficient firms. This creates the rising tail at the end of the supply function. The shape of the market supply function is similar to a function statisticians call an "ogive," a function which arises from adding up the elements of a frequency distribution–a cumulative distribution function.

Note the difference between the same cost and the bell-shaped cost market supply curves. As price rises, in the former the quantity supplied changes with great

Figure 7.6.   **The Market Supply Function as the Horizontal Sum of 1,000 Identical Suppliers**

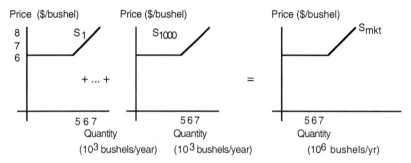

Figure 7.7.   **The Market Supply Arising from a Bell-Shaped Distribution of Average Variable Cost**

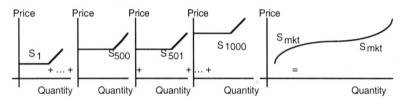

abruptness as we suddenly go from no firms to 1,000 firms producing. If the cost distribution is bell-shaped, once price reaches the average variable cost of the most efficient firm, there is some supply, and quantity supplied varies relatively smoothly as price increases.

Full Capacity Producing Firms with the Same Cost Functions

The example of firms producing at full capacity arises from the finding of Daniel B. Suits that:

> Because farms in agriculture tend to operate very close to capacity regardless of price, the principal supply response to falling price occurs when farmers find it no longer profitable to produce the crop. Similarly, the principal supply response to rising price comes when farmers find prices moving back into the profitable range and again take up production of the crop (1982, p. 16).

Nourse and Drury's observation is largely the same (1938, p. 90) with both basically at odds with the profit-maximizing neoclassical supply model.

The production of each firm is at full capacity, as long as the expected price is equal to or greater than average variable cost as seen in Figure 7.8. At such a price the output of each firm jumps to 7,000 bushels per year making the market supply jump to 7 million bushels per year.

Figure 7.8.   **The Market Supply Function for Firms with Identical Cost Functions Operating at Full Capacity**

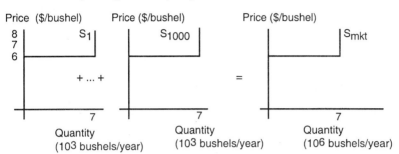

Full Capacity Producing Firms with a Bell-Shaped Average Variable Cost Distribution

With all firms working at full capacity, a maximum market supply of 7 million bushels per year is the most which is attainable. But with a bell-shaped distribution of cost, the quantity supplied will not change abruptly, as it does in Figure 7.8. Again, at relatively low prices the most efficient firms will market their product. Higher prices in the neighborhood of the mean of the distribution brings out the supply of the relatively high percentage of firms with near average efficiency and average variable costs. Finally, higher prices are accompanied by the marketed product of the relatively inefficient, high average variable cost firms.

In Figure 7.9 can be found an artful rendition of the market supply functions predicated on full capacity production with firms that have equal average variable costs and a bell-shaped average variable cost distribution. With the bell-shaped cost distribution shown, about 50 percent of the full capacity supply is obtained as the price goes from $10 to $25. But none comes in the equal average cost case until the price reaches $25 and that brings out the full capacity market supply.

Marginal and Average Variable Cost Are Equal and Constant

Marginal cost is equal to average variable cost in the common genus of linear total cost functions. This might be found in lumber mills which are plentiful in the United States. The relevant functions are given in Figure 7.10. Recall that the firm's supply function, based on profit maximization, is the range of the marginal cost function in which it is equal to or greater than average variable cost. But here marginal cost equals average variable cost. Both are $5 per 10 board feet of lumber for production rates from zero to the full capacity of 10,000 board feet of lumber per month. Were the supply function the marginal cost

Figure 7.9.   **The Market Supply Function for Firms Operating at Full Capacity with the Same and Bell-Shaped Average Variable Cost Distributions**

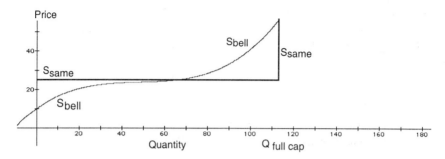

function, the firm would never have the revenue to pay a penny of total fixed cost—a fast route to bankruptcy. But there may be a way out of the situation in which the supply function is always less than average cost. Assume that the mill is operating at what is truly full capacity. If a dose of the variable resources used to produce marginal units were added to employment, no increase in production could take place. Instead, the total variable cost curve would become vertical at full capacity. Marginal cost, the slope of that function, would then approach infinity and average variable cost would increase more modestly. In this thought experiment (frequently referred to in German as a *gedanken* experiment) marginal cost becomes greater than average variable and average cost. The mill's supply function would then be of infinite elasticity at $5 per 10 board feet until full capacity is reached, whereupon it would become a vertical, zero-elasticity function.

If all mills had the same average variable costs, all 1,000 mills would have supply functions which go from infinite to zero elasticity. The market supply function would be the same except that the break in elasticity would occur at 1,000 times the rate of production of that of the mill.

Were the distribution of average variable costs bell-shaped among firms, the supply function would be ogive-like until full industry capacity is reached, at which point it would becomes vertical. The market supply functions would look quite like that of Figure 7.9.

Sell or Store

Producers of storable products, wood included, might expect the market price of their product to rise in the future. If the expected price rise, in percent per year, is greater than the interest rate, also in percent per year, storage would be profitable. If the current price of a product is $4 and is expected to increase by 6 percent in a year, the gain from storing the product one year is expected to be 24 cents. And if the interest rate is 5 percent, the interest foregone by not sell-

Figure 7.10.   **A Linear Total Cost Curve and Related Functions**

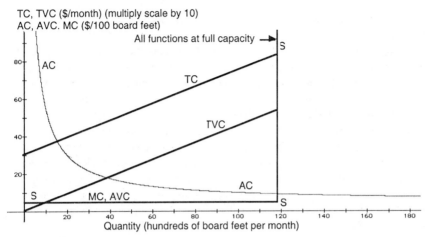

ing the product for a year, amounts to 20 cents. The net gain of storage is then 4 cents per unit per year or 1 percent of the price. That amount is "peanuts" but if you fail to exploit the storage option you are economically irrational.

But the cost of storage is not just foregone interest. There are also the sums which have to be paid to the warehouse which handles and stores the product, and there is frequently the loss of stores due to spoilage, theft, and rodents. Such costs can be added to foregone interest and compared to the expected price increase to determine whether to sell or store. Storage tends to take place when the price is relatively low and expected to increase; removal of product from storage tends to take place when the price is relatively high. Both actions tend to stabilize price.

Fixed Market Supply

Assume the existence of a product which cannot be stored and must, therefore, be sold very soon after production. Fish, flowers, tree-ripened fruits, and vine-ripened berries approximate this assumption. The firm's supply of such products tends to be vertical or of zero elasticity with the market supply function having the same shape. This conforms to Alfred Marshall's market period supply.

We all know examples of fixed short-run supply. The quantity of seats is fixed in auditoriums, stadiums, buses, trains, and planes. The price of these seats is set by producers, and this makes the supply function infinitely elastic up to capacity whereupon it becomes vertical, of zero elasticity. In Marshall's market period the supply function is vertical—at least in his *Principles*. In his lectures, however, he recognized the existence of "conventional prices"—implying a horizontal supply function.

Shifts in Marginal Cost and Supply

Shifts in the marginal cost function are caused by changes in factor prices and changes in factor productivity. An increase in the cost of a factor of production increases marginal cost and decreases supply. This is shown in Figure 7.11. The original marginal cost and supply are MC_0 and S_0. If a factor cost increases, marginal cost and supply will shift upward to MC_1 and S_1—which represents a decrease in supply. Assume that subsequently there is an increase in productivity such that marginal cost shifts back to MC_0 and supply to S_0.

If increases in variable costs are offset by increases in productivity, the marginal cost and supply function should be unaffected. This condition is better approximated in the production of goods than in the production of services, a matter of substantial significance to an economy in which growth of the service sector has long exceeded growth in manufacturing. An important reason for the relatively high growth in tuition and medical costs is the relatively low productivity growth in these important areas.

The Curtailment of Supply and the Increase in Profits

Why is it that producers in competitive markets frequently seek and profit from a curtailment or destruction of supply? It is because the market demand for what they produce tends to be inelastic. The demand for crude materials is derived from the demand for the finished products which use them with other factors of production. The cost of the crude materials is a fraction of the product price and this makes the elasticity of demand that fraction of the elasticity of demand for the product.

Consider the case of the demand for oranges which has a price elasticity of demand of -0.62. Assume that the citrus fruit growers receive 40 percent of the selling price to consumers. Their derived elasticity of demand is -0.248. Were their price cut by 4 percent, the quantity demanded would increase by slightly less than 1 percent. (Using the definition of the price elasticity of demand I calculated the percent change in quantity: $\Delta Q/Q = -0.248 \cdot -0.04 = 0.00992$.)

Given: (1) Citrus fruit growers destroy 1 percent of their crop. (2) E = -0.248
Find: The resulting change in their total revenue.
$\Delta P/P = \Delta Q/Q \div E = -0.01 \div 0.248 = 0.0403$
$TR = 1.0403P \cdot 0.99 \ Q = 1.03$
The 1 percent crop reduction yielded a 3 percent increase in total revenue.

That sort of crop destruction cannot be accomplished by the multitude of citrus fruit growers on their own. There would be a substantial incentive to cheat and not to destroy 1 percent of a crop, or a full 1 percent. But it can be accomplished by the issuance of a marketing order by the Secretary of Agriculture—

Figure 7.11.   **An Increase in the Cost of a Factor and the Decrease in Supply**

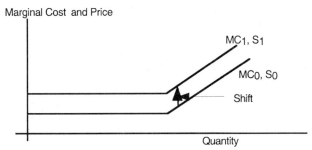

an order limiting marketing to a specified percent of a previous crop. While crop destruction adds to overall profits, bumper crops decrease them.

The Problem of Negative Marginal Revenue

As long as the market demand in a competitive market is inelastic at the market price, marginal revenue is negative. In the above example assume that oranges are sold to consumers for $10 a bushel with the grower receiving $4 a bushel. With an elasticity of demand of –0.62, the sale of the marginal bushel yielded a marginal revenue of –$6.13 (MR = P (1 + 1/E) = 10 (1 + 1/–0.62) = –$6.13). With the citrus grower receiving 40 percent of this, the marginal revenue received from growing the last bushel of oranges is –$2.45. (The derivation of the formula relating marginal revenue to price and the price elasticity of demand can be found in Appendix A.1.)

The graphical approach requires the proper location of the elasticity of -0.62 on the market demand function, as in Figure 7.12. The location is such that at this elasticity the ratio of the two segments of the demand function is 0.62 to 1. The second matter is that for a linear demand function, the marginal revenue function comes down at double the negative slope. Then a careful drawing shows that at the quantity sold at $10 a bushel, marginal revenue is –$6.13 per bushel. Citrus fruit growers would maximize their total revenue and profits if the crop destruction continued until the supply equaled demand at unitary price elasticity of demand.

It would be irrational for a firm to produce to the extent that its marginal revenue is negative. Does this become rational when the source of the negative marginal revenue is the market?

Efficiency and the Competitive Market

Efficiency, in a general sense, is the ratio of output to input. Most power generating plants transform fuel—coal, oil, and gas—into electrical energy. Their efficiency is the ratio of the energy they produce to the energy content of the fuels used. The efficiency of a light bulb is the ratio of the illumination to the energy

Figure 7.12.   **Determining Marginal Revenue from a Given Elasticity of Demand**

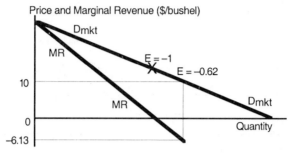

used to obtain that illumination. Maximum efficiency occurs when either maximum output is obtained from a given input or a given output is obtained from the minimum input.

The idea of efficiency is explicit in William S. Jevons's 1871 definition of economics. In his definition, the population, needs, and productive resources are given or fixed. Then, "the problem of economics" is the determination of "the mode of employing their labor which will maximize the utility of the produce" (p. 254). Jevons considers efficiency from the perspective of consumers. We now realize maximizing the production the income of a consumer can command requires two kinds of efficiency: allocative efficiency and technical efficiency.

Allocative Efficiency

Allocative efficiency occurs when the price of a product equals marginal cost: $P = MC$. This is the lowest possible product price a rational producer would require to make the marginal unit of production. It is the price which just covers the cost of the variable resources used in the production of the marginal unit. Assuming that firms in the competitive market vary their rate of production to maximize profits, they would increase production up to the point at which marginal cost equals the market-set price. Thus, firms in the neoclassical competitive market display allocative efficiency.

From the general perspective of efficiency, the ratio of the value of the output, P, to that of the input, MC, is 100 percent—at least for the marginal unit of production and in counting only the cost of the variable factors used in its production.

Production Efficiency

Production efficiency, a long-run concept, occurs when the price of a product equals its minimum average cost, $P = AC_{min}$. Average cost is a measure of the amount of resources used to produce a unit of production. If average cost is minimized, the resources used to produce the product, measured in units of dollars, are also minimized. And production at minimum average cost yields not only production efficiency but allocation efficiency, as well since marginal cost equals average cost at its minimum if the curves are "U"-shaped.

Were price greater than minimum average cost, economic profit would be experienced; if less, economic loss occurs. The former should entice the expansion of supply; the latter its contraction. Both tend to drive the price to minimum average cost whereupon there is no economic profit with the result that no net entries to or exits from the market should be experienced. The neoclassical competitive market alone yields both efficiencies.

Avoiding the Uncertainty of Future Market Prices

When farmers and ranchers are planning production they know the current price of crops and animals, but they do not know what the price will be when their products are marketable. There are several ways in which they avoid this uncertainty. One is to "negotiate" a price with a processor for the sale of future production. A large percentage of sugar beets, vegetables for canning, milk, broiler chickens, citrus fruit, potatoes, and turkeys are sold this way. Such negotiations usually involve the dictation of price by the processor, hence the quotation marks. The price, however, cannot be unrealistically low or the producer will opt to gamble on the future market price. (Those who sell to processors, in effect, leave the competitive market and its market set price.)

Other ways of avoiding or curtailing price uncertainty include the following: (1) Vertical integration of producers and processors is sometimes possible, particular if a crop is largely grown in a particular locale. The Sun Maid Raisin Cooperative integrated the activities from growing grapes to packaging and marketing raisins, a degree of vertical integration so extensive that the courts ruled the cooperative to be in violation of the anti-trust laws. (2) Certain crops-to-be can be sold on futures markets or to grain elevators. The producer then knows the price which will be received under contract for a certain amount of product to be delivered by a specified date. (3) Producers can join organizations which lobby to have governmental agencies set a minimum product price expected to be higher than the market price. Lobbying efforts can also be to curtail imports, to establish marketing quotas limiting supply, and the like.

Futures markets are of special interest. A wheat farmer can sell his crop on the futures market at the current price of futures contracts. Assume that, for example, it is March, the crop will be harvested in July, and the price of wheat to be delivered in July is $3.75 per bushel. Selling now at that future price would remove price uncertainty allowing the producer to set the profit-maximizing rate of production on the basis of a known price. This would be particularly attractive to producers who are risk averse. The July market ("spot" or "cash") price could of course be substantially higher or lower than the $3.75 March futures price.

Selling (and buying) in futures markets may also be attractive to producers who are risk-takers, gamblers, or speculators. That is so because over the course of time futures prices for delivery in a given month tend to have a substantial spread. On March 26, 1992 the price of wheat for July delivery closed at $3.49 a bushel but the futures price had varied from $2.79 to $4.295 per bushel over the course of the "season." The market price of wheat in July 1992 was substantially less than $4.295. Speculators who held contracts to sell at $4.295 in July could buy the wheat at the market price and sell it at the higher contract price. Their large profits would equal the losses of those who had contracted to buy at $4.295.

Some readers may realize that futures markets afford a wonderful locale for gambling and at far fairer odds than are generally found at race tracks and state lotteries. In truth, the percentage of trades consummated by the actual transfer of wheat or other commodity from seller to buyer amounts to only about 1 to 2 percent of the total quantity of futures contracts. Many of the other participants are betting on the future value of a piece of paper and are completely disinterested in actually buying or selling wheat or other commodities in the future.

Problems with the Competitive Model

There are a number of dubious aspects to the neoclassical competitive model: Do producers actually make decisions intended to maximize profit? Is the shape of the cost function that prescribed by the model? Does marginal cost pricing take place in this market? Is the tendency of the government to lend assistance to those in this market a sign of the badness of the market to producers?

Is the Rate of Production Set to Maximize Profits?

Return a moment to the cobweb model in which a low price of hogs is experienced, low hog production is commenced, and fours year years later the low supply of hogs is brought to market and with a stable demand for hog derived products, hog prices are relatively high. Then the high price stimulates high production and when these hogs come to market the high supply comes to and hog prices become low. I called this irrational, to counter an argument claiming rationality when there is so much undermining evidence. What should the hog farmers have done? Common sense indicates that they should have kept their growing stock at essentially a constant level.

Have you ever seen a vineyard? The grape vines are grown, not as vines but as small bushes. And the space between each vine is substantial. Consider the case of commercial apple orchards. The trees are kept quite small and not so close that they intertwine. What if profits from growing grapes for wine and apples for eating increased? Would they increase the density of vines or trees on their property. I think not. It would threaten the quality of the products.

How about a corn field with the corn ready for picking? It is no easy task to walk through the maze of corn—the vegetation is so densely packed. How can the field's operator grow more corn on it? I think that, too, is not very practical.

Return to the market for hogs. Did the low price and low profits cause decision-makers to raise fewer hogs? Again, I think not. The low hog price drove high cost hog farmers out of the industry and that is why the ensuing supply was low.

Or take a dairy farmer with twenty-four cows and twenty-four stalls in his cow shed. The price of milk goes up. Does he increase the size of his herd? He cannot in the short-run.

What I am getting at is that it is easy to talk about increasing the rate of production in response to higher profits on a given piece of farmland but I do not believe it to be practical or practiced.

What about low profits indicating that the rate of production should be curtailed. As indicated above, that decrease in supply called for seems to come from farmers moving out of the industry.

My answer to the question of this section is: No, farmers do not appear to change their rate of production, with land held constant, in response to profit incentives. For confirming views see Edwin G. Nourse and Horace B. Drury (1938, p. 90) and Daniel B. Suits (1982, p.16).

Profit Maximization: A Form of Schizophrenia

Consider the case of a manager. The neoclassical model portrays him as a hedonic consumer, a person whose decisions are intended to maximize his satisfaction or pleasure. Thus, we might expect the manager to have an attractive home, suitable rugs on the floor, a good array of electrical and electronic devices, a desirable car, and so on. But what about the manager in his office? He is now transformed into a miser who is supposed to minimize costs. His office is the smallest possible. Its walls are unpainted cinder block. The floor is asphalt tile, the color of which best conceals filth. The desk is ugly but functional; the illumination is from bare fluorescent bulbs, and so on. During workdays the manager may spend more waking hours in his decrepit office than in his pleasant home. How realistic is this model of schizophrenic Economic Man? And the same schizophrenia is expected of all managers who are profit maximizers.

A more realistic model appears in Chapter 9 under the heading "Utility Maximization as an Alternative to Profit Maximization." Farmers in air conditioned tractor cabs with television sets fit the mold of this model.

What About Efficiency?

Consider allocative efficiency first. If producers are utility maximizers, they will not set the rate of production such that the expected price equals the least possible marginal cost. And it is possible that they cannot, the argument of the previous section.

What about production efficiency? Laying aside costs enhancing utility rather than production, I suspect that the near full capacity operation of farms implies producing at or near minimum average cost. The almost unbelievable productivity growth in agriculture during the twentieth-century indicates either that increasing productivity is part of the culture of farming or that competition forces farmers to use increasingly productive equipment and methods of production, or some of both.

Government Involvement in Agriculture

Government involvement in agriculture contradicts the requirements of the competitive market that no person or institution can significantly influence the market price or quantity. There is a long history of governmental involvement in agriculture going back at least to the administration of Abraham Lincoln. In 1862 the Homestead and Morrill Land Grant Acts were passed by the Congress. The former allowed all citizens and citizens-to-be to claim 160 acres of government land, and after living on it for five years, to gain title to it on payment of a small fee. The Homestead Act increased supply. The Morrill Act gave the states 30,000 acres of public land for each representative it had in Congress—with the proceeds used for education in agriculture, engineering and military science. This led to the formation of state "land grant" colleges and universities—public institutions engaging in activities aimed at making farming more productive. The land grant colleges and universities have displayed ongoing influence on the efficient production and supply of agricultural products.

Substantial government involvement in transportation and its infrastructure converted local markets for agricultural products and manufactures into national markets. Railroad and warehouse-elevator charges were anathema to farmers. Farmers saw them as monopolies draining their income. Between 1870 and 1874, Illinois, Iowa, Minnesota, and Wisconsin passed laws regulating their rates. The Interstate Commerce Act was passed by Congress in 1887. It required the railroads to publish their rate schedules and to have charges which were "reasonable and just." Then came the disaster of the 1930s—the Great Depression, which hurt farmers even more than most other groups in the economy. This prompted numerous governmental attempts to assist the agricultural sector including the setting of minimum prices and the limitation of supply. In recent years disasters have struck farms in flood plains—farms frequently helped by government programs and agencies.

Governmental involvement in agriculture has been substantial throughout much of the history of the United States. Its actions and investments have helped to increase productivity per hour of labor and acre of land. This has greatly reduced the relative price of agricultural products leading to a concern to help farmers

Figure 7.13.   **Consumer and Producer Surplus**

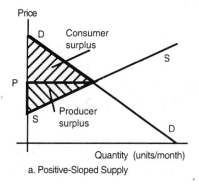

a. Positive-Sloped Supply

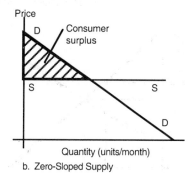

b. Zero-Sloped Supply

with one set of price supports or another.

Consumer and Producer Surplus

A number of government farm programs have affected consumer and producer surplus. Thus, this brief review of the analysis presented in Chapter 4.

Consumer surplus is the total utility obtained from the consumption of a product in excess of the total utility of the money used to pay for it. This makes consumer surplus the area under the demand function to the price line. And producer surplus is the total revenue received for a product in excess of the cost required for it to be produced. It is the area between the price line and the supply function.

Figure 7.13 shows both consumer and producer surplus for two cases. In both the demand function is negative sloped. In frame *a* the supply function has a positive slope; in frame *b* its slope is zero. As can be seen, the more vertical or inelastic a function is, the greater is the surplus. In addition, any and all price increases—from any and all sources—diminish consumer surplus.

A Government Set Minimum or "Parity" Price

Consider the effects of a government-set price which is above the market level. This is shown in Figure 7.14 for cases in which the supply function is positive-sloped, frame *a*, and mostly vertical, frame *b*.

Frame *a*, which corresponds to a durable crop, such as wheat, which can be stored when the market price is low and drawn from storage when it is high. The market price is P and the higher government set price, P_{min}. As a result of the price increase, consumers lose the amount of surplus covered by areas A plus B. Producers gain an amount of surplus equal to rectangular area A and lose the smaller triangular area C. The overall loss of surplus is B plus C and goes by the name of "deadweight loss."

Frame *b* is applicable to a perishable crop. Unless the market price covers the

Figure 7.14.   **Changes in Consumer and Producer Surplus due to a Government-Set Price Higher than the Market Price**

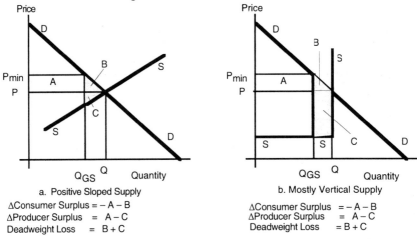

a. Positive Sloped Supply

ΔConsumer Surplus = − A − B
ΔProducer Surplus = A − C
Deadweight Loss   = B + C

b. Mostly Vertical Supply

ΔConsumer Surplus = − A − B
ΔProducer Surplus   = A − C
Deadweight Loss   = B + C

harvesting cost, the horizontal portion of the supply function, no crop will be marketed. Then the full crop is supplied to the market, the vertical-sloped portion of the supply curve. The resulting market price would be P. Assume, contrary to fact, that the government sets the price higher than the market price, P_{min} versus. P. There is then a loss of consumer surplus equal to the areas A plus B and a gain of producer surplus equal to area $A - C$. Note that with area C greater than A, there is also a loss of producer surplus. As in frame a, the sum of area B and C represents the deadweight loss. Note also that if demand is elastic, the higher price will yield lower total revenue and, assuming the whole crop is harvested, lower profits. Finally, government action did not help producers in this case and government parity pricing has not been applied to perishables.

A Government-Set Maximum Price: "Price Controls"

Price controls tend to be put into place during wartime periods in which commercial production is curtailed in favor of the production of goods required by the armed forces. Such periods then tend to be characterized by relatively high demand as compared to supply—the recipe for inflation. To stem the rate of inflation, "price controls," the setting of maximum prices, have sometimes been invoked as shown in Figure 7.15.

In frame a can be found the case in which the supply function is positive-sloped. At the lower-than-market government-set price, P_{max}, less is produced than at the market price, P. Moreover, the quantity demanded at that price can be substantially greater than the production. Consumer surplus is increased by areas A minus B; producer surplus is decreased by the sum of A and C; and a deadweight loss of B plus C is created. In frame b the supply function is first

Figure 7.15.   **Changes in Consumer and Producer Surplus due to a Government-Set Price Lower than the Market Price**

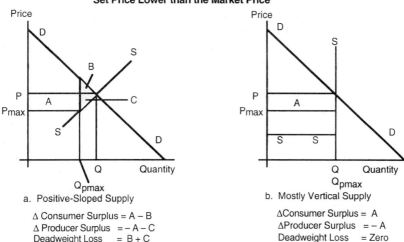

a. Positive-Sloped Supply

Δ Consumer Surplus = A − B
Δ Producer Surplus = − A − C
Deadweight Loss   = B + C

b. Mostly Vertical Supply

ΔConsumer Surplus = A
ΔProducer Surplus = − A
Deadweight Loss   = Zero

horizontal and then vertical. It could be the supply function of rental housing. No rental units are provided until the rent level is high enough to cover variable costs.

Once variable costs are covered, the function should be vertical. Note that there is no diminution in the quantity supplied in the short run. It is for this reason that rental housing affords a good target for controls. In addition, the increase in consumer surplus equals the decrease in producer surplus, and there is no deadweight loss.

A few words on the actuality of "price controls" are in order. The words have been put in quotation marks because price controls tend to be mainly wage controls with producers allowed to pass cost increases into price increases. By controlling wages the most important cost is restrained. Second, "rent controls," particularly as practiced in New York City, have not controlled the price of rental housing but its rate of increase. That rate over the past 40 years has averaged between 6 and 7 percent per annum—substantially higher than the general inflation rate but lower than that of rents not subject to controls.

By the way, with so many workers and employers and landlords and tenants, both the labor market and the market for rental housing should conform to the competitive market model. Were that the case there would be no unemployment and no surpluses or shortages of rental housing—except over short spans of time. But unemployment does exist and, particularly for the poor, there are shortages of housing at affordable prices. (Do not look for the private production of low-cost housing to resolve the problem. Housing for the poor is generally old housing with vacancies caused by better-heeled households moving out and into more modern homes and apartments.)

Summary

The competitive market, although uncommon, is the most important market in neoclassical economics. This is because: (1) Other markets are supposed to respond to changes in supply and demand as the competitive market does. So if you understand comparative statics in the competitive market, you understand it in all markets. (2) The competitive market is *the* efficient market. It sells its products at the lowest possible price, a price which just covers marginal cost. It, therefore, yields the most satisfaction per dollar to sovereign consumers—at least until monopolistic processors, such as cold cereal manufacturers, boost the price up by far more than their marginal cost.

It is expedient to consider producers as profit maximizers. This in conjunction with assumed "U"-shaped cost functions allows the derivation of a theoretical supply function, the positive-sloped portion of the marginal cost function where it is equal to or greater than average variable cost. Firms then plan to obtain an output rate at which expected marginal cost is equal to the expected price at which the crop is harvested and sold. If all guesses prove correct profits are maximized and the requirement for allocative efficiency is met, $P = MC$.

The reality seems to be that farmers tend to produce at or near full capacity rather than varying the rate of production to try to maximize profits. Behind positive-sloped supply functions are low prices which drive relatively high cost producers out of the market and decrease supply and high prices which allow those in the industry to expand and those driven from it to re-enter, increasing supply. A further reality is that since the Civil War, there has been important governmental involvement in agriculture—damaging its role as *the* free competitive market. This allows more farmers to engage in agriculture than would otherwise be the case and thereby brings more than an efficient amount of resources into agriculture.

Evaluation of the effects of government price setting has used the concepts of consumer surplus and producer surplus. Price increases, from whatever source, tend to decrease consumer surplus; price decreases increase it. Producer surplus is an excess in price over that required to bring a resource into use. For positive-sloped supply functions, non-cost-based price increases tend to increase producer surplus.

Two other markets which should be competitive are the markets for labor and for rental housing. Both have huge numbers of buyers and sellers. But without the auction markets of agriculture, their equilibrium is imperfect. They, too, have been subject to regulation under two misleading headings—price controls and rent controls. The former is largely wage controls; the latter rent increase controls.

Questions on Chapter 7

1. What are the characteristics of a competitive market?

2. Derive the firm's supply function graphically. Show that at any given price the function represents profit maximization.

3. Why is the demand for the product of a firm infinitely elastic and equal to market price?

4. Why is the demand function the firm's average and marginal revenue function?

5. Assume that at the market-set price, the market marginal revenue function is quite negative. Of what significance is this to the individual farmer?

6. Explain why the short-run market supply function might actually be related to the distribution of average variable cost functions rather than the marginal cost function.

7. Which is more consistent with profit maximization: the free competitive market or that market plus government subsidies? Discuss.

8. a. Show why, with a negative-sloped demand function and vertical supply function, a government-set minimum price would not be desirable to producers.
   b. Explain your answer from the perspective of rental income.

9. a. Define: consumer surplus, producer surplus, and deadweight loss.
   b. An increase in price decreases consumer surplus but it may not increase producer surplus. Explain.

CHAPTER EIGHT

Monopoly

The word *monopoly* wrongly seems to be the briefest of contradictions with *mono* meaning one and *poly* meaning many. In fact though, monopoly is a corruption of the Greek words *monos polein*, which can be translated as one seller. The one-seller monopoly faces a negative-sloping demand function, that of the entire market. This allows it to set the price of its product. But almost all of our gross domestic product is produced by firms which face negative-sloping demand functions and their market structure is *monopolistic*. The stress of this chapter is on monopolies, but I sometimes stray to include firms which are monopolistic.

The Characteristics of a Monopoly Market

The following characteristics of a monopoly market warrant examination: The market has one seller and many buyers. Entry into and exit out of the market are disallowed. The product of the monopoly is standardized and there are no close substitutes. Price is set by the monopoly. There may be a single price for the product or there may be price discrimination with one set of buyers (e.g., "residential") charged one price and a different set, for example, "business," charged another. The rate of production is essentially set by buyers who determine how much they wish to purchase at the monopoly-set price. Under monopoly there is no unique relationship between price and the rate of production and, as a result, no theoretical supply function exists.

There are two kinds of monopolies: natural and unnatural. The former owes its existence to production which exhibits increasing returns to scale, the latter to institutional power.

Figure 8.1.   **The Long-Run Planning Function and Expected Demand**

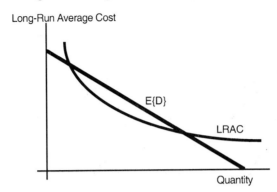

Natural Monopolies

Natural monopolies can be defined as follows:

> *Natural Monopolies* are monopolies which exist because they have exploited increasing returns to scale over the entire range of market demand. The price they set must be low enough to preclude entry by a rival.

The long-run average cost and expected demand functions of the natural monopoly can be seen in Figure 8.1. Note the following with respect to profits: There is a range of plant sizes in which expected demand is equal to or greater than long-run average cost. Over this range either normal or above-normal profits are attainable, and somewhere within the range there exists a plant size which will maximize profits. Finally, profit maximization may prove to be a dangerous goal.

In large markets, public utilities are the most common form of natural monopolies. I can purchase electrical energy from Consolidated Edison, natural gas from the Brooklyn Union, and local telephone services from Bell Atlantic. That's it. All three public utilities require and own large, expensive, infrastructures which are required to transport their services to customers. In small markets there may be many other monopolies: the town bank, plumber, doctor, dentist, general store, etc.

Let me show why it is that a market can be profitably served by one firm but not by two or more—why there are natural monopolies. Figure 8.2 shows the cost and revenue functions of a Small Town Monopoly Bank and what happens if the market is shared with a rival. Both have identical textbook "U"-shaped average cost functions, and they represent the least cost operations arising from the long-run planning function. Assume that at first only Small Town Monopoly Bank is on the scene. The demand is D_1D_1 and marginal revenue is MR_1.

Figure 8.2.   **Small Town Monopoly Bank Sharing the Market with Rival Bank**

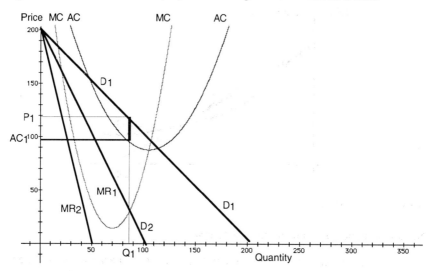

It equals marginal cost at an output rate of 86. The profit-maximizing monopoly price is P_1. That price is greater than average cost by the magnitude of the dark line shown, $P–AC_1$. And economic profit is substantial, namely, $(P_1–AC_1) \cdot Q_1$.

Then Rival Bank enters the market. Assume that it shares the demand with Monopoly Bank. Both banks now have a demand equal to D_2 and a marginal revenue of MR_2. At all quantities D_2, average revenue, is less than average cost so both banks are doomed to negative profits. Only one bank can profitably exist in the market. This does not mean that a profit-maximizing firm has a secure hold on the market. It can be done in by a smart rival, as will be seen in due time.

Natural Monopoly Planning: The Plant-Size Decision

In competitive markets producers can sell as much as they wish at the market-set price. As a result the choice of plant size was predicated on cost minimization. But a monopoly cannot sell as much as it wants—it has to contend with the negative-sloping demand for its product. As a result, a profit-maximizing monopolist chooses the plant which has the lowest average cost at the output rate defined by the equality of long-run marginal cost and the expected marginal revenue arising from expected demand.

The Long-Run Marginal Cost Function

Assume that we have the long-run average cost curve as the envelop of a set of short-run average cost curves. Consider a marginal cost curve associated with

Figure 8.3.   Deriving a Point on the Long-Run Marginal Cost Curve

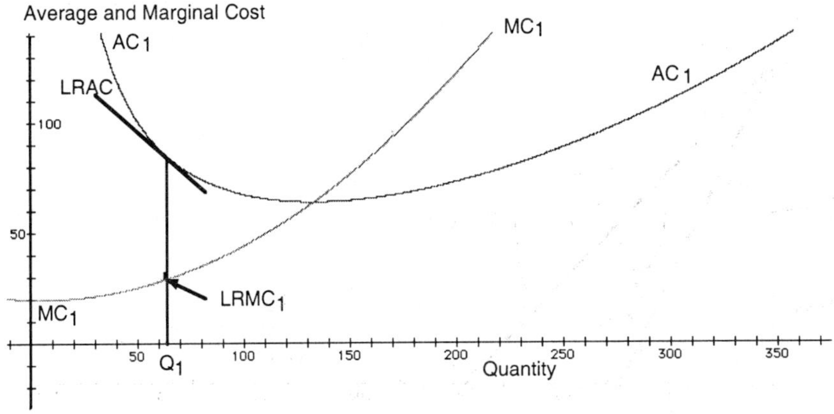

the short-run average cost curve. The magnitude of that marginal cost function, at the tangency of the two average cost functions, yields a point on the long-run marginal cost function. The determination of that point is shown in Figure 8.3.

That long-run marginal cost equals short-run marginal cost at the average cost tangency can be shown mathematically. What is given is that at the output rate Q_1 in Figure 8.3 average cost equals long-run average cost and their slopes are equal:

(1)   AC = LRAC

(2)   dAC/dQ = dLRAC/dQ

To show the equality of short-run and long-run marginal cost, at Q_1, the manipulation of the short- and long-range functions are given in tandem:

Short-Run	Long-Run

Write the equations for short- and long-run total cost:

(3)   TC = Q • AC   LRTC = Q • LRAC

Determine marginal cost by taking the derivative of the total cost functions:

(4) MC = dTC/dQ = d(AC•Q)dQ;   LRMC = dLRTC/dQ = d(LRAC•Q)/dQ

(5) = Q • dAC/dQ + AC•dQ/dQ   = Q • dLRAC/dQ + LRAC•dQ/dQ

(6) = Q • dAC/dQ + AC   = Q • dLRAC/dQ + LRAC

Figure 8.4.   **How a Profit-Maximizing Monopoly is Done In by a Normal Profit Rival**

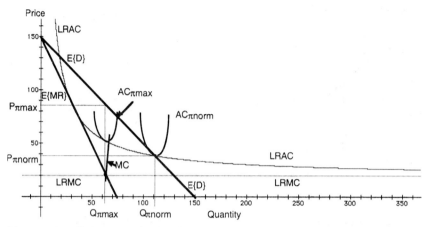

Since at Q_1 all the terms in the short-run marginal cost function equal comparable terms in the long-run function, MC then equals $LRMC$—at the tangency of the two average cost functions. Overall, long-run marginal cost is the locus of points on the short-run marginal cost functions at the output rates at which the average cost and long-run average cost functions are tangent. This is what has been shown for one average cost function in Figure 8.3.

Plant Size Under Profit-Maximization and Normal Profits: "Doing in" the Maximizer

Understanding the logic of the optimal plant-size decision should be helped by referral to Figure 8.4. Profit maximization takes place at $Q_{\pi max}$, where long-run marginal cost and expected marginal revenue are equal. The plant chosen, $AC_{\pi max}$, is that which minimizes cost at that rate of production—the plant with an average cost curve tangent to the long-range average cost curve at $Q_{\pi max}$. The profit-maximizing price at that quantity is $P_{\pi max}$.

The status of the profit-maximizing monopolist should be troubled by the possibility that Smart Rival, content with the average rate of return, might enter the market. It would have a plant built which has the lowest average cost at the rate of production defined by the equality of long-run average cost and expected demand. Smart Rival's plant, $AC_{\pi norm}$, would be larger than that of the profit maximizer, and its costs would be lower. Its price, $P_{\pi norm}$, is less than that of the profit maximizer—thus, doing it in. Note that, even if the profit maximizer dropped its price to the level at which it would have normal profits, 50 in Figure 8.4, it would still be destroyed by the larger, lower-cost Smart Rival.

Stigler's Study of Monopoly Pricing

The late George J. Stigler studied regulated and unregulated public utilities and found that there was no significant difference in their prices. But we know that regulated monopolies are held to "a fair rate of return on their prudently invested capital"—their average cost of production which includes the normal rate of return. Since unregulated monopolies tend to set the same prices, it appears that they, too, price on the basis of the normal rate of return. It consequently appears that monopolies which are public utilities are not profit maximizers but firms satisfied with the normal rate of return. Either consciously or not, this precludes their being destroyed by a Smart Rival willing to produce without receiving economic profits.

Efficiency with Volatile Demand

Natural monopolies owe their power to economies of scale, to production serving an entire market on the negative-sloped portion of their long- and short-run average cost functions. This means that marginal cost is less than average cost making marginal cost pricing irrational. As can be seen in Figure 8.4, greater production efficiency is attained by the largest plant possible—that predicated on normal profits.

There is, however, an unreality about the above choice of plant size and view of efficiency in the case of utilities. The demand for electricity, natural gas, and telephone services varies substantially over the course of the day. Moreover, public utilities are required to have substantial excess capacity to handle outages and unimaginable high demand. From this perspective of demand and efficiency, what is required is a low and flat set of average cost functions. Electrical utilities, for example, accomplish this by having a number of generators continually on line, continuously rotated by prime movers. When demand is low electricity is drawn from just one of them. As demand increases and the first generator approaches full capacity ("full load"), the marginal cost of the energy generated starts to increase, a second generator is switched on. And as demand increases still more additional generators are switched on. In this way, average cost, more precisely average variable cost, is kept low over a broad range of demand. This is one way of responding to the problem of efficiency in the face of large variations in demand.

The Sense of Negative-Sloped Average Cost Functions

In Chapter 6 it was pointed out that empirical cost studies indicate that average cost functions tend to decline until full capacity production is achieved. Why this is so warrants discussion. And it may not be possible to create an envelop of a set of such functions. This problem is also considered.

Some of the production processes best known to us have constant marginal cost over the range of possible rates of production. These violators of the law of diminishing returns have marginal and average variable cost functions which are equal and constant up to full capacity. This is exemplified by the case of Campus Pizza.

> Given: (1) 4 ovens, (2) a baking time of 15 minutes, (3) TFC = $16/hour
> (4). MC constant at $4 per pizza. (It is constant because each pizza requires the same amount of ingredients and oven and labor time.)
> Find: The average cost function.
>
> Average cost is the sum of average variable and average fixed cost.
> With marginal cost constant, average variable cost equals marginal cost: $4/pizza.
> Average fixed cost is total fixed cost divided by the rate of production:
> $$TFC/Q: (\$16/hour)/Q \ (pizza/hour) = \$16/Q$$
>
> Average cost is then AC = 4 + 16/Q. Here we have an average cost function which declines until full capacity production is reached. Were 1 pizza produced per hour, average cost would be $20 per pizza. But at full capacity of 16 per hour, it drops to $5 per pizza.

Consider, in addition to Campus Pizza, Campus Movie. Average fixed cost declines as more and more tickets are sold for a performance. And marginal cost would appear to be very small, rather constant and, therefore, equal to average variable cost. As a result Campus Movie should have a declining average cost function up to full capacity—just as Campus Pizza.

Robert E. Hall, of Stanford University, developed cost data on fifty industries. He concluded that "the typical firm in these industries is operating on a decreasing portion of its average cost curve" (1986, p. 286). To this might be added that perhaps typically the average cost function declines with the rate of production and has no increasing portion until three-shift full-capacity, or its equivalent, is reached.

The long-run average cost functions developed, thus, have been the envelopes of sets of "U"-shaped average cost curves. Here we are dealing with average cost functions which decline up to full capacity. Do such declining cost functions obviate the ability to create a long-run average cost function or the determination of the optimal plant size? The answer to both related questions is "essentially no" as can be seen in Figure 8.5. The long-run average cost planning function is the locus of points at the minimum of the negative-sloping average cost functions—points representing full capacity production. This long-run function,

Figure 8.5.   **Declining Average Cost and Long-Run Marginal Cost**

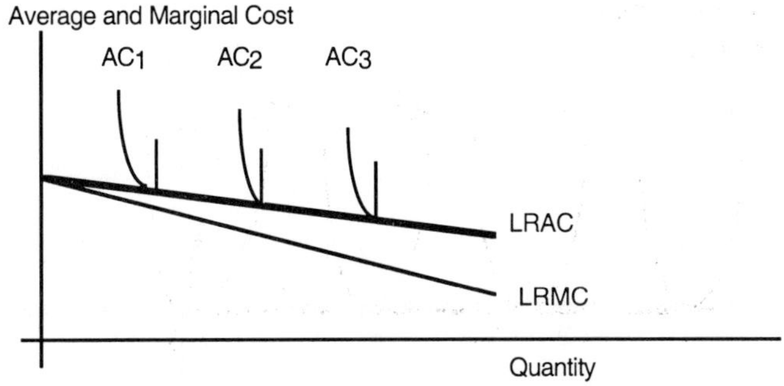

as the one derived from "U"-shaped functions, represent the lowest average costs achievable at various rates of production. Having expediently assumed that the long-run average cost function is linear, I can draw the long-run marginal cost function as initially equal to it and coming down at double its negative slope.

Unnatural Monopolies

Monopolies arising from economies of scale are "natural;" those with other origins would then appear to be "unnatural."

> *Unnatural Monopolies* are monopolies which exist as a result of institutional power.

The institutional power of unnatural monopolies is derived from government patents and franchises, the control of resources vital to the production or marketing of a product, or the creation of pools, trusts, holding companies, and cartels—creations intended to allow a number of firms to act as one. These various forms of institutional power are discussed below.

Profit Maximization and the Lack of Rivals

The unnatural monopoly need not fear the entry of a rival as long as the source of its monopoly power exists. Entry is forbidden, for example, because the monopoly controls resources required for production. This allows the unnatural monopoly to go for maximum profits without fear that a rival might usurp its monopoly status. But patents of various sorts can frequently be circumvented and this implies that consideration be given to average cost pricing and normal profits. The monopolist has to consider the possibility of the entry of rivals and the role that a high-profit policy has in that potential entry.

Figure 8.6.   **Long-Run Average and Marginal Cost Under Constant Returns to Scale**

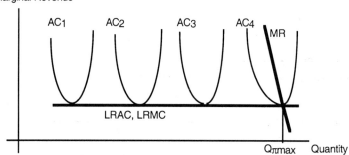

Average and Marginal Cost
Marginal Revenue

The Plant-Size Decision and the Amelioration of Decreasing Returns to Scale

Unnatural monopolies operate in the range of the long-run average cost function in which it is horizontal or positive-sloped. (A negative slope would change an unnatural into a natural monopoly.) The horizontal, constant returns to scale case, is straightforward and interesting. The positive-sloped long-run average cost function, diminishing returns to scale case, is complex and challenging.

In Figure 8.6 can be found a horizontal long-run average cost function which has equal to it the long-run marginal cost function. This holds under the condition of constant returns to scale. Expected marginal revenue equals long-run marginal cost at a rate of production equal to $Q_{\pi max}$. Profits could then be maximized by choosing the plant which has the cost function AC_4. Hold on, the existence of constant returns to scale changes the character of the plant size decision. Yes, AC_4 is fine, but what about two plants with minimum average cost at half of $Q_{\pi max}$ or three with minima at one-third of that figure, and so on? Planners must, before making a choice, consider the advantages and disadvantages of multiplant as opposed to single plant operations.

Assume that the long-run marginal cost equals marginal revenue in the decreasing returns range of the long-run average cost function. This is shown in Figure 8.7 where the profit-maximizing rate of production is 200 units per month and average cost with one plant, AC_{w1}, is $90 per unit—more than the average cost of many smaller plants. But planners know that it may be possible to avoid or ameliorate the higher costs arising from decreasing returns to scale by using more than one plant—plants which operate in the region of minimum long-run average cost.

How many plants can optimally do the job? The data have been rigged so that minimum cost is realized by building two identical plants, each of which has its

Figure 8.7.   **Counteracting Diminishing Returns by Using Smaller Plants**

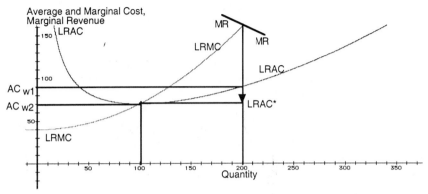

minimum average cost at 100 units per month. With two plants minimum average cost is reduced from $90 to $70 per unit. Assuming the planning function to be a minimum cost function, when corrected it would include the point $LRAC*$.

The assumption that 200 units would be sold each month was predicated on the existence of a single plant with a single profit-maximizing price. With two plants, costs would be lower, the profit-maximizing price would be lower, and more than 200 units a month would be sold. As a result, the size of the two plants would have to be somewhat larger than those with minimum cost at 100 units per month. How much larger would they have to be? The problem is iterative in character. This implies that numerous plant sizes have to be considered in such a way that plant sizes are varied until convergence yields a profit-maximizing size for a set of plants. This goes beyond the point made here, namely, that diminishing returns to scale can frequently be curtailed through the use of multiple plants.

Common Sources of Unnatural Monopoly Power

There are a number of common sources of monopoly power. They include patents, resource control, location, and organizational forms such as trusts. The sources are not independent. Having a patent on a product, for example, may lead a monopolist to gain control of the resources required for production. Sections on these sources of power follow.

Patents

Near the outset of our history as a nation, the value of patents was recognized. This can be seen in Article I, Section 8 of our Constitution:

> The Congress shall have the Power ... To promote the Progress of Science and useful Arts, by securing for limited Times to Authors and Inventors the exclusive Right to their respective Writings and Discoveries.

A patent is a seventeen-year monopoly grant awarded by the government for the discovery or invention of new products, processes, materials, or useful improvements of those in existence. It is usually renewable for an additional seventeen years. The monopoly grant benefits the inventor or his employer and this should tend to stimulate speculative investments in research and development.

 Some patents do in fact allow their holders to benefit from the monopoly grant for the length of the patent's existence; others merely give the firm which holds the patent a lead time. A wonderful example of the benefit obtained from a patent is found in the instance of tungsten carbide, an excellent tool steel. Walter Adams reports on this case as follows:

> In 1927, tungsten carbide sold in the United States at $50 per pound; but after a world monopoly was established by General Electric (GE) and Friedrich Krupp, A.G. of Germany, under which GE was given the right to set prices in the American market, the price promptly rose to $453 per pound. During most of the 1930s the price fluctuated between $225 and $453 per pound and not until 1942—when an indictment was issued under the antitrust laws—did the price come down. Thereafter it fluctuated between $27 and $45 per pound (1982, p. 478).

Why would GE charge about ten times as much for tungsten-carbide at one time as compared to another? My guess is that the higher price range represented profit maximization of an unnatural monopoly. The lower price range appears to be acceptance of the normal rate of return subsequent to government intervention in the "free monopoly market." This is pictured in Figure 8.8 where the two prices are roughly the midpoints of the ranges quoted above.

 Marginal cost is assumed constant at about $15 a pound. Average cost equals average revenue at a price of $35 and that would yield the producer the normal rate of return. But a profit-maximizing producer would have to charge $350 and such a price tempted General Electric—until a major war broke out and the government succeeded in having the price reduced by an order of magnitude.

Getting Around Patents

There are a number of ways through which rivals can get around patents, thereby reducing the value of the monopoly grant. They are cited by Martin Neal Bailey and Alok K. Chakrabarti in their fittingly innovative study: *Innovation and the Productivity Crisis* (1988). (1) What is patented is information available to the public. Rivals can obtain documents describing the product or process patented. This gives them information helpful in developing similar products, processes,

Figure 8.8.   **The Market for Tungsten Carbide with Normal and Maximum Profits**

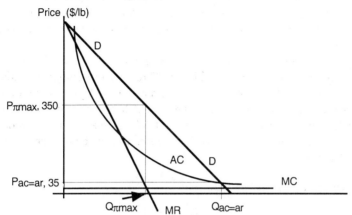

and materials. (2) Competitors can "reverse engineer" patented products: take them apart to determine their special aspects and then develop a similar product. (3) Competitors can hire key personnel involved in the development of the innovation. (4) Finally, key personnel can form their own companies where similar and more advanced innovations can be made.

Baily and Chakrabarti cite the work of Edwin Mansfield which indicates that "within four years of their introduction, 60 percent of the successful patented innovations have been copied" (p. 38). In a sense this crudely mediates the social dilemma patents pose. On the one hand we would like to stimulate innovation and a monopoly grant is an incentive to perform such work. On the other hand, we would like the broadest possible application of innovations which are socially beneficial—and this tends to be limited by patents.

Resource Control

At the age of 18, Cecil J. Rhodes, with his older brother, staked a claim in the newly opened South African Kimberly diamond field. He simultaneously attended to both his studies at Oxford University and his mining interests. In 1880 he founded the De Beers Mining Company, the second largest in the industry. In 1881 he graduated from Oxford. He joined with the owner of the larger diamond mining firm, in 1888, to form De Beers Consolidated Mines and was granted a monopoly for mining in the Kimberly field.

De Beers is not at all the only world producer of diamonds but it dominates the industry through its brilliant marketing strategy which gives it the power to be *the* seller of raw diamonds. Illustrative of De Beers's power was its victory over the Soviet Union. The Soviets decided to market their industrial quality diamonds directly thereby avoiding the cost of marketing through De Beers. Faced with this situation, De Beers used its substantial inventory to drive the price of industrial diamonds down to an unusually low level. The Soviets, not unmindful of the role of power, found it prudent to again have De Beers market their production.

Only 300 or so approved buyers are allowed to purchase from De Beers. They do so from a position of grave weakness. Three weeks before the "sight" they send in requests for the number of carats desired. Two days before they are told of the amount they are to receive. At the "sight," they see the diamonds they are expected to buy along with the price to be paid. Were a buyer to turn down the set of stones offered, he would risk the possibility of being purged from De Beers's list of approved buyers.

Patents Plus the Control of Resources

In 1863, Charles Martin Hall, a student at Oberlin College, discovered the electrolytic process used in the production of aluminum. The company he formed became the Aluminum Company of America (ALCOA). Not only did Hall's patent allow ALCOA to have a monopoly on the method of producing aluminum for a limited time, but it gave the company the time to gain control of the ores required for aluminum production and to place its plants near the cheapest source of energy—hydroelectric power plants. Production of aluminum is energy intensive. Thus, ALCOA was able to maintain a near monopoly position in the production of aluminum ingots eighty years after Hall's discovery.

It was not until 1945 that the Second Circuit Court of Appeals, acting as the court of final appeal in place of the Supreme Court, decreed that ALCOA was an illegal monopoly under the Sherman Act. This was largely due to the fact that Alcoa's' controlled more than 90 percent of the aluminum ingot market. The decision was written by the distinguished jurist, Learned Hand. The ruling of this lower court that 90 percent market share was in itself a violation of the Sherman Act reversed the Supreme Court's contrary position that size per se did not violate the Sherman Act but required examination of the pattern of business behavior leading to market domination and determination of whether the attempt was that of monopolization.

One of ALCOA's defenses was that its after-tax rate of return over the years of its existence, during which it experienced great growth, was only about 10 percent. Judge Hand's negative opinion on this is of some interest: "The ... issue is irrelevant ... for it is no excuse for 'monopolizing' a market that the monopoly has not been used to extract from the consumer more than a 'fair' profit." The "fair price" argument used by ALCOA may have been intended to protect its position as a producer of sheet aluminum since sheet producers which bought ingot from ALCOA found themselves unable to meet ALCOA's sheet price. The Court found that "it will be a disservice to break up an aggregation which has for so long demonstrated its efficiency." The expected remedy was that the federal government would dispose of the plants it had built for the production of aluminum for the conduct of World War II "to discourage monopolistic practices and to strengthen and preserve the competitive position of small business concerns in an economy of free enterprise"—as provided by The Surplus Property Act of 1944. In addition, ALCOA was enjoined to cease and desist its "price squeeze" under which it priced aluminum plate lower than was possible by plate producers who produced aluminum plate from ingots purchased from ALCOA.

Organizational Techniques

The post–Civil War period substantially changed the nature of the United States economy. A competitive agricultural economy experienced high industrial growth and ingenious approaches to stifle competition in key industries such as railroads, power generation, steel, tobacco, and petroleum. Free enterprise was, until the passage of the Sherman Act of 1890, free to do away with what major producers viewed as the destructive threat of competition. The four most popular organizational forms to establish control of a market were pools, trusts, holding companies, and cartels. The development of these approaches was well suited to the expansive spirit of the post–Civil War period.

The major industrialists—tycoons to some, "robber barons" to others—tended to believe in the "Protestant ethic," that they had a "calling" from the Almighty, and that their material success was a sign of the Almighty's evaluation of their performance. Max Weber, a distinguished German sociologist and political scientist contended that it was this ethic which formed the foundation for the development of capitalism. In his "The Protestant Ethic and the Spirit of Capitalism," Weber pointed out that under Calvin's extension of Martin Luther's view of a calling, the riches earned through a calling were not to be spent by the chosen. They were to lead ascetic lives. The riches were to be used in charitable ways including substantial gifts to the church. The post-Calvin attitude was "charity begins at home"—the open enjoyment of one's wealth.

Two examples of the view that wealth and power were God-given follow: First, John D. Rockefeller explained that "God gave me my money." Accordingly, Rockefeller's monopolization of the oil industry was merely a manifestation of the will of the Almighty. In the second example, the son of a striking coal miner, sent a letter to George F. Baer, the president of the railroad which owned the mine, pleading for a token face-saving offer to end the strike and the misery it created. Baer replied, "The rights and interests of the laboring man would be protected and cared for ... by the Christian men to whom God in His infinite wisdom has given the control of the property interests of the country."

Sanctioned by the Highest Authority, the post–Civil War tycoons felt unrestrained in seeking their fortunes. They tended to be ruthless in their handling of smaller firms which did not do their bidding. Defenders of the actions of these industrialists and bankers argue that the firms they crushed were no less ruthless. Several robber barons bought the votes needed in legislative bodies to reach their ends. It was reported that in the legislative struggle between Jay Gould and Cornelius Vanderbilt to control the Erie Railroad, the market price of a legislator was $15,000 with legislative leaders paid as much as $100,000 from one and $75,000 from the other antagonist. Rockefeller, whose initial monopolization efforts involved gaining control of the oil refineries of Cleveland, then quite important, was said to have done everything to the Ohio legislature but refine it. In this "free enterprise" context, the organizational forms of monopolization were developed.

Pools

The pool consisted of an agreement between a number of firms in an industry to cooperate in specified areas. Agreement might be on the share of the market to be allotted to each member of the pool or members might agree to market through a common agency. They were weak combinations because it was frequently advantageous to violate agreed-to rules and firms did just that. The actions once engaged in by pools are illegal.

Trusts

The trust is a combination which allows a set of corporations to act as if they were a single firm. Owners of voting stocks of the various corporations assign their shares to trustees who then have the votes to control the member corporations as one. Shareholders were given trust certificates that entitled them to their share of dividends of the corporation they owned. John D. Rockefeller, who had already done much to monopolize the petroleum industry, formed the first important trust in 1882. It consisted of seventy-seven companies which produced about 90 percent of the refined crude oil in the United States. It was organized in Ohio where Rockefeller had great political power. While the trust form of organization has disappeared, the expression "anti-trust" is still used to describe government agencies and statutes which are supposed to stop monopolization in its various forms.

Holding Companies

With the trust form coming under increasing media, public, judicial, and legislative attack, corporations moved to the anti-competitive device of the holding company. The holding company does not hold securities of shareholders in trust but actually owns shares of the corporations it controls or hopes to control. In

1899, Rockefeller responded to the pressure of the Ohio courts against his trust by obtaining a charter from New Jersey to form Standard Oil of New Jersey and thereupon purchased the shares of the companies controlled by his trust.

Cartels

Cartels are the most popular current organizational form used for the creation of what is, in effect, a monopoly:

> *Cartels* are associations of firms in the same field which agree to engage in activities intended to monopolize a market.

There are three types of cartels. (1) Some are formed to set the price of a commodity. All members agree to sell at the cartel-set price. (2) Others have the goal of restraining supply. Each cartel member agrees to restrict its rate of production to an agreed-to quantity. (3) Finally, each cartel member is given a territorial monopoly.

The most famous or infamous of cartels in recent years is the Oil Producing Export Countries (OPEC). Twice in the 1970s it was able to engineer large increases in the price of crude oil. Both triggered double-digit inflation in the United States and subsequent high unemployment to combat the inflation. The control of the price of crude oil required control of the supply with each member country given a quota to meet the supply goal. Cheating, producing more than promised, was profitable and tended to be counteracted by supply cutbacks by the Saudi Arabians. Once new major oil fields began production, in the North Sea and Alaska, OPEC lost control of the supply and with it its monopoly power.

Although cartels are generally illegal in the United States. an open exception can be found in major league sports. Organized baseball was exempted from coverage of the anti-trust statutes by the courts, which ruled that it was the national pastime and not a business. Football, basketball, and ice hockey leagues have followed baseball's lead. All essentially give each team a territorial monopoly. Entry into a league requires the approval of the cartel and such approval may be unattainable. But there is no way the majors can stop a new league from being formed. The new cartels also give members territorial monopolies—but usually in different metropolitan areas than the old league. The barriers to the creation of new leagues are formidable. There has to be a number of metropolitan areas (or Green Bays) with adequate demand for seats to games, entrepreneurs with command of the required funds willing to gamble them on a new team, in a new league, and the availability of the required practice and game facilities. More often than not, new leagues also require some big-name players to stimulate interest and attendance.

Roosevelt, the Trust Buster

Theodore Roosevelt, who became president upon the assassination of President William McKinley in 1901, is known as the "trust buster." He was an enemy of monopoly and monopolists at a time when they were not in high esteem, to some extent a result of the deep depression of the 1890s. Roosevelt started his anti-trust work with a proposal to Congress in 1902 for the establishment of a Bureau of Corporations. During the debate on this, Roosevelt took advantage of the fact that Rockefeller opposed such a bureau; Congress approved his bill. Reports of the bureau on monopolies in oil and tobacco led to the Supreme Court rulings of 1911 disolving the Standard Oil Company and the American Tobacco Company.

Price and Quantity Under Monopoly and Competition

Once a system has been built and production begins, the long-run function becomes irrelevant and immaterial—whether or not it ever really existed. Producers have to deal with actual production and costs including those required to "debug" the equipment and operations chosen by planners. Product demand becomes experiential rather than expected. And a selling price has to be set for each product with buyers determining how much to purchase at that price.

The price-quantity decision in monopolistic markets is just the opposite of that of the competitive market. In monopolistic markets producers set the price and buyers determine the quantity to be purchased at that price. In the competitive market the market sets the price and producers set the quantity to be produced at that price. This latter may actually be a binary decision with the quantity being that of full capacity production or none at all.

Two sets of cost functions, "U"-shaped and linear, are presented to show the different price and quantity outcomes in competitive and monopoly markets.

"U"-Shaped Marginal and Average Cost Functions

Figure 8.9 should help in making a comparison between the price-quantity results of a monopoly and the competitive market. The profit-maximizing price of the monopolist, $P_{\pi max}$, is based on the equality of marginal cost and revenue. It is the highest of the three prices and the quantity produced and sold is the lowest, $Q_{\pi max}$. Buyers are soaked by profit-maximizing monopolists. What about monopolists satisfied with normal profits? Their price is the lowest, $P_{ac=ar}$, and the quantity sold is the highest, $Q_{ac=ar}$. As Figure 8.9 has been drawn. positive economic profits are made in the competitive market. As a result the competitive price, P_{comp}, and quantity, Q_{comp}, fall between the other two. Only in the long-run does easy entry into the competitive market drive the

Figure 8.9.   **Price and Quantity Under Monopoly and Competition**

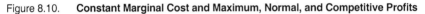

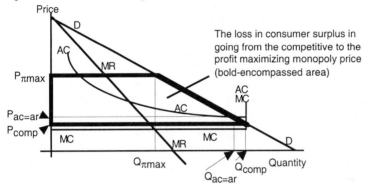

Figure 8.10.   **Constant Marginal Cost and Maximum, Normal, and Competitive Profits**

price down to equal the day-to-day price of the normal rate of return monopolist. There is an interesting condition in the normal profits case. The last unit produced and sold costs more to produce, *MC,* than its sale adds to revenue, *MR.* In addition, although *MR* is shown as zero it could be positive or negative.

Constant Marginal Cost and Declining Average Cost

The assumption in this section is that the total cost function is linear up to full capacity. As a result, average cost declines and marginal cost is constant up to full capacity. At full capacity total cost turns vertical making the marginal and average cost functions vertical, as well.

The average and marginal cost functions along with the market demand and marginal revenue functions can be found in Figure 8.10. Again the equality of marginal cost and marginal revenue determines the profit-maximizing rate of production, $Q_{\pi max}$, and the demand function determines the price which can be charged for that output, namely, $P_{\pi max}$. But the normal profit seeker sets price at the rate of production at which average cost equals average revenue or demand yielding the equilibrium price-quantity of $P_{ac=ar}$, $Q_{ac=ar}$. The competitive market supply in Figure 8.10 is the vertical, full capacity portion of the marginal cost function. It equals demand at full capacity production and yields a price of P_{comp}, which is below average cost. The negative profit tends to drive firms from the competitive market until the price reaches that of the normal profit monopolist, $P_{ac=ar}$. The loss of consumer surplus caused by monopoly profit-maximizing relative the competitive price is indicated by the bold-encompassed area of Figure 8.10.

The Failure to Consider Economies of Scale

There is a wonderful unstated assumption implicit in the comparison between the competitive and monopoly price. It is that there are no economies of scale associated with the case of monopoly. But natural monopolies are the offspring of economies of scale. With these economies, the monopoly price could be lower than the competitive price. Were this the case, the monopoly would yield a greater consumer surplus than the competitive market.

Abba Lerner and Monopoly Pricing and Power

Abba P. Lerner was a distinguished mid-twentieth-century economist whose analysis of monopoly pricing and measure of monopoly power are interesting. Lerner recognized that monopolists seem satisfied with less than maximum profits. He ascribed this to the desire of the monopolist to avoid the political opposition and the entry of new competitors. Lerner's observation is consistent with the comparable pricing of regulated and unregulated utilities.

He proposed that the measure of monopoly power be the ratio of the difference between price and marginal cost to marginal cost: *Monopoly Power = (P–MC)/MC*. The firm in the competitive market should have its marginal cost equal to price and that would yield zero monopoly power. If the firm's price is twice the magnitude of marginal cost, monopoly power is one; if three times marginal cost, it is two. That it is always one less than the ratio of price to marginal cost can be see by the following manipulation of Lerner's formula:

(7) $$(P - MC)/MC = P/MC - MC/MC = (P/MC) - 1$$

Robert Hall and others have, in effect, modified Lerner's approach by using just the ratio of price to marginal cost as a measure of monopoly power. Hall, by the way, obtained "meaningful estimates" on the price-marginal cost ratio in thirty industries. The seven with ratios greater than two, from highest to lowest, were chemicals, paper, railroad transportation, motor vehicles, primary metals, trucking, and warehousing.

While greater-than-one ratios indicate the absence of marginal cost pricing, the extent to which they indicate monopoly power is questionable. Take the case of Campus Movie. The marginal cost of seating another customer is close to zero. But its price has to be far higher. While the price-marginal cost ratio is very high it is surely no economic power. The problem may be that the definition of marginal cost is vague. Is it the cost of seating another viewer or is it the cost of running another performanc? If it is the latter the price to marginal cost ratio would be much, much smaller.

Kahn's Attempt to Make Marginal Cost Pricing Possible

With the norm of linear total cost functions, marginal cost is less than average cost, making marginal cost pricing impossible without massive government subsidization. But Alfred E. Kahn felt that marginal cost pricing was nonetheless possible. He used knowledge of economic analysis and the character of cost functions in regulated industries to invent the required approaches. This can be seen in his masterful two-volume 1970 work, *The Economics of Regulation*. Professor Kahn was in charge of the deregulation of the airline industry in the 1970s and his view of efficient pricing for airlines captures the elegance of his thinking.

In the case of the partly empty airplane, ... the "efficient price" would be zero as long as the response of travelers remained insufficient to fill the plane; then it would have to jump the moment the empty spaces fell one short of demand, possibly to the full cost of an additional plane.

Kahn estimates the marginal cost of transporting an additional passenger on a plane already in service to be zero up to the seating capacity of a plane. Marginal cost pricing seems very attractive to me—up to this point. Then, with a single passenger requiring an additional plane, marginal cost jumps to the full cost of flying that additional or marginal plane. What rough magnitude of price are we talking about? To get a feel for the figure I assume that a ticket for a flight from New York to San Francisco costs $400. Then if a plane with 250 seats requires 200 passengers on a flight to break even, the full cost of a flight is $80,000. Accordingly, the marginal cost of flying a single passenger on the second airplane is $80,000. Marginal cost pricing, "efficient pricing," would require that each passenger going from New York to San Francisco pay $80,000 for the trip.

Kahn realized that few of us would be able and willing to pay the entire cost of an additional flight and goes on to a second approach. He would auction off seats on a flight in such a way that the bid which fills the plane is charged to all. If this price did not cover average cost, capital should leave the industry and with fewer seats supplied, the price should be driven up until it reached average cost. Were the price higher than average cost, an increase in supply should lower it to average cost.

Kahn and My Alternate "Efficient Pricing" Approach

Consider taking a ride in a New York City taxi. You travel five miles, for example, and the charge, tip included, is $10. That is the total charge irrespective
of whether one, or two, or three people are being driven. Were two sharing the
bill, each would pay $5. Apply this reasoning to the pricing of the flight bet-
ween New York City and San Francisco, assuming that on the average, the
flight has 200 passengers. The marginal cost (efficient price) of the flight is
$80,000. That cost shared by 200 passengers yields an individual seat price of
$400.

Note that the complication here is that there are two different marginal units of
production—the marginal seat and the marginal flight. My choice for the problem of price-setting is the marginal flight. Actually, it is also Professor Kahn's
choice. I know that because of our communications on this matter. But the example was too good to avoid to illustrate that it is not uncommon to find that
there is some difficulty in identifying what the marginal unit of production is.
(What would you choose, for example, if you were deciding on the size of a
plane to be built?)

The Absence of a Theoretical Supply Function

A firm's supply function is the rate of production, Q^S, it will engage in at various prices, P—but such a relationship is *theoretically non-existent* for price-setters. The problem appears in Figure 8.11, which has two helpful demand functions. For the first, D_1D_1, and its marginal revenue function, MR_1, profit maximization occurs at the rate of production, $Q_{\pi max}$. The profit-maximizing price
is P_1. In other words, at a price of P_1 the firm is willing to supply $Q_{\pi max}$ units
of its product.

Now consider the more elastic demand function D_2. Its marginal revenue function is MR_2, and it, too, equals marginal cost at $Q_{\pi max}$. With the second demand function, however, the profit-maximizing price is P_2 which is less than-
P_1. So two different prices yield the same rate of production. That befuddles the
supply function which requires a single answer to the question: What price will
lead the firm to engage in a specified rate of production?

That price-setting firms have no *theoretical* supply function is ironic since it is
the instance in which the *actual* supply function is known at a glance: it is
horizontal at the price of the product.

Pricing with a Base Plus a Per Unit Charge

Public utilities frequently bill customers a fixed or base charge plus a charge for
the units consumed, usually per month. Assume that the monopoly electric

Figure 8.11.   **Two Different Prices Yielding the Same Supply Quantity**

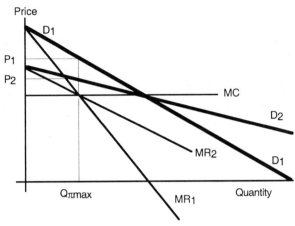

power company charges $5 per month plus $0.15 per kilowatt hour (kwh) of electricity. The total bill, *TB*, is then:

(8) $TB = 5 + 0.15Q$

The price of a kilowatt hour of electricity is:

(9) $P = 5/Q + 0.15$

The price is a rectangular hyperbola displaced upward by 15 cents. If you are away on vacation for the month the price approaches infinity. If a huge amount of electrical energy is used, the price approaches 15 cents per kilowatt hour.

   The base charge is largely a charge for fixed capital equipment which is there for you, used or not.

Price Discrimination

We have thus far assumed that a monopolist charges all buyers the same price. In fact, though, monopolists frequently charge different prices to different categories of buyers, a practice called *price discrimination*.

   Price discrimination is a fairly common phenomenon. Children and senior citizens often pay less than others as do females on "ladies day." Colleges and universities generally charge a great variety of prices for the educational services of a semester. Some students may be on full scholarship; others pay full tuition; many pay less than full tuition as a result of "financial aid." Monopoly utilities have different "rate schedules" for residential, business, and other groups of customers. Price discrimination makes economic sense to many firms because it can increase profits or surplus beyond that obtainable from a single price.

Figure 8.12.   **Profit Maximization with One Price* and with Perfect Discrimination****

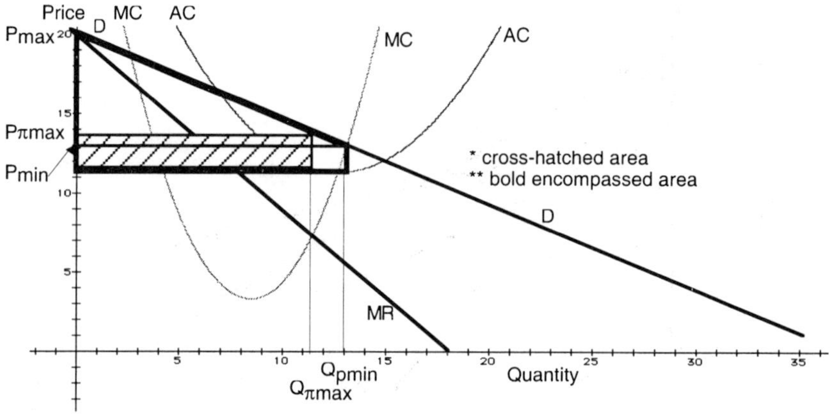

Perfect Price Discrimination

Perfect price discrimination requires the setting of a series of prices such that every buyer is required to pay the maximum he is willing to pay for the product in question. This yields a higher profit than that attainable through the use of one profit-maximizing price as is shown with the help of Figure 8.12. In it can be found the demand for the educational services of Fanciful University, the associated marginal revenue function, and Fanciful's marginal and average cost functions. Fanciful's new administration wants to compare the maximum profit that could be made charging a single price with that of charging each student the maximum that he would willingly pay.

Consider first the case of profit maximization. Marginal revenue equals marginal cost at enrollment level $Q_{\pi max}$. The price charged all students is $P_{\pi max}$. The profit, *surplus* in "not-for-profit" institutions, is the price, $P_{\pi max}$ minus the average cost at $Q_{\pi max}$, times that enrollment level. This comes to the area of the cross-hatched rectangle.

Let us now look at perfect price discrimination. Fanciful hires Dr. Psychic who is able to divine the maximum price that each student is willing to pay per semester and that is what each student is charged. The student willing to pay the most is charged P_{max}, which is an increment of total revenue. The next student is willing to pay slightly less and adds a slightly smaller increment to total revenue. These decreasing increments to total revenue go on until we reach the student just willing to pay $Pmin = MC$—just the marginal cost Fanciful experiences by virtue of his enrollment.

Under perfect discrimination the negative-sloping demand function serves as the marginal revenue function. Each additional student yields a marginal revenue equal to his demand price.

Figure 8.13.   **Profits with One and Two Prices**

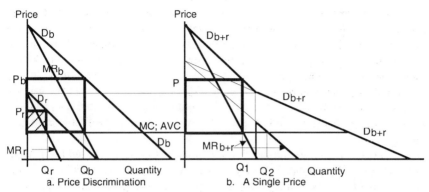

a. Price Discrimination   b. A Single Price

Now for profit under perfect discrimination. The area under the demand-marginal revenue function from $Q = 0$ to Q_{pmin} is total revenue. Total cost equals average cost at Q_{pmin} times Q_{pd}, the area under the bold horizontal line shown. The subtraction of total cost from total revenue leaves economic profit, the area boldly outlined. It shows that profits under perfect price discrimination are greater than profits under profit maximization. Perfect price discrimination pays, and Fanciful awards Dr. Psychic an honorary doctorate in esoteric studies as well as an esoteric honorarium.

Discrimination with Two Prices

Assume that there are two sets of buyers of electrical energy, residential and business, and that the demand of the latter group, D_b, is more inelastic than that of the former, D_r, at any given price. It will be shown using graphs and tabular information that profits are increased by having two profit-maximizing prices rather than one.

The Graphical Approach

The price discrimination case is shown in frame a of Figure 8.13, the single price case in frame b. Consider price discrimination first. The same constant marginal cost is experienced in producing for both the residential and business markets. The profit-maximizing output rates, Q_r and Q_b arise from the equality of marginal revenue of the residential sector, MR_r, and that of the business sector, MR_b, with marginal cost. The price in the business sector, P_b, is higher than that in the residential sector, P_r, since the demand function associated with the former is more inelastic at any given price.

Without data on total fixed cost, the closest we come to profit is profit plus total total fixed cost, $\pi + tfc$. In the residential market this is represented by the cross-hatched rectangle, in the business market, by the larger dark outlined rectangle which is inclusive of the cross-hatched rectangle.

In frame b the two demand functions have been added horizontally to form D_{b+r}. Due to the kink in the demand function, there is a discontinuity in the marginal revenue function so that marginal revenue equals marginal cost at two output rates, Q_1 and Q_2. The profit-maximizing monopolist chooses the former rate of production rather than the latter. This because in the region of Q_1 to Q_2, the area of the marginal revenue triangle under the marginal cost curve exceeds the area above the marginal cost curve. The former larger area represents a loss of revenue, the latter smaller area, a gain. It is, therefore more profitable to to produce Q_1.

At the profit-maximizing price, P, none of the output is purchased by residential customers. Total revenue minus total variable cost $(PQ - AVC \bullet Q)$ is the area covered by the bold-lined rectangle. The single profit-maximizing price, P, here happens to equal the price charged business in the two-price case, P_b. And the profits obtained from business are the same in both cases. What makes profits higher in the two price case is the addition of the profit obtained from residential customers, which is shown by the cross-hatched area of frame a.

A Tabular Approach

Table 8.1 and Figure 8.13 are based on the following business and residential demand equations: $P = 20 - Q_b$ and $P = 10 - Q_r$. The columns with the subscript b refer to the business demand, those with the subscript r to residential demand. The columns with the subscript $b+r$ refer to the kinked demand function obtained by the addition of the business and residential functions. The last column is the marginal revenue obtained from the kinked demand function and, more particularly, its total revenue function, TR_{b+r}.

The combined marginal revenue data for MR_{b+r} can be seen as declining to zero and, at the same quantity demand, increasing to five—a result of the discon-tinuity in the combined demand function. It then decreases again. This arises from the discontinuity in the demand and marginal revenue functions seen in Figure 8.12. The marginal revenues with a denominator of 2 have been so written to reinforce realization that marginal revenue equals $\Delta TR/\Delta Q$, and care must be taken to see that the proper magnitude of ΔQ is used. Recall that marginal cost is constant at \$4 per unit. Thus there is interest in uncovering marginal revenues which are also equal to \$4 per unit. At two output rates adjacent values of marginal revenue are \$5 and \$3. At an in-between output rate marginal revenue equals \$4 and that has been added to the original data in bold type.

We are now prepared to determine the profitability of the two cases: the first in which there is one profit-maximizing price; the second in which the profit-maximizing price is different for business and residential customers. The two boxed examples show how this can be done with tabular data.

Table 8.1.   **Hypothetical Data on Business, Residential, and Combined Demand**

Price	MC	Qb	TRb	MRb	Qr	TRr	MRr	Qb+Qr	TRb+r	MRb+r
20		0	0		0	0		0	0	
.										
.										
.										
13		7	91		0	0		7	91	
	4			5						5
12		8	96	4	0	0		8	96	4
	4			3						3
11		9	99		0	0		9	99	
	4			1						1
10		10	100		0	0		10	100	0
10		10	100		0	0		10	100	5
	4			-1			9			8/2
9		11	99		1	9		12	108	
	4			-3			7			4/2
8		12	96		2	16		14	112	
	4			-5			5			0
7		13	91		3	21	4	16	112	
	4			-4			3			-4/2
6		14	84		4	24		18	108	
	4			-9			1			-8/2
5		15	75		5	25		20	100	

Example 1: One Price

Given: (Data from Table 8.1) @ π_{+tfc} max MC = MR_b = 4 @ P=12; Q_b= 8; $Q_r = 0$

Find: Maximum Profit, π_{+tfc} max

π_{+tfc} max $= TR - TVC = P \cdot Q_b - (AVC \cdot Q_b) = 12 \cdot 8 - 4 \cdot 8$

$= 96 - 32 = 64$

Example 2: Two Prices

Given: (Data from Table 8.1)

MC = MR_b = 4 @ P = 12; Q = 8; MC = MR_r = 4 @ P = 7; $Q_r = 3$

P_b = 12, Q_b = 8; TR_b = 96; P_r = 7, Q_r = 3, TR_r= 21

Find: Profit, π_{+tfc} max

π_{+tfc} max $= 12 \cdot 8 - 4 \cdot 8 + 7 \cdot 3 - 4 \cdot 3$

$= 96 - 32 + 21 - 12 = 64 + 9 = 73$

The use of two prices is more profitable.

Heavy-Handed Price Discrimination—A Bad Example

The most extreme case of price discrimination I know of was that practiced by two chemical firms, Du Pont and Röhm and Haas. They sold a plastic molding powder, methyl methacrylate, to industrial firms for $0.85 per pound and to dental manufacturers for $22 per pound. This was a classic case for the intrusion of arbitragers, people who buy at a lower price in one market and sell at a higher price in another. This eradicated the price discrimination, but not gracefully. A rumor was circulated that arsenic had been added to the molding powder sold in industry to preclude its use in dentistry but this was denied by the producers when they were pressured into commenting on the rumor.

Arbitrage tends to equalize prices in different markets but the technique is not suitable for many markets. People or institutions who pay less than others for their telephone service, electrical energy, or natural gas cannot sell these products to others. Children cannot sell their cheaper movie tickets to those who are older, and so on.

Is Monopolization an Outgrowth of Profit Maximization?

The basic goal of the firm is survival. The basic threat to survival is competition. Monopolization diminishes competition and is, therefore, a basic goal of the firm. Monopolization yields the power to make more profits or to have a less turbulent life, or some of both.

Many firms lack the ability to measurably move in the direction of monopolization. But even those thought to be powerless can band together in a struggle against competition. A proposal to build a new shopping mall near an existing one frequently leads to the formation of a group opposed to the construction of the new mall. The group and it members, many of whom are outspoken fans of the free market, vigorously fight for their survival and against the free market threat of increased competition.

The breakup of a monopoly does not mean its end. The breakup of Rockefeller's Standard Oil empire did not end monopolization in petroleum. From the 1930s into the 1950s the seven major oil producers were able to control the supply oil in the United States and the price of oil throughout the world. That price was the price at Galveston, Texas, the *basing point,* plus the cost of transportation to the buyer. Ships of the British Navy fueled in the Persian Gulf from local producers, paid the price at Galveston plus the phantom costs to ship the fuel from Galveston to the Persian Gulf. Even if the Supreme Court dissolves a monopoly, the distaste for competition may stimulate actions intended to curtail or destroy price competition.

Could the de facto U.S. oil cartel have charged more and made greater profits during the period in which they controlled the price of crude oil? I suspect they could have but restrained prices and profits to lessen the probability that the federal and some state governments would overturn the legislation required for the cartel to function.

Maintaining Monopoly Power: IBM at Its Peak

Holders of unnatural monopoly positions have to devise strategies to assure the maintenance of their power. IBM's business strategy was as brilliant as its technological expertise and innovations. It had three crucial elements: (1) renting and not selling its equipment; (2) "bundling," the requirement that you buy a whole set or bundle of things from IBM; and (3) "blanketing the field" so that a producer of sophisticated or crude computers could not develop the expertise and reputation to move down or up into the space occupied by IBM's monopoly.

Since the equipment customers used was IBM's, it controlled basic aspects of its usage. You had to rent and buy a bundle of products and services from IBM. The input to IBM's equipment was through cardboard cards which had to be bought from IBM. The device used to punch information into the cards had to be rented from IBM. The output was on paper forms—paper which had to be bought from IBM. All maintenance and repairs had to be done by IBM employees. All peripheral equipment had to be rented from IBM. This was of special importance. It disallowed competition from a firm which produced better or less expensive cards, or card readers, or printers, or paper for printing, or devices for reproducing or collating cards. In other words all competitive inroads from peripheral areas were disallowed. Blanketing the field stunted the potential growth of competitors. If the Control Data Corporation (CDC) could develop a sophisticated scientific computer, it could go on to develop a less sophisticated mainframe which could compete with IBM. When CDC announced and showed that it had developed a computer more advanced than IBM's, IBM announced, contrary to fact, that it was developing an even better computer and that it should be available in a matter of months. CDC lost the orders for its computer and its corporate momentum.

IBM's dominance of the computer industry was undermined by the technology which led to the design and proliferation of desktop computers at prices affordable to many firms and individuals.

A relevant tangent. Microsoft currently designs the operating system for a large majority of IBM's and IBM-style personal computers. The operating system integrates the components of the computer system and provides the interface between external software and devices with the computer. Common examples of external software are application programs used in word processing, drawing and painting, creating spreadsheets, database handling, and Internet browsing. Bundling such software with the Microsoft operating system of course makes unnecessary the software of competitors—and that is just what Microsoft is doing as this is written (early 1998). If Microsoft's "Explorer" comes with your computer, why would you even think of buying Netscape's "Navigator" to interface with and browse the Internet?

Arguments for and Against Monopolies

There are those who oppose and those who favor monopolies or at least firms which are far larger than the norm. Adam Smith was one of those opposed to monopolies:

> The monopolist, by keeping the market constantly under-stocked, by never fully supplying the effectual demand, sell their commodities much above the natural price, and raise their emoluments, whether they consist in wages or profit, much above the natural rate (1937 [1776], p. 61).

But Alfred Marshall, in what could be interpreted as a rejoinder to Smith, was of a different mind:

> It may therefore appear as though the amount produced under a monopoly is always less and its price to the consumer is always higher than if there were no monopoly. But this is not the case. For when production is all in the hands of one person or one company, the total expenses involved are generally less than would have to be incurred if the aggregate production were distributed among a multitude of comparatively small rival producers (1961 [1890], p. 484).

Smith saw monopolies as exploiting their price-setting power to the detriment of buyers. Marshall saw monopolies, particularly natural monopolies, as being more cost effective than small firms. He implies that their prices tend to be lower than those of a competitive market to the benefit of buyers. And, as mentioned above, Abba Lerner believed that monopolies used little of their price-setting power in order to avoid government intervention in their affairs. John Kenneth Galbraith views monopolies as more profitable and more able to engage in research and development and thereby advance the economy. Others are of the opinion that monopolies are lethargic giants.

Thus, we have conflicting views regarding the effects of monopolies. I suspect that all the above contentions are true for some monopolies and untrue for others. General Electric charged an exorbitant amount for tungsten carbide and Du-Pont and Röhm and Haas charged dental manufacturers an exorbitant amount for methyl methacrylate. But ALCOA kept decreasing the price of aluminum and the Bell System asked to be regulated in return for the efficiency of monopoly status and showed great progress in advancing its technology and technology in general through the research activities of its Bell Laboratories.

Monopolies with the power to set price have the power to set it unreasonably high. That some unregulated monopolies charge no more than regulated monopolies may well be due to the fear that those which are unregulated may will lose that status if their prices are unreasonably high. There is in addition the profound problem of the political power of monopolies and big business in general. They have great influence on government at all levels and make a mockery of the essence of democracy which can be characterized as "one person, one vote." And if monopolies, big business, and banks seem to be sinking they tend to be bailed-out by the government in what appears to be an arrangement in which risk is socialized and profits privatized.

Summary

Monopolies and monopolization play an important role in our economy and its history. There are two kinds of monopolies, natural and unnatural. Natural monopolies exist because they can produce more cheaply than two or more firms in a market. They are the beneficiaries of economies of scale. But in choosing the most efficient size of plant, production is expected to take place in the declining range of the average cost function, the range in which marginal cost is lower than average cost. This precludes the efficient allocation of resources as manifest in marginal cost pricing. Moreover, if a natural monopolist wants to avoid being displaced by a rival, it must choose its plant size based on the normal rate of return rather than profit maximization.

Unnatural monopolies arise from numerous sources: government grants of monopoly status in the form of patents and franchises; the control of necessary resources; and the historic establishment of organizational forms such as pools, trusts, holding companies, and cartels. And while unnatural monopolies do not have the advantage of economies of scale, by going to multiplant operations they can largely avoid diseconomies of scale.

Price discrimination is practiced by monopolies (and other price-setting firms). This is obvious in the case of public utilities, which tend to have different rate schedules for residential, business, and religious institutions. Price discrimination can be a tool for increasing profits beyond that possible with a single price. Utilities frequently have a monthly base charge. This means that price varies with the rate of consumption: the lower the number of units purchased, the higher is the per unit price.

We tend to show monopoly price as being significantly higher than competitive price. But that actually may not be the case for natural monopolies which have their costs lowered by economies of scale. If monopoly price is lower, consumer surplus is augmented by the existence of the monopoly.

Arguments about monopoly bring into sharp focus the antagonism of the goals of laissez faire and competition. Monopolies are a manifestation of laissez faire and they are completely uncompetitive. If public policy favors competition vigorous application of the anti-trust statutes is required.

Questions on Chapter 8

1. a. Explain why there are "natural" monopolies.
   b. What is the threat to a natural monopoly which chooses to maximize profits? Explain.

2. Name the ways in which firms may be able to create unnatural monopolies.

3. Assume that a monopoly consists of 1,000 production units, has a total cost function which is linear up to capacity production, that the demand for its product is negative-sloping, and that the monopolist sells its production units to 1,000 different employees.
   Show the following:
   a. the competitive and monopoly price and quantity;
   b. the marginal revenue and cost functions and their relationship at the profit-maximizing rate of production;
   c. the changes to consumer and producer surplus.

4. a. Why might increasing monopolization be a goal of large firms in markets they dominate with a small number of other firms?
   b. Is increasing monopolization consistent with profit maximization? Explain.

5. What is the requirement for price discrimination between two groups? Explain.

6. ALCOA and IBM had near-monopoly positions in terms of the production of aluminum and digital computers. In what ways was their monopolization "desirable"; in what ways was it "undesirable."

CHAPTER NINE

The Firm

The firm is characterized succinctly in the neoclassical paradigm in essence as a black box which connects factor and product markets and, in the course of this, maximizes profits. But business, the collectivity of private firms, is much more than that. It is our dominant institution, and it is revolutionary in character. Such an important social complex deserves far more than just black box status.

What is attempted in this chapter is to present some idea of the nature of the firm. The first section gives a gloss of some of the work of the major "institutional economists"—Thorstein Veblen, John R. Commons, and Wesley C. Mitchell. Some of their work was on aspects of the activities of firms and related governmental activities. The second section covers some models of neoclassical economists interested in the emergence of the firm. The third considers how the firm differs from the market as the allocator of scarce resources. The fourth section is on the "culture of the firm," a subject of recent interest particularly to economists in schools of business attempting to understand the differences between productivity in firms in the United States and other countries. The final section involves what I am brash enough to describe as an updating of Alfred Marshall's "representative firm." Marshall's firm was representative in terms of its cost functions. The updating exploits empirical cost and demand studies.

Institutional Economics and the Firm

The post–Civil War period marked the start of great economic progress and turmoil. Railroads spanned the country and helped to create a national economy. Great trusts, pools, and corporations were created under the leadership of powerful entrepreneurs sometimes characterized as "robber barons." The very serious depression of the 1890s and a number of financial panics were experienced. Major strikes and worker riots occurred. Alfred Marshall's economics was largely irrelevant to the analysis of these important socioeconomic events.

In the context of the post–Civil War period, Thorstein Veblen (1857–1929) produced works quite different than those of Marshall. While neoclassical analysis is basically static, Veblen looked at and analyzed economic institutions from a long historical, evolutionary perspective. The first of his many books, *The Theory of the Leisure Class* (1899), traced the rise of the upper class from tribal to modern times. He coined phrases such as *conspicuous consumption* and *pecuniary emulation* in describing the activities of this leisure class, a class which had no need to work but nonetheless led the economy. Work by males of all classes was a matter of traditional behavior, but the elegance of the work clothes of the leisure class shielded its members from engaging in the manual work of the lower class, just as tribal males were shielded from the monotony of women's work. Another example of Veblen's work is *The Engineers and the Price System* in which he claimed that were firms run by engineers concerned with production, rather than businessmen concerned with profits, production and the standard of living would be far higher.

An institution to Veblen is a customary way of doing things, common habits which evolved from long practice and were acceptable to a broader community. Marriage is such an institution as is pride in workmanship and, as well, the business enterprise which embodies the customary and evolving way of producing goods and services.

Wesley C. Mitchell (1874–1948) devoted much of his professional life to the study of business cycles. Business cycles are a matter of great public concern. They seem contrary to the neoclassical model which has the outbreak of even a modest supply-demand disequilibrium create the force which results in equilibrium and full employment. Mitchell's massive empirical work was a precursor to the analytical work of John Maynard Keynes, the discoverer of macroeconomics. In his 1913 *Business Cycles and Their Causes,* Mitchell describes the "cumulation of prosperity" what macroeconomists were to call the "multiplier" and "accelerator." An indication of the high regard for Mitchell's work was his choice as president of the American Association for the Advancement of Science, the American Statistical Association, the Econometric Society, the Academy of Political Science, and the American Economic Association.

John R. Commons (1862–1945) studied the problems of the workplace and played an important historic role in framing labor legislation covering matters such as worker's compensation, social insurance, and work hazards. Commons stressed the economic role of collective action and defined institutions as "collective action in control of individual action." He is also somewhat responsible for the focus of two generations of institutional economists on the area of "the labor problem" including collective bargaining and industrial relations. Finally, he stressed the economic roles of political institutions, legislation, and the courts in *The Legal Foundations of Capitalism.*

To the institutionalists, the firm is a social institution engaged in production and profit-making with traditions or customs manifest in a "web of rules," which evolved over the course of time, rules which control and limit individual action.

One can arguably classify economic historians who study business (and other economic institutions) as institutionalists. Their studies cover the genesis of the firm, the rise and fall of firms—including plantations and the peculiar and odious institution of slavery. The two recipients of the 1993 Nobel Prize in economics, Robert W. Fogel and Douglass C. North are both economic historians. The *New York Times* report of their choice, on October 13, 1993, particularly the section on North is indicative of the broad evolutionary perspective of institutionalists:

> Professor North said yesterday that his work had gained greater currency in the wake of the collapse of Communism—and the struggle to build market economies where market-friendly institutions have not existed for half a century, if ever. 'Political institutions are as important as economic institutions. What happened in Central and Eastern Europe radically changed views about economic theory. Economists have no theory about that kind of change.'

North went on to suggest that there was a need for patent law, contract law, and laws with respect to property rights in order to develop market-based economies, an analysis in the spirit of John R. Commons. Add on legislation to limit the liability of investors, a crucial stimulus to investment in incorporated firms. The black box firm not only links factor and product markets but is a powerful political force at all levels of government.

Economic historians and others have also studied the lives of major entrepreneurs including their brilliance with respect to the development of new products (e.g., Thomas Alva Edison), new processes of production (e.g., Henry Ford), and the strategy and technique of monopolization (e.g., John D. Rockefeller).

Another group of economists, with some degree of institutional disposition, are those who serve firms as consultants paid to improve operations and to provide expert testimony before government agencies and the courts. Others study the operations of firms to develop case study problems aimed at advancing the skills of business school students

The Emergence of the Firm

There are a number of different models which attempt to explain the emergence of the firm as an economic institution. Nobel Laureate Ronald Coase's model stimulated contemporary interest in this topic and his analysis is presented first. Then I give the model of a famous follower of Adam Smith—Karl Marx. This is followed by the work of Armen Alchian and Harold Demsetz. Last but not least is the analysis of business historian Albert Chandler.

Coase and Transaction Costs

Ronald Coase, in his 1937 article on "The Nature of the Firm," hypothesized that firms replaced markets in organizing production because they have lower transaction costs:

> The main reason why it is profitable to establish a firm would seem to be that there is a cost of using the price mechanism. The most obvious cost of "organizing" production through the price mechanism is that of discovering what the relevant prices are. This cost may be reduced ... by the emergence of specialists who will sell this information. The costs of negotiating and concluding a separate contract for each exchange transaction ... must be taken into account (1986, p. 75).

Coase does not specify what the market-oriented alternatives to the firm were. The historical precursors were the guilds and the domestic or putting-out system with the latter being a more pliable institution and alternative to the firm.

It is not clear to me why transaction costs were high in dealing with the artisans of the domestic system. As Adam Smith observed in 1776, "In many places the money price of labour remains uniformly the same sometimes for half a century together"(1937 [1776], p. 74). The existence of traditional prices and ongoing relationships between the entrepreneur and the artisans of the putting-out system should have tended to make transaction costs quite low. And, as shall be explained, they are very high in modern corporations.

Karl Marx and the Division of Labor

Karl Marx, an admirer and follower of Adam Smith, based the emergence of the manufacturing firm on Smith's productivity-enhancing division or specialization of labor:

> Manufacture takes its rise in two ways. (1) By the assemblage, in one workshop under the control of a single capitalist, of labourers belonging to various independent handicrafts.... The tailor, the locksmith, and the other artificers, being now exclusively occupied in carriage-making, each gradually loses ... the ability to carry on, to its full extent, his old handicraft. But, on the other hand, his activity being confined in one groove, assumes the form best adapted to the narrowed sphere of action.... (2) Manufacture also arises in a way exactly the reverse of this—namely, by one capitalist employing simultaneously in one workshop a number of artificers, who all do the same, or the same kind of work.... The needlemaker of the Nuremberg Guild per-formed a series of perhaps 20 operations one after another, in England it was not long before there were 20 needlemakers ... each performing one alone of those 20 operations (1906,[1867], pp. 369–70).

As Adam Smith and Karl Marx saw it, the capitalist in assembling workers in a common workplace was able to organize work so that specialization and productivity increased. With lower costs the firm triumphed over the market.

Alchian and Demsetz and Teamwork

Armen Alchian and Harold Demsetz, in a 1972 article, contend that the development of technology involving team production was a basic reason for the formation of firms:

> When the "putting out" system was used for weaving, inputs were organized largely through market negotiations. With the development of efficient central sources of power, it became economical to perform weaving in proximity to the power source and to engage in team production.... The weavers did not simply move to a common source of power, ... purchasing power while they used their own equipment. Now team production in the joint use of equipment became more important. The measuring of marginal productivity, which now involved interactions between workers, especially through their joint use of machines, became more difficult while managing the *behavior* of inputs became easier because of the increased centralization of activity (1986, p. 120).

Teamwork is of course different than work which is individual in character and the firm does afford a setting in which supervisors can evaluate the relative merits of the work of the different members of a team. But just as an advanced form of power could be sold to individual artisans, the new technology could be sold or rented to them, or teams of them, as well. Teams, by the way, were usually the producing unit in the putting-out system—teams in the form of the family. And the captains and members of these teams, it would seem to me, would know which members were relatively productive and which were not. Moreover, why should the entrepreneur putting out the work care about this? His concern is getting from the team the specified product at an agreed-to price, time, and location. Are we concerned when we hire a team of painters, or carpenters, or plumbers, to do a job at an agreed-to price, how hard each of them works? Surely, not. Our only concern is that the job met our specifications regarding quality and timeliness. Note, however, the advantage of the firm which is very important but not stressed: "managing the *behavior* of inputs became easier." That is an important advantage of the firm whether or not work was by teams or individuals.

Chandler and the Growth of Technology and Markets

Albert Chandler, professor of business history at the Harvard Business School, in his 1977 prize-winning book, *The Visible Hand,* contends that:

> Modern business enterprise appeared for the first time in history when the volume of economic activities reached a level that made administrative coordination more efficient and more profitable than market coordination....
> [It] first appeared, grew, and continued to flourish in those sectors and industries characterized by new and advancing technology and by expanding markets (p. 95).

New technologies frequently involve economies of scale which are not divisible. The process of production could not be divided to suit the location of the households of workers. All had to work at the site of the productive equipment—for example, at the pin factory where the work of the many activities could be observed and coordinated. The capitalist firm evolved to support and exploit the lower unit cost of production made possible by new technology and larger scale of production. Lower costs were then at the root of the triumph of the firm over the market as the institution which coordinates production.

Resource Allocation by the Firm

Ronald Coase's analysis of the difference in the method of resource allocation by the market and the firm is wonderful:

> The price of a factor A becomes higher in X than in Y. As a result, A moves from Y to X, until the difference in the prices in X and Y ... disappears. Yet in the real world, we find that there are many areas where this does not apply. If a workman moves from department Y to department X, he does not go because of a change in relative prices, but because he is ordered to do so (1937, p. 73).

Thus, the allocation of resources by the firm, the institution of production, is by command and not by price incentive. A corollary to Coase's contention is that while we live in a democratic society, much of our lives are spent at work in an autocratic subsociety.

A qualification of Coase's generalization warrants mentioning. The move from Y to X by command sometimes involves the incentive of a pay increase. Examples of this include promotions to higher-paying jobs, work on higher-paying shifts, work on days which command premium pay, and work at remote locations with special travel and, perhaps, living allowances. The extent to which there are such incentives depends upon the rules of the "internal labor market," the internal-to-the-firm "market."

The Entrepreneurial Firm: *The* Revolutionary Institution

The entrepreneurial firm, in all industrialized societies, is *the* revolutionary institution. This is particularly recognized by Karl Marx and Friedrich Engels and Josef Schumpeter.

Marx and Engels and the Colossal Accomplishments of the Capitalistic Era

It is a wonderful irony that the most famous work attacking capitalism, *The Communist Manifesto,* dramatically portrayed it as a magnificent revolutionary force:

> The bourgeoisie, during its rule of scarce one hundred years, has created more massive and more colossal production forces than have all preceding generations together, Subjugation of Nature's forces to man, machinery, applications of chemistry to industry and agriculture, steam-navigation, railways, electric telegraphs, clearing of whole continents for cultivation, canalization of rivers (1932 [1848], p. 327).

While Marx and Engels ascribed these wondrous advances to the capitalist class, they were more particularly the joint product of inventors and entrepreneurs. The technological changes cited by Marx and Engels radically altered the lives of the populations of industrializing societies. No other force has had a comparable effect on changing the material conditions of life—and these technological changes are ongoing. The words *Industrial Revolution* slip from our tongues as does a host of trivialities. But this revolution, led by inventors and entrepreneurs, continually changes the character of the lives we lead.

Schumpeter and the Central Role of the Entrepreneur

Joseph Schumpeter, whose knowledge of economic doctrine was encyclopedic, was eclectic in terms of his personal view of economics. Schumpeter put the entrepreneur at the center of economic development, at the center of change. He saw invention as the *discovery* of new products and technological knowledge and *innovation* as the introduction and application of new technologies, products, sources of supply, and new forms of technical organization—with the innovator being the entrepreneur. He identifies the entrepreneur as the source of all economic change, disruptive included—the creator of the new and the destroyer of the old. In his opinion it is not possible to understand the capitalist system except in terms of the conditions giving rise to entrepreneurship.

Business as Our Dominant Institution

Business, the aggregation of private firms, provides much of the goods and services, jobs and income of our society. It has allowed us to attain the highest standard of living of any nation in the history of the world. Business responds to our material wants and, more important, creates new ones through the production for sale of new products. This tends to deepen the acquisitive character of our society. The acquisitive society tends to be far more influenced by the value structure of business and less by organized religion. And when business is depressed, the society is depressed. In an acquisitive society, a drop in the standard of living or a drop relative to that of others is depressing.

The government-supplied infrastructure of the society largely serves the needs and wants of business as does the related educational and political systems. The discipline and training obtained through schooling is intended to mold behavior to meet the disciplinary and training standards of the workplace. Much of the content of schooling is intended to yield skills required by business or those required for training by business. Many in the quest for college and university degrees expect that their degrees will be of assistance in getting higher-salaried and more secure jobs than could otherwise be obtained. A major reason for discontent with our school systems is the perception that they too often fail to adequately train students to meet the needs of business.

The imperfections of our infrastructure concern us largely because they affect business adversely. Systems of transportation, communications, banking, as well as education, are to a substantial extent in the service of business, and business, individual, and collective progress suffers from their faults.

The political system is also largely attuned to the interests of members of the business community. Woodrow Wilson, a distinguished political scientist, college president, governor, and president of the United States put the matter this way:

> The masters of the government of the United States are the combined capitalists and manufacturers of the United States. It is written over every intimate page of the records of Congress, it is written all through the history of conferences at the White House, that the suggestions of economic policy ... have come from one source, not from many (1961 [1910], p. 48).

Wilson knew both from scholarship and experience the power of business and money.

Nobel Laureate Milton Friedman, a wonderful proponent of laissez-faire capitalism, argues that government has replaced the church as our dominant social institution and that powerful institutions are threats to freedom. But government *at all levels* functions in the service of business. Perhaps the issue should be recast as: Is the power of business a threat to individual freedom?

As a result of its social importance, the collectivity of firms (business) plays a crucial role in determining the culture of the society. Perceptive readers will realize that this view reflects that of the classical economist Karl Marx, the founder of neoclassical economics Alfred Marshall, and scholar and president Woodrow Wilson.

The Culture of the Firm

An article in the *New York Times* of October 13, 1981, told of two identically designed Ford Motor Company plants with identical labor requirements. The plant in Germany produced 50 percent more cars per day and used 22 percent less labor than that in the United States. Obviously, the United States plant was far from being a profit maximizer. Why? The answer is that the culture, the norms and traditions, at Ford's German plant were quite different than those at its plant in the United States.

Utility Maximization as an Alternative to Profit Maximization

Adam Smith in 1776 clearly recognized that the managers of incorporated firms were not profit maximizers:

> The directors of such [joint stock] companies, however, being the managers rather of other people's money than that of their own, it cannot well be expected, that they should watch over it with the same anxious vigilance with which the partners in a private copartnery frequently watch over their own.... Negligence and profusion ... must always prevail ... in the management of the affairs of such a company (1937 [1776], p. 700).

In 1976, Michael Jensen and William Meckling added to the non-profit-maximizing behavior of employee-managers the perspective that even firms with owner-managers do not maximize profits:

> If a wholly owned firm is managed by the owner, he will make operating decisions which maximize his utility. These decisions will involve not only the benefits he derives from pecuniary returns but also the utility generated by various non-pecuniary aspects of his entrepreneurial activities such as the physical appointments of his office, the attractiveness of the secretarial staff, the level of employee discipline, the kind and amount of charitable donations, personal relations ("love," "respect," etc.) with employees, a larger than optimal computer to play with, purchase of production inputs from friends, etc. (1976 pp. 216–17).

The Jensen-Meckling model of utility maximization performs a great social service by destroying the schizophrenic manager of the neoclassical paradigm: the manager who as a consumer is a hedonist but hair-shirted at the firm in the quest for cost minimization. Under the Jensen-Meckling formulation, owner-managers, partial owner-managers, and non-owner-managers are utility maximizers in making their economic decisions both as consumers and managers.

Jensen and Meckling specify the owner-manager's utility as an increasing function of two variables: the firm's present value (the pecuniary benefit) and the level of non-pecuniary benefits. Maximum utility is reached when the gain of a dollar of pecuniary benefit yields the same marginal utility as the expenditure of a dollar on non-pecuniary benefits.

The optimization condition can be shown using an indifference map and that is done in Figure 9.1. In it can be found the case of the 100 percent owner-manager.It is a simplified version of a diagram used by Jensen and Meckling. Profit per year is on the vertical axis (in lieu of the present value of the firm) and non-

Figure 9.1.   **Maximization of Utility by an Owner-Manager**

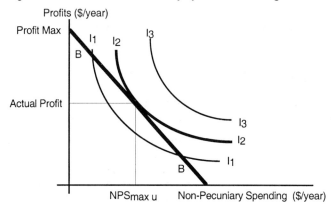

pecuniary manager's spending per year is on the horizontal axis (a simplification of the present value of the stream of manager's spending on non-pecuniary benefits).

The budget line is *BB* and its slope is –1: Every dollar of non-pecuniary spending by the owner-manager reduces profit by one dollar. Maximum profit occurs when non-pecuniary spending is zero. Maximum satisfaction is obtained by the tangency of the budget line and the highest utility indifference curve I_2I_2. It defines the mix of actual profits and non-pecuniary benefits which yields maximum utility.

Jensen and Meckling go on to point out that the lower the manager's share of ownership, the less a dollar of non-pecuniary expenditure subtracts from the partial owner's share of profit. A 50 percent owner-manager could spend a dollar on pleasure-yielding amenities at the cost of only a half-dollar of profit to him. The lower the share of ownership, the greater the tendency is for a manager to engage in non-pecuniary spending. This gives rise to the following types of actions:

> If both parties to the relationship are utility maximizers there is good reason to believe that the agent [the top manager] will not always act in the best interests of the principal [the owner]. The *principal* can limit divergences from his interest by establishing appropriate incentives for the agent and by incurring monitoring costs [costs to observe and control the agent's behavior].... In addition in some situations it will pay the *agent* to expend resources (bonding costs) to guarantee that he will not take certain actions which would harm the principal.... [Even then] there will be some divergence between the agent's decisions and those which would maximize the welfare of the principal.... We refer to this cost as the "residual loss" (1986, pp. 212–13).

The authors define the sum of the costs as *agency costs*. They go on to point out that "there are agency costs generated at every level of the organization." These agency costs are a reduction from maximum profits.

Managers and the Survival of the Firm

That managers make decisions on the basis of maximizing their utility is not meant to imply that managers are not concerned with the well-being of the firm which employs them. To the contrary, the most important of the goals of man agers may well be the maintenance of their jobs including their pay, perquisites, and power. That requires the achievement of a reasonable level of profitability. As Albert Chandler observed: "Once a managerial hierarchy has been formed and has successfully carried out its function of administrative coordination, the hierarchy itself becomes a source of permanence, power, and continued growth."

Missions

Firms tend to have missions or fundamental goals which evolve over the course of time. Institutional traditions tend to be consistent with the firm's mission. A college or university which evolves a research-oriented mission tends to employ people who have noteworthy research records or indicate such potential. Tenure, then, tends to be granted only to those who have excelled at research even though there may be lip service about the importance of teaching excellence.

Consider the evolving mission of the U.S. Steel Corporation. The steel industry was highly competitive during the 1870–1900 period—overly competitive according to powerful people such as Andrew Carnegie and J.P. Morgan. In this context the U.S. Steel Corporation, which was formed in 1901, involved the consolidation of firms with 65 percent of the industry's productive capacity. Its mission was to substantially attenuate competition. It succeeded in doing this for roughly sixty years. Then new technology manifest in minimills and foreign competition undermined its original role and led to the evolution of a new firm at least in name and mission: the USX Corporation whose mission seems to be that of profit-making.

IBM's mission, based on its record, had multiple goals: to blanket the market for electronic accounting machinery, to produce and maintain high-quality equipment, to reward shareholders with growth in share values rather than dividends, and to be paternalistic to its employees. The mission implied a number of important matters: the employment of high-quality people, particularly in marketing, research and development, production management, and equipment servicing, and their good treatment and loyalty to IBM. IBM's mission was successfully pursued under the paternalistic, entrepreneurial-managerial leadership of Thomas John Watson.

An interesting aspect of IBM's culture was the singing of praise to its leaders. At assemblies of employees, one could hear praise of Thomas John Watson:

Pack up your troubles, Mr. Watson's here   And smile, smile, smile.
He is the hero of our IBM   He's a man worthwhile

Songs of praise are currently uncommon in the culture of American firms.

In recent years IBM's role as the dominant firm blanketing the computer industry has been undermined by the advance of technology manifest in personal computers, by foreign competition, and by adverse court rulings. IBM's current mission seems to be to recapture some of its lost power and glory.

Evolution of a Web of Rules: The Norms of the Workplace

All societies have a web of rules which do much to define their character. They specify the standing and responsibilities of men, women, and children, and of religious institutions, as well as what is lawful conduct and what is not. Rules transformed into laws—municipal, state, and federal—are voluminous. Societies also set rules covering many of its institutions such as marriage, banking, and business. Rules specify what we can consume and what we cannot, how we should dress and the limits of undress, which toxins are legal to produce and consume and which are not, what can be built on privately owned land and what cannot, and on and on. These rules are so entwined with our lives that after adapting to them, we tend to be unconscious of their existence. Faced with the task of getting some groceries for dinner on a sultry day off, we do not consciously face the decision of whether or not to wear clothing on our trip to the grocery store; we automatically choose socially acceptable dress.

Market conduct is also replete with rules or norms. Fred Hirsh points out that:

> Informal social controls in the form of socialized norms of behavior are needed to allow the market process itself to operate. These range from social standards such as telling the truth to acceptance of the legitimacy of commercial contracts as a basis for transactions. An important aspect is implicit agreement on the sphere of market behavior: on what can be bought and sold, what interest may be pursued individually and collectively (1976, p. 121).

Market activities are a form of social activities. Social activities tend to be controlled by norms, and it should be no surprise that the subset of market activities are similarly constrained.

Rules Regarding Employees

Rules regarding labor are legion and indicative of the overall web of rules of business institutions. Rules tend to evolve to assure performance reasonably consistent with the welfare of the owners of the firm, the obligations of employees, and the reciprocal obligation of the employer.

The first set of rules involve the hiring of new employees into the various jobs with vacancies. One set of rules involve the mechanisms through which the search process is to be conducted. Should, for example, current employees be informed about the existence of openings? Should a job agency be used for initial screening and should it be told to screen out certain groups—an illegality the firm may wish to avoid? A second involves defining the education and experience requirements applicants must have—because of a job or a screening requirement. Related rules include defining who is to evaluate job applicants and who has the authority to grant them employment.

Other key rules include those which specify the following: the work particular people should perform and the compensation they are to receive in return, the times at which employees are to start and finish work, the role of seniority or tenure and how it is to be reckoned for various benefits, the grounds justifying pay increases and the standards required for promotions, the dress code, the holidays for which employees are to be paid but are not required to work, the life and health insurance and other benefits and the cost contribution to them made by employees, the rules for the layoff and the recall of employees, rules limiting movement in the workplace, rules regarding the requirement to follow the orders of a superior, rules which regulate or attempt to regulate work effort and quality, rules regarding the transmission of information within and external to the firm including those regarding the secrecy of salary information and plans of the firm, rules specifying or indicating the penalties for various rule infractions, and the process through which rules may be changed.

Firms of any substance tend to have "internal labor markets." This involves workers being hired at entry-level positions with one or more promotional directions available to them over the course of time. Some promotions may be basically predicated on seniority, others on seniority and merit, and some on merit alone—as evaluated by superiors. The higher a job is in the occupational hierarchy, the less likely it is that those promoted will be existing employees.

The myriad of rules reflect and help determine the culture of the firm. Rules, of course, limit the realm of decisions managers can make. Sometimes this saves the firm from indiscretions; at other times they may limit the ability to make profitable decisions.

Rule Setting

Rules are generally set unilaterally by management. They evolve historically and to some extent are the same as those set by other firms, particularly those in the industry and region in which the firm operates. When rules are being changed, consideration is often given to the expected reaction of employees, groups of employees, and sometimes rival firms. The latter is particularly so when compensation (or product price) is being changed. Rules about the pace of work are usually set by management. This is most obviously done by setting the speed of an assembly line. It is also done by management determining the size of a staff which has to complete a specified amount of work in a specified period of time. But the pace of work is not infrequently set by work groups. This, in a sense, overrides rules set by management. In fact, worker-set rules tend to follow historical practice—much of which was set by earlier managements.

Where workers are represented by unions, union representatives participate in the making and changing of rules which affect the terms and conditions of employment. Frequently the pay and fringe benefit parts of collective bargaining agreements with unionized blue-collar workers become the unilaterally set rules imposed by management on unorganized white-collar workers.

Neoclassical economists call the rules defining the culture of a firm, and particularly those relevant to layoffs and recalls, implicit contracts. But contracts are enforceable at law; implicit contracts are not. Moreover, they are not even *agreements* reached between managers and workers but usually managerial commands—as Coase indicated with respect to the allocation of labor. Thus my preference is for the descriptive term of the institutionalists, the *web of rules* of the workplace.

Government-Set Rules

Some of the most important rules of the workplace are the commands of government. These include rules limiting the work of women and children; specifying the hours of work per week required to obtain overtime rates of pay; exempting groups from overtime pay coverage; defining compensation for death and injuries; setting the social security contributions of firms and employees; defining the social security benefits available; prohibiting discrimination on the basis of race, sex, religion, and age; and specifying practices and equipment required in order to make the workplace safer. Government safety regulations are often obtained from industry publications on safety standards. Business opposition is frequently not against their own safety standards, but the temerity of the government attempting to enforce them.

Control by a Hierarchy of Managers

In a one-person firm, the barber or barrister is both manager and employee. As manager he decides what is to be done, as employee he does it. With only two people in a firm, one is normally the boss or manager and the other the worker, even though they may work shoulder to shoulder and even though they are "equal partners." One of the barbers and one of the barristers is in charge; the others are underlings. This represents the start of the managerial function: *to decide what is to be done and to see that it is done*. And for larger firms, at their formation and by growth over time, a managerial structure evolves to determine and control the processes of production and business, to orchestrate these processes and to develop plans intended to assure the preservation of the firm and its future advancement.

IBM and Ford both employed more than 300,000 workers in 1988. But IBM had seven levels of management while the Ford Motor Company had thirty-two. Does this reflect the fact that IBM workers, compared to those of Ford, do not have to be told what to do and need not have a high level of scrutiny of what they are actually doing? I suspect that this explains little of the difference and that much comes from the different cultures of the two firms, cultures which reflect their histories and the managerial philosophies of those in top leadership roles.

Control Through the Budget

The firm's budget is one of the most important control devices management has in firms of some size and substance. What it says to the various departments of the firm is essentially this: You are to perform the responsibilities of your department by expenditures of no more than the budgeted sum. That sum, as all standards set by management, has to be reasonable or it will be disregarded as a "joke." The budget also expresses the priorities set by management. If, for example, research and development is given a significantly larger share of the budget, it means that management believes that more R&D is required to attain the goals it has set.

Budgets are relatively easy to develop when products and production processes are the same or close to those of the past and the firm's profits have been satisfactory. The current budget then tends to be a reflection of previous budgets. But when a firm has experienced substantial losses and is intent on reversing its condition, budgeting becomes complex and difficult. On the one hand there is a need to carefully cut costs and, on the other, the need to allocate more resources to those areas expected to rectify its problems. But irrespective of how and why a particular budget was created, it serves as an important tool for short-run planing and the control of the groups which comprise the firm.

Who Controls the Top Management Team?

The existence of a management *hierarchy* implies that higher levels of management control lower levels. But who controls those at the top, the top management team? The higher authority which nominally controls the firm and its top executives is its board of directors. But some of the members of the board of directors are members of the top management team—not the best people for evaluating the work of top management. And many outside directors are de facto appointees of top management, rewarded with handsome fees for attending meetings of the board. It is difficult for the recipients of managerial largess to critically evaluate the performance of their benefactors. Moreover, these outside directors are frequently top executives who are not overly fond of having their work closely scrutinized by their boards of directors. They tend to do unto others as they would have others do unto them. Studies of outside directors indicate that they are frequently poorly informed regarding the problems a firm is encountering unless and until they become out of control. This should not be surprising since the information they receive almost always comes from the management members of the board. Thus, top management is frequently uncontrolled unless and until there is a perception that the economic viability of the firm is being threatened. Institutional investors, such has pension funds, are well aware of this problem. The significance of this will be known only over the course of time.

Why Layoffs Rather than Workweek Reductions

Why do American firms have layoffs rather than cuts in the workweek? Layoffs do make sense if laid-off workers can be expected to find comparable jobs in the external job market. A reduced workweek might be more sensible if comparable jobs are essentially unavailable. Why is it the tradition of overstaffed firms to lay off workers irrespective of the condition of the external job market?

Management has traditionally favored layoffs for a number of reasons: (1) Layoffs make it easier to determine or estimate the number of workers required to perform a given amount of work. (2) It avoids the coordination problem caused by the fact that certain workers and managers may not be on hand at the time they are needed by other workers or managers. (3) The morale and productivity of workers receiving full pay and benefits tend to be higher than those suffering an earnings reduction due to a workweek reduction. (4) It is cheaper to employ fewer workers mainly because expensive fringe benefit costs, such as the firm's health insurance costs, increase with the number of workers employed.

Neoclassical economists argue that there is an implicit contract between the firm and its workers to the effect that surplus workers are to be laid off and that if additional workers are required those laid off are to be recalled. To my knowledge, no believer in the existence of implicit contract has suggested the mechanism through which labor and management reached this "agreement." The rule favoring layoffs, seems to me, is a management cost-saving dictate advantageous to workers not laid off. Confirming this is a recent action by unionized automobile workers. They had been working overtime for a substantial amount of time and asked management to recall workers who had been laid off. Management refused, and the workers went on strike.

Blue- and White-Collar Workers

A long-standing historic norm involves breaking the labor force into two groups, blue- and white-collar-workers, and to treat them somewhat differently. Workers in production, maintenance, and related activities are categorized as "blue-collar" workers. All others are labeled "white-collar" or by a similar de scriptor. That blue- and white-collar workers are treated differently makes it a form of discrimination.

Production and maintenance workers are paid by the hour. White-collar workers tend to be "salaried"—to have annual salaries which are paid in weekly, twice-monthly, or monthly installments. The "place" of blue- and white-collar workers is quite different. Blue-collar workers tend to be laid off when the rate of sales and production declines; until recently, the ranks of white-collar workers tended to be reduced by attrition.

Traditionally, attempts to increase productivity have been focused on blue-collar work. White-collar work was relatively untouched by the productivity-cost-saving concerns of firms. Thus, a decade after the digital computer became ubiquitous at the work stations of white-collar workers, no data on a resulting increase in productivity could be found. That situation is now changing with many firms "downsizing" white-collar employment to make themselves more cost efficient and to structure themselves so that they can compete with rivals of the future—and increase profits along the way.

Why is it that in a typical firm the number of non-production workers roughly equals the number of production workers? Take the case of a college or university which produces educational and research services. The university employees engaged in producing these services include the faculty, some technicians, and teaching and research assistants; the staff of the library; and some of those in computer services. The rest of the employees, a majority in many universities, perform business-related functions. They work in the office of the registrar and that of the bursar, in purchasing and in facilities management, in accounts payable and accounts receivable, in payroll and fund-raising, in legal affairs and government affairs, in doing computer work for administration activities, and in the general management of the university.

The business functions are generally as essential to the operation of the university as the production of educational and research services. Faculties would not operate very long without the payroll department, or the office of the bursar, or the registrar, and virtually all the business-oriented groups.

Roy Radner estimated that in 1987, 46.9 percent of our full-time wage and salary workers were managers or assisted in the managerial process (1992, Table 5, p. 1386). It has become fashionable to call them "information workers." They can also be described as engaged in the business process and not the production process. Many seemed to be engaged in activities related to external and internal transactions. But whatever the description, for every production worker, there tends to be roughly one non-production worker employed by a firm. And it is what the production workers and facilities produce which yields the revenues of the firm. The products of those employed in business activities are not sold and, therefore, yield no revenues.

The Customer Base and the Relationship of Cost and Price

Firms not only produce products but they must also produce a base of custom-ers to buy their products. Brand loyalty and repeat sales tend to be of great im-portance. Blinder and associates have found that, on the average, 85 percent of sales go to regular customers (1998, p. 96). Firms consequently lean toward the dictum that "the customer is always right" and away from the market's *caveat emptor*, let the buyer beware.

Buyers are not overly fond of price increases. And sellers, concerned with their customer base, tend to avoid increasing price unless that is done by rivals, as well. This leads to sticky prices with the average firm changing its prices once a year or less. Only if the demand for the average company's products changes but once a year, can sticky prices conform to profit maximization.

Finally, producers do not normally sell to final buyers but to wholesalers, re-tailers, and dealers who do. This suggests the need for good relations between producers and these transaction intermediaries.

Workers and Production Norms

Economists and others who have been involved in the industrial relations pro-cess frequently observe the existence of norms of effort established by work groups. A firm which employed me for over a decade had "methods engineers" set up the procedures and the time required to fabricate, assemble, and wire their products. Almost without fail shop workers found ways to do the work in less time—but they never would. The rule of those workers was "never produce any-thing in less time than methods has set."

Production norms are also frequently set by piece-rate workers despite the fact that the nominal setting is by management. Management sets the length of time it should take to produce a piece of work and the price paid a worker for each piece produced. This serves as an incentive for workers to produce more and to earn more over the course of time. Piece-rate workers also frequently find quick-er ways to produce a piece than those envisaged by the rate setters—but they also find a disincentive to accomplish the high rates of production they are able to achieve. If management judges their earnings as being "too high" they "retime" the job, decreasing the length of time it should take to produce it. To combat such cuts in their piece rates, work groups tend to estimate what man-agement will allow them to earn and to accordingly quantify the maximum number of pieces those in the group should produce per day or week.

Even white-collar workers sometimes set work norms. The great Argentine poet, critic, and short story writer, the late Jorge Luis Borges, reported on this in a memoir published in the *New Yorker*. Early in his career, Borges got a job in a library and was assigned to cataloging acquisitions. He started doing 400 a day without undue strain and was soon reproached by senior members of the group who told him that he was going to cause co-workers to lose their jobs. "For the sake of realism, I was told that from then on I should do eighty-three books one day, ninety another, and one hundred and four the third" (1970, pp. 80–81).

While the workers of many countries lean in the direction of restraining production, Japanese, working for large firms, frequently recommend, directly or indirectly, ways to increase it. Why is this aspect of their work culture so different from our's? These Japanese workers have a lifetime employment commitment from their employers. This obviates the fear that their suggestions will lead to the loss of their jobs and those of co-workers.

Workers have trouble in regulating the pace of work when it is set by the likes of an assembly line. But if the pace is deemed excessive, workers will not complete all the work passing their work-stations. And slowdowns and strikes against assembly line speed-ups are not uncommon.

Equal Pay for Equal Work?

Workers who perform the same work frequently receive different pay as Adam Smith well knew:

> The price of labour, it must be observed, cannot be ascertained very accurately any where, different prices being often paid at the same place and for the same sort of labour, not only according to the different abilities of the workmen, but according to the easiness or hardness of the masters (1937 [1776], p. 77).

Almost half a century after its formation, U.S. Steel paid a variety of different rates of pay for the same work—a fact reflecting its history and mission. U.S. Steel was established by the amalgamation of many firms, firms which paid employees doing the same work a variety of wages. U.S. Steel left things as they were. Its mission was to decrease competition and not to provide "equal pay for equal work." And government occupational metropolitan area wage surveys continually show large wage differences among workers who seemingly perform the same work.

This is the context of the firm's pay-setting problem. It tends to be handled by management setting wages on the basis of a *system of job evaluation*. The goal of such a system is to develop a salary structure, usually involving a hierarchy of ten to fifteen different salary levels. All jobs are placed in one of these levels with the most valuable at the top and the least valuable at the bottom. Each salary level tend to have one or more key jobs. When the pay for a key job is set so too is the pay set for all jobs at its level. How jobs are rated to slot them into a salary level requires training in job evaluation.

The pay for key jobs is set by conducting to a survey of the wages paid comparable key jobs by a number of rivals in the industry of the firm. For each key job, the surveyed firms will be found to pay a variety of wages. This yields a distribution of pay for comparable jobs. A firm which has decided to be high a high wage payer will set the pay of key jobs in the high end of the distribution and the converse is true for those with a low wage policy. Once the pay of the key jobs has been set, the pay at the dozen or so levels of the salary structure have also been set.

The salary structure of a firm, to the extent it is known, becomes an important workplace institution. Much rancor is developed by attempts to raise or lower the salary level of a particular job. If a job is dropped to a lower level, workers in that job are enraged. If it is increased in position, those at the higher level are resentful since their work had always been evaluated as being of higher value that of the job elevated to their pay grade. Other jobs in the lower salary level tend to argue that they, too, should be upgraded since their work was always valued as highly as the job upgraded. As a result, the salary structures tend to be fixed in concrete. Shortages or surpluses of workers with the skills of a particular job, tend to have little, if any, effect on the pay of a particular job. Qualification standards tend to be lowered in the event of a shortage, and raised were a surplus to occur.

Competing Constituencies and Intrafirm Rivalries

The various major groups which comprise a firm frequently believe they should receive a larger "share of the pie" (of the revenues, net of external costs). The groups I have in mind are the shareholders, top executives, lesser managers, production workers, and white-collar workers. Shareholders may desire profit maximization but all the other groups have leanings in the opposite direction since increased rewards to them decreases profit. The way in which the pie is shared reflects the power structure of the firm and the ideology of those in power. In what might be called equilibrium, the shares of these constituencies tend to be constant, tend to become a rule. The firm which pays relatively high salaries at one time tends to pay high salaries at other times.

In recent decades, intrafirm shares have been changing. The compensation growth rate of those at the top has been far higher than that of others. Associated matters seem to be the decline in the strength and influence of labor unions, the increase in foreign competition, deregulation, and, what may seem strange, the destruction of the air traffic controllers union by President Ronald Reagan. In this historic setting, executives seem to have concluded that should be paid as they wish.

Departmental rivalries often occur in colleges and universities. And interdepartmental rivalries also exist. And this is true as well in industry. As an example, a firm I worked for had trouble selling an important product. Sales blamed engineering for failing to design the product so that it was attractive to buyers; engineering blamed production for the imperfections in the product; shop officials blamed engineering for the proliferation of change orders it had to cope with. There was no shortage of time spent on laying the blame elsewhere.

The Representative Firm's Cost Functions

What is done here is to determine the cost functions of the representative firm. Four items, all empirically based, are given: (1) The total cost function is linear. (2) The representative firm operates at 80 percent of full capacity. (3) Price is on the average 1.48 times the magnitude of marginal cost. (4) Profits before taxes are 7.76 percent of gross domestic product. Information on these is presented in a section called "data" at the end of this chapter.

What is to be found are equations for the three average cost function, the marginal cost function, and the three total functions.

The first function of interest is the relationship between price and marginal cost at the normal rate of production,

(1) $\qquad P = 1.48\ MC \qquad\qquad @\ Q = 80$

The next task is to determine the relationship between average cost and price at the normal rate of production. This is done using the data that the profit is 7.76 percent of gross domestic product at the normal rate of production.

(2) $\qquad (P - AC) \cdot Q/PQ = 0.0776 \qquad @\ Q = 80$

Rewrite equation (2) as

(3) $\qquad 1 - (AC/P) = 0.0776$

Solve equation (3) for average cost as a function of price and price as a function of average cost:

(4) $\qquad AC = 0.9224P \qquad\qquad @\ Q = 80$

Solve equation (4) for price.

(5) $\qquad P = 1.0841AC \qquad\qquad @\ Q = 80$

Substitute the right side of equation (5) for price in equation (1). Solve for marginal cost which equals average variable cost. And set average cost equal to 100.

(6) $\qquad 1.0841AC = 1.48MC \qquad @\ Q = 80$

(7) $\qquad MC = AVC = 0.7325AC = 73.25,\ \text{with}\ AC = 100\ @\ Q = 80$

Figure 9.2.   **The Total Cost Curves of the Representative Firm**

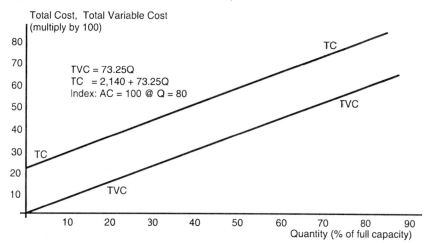

Note that since marginal cost and average variable cost are constant until full capacity is reached, they equal 73.25 for rates of production from zero to 100 percent.

Quantify the magnitude of average fixed cost at the normal rate of production.

(8) $AFC = AC - AVC = 100 - 73.25 = 26.75$ @ $Q = 80$

Use the value of average fixed cost in equation (8) to obtain the total fixed cost function.

(9) $TFC = AFC \cdot Q = 26.75 \cdot 80 = 2140$

Use the magnitude of marginal cost to obtain the total variable cost function.

(10) $TVC = MC \cdot Q = 73.25\ Q$

Total cost is the sum of equations (9) and (10).

(11) $TC = TFC + TVC = 2140 + 73.25Q$

Solve for average cost.

(12) $AC = TC/Q = 73.25 + 2140/Q$

Solve for average fixed cost.

Figure 9.3.   **Average, Average Variable, Average Fixed, and Marginal Cost of the Representative Firm**

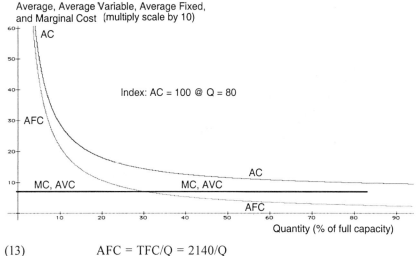

Average, Average Variable, Average Fixed, and Marginal Cost (multiply scale by 10)

Index: AC = 100 @ Q = 80

Quantity (% of full capacity)

(13)   AFC = TFC/Q = 2140/Q

Thus, we have obtained all of the cost functions of the representative firm. The total functions can be found in figure 9.2; the marginal and average functions in Figure 9.3.

The Required Price Elasticity of Demand

The price elasticity of demand required for profit maximization is calculated here. In the next section studies of actual elasticities seen by the firm are presented. The following information is at our disposal. First, price equals 1.48 times marginal cost, $P = 1.48MC$. Second, profit maximization is assumed. This requires that MC equals MR. As a result, $P = 1.48MR$. Third, we have derived the relationship between price, marginal revenue, and the elasticity of demand, and that will be redone to refresh memories. Then with the ratio of marginal revenue to price known, the elasticity of demand at profit maximization can be calculated.

Marginal revenue is the slope or derivative of the total revenue function.

(14) $MR = dTR/dQ$, or

(15) $MR = d(PQ)/dQ = P + Q \, dP/dQ$

Divide both sides of the equation by P.

(16) $MR/P = 1 + [(Q/P)(dP/dQ)]$

Figure 9.4   **The Demand and Marginal Revenue Functions Which Correspond with the Representative Firm's Price of 108.4 and Marginal Cost of 73.3 at a Quantity of 80**

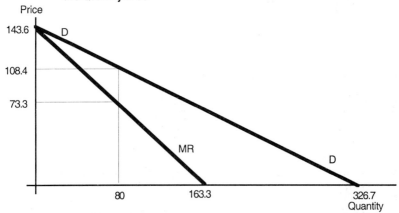

In brackets is the inverse of the price elasticity of demand. Thus,

(17) $MR/P = 1 + 1/E$ or $1/E = (MR - P)/P$

Solve for elasticity:

(18) $E = P/(MR - P)$

Substitute for price *1.48MR.* from equation (1):

(19) $E = 1.48MR/(MR - 1.48MR) = -3.08$

The linear demand function consistent with the above analysis has to go through a point defined by a price of 108.4 at a quantity of 80; marginal revenue has to be 73.3 at that quantity. It is shown in Figure 9.4. Can you show from the graph that demand curve has an elasticity of -3.08 at a quantity of 80?

If the representative firm is a profit maximizer, the derived demand for its product must be price elastic, otherwise marginal revenue is zero or less and a poor match for always positive marginal cost. But the demand for the final product must be substantially more elastic than the firm's derived demand. If the value added by the representative firm per unit of production is one-third of the price, the price elasticity of demand for the final product would have to be -9.0.

What Is the Actual Price Elasticity of the Demand?

Two estimates of the demand for a representative firm's products are given. The first is from researchers who used Profit Impact of Market Strategies (PIMS) data. The second is a survey of the estimates of the elasticity of demand for brand-name products.

Michael Hagerty, James Carmen, and Gary Russell have estimated the average price elasticity of demand experienced by 203 "strategic business units." The production units covered in the PIMS study produce consumer durables and nondurables, capital goods, raw/semi-finished goods, retail/wholesale services, and other services. PIMS data are from an ongoing survey of 1,500 "strategic business units." Their estimate of -0.985 (1988, table 2, p. 5) makes it impossible for the representative firm or any other firm to maximize profits.

Assume that the price elasticity of demand is -1, slightly more elastic that found by Hagerty and colleagues. Marginal revenue is then zero and the producer is maximizing total revenue—not profits. Profit maximization is then impossible unless the representative firm has a marginal cost of zero, which it does not.

Why do the PIMS firms fail to increase the price of their products to move into the elastic range of demand where they might be able to maximize profits? My best guess is that the "strategic business units" are making satisfactory profits at the existing price and fear that an increase would not be followed by rivals causing the loss of market share.

There are many estimates of the price elasticity of demand for generic products, but there are very few estimates of the product of a particular firm, for branded products. There are, for example, a number of studies which estimate the price elasticity of the demand for cars but I am unaware of any for brand X cars, the demand for the products of a firm which interests us here. Scott A. Neslin and Robert W. Shoemaker have reported on estimates of the price elasticity of demand for twenty-five brands of consumer nondurables. The average elasticity found is -1.82 (1983, table 1, p. 46), far short of the required -9.0. It again appears that it is not possible for the representative firm to be a profit maximizer.

Summary

The firm in the neoclassical paradigm is, in effect, a black box connecting factor and product markets in such a way that it maximizes profits. Over the course of time some work on the innards of the black box has been performed by classical economists, institutional economists, economic historians, and business economists, including Ronald Coase and others.

There are a number of different explanations regarding the evolution of the firm as *the* producing unit succeeding the market as manifest by the putting-out or domestic system. The one most persuasive to me ascribes the triumph of the firm to the advance in technology and economies of scale. This made the cost of capital equipment far higher than was affordable to ordinary workers and groups of workers and it made the cost of production significantly cheaper than that of the domestic system. Thus, the triumph of the firm over the market.

The nature of the technology tended to require workers to produce at a common site, at the site of the materialization of the technology. Workers produced at the mine, the smelter, the textile mill, the shipyard, and the ship—and not at home. By having workers at one site, production could be carefully scrutinized and further division or specialization of labor could be accomplished, cheapening the cost of production still more. Scrutiny and control requires managers and managers of managers. Thus, the evolution of the managerial hierarchy. The firm's budget is also an important instrument of control specifying the number of dollars a work group is to receive to accomplish a specified amount of work.

Adam Smith argued that firms managed by agents of its owners were inefficiently run and, in effect, were not profit maximizers. Jensen and Meckling's model suggests that this is also true for owner-managers. They have owner-managers maximizing utility, the arguments of which are profit and non-pecuniary benefits. Agents who are partial owners of the firm have even less incentive to maximize profit and more to increase their non-pecuniary benefits.

The firm is a social institution, with norms and traditions which tend to evolve and perhaps multiply over the course of time. They are manifest in its web of rules. Most rules are set by management; some are specified by government. If workers are unionized, union representatives participate in establishing and changing some of the rules. Rules regarding the pace of work are nominally set by management, but they must be reasonable. Rules are sometimes set by groups of workers—unionized and not. The same plants in different regions and countries have different cultures which are manifest in different productivities and profits.

Roughly half the employees of a representative firm are blue-collar workers engaged in the production of the product to be sold; the other half, the white-collar workers, perform business-related activities. Much of their work involves transaction costs between the firm and its vendors and customers, and the firm and its employees. The most important of all people to the firm are the entrepreneurs or entrepreneurial managers. Entrepreneurs start the firm, determine the products to be made and the markets to be supplied, choose the location of the firm, raise the required funds, organize the process of production, and lead it to the discovery of new products, new processes of production and new markets. Without their leadership, firms become victims of the progress of their peers.

Empirical cost data indicates that the representative firm has constant marginal and average variable cost. It has an average cost function which declines with the rate of production and is always greater than marginal cost. The firm tends to operate at 80 percent of full capacity, with full capacity defined by the firm, and to price its product, on the average, roughly 8 percent above average cost and about 50 percent above marginal cost.

For the representative firm developed on the basis of the data specified, an elasticity of demand of about -3.0 is required to maximize profits. With a firm's value added typically one-third of the final product price, implies that the elasticity of demand for the final product must be about -9.0.

The PIMS-based study of the demand for the products of strategic business units estimated elasticities of roughly −1.0 indicating that the goal of the representative firm may be revenue maximization. In addition this elasticity appears to be about one-ninth of that required for profit maximization. And studies of the demand for branded products yields estimated elasticities about one-fifth of that required for profit maximization.

All of this indicates that firms do not and cannot maximize profits.

Data

J. Johnston's *Statistical Cost Analysis* (1960) is the best single work on the subject of cost functions. In it Johnston presents his own work on six industries and thirty studies by others. The norm is the linear total cost curve with constant marginal cost and declining average cost.

The data relating price and marginal cost are from Robert E. Hall (1986, table 1, p. 296). Hall developed "meaningful estimates" for thirty industries. I omitted two which overlapped others, total durable and total nondurable goods.

The profit data consists of the the ratio of profits before tax to the gross domestic product of non-financial corporate business. It came from the 1993 *Economic Report of the President* (Table B–10, p. 360). The years used were from 1982 to 1991. The same source was used to obtain the capacity utilization rate (Table B–49, P. 403). For the 1982–1991 period it averaged 80.3 percent—which I rounded down to 80 percent.

Questions on Chapter 9

1. a. Give two models which attempt to explain the emergence of the firm in history.
   b. Explain why this represents the the domination of the firm over the market.

2. a. Briefly state Adam Smith's view regarding the management of firms by agents of their owners.
   b. How does the model of Jensen and Meckling relate to Smith's view?

3. a. Why is it that business can be called a revolutionary institution?
   b. Is business the most powerful force in the society? Discuss this issue.

4. What is the culture of a firm and why is it important?

5. Why do firms as societies develop a web of rules specifying the way various problems and responsibilities are to be handled? Give examples to illustrate your explanation.

6. Assume that at an output rate of 1,000 books per week, the average cost of a book is $40 and that its marginal cost is constant and equal to $30.
   a. What is the magnitude of total fixed cost per week?
   b. Write the equation for average fixed cost.
   c. What is the equation for total cost?

CHAPTER TEN

Imperfect Competition and Oligopoly

Two polar product markets have been examined thus far: the competitive and the monopoly markets. A major difference between them is that firms in the former market confront horizontal demand functions while firms in the latter experience demand functions which are negatively sloped. In the former the market dictates the price to firms; in the latter sellers have price-setting power. In both markets buyers have the power to purchase what they will at the existing price. These are the two kinds of markets found in Alfred Marshall's *Principles* over a century ago.

The problem with competitive and monopoly markets is that they cover a very small fraction of overall productive activity. Two other market forms have been developed to fill the void: imperfect competition (also called monopolistic competition) and oligopoly. The former is characterized by a large number of firms producing differentiated products, the latter by the domination of the market by a small number of firms. In both markets firms face negative-sloping demand functions—as does the monopoly. As a result firms in these markets are called *monopolistic.*

> *Monopolistic firms* are any and all which face downward-sloping demand for their products. This includes all firms which are monopolies, oligopolies, and imperfect competitors. Firms which face negative-sloping demand functions have some price-setting power.

A number of special characteristics of these markets-between-the-poles should be recognized. First, they produce most of the gross domestic product, by far. Second, *these are the markets in which competitive behavior is found.* Wheat growers do not take competitive actions to win over the customers of other wheat growers. Monopolists cannot acquire the customers of other producers since they are non-existent. Grocery stores and car manufacturers do compete for customers—sometimes by price and other times by non-price competition. Third and finally, the size of the market is important in determining whether a firm is an imperfect competitor, an oligopolist, or even a monopolist. The same supermarket is an imperfect competitor in a large city, an oligopolist in a small city which has only a few, and a monopolist in a town with only one.

Imperfect Competition

The concept of imperfect competition or monopolistic competition was independently propounded by Joan Robinson in her book, *The Theory of Imperfect Competition,* and Edward H. Chamberlin in his book, *The Theory of Monopolistic Competition.* Both books were published in 1933, the former in England and the latter in the United States. Both authors believed that their model better described the economy in general than the competitive model. Robinson and Chamberlin saw most producers as selling differentiated rather than standardized products. This gave them a measure of monopoly power. But that power is threatened by substitute products and the competition of other producers. Thus, firms generally had monopoly power threatened by competition.

Market Characteristics

Put in a more orderly fashion, the attributes of imperfect competition are the following: (1) There are many producers in the market. (2) There are many buyers in the market. (3) There is ease of entry into and exit out of the market. (4) The product is differentiated. (5) And firms face negative-sloping demand functions and have some price-setting power.
 The first three attributes of imperfect competition—many producers, many buyers, and easy entry and exit—are also characteristics of competitive markets. The crucial difference is the fourth element: Firms in competitive markets produce a homogeneous product but those in imperfect competition produce differentiated products. It is product differentiation which gives the imperfect competitor some control over the price of his product, some monopoly power. Control of price, of course, is a sign of the existence of a negative-sloping demand function. Finally, ease of entry implies the threat of additional competition—further limiting monopolistic power.

Industries with Imperfect Competition

The major example of imperfect competition is retail trade. There frequently are within reasonable reach many of the following: groceries; restaurants; do-it-yourself laundries; dry cleaners; liquor stores; and firms providing household help; painting and carpentry; selling, installing, and repairing air conditioners, television sets, and other electrical and electronic devices; and medical, dental, and educational services. The products associated with these fields tend to be differentiated.

Product differentiation and the resulting monopoly power comes from a variety of actual and perceived differences. Retail stores, alike in all other respects, differ in location. There may be a dozen and one groceries in a college town, but the one nearest to the campus is often the one residential students tend to patronize. There are, however, many other differences among grocery stores and other sets of producers in a market. There are differences in the ambience of show rooms, stores, and shops; in the personalities of people in contact with customers; in the promptness and courteousness of service; in the quality of the product sold; in the willingness to take returns; and make repairs. These differences yield negative-sloping demand functions and allow firms to charge different prices for the same product or set of products. Recall the *law of one price* which defines a market as the region over which a single price quickly prevails. With different prices set by different producers, the concept of the market is trivialized. A single retailer and his customers becomes the market for the products he sells.

Goals of the Firm

Different firms have different missions and goals. The goal of the neoclassical paradigm is the maximization of economic profit. Nobel Laureate Herbert A. Simon contends that decision-makers are *satisficers* not maximizers. In the area of profit their goal is to obtain satisfactory profits. Adam Smith claimed that hired managers would not maximize profits, and Michael Jensen and William Meckling's model has even owners maximizing utility rather than profits. William Baumol, of New York University, suggests that a common goal is the maximization of growth. That different firms have different goals should be kept in mind, particularly with respect to the effect on costs and pricing policy. The goals of profit, growth, and utility maximization are discussed below.

Maximization of Profits

Maximization of profits implies that all costs are minimized resulting in total cost curve *TC.* Cost minimization implies that we are all paid the least amount possible per unit of efficiency, that the facilities and equipment are the cheapest possible required to do the necessary work—with no exceptions. The spare character of the workplace could best be described by someone like Charles Dickens.
 In the neoclassical paradigm all firms are profit maximizers. They choose the rate of output at which marginal cost and revenue are equal. The price which they then set is the demand price at the chosen output rate.
 Firms do have good knowledge as to the magnitude of differential costs—especially so because they tend to be constant. But what do they know about the demand and price elasticities for their products? They also know how many units of each product were sold at the various product prices. But knowing a point on a demand function is a far cry from knowing what the marginal

revenue function looks like. A firm would have to know the quantity sold—not at one price but at several prices—to have a crude view of the demand function. This would allow calculating a small range of the total revenue and marginal revenue functions. If the marginal revenue segment is in the neighborhood of marginal cost, a price reasonably close to profit maximization could be set. But I suspect that the number of firms which do this are about as scarce as studies showing cost functions to be be "U"-shaped. Finally, almost all firms sell more than one product. Since there is no objective way of dividing fixed costs among them, there is no objective way of determining the profitability of each product.

I suspect that very few firms have the information which allows them to set a profit-maximizing price.

Growth Maximization

Consider the argument that the growth maximizer needs more money than others because it has to invest more in plant and equipment. If that is the case some attempt at profit maximization is in order. But the firm with a growth-oriented mission can pay minimal dividends, using the higher retained earnings to buy more plant and equipment than others. Shareholders would know that their prize should be expected in the future both in terms of the higher share prices and dividends of a larger corporation.

There is a basic issue overlapping profit and growth maximization. Are not profit maximizers required to have a growth orientation if growth is expected to make the firm more profitable?

Utility Maximization

Utility maximization implies higher costs, *TC,* than the minimum associated with profit maximization. These higher costs could be manifest in one or more of the following: higher pay, better employee benefits, a more humane work pace, a nicer work environment, more attractive space, a reluctance to lay off employees during periods of inadequate demand, and so forth.

Assuming the utility maximizer charges the same price as other firms, they sell as much as others and, as in the Jensen and Meckling model, the higher costs lower profits.

Negative Profits and Survival

There is no law requiring profits to be positive. Negative profits are not uncommon and their continuation threatens the very existence of the firm. Extraordinary actions are taken to control costs and enhance revenues. Why are great efforts taken to keep a firm alive, to take profit-maximizing actions?

Death of the firm has negative consequences, often of great severity, for a number of constituencies. (1) It can destroy much or all of the investments of

Figure 10.1.   **Total Revenue Before and After Price Has Been Set**

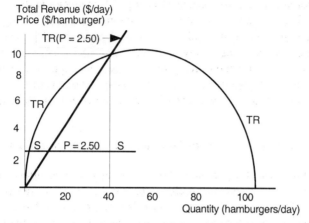

owners. (2) Lenders can lose a substantial percentage of the funds they put at the disposal of the firm. (3) Suppliers may not receive the revenues due them and lose what had been a valued customer. (4) Executives and managers lose their jobs, status, power, and income. (5) Finally, workers in losing their jobs, in effect, lose the most basic of their "property rights": the earnings which allow them to purchase property or products in a multitude of forms.

Sometimes efforts to save a firm work; often they do not.

Monopolistic Price and the Resulting Total Revenue Function

Once a firm sets the price of a product, it transforms the total revenue functions into the linear function defined by the given price. This is shown in Figure 10.1. As soon as the firm sets the price of a product, here the $2.50 price of a ham-burger, it creates a linear "total revenue function" with a slope equal to the price, $P = TR/Q$, and an infinitely elastic supply function at that price, SS. The total revenue experienced is at the intersection of the fixed price "total revenue function" with the demand-based total revenue function. The "total revenue function" plus a linear total cost function can be used to determine the break-even point—the rate of production required to yield the normal rate of return.

Note that at a price of $2.50 for a hamburger, forty are sold and the day's revenue is $100.

Monopolistic Implications of Location

The most common source of the monopoly power of an imperfect competitor is probably its location. The nearer a firm is to a customer, the lower is the cost of traveling to the firm to make a purchase. In like fashion, the further the customer is from the firm, the greater is the cost of delivering the purchase to the customer. As a result the liquor store down the block, in the middle of the New York City borough of Queens, is able to charge $2 more for a bottle of Freizenet than can be found in downtown Manhattan, the more famous borough. But if I travel to the remote store, it usually costs me far more than $2 to get there, in terms of the opportunity cost of my time and out of pocket transportation costs. Were I to buy a lot of liquor—for gifts and not consumption, of course—the savings would exceed the transportation cost and it would make it worthwhile to buy from the remote Astor Place Liquor Store rather than Bacchus, only a block away.

Customers Traveling to Different Locations and the Break-Even Condition

The transaction cost of a purchase, TrC, includes the opportunity cost of the time required to make a set of purchases plus the cost of the transportation to the location of the seller. Transaction cost is similar to total fixed cost in the sense that the greater is the value of goods purchased, the less is the transportation cost per dollar of purchase. Thus, if a distant supermarket has lower prices, it may make sense to go there for a large weekly shopping and to fill in during the week with purchases from a higher-priced neighborhood grocer.

Let me derive and show the *break-even condition,* the condition at which a consumer is indifferent to shopping in the neighborhood as opposed to shopping at a remote location where prices are lower.

The Break-Even Condition—The Algebraic Approach

The given or assumed conditions are the following: (1) The total bill in a neighborhood store is TB_N. (2) The total bill for the same goods at the remote store, TB_R, is k percent of that at the neighborhood store. (3) The transaction cost at the remote location, TrC_R, is greater than that arising from shopping in the neighborhood, TrC_N. What is to be found is the magnitude of the total bill at the neighborhood store which makes the buyer indifferent between buying there and remotely.

First, we have the relationship between the two total bills. The remote bill is k percent of the bill of the neighborhood store—for the same set of goods:

(1) $$TB_R = k \cdot TB_N$$

Second, the total cost of a purchase equals the total bill plus transaction cost: $TC = TB + TrC$. Break-even occurs when the total cost of the purchase in the neighborhood store equals the total cost of the same goods at the remote store:

(2) $$TB_N + TrC_N = TB_R + TrC_R$$

Substitute for TB_R, kTB_N, and solve for TB_N:

(3) $TB_N = kTB_N + (TrC_R - TrC_N)$

Solving for TB_N, the break-even magnitude of the neighborhood bill, yields:

(4) $TB_N = [TrC_R - TrC_N]/(1 - k) = \Delta TrC/(1 - k)$

What is the sense of the above equation? Consider the numerator of the right-hand side of the equation. It says that the greater the difference in transactions costs between the two locations, the higher is the dollar amount of the total neighborhood bill at break-even. Now consider the denominator. As the ratio of the remote total bill to the neighbor bill, TB_R/TB_N gets smaller, k gets smaller, $(1-k)$ gets larger and the right hand side of the equation gets smaller. The lower the relative price of the remote store, the lower is the total bill at the neighborhood store which yields break-even.

A numerical example should help in making the break-even concept clearer.

Given: (1) The transaction cost to the remote location is $6. (2) That to the near location is $2. (3) The remote seller charges 80 percent of what the neighborhood seller charges.
Find: The break-even bill at the neighborhood store.

$TR_N = \Delta TrC/(1 - k)$

$TB_N = [6 - 2]/[1 - 0.8] = \$20$

The monopolistic power of the neighborhood store is such that it can charge 25 percent more than a remote store for total bills up to $20. (The total bill in the neighborhood store is $20. In the remote store it is $16. The former is 25 percent more compared to the latter $(20 - 16)/16$; the latter is 20 percent less compared to the former $(16 - 20)/20$.)

The Break-Even Condition—The Graphical Approach.

A graphical version of the break-even approach can be seen in Figure 10.2. Total cost at the near and remote locations are plotted as a function of the total neighborhood bill. The vertical intercepts are the transaction costs of $2 and $6. The slope of TC_N is unity; that of TC_R is k, which equals 0.8. The functions are equal when the bill at the neighborhood location is $20. At other bills, the vertical differences between the functions give the magnitudes of the dollar advantage of shopping in the neighborhood and then at the remote store. The monopoly power of the firm located in the neighborhood, in this example, is such that it can charge 25 percent higher prices than a remote rival and expect economically rational people in the neighborhood to buy from it for expected purchases of $20 or less. (Note that if $P_R = 0.8P_N$ then $P_N = 1.25P_R$.)

Figure 10.2.   **The Break-Even Point Between Shopping in the Neighborhood or at a
Cheaper Remote Store**

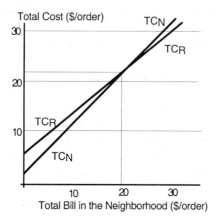

Firms Delivering Products to Customers at Different Locations

Three different transaction or shipping and handling charges are examined: (1)
Costs are proportionate to the distance of the customer from the producer. (2)
Customers are placed in three zones with differing zonal charges. (3) The deliv-
ered price is the same irrespective of the location of the customer.

Shipping and Handling Costs Proportionate to Distance

Assume the following: (1) There are two firms which sell and deliver the same
set of products. (2) The firms charge the price of the product and a shipping
charge which is proportionate to the distance of the customer from the firm. (3)
The more remote firm's prices are k times that of the nearer firm, with k a constant less than 1 and greater than zero. This case is analytically the same as that
of the customer deciding whether to purchase from the nearby or remote store.
All that need be done is to substitute the mileage charges of the firm for the
transaction costs of the customer. There is a break-even total bill between the total bill from the neighborhood and remote firms. At total bills less than break-
even, it is cheaper to buy from the nearer seller which delivers; for bills above
break-even, it is cheaper to buy from the remote seller which also delivers. The
locational monopoly condition is alive and well when delivery costs are a function of distance.

Delivered Price as the FOB Price Plus the Cost to Deliver to a Zone

Many firms find it expedient to base their delivery charges not on the basis of
the precise mileage to each individual customer but on the basis of the mileage

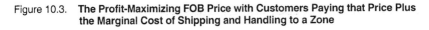

Figure 10.3.   **The Profit-Maximizing FOB Price with Customers Paying that Price Plus
the Marginal Cost of Shipping and Handling to a Zone**

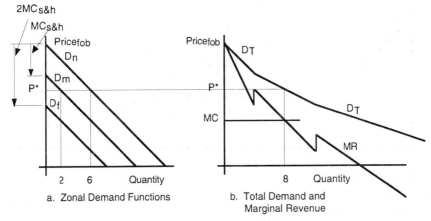

a. Zonal Demand Functions

b. Total Demand and
Marginal Revenue

to a region or zone which encompasses a set of customers. The implications of
this common approach deserves consideration. The abbreviation FOB or fob
means free on board. A car which is fob Detroit is free of shipping charge if
picked up at a designated location in Detroit. And it is the starting point from
which the charges are made.

The assumptions are these: (1) The firm is a profit maximizer which sets its fob
price on the basis of the marginal cost of production and the marginal revenue of
the total demand function. (2) It has customers in three zones—the near, mid-
range, and far zones. (3) Each zone has the same demand for the firm's product.
(4) Delivery costs and charges are as follows: Those in the near zone are so close
to the producer that there is no delivery charge; the shipping and handling cost
for mid-range-zone deliveries is $MC_{s\&h}$; and the delivery cost to the far zone is
$2MC_{s\&h}$. (5) The delivered price is the fob price plus the marginal cost of delivering the product to a zone.

The zonal demand functions can be found in frame *a* of Figure 10.3. Note that
the vertical axis is the fob price and *not* the delivered price to the mid-range and
far zones. As a result, the mid-range demand, D_mD_m, is equal to the near-range
demand, D_nD_n, downshifted by the delivery charge of $MC_{s\&h}$ per widget. This
is because the delivered price to mid-range zone X is $MC_{s\&h}$ more than that
shown on the price axis in frame *a*. In like fashion, the demand arising from
customers in the far zone, D_fD_f, is equal to the near range demand downshifted
by $2MC_{s\&h}$ per unit.

The horizontal sum of the three demand functions appears in frame *b* as
D_TD_T, along with its marginal revenue function and a flat marginal cost function. The discontinuities in the marginal revenue function arise from total demand being linear with three different slopes. The profit-maximizing rate of production, at the equality of marginal revenue and cost, is eight and the profit-

Figure 10.4.   **Profit Maximization with a Single Delivered Price**

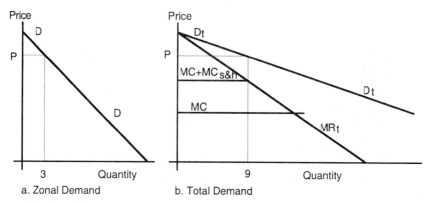

a. Zonal Demand   b. Total Demand

maximizing fob price is P^*. Six units are purchased in the near zone, two in the mid-range, and none in the far zone.

The implications of the zonal pricing case are these: (1) The locational based monopoly power of the seller is maintained, particularly in the near zone. (2) There is some price discrimination in that buyers more remote in a zone pay the same price as those less remote in the zone. (3) Penetration into remote zones is limited by the higher price the firm charges to cover zonal shipping and handling costs.

One Delivered Price for All Customers

To purchase a product using a mail order catalog generally requires that you pay the (fob) price of the product plus a shipping and handling charge. The latter is often the same amount whether you live in Bangor, Maine, or San Diego, California, or anywhere in between. With one price the producer can compete with others throughout the country—but it does lose its locational monopoly power.

For the sake of expediency, assume the existence of the same demand functions and shipping costs as assumed in the previous example in which different shipping and handling costs were assigned to three different zones. Since demand and price are, here, the same in all three zones, so, too, will be the number of products sold. The average shipping and handling cost is charged to all customers irrespective of location. This amounts to the sum of the costs to the three zones divided by 3: $(0 + MC_{s\&h} + 2MC_{s\&h}) / 3 = MC_{s\&h}$. This makes total marginal cost equal the sum of the marginal cost of production and the marginal cost of shipping and handling, as is shown in Figure 10.4. Profits are maximized at an output rate of 9 with each of the three zones buying 3 units.

Note that more is sold with a single delivered price than with multiple delivered prices and the increase in sales is a manifestation of price discrimination.

Price Discrimination

Price discrimination has been previously defined as charging different prices to different buyers or categories of buyers. Here the claim appears to be just the opposite—namely, that charging the same *delivered* price to the three groups of buyers is a form of price discrimination. How can this seeming contradiction be explained? The answer is that those near to and those far from the firm are *not* buying the same product. What is being bought is the good which is desired *plus* the shipping and handling services required to deliver it to the desired locations.

The implications of the single delivered price case follows: (1) The firm foregoes its local monopoly so that it can market its products competitively over a larger region. (2) It discriminates against nearby buyers and in favor of remote buyers. (3) Its overall sales increase and, although not shown, so do its profits. Note the wonderful statement in a mail order catalog which follows:

> In order to provide the fairest possible shipping and handling charges, we base them on average weight and distance for outgoing packages. If you purchase a light item and live close to us, the charge may be a little high. If you live a great distance [from us] and the item is heavy, the charge may be low. We believe our method is fair for everyone and our total shipping and handling charges are less than our actual costs (Trend-Lines, Catalog 512A, [1994]).

Who could give Trend-Lines description of the price discrimination implicit in a single shipping charge anything less than an *A*?

Locational Monopoly as a Metaphor for Other Monopolistic Attributes

Logic entails buying from the closer and more expensive store, up to some dollar value of spending. This is because until that amount is reached its location makes it cheaper than a lower-priced remote store. This is due to the greater cost of going to the remote store. But you may actually buy in a higher-priced establishment for a number of reasons other than its closer location. You may buy there because it is kept cleaner, has a nicer design, is more customer friendly, has help who know you or who are attractive to you, or whatever. Locational monopoly can be thought of as a metaphor for attributes such as those mentioned above. Moreover, there is probably some point at which the monetary savings at another store offset the value of the differential utility of the more attractive store—a break-even point similar to the locational break-even point. Beyond that point, buying would take place in the less attractive but cheaper store.

Figure 10.5.   **Imperfect Competition and the Long-Run Equilibrium**

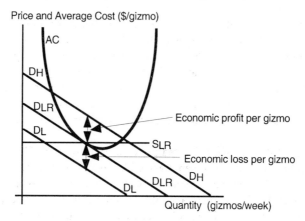

Profits in the Short- and Long-Run

The expository assumptions are that all firms in a market have the same cost functions and they are all profit maximizers. Figure 10.5 shows that in the short-run a profit-maximizing firm is in one of three situations: (1) If the demand for its product is $D_L D_L$, less than average cost, AC, it is suffering an economic loss. This loss will drive firms from the market increasing the demand for those which stay. With fewer firms the demand for the product of each increases to $D_{LR} D_{LR}$, whereupon all firms experience the normal rate of return, and there are then no net entrants into the market. (2) The demand is D_{LR}, tangent to the average cost function, AC, so all firms receive the normal rate of return, zero economic profit. There is, as a result, no incentive to enter into or exit from the market. (3) Demand is $D_H D_H$. Economic profits are experienced. Those in the market consider expansion; those outside, with the required expertise, have an incentive to enter the market. The increase in the number of producing units reduces the demand per unit until long-run demand is reached, $D_{LR} D_{LR}$.

Note that the long-run demand function is always tangent to the average cost curve on its downward-sloping portion. Thus, long-run equilibrium does not yield production efficiency (operation at minimum average cost in the long-run).

Should Rational Expectations Make the Profit Motive Ineffectual?

According to the rational expectations model, decisions are made on the basis of past experience, current information, and future expectations which exploit all relevant information. Assume that the demand is high at $D_H D_H$. Economic actors should then know that there are economic profits and that they will be driven to zero in the long-run. With economic profits high now but doomed to zero in the long-run, is it rational for insiders to expand and outsiders to enter the market? Hold your answer while we see if another application of rational expectations yields some helpful information to us.

Nobel Laureate Robert Lucas is a great fan of the rational expectations model. He has applied it to expansionary monetary policy intended to stimulate the economy. His hypothesis is that decision-makers will take note of the X percent increase in the money supply and rationally expect that it will, in the long-run, lead to an X percent inflation rate. But rather than wait for the long-run, they promptly increase wages, prices, and interest rates by X percent. These price increases absorb the increase in the money supply so that the intended economic stimulation never occurs.

How does Lucas's reasoning apply to the case of economic profits which in the long-run will be brought to zero? If long-run rational expectations deter expansion, economic profits should persist. Their persistence could ultimately serve as an effective stimulus to expansion in the market, driving down the demand per producing unit to the long-run demand, $D_{LR}D_{LR}$, and economic profits of zero.

Return a moment to Lucas's model. If everyone else is going to raise their price, why not keep price constant thereby obtaining a greater market share? Others anticipating or seeing such actions might resist increasing their prices thereby undermining the transformation of the long-run into the short-run price increase. And what about reality—do price-setters actually increase prices as a function of growth of the money supply? I, in effect, asked that question of Alan S. Blinder of Princeton University who recently performed some wonderful research on various aspects of price-setting. His answer follows:

> As to the money supply, in pretesting the questionnaire, we did ask a series of questions about whether price-setters take into account macro variable X; and money supply was one candidate for X. Since no one we asked paid any attention to the Ms [the various measures of the supply of money] we deleted this in the final questionnaire that went into the field (Letter from Alan S. Blinder dated May 16, 1994).

This, of course, badly undermines Lucas's rational expectations ineffectual monetary policy hypothesis.

Entry and the Need for Price and Quantity Information

In the neoclassical paradigm the price system is supreme and the only economic information potential entrants require is that on prices—albeit *future* prices. Is this enough information for those with the required technological and business expertise? The answer is *yes* in competitive markets and *no* in all others—hat is, it is generally *no*. *The answer is yes in the competitive market only because the price is also the demand function.*

That the price of hamburgers will be $2.50 next year and will increase at the rate of 10 cents a year for the next decade is close to worthless information to someone interested in opening a fast food store. It fails to provide information on the quantity of sales anticipated at this price. Should I expect to sell 1 or 1 million per year? Decision-makers need information on expected demand, price-quantity information, to make rational entry decisions. The price system fails to provide the required information. It is inadequate. What is required is a market survey which starts with buying hamburgers from luncheonettes in the area you are considering. If they are not overcrowded during the lunch hours, you should consider setting up somewhere else. Or you might try buying one of those over-crowded luncheonettes.

Summary on Imperfect Competition

Here is a market structure with many sellers and many buyers. The product is differentiated and producers face negative-sloping demand functions. The source of this differentiation which allows some to charge more than others for the same profit is location. Location is a metaphor for all things which differentiate one producer from another. It includes location, appearance of the store, speed and quality of service, the attitude of the staff toward customers, and any other attribute drawing people to one producer rather than another. Some of its managers would like to maximize profits. Others prefer maximizing utility, growth, or total revenue. Some goals imply cost minimization; others do not. Firms with different goals and costs may charge more or less than others do for the same product. And prices may be adjusted to respond to competitive pressures or the lack thereof. This implies that demand is negative sloped for the products of firms under imperfect competition.

Logic has it that we buy from a better-located but more expensive firm *up to a point*— the break-even point which is a dollar figure beyond which it pays to buy from a worse located seller whose prices are lower.

Sometimes products are bought by phone, mail order, or on the Internet. What is purchased is the product plus the shipping and handling services required to deliver it to the buyer. Again it might be cheaper to buy from a more expensive local seller because the price with the low shipping charge is lower. But as the total bill increases a break-even point is reached beyond which purchases from a remote lower-priced seller are cheaper.

If firms sell on the basis of price plus the shipping costs to an individual customer proportionate with distance, different customers pay different delivered prices—but this is *not* price discrimination. It is the other way around. Charging the same delivered price to customers located near and far is discriminatory. This is because what is being bought is the product plus delivery services. Charging all the same delivered price is a common form of price discrimination favoring those far off against those nearby. In doing this the seller forsakes his locational monopoly for the ability to compete over a broader market area.

A final matter is that price-quantity signals, demand signals, are required to make rational entry and production decisions. But the market does not provide such information.

Oligopoly

An oligopoly is an industry dominated by a small number of firms which are rival conscious. Stable oligopolies are those in which the same firms dominate an industry for a substantial period of time. Competitive oligopolies have different firms dominating an industry at different times. Models of stable oligopolies are substantially better than are those which are competitive.

Market Characteristics

The attributes of the oligopolistic market are the following: (1) The market is dominated by a small number of large firms, large relative to the size of the market. (2) The firms are rival conscious. In making decisions they give due weight to the expected responses of rivals. (3) Entry into and exit out of the market is difficult. (4) In some oligopolistic markets the product is homogeneous; in others it is differentiated. (5) Oligopolies face negative-sloping demand functions and have some control over price. (6) Where the industry is stable price leadership and some non-price competition tends to be the norm. (7) When competition arises both price and non-price competition are practiced.

Oligopolistic Industries

There is a long list of industries which are categorized as oligopolistic. The steel and automobile industries are popular examples. In the former products are standardized; in the latter they are differentiated. Other oligopolistic industries produce breakfast cereals, long-distance telephone service, beer, glass, network entertainment, movies, cameras and film, certain chemicals, many drugs, soap, toothpaste, brokerage houses, and so on.

Rival Consciousness

Rival consciousness means that an oligopolist, in contemplating actions which will be more or less known to rivals, gives due consideration to their expected reactions. Stable oligopolies tend to have an industry-wide culture defining the relationship between the rivals. The Supreme Court has called the price relationship of the oligopolists, a manifestation of price leadership, "conscious parallelism." Non-price competition is frequently used to maintain or slowly advance market shares.

In the case of competitive oligopolies non-price actions are complemented by price competition—some of which is hidden from view. Tell long-distance phone company X that you are switching to Y, and hidden prices sometimes arise so that you will see the good sense of staying with X.

But whatever the competitive maneuvers might be, decision-makers consciously consider the ways in which they expect rivals to respond.

The Cournot Model

Antoine Augustine Cournot, a distinguished French mathematician who lived from 1801 to 1877, started his economic analysis with the theory of monopoly. He then increased the number of firms in a market until he reached the case of competition. Along the way Cournot passed what we now call oligopoly. For illustrative purposes he exploited the special case of the two-firm market, the duopoly, with a model which stressed the reaction of one producer to the actions of its rival. All of this appears in his 1838 work, *Mathematical Principles of the Theory of Wealth.*

The assumptions of Cournot's duopoly model are these: (1) There are two firms in the market—A and a new firm B. (2) Both are profit maximizers. (3) They produce the same product. (4) They have the same costs. (5) Both know the market demand function which is linear. (6) Each firm expects its rival to produce in the oncoming period just what it produced in the previous one. (7) Equilibrium occurs when firms produce the same output in two consecutive periods. Figure 10.6 should help in seeing how the reactions assumed by Cournot unfurl over the course of time.

The process starts in period 1. The market demand function in this period is the demand for the production of A. Marginal cost is constant. The marginal revenue curve comes down at twice the negative slope of the demand function and is equal to marginal cost at an output rate of 300 magnums per month and that is what A produces.

The demand B expects is a reaction to the output of A, namely, the residual of the market demand remaining after A has sold the 300 magnums. The residual demand could be shown be shifting the market demand function 300 units to the left. Instead, I have shifted the price axis 300 units to the right and darkened the portion of the market demand function available to B. The residual demand at a price equal to marginal cost is 300 magnums. Under profit maximization, B produces half of that, 150 magnums per month.

In the second month A expects B to produce 150 magnums. The remaining demand is the darkened portion of the market demand function. At marginal cost it amounts to 450 magnums. At profit-maximization A's output for the month is 225 magnums, down from 300. With this amount subtracted from market demand, the residual demand is 375 magnum at marginal cost. B maximizes profit by the production of half of the residual, 187.5 magnum, up from 150.

In the third month A expects B to produce 187.5 magnum. It sees the darkened

Figure 10.6.   **The Cournot Duopoly Model**

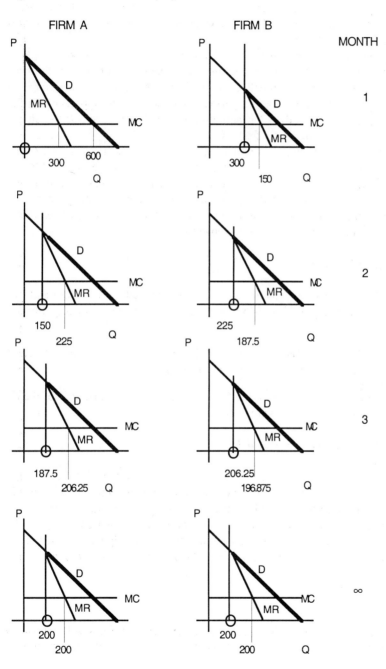

portion of the market demand function as remaining and maximizes production by making 206.25 magnums (down from 225). Armed with this information, *B* calculates the residual demand and based upon it maximizes profit by the production and sale of 196.875 magnums.

At equilibrium each firm produces 200 magnums. Thus, the market supply is 400 magnums per month—up by one-third from the output of 300 which existed when the market was monopolized by *A*. Although reaching this equilibrium would take an infinite number of periods, it is possible to approach it quite quickly. After three periods *A* has an output rate of 203.125; and *B* has an out put rate of 193.75, both not far from 200.

The major contribution of the model is that it shows one firm reacting to the action of a rival. But there are two major weakness. One is the absence of learning. Until equilibrium is reached, *A* expects *B* to produce less than it always does and *B* continually expects *A* to produce more than it actually does. The model also implies that until equilibrium is reached, more is bought from *A* at a higher price than is bought from *B* at a lower price.

A Nash Equilibrium

The 1994 Nobel Prize in economic science was awarded John F. Nash and two other game theorists. Nash is famous to many economists for his equilibrium criterion:

> *A Nash equilibrium* is one in which decision-makers choose the best action possible, given the actions of rivals.

This is precisely the strategy of the Cournot model. Given the output of the rival, the producer acted to maximize profit.

The Kinked Demand Curve Model

Paul W. Sweezy while teaching at Harvard University in the 1930s, developed the kinked demand curve model which is helpful in explaining the relationship between rival consciousness and the stickiness of prices in mature oligopolies. It is assumed that *A's* oligopoly price is P_1. The demand function envisaged by Oligopolist *A* is kinked at that price, as can be seen in Figure 10.7. It is relatively elastic at prices higher than P_1 and relatively inelastic at prices lower than P_1.

Why the Kink?

If Oligopolist *A* increases price above P_1, she expects that rivals will not follow the price increase. With rivals not following, *A* expects the function to be rela-

Figure 10.7.   **The Kinked Demand Curve**

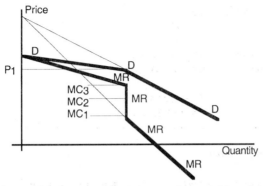

tively elastic–for a given increase in price a substantial loss in sales and market-share is expected. What if price is decreased? Here *A*'s perception is that rivals will follow the decrease. As a result the gain in sales is modest, the demand function is relatively inelastic in the region of decreasing price. Thus the kink at the existing price.

Why Stable Prices?

Oligopolist *A*'s kinked demand function yields a marginal revenue function with a discontinuity—a discontinuity which helps to stabilize prices. The discontinuity acts as an additional factor in keeping prices sluggish. Assume that at the outset marginal cost is MC_1. It equals marginal revenue at the original rate of production and yields the original profit-maximizing price—at least for a profit-maximizing price leader. Then assume that marginal cost increases to MC_2. The same output rate and price would be maintained. This is true for the still higher marginal cost of MC_3. The same would be true if the shifts in marginal cost in the region of discontinuity came about from productivity changes. Thus, the discontinuity in the marginal revenue function helps to keep price constant as marginal cost varies over the range of the discontinuity.

Game Theoretic Models

In relatively recent years, game theory has been exploited in an attempt to better understand oligopolistic behavior. It creates a logical framework for the consideration of the implications of the alternative reactions of rivals to actions of a firm. It could, for example, show profits if a rival responds to a price increase and if it did not. This could help in understanding whether or not a price change is expected to be profitable. Games are generally assumed to be played by two rivals. They sometimes yield equilibrium solutions; sometimes not. These models are applicable to both stable and competitive oligopolies.

Table 10.1. **The Dominant Strategy Payoff Matrix: Decisions on Product Quality**

A's Strategies	B's Strategies	
	1B	2B
1A	A's profit: $4 million B's profit: $6 million	A's profit: $2 million B's profit: $4 million
2A	A's profit: $6 million B's profit: $4 million	A's profit: $4 million B's profit: $2 million

A Dominant Strategy Game

A Dominant Strategy Game is one in which both firms can decide upon the better or best course of action irrespective of the reaction of the rival. This is shown in the example of the *payoff matrix* of Table 10.1. The two players are firms A and B and each must decide on one of two strategies: *1A* or *2A* for firm A and *1B* and *2B* for firm B. The lower-numbered strategies involve producing lower-quality widgets; the higher-numbered, higher-quality widgets.

Consider A's payoffs first. If it produces a lower-quality product, *1A,* it will earn $4 or $2 million, and if it produces a higher-quality product it will earn $6 or $4 million. Since it can do no worse and may do better by producing a higher-quality product, A chooses strategy *2A,* irrespective of what B might choose. While A is rival conscious, the action or reaction of its rival is of no consequence to its decision in this dominant strategy case.

What will B do in this game? If it produces the lower-quality product, strategy *1B,* it will experience either $6 or $4 million in profits. If the higher-quality product is made under strategy *2B,* it will obtain either $4 or $2 million in profit per year. It, therefore, decides on the lower-quality production strategy, *1B,* irrespective of what A does. Thus, the criterion of the dominant strategy game is met—a strategy under which the actions of the rival player turns out to be irrelevant to the other player or players. And as a result of the *2A* and *1B* choices, A's profit is $6 million and B's is $4 million.

Note that although the example was said to involve product quality, it could have involved any other variable, price or non-price.

Non-Dominant Strategy Games

Two examples are given. In the first, one of the two firms has a dominant strategy. In the second, neither firm has a dominant strategy.

The payoff matrix for the first example appears in Table 10.2. If A chooses *1A,* its profits are either $6 or $2 million. If it chooses *2A,* its profits are either $5 or $4 million. It can have no dominant strategy. If B chooses *1B,* its profits are either $6 or $4 million; if it chooses *2B* its profits will be either $4 or $2 mil-

Table 10.2.   **A Payoff Matrix in Which *A* Has No Dominant Strategy: Decisions on Product Quality**

	B's Strategies	
	1B	2B
A's Strategies		
1A	A's profit: $6 million	A's profit: $2 million
	B's profit: $6 million	B's profit: $4 million
2A	A's profit: $5 million	A's profit: $4 million
	B's profit: $4 million	B's profit: $2 million

Table 10.3.   **A Payoff Matrix in Which Neither *A* Nor *B* Has a Dominant Strategy on Product Quality**

	B's Strategies	
	1B	2B
A's Strategies		
1A	A's profit: $6 million	A's profit: $2 million
	B's profit: $4 million	B's profit: $5 million
2A	A's profit: $5 million	A's profit: $4 million
	B's profit: $6 million	B's profit: $3 million

lion. *B*, therefore, has a dominant strategy of *1B*. With *B* choosing *1B, A* does best with strategy *1A*. The result is that both firms earn $6 million.

Now consider an example in which neither *A* nor *B* has a dominant strategy. The payoff matrix is that of Table 10.3. The results depend on who goes first. Since both *A* and *B* know the matrix then can determine just what will happen if *A* or *B* goes first. The results found in Table 10.4 show that the firm which goes second always does better. With *A* going first, the best choice combination for *A* and *B* is: *2A,1B* under which *A* obtains $5 million and *B* $6 million in profits. When *B* goes first, the best combination is *1B,1A*. This yields $6 million to *A* and $4 million to *B*. Were they to alternate who goes first, *A* would average $5.5 and *B* would average $5 million. And if *B* is a good bargainer, it might convince *A* to split the $0.5 million difference. Finally, since *A* and *B* choose the best course of action predicated on the action of its rival, all results are Nash equibria.

Are the Matrices Realistic?

Oligopolies are large corporations which are required to make public their annual statements. So the pre-game profits of a rival are known—although it may bedifficult or impossible to relate profits to a particular product or product line. But strategists are employed to do difficult things so grant that they can estimate the profits of a product. They can also suggest a set of strategies. For those strategies which are variants of previous strategies used, the previous responses of ri-

Table 10.4. **The Results of the Payoff Matrix of Table 10.3**

A goes first.	Choice	Profit
	1A	$2 million
B's best choice	2B	$5 million
	2A	$5 million
B's best choice	1B	$6 million
B goes first		
	1B	$4 million
A's best choice	1A	$6 million
	2B	$3 million
A's best choice	2A	$4 million

vals are known. If they appeared to be acceptable to rivals and successful to the subject oligopolist, then variants of those responses can be anticipated and the numbers placed in the matrix should be reasonable. But the more the new strategy departs from old strategies, the greater is the problem of forecasting what the response will be and the magnitude of the numbers in the matrix. Viewed from a slightly different perspective, responses in a stable oligopolistic market are far easier to anticipate than responses in a competitive oligopolistic setting.

Concentration Ratios

The purpose of a concentration ratio is to create an empirical measure which indicates the extent to which large firms dominate the sales of an industry. There are two popular measures of concentration: the x-firm concentration ratio and the Herfindahl-Hirschman Concentration Index.

The X-Firm Concentration Ratio

The x-firm concentration ratio is the percentage of the sales or shipments of an industry accounted for by the industry's x largest firms. The four-firm concentration ratio is the most popular. The eight-firm concentration ratio is also used both as a measure of concentration and a measure of the relative size of the second echelon of large firms. The ratios normally used are those published by the U.S. Department of Commerce and they are based on national statistics.

  The x-firm ratio is an imperfect measure of concentration for a number of reasons. (1) The most obvious problem is that an x-firm concentration ratio masks the relative size of the x firms. A four-firm concentration ratio of 40 percent might refer to one firm having 37 percent of market sales with each of the others having 1 percent. It might, as well, refer to the four largest firms each having 10 percent of sales. Having one dominant firm in a market is quite different than having four of equal stature. (2) The ratio is based on national statistics whereas many markets are local, regional, or international in character. (3) There is a problem in specifying the product which is relevant for concentration ratios. Are tea and coffee, for example, such close substitutes that their markets should be considered as one? On the other hand, should producers of terribly expensive cars or computers or other products be included in the same calculation with producers who manufacture more plebeian forms of the products? (4) Production of a product frequently involves the production of a set of industries—some of which are far more concentrated than others. The petroleum industry, for example, consists of four rather different subindustries. One involves the production of crude oil. The second handles the transportation of that crude oil to refineries, frequently by pipeline. The third involves the refining of the crude oil, and the fourth its distribution to final users. The concentration ratio is radically different in these different related subindustries. (5) Finally, a concentration ratio does not indicate the amount of "churning" which has taken place—the turnover of firms which comprise the leaders in an industry. The nature of an industry continually dominated by the same four firms might be quite different in terms of performance than an industry in which the top four of one decade is poorly correlated with the top four of another decade. I say "might be" largely because some market share changes are due to mergers and acquisitions of firms which have a history of "working together." Merging them would have little, if any, effect on the power structure of an industry.

The Herfindahl-Hirschman Concentration Index

The Herfindahl-Hirschman index, H, measures the concentration in an industry or market by taking the sum of the squared values of the market share, MS, of all firms in a market or industry:

(5) $$H = (MS1)^2 + (MS2)^2 + ... + (MSN)^2$$

If a monopoly controlled a market, H would equal 10,000 ($H = MS2 = 1002 = 10,000$). If their were two firms in a market and they had equal shares H would equal 5,000 ($H = 50^2 + 50^2 = 5,000$). But if there were two firms in a market and one had 80 percent and the other 20 percent of its sales revenue, H would equal 6,800 ($H = 80^2 + 20^2 = 6800$). Thus it is that the Herfindahl-Hirschman index solves the relative size problem inherent in the x-firm index. It also captures the importance or unimportance of the shares of those beyond the x firms. It solves the first problem mentioned above but not the other four.

Price Leadership

Price leadership is common in stable oligopolies. It is an important part of the industry's culture. It has two related forms. A typical set of rules are the following: (1) Oligopolist X is the price leader. (2) It announces new prices or percentage increases on or about October 15. (3) Followers' price changes appear in staggered announcements over the course of a month or so. If the products are homogeneous, the followers' prices are those of the leader. If products are differentiated, the percentage changes in price announced by the leader are are closely followed. (4) All price changes go into effect on a specific date, such as January 1 of the upcoming year. (5) The price changes are close to those expected by the oligopolists and their customers. The firms are rival and customer conscious.

Sometimes a major follower will grow impatient waiting for the leader to act and will itself increase prices. But when the leader does announce its price increase, if a discrepancy exists, the original price-setter and other followers tend to change their prices to come into conformance with the leader.

Non-Price Competition

Monopolistic firms, particularly oligopolists in stable oligopolies, tend to prefer non-price to price competition. Areas in which non-price competition takes place include the following: (1) the brand naming of products; (2) advertising and marketing; (3) the quality and performance of products—in fact and claims; (4) the time between the placing of an order and its delivery; (5) the coverage and duration of warranties; (6) the time allowed for the payment of bills; (7) the interest rate charged on overdue bills; (8) delivery, assembly, and installation charges; (9) discounts; and (10) the styling and packaging of products. There are numerous other forms of non-price competition. Saul Nelson and Walter G. Keim outline more than 200 in their paper "Methods of Non-Price Competition," reprinted in Backman (1953, pp. 96–115).

Why do firms in stable oligopolies tend to prefer non-price to price competition? A price cut is easy to emulate and, therefore, of little if any value to its initial maker if rivals quickly adopt it. Moreover, it may provoke a larger price cut, a cut intended to punish the firm which originally cut prices. It is more difficult to respond to some of the techniques of non-price competition. (1) An oligopolist may improve the styling or performance of a car but it may take two or three years for rivals to emulate the changes. (2) Brilliant advertising slogans, songs, and cartoon characters can be developed. The "Joe Camel" advertisements were so popular that they were banned in the mid-1997 negotiations between thirty attorney generals and the cigarette manufacturers. (3) Other forms of non-price competition may be under the table and unknown to rivals. Salespeople may have the authority to grant longer periods to pay for a product to valued customers and potential customers—with the understanding that the concession is top secret. (4) Warranties can be made less restrictive and longer in duration. Although this is easy to replicate, it might be too risky and costly to do so for a firm which fears the potential costs of the improvement.

The evidence in support of the relative preference of business for non-price rather than price competition rests on the more frequent occurrence of the former and the frequent absence of the latter.

Barriers to Entry

High barriers to entry deter new firms from entering a market and, therefore, allow the maintenance of an oligopolistic market and the monopoly power of its strongest members. Some of the most important barriers are: economies of scale, financial requirements, the control of special resources, and special know-how.

Economies of Scale

A small set of resources can suffice for the production of a modern retail store, dentist's office, pizza parlor, and carpenter's shop. But much is required to run an automobile factory, an integrated steel mill, or a nuclear power plant. The difference is largely due to the fact that the production process of the former do not involve economies of scale while the latter do. Assembling cars in a plant the size of a pizza parlor would create costs so high that cars would become unaffordable. The usual measure of the scale required for a certain form of production goes by the name minimum efficient size. It is the lowest rate of production which yields minimum average cost—the rate of production at which the declining long-run average cost planning function becomes flat.

Economies of scale are important in determining the number of firms which can profitably exist in an industry. If the minimum efficient size automobile production is two million cars per year and the quantity of new cars demanded is eight million cars per year, the market can support no more than four producers.

Financial Requirements

It may appear that financial requirement are much the same as scale requirements, but that is not always the case. The minimum efficient size required may be two million a year for both the production of autos and pins but the financial requirements will be quite different. The greater the financial requirement is, the greater is the barrier to entry.

Special Resources

Special resources required to enter a market may be unavailable. The least cost method of production is required by an entrant but it may be patented and unavailable. Fabricating a product may be proscribed by patents. An airline may find it impossible to enter a market because it lacks the "slots" required to offer flights to or from a particular airport. A new steel producer might not be able to obtain the iron ore required because the iron ore deposits are owned or controlled by the existing steel producers. New broadcasters require a suitable frequency in the electromagnetic spectrum, but none may be available. Street vendors in New York City require licenses, but no more are currently available. The other side of the problem is the tendency of those already in a market to develop strategies to control special resources and, as a result, to limit competition.

Special Know-How

Not all production meets reasonable quality standards. Many aspects of production have an artful component known to those with talent and experience in the particular production process. The steel industry of the late nineteenth century produced many "seconds" and one of the accomplishments of the steel tycoon Charles M. Schwab was in substantially lowering that failure rate. Workers in the mill had the know-how to accomplish this, and Schwab had the know-how to get them to use it. As a young engineer I quickly learned that highly accurate machining was best done by Joe P; delicate assembly was best done by Johnny N; and highly accurate grinding by Henry R. Colleagues who were "product engineers," recommended transistors from company X because their quality was better than required by the industry's specifications. A Harvard Business School case study found that the reason for an explosion of the failure rate a firm experienced in the manufacture of a special kind of glass was the simultaneous loss of three of its foremen engaged in its production. Much production requires experiential know-how and the more required, the greater the barrier to entry. A company I worked for was expert in the design and production of analog computers but lacked any special digital computer know-how. This led to its "creative destruction."

Imports and Foreign Firms: Anti-Barriers

The barriers to entry mentioned above wrongly imply that existing firms in an oligopolistic industry need not fear an increase in competition. In some of our most important oligopolies—auto and steel, for example—imports have badly eroded the monopolistic power of the leading firms. And in the case of the automobile industry, some foreign firms, successful in marketing here, have built and are building production facilities in the United States.

Technological Advances

Technological advances have been an important force in both increasing and decreasing monopolization. Charles Martin Hall's discovery of the electrolytic process for the production of aluminum represented a major advance in the process of producing aluminum. His operating company, which became the Aluminum Company of America (ALCOA), was largely responsible for the ability to produce aluminum products at costs sufficiently low to make aluminum a viable substitute for other metals. ALCOA's initial monopoly stemmed from Hall's patent on the production process. Its continued domination of the aluminum industry reflects its increasing know-how regarding the production of aluminum.

Intel and Motorola have emerged as *the* semi-conductor chip manufacturers. The industry has become more highly monopolized as other semi-conductor manufacturers increasingly failed to make the major investments required to develop and produce switching devices of ever-increasing speed.

Technological advances also destroy monopoly power. The development of the minimill for the production of steel from scrap increased competition in that industry. The development of personal computers destroyed IBM's domination of the computer industry. And the application of microwave technology to long-distance telephone services converted the AT&Ts monopoly into an oligopoly.

Mergers and Acquisitions

Mergers and acquisitions have played an important role in the development of the market structure of many of the key industries in the economy. In 1882, John D. Rockefeller utilized acquisitions to create Standard Oil as the dominant firm in the petroleum industry. In 1908, William C. Durand formed General Motors by the merger of about twenty-five automobile and parts manufacturing companies. The creation of the U.S. Steel Corporation in 1901 by Andrew Carnegie and J. Pierpont Morgan converted the steel industry from one which was highly competitive to one which was oligopolistic.

Why would one firm want to sell its assets, history, and good will to another firm? In the case of oligopolies or large widely owned firms the logical answers are quite straightforward. An offer is obtained which is too good to refuse. What is meant by sellers receiving an offer too good to refuse? Who are the sellers? The sellers consist of two distinctly different groups: the executives and the shareholders of the target firm. The executives of a target firm in a friendly takeover, tend to receive a package of wonderful benefits sometimes dubbed "golden parachutes." And the shareholders tend to receive, in one form or another, substantially more than the stock market valuation of their shares. This is the essence of an offer too good to refuse.

Why do acquiring firms make such generous offers? David J. Ravenscraft and F. M. Scherer offer three possible reasons: (1) Buyers are more optimistic than sellers about the future profit prospects of the firm. (2) They believe they can run the firm more efficiently and profitably than the current managers. (3) Those in control of the acquiring firm feel that the acquisition will lead to increasing their prestige and income (1987, p.3).

Types

Mergers and acquisitions can be categorized as horizontal, vertical, and conglomerate. The horizontal merger involves the purchase of a firm which makes products which are the same as or similar to those made by the acquiring firm. Vertical mergers cover cases in which the target firm is in the chain of production of the acquiring firm. An oil refinery may acquire a firm owning land rich in oil deposits or a firm which controls many gas stations. Conglomerate acquisitions involve the purchase of firms whose products are not related to those of the acquiring firm such as a large retailer purchasing an insurance company. While in the case of horizontal mergers the acquiring firm has production and business expertise of substantial relevance to the operation of the targeted company, this is less true in the case of vertical mergers, and still less true when it comes to conglomerate acquisitions.

Do Mergers and Acquisitions Tend to Be Profitable?

Different economists have different views as how successful mergers have been. This is due in part to considering effects on different constituencies of the corporation.

Ravenscraft and Scherer have examined profitability from the perspective of the acquiring firm and found the results to be on the dismal side.

> A sizable fraction of the acquisitions made during the 1960s and early 1970s were subsequently resold. Our best estimate within a high range of uncertainty is one-third [within ten years of acquisition].... Poor and declining profitability ... characteristically preceded sell-off.... Our case studies reveal that substantial efficiency increases occurred ... following divestiture (1987, pp. 190–191).... Our research indicates ... the failure to manage acquired companies as well as they were managed before acquisition. ...Merger-makers of the 1960s and 1970s suffered from massive hubris (p. 212).

In general, it appears that the managers who acquire a company fail in that they do not run it more efficiently and profitably than its previous managers.

Michael C. Jensen looks at takeovers from a rather different perspective. He finds that "the market for corporate control" benefits shareholders, society, and the corporate form of organization. The clearest beneficiaries are the shareholders of the firm which is sold:

The gains to selling firm shareholders from merger and acquisition activity in the ten-year period 1977–1986 total $346 billion (in 1986 dollars). The gain to buying firm shareholders ... will add another $50 billion to the total. These gains ... equal 51 percent of the total cash dividends (valued in 1986 dollars) paid to investors by the entire corporate sector in the past decade (1988, p. 21).

Strangely enough, Jensen's figures seems to reinforce the hubris hypothesis of Ravenscraft and Scherer. Merger-makers' incorrect belief that they could run target companies more profitably than their existing managements led to their purchases of firms at prices far above their current market value.

Forces Leading to Competitive Oligopolies

What are the forces which bring competition to an industry in which cooperation seemed the norm? There are three: (1) the entry of foreign oligopolists into the market, (2) technological progress which undermines the power of those in a field, and (3) deregulation which destroys important aspects of the culture of an industry.

General Motors, Ford, and Chrysler have been affected by foreign manufacturers, particularly those from Japan. The steel oligopolists have been badly perturbed by technology which allows the profitable production of steel in mini-mills using a scrap metal charge. Foreign competition has also eroded the stability brought to the industry by the formation of U.S. Steel a century ago. Long-distance telephone service, synonymous with AT&T for many decades, has been radically affected by microwave technology replacing hard wiring. Airline industry stability has been badly upset by deregulation. The stability of government guided price-setting has been replaced by competitive price-setting by the individual airlines. And low-cost airlines, unencumbered by desirable wage scales which were covered by government price-setting, have become a competitive force. Whereas airline rates were the same for all passengers in a given class of service, one can sometimes find on a given flight people who have paid over three times what others have paid for the same service.

Quasi-Oligopolies: Small Firms in Small Markets

Imperfect competition involves many, many firms which produce differentiated products. The best example is that of retail stores. In major metropolitan areas there are many banks, supermarkets, restaurants, dry cleaners, doctors, dentists, troublemakers, and so on. But what about a town which has a small number of retail establishments of the kinds alluded to above? With the number in a market being small, the firms tend to be rival conscious. These firms are oligopoly-like except for the fact that there is ease of entry into and exit out of the market—thus the name "quasi-oligopolies."

Consider more deeply the boundaries of a market. There may be hundreds and sometimes thousands of retail stores selling the same product in a metropolitan region such as New York City. But much shopping takes place in a given neighborhood in which there are only a small number of stores for various kinds of common products: a few groceries, a couple of bakeries, three green grocers, a few banks, a couple of hardware stores, two gas stations, two auto repair shops, and several restaurants with only one or two of a particular culinary type. Each knows the existence of rivals selling close substitutes and, I suspect, pays some attention to their activities. These very small firms are also quasi–oligopolies.

By the way, Adam Smith was well aware of the significance of the size of the market. His chapter "That the Division of Labour is Limited by the Size of the Market" indicates this. In a small market, he asserted, the country carpenter "is not only a carpenter, but a joiner, a cabinet maker, and even a carver in wood, as well as a wheelwright, a ploughwright, a cart and waggon maker" (1937, [1776], p. 17).

Summary on Oligopoly

Oligopolies are large firms which dominate an industry and are rival conscious. Some of our most important industries are dominated by oligopolies. Cournot's duopoly model is the oldest of those attempting to indicate the effect of a rival on the decision-making of a firm. Sweezy's kinked demand function, based upon the assumed reactions of rivals, helps to explain the tendency of oligopoly prices to be sticky—to respond slowly to changes in supply and demand. Game theoretic models attempt to add to our understanding of the strategic actions made in the context of expected responses and sometimes independent actions of rivals.

Concentration ratios are a measure of the extent of monopolization in a market. The traditional four largest firm measure has many imperfections, some of which are resolved by the Herfindahl-Hirschman concentration index.

Price leadership frequently evolves in lieu of price competition. Non-price competition is the norm in stable oligopolies. Their advantage is that some forms of non-price competition are difficult to emulate, some can be hidden from view, and none are as threatening as price competition.

Oligopolistic markets have barriers to entry. These arise from the economies of large-scale production, large financial start-up requirements, the need for special hard-to-get resources, and the requirement of special know-how. Technological advances have mixed effects on the development of this market form. Discoveries of value can, on the one hand, lead in the direction of monopolization and, on the other hand, allow for easier entry and an increase in competition.

Mergers and acquisitions have played an important historic role in converting more competitive into more monopolistic industries. In recent decades, they have frequently involved payments by an acquisitor substantially above the market value of the targeted firm. The reason for this is largely grounded in the conceit that the targeted firm can be more profitably run by the purchasing firm. In fact, acquired firms tend to be run less profitably than was the case before their acquisition—a manifestation of the winner's curse.

The forces leading to the conversion of monopolies and stable oligopolies to competitive oligopolies are foreign competition, technological advances, and deregulation. I suspect that one day competitive oligopolies will become stable but lack the slimmest idea of how long this will take.

Finally, small firms in small markets tend to be rival conscious. The markets they are in are oligopolistic in character except for the existence of ease of entry and exit.

Questions on Chapter 10

1. a. Explain what the monopolistic elements are with reference to the grocery store which is closest to your residence.
   b. Show how you can determine the size of a grocery bill which would justify patronizing a more distant store.

2. Assume that there are (i) two gasoline stations rather close together, (ii) each of which sells a major brand of gasoline, and (iii) one of them could sell the amount of gas currently sold by the two.
   a. Why are there two stations?
   b. What are the efficiency implications of the problem?

3. a. Draw a kinked demand curve seen by an oligopoly and explain why the kink is supposed to exist.
   b. Draw the marginal revenue function associated with the kinked demand curve. Explain the reason for the discontinuity and its supposed implication.

4. a. Why do oligopolies frequently prefer non-price to price competition?
   b. What are some of the forms of non-price competition in the car industry?
   c. Is "price leadership" consistent with the avoidance of price competition? Explain.

5. a. What is the logic of a firm acquiring another firm at a price substantially higher than that indicated by the value of its shares on the stock market?
   b. Acquisitions either produce the same kind of products as the buyer or they do not. Which kind of acquisition tends to be more successful? Explain.

6. Assume that there are two competitive oligopolists and they play a non-dominant strategy game in which going second is more profitable than going first. How might this evolve into a stable duopoly?

7. Name three industries that have been made more price competitive—one by foreign competition, one by technological progress, and one by deregulation. Discuss.

CHAPTER ELEVEN

Product Price Setting and the Economics of Advertising

Some product prices are set by markets; some are set by various government agencies; a relatively small number are set by powerful buyers; and far more are set by sellers. A main concern of this chapter is the common ways prices are set by sellers. A second but vital concern is with price behavior, the speed or slowness of the response of prices to shifts in demand and supply. If prices quickly respond to changes in supply and demand markets quickly equilibrate and price is the important allocator of resources. But if prices change only once a year, for example, markets may not quickly equilibrate and the role of price in allocating resources is terribly diminished.

In addition to determining product prices, many firms must decide the extent to which they will advertise and the economics of that decision is confronted in this chapter, as well.

Common Price-Setting Approaches

Price-setting approaches run the gamut from those which are demand-oriented to those which are supply or cost oriented. But approaches leaning toward demand must give consideration to supply and costs; those which lean toward the supply or cost side must also take some cognizance of the state of demand. Demand -oriented price setters must recognize that costs must be covered for a firm to continue its existence. Supply-cost-oriented decision-makers cannot blithely add up a set of costs to determine a price. Such a price could be high enough to make sales dangerously low.

Demand-oriented price-setting is examined first. That is followed by the more popular price-setting approach which emphasizes the supply or cost side.

Figure 11.1.   **Demand-Oriented Price-Setting at a Wholesale Fish Market**

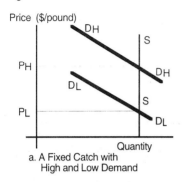
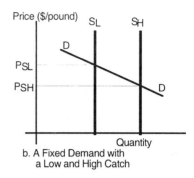

a. A Fixed Catch with
High and Low Demand

b. A Fixed Demand with
a Low and High Catch

Demand-Oriented Pricing

Demand-oriented pricing is found in a number of different settings: (1) Products or resources are fixed in supply. (2) The output of the production process is a set of joint products such as meat and hides. (3) Prices are discriminatory—based on differences in the demand of various groups. (4) Different prices are charged for different space in the same structure. (5) Strong consideration is given to the reaction of buyers to price and price changes. All of these conditions lead to changes in demand being the source of changes in price.

Price Setting with Fixed Supply

Our classical economic forebears saw land as a unique resource because it was fixed in supply. Alfred Marshall extended this to cover an unspecified set of products during the "market period," a period in which by definition the supply is fixed. He also recognized that structures and major forms of capital equipment were fixed in supply for considerable periods of time and called the returns they receive "quasi-rents." The supply of the work of deceased artists and artisans is fixed and this tends to be true as well of the number of stocks and bonds a firm has outstanding. Special talents tend to be fixed in supply.

New York City's Fulton Street wholesale fish market affords a good example of pricing with a fixed supply arriving near the outset of the day. Vendors must set their prices so that the catch of the market day is sold by that day's end. The supply of and demand for fish in this market is shown in frame *a* of Figure 11.1. With the demand thought to be relatively high, fish mongers would tend to set prices relatively high as at P_H. If the start of the day hunch was that it was relatively low, the price would be set at P_L. During the hours of the market day evidence of the actuality of demand would be found and the price adjusted so that the entire supply is sold by day's end. From the perspective of sellers, "sell it or smell it," becomes the pricing credo.

Figure 11.2.   **Ms. Jones's Home Supply Function**

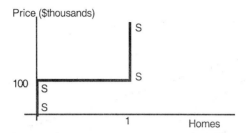

While the supply of fish is fixed for the market day, the catch of each day is different. On a good day for fishing the supply of fish tends to be relatively high. On a stormy day many ships may forego fishing and the catch would be relatively low. In frame b of Figure 11.1 the high catch, $S_H S_H$, leads sellers to set the initial price relatively low, P_{SH}; the high price of P_{SL} accompanies the low catch, $S_L S_L$. But as the actual demand manifests itself the price is adjusted to clear the market of the supply.

Not all products fixed in supply are sold at any attainable price. Owners looking to sell a Picasso or a home frequently set a minimum or reservation price for the item they would like to sell. But that minimum price is generally demand-oriented. Assume that Ms. Jones, the owner of a house, has in mind a minimum price at $100,000 for the sale of her home as can be seen in Figure 11.2. She probably set that minimum at or near the level buyers have paid for comparable homes in the recent past. Then, the highest bid at or over the reservation price would win the house. If, after a while such a bid is not received consideration may be given to lowering the reservation price. But whatever her course of action, the supply is fixed and demand is crucial in determination of the selling price.

Joint Product Pricing

Joint products are exemplified by the multiplicity of products obtained from livestock and refined crude oil. The butcher who buys a "side of beef" at one and the same time buys a variety of kinds of beef in fixed proportion—each of which requires a price. The refining of crude oil yields a large set of different products ranging from liquefied petroleum gases and gasolines of various octane levels to residual fuel oil and petroleum coke. The hundreds of products of a refinery require hundred of prices. Relative demand for each of the joint products as related to its supply is at the root of the price set.

Figure 11.3 should help in showing the price determination of two kinds of jointly produced beef—call them grade A and grade C. The three demand functions are for grade A meat, D_A, grade C meat, D_C, and the total demand, D_T. The quantity axis has three scales. The topmost is for the quantity of grade A

Figure 11.3.   **Profit-Maximizing Prices for Joint Products A and C**

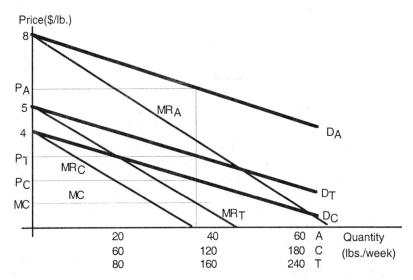

beef; the middle scale is for the quantity of grade C beef; the bottom scale is the sum of the weight of grade A and C beef demanded. All quantities are in pounds per week. If the butcher sells 40 pounds of A and 120 pounds of C beef, he would have to buy 160 pounds of beef (net of waste)—a demand derived from the demand for the two kinds of beef. Its demand price is the quantity weighted average of the two grades of beef demanded. Where P_C equals $4 and P_A equals $8, P_T equals $5. This arises from the lower grade of meat being weighted three times that of the higher grade.

The marginal cost of a pound of beef is the cost of an additional pound to the butcher plus his processing, inventory, and transaction costs. It is shown as constant. The intersection of the marginal cost function with the marginal revenue of total demand, MR_T, determines the profit-maximizing amount of meat which should be bought and sold. At that quantity, the demand prices of the two grades of meat are P_A and P_C.

Note that in Figure 11.3 the marginal revenue obtain from the sale of grade C beef at profit maximization is zero. Were the demand for it somewhat lower and the demand for grade A beef somewhat higher, the marginal revenue would be negative and profits would not be maximized. Heartless profit maximizers could solve this problem by increasing the price of grade C meat until its marginal revenue became zero. The unsold meat would be discarded.

The actual price-setting problem is even far messier than shown since the butcher gets a dozen or so different cuts of meat from a side of beef and that requires setting a dozen or so prices. Picture a butcher estimating the dozen demand functions, their marginal revenue functions, the total demand function, and so on. It is far easier to set all prices as some lesser or greater ratio of those of others and by experience to adjust the relative prices to clear the refrigerator of all of the cuts of meat. The butcher would buy the number of sides of beef which corresponds to the amount sold. Profit maximizers could move the whole set of prices up and down to determine the prices which would maximize profits.

Time of Day Pricing

Restaurants, motion picture theaters, telephone companies, and electrical power utilities frequently charge different prices at different times of the day. This is because their productive facilities are available for use during the relatively low and high demand periods of the day. With two different demand functions, the time of day pricing becomes quite the same as the price discrimination problem. It is a more profitable form of pricing than that which uses a single price. Time of day pricing also tends to even out the demand or loading of productive systems over the course of the day. This lowers the per unit cost of production in two ways. First of all, with lower peak loads, less capital equipment is required. Secondly, the more constant demand is over the course of a day, the greater is the time that equipment can be run at their most efficient rates—at their least cost rates per unit of production.

Let me cite an example to indicate the advantage of the efficiency gained by operation at a more stable demand. A modern generator of electricity with a capacity of 46 megawatts produces that power using only twice the fuel it requires to produce a single megawatt of power. Average fuel cost per megawatt at capacity is then one-twenty-third of that at minimal load. If the load is better equalized by time of day pricing, generators can be operated more of the time in the region of full capacity and low cost. By the way, the marginal cost to drive a generator is essentially constant from zero to full capacity load. Score one more for constant marginal cost.

An important attribute of products with time of day pricing is that they are not storable, in a practical sense. You cannot, for example, buy a cheaper evening telephone call and use it at some time at which the price is higher. Nor can cheaper electricity be practically stored. You can, of course, store electrical energy in batteries, but their is a fundamental rub: Batteries yield direct current while virtually all the power-hungry electrical devices we use operate on alternating current.

Spatial Price Differentials

Different prices are assigned to different locations in auditoriums, stadiums, digs in apartment houses, and rooms in hotels. The costs of production are the same for the differently located seats, apartments, and rooms of standard configuration in a given structure. The price differentials are responses to differences in demand. It is nicer to have a seat on the fifty-yard line at the Super Bowl rather than one which is almost out of the stadium.

Multiple Pricing Not Based on Cost

It costs as much to produce product X irrespective of who the buyer is. Nonetheless, discounts are sometimes offered to "senior citizens," children up to a specified age, and women on "ladies' night." But the most wonderful form of multiple pricing I know of, outside of higher education, can be found in the theater.

As can be seen in Table 11.1, there were nine different prices for a midweek orchestra ticket to the Broadway musical *She Loves Me*. The tickets which cost more than $65 are essentially $65 tickets marked up by commissions which go to the sellers. That aside, the spread of ticket prices is about four to one with tickets bought at the TKTS booth about half that of the box office price, while those obtained through a Theatre Development Fund mailing are half that of the TKTS booth price. One should not jump to the conclusion that this wide range of prices is irrational. That a set of two to one price ratios makes sense is shown below.

The following assumptions are made: (1) The producers are profit maximizers. (2) The demand for theater tickets is linear. (3) At the profit-maximizing price the theater has empty seats. (4) Two additional prices, lower than the single profit-maximizing price, are sufficient to obtain a capacity audience. (5) And the marginal cost of seating another warm body is negligible. The challenge is to show that the first lower price is half of that of the box office and that the second lower price is half of that.

The weekday demand for seats to *She Loves Me* is shown in Figure 11.4 as D_1D_1. Its price intercept is P_0. Since marginal cost is negligible, profit maximization takes place at the rate of production at which marginal revenue is zero and total revenue is at its maximum. This is midway on the demand function and the result is that the box office price, P_{BO}, equals 0.5 P_0.

Many seats are now unoccupied and revenues and profit will increase if tickets for them can be sold. We now face the residual demand curve D_2D_2 comprised of people who are willing to pay less than P_{BO} for seats. That residual could be shifted to the price axis or, less graphically messy, the price axis can be mentally shifted to it. The price axis intercept of D_2D_2 is 0.5 P_0. Profit is maximized for this residual demand midway on the function—at price P_{TKTS} equal to 0.25 P_0. The TKTS booth price is half of the box office price.

With seats still empty, a third profit-maximizing price warrants consideration. What remains of the original demand function is D_3D_3. Its price intercept is 0.25 P_0. Revenue and profit are maximized at the midpoint of this residual function giving us a revenue and profit-maximizing price, P_{TDF}, equal to 0.125

Table 11.1.   **Prices for an Orchestra Seat for the Broadway Musical *She Loves Me***

Wheelchair seating	$15.00
Theater Development Fund (TDF)	15.50
TKTS booth	35.00
"Twofers"	40.00
Group sales	58.50
Box office	65.00
Ticketmaster	72.50
Legal broker	up to 75.00
Illegal broker	up to 190.00

Source: New York Times, March 18, 1994, p. C1.

Figure 11.4.   **The Use of Multiple Prices to Maximize Profits**

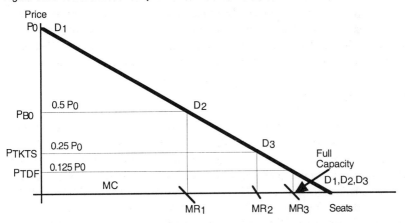

P_0. This TDF price is half that of the TKTS booth, and expediently with it in place all seats are occupied.

I have obviously slipped by a fundamental problem. Why would people pay the box office price when they might be able to get tickets at one-half and even one-quarter of that price? The important word in the question is *might.* There is substantial uncertainty about an individual being able to get discount tickets to a popular show and whether they are available at an opportune time. This uncertainty is eliminated by box office purchases.

Automobile Industry Pricing: From Demand to Cost Orientation

One of the most interesting areas of pricing can be found in the automobile industry–as reported by high officials in the industry. Illustrative of this is a running quotation from a speech by Ernest R. Breech, former chairman of the board of the Ford Motor Company:

> We start by estimating the quantities of our products customers will take at any one price or in any price class. Then, looking three years ahead, we design to that tentative price.... All the way through [the] process of designing, engineering, purchase and manufacturing to a cost pattern we have to arrive at some reasonable anticipated volume of sales. The term we used is 'Standard Volume,'... generally about 80% of capacity, calculated on a two-shift basis....The idea of standard volume is a useful one in price setting, for it is directly related to the profit we expect to average over a period. This 'standard return' is the rate required for the company to cover its risks, to meet its obligations, and to continue to grow soundly. Finally, this method of pricing assures the customer that he will not pay for idle plant facilities if standard volume is not realized (1961, pp. 81–82).

Breech's statement is fascinating in several respects: first, an estimate of demand three years from the present is made; second, three years are required to develop a set of new models; third, documentation of the two-shift tradition of the industry; fourth, the implication that average cost decreases with the rate of production; fifth, and final, the transition from demand to cost orientation.

Supply-Oriented Pricing

Supply-side pricing tends to be "cost plus" in character. By that I mean that the price set tends to be the estimated direct or variable cost *plus* some share of overhead or fixed costs. The most common form of cost plus pricing is in the markup pricing of retail stores. But cost plus is much more prevalent. Manufacturers, as seen in the auto industry, use this approach, and so do, for example, auto repair shops, lawyers, consultants, and college professors in setting a price on their grant proposals. This is not to say that there are no deviations from cost plus to respond to the realities of demand. That can be done by controlling constituent costs so that their addition yields a price not unattractive to buyers. More often, the overhead rate is reduced on a product with the result that it increased on other products.

Much of what follows is on the subject of markup pricing; some is on other forms of cost-oriented pricing.

Markup Pricing

Under markup pricing the seller sets the price, P, as the unit cost of the product, C, increased by the magnitude of the markup ratio, M:

$$(1) \qquad P = C (1 + M)$$

Generally, C is the average variable cost of the product and the markup is intended to cover fixed or overhead costs and profits. If average variable cost is

Figure 11.5.   **The Markup at Profit Maximization**

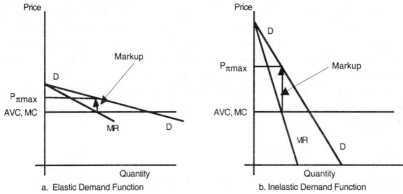

a. Elastic Demand Function   b. Inelastic Demand Function

constant as the rate of production and sales vary, C also equals marginal cost. Consider how markup pricing works:

Example 1:
Given (1): Cost of a watch to a retailer is $10. (2) The *markup ratio* is 75 percent.
Find: The retail price of the watch and the sellers markup.

$P = 10 (1 + 0.75) = \$17.50$
The seller's *markup*, the difference between cost and selling price, would then be $7.50.
Example 2:
Given: The cost is increased to $11.
Find: The selling price.

$P = 11 (1 + 0.75) = \$19.50$
Both the cost and price increased by 10 percent.

If equation (1) is solved for the markup ratio, M, it is found equal to the difference between the selling price and cost divided by cost.

(2) $M = (P - C)/C$

Note also that another method of formula pricing uses the *gross margin ratio*, G, which equals the difference between price and cost divided by price:

(3) $G = (P - C)/P$

Pricing by markup formulas is just about essential when sellers are required to set and change large numbers of prices. It is unrealistic to believe, for example, that a retailer could and does estimate demand, marginal revenue, and marginal cost functions for the hundreds and thousands of products she sells. Markup formula pricing is required.

Markup pricing is not inconsistent with profit maximization—but to make the connection the price setter has to know the elasticity of demand for every product she prices. That this is so can be seen in Figure 11.5 in which the demand function of frame a is more elastic than that of frame b. Marginal cost is constant and the same in both cases. The more inelastic the demand, the greater is the profit-maximizing markup. The profit-maximizing markup ratio can be shown to be a function of the price elasticity of demand, E.

The derivation of the relationship between the profit-maximizing markup ratio, $M_{\pi max}$, and the price elasticity of demand, E, starts with the definition of total revenue:

$$(4) \qquad TR = PQ$$

Marginal revenue is the slope or derivative of the total revenue function:

$$(5) \qquad MR = d(PQ)/dQ = P + QdP/dQ$$

Divide both sides by P:

$$(6) \qquad MR/P = 1 + 1/E \text{ or } P = MR/(1 + 1/E)$$

At profit-maximization MC equals MR, thus:

$$(7) \qquad P = MC/(1 - 1/E)$$

With average variable cost equal to marginal cost, the formula for markup pricing is:

$$(8) \qquad P = MC(1 + M)$$

Substitute for $(1 + M)$ in equation (8), $1/(1 - 1/E)$ in equation (7):

$$(9) \qquad (1 + M) = 1/(1 - 1/E) = E/(E - 1)$$

Subtract 1 from both sides and solve for M, the profit-maximizing markup is:

$$(10) \qquad M = 1/(E - 1)$$

Thus, we have the profit-maximizing markup as a function of the elasticity of demand. As a result, a seller who can crudely estimate the elasticity of demand, is able to crudely maximize profits.

Figure 11.6 is a plot of the profit-maximizing markup ratio as a function of the price elasticity of demand. If the elasticity of demand is –1.5, the markup ratio is 2. This can be seen in Figure 11.6 and by inserting this elasticity into equation (10). This would yield a price three times marginal cost. If the elasticity is

Figure 11.6.   **The Profit-Maximizing Markup Ratio as a Function of Demand Elasticity**

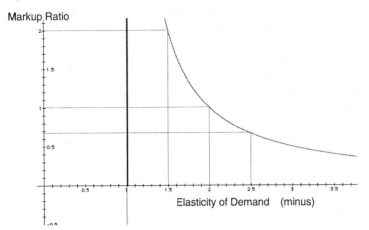

−1, the markup approaches infinity. Think why this is so—why at this elasticity marginal cost would have to be zero. Since it is not possible to maximize profits in the inelastic range, in which marginal revenue is negative, equation (10) cannot function in this range. This is not to say that firms cannot function in this range. They may have no alternative.

Full-Cost Pricing: The Research of Hall and Hitch

Full-cost pricing is pricing products on the basis of the average cost of production at the expected rate of production. The price is the sum of the average variable cost plus an estimate of the share of fixed cost to be charged to that product. A common and crude way of assigning fixed costs to a product is do it on the basis of its expected share of total revenue. A product which is expected to bring in 10 percent of total revenue in the coming year would be burdened with 10 percent of the total fixed cost. While I have put the costs in economic categories, business categories would have full-cost equal to direct cost plus a share of overhead costs. While average variable and direct costs are not the same, and so to with respect to fixed costs and overhead, both approaches should yield a price intended to equal average cost. In 1939, R.J. Hall and C.J. Hitch published a study in which they claimed that business sets prices on the basis of full-cost.

The supply-side contention created a furor in the ranks of economists who taught that price was either set by markets or monopolists.

Hall and Hitch based their findings on interviews of thirty-eight British businessmen plus broader discussions with others. The furor Hall and Hitch created among economists was unwarranted. Business school textbooks of the 1930s generally had price based on cost. Moreover, many knew that cost-oriented price-setting was common in the distributive trades, in wholesale and retail trade. And some knew it to be common in construction and manufacturing. For a while in the 1930s, it looked liked full-cost pricing might replace the marginally based pricing of the neoclassical paradigm.

A major issue confronted by Hall and Hitch was the extent to which variations in demand led to variations in price. Their main contention was that over the business cycle "there will be no tendency for [prices] to fall or rise more than the wage and material costs" (1939, p. 12). But Hall and Hitch did present some exceptions: "A few [businessmen] admitted that they might charge more than full-cost in periods of exceptionally high demand, and a greater number that they might charge less in periods of exceptionally depressed demand" (p. 19). Thus, the picture Hall and Hitch create is one in which price is largely based on costs and is not very responsive to shifts in demand—even large ones.

Machlup's Critique of Hall and Hitch

Fritz Machlup's successful defense of marginal analysis against full-cost pricing is largely predicated on his analysis that average cost pricing and the failure to increase price in response to increases in demand are manifestation of marginal analysis. To come to such conclusions requires quoting somewhat extensively from his article "Marginal Analysis and Empirical Research" (1946).

> ...A goodly portion of all business behavior may be non-rational, thoughtless, blindly repetitive, deliberately traditional, or motivated by extra-economic objectives (p. 520)....Maximization of salaries and bonuses to professional managers may constitute a standard of business conduct different from that implied in the customary marginal analysis of the firm (p. 528).
>
> Instead of giving a complete explanation of the "determination" of output, prices, and employment by the firm, the marginal analysis really intends to explain the effects which certain *changes* in conditions may have upon the action of the firm. What kind of changes may cause a firm to raise prices? to increase output? to reduce employment? (p. 521).
>
> If a firm were to regard a certain price change as a desirable step for the time being, but feared that a later reversal might be difficult or costly, it would weigh this anticipated future cost or loss against the short-run benefit. Anticipations of this sort ... are not exceptions to marginal analysis but are part and parcel of it (p. 524).

By now we have have gone full circle. Marginal analysis is concerned with change. The change in condition is an increase in demand. What is the consequential change by the firm according to marginal analysis which provides us with a positive-sloped supply function? The answer we have been taught is that the firm will increase its price. But Professor Machlup argues that this contention may be wrong. By considering future matters, the firm may decide not to increase price in response to an increase in demand—the contention of full-cost pricing. This does away with the value of and need for full-cost being used to describe much of business pricing.

If it is claimed that the neoclassical paradigm, in general, covers all possible responses to changes in conditions, it totally insulates itself from potential criticism. But it also suggests that there is not very much value to the analysis it provides about the responsiveness of economic actors and institutions to changes in supply and demand. This does not mean that the analysis is of no value. It does mean that its value is essentially the logical training it provides.

Heflebower's Critique of Full-Cost Pricing

A more measured critique of full-cost pricing can be found in Richard B. Heflebower's "Full Costs, Cost Changes, and Prices" (1955). At the outset Heflebower cites several American empirical studies which contend that price is set on the basis of average cost at some assumed rate of production and some notable economists who "would assign to full-cost a definite role in economic doctrine" (p. 362).

The Constancy of Marginal Cost

A major area of interest is how do costs vary with the rate of production and, particularly, how marginal cost varies with the rate of production. Heflebower sums up the evidence as follows:

> There is now considerable evidence to the effect that, in manufacturing operations at least, marginal costs do not vary for a fairly wide range of output rates. The area of flatness of marginal costs extends downward from the neighborhood of the output for which the plant was designed to as much as 30 percent below that point. That marginal costs are horizontal has been demonstrated almost without exception in statistical investigations of cost experience (p. 370).

Although it was known more than four decades ago that marginal cost was constant over the usual range of rates of production, textbook writers have remained loyal to the scarce "U"-shaped function.

Full-Cost Pricing Is Common

Heflebower informs us that full-cost pricing is practiced where firms have to set many prices:

> In a number of manufacturing industries and in the distributive [wholesale and retail] trades generally, the variety of items sold or the frequency of change of what is sold requires that many prices or output decisions be

made. Typically some kind of formula is adopted as a procedure in which part or all of direct cost ... constitutes a base upon which is superimposed a margin, usually in percentage form, to cover other costs and profit (p. 378).

Thus, we are provided with information indicating that full-cost pricing, rather than pricing based on marginal analysis, is common. The remaining issue is whether pricing is exclusively supply-cost-sided or is responsive to demand.

A Casual View of the Responsiveness of Price to Demand Shifts

Heflebower presents information on price changes which respond to demand changes in manufacturing and in some areas of retail trade.

The Case of Manufacturing

Two examples are given in which firms tend to charge less than the formula price in response to demand shifts. In both the price is cut. In one the price decrease is in anticipation of a large increase in demand, in the other, in response to a decrease in demand! In the first a firm cuts its price to obtain a large profitable contract. In the second, "in times of low demand, ... after-the-fact proof would show, I think, ... smaller markups on direct cost." My own view is that in the first case the price cut is due to an anticipated decrease in average cost as a result of the large increase in demand. In the second case the price decrease was, as stated, the result of the demand decrease. In this example the firm seems to be trying to limit the loss of sales and customers.

The Case of Retail Trade

For this case Heflebower presents an interesting set of data on *gross* margins in men's and boys' clothing stores, department stores, and large furniture stores. It is reproduced as Table 11.2 here. Note that I have added some data to Heflebower's: Calculated *changes* in the gross margin (shown in brackets), and data on the annual percentage change in real gross national products or real aggregate demand—for later use.

Full-cost pricing, supply-sided pricing, should not be responsive to changes in demand (except, perhaps, if the changes imply changes in full-cost). Heflebower states that the responsiveness to demand undermines the contention that "full-cost pricing" is only based on costs. This is demonstrated by the fact that in two of the three industry groups examined the gross margin fell in the recession of 1938 and that all increased in the 1938–1941 expansion—an expansion stimulated by the increased production of armaments supplied to our World War II allies fighting the Nazis. Heflebower could have done more with the data by making an empirical estimate of the responsiveness of price to changes in demand. If demand decreased by 1 percent, would price decrease by 10, by 1, by 0.1 percent, or by what?

My Estimate of the Responsiveness of Price to Changes in Demand

My estimate uses most of the data of Table 11.2. The 1937–1941 statistics on large furniture stores are flawed and have been omitted. (See note *d* of Heflebower's Table 1.) The model used is that the percentage change in gross margin is an increasing function of the percentage change in real gross national product (a proxy for changes in consumer demand) and a stochastic disturbance term:

(11) $\Delta GM/GM = a + b\ \Delta RGNP/RGNP + u$

where *GM* is the gross margin, *RGNP* is real *GNP, μ* is a stochastic disturbance term, and *a* and *b* are the parameters to be estimated. The model says that if demand changes by 1 percent, the gross markup ratio changes by *b* percent. An estimate of the magnitude of *b* is required. It was obtained from the following simple regression equation:

(12) $\Delta GM/GM = -0.7293 + 0.1994\ \Delta RGNP/RGNP$ Adjusted $R^2 = 0.2080$
$$(t = 2.2225)$$

Thus it is seen that if demand changes by 1 percent, the gross markup is estimated to change by 0.20 percent. Consider the effects of this on price.

Given: (1) $GM_1 = 0.355$ (the average in Table 11.2). (2)Demand increases by 1
        percent, GM by 0.2 percent.
Find: Percent increase in price.

$P_1 = C/(1 - GM_1) = C/(1 - 0.355) = 1.550C$
$GM_2 = 1.002GM_1 = 1.002 \cdot 0.355 = 0.3557GM_1$
$P_2 = C/(1 - .3557) = 1.552C;$ $P_2/P_1 = 1.552/1.550 = 1.0014$

A 1 percent increase in demand leads price to rise by 0.14 percent. Heflebower is correct, full-cost prices do respond to demand—but not by very much at all.
  Heflebower makes an interesting observation when he points out that different firms have different cost structures. As a result, in the case of price leadership, if the leader sets price at full-cost, followers cannot. His point is quite valid. It also suggests that if a price leader is a profit maximizer, followers are not.

Other Examples of Cost-Oriented Pricing

My car dealer's service department charges $72 per hour for the time a mechanic works on a job. The mechanic's pay, however, is a minor fraction of this figure.

Table 11.2. **Gross Margins of Selected Types of Retail Stores as a Percentage of Net Sales and Percentage Change in Margins and Real GNP, 1936-41 and 1947-51**

Year	Men's and Boys' Clothing Stores	Department Stores	Large Furniture Stores	RGNP Growth
		(all data are in percent)		
1936	37.0	36.5		
	[-2.2]	[-0.3]		5.3
1937	36.2	36.4	32.4	
	[-1.7]	[0.0]	[-12.0]	-5.0
1938	35.6	36.4	28.5	
	[3.1]	[1.4]	[0.3]	8.6
1939	36.7	36.9	28.6	
		[0.3]	[1.4]	8.5
1940		37.0	29.0	
		[3.2]	[9.7]	16.1
1941	37.3	38.2	31.8	
.				
.				
.				
1947		35.4	39.7	
		[0.5]	[-2.0]	4.5
1948		35.6	38.9	
		[-1.1]	[-1.0]	0.1
1949		35.2	38.5	
		[3.1]	[3.4]	9.6
1950		36.5	39.8	
		[-3.3]	[-2.2]	7.9
1951		35.3	38.9	

Sources: All gross margins are from Heflebower, Table 1, p. 384; percentage change in gross margins, calculated by me, are in brackets; changes in real GNP, in percent, are from *Historical Statistics of the United States,* September 1975.

The $72 is the mechanic's pay marked up to cover all other costs associated with servicing cars. The "hours" charged are not the actual clock hours spent on a tuneup, for example, but the "standard hours" it should take to perform the job according to the dealer or some external group. The result is a standard cost for each repair that the shop makes—the standard hours time $72 per hour plus the price of parts and lubricants.

In like fashion, the hundreds of dollars charged by prestigious law firms for an hour of legal work is not the wage of the attorney on the case. It is the attorney's wage marked up to cover non-billable hours and all the other costs of the law firm, calculated on a per hour basis.

Years ago, a substantial amount of the research and development contracts, awarded by our Defense Department, were on a "cost-plus" basis. There was and

Figure 11.7.   **The Price of Electricity as a Function of Monthly Consumption**

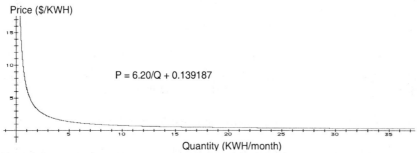

Price ($/KWH)

P = 6.20/Q + 0.139187

Quantity (KWH/month)

is great uncertainty about the costs which will be experienced in advancing the state-of-the-art of concern to the armed services. Moreover, contract specifications changed frequently during the course of a contract. These changes tended to be disruptive and costly. Thus, the case for "cost-plus." But in recent years, contracts are awarded on the basis of fixed-fee. Changing the form of the contract, however, does not change the uncertainty associated with advancing the state-of-the-art nor does it change the problem of meeting changing specifications. The result is negotiated changes to the fixed-fee—changes which reflect costs prudently incurred by the contractor. With negotiated changes, I suspect that fixed-fee contracts are not far removed from cost-plus.

The Price of Electrical Energy

The price structure set by public utilities under regulation is cost oriented. Regulatory agencies allow a price, actually an average revenue which covers costs including a fair rate of return on prudently invested capital. In other words the average revenue allowed is limited to average cost which includes the normal rate of return. The electrical energy bill I recently received (the check is in the mail) consisted of a "basic service charge" of $6.20 for a 30 day month plus a charge of 13.9187 cents per kilowatt hour (KWH) for each unit of energy used in the month. As a result the total bill, TB, is:

(13) $TB = 6.20 + 0.139187 \, Q$

where the units of Q are kilowatt hours per month. Seemingly the basic service charge is to cover fixed costs with the additional sum covering variable costs. The price for a kilowatt hour of electrical energy is obtained by dividing the total bill by the amount of energy consumed, Q:

(14) $P = 6.20/Q + 0.139187$

as shown in Figure 11.7. It is a rectangular hyperbola translated upward by

13.9187 cents per kilowatt hour.

Were no electricity used in a month, the price would approach infinity and the greater the usage, the lower the price which ultimately approaches 13.9187 cents.

The user of 50 KWH in a month pays 25.6 cents per kilowatt hour; the user of 200 KWH pays 16.3 cents per KWH. Thus, those who use electrical energy sparingly, the aged I suspect, pay a higher price than profligate users.

Cost-Based Pricing and the Negative-Sloped Supply Function

The empirical average cost function tends to be negative-sloping. This means that firms which have to or just want to cover their costs tend to charge more when demand is low and less when it is high. You need not go far to find this kind of price-setting. Private colleges and universities tend to have high fixed costs and constant marginal and average variable costs. The result is the common negative-sloping average cost function. Schools with limited reserves and borrowing power and those reluctant to use them have to or opt to cover average cost. Thus when enrollment drops, tuition tends to increase to cover the higher average cost. They are full-cost price-setters with the negative-sloping average cost function serving as their supply function.

Pricing with Negligible Consideration of Demand

Many entertainment events are underpriced from the perspective of supply and demand. Rationing is then done not only by price but by queues of enormous length. Some fans are in line to buy tickets days before they go on sale.

The extent to which price setters may have neglected demand is indicated by the following report of Peter Alfano:

> The face value of a Super Bowl ticket is $75, but agencies that legally deal in buying and selling tickets on the open market say that prices may go as high as $1,500 for a prime seat (1989, p. 1).

Note that I said "may have neglected demand." Charging what the traffic can bear may antagonize the fans who buy tickets during the regular season and those who watch games on television. This could be more costly than the loss of potential revenue due to under pricing. In addition, in all likelihood many seats would be empty at the profit-maximizing price and that might lead to a good deal of negative publicity and diminished demand.

Top rock stars, in like fashion, may knowingly set their concert prices below equilibrium so as not to jeopardize recording sales. They may also be allergic to empty seats, a sign of being "over the hill."

Price-Based Pricing

Many prices and price changes are based on other prices and price changes. The most important of these are the prices of followers based on the price or price changes of leaders—the former for standardized products, the latter for those which are differentiated.

In liability cases, lawyers frequently charge litigants one-third of the settlement award. Real estate brokers, agents of the seller, generally charge 6 percent of the selling price of a house. Salespeople working on commission receive a scheduled percentage of the price of the products they sell. Many architectural firms set their fees as a percent of the estimated cost of building a structure. The fees of interior decorators and designers are frequently a percentage of the prices paid by clients for various purchases. Long-term leases of commercial structures frequently have the level of rent geared to a rental price index. And some collective bargaining agreements include cost of living adjustments geared, more or less, to the consumer price index.

Price-Setting Strategies

The price-setting strategy of neoclassical theory is that under which profit is maximized. In more sophisticated neoclassical form, price is set to maximize the present value of the future stream of profits or the value of a firm. Price strategy is usually tied to wage strategy—with an interesting exception noted below. It is also related to cost strategy in general and to the utility functions of those who determine what strategies should be followed. Consider some examples of price strategy:

1. It was pointed out, in Chapter 8, that natural monopolies interested in maintaining their monopoly status should opt for average cost pricing. There would then be no incentive for another firm to attempt to wrest monopoly status from the existing monopolist. And very low prices are occasionally the strategy used by powerful firms to discipline firms charging "too little."

2. Henry Ford's price strategy was to drive the price of the Model T Touring Car as low as possible through the use of his production policy. The cost of production was to be minimized through the use of standardized parts, production of a standardized car and, rationalization of the process of assembling parts. In 1909 the price of a Ford was $920. By 1923 it had dropped to $290. But Ford's wage policy contradicted his price policy. In 1914, Ford made headlines by paying his production workers $5 for an eight-hour day. The hourly rate of $0.625 was almost three times the average of $0.22 per hour found in manufacturing at that time. Ford, in this complex of strategies was a wonderful example of a utility maximizer; surely not a profit maximizer.

There tends to be more leeway in the setting of the price of new rather than customary products—particularly if there are no good substitutes for the new product. Two new product pricing approaches at the extremes are given in the following two examples.

3. One new product price strategy charges high prices at the outset, ostensibly to quickly recover research and development costs. Price is then lowered over the course of time. This can be characterized as "skimming the market," taking advantage of the segment of the market relatively insensitive to price and then selling to those who can only afford to pay a lower price. Many new drugs have been very high priced at the outset with lower prices set over the course of time.

4. The second new product strategy is to set a low price at the very start to develop a large market for the product as quickly as possible. If large sales are attained, the firm may be able to dominate the market and to take advantage of economies of scale and declining average cost. DuPont used a low-price strategy when it developed cellophane, a product which dominated transparent packaging for many years.

In a sense, all of the examples of price strategy cited involve new products and markets. As a product and its market matures, the extent of price strategy narrows.

Sticky Prices

Supply functions are generally shown as positive sloped and demand functions as negative sloped. Changes in demand and supply tend to be shown as parallel shifts. Then, for example, if demand increases, price and quantity also increase. But it has already been shown that markup-based pricing may be very unresponsive to shifts in demand. And with functions drawn differently, a change in demand can result in a change in quantity alone. I will start with a model under which price is absolutely sticky as demand shifts. After that can be found some wonderful research on sticky prices by Alan S. Blinder of Princeton University.

A Constant Price Model

Recall the formula for the profit-maximizing price:

(15) $P_{\pi max} = MC/(1 + 1/E)$

If marginal cost is constant and demand shifts in such a way that the price elasticity of demand remains constant, the profit-maximizing price will be unchanged. Constant marginal cost is commonplace. But what kind of a shift will

Figure 11.8.   **A Demand Decrease Yielding the Same Profit-Maximizing Price**

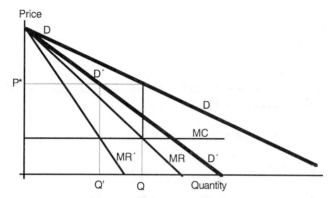

yield the same price elasticity of demand at a given price? That shift occurs if demand rotates around its original price intercept as shown in Figure 11.8—along with a constant marginal cost function.

The original demand function is *DD*. Its marginal revenue function is *MR*. It equals marginal cost at an output rate of *Q* and the resulting profit-maximizing price is *P**. Demand then decreases to *D'D'*—a function which has the same price axis intercept as *DD*. Its marginal revenue function, *MR'*, equals marginal cost at an output rate of *Q.'* And profit-maximizing price is again *P**.

Thus, it is theoretically possible for the profit-maximizing price to remain constant as demand shifts.

The Relationship of Marginal Cost Changes to Price Changes

Just how much should the profit-maximizing price increase if marginal cost increases by a given amount? To answer the question the relationship of the profit-maximizing price to marginal cost must be obtained. This is done for the case of the following linear demand function:

(16) $P = P_0 - mQ$

where, P_0 is the price intercept of the demand function and its slope is $-m$. The marginal revenue function has the same price intercept as the demand function and comes down at double its negative slope:

(17) $MR = P_0 - 2mQ$

At the profit-maximizing rate of production, Q^*, marginal cost equals marginal revenue. Thus,

(18)   MC = P_0 – 2mQ*

Solve equation (18) for Q. *

(19)   Q* = $(P_0$ – MC)/2m

To solve for the profit-maximizing price substitute Q* of equation (19) into the demand function, equation (16).

(20)   P* = P_0 – m [$(P_0$ – MC)/2m]

Simplify equation (20).

(21)   P* = $(P_0$ + MC) / 2 = $0.5P_0$ + 0.5MC

Take the first difference of equation (21) to show how the profit-maximizing price changes, ΔP*, with a given change in marginal cost, ΔMC.

(22) ΔP* = $0.5\Delta MC$

For a given change in marginal cost, the change in the profit-maximizing price is half as much—for a linear demand function.

Blinder and Associates' Empirical Work on Price Behavior

In March 1992, Princeton's Alan S. Blinder had completed an outstanding sur-vey of price behavior. Thereupon, he was called to serve on President Bill Clin-ton's Council of Economic Advisers and then as assistant chairman of the FED's Board of Governors. These responsibilities slowed progress on getting his work into press but with the help of three associates—Elie R. Canetti, Da-vid E. Lebow, and Jeremy R. Rudd—we now have *Asking About Prices: A New Approach to Understanding Price Stickiness* (1998). His study is based on a sample of firms which are representative of the private, nonfarm, for profit, un-regulated sector of the United States economy. This covers firms producing about 85 percent of the gross domestic product. His data were obtained through the use of a questionnaire survey. Princeton graduate students and some others read a battery of questions to price-setters, or those knowledgeable in their firm's price behavior, and coded their responses.

The Frequency of Price Changes

How often do the prices of your most important products change in a typical year? The answers to this question can be seen in Table 11.3. Firms producing

Table 11.3.   **The Frequency of Price Changes**

Frequency of Price Adjustment (times per year)	Firms (percent)	(cumulative percent)
Less than once	10.2	10.2
Once	39.2	49.4
1.01 to 2	15.6	65.1
2.01 to 4	12.9	78.0
4.01 to 12	7.5	85.5
12.01 to 52	4.3	89.8
52.01 to 365	8.6	98.4
More than 365	1.6	100.0

Source: Blinder et al., Table 4.11.

Table 11.4.   **Why Firms Do Not Change Prices More Frequently**

Reason	Firms	Percent
It would antagonize or cause difficulties for our customers	41	21
Competitive pressures	28	14
Costs of changing prices	28	14
Our costs do not change more often	27	14
Coordination failure, price followship	15	8
Explicit contracts fix prices	14	7
Custom or habit	11	6
Regulations	7	4
Implicit contract with regular customers	5	3
Miscellaneous other reasons	20	10
Total	196	100

Source: Blinder et al., Table 4.2, p. 85.
Notes: (1) The percentage calculations are mine. (2) The data represents 196 responses from 151 firms.

half of the private nonfarm output typically change their prices once a year or even less frequently. Firms producing over three-quarters of the national output change their prices quarterly or less frequently. But 10.6 percent of our national output is priced weekly or more frequently—a reflection of the high frequency ofprice changes in competitive markets.

Why the Low Frequency of Price Changes?

Blinder's team tried to determine the reasons for the low frequency of price changes by many firms. The responses and their frequencies can be found in

Table 11.4. Many different reasons were cited for not changing prices more frequently. The most common was that it would antagonize or cause difficulties for customers. Note the importance of regular customers to a firm—an irrelevancy in a true faceless market. Next in importance can be found three different reasons: competitive pressures, the cost of changing prices, and the stability of the cost of production. Of somewhat lesser importance to respondents are the failure of price leaders to change price more frequently, contracts with customers, and custom or habit.

 It should be noted that some of the reasons for not changing prices more frequently are somewhat related and that may be why some firms responded positively to more than one of the reasons. Competitive pressures and coordination failure seem to have a close kinship. And implicit contracts may be closely related to the desire to avoid causing difficulties for customers.

 There may be some reluctance to say that you change prices once a year because of custom or habit since this might be interpreted as a failure to analyze the basis for a very important business practice. But it seems that custom or habit is at the root of the common practice of changing wages once a year, which may be an important factor lurking behind the frequency of price changes.

More Hypotheses Regarding Stickiness

One of the most apparent generalizations regarding price behavior is that raw material prices are more flexible than the prices of finished goods. Other price stickiness generalizations or hypotheses are related to demand and supply factors and industry structure.

Demand Factors

Experience seems to point in these directions: (1) The price of durable goods appears to be stickier than the price of nondurables. As demand and the economy declines, consumers and producers lose interest in purchasing durable goods since they can often make additional use of those they already have. Price-setters seem to believe that price cuts would be unavailing. Durable goods which have experienced large price cuts have not experienced relative production stability. Large cuts in the price of building materials have not helped very much in increasing the sale of structures when demand for them is depressed. (2) The price of products subject to joint demand tends to be stickier than others. The products used in construction, for example, tend to have sticky prices. The cost o each material covers a very small portion of the total cost of building a structure so that variation in the cost of any one of them would have little, if any, effect on the price and quantity of buildings produced. (Structures are, of course, the quintessential durable good.) (3) The lower the availability of close substitutes the greater is the tendency toward price stickiness. (4) The price of luxuries, furs aside, tends to be stickier than the price of necessities.

Supply Factors

Several supply characteristics have been hypothesized as related to price stickiness. (1) The negative-sloped average cost function discourages price changes with demand. An increase in demand increases the profit per unit of production and the number of units sold. With profits increasing well there is little need for a price increase. If demand falls, the cost per unit increases and this discourages decreasing price. (2) The more quickly the rate of production can be changed, the greater is price stickiness: quantity changes obviate the need for price changes. Manufacturers can quickly change the rate of production and manufacturing prices tend to be sticky. An increase in demand brings forth more production, a decrease less production. But farmers cannot quickly change production and shortages and surpluses are equilibrated by increasing and decreasing prices. (3) Perishables tend to have more flexible prices as compared to products which can be stored.

The Structure of an Industry

A common claim is that the higher the concentration of production in an industry, the stickier are prices. On one hand, highly concentrated markets tend to have an established price leader and followers and this should solve the price change coordination problem—the fifth most important bar to price changes in Blinder's study. On the other hand, there seems to be little evidence supporting the industry concentration hypothesis independent of the product supply and demand characteristics mentioned above.

Summary on Price-Setting

Demand-oriented price-setting tends to take place in circumstances in which costs are unknown, irrelevant, or difficult to identify. The cost of producing land is unknown. The cost of a house thirty years ago is irrelevant to its current value. The cost of producing a sheep may be known but the cost of producing its coat, hide, and various cuts of meat are not—but they all require pricing. In these circumstances, demand-oriented pricing takes place. Demand is also frequently an important component of what becomes cost-based pricing. This occurs when a firm first considers what buyers are willing to pay for a product, then attempts to constrain costs so that when added up they are near that price, and finally bases price on those costs.

The circumstances leading to cost-based pricing are the large number of products which must be priced, the relative good knowledge of the cost of each of them, the belief that these costs should be covered, and relative poor knowledge of demand and its price elasticity. True believers in full-cost pricing contend that such prices are immune to demand changes. And Machlup claims that the failure of price to change as demand changes is consistent with marginal analysis. A demand increase implies a price increase—but it may or may not occur, depending on the price-setter's view of the future.

Critics argue that those who engage in markup or full-cost cost pricing actually respond to demand. A simple regression on data used by Heflebower indicates that markup pricing, in three industries, does respond to demand—but not by very much.

A change in demand, in theory, need not cause profit-maximizing price-setters to change price. This is the case if the elasticity of demand is the same for the original and the shifted demand function, at the original price. The change in price related to a change in marginal cost tends to be attenuated. For a linear demand function, the price change should be half that of a marginal cost change.

A debt is owed Blinder for his research on sticky prices. Blinder found that some firms vary the price of their most important product once every few years and that others varied it more than once a day. The representative firm, changes it once a year or less. The lower the frequency of price changes, the less is the importance of price in the allocation of resources.

Respondents to Blinder's survey indicated a number of reasons for their failure to change their prices more frequently. The most important was the desire not to antagonize customers or cause them difficulties. Closely ranked below this were competitive pressures, costs of changing prices, and a comparable frequency of cost changes.

Casual observation indicates that certain classes of goods have more flexible pricing than others. Raw material prices are more flexible than those of finished goods, nondurables more flexible than durables.

The Economics of Advertising

The firm's purpose in advertising is to increase the demand for its product. Then, at any given price more can be sold or at any given quantity a higher price can be charged—or some of both. The question addressed here is how much should be spent on advertising by a profit-maximizing firm? The answer, at first, seems to be merely a variant of the "golden rule of profit maximization": Keep spending until marginal cost equals marginal revenue.

Advertising spending is considered here like a factor of production in that it has a marginal product, the change in the quantity demanded per dollar of advertising spending. Two cases are presented. In the first, quantity is held constant and the increase in demand is manifest in an increase in the demand price. In the second, the price is held constant and the increased demand is used exclusively

Figure 11.9.   **The Advertising Production and Marginal Productivity Functions**

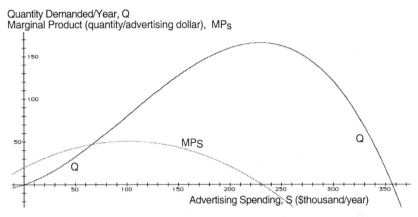

Quantity Demanded/Year, Q
Marginal Product (quantity/advertising dollar), MPₛ

to increase the quantity demanded. The final section questions the static analysis used. Studies of advertising indicate that it is cumulative in nature; its marginal productivity increases with time. As a result, spending on advertising should be thought of as a form of investment.

The Advertising Production Function

The advertising production function has quantity demanded as a function of advertising spending, both per unit of time. This is shown in Figure 11.9. Since quantity demanded is also a function of price the production function is $Q = f(P; S)$. The slope of the advertising production function, $\partial Q/\partial S$, is the marginal product of advertising—the change in the quantity demanded per dollar change in advertising spending.

The reason for the shape of the advertising production function follows. A small amount of spending will be largely unnoticed and will, therefore, do little to shift the demand function. As more is spent each additional dollar of spending has an increased effect on the quantity demanded. But as spending increases still more, a process of saturation starts to take place. The additional dollar per year of advertising becomes increasingly repetitive and tiresome and has a reduced impact on increasing the quantity demanded. This continues until the peak of the production function is reached. Finally, additional spending turns customers off so that the quantity demanded declines.

The marginal product of advertising spending is the slope of the advertising production function, the ratio of the change in the quantity demanded to the change in advertising spending. It reaches a peak where the magnitude of spending is such that the increasing slope ends and begins to decrease. Its zero value corresponds to the peak of the production function.

Profit Maximization with Quantity or Price Held Constant

From an incremental perspective, profit maximization takes place when the differential of total revenue, $d(PQ)$, equals the differential in total cost. With quantity held constant the differential of total revenue is QdP and the differential in total cost is dS. Assuming that at slightly lower rates of spending the differential of total revenue was greater than that of cost, the profit-maximizing condition is:

(23) $QdP = dS$

At profit maximization, the differential in total revenue just equals the differential in advertising spending.

  With price held constant, the differential in total revenue is PdQ and the differential in the cost of advertising, dS. In addition there is the differential cost of production, $MCdQ$, arising from the advertising created demand increase. Thus:

(24) $PdQ = dS + MCdQ$

Solve equation (24) for the differential in advertising spending:

(25) $dS = PdQ - MCdQ$

Profit is maximized when the differential in advertising spending equals the resulting differential in total revenue minus the differential cost of production arising from satisfying the increased demand for the product.

The Dorfman-Steiner Analysis

Robert Dorfman and Peter O. Steiner carried the above profit-maximization condition further in their paper "Optimal Advertising and Optimal Quality" (1954). (The inclusion of spending on quality arises from the fact that it can be analyzed in the same way as spending on advertising.) The analysis covers advertising-created demand taken as a price increase and then as an increase in quantity demanded.

Quantity Held Constant

Divide both sides of the profit-maximizing condition of (23) by $P \cdot dQ$,

(26) $(QdP)/(PdQ) = dS/(PdQ)$

Then invert both sides to get,

(27) $$(dQ \cdot P)/(Q \cdot dP) = P \cdot dQ/dS$$

The left side of the equation is the price elasticity of demand. The right side is the value of the marginal product of advertising spending, μ.

(28) $$E = \mu$$

Thus, with the increase in demand taken as an increase in price, the profit-maximizing condition occurs at the rate of spending, S, at which the value of the marginal product of advertising spending equals the price elasticity of demand.

Price Held Constant

With the price held constant the increase in demand arising from a differential increase in advertising spending is manifest in an increase in the quantity produced and sold. Again, at profit-maximization the differential in total revenue equals the differential in total cost. The latter is now the sum of the differential in advertising spending, dS, plus the differential cost of production, $MC \cdot dQ$:

(29) $$dTR = dTC, \text{ or}$$

(30) $$PdQ = dS + MCdQ$$

Solve for dS:

(31) $$dS = (P - MC)dQ$$

At profit maximization the differential of advertising spending equals the differential in total revenue, PdQ and the differential in total cost, $MCdQ$.

Finally, since the value of the marginal product of advertising spending, μ, equals $P \cdot dQ/dS$, equation (29) can be written as:

(32) $$\mu = P/(P - MC)$$

At profit maximization $MC = MR$ and the above equation then becomes:

(33) $$\mu = P/(P - MR)$$

The right side of the above equation can be shown as equal to the price elasticity of demand. Thus:

(34) $$\mu = E$$

The profit-maximizing condition is again the equality of the value of the marginal product of advertising spending and the price elasticity of demand.

The Problem of the Duration of a Firm's Advertising

The problem with the above marginal revenue–marginal cost based analysis is that it is static. It fails to recognize that the advertising production function is dynamic. The effect on demand of a given rate of advertising spending tends to increase over the course of roughly seven to ten years. Advertising spending, consequently, is a form of investment spending. As a result, present value calculations should be used in determining its rate of return. It is this rate of return, suitably adjusted for risk and uncertainty, which should determine whether or not the investment is expected to be profitable.

  Do firms which advertise actually make calculations of the marginal product of advertising and the price elasticity of demand, calculations which appear both difficult and suspect over the course of time? What is known is that in some industries a good deal of advertising takes place, while in others there is very little. These are manifestations of the culture of an industry. If its rivals advertise, firm feels compelled to advertise, as well. My guess is that advertising budgets—as the Cournot model—are related to the firm's perception of the previous year's advertising spending of its principal rivals.

An Aside on the Economics of Quality

Spending on the quality of a product, X, can be handled in much the same way as spending on advertising has been handled. Here the quantity demanded is a function of the price of the product and spending on its quality: $Q = f(P; X)$. The marginal product of spending on quality is dQ/dX.

  For the quantity-held-constant case, profit is maximized when:

(35) $QdP = dX$

For the price-held-constant case, the profit-maximizing condition is:

(36) $PdQ = dX + MCdQ$.

As can be seen in the case of quality improvement, advertising spending and the associated analysis can be used as a metaphor for all sorts of spending intended to increase the demand for a firm's product.

A Brief Critique of Advertising

Does spending on advertising represent an efficient allocation of resources? The answer to the question is quite different to sellers as opposed to buyers. Sellers, as discussed above, are interested in shifting demand. The interest of buyers in advertising is quite different. They would like factual information on quality and price. They do not want misinformation nor do they want the same information, the same commercial, presented over, and over, and over again.

Much advertising is valuable to consumers. The weekly ads of supermarkets are helpful in informing them of the prices of products which interest them. Ads on homes and apartments for sale and rent are helpful to those seeking living space. Bona fide ads on job vacancies can be terribly important to unemployed and some employed workers.

But much of advertising seems to involve zero-sum games. The more of brand X toothpaste purchased, the less of brand Y toothpaste purchased. And the more brand X advertises, to increase its market share, the more brand Y is prone to advertise, to protect its market share. If an advertisement does not add to the knowledge of consumers, it represents a waste of resources. And this is true of the advertisements of many branded products.

I am of the opinion that, on an overall basis, the advertising of consumer goods represents a substantial overallocation of resources.

An area of advertising which appears to be of substantial social value is advertising to producers. Medical practitioners become aware of the curative power of new drugs and their undesirable effects through the marketing of the producers. Office and production managers learn of better ways of tying their computers or work stations together by the ads of producers of networking equipment. Shop managers become aware of the availability of equipment advances and so forth.

Summary on the Economics of Advertising

Optimal advertising spending can be analytically determined for the case in which price is held constant and that for which quantity is held constant. Both can be specified by formulations in which differential revenue equals the differential in costs. Dorfman and Steiner carry this further and show that in both cases the equilibrium condition occurs when the absolute value of the price elasticity of demand equals the value of the marginal product of advertising spending. They also show that advertising spending can be considered as a metaphor for all types of spending intended to increase the demand for the product of the firm doing the spending

Unfortunately, the analysis, based on differential revenue and cost, fails to take into consideration the fact that the effect of a given rate of advertising spending on demand varies with time. This makes advertising spending an investment deserving the same rate of return consideration as other investments.

Does advertising spending represent an efficient allocation of resources? This seems to be more the case in producer, labor, and housing markets than in markets for consumer products.

Questions on Chapter 11

1. Explain the idea of demand-side pricing. Give examples.

2. Explain the idea of supply-side pricing. Give examples.

3. a. The price of almost all consumer goods are markup prices. Why?
   b. Write the markup price formula and define the variables.
   c. What is the markup intended to cover?

4. Blinder's research indicates that product prices are changed, on the average, once a year or less frequently. What are some of the more common reasons for prices being sticky?

5. What are some of the factors which lead to sticky prices on (a) the demand side and (b) on the supply-side?

6. What are the implications to the allocation of resources of price changing once a year on the average?

7. About 10 percent of prices change weekly or more frequently.
   a. What should be the effect of this on the value of the marginal product of labor—on the wage rate?
   b. Assume that the wages of a worker are set once a year. How might she be affected by a product price which continually varies?

8. a. Present the marginal condition for profit-maximizing advertising spending or the following two cases: (i) Quantity is held constant. (ii) Price is held constant.
   b. Explain why the assumption of a static marginal productivity function is wrong.

CHAPTER TWELVE

The Labor Market: Supply and Demand

The labor market is the most important of all factor markets. Producers spend more on labor services than on everything else combined. On the other side of the coin, more income is derived from the sale of labor services than from all other sources combined. Adam Smith and his followers, in effect, started their models of the supply of labor from models of population or fertility, the most famous of which is arguably credited to the Reverend Thomas Robert Malthus. Fertility and population models are fun to play with and I will start there. As time goes on the new born reach working age and decide the extent to which the hours of their lives will be devoted to marketed work. This is the source of the basic inflow into the existing stock of labor. The most important outflow is retirees. Given the natural resources, technology, and fixed capital available to the economy, the labor supply is crucial in determining the magnitude of its production. But it is not merely the number in the supply which counts; it is the number of them who are *employed,* the *hours* they work, their *skill,* and the level of their *effort.*

The abstraction of the aggregate supply becomes more concrete as incentives draw workers from this supply to smaller constituencies: the supply to regions, industries, occupations, and firms. Generally, the smaller the supply going to a user, the greater is the wage elasticities of supply. Thus, while the overall supply of labor has close to zero elasticity, the supply to the firm in the competitive labor market is infinitely elastic. Atomistic firms can employ as many workers as they want without raising the price paid for labor services.

The demand for the factors of production is derived from the demand for products. The neoclassical model of factor demand is based on the marginal productivity of each particular factor of production. Product price or marginal revenue is used to transform demand from product to dollar terms. Much information about production functions and marginal productivity was presented in Chapter 5. Some of that presentation will be reinforced and critically viewed here.

It would be nice to say that the overall supply and demand functions equilibrate and, as a result, yield the average wage rate and the amount of employment in the economy. But the matter is more complex than that. In the presence of equilibrium there should be zero unemployment. But there is always some and sometimes large amounts of unemployment and other forms of disequilibrium. Unemployment is generally assumed to be non-existent in microeconomics texts but this aspect of the labor market is too important, sometimes too tragic, to ignore. Labor market equilibria and disequilibria are covered in the following chapter.

Population and Fertility Models

The models presented are those of Adam Smith, Thomas Robert Malthus, Gary S. Becker, Harvey Leibenstein, and that of demographers—the theory of demographic transition.

Adam Smith's Model

Here is my favorite population model from my favorite economist:

> If this demand [for labor] is continually increasing, the reward of labour must necessarily encourage ... the marriage and multiplication of labourers, as may enable them to supply that continually increasing demand by a continually increasing population.... The demand for men, like that for any other commodity, necessarily regulates the production of men; quickens it when it goes on too slowly, and stops it when it advances too fast. It is this demand which regulates and determines the state of propagation in all the different countries of the world (1937 [1776], p. 80).

The substantial decrease in the birth rate during the Great Depression conforms to Smith's model. In the case of the poor, Smith seems to anticipate the population model of his follower, Thomas Robert Malthus:

> Every species of animals multiplies in proportion to their means of subsistence, and no species can ever multiply beyond it. But in civilized society it is only among the inferior ranks of people that the scantiness of subsistence can set limits to the further multiplication of the human species; and it can do so in no other way than by destroying a great part of the children which their fruitful marriages produce (1937 [1776], p. 79).

What we have is inadequate demand for the skills of the poor, unemployment and low wages, inadequate sustenance, and a high infant and child mortality rate. Does this sound familiar?

The Malthusian Theory of Population

The first edition of the population model of the Reverend Thomas Robert Malthus was published in 1798 with the informative title, *"An Essay on the*

Principle of Population, as it Affects the Future Improvement of Society: with Remarks on the Speculations of Mr. Godwin, M. Condorcet, and Other Writers." Malthus's 1798 book was a political tract. It opposed the arguments of Godwin and Condorcet who supported the proposal of England's prime minister, William Pitt, that the dole, welfare payments doled out to the poor, be increased. The essence of Malthus's model can be found in the following statement:

> Taking the whole of the earth ... and supposing the present population equal to a thousand millions, the human species would increase as the numbers, 1, 2, 4, 8, 16, 32, 64, 128, 256; and the subsistence as 1, 2, 3, 4, 5, 6, 7, 8, 9. In two centuries the population would be to the means of subsistence as 256 to 9 (1926 [1798], p. 21).

Of course, population could not expand by a factor of 256 if the food supply grew by only a factor of 9. Malnutrition, starvation, and high infant mortality would keep the growth in numbers of those who are poor within the limits posed by the supply of food they could command.

Malthus believed that the more welfare given the poor, the more of their children would live, with the standard of living remaining at the subsistence level. He was not only opposed to the improvement in the poor law proposed by Pitt but opposed the very existence of such a law. His view was that if a man could not support his children they must starve. Here was a clergyman neither overly concerned with charity nor the biblical imperative to "be fruitful and multiply."

I have previously pointed out that Malthus's model was essentially that of Adam Smith. Karl Marx, who seemed to hate the cleric-turned-economist, deemed Malthus's model a form of plagiarism:

> This work in its first form is nothing more than a school boyish, superficial plagiary of De Foe, Sir James Steuart, Townsend, Franklin, &c., and does not contain a single sentence thought out by himself (1906 [1867], p. 675).

Beyond Marx though, Malthus's model had a terrible forecasting record. Instead of the misery caused by excessive births as compared to the food supply, the living standards of workers improved during the years, decades, and centuries following the essay.

Interest in the model reflects our concern for history, the history of economic thought, and classical economic analysis in which it played a crucial role.

Becker's Fertility Model

Nobel Laureate Gary S. Becker's model can be found in his article "An Economic Model of Fertility" (1960). Becker points out that with the growth in knowledge and the availability of contraceptive devices, people are now reasonably able to determine the size of their families.

What economic variables are relevant to the family-size decision? Becker states that children can be considered, in effect, as a durable producer good or a durable consumer good. Producer goods represent an investment intended to yield net returns over the course of time. Investing in large numbers of children in poor agrarian societies should yield some who will assist in agrarian work and at least one who will shoulder the responsibility for the care and feeding of parents in their post-productive years. Since the costs of raising a child in recent times exceeds the returns, Becker categorizes them as consumer durables and likens them to cars, houses, and refrigerators.

Becker's fertility-related hypothesis is this: "an increase in income should increase both the quantity and quality of children, but the quantity elasticity should be small compared to the quality" (p. 212). By elasticity, Becker means income elasticity. The word "quality" is defined as being more expensive and has no judgmental connotation. Just as the quality of a car is measured by its relative price, the quality of a child is measured by the relative amount of money spent on it. Of course, the relatively rich do spend more on their children than the relatively poor.

The real rub is Becker's contention that the higher the income level, the greater the demand for children. Many would rightly hypothesize just the opposite: that the rich get richer and the poor get babies—an aphorism supported by the facts. Then, how does Becker maintain his children as consumer durables hypothesis? He does this by claiming that there is a good deal of general evidence that contraceptive knowledge is positively related to income and through the use of data on two small groups. One survey showed that richer people desire larger families than poorer people. Another was a survey on the family size of a group which graduated from Yale in the same years. Becker assumes that their knowledge of contraception is unrelated to income. The data showed that higher-income graduates had more children than those with lower incomes.

Becker finds that birth rates diminish in recessions and increase in prosperous times, matters which accord with his income-oriented model. Note, however, that as our society has gotten richer over the course of our history, the birth rate has declined. This seems to contradict Becker's model—at least during that part of our history in which children could no longer be thought of as investments.

Leibenstein's Fertility Model

Harvey Leibenstein's fertility model appeared in his "An Interpretation of the Economic Theory of Fertility" (1974). In it he criticizes Becker's model and then presents his own.

Leibenstein argues that Becker failed to explain two of the most important aspects of variations in family size: the tendency of higher-income families to have fewer children than lower-income families and the tendency, over the course of time, for the birth rate to fall as family income increases. Leibenstein contends that higher-income people do not want more children than those with lower incomes. Survey data he provides shows that both rich and poor want just about the same number of children. This contradicts information used by Becker.

Leibenstein also argues that the children of higher-income parents are not more costly than those of lower-income parents. He bases this on the opportunity cost of child rearing, finding that higher-income mothers have a greater propensity to work than those with lower incomes. This is not completely persuasive because Leibenstein fails to consider the direct spending on behalf of children. Richer families spend more for their children on food, clothing, toys, and education. I suspect that adding the present value of such costs to the opportunity cost of child rearing would make a child of the rich substantially more expensive than a child of the poor.

Leibenstein starts his competing model with this conundrum:

> In general, if we choose socioeconomic groups, such as occupational groupings ... we find that the empirical evidence supports the generalization that the higher the income level of the group (except for extreme groups) the fewer the average number of children per family, but *within* such groups, the reverse holds (p. 474).

This moves him into explaining both somewhat contradictory phenomena.

A key assumption of Leibenstein's model is that each household is a member of a *social influence group:*

> A social influence group, *SIG,* consists of a group of households so interrelated that the group influences the target living standards and family size of its members (p. 472).

A social influence group is similar to a socioeconomic group except that it is more closely knit and more influential in the setting of norms.

If the individual family tends to conform to the norms of the social influence group, why do higher-income families in the group have more children than those with lower-income? The reason, as Leibenstein explains it, is that the group has many norms—such as a house in the suburbs, two cars, tickets to the local concert series, membership in the pool club, three children all of whom should be college educated, and so on. The lower the income of the family in the group, the harder it is to meet all of the norms. A possible consequence is having fewer children than the norm. Note the wonderful similarity between Becker's and Leibenstein's models. In both higher-income families tend to have more children and of higher "quality"—but for Becker this happens in general while for Leibenstein it happens only within a social influence group.

The really difficult analytical chore is to explain why households in higher-income SIG's tend to have smaller families than those in lower-income groups. Leibenstein's complex argument comes to this. The higher the income level of a SIG, the greater is the need for its members to display their status. This occurs through what Thorstein Veblen called "conspicuous consumption" as displayed by each family member. This "upward drift in commitments" is costly and allows less income to be available for the large expense of having as many children as is the norm in lower-income groups. The explanation may be quite correct but I cannot help being uncomfortable with the idea that the relatively rich are less able than the relatively poor to afford more children.

The Theory of Demographic Transition

In the long interregnum between Malthus and Becker, population models were left in the hands of demographers—people who specialize in the subject of population, its growth, migration patterns, and distributional changes. Here, thanks to Leibenstein, is their theory of demographic transition.

The Transition theory has three historic periods with different fertility propensities: In the first stage life is primitive and death rates are high. The very survival of a society requires the maintenance of a very high birth rate. Be fruitful or perish. In the second stage there is an advance in hygienic techniques and nutritional levels, generally concomitant with technological progress. This reduces the mortality rate, particularly of infants, and this, in conjunction with a high birth rate, leads to population growth. In the third stage there is a decline in the desired and actual fertility rates both in the absence and presence of advances in contraceptive technology.

This is a wonderful expansive view of what might be called population history. Why is there a decline in the fertility rates in the third stage—in our current stage? Demographers cite the following behavioral determinants: (1) The rise in the education of women and associated changes in their goals. (2) The increased participation of women in the non-agricultural workforce. (3) The reduction of infant mortality. (4) A decline in the power of traditional religious fertility norms. (5) Urbanization and its secularizing tendency. (6) The rise in compulsory education and the decline in child labor. (7) The advance of women's rights. (8) The development of retirement income programs. (9) The development of medical care programs. (10) An increase in socioeconomic mobility. (11) And finally, the development of improved contraceptives. All of these factors are rich in economic as well as anti-fertility content.

Population and the Labor Force: Stocks and Flows

Stock-flow analysis is an important device in many circumstances. It can be used to account for and predict or project changes in population, population in a state, school age population in a city or a school district, the size of any inventory from gold to garbage, the number of people in the labor force, and much more. What is common to all of these items is that they are stocks at a given point in time increased over the course of time by inflows, and decreased by outflows. Take the case of population. The size of the population, or stock of people, at the end of 1997, POP_{E97}, equals the stock at the end of 1996, POP_{E96}, plus the flows into, $in97$, and minus the flows out of the stock, $out97$.

(1) $$POP_{E97} = POP_{E96} + in97 - out97$$

The stock-flow approach has broad application in relating a current to a past inventory, stock, or population.

Population Inflows and Outflows

The inflows into the population are births and immigrants; the outflows are deaths and emigrants. The corresponding stock-flow diagram is shown in Figure 12.1. Interestingly enough, friends in systems engineering call the stock-flow approach birth-death analysis. Some flows are more important than others and, as a result, warrant more attention and special model building. If the flows are constant the population will be either increasing, staying constant, or decreasing at a constant rate. Even in this tame sort of situation crucial changes may be indicated by the analysis. Assume that births and deaths are the important flowsand that both births and deaths have declined substantially as compared to recent times. With a decline in the inflow of births, the population will be aging, and with a decline in the outflow of deaths it will be aging still more. An aging population causes a number of important social problems including: (1) a decline in the labor force participation of the population, (2) a decrease in production per capita and the standard of living, (3) and, the need to allocate more resources to activities required and wanted by the aged including hospitals, medical services, nursing home, and home health care services. And to the extent that government provides retirement and health services to the aged, these systems will be strained. If key inflows or outflows are variable, as is the case with births and deaths, appropriate models are useful.

Labor Force Inflows and Outflows

Just as the population of a state is a subset of the population of the nation, the labor supply is a subset of the nation's population. The subset is largely composed of those in the population with roughly the following characteristics: (1) membership in the 16–65 age group, (2) with completed full-time schooling, (3) not disabled, (4) and not institutionalized. The same stock-flow approach can be used with respect to variations in the overall supply or stock of labor. The

Figure 12.1.   **Population Stock and Flows**

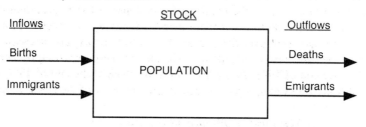

$$\text{POPULATION}_{12/31/00} = \text{POPULATION}_{12/31/99} + \text{Inflows}_{1999} - \text{Outflows}_{1999}$$

Figure 12.2.   **The Stock of the Labor Supply and Its Inflows and Outflows**

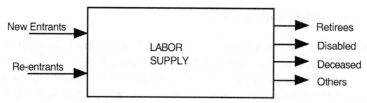

names of the in and outflows are just somewhat different as shown in Figure 12.2.

The flows into the labor force as shown are new entrants and re-entrants—the latter being people who had been in the labor force, left it as "others" and return to it. The outflows from the stock are those who retire, are disabled, die, and others who leave the labor force for a variety of other reasons.

Production for the entire population comes from those in the labor force who are employed, working with the other factors of production. In 1950, 41.6 percent of the population was in the labor force; in 1990 the percentage was 50.6 —a 21.6 percent increase in the ratio. The dramatic increase comes largely from the secular increase in the propensity of women to enter the labor force. Women's liberation has allowed them to do much of the work of the household and to do marketed work, as well.

Estimating the Future Size of the Labor Force

In the mid-1970s, Robert J. Lampman, a distinguished member of the University of Wisconsin's faculty, predicted that early in the twenty-first century there would be problems in funding social security retirement benefits and medicare health benefits. He apparently did this through a stock-flow analysis which recognized the importance of the baby boom of the 1950s and 1960s and the subsequent baby bust. Allow such an analysis with a simple example.

Assume that there is a primitive society with the following attributes: (1) at the age of 12 males begin working alongside of older males; (2) males work until they die or reach 70 years of age; (3) and, the population and mortality rate is known for each year of age. The problem is to determine for each of the next 12 years the number of males in the workforce.

By virtue of knowing the number of males age 12 through 69 we know the size of the labor force on December 31, 1997. To estimate the size of the labor force on December 31, 1998, we have to estimate the 1998 inflows and out-flows. The inflow is the number of males who are 11 on December 31, 1997, minus the number of them expected to die in the course of 1998. The outflow is the expected death for those in the labor force between the ages of 12 through 68 plus all of those who are age 69 on December 31, 1997. Subtracting the outflow from the inflow and adding it to the size of the labor force on December 31, 1997 yields the size of the labor force on December 31, 1998.

The size of the labor force on December 31, 1999, is estimated the same way. The inflow is the number who are 10 years of age on December 31, 1997, minus those expected to die during the course of 1998 and 1999. The 1999 outflow is the number of deaths expected among those who on December 31, 1998, were 12 through 68 plus all of those who were age 69—according to our calculation. Adding the net inflow to the population of December 31, 1998 yields the end of 1999 population

This accounting can be carried on for 12 years since we know the number of males born in 1997 and with our mortality statistics we can estimate the number of them who will be entering the workforce 12 years later. And we can estimate even further into the future if the birthrate is stable or if it shows a clear trend.

Return to the United States for a brief impressionistic view of what can be called the social security problem. During the 1950s and 1960s the birthrate was unusually high. Thereafter it was on the low side. The baby boomers will be re-tiring in the 2015–2035 period, and as a result there will then be an unusually large number of retirees on social security. But because post-1960s birthrates were low, there will be a relatively small number of workers contributing to the support of this relatively large number of retirees. Even more fundamental is the expectation that a relatively small workforce will be producing for a relatively large non-working population.

The Work-Leisure Decision

Individuals anticipating work are supposed to decide on the number of hours per unit of time they want to work: the work-leisure decision. The hours of work decision is influenced by the wage rate the individual can obtain and his attitude toward work. At a given wage rate, workaholics would be prone to work more hours per week, for example, than those who are somewhat allergic to such an activity. *Leisure,* by the way, encompasses all non-work hours. A person choos-ing to work 40 hours per week at the same time chooses 128 hours of leisure per week.

Figure 12.3.   **The Hours of Work Decision via Marginal Utility Analysis**

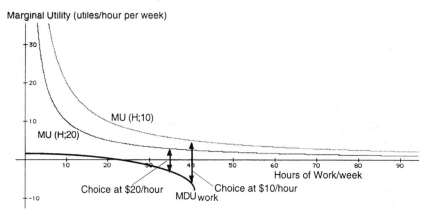

Marginal Utility (utiles/hour per week)

Marginal Utility and the Hours of Work

The use of marginal utility analysis to determine the hours a person would work is the 1871 discovery of William Stanley Jevons. Jevons applied a transformed version of what is now called the law of diminishing marginal utility to the problem of the choice of hours of work. Marginal utility is a function of the rate of consumption and the law of diminishing marginal utility postulates the decline of marginal utility with the rate of consumption. Jevons transformed marginal utility from being a function of the rate of consumption to being a function of the hours of work per unit of time. The more hours worked, the higher is income and the rate of consumption, and the lower is marginal utility. This declining marginal utility function, $MU(H; 10)$, is shown in Figure 12.3. The symbols in parentheses indicates that marginal utility is in this example a function of hours, H, hours per week of work, and that the assumed wage rate is $10 per hour.

To this marginal utility function, Jevons added the concept of what is now called the marginal disutility of work. Jevons called it "the degree of painfulness" of labour." He put the matter this way:

> Experience shows that as labour is prolonged the effort becomes as a general rule more and more painful. A few hours of work may be considered agreeable rather than otherwise; but so soon as the overflowing energy of the body is drained off, it becomes irksome to remain at work. As exhaustion approaches, continued effort becomes more and more intolerable (1970 [1871], p.190).

Jevons's marginal disutility of work function, MDU_W, also appears in Figure 12.3. As the figure is expediently drawn, until 40 hours of work a week, the marginal utility obtained from the marginal unit of work, at a wage of $10 per hour, exceeded the marginal disutility of work. This made it sensible to work more hours. At 40 hours per week marginal utility and disutility are equal and the satisfaction obtained from work is maximized. Assuming that this worker sets the amount of hours he will work, it would be 40 hours a week.

Increase the Wages Rate and the Hours Decrease

The above example assumes that the wage rate is constant at $10 per hour. What happens if it increases? For simplicity assume that pay is increased from $10 to $20 per hour. What happens is also shown in Figure 12.3. In going from a wage of $10 to $20 per hour, all magnitudes of income and marginal utility are reached in half the hours shown in the original marginal utility function, $MU(H;10)$. The resulting marginal utility function is $MU(H;20)$. There is no change in the marginal disutility of work function. This assumes that pay has no effect on the pain or pleasure intrinsic to work itself. As is shown, at the higher wage, workers prefer to labor fewer hours per week—instead of choosing to work 40 hours a week, 36 hours of work per week maximize utility and that is the worker's choice. The generalization obtained from the marginal utility approach is that the higher the (real) wage, the fewer the hours people will choose to work. What a wonderful irony: The incentive to work is the pay we receive—but the higher it is, the fewer the hours we are willing to work.

Increase Taxes and Working Hours Increase

An interesting aspect of the marginal utility approach is that an increase in the tax on earnings should lead people to work more hours. This can be seen by consideration, in reverse sequence, of the example used with Figure 12.3. With a wage rate of $20 per hour the individual chooses to work 35 hours per week. If taxation comes along so that the after-tax wage rate is $10 per hour, lo and behold, the choice is for a longer workweek.

Increase Asset Income and Hours Decrease

The above examples assume that the only source of income is work. Consider now the addition of income derived from the ownership of assets. Asset income allows an individual to attain a given marginal utility working fewer hours per week. This should cause the individual to desire to work fewer hours a week as did higher pay.

Jevons's Model and the Empirical Record

The 1920–1935 record is consistent with Jevons's model which should show the hours of work per week decreasing with increases in the real wage. A simple regression of the average hours of work per week, H, as a function of the real wage, RW, yields the following results:

(2) $H = 74.65 - 30.125RW$ adj. $R^2 = 0.7437$ DW = 0.90
                    (t = 6.72)

For the average hours of work per week and the real wage, I used data from manufacturing as published in the 1964 *Economic Report of the President*. The mean real wage in this period was $1.077 per hour in 1967 dollars (Table C–27 wage data with my adjustment using the consumer price index, 1967 = 100.) And at that real wage 42.2 hours were worked per week—on the average (Table C–26, p. 239). Were the real wage increased by $0.10 per hour, roughly 10 percent, the workweek would decrease by 3.01 hours per week–according to the above estimating equation.

But consider the period covered—from the roaring twenties to the worst part of the Great Depression—period in which social and political concerns were for sharing work.

Students of industrial relations know that the hours of work, H, varies negatively with the unemployment rate, U. A regression of this model, again using 1920–1935 data, yields the following estimating equation:

(3) $H = 46.45 - 0.4200U$ adj. $R^2 = 0.7987$ DW = 0.76
                    (t = 7.78)

Here, an increase in the unemployment rate of 1 percent would lead to a decrease in the workweek of 0.42 hours. The model that hypothesizes hours of work are a decreasing function of the unemployment rate has a better fit to the data, a higher adjusted R^2, than the model in which hours of work are a decreasing function of the wage rate. Using both the real wage and unemployment as explanatory variables yields better results, but enough is enough.

The post-1935 record does not conform as well to Jevons' model as did the 1920–1935 data. The real wage increased fairly steadily from 1935 through 1978 and this, omitting the 1940–1946 war-related period, was accompanied by a slight decrease in average weekly hours. The real wage in manufacturing decreased during the 1978–1990 period. According to Jevons, the length of the workweek should have increased—but it did not.

Marshall's Modification of Jevons's Model

Alfred Marshall realized that a worker frequently had little, if any, power to set the number of hours in his workweek. His solution to the departure from Jevons's model follows:

> If a man is free to cease his work when he likes, he does so when the advantages to be reaped by continuing seem no longer to over-balance the disadvantages. If he has to work with others, the length of his day's work is often fixed for him; and in some trades the number of days' work which he does in the year is practically fixed for him. But there are scarcely any trades, in

which the amount of exertion which he puts into his worked is fixed. If he is not willing or able to work up to the minimum standard that prevails where he is, he can generally find employment in another locality where the standard is lower (1961 [1890], p. 527 , n. 2).

Marshall seems to be saying that Jevons's model is applicable to self-employed workers. Many doctors, dentists, lawyers, and plumbers can set their own hours, but not others. But then Marshall thinks he has a way around the problem that work groups have their hours set for them. He does this by substituting for the desire to work fewer hours, the wish to engage in less exertion. But the desire to work fewer hours may be coupled with just the opposite desire—namely, to work harder. I would like to get the eight hours of work done in seven, get paid for the eight, and go home. Marshall's use of less exertion as a substitute for fewer hours may be in error.

Indifference Curve Analysis and the Work-Leisure Decision

The application of indifference curve analysis to the hours of work decision is shown in Figures 12.4 and 12.5. The vertical axis is income per week. The horizontal axis is hours of leisure per week. Both income and leisure are postulated as desirable. Almost everyone prefers more to less of them. Where do the hours of work come into the picture? They are the conjugate of hours of leisure. There are 168 hours in the week and if the individual opts for 128 hours of leisure he, at the same time, decides to work 40 hours per week: *Hours of work per week = 168 – Hours of leisure per week.* Hours of work increase in the leftward direction. The income lines are based on an hourly wage of $10 and $20, respectively. In Figure 12.4 an increase in the wage rate leads to a decrease in the hours of work; in Figure 12.5 it is the other way around—an increase in the wage rate leads to an increase in the hours of work decision. Both are shown by dark lines with arrowheads indicating the change in the hours required to maintain maximum satisfaction.

The Income and the Substitution Effects

Why an increase in pay could cause a worker to want to work more or fewer hours requires examination of the income and the substitution effects.
 Using indifference curve analysis, an increase in the wage rate can lead to either an increase or a decrease in the hours a worker would like to labor. This ambiguity arises from the contrary income and substitution effects.

> The Substitution Effect. A wage increase makes the opportunity cost of leisure more expensive. As a result, the worker substitutes work for leisure.

Figure 12.4.   **A Wage Increase Yielding a Shorter Workweek**

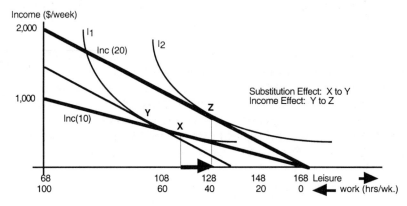

Figure 12.5   **A Wage Increase Yielding a Longer Workweek**

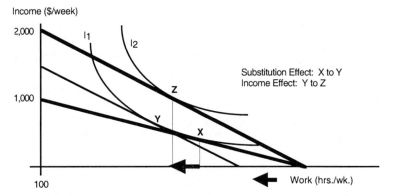

The Income Effect. A wage increase results in an increase in income. With greater income, the consumption of normal goods increases. Leisure tends to be a normal good. As a result, an increase in income tends to lead workers to choose more leisure.

With the substitution effect leading to more work and the income effect leading to less work, the effect of a wage increase on the hours of work decision is ambiguous. In Figure 12.4 the income effect, YZ, is greater than the substitution effect, XY, and, as a result, fewer hours are worked. But in Figure 12.5 the income effect is less than the substitution effect. Thus, more hours are worked per week.

The Negative Income Tax Experiments

The largest set of social experiments in the history of the United States involved replacing welfare support with a negative income tax—periodic payments to families in poverty which diminish as the income of the family increases. Many of these were families of the working poor with poorly paid males and a relatively large number of children. The fear of the members of the Congress and researchers was that the program would tend to discourage people from working. To determine what the effect would actually be, experiments with the negative income tax were conducted in different areas of the country.

The following example is intended to help explain how the negative income tax worked and why it was feared that it would discourage work. Assume that before the onset of the program, the typical head of household earns $5 an hour, works 40 hours a week, and enjoys the satisfaction implied by indifference curve I_1—as is shown in Figure 12.6. Before the negative income was applied the worker earned $200 in a week—$5 an hour times 40 hours per week.

Then the program is put into place. Using typical figures, it provides $150 a week in base income. This is the income, the negative income tax, the family gets from the government if it has no other source of income. The government reduces its subsidy by 50 cents for every dollar of income earned. As a result the covered worker's pay of $5 an hour drops to an after-tax net of $2.50 an hour, making the opportunity cost of leisure drop from $5 to $2.50 per hour. The income line shifts from *Inc(5)* to *Inc(150, 2.50)*. Note also that with the arbitrary way I have drawn the indifference map, the worker now has an income of $200 a week through only 20 hours per week of work—$150 plus $2.50 per hour times 20 hours per week of work.

What actually happened? In general, the effects were very small. In the New Jersey experiment, for example, the following results were found after three years: white male household heads worked fewer hours; the unemployment rate of Spanish-speaking male heads of households increased; and white wives decreased their labor force participation substantially. (Recall that women in the experiment had large families and large family responsibilities. Only a small percentage worked before and during the experiment.) There was no effect on the labor supply of Black households. The changes which took place were very small in terms of changes in the hours worked per week. The set of commendable negative income tax experiments took place during the Nixon administration. The demise of the program can be attributed to his increasing interest in the Vietnam War, the Watergate Scandal, and the resignation of the President.

The Eight-Hour-Day Movement

In the neoclassical model workers are able to choose the number of hours they work. This must be a surprising hypothesis to students of American history and particularly those who know the history of our labor union movement. The eight-hour-day movement played an important role in that history. The first national labor federation was founded in 1866 under the leadership of William H. Sylvis. One of the top goals of the National Labor Union was the achievement

Figure 12.6.   **The Negative Income Tax and the Hours of Work**

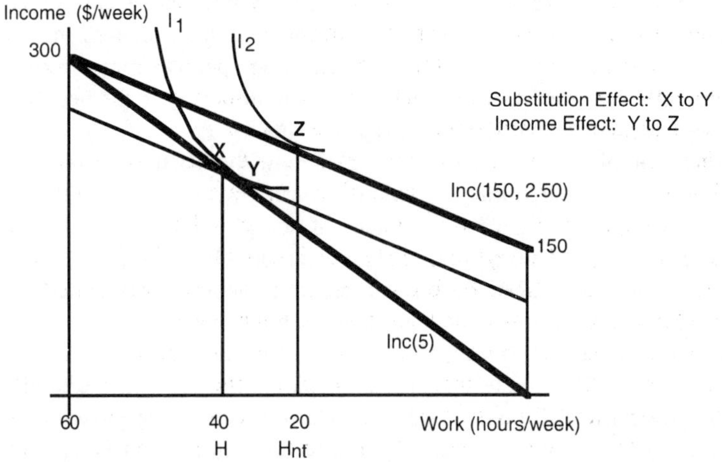

of an eight-hour workday. The Knights of Labor, another post–Civil War labor federation, championed the eight-hour day. The American Federation of Labor, founded in 1881, demanded the attainment of an eight-hour day by May 1, 1886, and threatened a general strike to bring it about. While there were some victories along the way it was not until the Great Depression of the 1930s that the eight-hour-day became the norm. The long and deep depression lowered the power of business, and a pro-labor Congress passed the Fair Labor Standards Act of 1938 which, in effect, created the eight-hour-day.

Marx's Hours-of-Work Model

In 1867, Karl Marx modeled the setting of the hours of the workday as follows:

> Between equal rights force decides. Hence it is that in the history of capi-
> talistic production, the determination of what is a working day, presents it-
> self as a struggle, a struggle between ... the class of capitalists, and ... the
> working class (1906 [1867], p. 259).

The determination of the hours of work as indicated by the history of the eight-hour-day movement seems better correlated with the model of Marx than with that of the neoclassical paradigm.

Education as an Investment in Human Capital

A major reason for the failure of people of working age to participate in the labor force, or to participate fully in the labor force, is that they are attending school. Economists have long viewed education as what is now called an *investment in human capital*. There are two basic kinds of investments in human capital: one involves individuals investing in education; the other involves on-the-job training.

Investments in Education by Individuals

Adam Smith analyzed occupational-oriented education as follows:

> When an expensive machine is erected, the extraordinary work to be performed by it before it is worn out, will replace the capital laid out upon it with at least the ordinary profits. A man educated at the expence of much labour and time to any of those employments which require extraordinary dexterity and skill, may be compared to one of those expensive machines. The work which he learns to perform, it must be expected ... will replace to him the whole expense of his education, with at least the ordinary profits of an equally valuable capital (1937 [1776], p. 101).

Economists in categorizing education as an investment in human capital are just following the analysis of Adam Smith.

How do we go about determining whether or not an investment, in general or in education, is expected to be profitable? It is done by calculating the expected rate of return on the investment. That will be done here with the help of an example.

Consider a hypothetical 18-year-old high school senior deciding whether to go to work or to college. The problem is shown in Figure 12.7. Assume that in both cases the senior expects to work until attaining age 65. The alternatives are then forty-seven years of work and income or a four year investment in a college education followed by forty-three years of work and income. What guesstimates are required in order for the 18-year-old to determine the expected rate of return on a four year college education? (1) The annual income that would be received as a high school graduate for each of the forty-seven years, *HS*. (2) The direct costs of going to college for each of four years, *DC*. (3) Income figures for each of forty-three post-college years, *CG*. In addition, there is the need for the technical knowledge required to calculate the rate of return based on the three items specified above.

The investment in a college education appears in the negative-sloped cross-hatched area of Figure 12.7. It consists of two parts. The first is the opportunity cost of college attendance, the earning foregone as a result of attending college. The second part of the investment is the direct cost of attending college: tuition and fees, room and board, books and supplies, perhaps the cost of a computer, and so forth.

Figure 12.7.   **An Investment in a College Education**

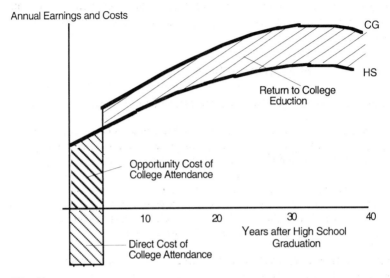

Annual Earnings and Costs

CG

HS

Return to College
Eduction

Opportunity Cost of
College Attendance

10   20   30   40

Years after High School
Graduation

Direct Cost of
College Attendance

The Returns

The returns are the difference between what is earned with a college education minus what would have been earned without that education—the positive-sloped cross-hatched area in Figure 12.7. Unless the area encompassing returns is greater than that of costs, no positive rate of returns will be experienced—a not terribly uncommon experience.

The Rate of Return

The rate of return is the interest rate used in discounting future returns and costs, which yields a present value of zero. A cream puff example will be used to show that this is something you really know. Assume that you loan me $100 and I promise to repay you with $200 a year from now. What is the rate of return you earned on your $100? Hopefully, the answer given is 100 percent per year as a result of the receipt of $100 of profit on a $100 investment. What you have done, in effect, is to solve for the rate of return r, in the following present value formula:

(4) $PV = -C + R_1/(1 + r)$

where, PV is the present value of a future stream of costs and revenues—in dollars. C is the cost of the investment made right now— that is, made in the present. As a result it needs no discounting. R_1 is the revenue to be received a year from now discounted by $(1 - r)$; and r is the rate of return on the investment, in percent per year. It is the interest which brings the present value to zero.

Substituting the numbers of our example into the above formula yields:

(5) $PV = -100 + [200/(1 + r)]$

The present value equals zero if the bracketed terms equal 100 and that happens if the denominator $(1 + r)$ equals two. In that case r equals 1 or 100 percent. Both common sense and the present value calculation yield the same results.

But what if our agreement is that for the $100 you lend me now, I will give you $200 in two years. The present value relationship for this case is:

(6) $PV = -100 + [200/(1 + r)^2]$

Because the return is to be received two years from now, the discounting of the 200 return is to the power of 2. To make the right-hand side of the equation equal to zero, the terms in brackets must equal 100: $200/(1 + r)^2 = 100$; $(1 + r)^2 = 2$; $(1 + r) = 1.4142$; $r = 4$ 1.42 percent per year.

In line with the above superficial presentation, the present value formula required for our 18-year-old high school senior to determine the expected rate of return is:

(7) $PV = - (HS + DC)_1/(1 + r)^1 \ldots - (HS + DC)_4/(1 + r)^4] +$
          $+ (CG - HS)_5/(1 + r)^5 + \ldots + (CG\text{-}HS)_{47}/(1+r)^{47}$

Assuming unemployment in the years of college attendance, the bracketed first four years consists of costs alone: the direct cost of attending college, DC, plus the opportunity cost of going to college—the foregone earnings of a high school graduate, HS. Years five through forty-seven have the college grad getting a return on his investment equal to his earnings, CG, minus what he would have earned without college, HS. All of this is discounted by 1 plus the rate of return raised to the power conforming to the number of years from college entry.

The remaining task is to determine the rate of return, r, which brings the present value to zero. The most obvious way of accomplishing this is by trial and error. Guess at the magnitude of the rate of return. Then calculate forty-seven discount factors: $(1 + r)$ to $(1 + r)^{47}$. Then take the forty-seven numerators and divide each one by the appropriate discount factor. Subsequently, add up the forty-seven discounted returns. Then, if their sum is positive, try a higher rate of return; if it is negative, try a lower rate of return. Do this until you get the rate which brings present value to zero.

I know of no 18-year-old, or parent, or guidance counselor who has made the required set of income forecasts and calculated the expected rate of return. It, therefore, appears that the analysis of investing in a college education is an example of normative and not positive economics.

A number of economists have made the required calculations for the purpose of determining if, on the average, investing in college makes sense.

X Makes Some of the Investment; Y Pockets All of the Returns

Recall that in the analysis of consumer behavior we slipped by the point that consumers and households are not the same and that someone forced to eat broccoli may not be maximizing his satisfaction. A similar problem exists here. The investors in the direct cost of a college education frequently receive no monetary return on their investment. These irrationals are called parents. The return on their investments goes to an alien group, those brilliant recipients of parental irrationality called children.

Why do parents feed infants? Because they enjoy it and there is a social obligation to do it. Why do they spend money on sending children to college? Because they enjoy it and there has evolved a social obligation to do it. Parental spending on the education of their children is a form of parental consumption. And children receive a windfall rate of return on their part of the investment.

What Is the Rate of Return on an Investment in a College Education?

Gary Becker estimated the average rate of return of urban native white males graduating in 1939 to be in the range of 13.0 to 15.3 percent per year after taxes. For 1949 graduates his single best-guess estimate is 13.0 percent per year. Moreover, he felt these figures stood up so well that he maintained the same figures in his 1975 second edition of *Human Capital*. Becker felt that these rates of return are indicative of a reasonable allocation of resources to higher education. Richard B. Freeman, on the other hand, calculated the rate of return in 1973 as being lower, namely, between 7.5 and 10.0 percent. He evaluated this as indicative of the excess allocation of resources to higher education, hence, the title of his book: *The Overeducated American* (1976).

Tuition, by the way, is frequently subsidized making the social less than the private rate of return. This moves the conclusion more in the direction of the overallocation of resources to education. Whether this should be of personal or social concern is another matter. To many of us, college attendance is more than an investment.

Investments in On-the-Job Training

Gary Becker popularized the idea of on-the-job training as an investment in human capital in the first edition of *Human Capital* (1964). In it he differentiates between *general* and *specific* training.

Figure 12.8.   **The Aggregate Supply of Labor**

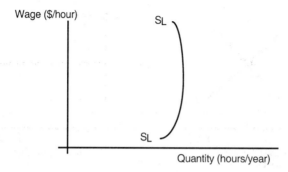

Wage ($/hour)

SL

SL

Quantity (hours/year)

General Training

General training is defined by Becker as training of value to the firm giving the training and also to other firms. As a result he postulates that general training by a firm is an investment made through the reduction in the pay of trainees. Subsequently, the higher skills of the trained workers should result in higher pay allowing the trained workers to regain the cost of the investment and a re-turn on it. An example of general training is the apprenticeship programs of the construction industry. The carpenter who is taught to hang a door or to build the frame of a house can do that for a large number of firms which perform that sort of work. His low wage as an apprentice and the big jump in pay when he becomes a journeyman are in line with Becker's model.

Specific Training

Specific training is only useful to the firm employing the trained workers. Here Becker has the firm paying for the cost of the training with its investment repaid through the added productivity the training affords its workers during their post-training employment by the firm. Another firm cannot exploit the training of a worker in the manufacture of a kind of glass made only by his employer.

The Supply to the Economy

What has been done thus far regarding the supply of labor? Workers have been born, whether or not in conformance with one fertility theory or another, grown to school age, invested in more or less schooling, decided to enter the labor force, and decided how many hours they were willing to work per day, week, month, and year. This puts those hours of labor services in the supply of labor, a function shown as Figure 12.8.

It is usually assumed that at relatively low wage rates an increase in the wage rate brings about an increase in the quantity of labor hours supplied and that at

Figure 12.9.   **The Competitive Labor Market and the Supply to the Firm**

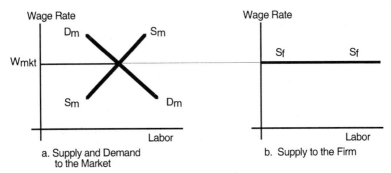

a. Supply and Demand
to the Market

b. Supply to the Firm

relatively high wage rates an increase in the wage rate leads to a decrease in the number of hours supplied. This means that the substitution effect is stronger than the income effect at low wages. Then for a substantial range of higher wages the quantity supplied is roughly constant implying the offsetting of the substitution effect by the income effect. Finally, supply becomes "backward bending" implying that the income effect is greater than the substitution effect at relatively high wage rates.

Why would a person have almost the same propensity to work when wages were quite low as when they are higher? A number of reasons are suggested: (1) It may be a question of work or starve. (2) There is a social imperative that males work after schooling and before being aged. The somewhat weaker social imperative holds for unmarried women without children. For those with children there is some expectation that they will enter the labor market once the children can fend for themselves. (3) Many work because there are those who depend on them. (4) Finally, many of us are imbued with a work ethic.

The Supply to Firms, Occupations, Industries, and Regions

Workers in supplying their services to the economy have only one alternative to work, not to work. But there are many alternatives when decisions involve supplying labor services to one among many firms, occupations, industries, or regions. As the number of alternatives increase, the supply becomes more elastic. Why should the individual work for a firm which pays less than "the going rate" if jobs at or above that rate are available?

The Competitive Labor Market

Take the case in which many, many firms demand labor services in a given labor market. This is the competitive labor market. In it the wage rate is set by the market supply and demand functions as is shown in frame *a* of Figure 12.9. The equilibrium wage is W_{mkt}. Each firm in a competitive labor market sees an

Figure 12.10.   **Monopsony Supply and the Marginal Wage**

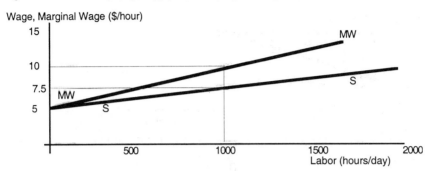

infinitely elastic labor supply function, S_fS_f at that wage as shown in panel b. This is because each firm demands and employs a negligible part of the market supply and can, therefore, buy as many hours of labor services per unit of time as it desires at the market wage rate.

The Monopsonistic Labor Market

Monopsonistic buyers confront positive-sloped supply functions—here, that of labor services. For this to occur, the firm must employ a measurable portion ofthe market supply of labor. Then, to procure additional labor services it must draw workers away from other firms. To do this it must raise the wage it pays.

Sometimes the monopsonist is a very large firm employing many thousands of workers in a labor market. Monopsonists can also be smaller-sized firms operating in markets in which the supply of workers with the talents desired is relatively scarce.

An example of a large monopsonist is the Boeing Corporation. It employs far more engineers and scientists than the Tacoma, Washington area would normally provide. An example of a small monopsonist is the New York Yankees which employs twenty-five very highly skilled "production workers," a number greater than that attainable in the local labor market. In both cases, somewhat higher pay tends to be required to obtain more highly skilled and talented employees.

The positive-sloped labor supply function seen by the monopsonist is shown in Figure 12.10. It is of the form:

(8) $W = W_0 + mL$

In figure 12.10, $W_0 = 5$ and $m=0.0025$.

The total wage function, TW, is the total cost of labor services as a function of employment—during a given period of time. It is the wage rate times the

Figure 12.11.   **The Supply of Academics Showing Rental and Transfer Income**

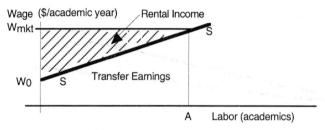

number of hours employed at that wage: $TW = W \cdot L$. With the supply function: $W = 5 + 0.0025L$, the total wage function is:

(9) $TW = WL = 5L + 0.0025L^2$.

The marginal wage function, MW, is the slope of the total wage function, dTW/dL. For the example being used, the marginal wage function is:

(10) $MW = 5 + 2(0.0025)L = 5 + 0.0050L$

It has the same wage intercept as the supply function and double its positive slope—as shown. The marginal wage embodies a deterrent to employment. If, for example, the monopsonist is employing 1,000 hours of labor a day the wage rate would have to be $7.50 per hour, according to equation (8). The 1,000th hour added not $7.50 but $10 to the total wage bill, in equation (10).

Rental and Transfer Earnings

Rent is generally thought of as the price charged for the use of a factor fixed in supply—as for the use of a parcel of land for a specified amount of time. It is a payment which is not required to draw a factor into productive use. In the latter sense, economic rent can be applied to the factors of production.

> Economic rent is the difference between what a factor is paid and the minimum amount necessary to obtain its services.

Consider the positive-sloped supply of academics shown in Figure 12.11. The market wage is W_{mkt}. Both rental and transfer income are shown. Note the academic who is willing to take the lowest salary shown, W_0. He is paid W_{mkt}. This amounts to $W_{mkt} - W_0$ more than is required to transfer his services to the academic market. That unnecessary payment is rental income. Slightly less rental income would be received by the person who would willingly work at a slightly higher salary. All of those employed would be recipients of rental income except for the marginal academic who would willingly work for the market wage and nothing less. The amount of rental income paid in this market is the cross-hatched area between the supply function and the market wage.

While I show the first academic as willing to work for about half of the market wage, I suspect that once paid the market wage he would be reluctant to work for any less. This implies the supply function quickly becoming more elastic and rental income quickly disappears.

The Demand Function

The demand for labor can be shown in the aggregate, although it virtually never is, and at the level of the producing organization. John Stuart Mill had the aggregate demand for labor coming from a "wages fund"—a fixed amount of money. Neoclassical demand is generally based on the negative-sloping portion of the marginal productivity function. That negative-slope is a consequence of the law of diminishing marginal productivity. Marginal-productivity-based demand has three variants, all of which assume that the employer is a profit maximizer. In the first workers are paid in units of the product they help to produce, beer for example. The second covers the competitive product market and has workers paid in dollars, to many an advance over beer. The value of the beer is transformed to dollars by virtue of its price. The third approach handles monopolistic product markets. Here the transformation from product to dollar terms is handled through the marginal revenue of the product. All of this is presented, shortly.

The critique of neoclassical factor demand theory starts with the fact that roughly half the labor force have their production marketed; half do not. Only the former half should be paid under the model making it at best a half-truth. Then analysis of its inventor, John Bates Clark comes next. Clark essentially denies the existence of the short-run production function undermining the factor demand theory associated with his name. Clark varies not only the employment of labor but also physical capital. Two ways of solving the lack of capital problem are presented and found wanting. The final attempt at the development of a factor demand function exploits information implied in the cost-oriented model of production.

The Aggregate Demand for Labor

The aggregate demand for labor is implied by John Stuart Mill's wages fund doctrine:

> Wages (meaning, of course, the general wage rate) cannot rise, but by an increase in the aggregate funds employed in hiring labourers, or a diminution in the number of the competitors for hire (1961 [1848], p. 344).

It can be argued that national income statistics are reasonably in accord with Mill's wages fund doctrine since throughout the century the employee compen-

Figure 12.12.   **The Production Function and the Marginal Product of Labor**

Quantity, Q (thousands of six-packs per day)
Marginal Product of Labor (six-packs/month)

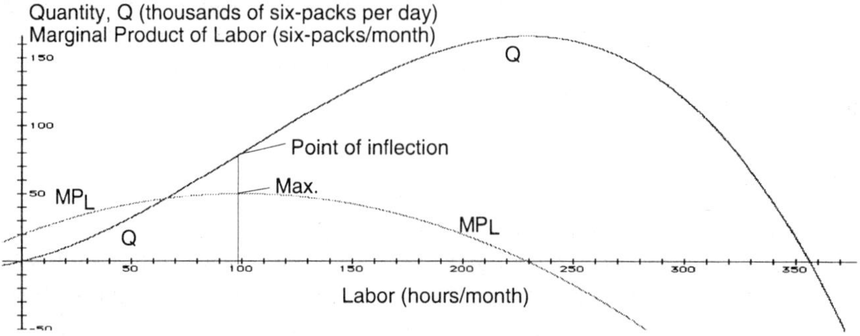

sation share of nation income has been reasonably constant—largely in the 70 to 75 percent range.

With employee compensation a reasonably stable portion of national income the implication is that the wage elasticity of demand is roughly minus 1—but that would be grossly misleading. The demand for labor is highly inelastic.

The Production and Marginal Productivity Functions Briefly Recalled

The production and marginal productivity functions were discussed in Chapter 5. For the sake of convenience a very brief review is presented here. A theoretical production function, QQ, is shown in Figure 12.12. Production of six-packs is on the vertical and the employment of labor on the horizontal axis. Start at zero employment where there is no production. As more hours of labor services are employed, all other factors of production held constant, each at first adds more to production than the previous one. This is because better organization of the work process can be obtained with more hours of work and workers. This process of increasing marginal productivity continues until the "point of inflection" on the production function is reached. It is the point at which the increasing slope of the function ends and the decreasing slope begins—the point at which the marginal product of labor is greatest. Why does marginal productivity decline? As the employment of labor increases, the other factors which are assumed fixed in supply become relatively scarce and their increasing lack of availability to labor lowers labor's marginal product.

Consistent with profit maximization, the production function represents the maximum amount of production attainable with given amounts of capital and labor.

The slope of the production function, $\partial Q/\partial L$, is the marginal product of labor. It is the rate of change of the quantity produced with respect to the employment of labor. Its units are here six-packs per hour of labor. Marginal productivity is maximized at 100 hours per day in Figure 12.12. The marginal product of labor is a close cousin of the differential product of labor, $dQ, = \partial Q/\partial L \cdot dL$: the change in the rate of production arising from a differential change in the employment of labor. Its units are the same as that of the quantity produced, here six-packs per month. Again, in normal discussion we tend to speak of the marginal product as a change in (the rate of) production—but, in fact, that is the differential product.

Demand with Competitive Labor and Product Markets

The development of the marginal-productivity-based demand function is given in two stages. In the first workers are paid in units of what they produce. In the second they are paid in dollars.

Workers Paid in Units of What They Produce

Assume that (1) a firm produces six-packs (don't ask "of what"), (2) its employees are paid in six-packs, (3) the employer is a profit maximizer, (4) the employment of labor is varied as the wage rate is varied, and (5) all other factors are held constant. The problem is to show that at the profit-maximizing rate of employment, the marginal product of labor equals the wage rate, $W = MP_L$—a condition not far removed analytically from the maximization condition in the competitive product market, $P = MC$. That the maximization condition is $W = MP_L$ is shown mathematically and graphically.

The Mathematics of Profit Maximization

In this wondrous example, all factors are paid in units of the product. Profit is the difference between the total product, Q, and the amount of product the firm pays to labor, WL, and capital, RK:

(11) $$\pi = Q - (WL + RK)$$

To find the condition for profit maximization (and minimization), take the first derivative of the profit equation, with capital held constant, and set it equal to zero.

(12) $$\partial\pi/\partial L = \partial Q/\partial L - W = 0$$

Solve for W in equation (12):

(13) $$W = \partial Q/\partial L = MP_L$$

The condition that the wage rate equals the marginal product of labor, $W = MP_L$, is a maximum if the second derivative of the profit equation is negative.

Figure 12.13.   **The Marginal Product and the Product Demand for Labor**

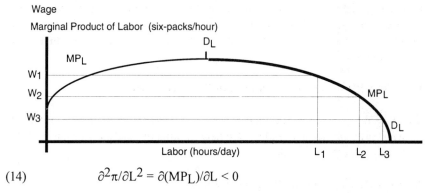

(14) $\partial^2 \pi / \partial L^2 = \partial(MP_L)/\partial L < 0$

The term $\partial(MP_L)/\partial L$ is the slope of the marginal product function and it must be negative for the second derivative to be less than zero. Requiring that it be negative means that the demand for labor function must be negative-sloping—the norm for demand functions.

Profit Maximization Shown Graphically

An appropriate marginal productivity function is shown in Figure 12.13. It is at first positive-sloped. When the law of diminishing marginal productivity takes over, its slope becomes zero and then negative. Marginal productivity is maximum at the inflection point on the production function and zero at maximum production.

Assume the wage rate is W_1 and that the worker is paid in six-packs per hour. Starting at zero employment, the wage rate is greater than the marginal product of labor and this occurs until they are equal. Up to that point, the employment of marginal units of labor increased the loss incurred by the firm. That loss is maximized by the employment at which the wage equals the marginal product of labor where its slope is positive.

As employment is increased further, the marginal product exceeds the wage rate and profit is made on the marginal units of employment. Additions to profit, continue until the employment L_1 is reached. There the wage rate equals the negative-sloped marginal product of labor, $W = MP_L$. This yields a point on the demand function: the number of units of labor to be employed, L_1, at the wage rate, W_1. The same reasoning holds at other wages; for example, at the lower wage rates of W_2 and W_3 profit-maximizing employments are obtained by employing L_2 and L_3 units of labor per day. This yields two more points on the demand-for-labor function. Pursuing this process yields the entire demand function: the downward-sloping portion of the marginal productivity curve, $D_L D_L$.

Note that the shape of the marginal productivity function is "inverted U-shape."

Figure 12.14.   **The Conversion of the Wage Rate from Product to Dollars per Week**

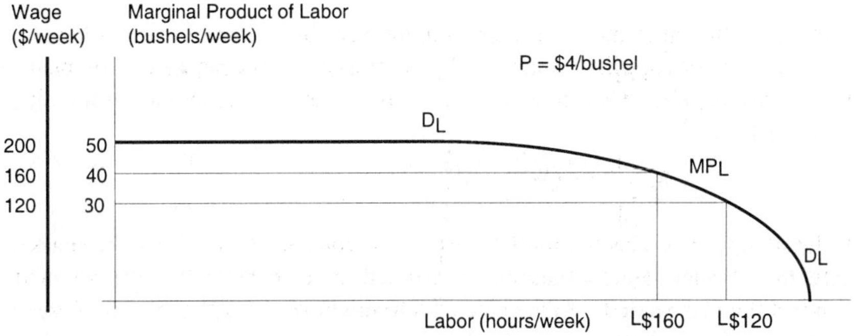

Workers Paid in Dollars: The Value of Their Marginal Product

In the competitive market, it is not very difficult to go from paying in six-packs to paying in dollars. This can be shown as follows.

Profit is the difference between total revenue and total cost (total variable factor cost plus total fixed cost).

(15) $\pi = PQ - (WL + RK + TFC)$

where π is profit, P is the price of the product, Q is the quantity of the product produced and sold, W is the wage rate in dollars per hour, L is the number of units of labor employed, R is the return to a unit of capital, K is the number of units of capital employed, and TFC is total fixed cost. If capital and product price are constant, the first derivative of profit with respect to the employment of labor is:

(16) $\partial\pi/\partial L = P \cdot \partial Q/\partial L - W$

At maximum $\partial\pi/\partial L$ is zero. Substitute MP_L for $\partial Q/\partial L$ and solve W:

(17) $W = P \cdot MP_L = VMP$

Profit maximization takes place at the rate of employment at which the wage rate equals the price of the product times the marginal product—the value of the marginal product, *VMP*.

In Figure 12.14 the conversion from pay in units of product to pay in units of dollars is shown. The price of the product is $4 per bushel. To transform the wage from product to money units multiply the marginal product of labor, for example, forty bushels per week, by the price of the product, $4/bushel. The result is $160 per week, The dollar per week axis is merely the bushels per week axis multiplied by $4/bushel.

Demand with a Monopolistic Product Market

In this case the labor market remains competitive but an employer markets her product in a monopolistic market. Again start with the equation for profits which consists of total revenue minus the cost of variable labor and capital plus total fixed cost.

(18) $\pi = PQ - (WL + RK + TFC)$

In the competitive product market, price is a constant dictated by the market. Here, the product demand function is assumed to be constant. The monopolistic firm has the task of setting the price which maximizes profit. The *variables* in the above profit equation are accordingly price, the rate of production, and the employment of labor. It is assumed here that the wage rate is given. The first derivative of the profit equation is then:

(19) $\partial\pi/\partial L = P \cdot \partial Q/\partial L + [Q \cdot \partial P/\partial L] - W$

Equation (19) is the same as that for the competitive product market, equation (16), except for the troublesome bracketed term—troublesome because we do not have a function in which price varies with the employment of labor. To get around this we can use what is equal to $\partial P/\partial L$: the "cross product" $\partial P/\partial Q \cdot \partial Q/\partial L$ (the slope of the demand function times the slope of the production function). Then:

(20) $\partial\pi/\partial L = P \cdot \partial Q/\partial L + Q(\partial P/\partial Q \cdot \partial Q/\partial L) - W$

Collecting terms, the above equation can be rewritten as:

(21) $\partial\pi/\partial L = \partial Q/\partial L \, (P + Q \cdot \partial P/\partial Q) - W$

The terms within the parentheses equal marginal revenue: $MR = d(PQ)/dQ = P + Q\partial P/\partial Q$. Thus, at profit maximization (and minimization):

(22) $\partial\pi/\partial L = MP_L \cdot MR - W = 0$

Solve equation (19) for W:

23) $W = MR \cdot MP_L = MRP$

Unfortunately, marginal revenue is a function of the rate of production, Q, and not the rate of employment, L, as is required here. In other, words, for the de-

Figure 12.15.   **The Value of the Marginal Product of Labor Versus Its Marginal Revenue Product**

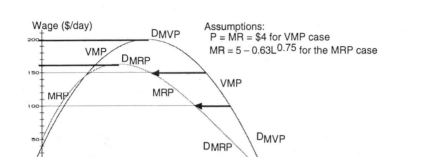

mand for labor we have to know the magnitude of marginal revenue at various rates of employment. The marginal revenue function, $MR=f(Q)$, can be made a function of L, by substituting for Q the right hand side of the production function, $Q=f(L,K)$. This yields marginal revenue as a function of the employment of labor and capital, with the latter held constant.

Let me make this abstraction concrete through the use of an example in which the marginal revenue and production functions are known and the latter function is used used to transform marginal revenue from a function of quantity demanded, Q, to marginal revenue as a function of the employment of labor, L.

Given: (1) The marginal revenue function, $MR = 5 - 0.063Q$.
       (2) The production function, $Q = L^{0.75}$.
Find: Marginal revenue as a function of the employment of labor.

Substitute the right-hand side of the production function for Q in the marginal revenue function given:
$$MR(L) = 5 - 0.063L^{.75}$$
Thus, we have marginal revenue as a decreasing function of the employment of labor.

Again, to obtain the marginal revenue product demand for labor function, equation (23), multiply marginal revenue (as a function of the employment of labor) by the marginal product of labor.

In Figure 12.15, the demand based upon the value of the marginal product can be compared to demand based on the marginal revenue product. To transform the marginal product function into the value of the marginal product function I assumed that the price of the product was $4 and the producer could sell all that was desired at that price. For the monopolistic market case I arbitrarily chose a demand function which yielded a product price of $4 at the rate of employment of forty hours per day—as you can see. Its marginal revenue function, $MR(L) =$

$5-0.063L^{0.75,}$ multiplied by the original marginal productivity function yields the marginal revenue product function of Figure 12.15. As you see it creates a noteworthy decrease in the demand for labor, particularly as indicated by the lower employment found at wages of $100 and $150 per day.

Do Marginal Revenue Product Payments Exhaust the Product?

Recall that the Cobb-Douglas production function exhausted the product if the sum of the factor elasticities of production, a and b, were equal to 1 and the factors were paid the value of their marginal products. Actually, that was shown Chapter 5 for the case in which factors are paid in units of what they produce as shown in equation (24) where aQ is labor's share and bQ is capital's share of production:

(24) $Q = aQ + bQ$

If the price of the product is P and labor and capital are paid the value of their marginal products both sides of equation are properly multiplied by that variable:

(25) $PQ = P \cdot aQ + P \cdot bQ$

Now we have total revenue exhausted by having the value of the marginal products paid the factors.

The case in which the factors are paid their marginal revenue products is shown in equation (26):

(26) $PQ > MR (aQ + bQ)$

Total revenue is greater than marginal productivity based factor payments because product price is greater than marginal revenue for all negative sloping product demand functions. There are two interesting aspects to this situation. First, what happens to the excess in total revenue which is not paid to the factors. Second, a firm generally produces a value added which is a fraction of the total revenue received for the final product. This makes the demand for the firm's product more inelastic than the demand for the product. The result could be that the firm's marginal revenue is negative. How, then, are factor payments determined and do they exhaust the total revenue?

What About the Demand for Workers Whose Products Are *Not* Marketed?

In a representative firm roughly half of the workers are employed in the production of the products the firm sells. Their labor yields a marginal revenue pro-

Figure 12.16. **The Monopsonistic Labor Market and the Absence of a Demand Function**

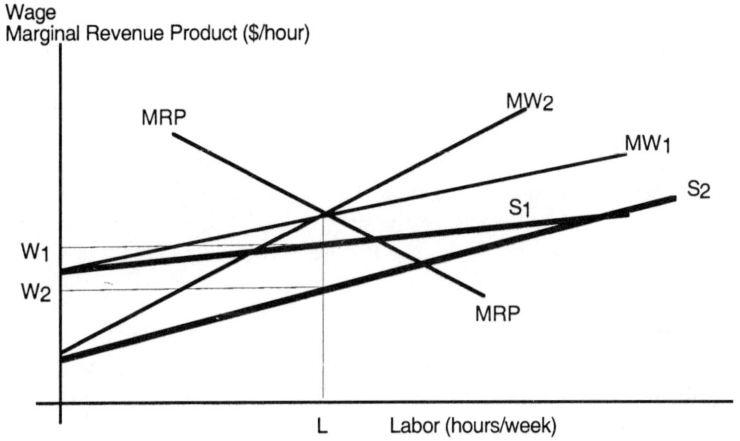

duct. And about half of the employees produce products which are not sold by the firm. Were workers paid their marginal revenue products half the employees of the firm would be paid; half would not.

I am unaware of any attempts to mend this enormous hole in the model.

Monopsony and the Non-Existence of a Labor Demand Function

There is no theoretical factor demand function when the employer is a monopsonist—just as there is no theoretical product supply function if a firm is monopolistic. The monopsonist's demand for labor depends upon the state of the supply of labor. This is shown in Figure 12.16. Profit maximization occurs at the rate of employment at which the marginal wage equals the marginal revenue product of labor. For both supply function S_1 and supply function S_2, profit is maximized at the same employment rate, L. But the wage paid with S_1 in force is W_1. Were the supply of labor S_2, the wage would be lower, namely, W_2. At two different wage rates the same quantity of labor is demanded: Thus, the absence of factor demand functions in monopsonistic markets.

Marshall's Rules and the Elasticity of Factor Demand

One of the most interesting analytical contributions of Alfred Marshall is his rules regarding the elasticity of derived demand. Marshall put it this way:

> Let us inquire what are the conditions, under which a check to the supply ... of a factor of production may cause a very great rise in its price.
>   The first condition is that the factor itself should be essential, or nearly essential to the production of a commodity, no good substitutes being available at a moderate price.

> The second condition is that the [product] ... should be one for which   the demand is stiff and inelastic; so that a check to its supply would cause consumers to offer a much increased price for it....
>
> The third condition is that only a small part of the expense of production ... should consist of the price of the factor. [Recall that the elasticity of derived demand is the factor's share of the product price times the elasticity of demand for the product.]
>
> The fourth condition is that even a small check to the amount demanded should cause a considerable fall in the supply price of other actors of production.... This will increase the margin available for paying [higher prices to the factor whose supply has been checked] (1961 [1890, pp. 385–386).

Marshall used his analysis to explain the considerable strength of the plasterers' union in wage bargaining. But that strength has been badly eroded by the development of wall-board as a substitute for plastered walls, and this correctly implies the union's weak bargaining power.

John Bates Clark and His Marginal-Productivity-Based Demand Model

John Bates Clark is generally credited with the discovery of marginal productivity factor demand analysis. But I submit that a careful reading of Clark will yield a different view than the neoclassical demand model presented above. The reason is that Clark recognized that very little additional production could be accomplished by the increased employment of labor if capital is held constant. His analysis can be found in his 1899 work, *The Distribution of Wealth: A Theory of Wages, Interest, and Profits.*

Advancing from Wages Set on No-Rent Land to No-Cost Capital

The only precursor acknowledged by Clark is Henry George who had all labor paid on the basis of the product added by a farmer to no-rent land—land so poor that it could draw no rent:

> If the theory [of Henry George] is advanced that the wages of labor are permanently fixed by the gains that men can realize by tilling no-rent ground, this theory must mean that the mere occupiers of pieces of land that cannot be let for any appreciable rent are the men to whose gains the wages of everyone conforms. This is a theory of "squatter sovereignty" over the labor market.... With all its absurdity, this theory does at least appeal to the principle that wages tend to equal what labor itself can produce (1965 [1899], pp.88–89).

Note the words "what labor itself can produce." The problem faced by Henry

George and John Bates Clark was to identify just what was added to production by increments of labor alone even though this usually cannot be done since labor normally works with other cooperating factors of production. Agricultural production is often portrayed as the product of labor and land. George "solved" the problem of identifying the contribution to production of labor alone by defining away the contribution to production of land. He did this by labeling it "no-rent land."

Clark's advance over George's approach was to employ labor with "no-cost capital." Clark felt this to be an important advance because the use of no-rent land is relatively rare but the use of no-cost capital is reasonably common—or so he claimed. This is because all capital equipments, before they are scrapped, supposedly yield no return to their owners. The following example should give you a feel for the kinds of operations which set the wages for all of labor, according to Clark:

> There are mills and furnaces so antiquated, so nearly worn out or so badly located that their owners get nothing from them; and yet they run, so long as superintendents can earn their salaries and ordinary workers their natural wages. There are machines that outlived their usefulness to their owners, but still do their work and give the entire product they help to create to the men who operate them....There are stocks of merchandise so full of remnants and unstylish goods that it barely pays salesmen to handle them. Everywhere, in indefinite variety and extent, are no-rent instruments, and, if labor uses them, it gets the entire product of the operation (1965, p. 96).

Note that both George and Clark move from the realm of production to that of cost to justify the neglect of the marginal product of land and capital. This questionable approach then assigns all productivity to labor. But no production could have taken place without the no-rent land of George and the no-cost capital of Clark. Moreover, were George's land or Clark's capital applied to "no-wage labor," the very same product would be identified as the product of land or capital. Thus, it seems to me that neither George nor Clark was able to identify the product of labor alone. Note also recognition of the need for circulating capital, the remnants which labor and equipment turn into textiles or clothing.

Adding the Intensive to the Extensive Margin

Clark adds to the extensive margins of no-rent land and no-cost capital the intensive margins. In agriculture the marginal worker could (1) help in planting more quickly which gives the crop a longer growing period, (2) assist in harvesting the crop more quickly saving it from the storms of autumn, and (3) glean behind the reapers. He finds the intensive marginal productivity to exist throughout the industrial system: 105 men can sail a steamship better than 100.

The Character of Fixed Versus Circulating Capital

Clark is insightful in his discussion of the classical categories of capital goods: fixed and circulating. "Buildings, machinery and the like represent the former genus; and raw materials, unfinished goods, etc., the latter" (1965, p. 141). The former are fixed in the short-run while the latter are variable.

Another basic difference between fixed and circulating (or variable) capital is that the former is unchanged while the latter is changed in character in the process of production. The fixed capital assembly line remains unchanged in character by the process of production. But circulating capital, mainly in the form of parts, changes character upon transformation into a car. He also explains that fixed capital is active while circulating capital is passive in character. It is the fixed capital which participates in the transformation of the circulating capital into useful forms.

How More Is Produced While "Capital" Remains Constant

Recall the example I gave in Chapter 5 challenging the existence of the production function and the marginal productivity of labor. The example had 100 production workers laboring a standard workweek and a variable capital input of 1,000 kits per month from which 1,000 cars a month were assembled. With capital held constant and an additional worker employed, no more than 1,000 cars per month can be built in a month. Additional units of labor cannot be substituted for the parts of a car. The marginal product yielded by the employment of the 101st worker must then be zero. Clark also claims that with capital held constant precious little additional production can be accomplished, although he seems pointed at fixed capital while I stress circulating capital:

> In the industrial system it may be that five men can be added to a gang of a hundred, without requiring a change in the amount of capital employed and without changing the form of it. Elsewhere only one man in a hundred can, in this way be added or subtracted (1965, p. 101).

How then does Clark get greater output as the employment of labor increases, with capital held constant. He does it *not* by keeping physical capital constant but by keeping money capital constant. Consider the case in which Clark starts with the employment of 1,000 workers each with $100 worth of capital equipment at his disposal:

> Add, now, a second thousand workers to the force.... This second increment of labor has at its disposal capital amounting to only half a hundred dollars per man.... Where one of the original workers had an elaborate machine, he now has a cheaper and less efficient one; and the new workers by his side also have machines of the cheaper variety (1965, p. 175).

So each time there is a change in the rate of production, Clark would liquidate the existing plant and equipment and with that sum of money build a new one with the mix of fixed and circulating capital which can handle the desired rate of production. There is not a hint of reality in Clark's approach. A firm which increases its employment from 1,000 to 2,000 tends to have greater profits and the ability to increase the amount and quality of capital equipment available to the average worker. *Nor does Clark recognize the inability to produce more without more circulating capital.*

Other Attempts to Resolve the Zero-Marginal-Productivity Problem

Keeping capital constant quickly brings the marginal productivity of labor to zero—except for trivial no-rent and no-cost capital cases. Two models attempt to resolve this problem. Both involve increasing the quantity of the factor held constant in marginal productivity analysis. Alfred Marshall does this in his joint demand model. Milton Friedman and others do it in a model in which capital is not held constant but is varied.

Marshall's Joint Demand Approach

In the neoclassical factor demand model, one factor is varied and all others are held constant. This allows identification of the magnitude of the contribution to production of the variable factor—and the profit-maximizing demand price of the factor. This is problematic because joint inputs are generally required to increase production. Alfred Marshall posed the problem in the following way:

> Bread satisfies man's wants directly: and the demand for it is said to be direct. But a flour mill and an oven satisfy wants only indirectly ... and the demand is said to be indirect.... The services of the flour mill and the oven are joined together in the ultimate product, bread: the demand for them is therefore called a joint demand. Again, hops and malt are joined together in the common destination of ale.... Thus the demand for each of several complementary things is derived from the services which they *jointly* render in the production of some ultimate product (1961, p. 381).

Note that the factors are not substitutes; they are complements. They are not demanded individually; they are demanded jointly. And they are forms of circulating capital—their character is changed by the process of production.

Marshall's method of determining the demand for each of the joint factors is stated with great clarity:

> The demand schedule for any factor of production of a commodity can be *derived* from that for the commodity by subtracting from the demand price of each separate amount of the commodity the sum of the supply prices for corresponding amounts of the other factors (1961, p. 383).

Figure 12.17.   **The Demand for Blades and Handles Incorrectly Derived from the Demand for Knives and the Supply of Blades and Handles**

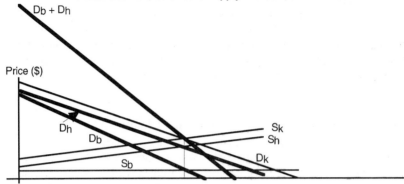

In illustrating the approach, Marshall has as the factors of production blades and handles which join together to make knives. Keep in mind that neither a blade alone nor a handle alone can produce the product. You cannot substitute a blade for a handle, an assembler for the parts to be assembled, a typist for paper, or a carpenter for a hammer, nails, and wood. Joint demand is terribly common.

Marshall's solution to the joint demand problem is shown in Figure 12.17. The three functions given are: (1) the demand for knives, D_kD_k; (2) the supply of blades, S_bS_b; and (3) the supply of handles, S_hS_h. What Marshall attempts to find is the derived demand for the factors of production, handles and blades.

The demand for handles, D_hD_h, is derived in this way. At various quantities, the supply price of blades, P_{sb}, is subtracted from the demand price for knives, P_{dk}, with the remainder being the demand price of handles, P_{dh}:

(27) D_hD_h: $P_{dh} = P_{dk} - P_{sb}$

The demand for blades, D_bD_b, is derived in like fashion. At any given quantity the demand price of blades, P_{db}, equals the demand price for the product, P_{dk}, minus the supply price of handles:

(28) D_bD_b: $P_{db} = P_{dk} - P_{sh}$

Both of Marshall's derived demand functions appear in Figure 12.17. If Marshall's method is correct, the vertical addition of the demand for handles, D_hD_h, and the demand for blades, D_bD_b, should equal the demand from which they are derived, the demand for knives, D_kD_k.

Why the vertical sum of the factor demand functions should equal the demand for knives is easily seen. If, for example, you are willing to pay $10 for a knife, you are willing to pay $10 for the factors which produced the knife. The vertical sum of the factor demand prices accordingly must equal the demand price of the product. The vertical addition of Marshall's factor demand functions appears as

$D_b + D_h$. It bears little relationship to what it should equal, the demand for knives, except at one point—that at which the original or given demand for and supply of knives equilibrate.

How did Marshall go wrong? Marshall went wrong in his original formulation of the joint demand problem. Correctly put, derived from the demand price for knives, P_{dk}, are the demand prices for the factors: blades, P_{db}, plus handles, P_{dh}:

$$(29) \qquad P_{dk} = P_{db} + P_{dh}$$

Solving equation (28) for the demand price of blades yields:

$$(30) \qquad P_{db} = P_{dk} - P_{dh}$$

But in Marshall's formulation, the demand price of blades equal the demand price of knives minus the *supply price* of handles in equation (28)—and that is incorrect

$$(28') \qquad P_{db} \neq P_{dk} - P_{sh}$$

Of what broader significance is the error of subtracting a factor supply price from the product demand price to obtain another factor's demand price? Allow me the liberty of answering this question by posing two hypotheses in the form of questions. Consider the production of cars as involving two stages. In the first stage, firms produce the parts for cars. In the second stage firms assemble the parts, transforming them into cars. What are the factors at the second stage? They are labor capital, and the circulating capital of parts. But since the parts were produced by other firms we subtract out the cost of the parts— their supply price times the quantity purchased at that price. We now have what is essentially value-added by assembly of the parts—what the parts assembly plant added to the value of the parts. The two questions I have are these: Having subtracted out the supply price time quantity of parts, can we obtain a valid parts assembly production function? And assuming that a valid production function can be obtained, can we derive valid factor demand functions from value added production functions recognizing that their creation required supply price times quantity subtractions?

The Demand for Labor as Capital Is Varied

The problem of zero or near-zero marginal productivity arising from keeping capital constant is solved in textbooks by Noble Laureates Milton Friedman and Gary Becker. They do this by varying capital. Let us examine Friedman's formulation (1962). He specifies competitive product and factor markets with fac-

Figure 12.18.   **The Demand for Factor A as Factor B Is Varied**

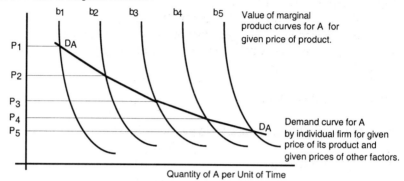

Price of A: Value of Marginal Product of A

Quantity of A per Unit of Time

Source: Friedman, Fig. 73, p. 177.
Note: I have added the specific prices, P_1... P_5.

tors A and B. The profit-maximizing equilibrium has the prices of the factors equal their value of marginal products: $P_a = P_x \cdot MP_a$ and $P_b. = P_x \cdot MP$. Then Friedman surprisingly says:

> It is tempting to interpret this [$P_x \cdot MP_a$] as the demand curve of the firm for A, and, indeed, the demand curve for A is often loosely described as given by the value of marginal product for A. But this is strictly correct for only one special case: that in which the firm is not free to vary the quantity of any factor other than A; i.e., all other factors are "fixed" (p. 176).

This is a wonderful statement doing away with the contradiction between the two production parables: (1) When costs are the primary concern, with factors A and B used to produce X, neoclassical cost analysis varies both (in such a way that their marginal products per dollar are equal). (2) But when production is the focus producers increase the rate of production by increasing the employment of only one factor at a time, either A or B. Friedman varies both factors and obtains the demand for one of them.

Friedman's demand for labor function evolves along these lines. He shows the value of marginal product functions to be very inelastic. With B held constant, not very much additional employment of A is required to bring marginal productivity to or close to zero—as can be seen in Figure 12.18.

But as the price of A declines from P_1 to P_2, more units of A are employed. The availability of more units of A causes the marginal product of B to increase. This leads to the increase in the employment of B from b_1 to b_2 which brings about a large increase (upward shift) in the marginal productivity of A and an increase in its employment. Further decreases in the price of A—to P_3, P_4, and P_5—bring about the additional employment of B, additional increases in the

Figure 12.19.   **The Production and Marginal Productivity Functions Consistent with Constant Marginal Cost**

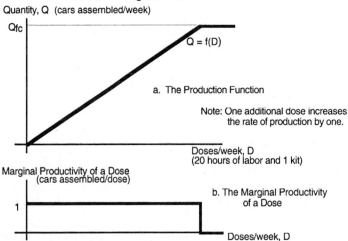

Quantity, Q (cars assembled/week)

Q_{fc}

Q = f(D)

a. The Production Function

Note: One additional dose increases the rate of production by one.

Doses/week, D
(20 hours of labor and 1 kit)

Marginal Productivity of a Dose
(cars assembled/dose)

b. The Marginal Productivity
of a Dose

1

Doses/week, D

marginal productivity of A, and the additional employment of A far beyond that indicated by its prior marginal productivity functions. The result is the smooth darkened demand for A function, $D_A D_A$. Its smoothness implies, contrary to his descrip-tion, the continuous increase in the use of B as the price of A falls and the employment of A increases.

Note the following: (1) The value of the marginal product of A is arbitrary in character. In all instances it depends on the quantity of B at its disposal. This is true for all factors. (2) The price of A determines not only the amount of A but also the amount of B employed. (3) No consideration is given to the derived de-mand of circulating capital. When you demand a shirt or a blouse, derived from it is the demand for the required material and the time it takes an operator and a sewing machine to transform it into the shirt or blouse. Why economists dis-criminate against circulating capital is a mystery.

A Marginal Productivity Function Consistent with Constant Marginal Cost

Empirical studies indicate that marginal cost tends to be constant over the range of actual rates of production. The constancy of marginal cost implies that the factors are employed in fixed proportions, in doses, and the marginal productiv-ity of a dose is constant This means that the production function is a linear function of factor doses over the range of constant marginal cost. The relevant production and marginal productivity functions can be found in Figure 12.19.

The rate of production is shown as proportionate to the employment of doses of the factors until full capacity, Q_{fc}, is reached. A dose is the set of factors employed to attain a unitary increase in the rate of production. The dose required to assemble a car consists of twenty or so hours of labor and a kit, the parts and other capital required for that assembly.

In the realm of costs, the cost of a marginal dose represents an addition to total cost ΔTC, in units of dollars per unit of time. And since a unitary increase in the rate of employment of doses brings about a unitary increase in the rate of production, the marginal cost of a dose is the same magnitude as its incremental cost except that its units are dollars per unit of production: ΔTC *($/year) = MC ($/unit of production)* • ΔQ *(units of production per year)*.

Hicks and the Scale and Substitution Effects

It was pointed out in Chapter 5 that Sir John Hicks who did much to popularize marginal productivity theory in the 1930s renounced it in the 1960s. He did this because of the realization that producers had to change the method of production in order to change the marginal productivity of labor—a long-run planning phenomenon rather than one related to actual production and employment. This caused him to replace factor demand based on marginal productivity with factor demand based on scale and substitution effects:

> Under the scale effect the quantity of the factors demanded is an increasing function of the rate of production.

> Under the substitution effect increases in the relative price of a factor stimulates the substitution of other factors.

The scale effect shifts the factor demand function rightward and the greater the availability of substitutes, the greater the demand function's elasticity. This approach is terribly sensible but lacks the mathematical elegance surrounding the marginal-productivity-based demand model.

Summary

Population theory is important from a historical perspective. Armed with data on the population by age, and mortality statistics and the propensity to work by age, one can make good annual estimates of the flows into and out of the labor force decades ahead. That aggregate supply of labor is portrayed as highly inelastic and somewhat backward bending. The inelasticity indicates that people will work over a considerable range of wages. But once in the labor force people can supply their labor to different firms, occupations, industries, and regions. The large number of alternatives makes the supply of the constituents of the aggregate supply far more elastic.

The supply of labor is quite different if people, on the average, work twenty rather than forty hours a week. Jevons contends that the choice of hours is that of workers and then applies marginal utility—disutility analysis to the problem. Under Jevons's model the higher the wage rate the lower the hours worked per unit of time. This is because the higher the wage the sooner a worker reaches the equality between the marginal utility obtained from earnings and the marginal disutility of work. Indifference curve analysis is ambiguous about the effects of a pay increase on the hours of work decision. This is because the income effect stimulates less work and the substitution effect more work. Models claiming that individual workers decide how many hours they are to work a day, week, and so on assume that this is a matter of indifference to employers. On the contrary, they are frequently very concerned about the hours their employees work and the norm is for employers to make that decision.

The lengthy history of the eight-hour-day movement is quite at odds with the contention that workers choose the amount of hours they will labor. Marx's power-based model seems more in accord with the facts.

The quality of the workforce is an important aspect of the supply. It is improved by schooling and on-the-job training. Related spending can be considered to be investments in human capital. The rate-of-return approach makes great sense with respect to evaluating whether or not a reasonable amount of resources have been allocated to the production of schooling. Empirical studies have tended to show it to be comparable to that of other investments of comparable risk and uncertainty. To what extent, if any, individuals estimate their expected rate of return is another matter.

The intensity of work reflects the culture of the workplace which is related to the cultures of the industry, region, and society. Of some relevance is the perception that management cares about the worker's welfare.

The theoretical demand for labor function is based on the assumption that production can be increased by the increased employment of labor alone. This allows identification of its marginal product, the slope of the production function. Three variants of demand based on marginal productivity are commonly presented. In one, workers are paid in units of the product. In the second labor and product markets are assumed to be competitive and workers receive the dollar value of the marginal product. In the third the product market is monopolistic and workers are paid the marginal revenue product. All of the variants require that the worker's product is sold. That is the case for the half of the firm's employees who are production workers; it is not true of the other half whose marginal revenue products are zero, but are paid nonetheless—sometimes extravagantly. In addition, there is no theoretical demand function if the employer is a monopsonist.

Whether varying one factor alone can increase production is arguable. In Chapter 5 mention was made of the fact that Josef Schumpeter and Sir John Hicks did not believe in the existence of a short-run production function. John Bates Clark, the inventor of the marginal productivity-based factor demand model, appears to be of a similar mind. To increase production Clark varied labor and capital while *money* capital was held constant. Nonetheless, almost all textbooks and empirical studies of the production function assume that substantial additional production can be attained by the increased employment of a single factor of production. How this is done is never explained and it is maintained here that such production is impossible except in trivial pursuits. And the wages paid for trivial activities do not set the wages paid all of us.

How do economists handle the problem of production and demand if the marginal productivity of labor is at or near zero because capital required is unavailable? There are three ways—all of which confront the shortage of "fixed" capital. Clark sets money capital constant and has the dollar value of the capital equipment per worker varying inversely with a firm's employment. Marshall varies the two required factors subtracting the supply price of one from the product demand price to derive the demand of the other. Marshall was shown to be wrong because the vertical sum of the derived factor demand functions did no equal the product demand function from which they are derived. (Empirical value added–production functions also subtract out costs, namely, the cost of what is bought from other firms or sectors of the economy. The demand functions derived from them are, therefore, suspect.) The third way of solving the need-for-capital problem involves varying capital inaccurately classified as "fixed." But then the demand for labor is based not upon the marginal product of labor but a blend of the marginal product of labor and capital. In none of these is recognition given to circulating capital and to how it is handled in the model even though no production can take place in its absence.

Empirical studies generally indicate that marginal cost is constant. This implies that production is accomplished through the use of factors which are fixed in proportions. As a result, the productivity of individual factors cannot be identified. Constant marginal cost also implies constant marginal productivity of the dose of factors comprising marginal cost, and a linear production function up to the full capacity of the producing unit.

Questions on Chapter 12

1. Explain the idea of stocks and flows by showing the flows which bring about a change in the total enrollment at your school.

2. a. What is Adam Smith's population model and to what extent, if any, is it relevant at a time of considerable unemployment?
   b. The post–World War II period experienced a baby boom and a subsequent bust. How might this be explained?

3. a. The hours people would like to work can be shown using marginal utility and indifference curve analysis. Show how they both work.
   b. Why do I say "would like to work" and not "the hours a worker decides to work"?

4. Explain the marginal productivity model of the demand for labor paid in
   a. units of the product
   b. in dollars.

5. a. Why does keeping capital constant create a problem in producing more by the increased employment of labor alone?
   b. Why is varying labor and capital together a good thing for production but a bad thing for determining the demand for labor?

6. Assume that: (i) In order to assemble another car, at all rates of production, twenty hours of labor and a kit of capital, including parts, are required. (ii) The price of the car to dealers is $10,000. (iii) And the price of a kit is $6,000.
   a. Explain how Alfred Marshall would have used the above information to attain the demand for labor function.
   b. Explain why the approach is wrong.

CHAPTER THIRTEEN

Employment, Unemployment, and the Real Wage

Employment and the related wage payments give workers earnings which amount to about 70 percent of national income and, at the same time, 70 percent of the nation's purchasing power. By this measure, the earnings of labor are the most important of factor payments and labor the most important of factors.

The neoclassical paradigm treats all markets the same with supply and demand yielding a stable equilibrium, stable in the sense that the force of disequilibria causes equilibria to be regained. Were labor markets in accord with the theory, the smallest outbreak of unemployment or labor shortage would force the market toward equilibrium and eradication of the labor shortage or surplus. With its high stress on this theory, unemployment in the neoclassical paradigm, is of little, if any, concern. Some distinguished leaders of the school even deny the existence of involuntary unemployment contending that people normally categorized as unemployed have actually chosen leisure over work. This is congenial to the equilibrium thrust of the paradigm—but not to me and others. Unemployment and other labor market disequilibria receives due coverage here.

The existence of unemployment has given rise to a substantial number of models explaining its existence. Old an new ones are examined. Almost all economists believe that were the real wage less sticky, unemployment would be attenuated. But an empirically based model is presented which indicates that decreases in the real wage would probably worsen unemployment due to the real earnings loss it would create. Disequilibrium in the labor market covers more than unemployment. There is disequilibrium, for example, when workers want to work more or fewer hours than they actually work. All disequilibria considered, about 40 percent of workers are in disequilibrium.

The labor market is characterized by multiple prices for what seemingly is the same kind of work performed by the same quality workers. This is frequently a manifestation of the existence of high- and low-wage firms and high- and low-wage industries. Models of wage differentials are presented in an attempt to explain this phenomenon. At the end two "bottom lines" are considered. One is the growth record of real earnings during the post–World War II period. The other refers to the distribution of earnings and the worsening position of low-wage workers.

The Labor Market and Its Operation

In some ways the so-called labor market has the characteristics of a competitive market. There are about 130 million suppliers of labor services and about 14 million producers who demand labor services. This is an important matter since the competitive market, particularly organized competitive markets, quickly wipe out shortages and surpluses. Alternatively put, were labor services sold in an organized market unemployment and shortages might be of short duration and little consequence. But the competitive market requires the product exchanged to be homogeneous and labor is anything but that. Few of us have the expertise to do heart transplants or to pitch a World Series game, or to run a jack-hammer, or to pick a crop, or to teach topology, or to erect the steel frame of a skyscraper. Moreover, some labor markets are national, others local, and many exist in the innards of firms and government agencies, internal labor markets. All of this implies that the setting or wages, employment, and unemployment are the products of many labor markets derived from the demand for a multitude of different products. But whatever our skills and inclinations, all in the workforce are covered by the abstractions *labor* and the *labor market*. Moreover, it is perhaps the best vehicle to use for determining what may be the most important performance of the economy—the real wage and annual earnings and their growth, employment, and unemployment.

In the previous chapter, the development of the labor supply and demand functions have been considered both in terms of neoclassical models and some alternatives. That long presentation need not be repeated here. However formed, we have the aggregate supply of and demand for labor functions. Now the focus is on the *operation* of the labor market. First, brief consideration is given to the character of a stable equilibrium. Second, the Great Depression is used as a laboratory test particularly with respect to the problem of transforming the money wage cuts of that period into real wage cuts. The final section confronts the question: Can reduction in the real wage increase the employment of labor? Almost everyone believes that the answer to this question is "yes." But please hold your answer until you have read the section addressing this question. You might then conclude that the answer is "no."

Figure 13.1.   **Equilibria with the Growth of Demand Exceeding Supply and then the Growth of Supply Exceeding Demand**

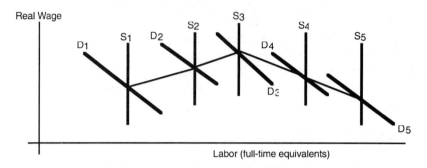

Stable Equilibrium

Why is the equilibrium between quantities supplied and demanded a stable equilibrium:

> A stable equilibrium has the characteristic that when driven from equilibrium, forces automatically develop to drive the system or market back to equilibrium.

Assume that a market is in equilibrium. A random event or shock then increases the wage (or price) so that it is higher than its equilibrium value. This automatically creates a surplus which provides the force to drive the wage (or price) back down to its equilibrium level. Had the shock driven the wage (or price) below the equilibrium level, a shortage would occur and that would create the force to drive the wage (or price) back to the equilibrium level.

Do not lose sight of the fact that if the quantity supplied in the labor market equaled that demanded, full employment of labor would exist. There would be no unemployment. The fruits of stable equilibrium are especially important to dynamic economies, economies in which supply and demand are just about always shifting and at times with some irregularity. The stability system is dumb to the cause of disequilibrium. As the smallest disequilibria occurs between quantities supplied and demanded, in the form of a shortage or surplus, it responds with the force to eradicate it.

As demand and supply shift over the course of time the stable equilibrium yields the kind of relationship assumed by David M. Blank and George J. Stigler for the market for engineers as shown in Figure 3.5. In Figure 13.1, equilibria are attained both as demand growth is greater than that of supply and when supply growth is greater than demand. The former is characterized by labor shortages; the latter by surplus—with the real wage responding to maintain equilibrium or full employment.

Table 13.1.   **The Labor Market, Selected Variables, 1929–1934**

Year	Labor Force (millions)	Unem- ployment (percent)	Employ- ment (millions)	Wages ($/hr.)	GNP Price Index (1958=100)	Real Wage W/P$_{gnp}$
1934	51.91	21.7	40.64	0.53	40.1	1.26
1933	51.13	24.9	38.40	0.44	38.8	1.12
1932	50.35	23.6	38.47	0.41	40.9	1.02
1931	49.59	15.9	41.71	0.51	45.6	1.14
1930	48.78	8.7	44.54	0.55	50.0	1.12
1929	48.02	3.2	46.48	0.56	51.3	1.11

Source: *Historical Statistics of the United States.* The calculation of employment and the
real wage are mine.

The Great Depression and the Absence of a Stable Equilibrium

Consider the case of the Great Depression. Relevant data appear in Table 13.1.
Note first the progress of the unemployment rate and the real wage It started at
a low of 3.2 percent in 1929. It became quite high, 8.7 percent in 1930, and the
real wage *increased* by about 1 percent. From 1930 to 1931 the surplus almost
doubled and the real wage *increased* by 1.8 percent. Between 1931 and 1932 the
money wage dropped by almost 20 percent, hardly sticky, and the real wage decreased by 10.5 percent. Despite this large decrease in the real wage, another
major increase in unemployment took place as the rate went from 15.9 to 23.6.
The unemployment rate was highest in 1933, just short of 25 percent. Both the
money and real wage increased despite the massive unemployment. The real
wage in 1933 was just about what it had been in 1929—but 8.1 million fewer
workers were employed. Finally, in 1934 the real wage increased by over 12
percent, employment increased and the unemployment rate decreased. Obviously, the labor market was not one with a stable equilibrium particularly in the
context of a collapse in demand.

The 1929–1933 collapse in demand is shown in Figure 13.2. The data are from
Table 13.1. The lessons coming from the laboratory experiment of the Great Depression are these: (1) The equilibrating force of relatively huge amounts of surplus labor is quite modest. (2) This may be due in part to the fairly tight gearing between wages and prices which kept the real wage rather constant despite
relatively large changes in money wages. (3) And the substantial constancy of
the real wage and substantial declining employment indicate a collapse in aggregate demand and the derived demand for labor. With the demand for labor
highly inelastic, decreases in the real wage could have little, if any, effect on unemployment.

Figure 13.2.   **Supply of and Demand for Labor, 1929 and 1933**

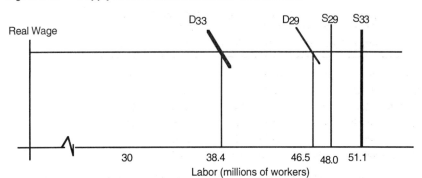

Labor (millions of workers)

Categories of Unemployment

There are three common categories of unemployment: frictional, structural, and deficient demand or cyclical. Seasonal unemployment is no longer considered to be an important source of overall employment and the replacement suggested is anti-inflation unemployment. Statistical discrimination, which affects the distribution of unemployment, has been included for good measure.

Frictional Unemployment

A person is frictionally unemployed when a job exists for a person with her qualifications but the unemployed worker is unaware of its existence and the employer with the opening is unaware of the existence of the qualified unemployed person.

   The obvious solution to the problem of frictional unemployment is an improvement in the transmission of job openings information to the unemployed and the qualifications of the unemployed to employers with job openings. A number of countries handle this problem by requiring employers to register job openings with a government employment agency. United States employers have resisted this as a potential intrusion into their right to hire as they will. Skeptics suggest that auxiliary reason might be that government involvement would tend to reduce the ability of employers to discriminate in their hirings.

Structural Unemployment

Structural unemployment occurs if there is a mismatch between the skills required by employers and the skills of the unemployed. It also occurs when there is a mismatch between the location of jobs and the unemployed with the skills required for the job. There would be jobs for the structurally unemployed if they only had the right skills or lived in the right area.

Structural unemployment has been related to the poor scholastic achievements of many of the young unemployed and the out-of-date skills of older workers who are the victims of downsizings. Another claim is that we have advanced from having an economy in which much work required only a strong back to one in which workers require good verbal and mathematical skills.

The solution to the structural skill mismatch is to make available to unemployed workers the training required to qualify for existing job openings and to provide relocation assistance to those who qualify for remote jobs.

There are two major arguments against the contention that the structural problem is an important source of unemployment. The first is the experience of low unemployment. When the demand for labor is high, the structural unemployment problem seems to disappear. The second has to do *not* with the lack of skill of the labor force but with their excess skills relative to the work they perform. The Bureau of Labor Statistics estimates that a quarter of college graduates in their late 20s and early 30s are employed in jobs requiring no more than a high school education. This indicates that many are unemployed not because they lack required skills but because they lack the required credentials.

But why are college graduates hired to perform work which requires the skills found in high school graduate? On the supply side, the answer is that college graduates are willing to take these jobs. On the demand side, there is the expectation of employers that, as a group, college graduates are more productive than high school graduates. There are, however, some high school graduates who would actually be substantially more productive than some college graduates. The generality of choosing college graduates over high school graduates is an example of statistical discrimination.

Deficient Demand or Cyclical Unemployment

Deficient demand or cyclical unemployment arises from a shortfall in the demand for labor as compared to the size of the labor force. This is the most important, troubling, and depressing form of unemployment. The creation of the additional demand required to end this form of unemployment is a major topic in macroeconomics.

Anti-Inflation Unemployment

Another form of unemployment is *anti-inflation unemployment.* Frequently when the unemployment rate drops stock market prices drop as there is speculation that the FED will raise the interest rate to protect us from inflation. And sometimes the FED does take steps intended to increase the interest rate. Increases in the interest rate are inflationary in and of themselves. But the deeper intention is to curtail interest-sensitive spending, to increase the unemployment

Figure 13.3.   **Frequency Distributions of the Expected Value of Members of Group A and Group B**

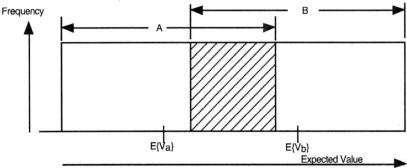

of workers who help produce homes, cars, and other big-ticket items and to have this unemployment depress oncoming wage increases. The conscious creation of unemployment by the FED may be discomforting to those who view unemployment as *the* economic failure.

Statistical Discrimination and Unemployment

Statistical discrimination in labor market hirings involves evaluating job applicants on the basis of the expected value an employer assigns to a group—instead of the expected value of an individual. Figure 13.3 illustrates this kind of discrimination. It shows the hypothetical distribution of the value of people in group A and people in group B. Those in A could, for example, be high school graduates, those in group B college graduates. The job might be one which used to be performed by high school graduates and is now performed by college graduates. The reason for hiring college graduates rather than high school graduates is that the expected value of their work, $E\{V_b\}$, is higher than the expected value of the work of high school graduates, $E\{V_a\}$.

If employers judge individuals in group A and B on the basis of the expected value of the group they are in, college graduates are always preferred to high school graduates. But note the cross-hatched overlap of the two distributions. There is a substantial percentage of high school graduates whose value is equal to or greater than that of college graduates—but the statistically based stereotyping of members of both groups obscures this. As a result less valuable college graduates will be hired and more valuable high school graduates will not. Statistical discrimination is practiced not only with respect to levels of education but also with respect to gender, race, age, and school reputation. Just as structural unemployment tends to lessen as demand increases, so, too does statistical

Figure 13.4.   **The Unemployment Rate, 1950-1990**

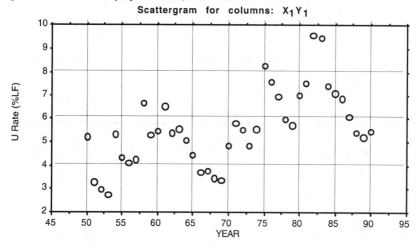

Scattergram for columns: $X_1 Y_1$

discrimination. When employers have trouble filling job openings they are
prone to look more at individual attributes rather than group norms or ster-
eotypes.

Some Unemployment Statistics

In the first chapter I mentioned that ordinal information is close to useless and
that economics requires more quantification. Unemployment is a word with
negative implications to many of us. But it would not be terribly important if
unemployment rates tended to be "low" and the unemployment was shared fairly
equally among those in the labor force. In line with this, information on the unemployment rate and the duration of spells of unemployment are presented.

The Unemployment Rate

Figure 13.4 shows the unemployment rate during the 1950–1990 period. The
low of 2.9 percent was in 1953, during the Korean War. Less than a 4 percent
unemployment rate was attained in 1966, 1967, 1968, and 1969, the Vietnam
War years. The high of 9.7 percent occurred in 1982. Some of this high rate was
anti-inflation unemployment. It followed three years of double-digit inflation.
Note the irregular cyclical pattern of unemployment, the increasing trend in the
unemployment rate and the large jumps in the rate as it reaches its peaks. The
average unemployment rate during the 1950–1990 period was 5.8 percent. Had
unemployment been evenly distributed, each of us would have been idle 2.9

Table 13.2.   **The Distribution of Unemployment by Duration, 1984**

| Weeks | Duration of Unemployment (weeks) | | | | |
| | less than 5 | 5–14 | 15–26 | 27 or more | Mean Duration |
	(percentage in category)				
	39	29	13	19	18.2

Source: Economic Report of the President, 1996, Table B–40, p. 326; for the number of unemployed by duration; my conversion to percentages.

weeks of the year. Were that the case no individual worker would have been badly hurt. On the other hand, if the same 5.8 percent of the labor force remained continually unemployed, we have a social problem of concern.

The Distribution of Unemployment by Duration

The data of Table 13.2 are indicative of the distribution of unemployment by duration. The information is for 1984, a year in which the unemployment rate averaged 7.5 percent. The Bureau of Labor Statistics puts the unemployed into the following duration of unemployment categories: less than five, five to fourteen, fifteen to twenty-six, and twenty-seven weeks or more. The average number of unemployed people in 1984 was 8.54 million. The average duration of unemployment was 18.2 weeks. For the 19 percent unemployed for twenty-seven or more weeks, the average duration of employment was sixty-two weeks—a frightening figure to me. (I assumed that, for the three lower-duration categories, the average length of unemployment was at the midpoint of the group:and solved for the average duration in the highest duration group: *18.2 = 0.39 • 2.5 + 0.29 • 9.5 + 0.13 • 20.5 + 0.19X; X = 62.13.*)

The distribution of unemployment is highly unequal. About half of the unemployed find jobs within two months, but roughly one-tenth have spells of unemployment greater than a year—a personal and social problem of concern.

Recent Models of Unemployment

Models explaining the existence of unemployment are placed under two headings in this section. The first set consists of models of unresponsive wages—wages which do not drop enough to eradicate unemployment. Following these are calculations which indicate that flexible wages cannot resolve unemployment. The second set of models postulate the existence of jobs for the unemployed and theorize why workers do not accept them. This is followed by a study by the current commissioner of Labor Statistics indicating that the number of unemployed workers tends to be substantially greater than the number of job vacancies.

Figure 13.5.   **The Efficiency Wage and Profit Maximization**

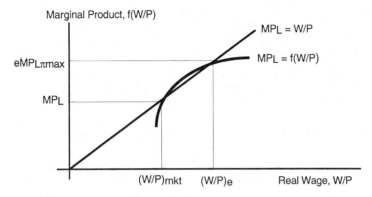

Models of Unresponsive Wages

Models explaining the unresponsiveness of the wage rate to unemployment imply that decreases in wages would substantially reduce unemployment. The most important contemporary models which attempt to explain the stickiness of wages are the efficiency wage model, implicit contracts model, and the insider/outsider model.

The Efficiency Wage Model

The efficiency wage model posits productivity as an increasing function of the real wage with the efficiency wage being that at which profit is maximized. The idea can be found in Adam Smith's observation that:

> Where wages are high ... we shall always find the workmen more active, diligent, and expeditious than where they are low (1937 [1776], p. 81).

The logic of the efficiency wage can be understood with the help of Figure 13.5. It shows the marginal product of labor as an increasing function of the real wage. All points on the 45 degree line from the origin, an identity line, represent the equality of the marginal product of labor and the real wage, $MP_L = W/P$. The first equilibrium is the conventional one in which the real market wage equals the marginal product of labor. I show it to be unstable because more profits can be made by increasing the real wage until the marginal product of labor as a function of the real wage again equals the marginal product on the real wage equality line. This is the efficiency wage, the true profit-maximizing wage. Note that the logic of this depends on increases in marginal productivity being greater than the real wage in the interval from the market to the efficiency wage. This is a stable equilibrium because profits are lost in paying either less than or more than the efficiency wage.

There are two reasons for the association of the efficiency wage with unemployment. First, it allows an employer to attain a given rate of output with fewer employees. Second, assuming unemployment exists, the efficiency wage is not reduced to equilibrate the market because that would lower both productivity and profits. Thus, the maintenance of unemployment.

Fair questions regarding the efficiency wage model are: If the efficiency wage is more profitable than the market wage why is the market wage not increased to the efficiency level? Is the failure to pay the efficiency wage irrational?

The Insider-Outsider Model

The insiders in this model are the employed. The outsiders are the unemployed. The insiders have more bargaining power than the outsiders, power which allows them to obtain a higher-than-market wage. The power of the insiders is in the area of transaction costs. The termination of an insider tends to involve severance and morale costs. The employment of an outsider tends to require spending on search and on-the-job training. The greater these transaction costs are, the greater is the ability of insiders to attain above-market wages. This creates an incentive for insiders to increase transaction costs. If workers are represented by a union, for example, an increase in severance pay would do just that as would an arbitration or work stoppage challenging the termination of an insider.

What about unemployed workers willing to work for lower pay than insiders? To successfully underbid insiders, outsiders would have to accept pay lower than insiders by at least transaction costs. And, if they did, insiders might take steps costly to the employer. Senior workers are frequently used to informally train new hires in the most efficient ways of accomplishing work tasks. That informal help could be curtailed. And production is frequently accomplished by teams, and aspects of teamwork could be reduced. As a consequence of the transaction and other costs, insiders are hypothesized as being able to obtain and maintain a wage higher than market clearing.

The Implicit Contract Model

The implicit contract model starts with the assumption that workers are more risk averse than employers—the latter because shareholders tend to hold diversified portfolios which allow them to be unconcerned with firm-specific risks. The model contends that the manifestation of risk which workers want to avoid is that of fluctuating wages. It is in their interests to have sticky wages and temporary layoffs with a significant portion of their wage loss covered by layoff pay, unemployment compensation, and the value of leisure.

The model assumes that employers benefit from having sticky wages. This allows them to curtail quits and to retain workers with the skills they require.

Over the course of time, employers reduce their costs by *not* varying wages in response to fluctuations in demand but by having temporary layoffs. Thus, the implicit contract of sticky wages, layoffs, and recalls is also in the interests of employers.

In this model the wage paid is independent of variation in the demand for labor. When the dollar value of the marginal productivity of a firm's workers is relatively high, workers are paid less than the value of the marginal product; when it is low, they are paid more than their marginal product. No such trade-off exists with respect to the layoff of workers when demand is low. The firm, for example, cannot be convinced to employ more than is required when demand is low and less than is required when it is high.

Problems with the Insider-Outsider and Implicit Contract Models

Allow me to suggest that the tradition of keeping pay fixed and laying off redundant blue-collar workers and some white-collar workers represent the self-interest of management and not an agreement worked out with unorganized work groups or the power of insiders over their managements. (1) By keeping wages constant, executives and managers need not set an example justifying the pay cuts of employees. (2) After the layoffs, sometimes tearful, the maintenance of wages and basic hours helps to uphold the morale and productivity of those whose employment is maintained. (3) It also allays the fear that with lower pay the best workers will leave their service. (4) While some work groups may prefer work-sharing, managements resist this. It costs more to staff a plant with more workers and a shorter workweek because of additional fringe benefit costs. (5) Wage maintenance and layoffs allow managements to avoid confronting a question the answer to which implies two different policies when demand decreases: Would redundant workers benefit by being laid off because job openings at other firms are plentiful or would they be better off working a shorter workweek because of the scarcity of comparable jobs? The tradition of fixed wages and layoffs makes good sense to employers and that is why it is such a common practice. (6) Finally, not all redundant workers are laid off. Managers are part of the "team" making them somewhat insulated from immediate demand shortfalls. So, too, with their staffs. And there are those, particularly professionals, who represent investments intended to yield greater profits and growth.

Would Employment Increase If the Real Wage Decreased?

The implicit contract and insider-outsider models assume, in effect, that decreasing the real wage would increase the employment of labor and, of course, hypothesize why that fails to occur. But I have the peculiar view that decreasingthe real wage would increase the *unemployment* of labor. Figure 13.6 affords a preview of the calculations which follow. It includes a demand function and a total

Figure 13.6.   **The Demand for Labor and Total Earnings**

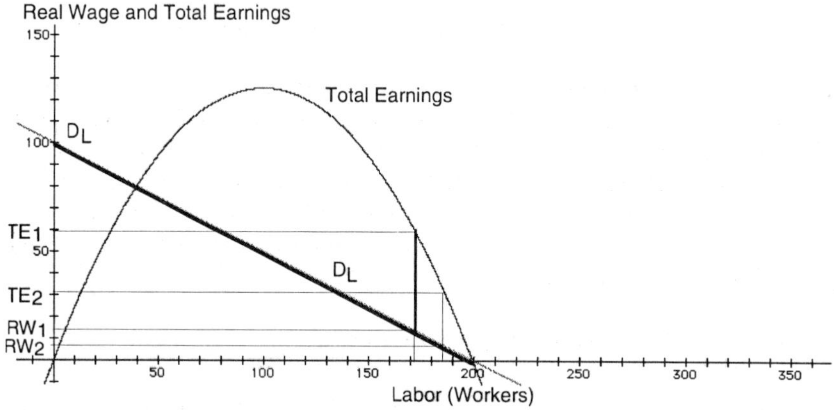

Real Wage and Total Earnings

earnings function, analogous to the total revenue function. The absolute value of the numbers on the graph are arbitrary but the changes shown are in the realm of reality.

The initial real wage is RW_1 and that puts us in a highly inelastic range of the demand for labor function. Employment is 172 and total earnings, TE_1, are 60. Then the wage is cut in half to RW_2. Employment increases to 185, an increase of 7.6 percent. But total earnings decrease from TE_1 to TE_2—from 60 to 33. The drop in earnings is 45 percent. With the real earnings of labor decreased by 45 percent, there will be a massive decrease in consumption, aggregate demand, the derived demand for labor, and the employment of labor. A cut in the real wage accordingly decreases rather than increases employment. This claim warrants some detailing.

The Inelasticity of the Demand for Labor and the Effect on Earnings

Daniel Hamermesh's survey of the empirical work on the elasticity of demand for labor (1976) found that the mean was about –0.15. This indicates that to increase employment by 1 percent, the real wage has to decrease by 6.67 percent. What is the effect of the wage decrease on total earnings? Total real earnings, initially TE_1, equals the real wage times the number employed at that wage:

(1) $TE_1 = RW_1 \cdot L_1$

Then decrease the real wage by 6.67 percent and increase employment by 1 percent. Total earnings are then:

(2) $TE_2 = 0.933\ RW_1 \cdot 1.01\ L_1 = 0.942\ TE_1$

The pay cut required to increase employment by 1 percent decreases total earnings by 5.8 percent. The issue becomes: How much will employment decrease as a consequence of a 5.8 percent decrease in total real earnings?

Spending as a Function of Earnings

Earnings amount to about 73 percent of national income. As a result, if earnings decrease by 5.8 percent, income decreases by 4.23 percent. The issue is then: Will a 4.23 percent decrease in national income cause more than a 1 percent decrease in employment? The assumptions used in attempting to answer this question are these: (1) The percent of decrease in spending equals the decrease in national income (4.23 percent) times the marginal propensity to spend, MPS_p. (2) The "multiplier" equals 1. There is no cumulation in the decrease in spending. (3) The decrease in the demand for labor is proportionate to the decrease in spending. A 1 percent decrease in spending decreases demand and employment by 1 percent.

What we have is this: the percentage change in national income, $\Delta NI/NI$, times the marginal propensity to spend, $MPSp$, equals the percent change in aggregate spending, $\Delta Sp/Sp$, which equals the percent change in the employment, $\Delta Emp/Emp$:

(3) $\Delta NI/NI \cdot MPSp = \Delta Sp/Sp = \Delta Emp/Emp$

What I would like to find is the magnitude of the marginal propensity to spend which causes the 4.23 percent decrease in income to decrease spending by 1 percent—just canceling out the increase in employment rate brought about by the 6.67 percent cut in the real wage.

(4) $-0.0423 \cdot MPSp = -1;$ $MPSp = 0.236$

If the marginal propensity to spend is less than 0.236, the real wage cut increases employment. If it equals 0.236, employment is unchanged. And, if it is greater than 0.236, the real wage decrease will decrease employment. The marginal propensity to spend is typically estimated to be roughly 0.6. (A $100 income change yields a spending change of about $60.) Accordingly, a decrease in the real wage can be expected to decrease employment.

Money Wages and Prices Geared Together

While it is easy to decrease the real wage in a textbook, it is much harder to decrease it in actuality. This is because of the gearing between wage and prices. During the 1929–1933 period money wages dropped by about 25 percent—as did prices. The tighter the gearing between money wages and prices, the greater is the percent drop in money wages required for each percent change in the real wage. And the more impractical is the use of money wage decreases to resolve the unemployment problem.

To quantify the more recent relationship between prices and wages I have used more recent data, namely, annual data for the 1947–1990 period. The model used follows:

(5) $\ln P = A + B \ln W + u$

where: P is the gross national product deflator; W is money compensation (the money wage inclusive of the cost of fringe benefits); and u is a stochastic disturbance term with an expected value of zero. It includes all the other variables which affect price such as the cost of non-labor factors, the productivity of labor. the wage-price controls of the Nixon administration, and the state of demand as indicated, for example, by capacity utilization rates. In the logarithmic form, the estimated value of B is the elasticity of price with respect to the wage rate.

The following estimating equation was obtained:

(6) $\ln P = 1.2885 + 0.7094 \ln W$ $R^2 \text{adj.} = 0.9822$
                      $(t = 48.73)$

According to the regression equation a 1 percent drop in compensation yields a 0.71 percent drop in the price level. With this relationship, it might be of some interest to estimate the decrease in the real wage which would accompany a depression-like cut in the money wage of 25 percent.

Given: (1) The percent change in price equals 0.7 of the percent change in the money wage. (2) The money wage drops by 25 percent.
Find: The percent change in the real wage.

The real wage is initially, $RW_1 = W_1/P_1$. If the money wage decreases by 25 percent, $W_2 = 0.75 W_1$.
The price decrease is 0.7 of the money decrease, $0.7 \cdot 25 = 17$.percent. Thus, $P_2 = 0.825 P_1$
As a result: $RW_2 = 0.75\ W_1 \div 0.825\ P_1 = 0.909\ RW_1$, a 9.1 percent decrease.

The 25 percent drop in the money wage yields a 9.1 percent decrease in the real wage. From the perspective of the elasticity of demand, this should decrease unemployment by roughly 1.5 percent—with no consideration of the increase in employment arising from the decrease in total income accompanying the pay cut.

Models of Unemployment Based on the Search for Higher-Paying Jobs

Models involving the search for a higher-paying job imply unemployed workers have been offered one or more jobs but have chosen to remain unemployed in order to find one which pays more. The two models in this category are the search (for higher pay) and the reservation wage model.

The Search Unemployment Model

Unemployment models involving search assume that there are job openings for the unemployed; the unemployed have found and been offered one or more of them; but they are looking for one which pays better. They have, therefore, chosen to remain unemployed and are not involuntarily unemployed. Employers are also searching. They are trying to find workers who meet their standards and will accept the wages and benefits they offer. If they fail, they may have to increase their compensation package.

The development of interest in wage search models can be attributed to the work of George J. Stigler. Recall Stigler's price search model presented in Chapter 6. It involved buyers searching for the cheapest price where the cost of the search is a transactions cost. The model was demand sided with buyers knowing the distribution of prices but not the price at which each firm was selling. Buyers should search until the marginal cost of search equaled its expected marginal benefit which declines with the number of canvasses.

Stigler's analysis of labor market search is basically the same. The main differences between the price and wage search models are these: (1) The wage search model is supply sided. (2) Workers search for the highest wage but, with the future job expected to be a continuing relationship, the marginal benefit or gain is the expected present value of the increase in wages obtained by the investment in the marginal canvass. (3) The marginal cost of continuing a search is the foregone wage of the best job offer turned down minus the value of leisure and unemployment compensation. Note that the model assumes that jobs are plentiful. The search is not for a job but for a better-paying job.

An example applying Stigler's model follows: Assume that one-third of all job openings for engineers with three years of experience in the design of computer networks, pay $20 an hour, one-third $25 an hour and one-third $30 an hour. In Table 13.3 can be seen the probability of finding the maximum wage, in bold faced type, and the others in regular type; the expected wage arising from each of three canvasses; and the expected marginal increase in the wage obtained by an additional canvass.

Some words on how the probabilities were obtained. It is assumed that there are the same number of job openings at $20, $25, and $30 an hour. As a result, on the first canvass there is a one-third probability of finding each of the three wage rates. On the second canvass, there are nine alternatives arising from the two tries: $20, $20; $20, $25; $20, $30; $25, $20; $25, $25; $25, $30; $30, $20; $30, $25; $30, $30. The probability of finding no better than a $20 job is 1 out of 9. The probability of finding no better than the $25 job is 3 out of 9. And the probability of finding the $30 job is 5 out of 9. The third canvass involves 27 alternatives and working them out is left to the reader.

The expected wage rate for each canvass is the mean found in the canvass: the probability, *pr,* of attaining a wage times the wage for each of the three wages:

Table 13.3.   **Search, the Expected Wage, and Marginal Wage**

Canvass	Probability of Finding Each Wage $20 $25 $30			Expected Wage	Marginal Wage
				(dollars per hour)	
1	1/3	1/3	**1/3**	25.00	
					2.22
2	1/9	3/9	**5/9**	27.22	
					1.11
3	1/27	7/27	**19/27**	28.33	

$E\{W\} = pr20 + pr25 + pr30$. The expected marginal wage, $E\{MW\}$, is the difference between the expected wage in two successive canvasses or the additional expected wage rate obtained from one additional canvass.

The present value of the marginal gain is calculated as follows: The marginal gain, MG, of a canvass is the present value of the discounted value of the marginal wage for the length of time the individual worker expects to maintain that differential. Take the marginal wage of $2.22 per hour or $384.80 per month. Assume that the individual expects to maintain that marginal monthly wage for 60 months and discounts future wages by 1 percent a month. The present value, PV, is then:

(7) $MG = PV = 384.80/(1.01) + 384.80/(1.01)^2 + ... + 384.80/(1.01)^{60}$

The above equation is that of the sum of geometric series, S, of the form:

(8) $S = PV = aR + aR^2 + ... + aR^n$

In our example $a = 384.80$, $R = 1/1.01$, and $n = 60$. The sum of such a series is given by the formula:

(9) $S = aR(1 + R^n)]/(1-R)$

The sum is close to $17,300. That is the present value of marginal wage of $2.22 per hour received for five years. (Without discounting the sum amounts to $23,088.)The present value of the third canvas would be half of that and additional canvasses would be of diminishing value.

What about the cost of attaining the higher-present-value job? Assume that it took a month to find a $25 per hour job and that the expected value of the wage to be found in another month is $27.22 per hour. What was the cost of obtaining the expected marginal wage increase of $2.22? The marginal cost was the loss of a month's pay at $25 per hour. This amounts to $4,350 ($25 hour • 40 hours/week • 4.35 weeks/month). Deduct from this amount, unemployment compensation for a month, and the value of a month of leisure. Discount these net marginal costs by one month and you have the present value of the costs associated with the present value of the marginal gain which equals $17,300. With the marginal gain greater than the marginal cost, additional canvasses should be made until the expected marginal gain equals marginal cost.

The search model implies a wonderful contradiction to neoclassical theory. The quantity of labor services supplied to high-wage firms should be relatively high; that to low-wage firms relatively low. In theory, the surplus of job applicants should lower the wage of high-wage firms; the relative shortage should raise that of low-wage firms. With workers searching for higher-wage jobs, the wage differential between firms should be driven to zero thus destroying the search rationale in this model. I call the contradiction *theoretical* because empirical studies indicate that high- and low-wage firms remain high- and low-wage firms over the years and are unmoved whether or not greater and lesser quantities of labor are supplied to them.

Another problem of the search model is that it is completely supply sided. No recognition is given to the search activities of firms anxious to find desired employees.

The Reservation Wage Model

The reservation wage model assumes that jobs are available for the unemployed and is a variant of the search model discussed above. The reservation wage is the minimum wage an individual worker will accept in exchange for his labor services. An unemployed worker who had been earning $20 an hour might have a reservation wage of $18 an hour. In searching for a job he rejects offers under $18 an hour and accepts any which pay $18 or more–even though better-paying jobs may be found by additional canvasses.

The unemployment caused by the reservation wage is a function of the mismatch between the distribution of reservation wages and the distribution of job offers by wages. Both distributions cover jobs of a particular type and workers qualified to perform the duties of that particular type of work. The distributions are shown in Figure 13.7. The vertical distance on the job openings function is the number of job openings at a particular wage. The vertical distance on the unemployed workers function is the number of workers with a particular reservation wage. The area under the job openings functions is the number of openings in a particular job. The area under the unemployment function is the number of unemployed who are qualified to perform that job. The distributions are so oriented that employers would like to pay less than workers would like to receive—except for the cross-hatched overlap of the functions. The failure of the unemployed workers to accept the wages of the job offer is the reason for the ex-

Figure 13.7.   **Distributions of Wage Offers and Reservation Wages**

Distributions of Job Openings and Unemployed Workers, by Wages

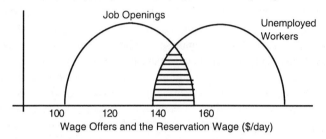

Wage Offers and the Reservation Wage ($/day)

istence of unemployment.

The cross-hatched area represents the maximum number of unemployed workers who can find a job paying the workers' reservation wage or more. Reaching the maximum requires perfect matching of wage offers and reservation wages. This requires that a $30 job offer, for example, is matched with unemployed workers with a $30 reservation wage and not with one who would have been willing to work for $25 an hour. The more workers receive offers equal to or greater than their reservation wage, the lower is unemployment and the number of job openings to be filled.

As unemployment continues, workers tend to lower their reservation wages. The result is a greater overlap of the job offer and reservation wage distributions and greater employment of the unemployed.

The Limited Relevance of the Search and Reservation Wage Models

To what extent do workers actually reject job offers to search for better-paying jobs? Harry J. Holzer's research on teenagers found that they accept about 80 percent of the job offers they get. And C. Rosenfeld found that only about 10 percent of workers in general, searching for employment, turn down a job offer. That a great majority of the unemployed accept the first job offer is at odds with both the search and reservation wage models. It implies that search and reservations wages are not important determinants of unemployment.

Is There Really No Involuntary Unemployment?

The most radical of the unemployment models is the neoclassical one in which *involuntary* unemployment is non-existent. It is a convenient way to do away with unemployment and is based on the contention that all those without jobs have opted for leisure rather than work. Its most recent prominent adherent is the 1995 recipient of the Nobel Prize in economic science, Robert E. Lucas, Jr. In his 1986 paper, "Models of Business Cycles," Lucas put the matter this way:

> To explain why people allocate time ... to unemployment we need to know why they prefer it to all other activities.(p. 36). By dogmatically insisting that unemployment be classified as 'involuntary' ... [the Keynesian approach] simply cut itself off from the actual options the unemployed are faced with (p. 47).

According to Lucas, to understand the unemployment of the Great Depression we have to explain why many workers decided that they prefered unemployment to work.

Robert Aaron Gordon in his presidential address to the American Economic Association has responded to the no-involuntary-unemployment claim this way:

> The persistence of unemployment contradicts the neoclassical model which contends that there is an inexorable tendency toward the equilibrium of supply and demand. Sophisticated neoclassicists have assumed the problem away by means of an argument that flies in the face of facts such as the one that all unemployment is a voluntary activity as part of a search activity in which workers are continually equating costs and prospective benefits (1976, p. 5).

As a child of the human tragedy, the Great Depression, I cannot grasp the contention that its unemployment represented the choice of leisure over work.

Abraham's Study Indicating that Involuntary Unemployment Exists

Every once in a while newspaper headlines report on a large number of people queuing up to get a small number of jobs. An article in the *Columbus Dispatch* of September 27, 1983 stated that 9,500 workers applied for 150 openings at the local Western Electric plant. The *New York Times* of October 23, 1995 reported that 17,200 people applied for 320 jobs at the new Omni Hotel in downtown Manhattan. Stories like these give the impression that there are usually substantially more people who are unemployed than there are job openings. That such a casual impression tends to be true can be seen in the systematic work of Katharine G. Abraham, now commissioner of the Bureau of Labor Statistics. Abraham's work on the ratio of unemployment to job openings can be found in her article "Structural/Frictional vs. Deficient Demand Unemployment: Some New Evidence." Her conclusions, which follow, were based on six studies of "unemployment versus vacancy and job seekers versus vacancy estimates."

> ...The information compiled suggests that both the number of unemployed persons and the number of job seekers have consistently been much larger than the number of vacant jobs. If it could be assumed that the vacancy rate/unemployment rate relationships observed in the available survey data mirrored the vacancy rate/unemployment rate relationship prevailing in the United States over the same time period, reasonable estimates would be that there were roughly 2.5 unemployed persons for every vacant job during the middle 1960's, an average of close to 4.0 unemployed persons per vacant

job during the early 1970's, and an average of 5.0 or more unemployed persons for every vacant job during the latter part of the 1970's (1983, p. 712).

Thus, the predominant form of unemployment has been that of deficient demand. With a norm of almost four unemployed people for each job vacancy it makes sense that a great majority of first job offers are accepted and that the search process mainly consists of attempting to find a job. Abraham's study contradicts the no-involuntary employment model. If workers were immediately hired at the birth of each job opening, instead of the average ratio of four to one between the unemployed and job openings, it would be about three to zero. In other words, three-quarters of the unemployed would remain involuntarily unemployed due to the absence of any job openings at all.

Why the Neoclassical Model Rejects the Reality of Unemployment

The reality of unemployment is anathema to the neoclassical paradigm. Why is that? (1) No earnings are foregone by the employment of an unemployed worker. The opportunity cost of labor is then zero, making labor in theory a free resource. (2) If surplus labor exists it undermines the fundamental contention of the neoclassical school that the role of economics is to study the allocation of *scarce* resources. (3) Recognition of unemployment in the labor market createsan opening for consideration of the unemployment of capital—of the surplus of this resource that tends to lie idle two-thirds of the hours of a week. (4) There is substantial worldwide overcapacity in a number of important industries including those making cars, steel, airplanes, semiconductors, and armaments. (5) Surplus commercial space exists in some major cities. There are, of course, opportunity cost problems implicit in items (4) and (5).

Allow me to paraphrase the statement of Lucas quoted above: By dogmatically insisting that the unemployment of productive resources is non-existent, the neoclassical paradigm has cut itself off from some of the most compelling problems which exist in our economy and society—that of the surplus of workers, capital, and capacity in important industries.

A Broader View of Labor Market Equilibrium

Labor market disequilibrium figures can be found in Table 13.4. The forms of disequilibrium follow: (1) unemployment, (2) discouraged workers, workers who want jobs but cannot find them and leave the labor force, (3) workers who want to work fewer hours and are willing to earn less, and (4) workers who want to work more hours and earn more. (There are also those working below their capabilities, but I have no estimates on their number.) Were the neoclassical paradigm accurate in its description of the labor market, none of these disequilibria would exist.

Table 13.4.   **An Estimate of the Percent of Workers in Disequilibrium in the Labor Market**

Form of Disequilibrium	Percent of the Labor Force	
Unemployment	6.0	
Discouraged workers	0.6	
Desire to work more hours	26.3	
Desire to work fewer hours	10.6	
Total		43.5

Sources: See text.

The 6 percent unemployment figure is my choice as one which roughly approximates the experience of recent decades. Discouraged workers, those driven out of the labor force because of the failure to find jobs, tend to comprise roughly 10 percent of the unemployment rate, hence the 0.6 percent figure. Finally, Fred Best in his "Exchanging Earnings for Leisure" found that 28.0 percent of the *employed* (26.3 percent of the labor force) wish to work more hours at their base wage rate and 11.3 percent (10.6 percent of the labor force) want to work fewer hours and earn less. The total indicates that 43.5 percent of those in the labor force are in disequilibrium—a far cry from the zero percent of the neoclassical paradigm. Of special interest is that slightly over one of four workers wants to work more hours at the existing rate of pay.

The Law of Many Wages, More Disequilibrium

Students of labor markets find that workers doing the same kind of work frequently get quite different rates of pay. Adam Smith reported on this as follows:

> The price of labour, it must be observed, cannot be ascertained very accurately any where, different prices being often paid at the same place and for the same sort of labour, not according to the different abilities of the workmen, but according to the easiness or hardness of the masters (1937 [1776], p. 77).

Smith's finding is alive and well today, a continuing form of disequilibrium. An extreme version of the multiplicity of pay for the same kind of work occurred in the pre-union steel industry. Workers in the same mill doing the same work often received substantially different pay—pay determined by their respective foremen who received the money budgeted to perform a specified kind and amount of work. This budget was paid out at the discretion or indiscretion of the supervisor.

The Magnitude of Differentials Within an Occupation

Allow me to exploit Erica L. Groshen's 1989 research to indicate the magnitude of differentials within an occupation in a single metropolitan area. Groshen's work is based on data from a sample of firms in a standard metropolitan area during a six-year period, covering individual workers and establishments. It includes the following information: straight time-wage rates, gender, occupation, establishment identification of workers, size class of the establishments, and identification of their industry (by the two-digit form of the Standard Industrial Code).

Groshen found that there was a substantial difference in what employers paid workers in a given occupation:

> The most conservative estimate of establishment wage differentials in this sample (controlling for very detailed job classification) yields a standard deviation of 12 percent within industry, or 18 percent, including interindustry differentials (p. 1).

Assume that the distribution of wages in an occupation is normal or bell shaped. If the average wage in an occupation were $10 per hour, a bit less than two-thirds of those in the occupation would be getting paid in the range of $8.20 to $11.80 per hour. The latter wage is 44 percent higher than the former. At the rate at which the real wage is advancing, it would take a complete work-life to progress from the lower to the higher figure. Close to 95 percent of the workers in an occupation should be covered in the range of plus or minus two standard deviations from the mean. For the above example this comes to a range of $6.40 to $13.60 per hour. The differential is greater than the lower wage.

The Constancy of the Ranking of Employers by Wages

Groshen found "that interemployer wage differences and rankings of employers by wage are virtually stationary over six years" (p. 3). In comparing employers ranked by wage rate in the first and sixth years, Groshen obtained rank order correlation coefficients greater than 0.9—a figure comparable to that found in other studies. High-wage firms tend to have a continuing high-wage policy. And the same is true for other firms throughout the wage distribution. The high constancy of the rankings of employers, by wage, rules out a common claim that the wage differentials between firms are random—implying that the rankings of the firms are constantly changing. They are not.

The large wage differentials found for seemingly the same work and their con stancy makes hash out of the law of one wage. And the ranking constancy is in keeping with Smith's contention that wage differentials depended upon the easiness or hardness of employers.

Models of Wage Differentials

The standard generalizations are that wages are higher in: (1) some industries, (2) large firms, (3) unionized firms, and (4) firms not in the previous categories which have high-wage policies. Models intended to explain large wage differentials, where none would be expected under basic theory, include some used to explain the existence of unemployment.

The Search Cost Model

The search cost model contends that current employees can be paid less than the market wage. This is because search costs are incurred in finding another job. Subtracting search costs from the market wage makes the value of a job somewhat greater than its wage. The expected magnitude of search costs allows firms to pay a negative differential up to that magnitude.

The model is quite naive in that low-wage workers frequently know the firms and industries which pay more for the same kind of work they are doing. But if these firms and industries are not hiring, or not hiring their kind, such knowledge is of no value. It also neglects confronting the issue of why some employers and industries pay more than others, sometimes substantially more.

The Efficiency Wage Model

The argument that the efficiency wage is a source of wage differentials goes like this: While it is more profitable for firms to pay an efficiency wage which is higher than the market wage, different firms may find that they have different efficiency wage rates for the same kind of work. This is because different firms organize work differently and place different forms and amounts of capital equipment at the disposal of workers and work groups.

Larger firms and firms in high-wage industries do tend to provide more capital per worker and to pay more than others for the same forms of work. I am unaware of any research indicating that these firms tend to organize work in a way that makes their efficiency wage higher than that of other firms.

Extra High Quality Workers

Higher-paying firms may employ workers whose quality is higher than that implied by measurable variables such as age, experience, and education. Because of this non-measurable quality, extra high quality workers would be more productive than standard quality measures imply and they would command positive pay differentials.

Two researchers whose work I am aware of have attempted to quantify quality through the use of test scores. One found that typists with better scores received higher starting salaries; another found that test scores and education were poor predictors of the pay of clerical workers—but experience was. In addition, are workers of higher quality in the high-wage automobile, steel, and construction industries? I have my doubts.

The Random Events Model

The random events model contends that wage differentials represents random occurrences arising from the lack of current information about the wage rates paid by other firms in the market. A consequence of this lack of information is that some firms pay their employees more and others less than the average. But when employers become better informed, firms paying too much drop their wages or the amount of the annual increase granted workers and those paying too little increase their wages relative to others. As a result of this, substantial variation in the wage hierarchy of firms takes place as they learn what others are paying and take corrective actions.

Unfortunately, the model is contrary to actuality. As Groshen's research found, and many workers know, high-wage firms tend to remain high-wage firms.

The Insider-Outsider Model

The insider-outsider model has workers bargaining to receive as much as possible of the transaction costs of employing new workers. Two factors could lead to the workers at different firms getting different wages. The first is that transaction costs may be higher at some firms than others. This may be related to the way work is organized and, therefore, the way in which new employees learn the methods used by the firm. The second depends upon bargaining power within each firm as compared to others. A consequence of this power is that at some firms little, if any, of transaction costs will reach the paycheck of insiders while at other firms workers can capture the entire sum.

Since trade unions are only able, on the average, to obtain about 10 percent more pay than non-unionized workers, I would be shocked to find that non-union insider bargaining increased the wage by a significant portion of the existing wage differentials. And why should this approach be more successful in high-wage industries and in large firms than in others?

Rent Sharing

The rental income of a firm is the profit it earns in excess of that required to maintain the employment of its capital goods, the facilities and equipment of the firm. Firms with high rental income per worker may share this income with their employees thus paying them more than employees of other firm. This, of course, represents a departure from profit maximization.

Some studies do indicate that firms with higher profits per employee pay more than the average; other studies have found no relationship of pay to profits.

Labor Unions

Trade unionists know that the major function of unions is "to take labor out of competition." Alfred Marshall's "rules" regarding the elasticity or inelasticity of the labor demand function, discussed in Chapter 12, shows the extent to which this can be done or why some unions have substantial power and others little, if any. In any event, recent surveys of studies of the effect of trade unions on wages indicate that unionized workers, on the average, earn about 10 percent more than comparable non-union workers. Recent studies also indicate that unionized workers tend to have more capital goods at their disposal and that they are more productive than non-union workers. About 15 percent of the labor force is currently represented by unions.

In theory the limitation on the differential an employer can pay, here to unionized employees, is limited to its rental income. Otherwise, the return to capital would be decreased below the normal rate—destroying the incentive for continuing investment in the firm.

The Standard of Living Derived from Work

Much of our standard of living comes from work-based earnings and that is examined here. The standard of living derived from work can be quantified by annual real earnings per person, RE/Pop. This is the product of the following variables: the average real wage per hour, RW; the average number of hours worked in a year, L; and the employment-to-population ratio, Emp/Pop:

(10) $RE/Pop = RW \cdot L \cdot Emp/Pop$

The common sense of the formula should be recognized. The per capita standard of living can increase as a result of an increase in (1) the real wage, (2) the hours worked in a year, and (3) the number of people who are employed in a given population. Each of these items warrants consideration.

The Ambiguous Real Wage Record

What is the real wage? Let me suggest four variants: (1) The money wage rate deflated by the consumer price index. This is the best measure of before tax consumer purchasing power. (2) The money wage rate modified by the gross domestic product deflator. (3) The money compensation package deflated by the consumer price index. (4) The money compensation package modified by the gross domestic product deflator. This is the best measure of the real cost of labor to employers.

Data on two measures of real compensation can be found in Figure 13.8. Both start with money compensation in current dollars. One is deflated by the consumer price index; the other by the gross national product price deflator. What we have here is a tale of two graphs.

The circles are the money wage deflated by the consumer price index. The

Figure 13.8.   **Compensation Deflated by the Consumer Price Index, o, and the GNP Deflator, □,1947–1990**

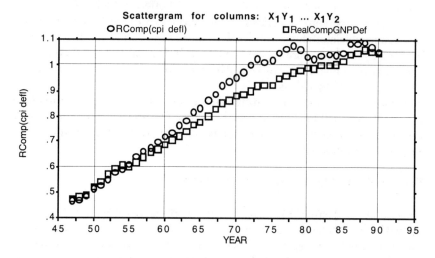

squares are the money wage discounted by the GNP deflator. Both graphs indicate that rather steady growth in real compensation took place from essentially the end of World War II until 1973. The data of greater interest to workers, the consumer price index deflated data, show that after 1973 progress in real compensation was both volatile and far below the previous trend. Real compensation in 1990 was the same as it had been in 1976, fourteen years earlier. Had the 1947–1973 growth rate continued to 1990, real compensation would have been about 50 percent more than was experienced! That can be thought of as the cost of the productivity growth slowdown.

 The graph of greater interest to employers, compensation adjusted by the GNP deflator, shows lower growth, less volatility, and a decrease in the growth rate starting about 1969. By 1990, real compensation was essentiallly equal, whether deflator was the consumer price index or the gross national product deflator.

The Length of the Average Workweek

Although the average workweek in manufacturing shows no trend during the post–World War II period, the average workweek in private nonagricultural industries has been decreasing as is shown in Table 13.5. According to these data, weekly hours have been decreasing at the rate of 0.13 hours per year. I am unsure regarding how much this is due to (1) the increasing share of employment in nonmanufacturing industries, (2) the reduction of the length of the workweek for full-time employees in these industries, or (3) the increased use of part-time workers, some of whom do not want to work part-time. My guess is that the declining hours are related to the relative growth in the service sector and an in-

Table 13.5.   **Average Weekly Hours of Work, Nonagricultural Industries, Selected Years, 1950–1990**

Year	Average Weekly Hours
1950	39.8
1955	39.6
1960	38.6
1965	38.8
1970	37.1
1975	36.1
1980	35.3
1985	34.9
1990	34.5

Source: Economic Report of the President,1991, Table B–44, p. 336.
Note: The data include full- and part-time workers.

crease in the use of part-time workers.

The Employment to Population Ratio

It is not hard to fathom that the ratio of employment to the population is an important variable. Were the ratio 1 to 100, one worker would be laboring to produce enough to cover the needs and wants of a hundred. If, however, 50 were employed in a population of 100, the task would be much smaller—and the standard of living inevitably much higher. Today and into the foreseeable future, the employment to population ratio is of substantial concern. This is because the baby boomers of the 1960s will soon be retiring. But their procreation rate was low. With a low worker to retiree ratio it may be difficult for the social security system to handle the existing pension and health benefits.

In 1950, 39.5 percent of the population were employed. The ratio dropped to 37.4 percent in 1961 and was essentially constant through 1963. The trend since then has been for the ratio to increase. It reached 47.8 percent in 1989, 27.8 percent higher than it had been in 1961. Such an increase in the percent of the population who are working is remarkable. The major reasons for the increase in the employment to population ratio have been the increase in the long run tendency of women to enter and remain in the labor force and the inflow of the baby boomers into the labor force.

The labor force participation of women has been stimulated in recent decades by the women's liberation movement, the increase in the education of women, the delay in marriage and child bearing, the increased tendency of marriages to dissolve, and the stagnancy of the real wage. Multiple wage-earners are frequently required for a family to attain its desired standard of living. The modest increase in real family or household earnings is clearly due to the additional earn-

Figure 13.9.   **Real Per Capita Weekly Earnings, 1950–1990**

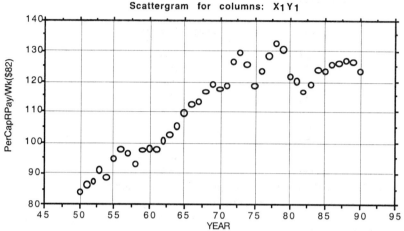

ings of women.

 The baby boom of the 1950s and 60s is related to the end of World War II in 1945, the end of the Korean War in 1952. The goals of many males, both former members of the armed services and others, were to quickly complete their education, obtain better jobs than their parents, form families, and raise children in idylic suburbs. The subsequent baby bust appears to be in part a reaction to the boom and to the greater vagaries of economic performance.

Real Weekly Earnings per Capita

Real weekly pay per capita is to me, unemployment and distribution of income aside, the bottom line of economic performance. It is a measure of the purchasing power of the average person in the economy. Economics has been called a dismal science and Figure 13.9 shows the dismal economic record of recent years. That real weekly pay per person, deflated by the consumer price index, was less in 1990 than in 1972 gives the best economy in the world little to brag about. If only the trend of the first half of the 1950–1990 period had continued into the second half, our standard of living would have been over 50 percent more than that experienced in 1990.

The Increased Inequality of the Distribution of Earnings

The increasing inequality of the distribution of wages is presented in two sections. The first is intended to give readers a feel for the problem by showing the increase in the ratio of high to low pay in recent years. The second examines a study by John Bound and George Johnson which attempts to explain why the

Table 13.6.   **Weekly Earnings Ratio of Males at the 10th and 90th Percentile of the Distribution**

Year	Ratio of Weekly Earnings of Males at the 10th to the 90th Percentile of the Distribution
1963	0.34
1969	0.33
1979	0.29
1989	0.23

Source: Marvin H. Kosters as cited in Gary Burtless (1995).

wage disparity has substantially increased.

 Perhaps the most troubling aspect of the changes in the distribution of wages in recent decades is the fall in the relative position of low-wage workers. On the average real per capita earnings in 1990 were no more than they had been in 1972. But low-wage workers, those most in need of earning, have done far more poorly than the average since the 1960s. This is indicated by the declining ratio of the weekly earnings of males at the 10th percentile to males at the 90th percentile of the earnings distribution as shown in Table 13.6 for selected years from 1963 to 1989.

 Over the span of twenty-six years, the ratio of the weekly pay of low-wage to high-wage males dropped from slightly more than one-third to slightly less than one-quarter. If low-wage workers in 1989 earned 34 percent of the weekly wage of high-wage workers, as they did in 1963, their real weekly earnings would have been one-third higher than they actually were. Again the change or disruption seemed to have started in the early 1970s and worsened in the 1980s.

The Analysis of Bound and Johnson

As indicated above, the 1980s saw a substantial increase in the disparity between the real wage of those who are relatively well paid and those who are relatively poorly paid. In 1979 male college graduates with an average of five years of experience received 27 percent more pay than high school graduates with the same work experience. By 1988 that differential had increased to 66 percent! (See Table 13.7.) Moreover, the real wage of both groups was less in 1988 than it had been in 1979. The real wage of the college graduates being discussed had dropped by 4.2 percent while that of the high school graduates was down by 24.6 percent! The data are from a brilliant and complex work by John Bound and George Johnson (1992).who attempt to explain the 16.3 percent average relative wage decline of high school to college graduated from 1979 to 1988. They break the decline into three categories: relative supply and demand, rents, and technology bias in favor of college graduates.

Table 13.7. **The Real Wage of Males, by Education and Experience: 1973, 1979, and 1988**

Experience	Education	Real Wage ($1988)			[Real Wage Change] 1973-1988
Years		1973	1979	1988	(percent)
0–9	college	12.69	11.38	12.16	–4.2
	high school	9.69	9.89	7.31	–24.6
	[Ratio	1.31	1.27	1.66]	
10–19	college	16.95	15.29	14.81	–12.6
	high school	12.69	12.09	10.31	–18.8
	[Ratio	1.34	1.26	1.44]	
20–29	college	18.62	17.10	17.08	–8.3
	high school	13.92	12.81	11.91	–14.4
	[Ratio	1.34	1.33	1.43]	
30+	college	18.26	16.88	17.64	–3.4
	high school	13.65	13.02	12.05	–11.7
	[Ratio	1.34	1.30	1.46]	

Sources: The data are from Bound and Johnson (1992), Table 1, p. 373. Information in brackets are my calculations.

The 1979–1988 change in relative supply and demand forces should have increased the relative pay of high school graduate by 10.0 percent.

The change in rents should have decreased their relative pay by 4.9 percent. (The change in rents covers the following: the industry of employment, industrial differentials, and the decling effect of trade unions on wages.) What remains to be explained is a 21.4 percent change in the differential: the 16.3 percent differential + 10 percent ascribable to supply and demand – 4.9 percent associated with rents.

Bound and Johnson, in fact, find a relative differential in favor of college graduates of 21.3 percent due to technological bias in favor of college graduates. The lion's share of this, 19.4 pecent, comes from regressing the change in the relative pay on the factors explained and assigning the residuals to technological bias in favor of college graduates.

It is from the Bound and Johnson study, more than any other, that many economists and others believe that the broadening of the distribution of income is due to technological bias in favor of college graduates.

An Alternative View

Allow a crude analysis merely based on the data of Table 13.7. Note that every one of the eight male groups moved backward in real earnings during the 1973–1988 period. This would seem to imply that every group of males displayed decreased productivity from 1973 to 1988. In fact, in the business sector output per hour increased by 21.9 percent during this period. It went up from 77.6 in 1973 to 94.6 in 1988 (1996 EROP, Table B-45, p. 332), an increase of 21.9 percent. Why the real wage declined is somewhat of a mystery.

In addition, it is important to recognize that in the 1973–1979 period the real earnings changes were quite the opposite of those of which took place in the 1979–1988 period. During the earlier years, male high school graduates did better than college graduates in all four experience groups. It stretches the imagination to believe that in one period there was technological bias in favor of the less well educated and just the opposite in the subsequent period. It is suggested, alternatively, that the fall in both the relative and the absolute real wage of the better educated in the earlier period was a wakeup call to reconsider the issue of relative pay.

In this setting the alternate hypothesis is this: In a period of falling real wages, management had to consider the "need" to treat relatively well in pay, the most important of their work groups—those with greater education and those with greater experience.

Test this hypothesis with the data on real wage change (in percent) 1973–1988, in Table 13.7. Consider first high school graduates by experience. There are four groups by experience so that three adjacent comparisons can be made. In all three the group with higher experience did better (less poorly) than the group with lower experience. There are also four college groups by experience so three comparisons can be made. In two of three comparisons, the higher experienced group did better than the lower experienced group. With respect to education, in all four experience groups, males with college degrees did relatively better than high school graduates. Out of ten comparisons, nine are consistent with the alternative hypothesis.

Summary

The neoclassical paradigm treats all markets the same—analytically. There are individual supply and demand functions which can be added up to form the market supply and demand functions. The market functions equilibrate to yield the market-clearing price and quantity, here the real wage and full employment.

Equilibrium is stable because departures from it, shortages and surpluses or unemployment, force the real wage to the market clearing equilibrium. Whether for good or ill, the labor market is quite uncongenial to this basic model, both in terms of ongoing quantity and price disequilibria.

Unemployment is the major pathology of the labor market. Traditional categories of unemployment are frictional, structural, and deficient demand. with the latter by far the most important. Aside from frictional unemployment, these phenomena contradict the neoclassical model. If demand is inadequate the real wage should drop, eradicating the problem. But substantially more than frictional unemployment often persists for years on end.

Two sets of unemployment models have been created to explain the cause of the failure to do away with unemployment in a timely fashion. The first set relates unemployment to practices which raise the real wage above the market-clearing wage. The efficiency wage model is perhaps the most interesting of them. These models assume that without such practices the real wage would drop to a full employment equilibrium.

But would wage decreases increase employment? The demand for labor is highly inelastic. As a result large percentage decreases in the real wage are required to yield small percentage increases in employment. But the large decreases in the real wage yield decreases in earnings almost as large. This tends to reduce the demand for products and the derived demand for labor. As a result, real wage decreases may actually decrease employment!

The second set of unemployment models has workers refusing job offers so that they can search for higher-paying jobs. By turning down job offers, these workers have chosen leisure over work and are, therefore, not involuntarily unemployed. But these models are undermined by research which shows that a large majority of workers accept the first job offer they receive and the number of unemployed workers tends to be far greater than the number of job openings.

Despite the general lack of job vacancies as compared to the number of unemployed, the neoclassical model seems compelled to blind itself to unemployment. This is because unemployment turns labor from an economic to a free resource. And the same with all other factors not fully employed. In addition, the stress on the tragedy of unemployment contradicts the neoclassical singular focus on scarcity.

The violation of the law of one wage by substantial wage differentials for people doing the same kind of work has stimulated the production of a number of more or less interesting models. These models have to explain why: (1) pay is higher in some industries than in others; (2) large firms tend to pay more than others; and (3) some firms pay more than comparable firms. But this appears to be beyond their reach.

The standard of living derived from work can be measured by real weekly pay per capita. Real hourly pay grew substantially in the 1948–1973 period. Its growth has been erratic since then. What has held the standard of living up has been the increase in the proportion of the population in the labor force. More specifically, what has held the standard of living up has been the increasing propensity of women to be in the labor force.

While virtually all groups of workers have been moving backward in terms of their real per hour wage, the ones who have been hit the hardest are those who need money the most, low-wage workers. The real pay of those with relatively low education and experience has declined badly. There are many models which attempt to explain why this has happened. The most sophisticated ascribes the change mostly to the bias of new technology in favor of better educated, higher-paid workers. In fact, however, we have no data on the technology afforded workers by managements as a function of their age and education. An alternative hypothesis contends that with the real wage going backward management has been most sympathetic to those with higher experience and education and this largely comports with the data.

Questions on Chapter 13

1. a. Name three departures from equilibrium in the labor market.
   b. Present the neoclassical models which should resolve these disequilibria.

2. a. Explain what price disequilibrium is.
   b. Present three models which explain why one group of workers earns more than another doing the same work and as well.

3. Many colleges and universities are increasingly replacing retired full-time faculty with part-time faculty ("adjuncts").
   a. Explain why this is "rational."
   b. What is the equilibrium implication of this, if any?

4. Assume that three months after commencement X percent of the graduating class have been unable to find jobs. (X should be your best guess.)
   a. Present the argument that they have chosen leisure over work—why there must be jobs for them even though no one knows of their existence.
   b. Present the opposite argument—that they are involuntarily unemployed.

5. It is frequently argued that were wages more flexible, unemployment would be substantially lower.
   a. What problem would flexible prices impose?
   b. Explain with some arithmetic why a highly inelastic demand for labor also poses a problem.

6. a. How is it that when a producer sets the rate of production at a specified quantity, he has determined the quantity of labor and circulating capital demanded?
   b. What is gained by solving the problem in the labor market? (Hint: One potential gain might be external to the firm.)

7. The real wage of male high school graduates with 0–9 years of experience fell by 24.6 percent between 1973 and 1988. Why might this have happened? (Hint: One consideraton should be how much the price level increase over this period.)

8. Assume that when the marginal productivity of labor increases by 1 percent, real compensation, W/P, increases by 0.75 percent. Show mathematically why this undermines marginal productivity labor demand theory.

CHAPTER FOURTEEN

The Market for Capital Goods

The market for capital goods is crucial to the economy. Since Adam Smith we know that capital goods are *the* important source of productivity growth, growth in the standard of living, and the wealth of nations. But capital goods may also have a negative effect on the economy. John Maynard Keynes contended that spending on capital goods, investment spending, is volatile and *the* cause of the business cycle. The market for capital goods is, accordingly, of great interest and importance. A basic assumption is that the supply of capital goods responds demand. As a result, the concern of this chapter is with the demand for capital goods.

The demand for capital goods can be called the demand for investment goods. This is because spending on capital goods often requires large monetary outlays with profits dependent on the flow of future revenues and costs. Because of the magnitude of the funds required, investment spending tends to be shown as a function of the interest rate. As a result the market for capital goods and the markets which set interest rates are examined here.

Categories of Capital Goods

Recall the two forms of capital goods as delineated by our classical forebears: fixed and circulating. Structures and equipment are categorized as fixed capital–even though the purchase of much equipment is more quickly accomplished than the employment of additional labor. A capital good which is transformed into the final product goes by the name of circulating capital—but the word circulating is less than descriptively ideal. Thus, allow another look at the three forms of capital goods: structures, equipment, and inventories.

Structures

Structures are categorized as non-residential and residential. The former generally serve as the locus of work of one sort or another. The latter structures comprise the indoor living space of the populace. Structures are basic to production and the conduct of family life.

Business structures provide the space and ambience for work. Once the space and ambience requirements are met the structure plays a passive role with respect to the process of production. The size of a structures limits the amount of production which can take place. Sometimes this limitation can be quickly overcome by finding and employing the additional space required and sometimes this is not possible. More space can be found for the drafting room. It cannot be readily found for a refinery which would like to produce more than its full capacity.

There is, however, an aspect of structures which can affect the rate of production and that is the *allocation of space* within a structure. Space allocation should integrate equipment and personnel in such a way that efficiency is maximized. But that is not always an easy task because of the territorial claims of workers, managers, departments, and tradition.

The quality of residential structures and the amount of space available to a family or household play an important part in determining the family's or household's standard of living.

Equipment

Adam Smith described the role of equipment in increasing productivity and his analysis is as valid today as it was two centuries ago. Equipment is frequently available off-the-shelf. Such equipment is accordingly as variable as labor. But specialized equipment may take extended amounts of time to design and build. The productivity potential of equipment is not always accurately envisaged. On one hand, thoughtful workers are often able to do things with a crane or a computer which their designers never envisaged. On the other hand, the claimed advantages of some new equipment are hard to find in practice.

Overall, the amount of capital available to each worker, its vintage, and productive potentialities are important elements in advancing productivity and the standard of living.

Inventories

Inventories are a catchall category for a number of different important kinds of capital. It includes products to be used as inputs to the process of production and outputs of that process, finished products to be marketed. As a result, a firm typically has two inventories. A car assembly plant has an inventory of "kits" to be transformed into cars and an inventory of the finished product, cars.

In many firms, the largest type of investment is in the form of inventories. This can be seen most easily in supermarkets where much of the inventory is in the view of customers. That is also true of many manufacturing firms. A former student of mine, who headed up production for a firm which manufactured printing equipment in several countries, told me that their largest investment was the firm's parts inventory—parts required to repair the equipment that they had produced over the years.

In 1990 the dollar value of the stock of inventory in the United States was roughly $1 trillion while the gross domestic product was $5.7 trillion. Carrying this much inventory is a considerable expense, and minimization of inventory costs makes much sense. Changes in the aggregate of inventories, particularly as manifest in the inventory to sales ratio, is one of the most important macroeconomic leading indicators. Increases in the inventory to sales ratio are a sign of oversupply and the possibility of future decreases in production and employment.

Inventory costs consist of transactions costs and carrying costs. Both are briefly discussed before the problem of inventory cost minimization is examined.

Transaction Costs

Transaction costs, *TrC,* can be assumed to include two cost items. The first is a fixed ordering cost, *F,* per transaction. This is essentially the cost of the performing paperwork, the bookkeeping of an individual order. There is also a per unit shipping and handling cost, *S.* This makes the transaction cost of an order $F + SQ$, where Q is the number of units in an order. The number of orders per year, *N,* is the annual demand, *AD,* divided by the size of each order, Q. Thus, the annual transaction cost is:

(1) $$\text{TrC} = (F + SQ) \cdot AD/Q = F \cdot AD/Q + S \cdot AD$$

Carrying Costs

Carrying costs involve the foregone income on the funds tied up in the cost of the inventory and the cost of warehousing the inventory. Let P equal the cost of carrying a unit of inventory for a year. It is assumed that the maximum number of units in inventory is Q, the amount of an order, and that the inventory falls linearly to zero, whereupon Q more units are placed in inventory. The average number of units in inventory is, therefore, $Q/2$, and the annual carrying cost is $P \cdot Q/2$.

Minimizing the Cost of an Inventory

The total inventory cost, *TIC,* is the sum of the carrying and transactions costs:

(2) $$\text{TIC} = (PQ)/2 + (F \cdot AD)/Q + S \cdot AD$$

The variables are total inventory cost, *TIC,* and the number of units in each order, Q. The cost minimizing Q is obtained by taking the derivative of the above equation with respect to Q, setting it equal to zero, and solving for Q.

(3) $dTIC/dQ = P/2 - (F \cdot AD)/Q^2 = 0$

Solve for Q^2 and Q:

(4) $Q^2 = 2(F \cdot AD)/P;$ $Q = \sqrt{2F \cdot AD/P}$

Thus, to minimize the annual cost of an inventory each order should equal the square root of twice the ordering cost times the annual demand divided by the annual carrying cost of a unit of inventory. The higher is the fixed cost of each transaction, F, the larger is the maximum size of the inventory, Q, and the higher the carrying charge, P, the smaller the least cost size of the inventory. The two examples below are intended to give readers a better feel for the problem of minimizing inventory costs.

Example 1:
Given: (1) Fixed cost = $100 per order. (2) Annual demand = 10,000 computers/yr.
        (3) Cost of carrying a unit in inventory per year = $80.
Find: Number of computers per order and the total inventory cost.

$Q = \sqrt{2} \cdot 100 \cdot 10,000/80 = 158$ computers per order; 10,000/158 = 63 orders/yr.
TIC = $100/order $\cdot$ 63 orders/year + $80/computer–yr $\cdot$ 79 computers = $12,620/yr.

Example 2:
Given: All data as in example 1 except that the size of all orders is 200 computers.
Find: The Total Inventory Cost.

The number of orders, N = 10,000/200 = 50
TIC = $100/order $\cdot$ 50 orders/yr + $80/computer–yr$\cdot$100 computers = $13,000/yr.

While the number of orders per year are quite different in the two cases, the total inventory cost is fairly close. This is because the two kinds of costs tend to offset each other: Reducing the number of orders per year reduces transaction costs but the higher average inventory increases carrying costs.

Just-in-Time Inventories

Japanese manufacturers have pioneered the use of what approaches a zero inventory of inputs. They arrive *just in time* to be used. This is not contradictory of the seemingly finite inventory suggested by equation (4). Computers, communications devices, and a reasonable scheduling horizon should allow vendors to be made aware of the products required by the buyer far enough in advance to adjust their normal rate of production to that which is required. I do not know whether or not vendors keep inventories or also produce in a just-in-time manner. The latter implies that a very short period is needed to produce the required units of output.

Figure 14.1.   **The Stock of Capital and Its Inflows and Outflows**

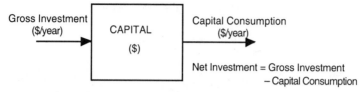

Capital: Its Stock and Flows

The capital stock is the amount of structures, equipment, and inventories which exist at a given point in time. Because of the great heterogeneity of the stock it is denominated in dollars. And to compare the size of the stock at one time to another, the use of dollars of constant value is desirable. Over the course of time the inflow of *gross investment* adds to the stock and the outflow of *capital consumption* subtracts from it, as shown in Figure 14.1. Stock-flow accounting is exemplified by the dollar value of the stock of capital on December 31, 1998, being equal to the dollar value of the stock of capital on December 31, 1997, plus the inflows minus the outflow which took place during the course of 1998.

The difference between the inflow, gross investment, and outflow, capital consumption, is *net investment.* It is the amount by which the capital stock changes over the course of a year. For the capital stock to increase requires gross investment to be greater than capital consumption (including obsolescence). For the capital to labor ratio to increase, an important aid to productivity growth, the growth of the capital stock must be greater than the growth of employment. A final aspect of the capital stock of importance is its vintage. For two stocks of capital of the same real dollar magnitude, one with an average age of six and the other with an average age of three years, the latter will be the more productive.

The above stock-flow diagram implies the inclusion of all forms of capital. Alternatively, a larger number of different stock-flow diagrams can be more informative—one for cars, another for trucks, a third for computers, and so forth.

Gross and Net Private Domestic Investment

Through the figures in Table 14.1 we can get a feel for the relative magnitudes of gross investment spending by business and consumers and the extent to which capital spending represents the replacement of capital which has been consumed, an outflow from the stock, and how much represents an addition to the stock, net private domestic investment.

Gross investment spending is an important segment of aggregate spending and the related employment. Net business spending on structures and equipment is an important source of productivity increases but this represents only about 20 percent of the gross. About 80 percent of gross non-residential spending used for

Table 14.1.   **Gross and Net Domestic Investment 1990, billions of 1987 dollars**

	Gross	Net	(Percent of gross)
Non-residential			
Structures	179.1	46.9	(26.2)
Producers' durable equip't	359.0	55.7	(15.5)
Change in inventory	6.2	6.2	
Subtotal		544.3 108.8	
Residential	194.8	75.5	(38.8)
Total	739.1	184.2	(24.9)

the replacement of structures and equipment. Only 20 percent of it adds to the existing stock of non-residential capital.

The Criterion for Riskless Investment

The theoretical criterion for profit maximizing investment is that investment spending should take place until the expected rate of return, $E\{r\}$, is equal to the interest rate, i. Which interest rate is it? (There are so many of them.) Were the investment truly risk-free, the correct interest rate would be that of U.S. government securities of the same duration as the expected life of the capital good.

The Rate of Return and the Rate of Interest

If the estimated cost and revenue figures used to calculate the expected rate of return are in current dollar figures (figures which are *not* adjusted for the expected increase in prices of future years) then we are dealing with real dollars, the dollars of the base year. What we have then are the data arranged in the form of the present value equation where the present value, the cost of the equipment, is known, future revenues and costs are estimated, and the unknown variable is the expected rate of return–the magnitude of which is calculated:

(5) $PV = (R_1 - C_1)/(1 + r) + (R_2 - C_2)/(1 + r)^2 + ... + (R_n - C_n)/(1 + r)^n$

Expected Revenues and Costs

Expected revenues can be specified in a few different ways. For equipment used in production, the annual revenue is either the expected value of its marginal revenue product or the monetary value of the savings in labor costs if affords. For equipment used by non-production workers, the latter form of annual revenue is appropriate. But there are cases in which the marginal benefit can be alternatively defined. The addition of a computer in the department of delinquent accounts is, for example, estimated to allow $100 thousand more a year to be collected and that would be its marginal benefit.

We are here planning to buy a piece of equipment and the proper and somewhat complex way to defining its cost has been imposed upon you in chapter five. It is the expected rental cost plus the expected costs of energy, maintenance, and repairs.

Calculating the Expected Rate of Return

All of the data of the present value equation (5) have been estimated except for the expected rate of return, r. By definition, the rate of return r is the interest rate which brings the right side of the present value equation to zero. With one unknown, the value of r can be calculated–but there are two problems. One, is that there is no way to put the equation into a form in which r equals a mathematically manipulated array of revenue and costs. As a result the magnitude of r must be calculated by trial and error, that is by an iterative process which tries to find the magnitude of r which brings the future flow of costs and revenues to zero. There are computer programs which can do this. Otherwise it requires more or less dog work. The second problem is one almost invariably avoided—and with good reason. If, as can be be seen in equation (5), there are n discounting of costs and revenues, there are n values of r which bring the right side of the equation to zero. The expediency is to use a value of r which seems in accord with the norm of the annual ratios of revenue to costs. If, for example, the ratio of expected revenues to costs is about 1.1 and a calculation of the expected rate of return is about 10 percent, a calculated rate of return in the neighborhood of 10 percent per annum would be chosen as a reasonable estimate.

The Appropriate Interest Rate

As mentioned above, the appropriate interest rate is that of federal government securities. If there is no duration of government bonds which corresponds to the expected life of the capital good, a yield curve can be utilized. It is a curve which relates the rate of return (i.e., yield) here on federal securities, as a function of the duration of the loan. Choose the interest rate on the yield curve corresponding to the years the expected life of the capital good.

The investment spending is profitable if the expected rate of return is equal to or greater than the appropriate interest rate. And profit is maximized when $r = i$ for the marginal unit of investment spending.

An Investment Hierarchy and Investment Spending

Assume that the firm has a number of proposed investments in capital goods. Each should be accompanied by an estimate of the expected rate of return. A hierarchy of investment projects can then be established with the investment ex-

Figure 14.2.   The Hierarchy of Investments Ranked by the Expected Rate of Return

Expected Rate of Return and the Interest Rate (percent/year)

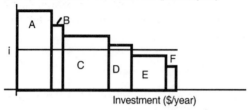

Investment ($/year)

pected to yield the highest rate of return at the top. Some projects may be changed to improve their standing in the hierarchy. A proposal that everyone should have a new computer, for example, could be changed to one limiting the number to employees whose productivity would clearly improve with faster devices and more storage. This would decrease the dollars spent on the project and increase its rate of return and standing in the hierarchy.

The rate of return hierarchy is shown in Figure 14.2. To simplify things one interest rate is shown rather than one which is tied to the length of each investment. At that interest rate, investments in A, B, C, and D are expected to add to profits; E and F are not. Were the interest rate somewhat higher, no investment in D would be made; were it sufficiently lower, investment spending would be increased to cover project E. Thus, the firm's investment demand function is negative sloping with the interest rate. As the rate of interest declines, the quantity of investment spending increases.

The market investment demand function is the horizontal sum of the investment function of all firms. It, too, is negative sloping.

Adjustments for Risk

With no consideration for risk the marginal criterion for making an investment is the equality of the expected rate of return and the interest rate, $E\{r\} = i$. But the riskier an investment is, the higher the risk premium. Since we would like to maintain the marginal conditions the risk premium is added to both sides of the equality: $E\{r + r_{rp}\} = i + i_{rp}$, where r_{rp} is the expected risk premium on an investment. If, for example, the interest rate is 8 percent and the risk premium is 10 percent, the expected rate of return, including the risk premium, would have to be 18 percent or more to justify the investment.

To determine the risk premium, assume that we have two rate-of-return distributions on investments which are believed to have had comparable risks to the one under consideration. One distribution is on the expected riskless rates of return on these investments; the other distribution is that of the actual rate of return experienced. The difference in the expected values of the two distributions is an estimate of the expected risk premium.

Diversifiable risk is risk lessened by the investment in many different projects. This, at first glance neutralizes risk and obviates the need for a risk premium—just as a diversified stock portfolio at first glance neutralizes risk. But the risk limiting nature of diversification cannot overcome the risk engendered by variations in the state of the economy—a non-diversifiable risk. Non-diversifiable risk occurs if all investment in a firm is tied to a single project and the required capital goods. Similarly stockholders with "all their eggs in one basket" have no diversification, a non-diversifiable risk. The risk premium applies here.

Risk Based on the Capital Assets Price Model

A popular way of estimating a risk premium uses the *capital assets price model*. The model has the risk premium as the difference between the rate of return with risk, r, and the risk-free rate of return, rf, This risk premium is quantified as the difference between the stock market rate of return, r_m, and the risk-free rate of return, rf times a parameter β, the asset beta.

$$(6) \qquad \text{risk premium} = r - r_f = \beta\,(r_m - r_f)$$

The meaning of asset beta can be seen by taking the first difference of equation (6) with the assumption that the risk-free rate of return is constant: $\Delta r = \beta\Delta r_m$ or $\beta = \Delta r/\Delta r_m$. Asset beta is the amount of the change in the rate of return of an asset relative to a given change in the market rate of return. If the stock market rate of return changes by 1 percentage point and, on the average, the rate of return of an asset changes by 2 percentage points, the asset beta equals 2.

We are now close to the end of the line. The appropriate real risk-adjusted rate of return for an investment, r, is the risk-free rate plus the risk premium:

$$(7) \qquad r = r_f + \beta(r_m - r_f)$$

To obtain the risk-free and stock market rates the work of Jeremy J. Siegel is exploited. In his mid-1997 article, "Is the U.S. Stock Market Overvalued?" he reports that:

> The average annual after inflation rate of return on U.S. stocks from 1871 through 1966 is 6.8 % ... [and the] return on government bonds has been only 2.7 % per year (p. 9).

Exploiting Siegel's figures, the equation for the risk-adjusted real rate of return follows:

$$(8) \qquad r = 2.7 + \beta(6.8 - 2.7) = 2.7 + \beta(4.1)$$

All that need be done is to plug in the asset beta of a particular investment and calculate the risk-adjusted rate of return.

Government bonds with a β of zero, have an expected real rate of return of 2.7 percent. A mutual fund indexed to the overall stock market would have a β of 1 and a risk-adjusted real rate of 6.8 percent $(2.7 + 1 \cdot 4.1)$.

The logic of the matter is this: If the expected real rate of return on U.S. bonds is equal to or greater than 2.7 percent, the purchase of such bonds is profitable. And if the expected real rate of return on an indexed stock market fund is equal to or greater than a real rate of 6.8 percent, make that investment. You should not invest in the indexed stock fund if the expected return is 6.7 percent. Why is that? It is because 6.7 percent minus the risk premium of 4.1 percent is 2.6 percent risk-free. With an expected rate of 2.7 percent from risk-free government bonds, you are better off buying the bonds.

The data required to calculate the asset beta of a new investment is non-existent. You can, of course, guess at the extent to which the expected rate of return will vary with the stock market's rate of return. Alternatively, if the asset betas of some old capital goods are known and the new one can be related to one of them, one can apply that asset beta to the new investment to estimate its risk premium.

Problems with the Capital Assets Price Model

The capital assets price model has some problematic aspects: One problem is the difficulty in finding what the market rate of return is. The formula for its annual market rate of return over a calendar year t is:

$$(9) \qquad r_{mt} = \{(P_{12/30/t} + \text{average dividend}_t - P_{12/30/t-1})/P_{12/30/t}\} - 1$$

All stock indexes are price indexes and they yield information on the average price of a certain set of shares on the last day of the year and all others the market is in operation. But they give no information on dividends and without that the market rate of return cannot be calculated.

A second problem is the choice of the period to use for determining the risk-free and market rates of return. Professor Siegel arbitrarily used the 1871–1966 period to obtain the figures used above. Are figures from this period those which are currently relevant for calculations of risk premiums? If not, what is the appropriate period?

A third problem is the specification that the difference between the return on the stock market and return on government bonds, here 4.1 percent, The argument is that were the differential higher, bond holders would sell their bonds and buy shares of stock. With a lower demand for bonds, their price decreases increasing their interest rate and returning the risk premium to the equilibrium of 4.1 percent. But some buy government bonds for reasons other than the inadequacy of the differential luring them into the stock market. Some buy them because: (1) they are required to by law or regulation, (2) they afford a tax advantage, or (3) they are unaware of the differences in long-run value arising from seemingly modest difference in interest rates. One thousand dollars invested in 2.7 percent government bonds would have yielded $1,947 after twenty-five years. The same sum invested in the stock market at 6.8 percent would have yielded $5,179. Were the twenty-five year bond holders aware that the cost of receiving their risk-free $1,947 was typically $3,232 ($5,179–1,947)?

Risk and Uncertainty

Risk is theoretically insurable. This is because there is supposed to be a risk distribution function which allows insurance companies to offer risk insurance—just as they are able to offer life insurance because of the existence of a mortality distribution function.

Uncertainty arises when there is no experience that can be drawn upon to create a rate-of-return distribution. Either the process of production is new or the product is new, or both. Can the robot, Production Man, really make the product without human intervention? What is the number of newfangled widgets that can be sold at various prices? Will more sales occur if classic Coke is replaced by caffeine-free Coke? The answer to the above questions are uncertain.

Guessing correctly in the arena of uncertainty is at the core of the entrepreneurial function. There are no formulas which can be appropriated to handle the problem. In determining the magnitude of the uncertainty premium, the entrepreneur, in effect, creates the expected value from a subjective uncertainty distribution function. Assume that what starts as an 8 percent risk-free rate of a return has a risk premium of 10 percent. The expected rate of return then had to be 18 percent or more to justify the investment. Add perhaps 20 percent for uncertainty and the required rate becomes 38 percent. That is roughly the expected rate of return a major manufacturer required to justify investment in innovative project.

Investment decisions are somewhat eased by the establishment of a capital budget. Much of it is allocated for plant and equipment replacement. The rest tends to be spent on the basis of entrepreneurial intuition, the inclinations of informed department heads, and the firm's power structure.

How Is the Interest Rate Set?

There are several answers to the question of how the interest rate is set. One answer is that it is set by the FED through its control of the *federal funds rate*. Another is that it is set in the market for money. The third is that the interest rate is set in the market for loanable funds.

The Federal Funds Rate

The federal funds rate is an interest rate set by the Open Market Committee of the Federal Reserve System, the FED. It is the interest rate banks pay for overnight loans made by other banks. These funds are used to cover the reserve requirements of the borrowing bank. This cost is usually covered by it serving as the base upon which banks set their short-term interest rates. When the federal funds rate increases, short-term interest rates increase. But investment is long-term in character making the federal funds rate of limited interest here. There is little evidence that increasing the rate for overnight loans has an impact on long-term rates.

The Market for Money

Money has several important functions. It is (1) the medium of exchange, (2) the unit of account, (3) a store of value, (4) and, the standard of deferred payment. The form used as the medium of exchange consists of coins and currency and checking account balances. These are used to pay for goods and services purchased by individuals and institutions. In the money market, the interaction between the demand for and supply of money sets the interest rate—the rental price charged for the use of a dollar for the period of one year.

The Demand for Money

John Maynard Keynes broke the demand for money into three "motives": The transactions, precautionary, and speculative motives.

The transactions demand is the demand for money to pay for purchases of goods and services. It varies with income; the larger income is, the larger the number and magnitude of the transactions made, the higher is the transactions demand.

The precautionary demand is for unexpected money needs. The individual or firm wants to avoid the embarrassment of not having enough money to pay an unexpected bill. Holding money as a precaution has an opportunity cost in the form of foregone interest. The quantity of precautionary money demanded, therefore, varies inversely with the interest rate.

The third area of demand arises from the speculative motive. Here the alternatives Keynes considered were holding money which yielded no interest or investing it in interest-bearing bonds. The higher the interest rate, the greater the opportunity cost of holding speculative money. Again the quantity demanded varies inversely with the interest rate. Why hold money bearing no interest rather than bonds which bear interest? A problem arises if the interest rate on bonds is expected to increase. This causes the value of existing bonds to decrease. The speculative demand for money is, therefore, inversely related to the interest rate and directly related to expected increases in the interest rate.

Figure 14.3.   **The Supply of and Demand for Money**

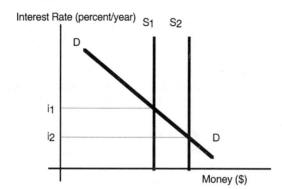

The Supply of Money

The supply of money is the stock which is available at a given point in time. Its magnitude is set by the FED assuming the cooperation of banks and borrowers. The FED's Open Market Committee buys government bonds on the open market. Sellers deposit the checks received from the FED. The checks are cleared back to the FED, which increases the reserve accounts of the banks by the amount of the checks. This increases banks' excess reserves—funds which can be loaned with interest. Were the market initially in equilibrium, to loan more money requires the bank to reduce its interest rate. The additional loans appear as additional money in the borrower's checking account.

 Note the assumptions upon which the money expansion scenario is built: that banks will attempt to lend their excess reserves and that borrowers will try to borrow these reserves. That is *almost always* what happens but the assumptions can be incorrect. If banks are insecure about loan repayments, they may not loan all of their excess reserves, or if borrowers fear that they will not be able to repay their loans (driving them into bankruptcy), they might not engage in borrowing. In the Great Depression, as a result of these fears, the banking system was awash with excess reserves..

Monetary Stimulation and the Equation of Exchange

The demand for and supply of money is shown in Figure 14.3. With the FED-set supply S_1S_1, the interest rate is i_1. Assume that the FED wished to stimulate the economy—a manifestation of *monetary policy*. It could buy government bonds on the open market which generally leads to the supply of money increasing, here to S_2S_2, driving the interest rate down to i_2. At this lower interest rate more investment spending would be profitable.

 Critics of monetary policy claim that the increase in the stock of money is inflationary. Their argument can be seen using the *equation of exchange:*

(10)   PQ = MV

where P is the overall price level; Q is real gross domestic product; PQ is the gross domestic product in current dollar, M is the stock of money; and V is the velocity of circulation, the average number of times a dollar is used for the purchase of final goods and services in a year.

Critics argue that if the stock of money, M, increases, the price level, P, increases. The latter leads to the interest rate increasing. The effect on the economy is then only inflationary.

One could just as rationally argue that all of the increase in the stock of money leads to an increase in real output, Q. The lower interest rate would increase spending on interest-sensitive goods increasing employment and productivity.

Putting the equation into ratio or percentage form is a convenience. Take the first difference of the equation of exchange:

(11) $\Delta(PQ) = \Delta(MV)$

Dropping the second-order terms, $\Delta P \Delta Q$ and $\Delta M \Delta V$, we have

(12) $P\Delta Q + Q\Delta P = M\Delta V + P\Delta M$

Divide the left side by PQ and the right side by MV:

(13) $\Delta P/P + \Delta Q/Q = \Delta M/M + \Delta V/V$

A 10 percent increase in the money supply ($\Delta M/M = 0.1 = 10\%$) with velocity held constant must register on the left side of the equation as a 10 percent increase divided between inflation and real output. The issue is, as stated above, how much of the 10 percent manifests itself in an increase in real output and how much in inflation. There is a good deal of evidence that prices are sticky, that they respond slowly to cost and demand changes. Thus, my opinion is that an increase in the money supply largely reflects itself in an increase in real output. What happens in the long-run is less clear. This is because after the recovery from a depression the level of economic activity tends to rise to the level it would have attained had the depression never existed. The extra money would then create inflation—but only if the ratio of money to real output increased.

The Market for Loanable Funds

In this analysis loans are flows, usually annual. The supply and demand appear in Figure 14.4. The demand for loanable funds comes from all borrowers: business, government, consumers, and foreign borrowers. Note how this demand differs from the demand for money. The demand for money is a demand *to hold money*. The demand for loanable funds is a demand *to use* the money borrowed.

Figure 14.4.   **The Supply of and Demand for Loanable Funds**

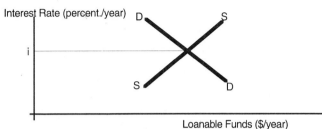

Loanable Funds ($/year)

The supply of loanable funds, in turn, comes from the savings of corporations, state governments, consumers, foreign dollar holders, plus a FED-generated increase in the lending power of banks. Here the FED appears to have a more modest interest-setting role than in the market for money. Does this compromise the power of the FED to control the interest rate? Day-to-day changes in the interest rate would arise from non-policy-related shifts in supply and demand. But if the FED wanted to tighten or loosen credit it could still decrease or increase the share of the supply it usually controls.

The Nominal and the Real Interest Rate

Start with definitions of the nominal and the real interest rate. The nominal interest rate is the interest rate as we normally know it: the interest rate banks pay on savings; the interest rate charged on mortgages; the interest rate charged on car and credit card loans, and the interest rate called-out on bonds. This interest rate is sometimes called the nominal interest rate.

> *The (nominal) interest rate* is the rental price paid for the use of a dollar for a year. Its units are percent per year.

The word *nominal* implies a put down, that it is the interest rate in name only. Allow an example to show why this is so. Suppose I were to lend some money for a year at 6 percent and that the inflation rate turns out to be 8 percent. The real rate of interest I would actually get would be about minus 2 percent—the money I received for the loan a year later was 2 percent less in purchasing power than the money initially loaned. Of course, things could go just the other way. The loan could have been at an interest rate of 10 percent with the lender and the borrow expecting an inflation rate of 6 percent. The repayment to the lender would then yield to him 6 percent more purchasing power. If, however, the price level went up by only 1 percent, the value of the repaid money would be 9 percent higher than that loaned out.

For a loan of a given magnitude, duration, and interest rate, the number of dollars which must be paid in each period and at the end of the loan. But unless borrowers and lenders know the inflation rate, they do not know the value of these dollars. and the real rate of interest.

> The *real interest rate. Ri,* is the rent paid for the use of a dollar for a year, in dollars of constant purchasing power. It is the interest rate deflated by the annual increase in prices, $p*$, in percent:
>
> $$Ri = [(1 + i)/(1 + p*)] - 1 \text{ or } (i - p*)/(1 + p*).$$

Note that the conversion of an interest rate into a real interest rate by by discounting the rate by 1 plus the percentage change in prices is the same conversion used to change wage payments into real wages, wages which are a measure of purchasing power.

Consider two examples to get a better feel of the calculation of the real interest rate with the interest rate and the inflation rate given.

Example 1:
Given: $i = 6$ percent/year; $p* = 8$ percent/year.
Find: The real rate of interest, Ri.

   $Ri = [(1 + i)/(1 + p*)] - 1 = [1.06/1.08] - 1 = 0.98148 - 1 = -1.85$ percent/year.
      $= (i - p*)/(1 + p*) = (6 - 8)/1.08 = -1.85$ percent/year.
Example 2:
Given: $i = 6$ percent/year; $p* = 2$ percent/year.
Find: Ri
      $Ri = (i - p*)/(1 + p*) = (6 - 2)/1.02 = 3.92$ percent/year

---

The Real Interest Rate and the Problem of Inflationary Expectations

It is convenient to approximate the real rate of interest by subtracting the inflation rate from the interest rate and that will be done here—but remember that it is an expedient approximation and that it almost always yields higher real rates than the actuality: $r - p* > (r - p*)/(1 + p*)$ if $p* > 0$.

(14) $Ri \approx i - p*$

The approximation can also be written as

(15) $i \approx Ri + p*$

Equation (15) shows that the interest rate has two components: one tends to cover the real interest rate; the other the rate of inflation. If the real rate is reasonably constant, the variability of the interest rate largely reflects the variability of the inflation rate. The extent to which this is true will be seen shortly as interest rate data are examined.

Figure 14.5.   **The Nominal and Real Interest Rate, Moody's Baa Corporate Bonds, 1947–1990**

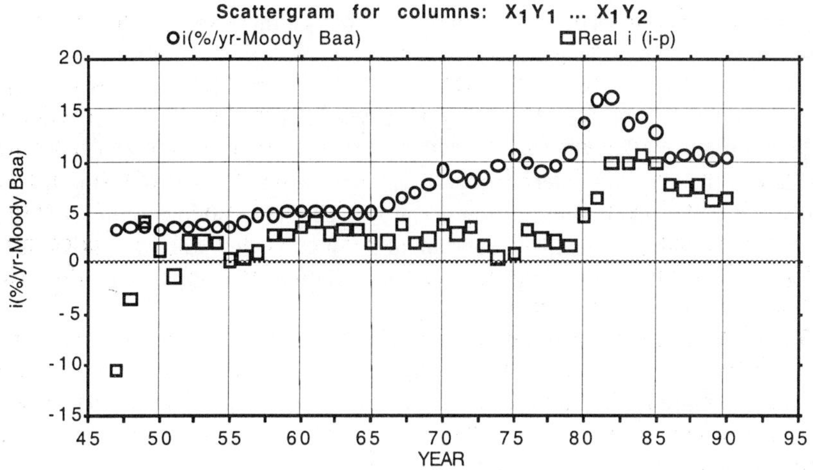

Scattergram for columns: X_1Y_1 ... X_1Y_2

○i(%/yr-Moody Baa)   □Real i (i-p)

Interest and Real Interest Rate Data

Plots of the nominal and the real interest rates from 1947 to 1990 can be found in Figure 14.5. The interest rate is that of corporate bonds rated Baa by Moody's. The reason for the choice is that the Baa bond rates are those commonly paid by ordinary corporations, with the lower rates of Aaa bonds largely confined to those of "blue chip" status. The circles represent the interest rate, the squares the real interest rate.

Interest Rate Data

During three subperiods the interest rate was reasonably stable: 1947–1955; 1959–1965; and, 1970–1978. A fourth period, 1979–1990 is characterized by a cyclical pattern of increases and then decreases in the interest rate.
 Overall, the interest rate showed a tendency to increase from relatively low post World War II figures to higher rates.

Real Interest Rate Data

As can be seen in Figure 14.5, from 1952 to 1979, the real rate of interest was in the range of zero to 4 percent with little, if any, discernible trend. This was in keeping with the view or hypothesis that the real rate of interest tends to be constant, whereas the nominal rate reflected changes in inflation. This relative constancy of the real rate took place despite the fact that the nominal interest during the 1970–1979 period was roughly double that of the 1952–1965 period. However, there were times during which the real interest rate was far from the zero to 4 percent per annum range.

If future inflation is underestimated, as in 1947, the real rate of interest will be low. The failure to recognize the high post–World War II inflation rates reflected a belief by many that after the war we would return to the prewar economic malaise and the very low interest rates of the depression of the 1930s. But instead, of a substantial depression, prosperity arose. The large savings built up during the war created great demand, substantial production, and wage and price inflation. As a result of this high unexpected inflation, real interest in 1947 and 1948 was substantially negative.

Rather the opposite occurred in the 1980s. The rising trend in inflation in the late 1970s led to the expectation of its continuance. As a result interest rates were relatively high compared to the actual inflation rates. Real interest rates were then unusually high. In 1986, for example, the real rate of interest was 10.5 percent—about four times the earlier norm.

Reasonably accurate inflationary expectations seems to yield a real rate in the 2–4 percent range. In the late 1990s with its very low inflation rates, the real rate has returned to its earlier range.

Funds for Capital Spending

There are a number of different sources of funds to buy capital goods. Two of them allow the firm to avoid borrowing and the need to repay money on a contracted schedule. One is to use retained earnings. The second is to raise money by issuing new shares of stock.

Funds required for investment spending are frequently borrowed—through the use of bond issues, from insurance companies, pension funds, other corporations, and some banks. Payments on loans are a fixed cost. The amount borrowed does not change as the production rate changes.

The repayment of loans is generally done in one of two ways: one is exemplified by bond, the other by mortgage payments. The former requires paying interest on the amount borrowed, usually semi-annually, plus repayment of the entire principal sum borrowed on the very last day of the loan; the latter involves equal payments throughout the duration of the loan so that it is completely paid at the end of its term of the mortgage.

Bonds and Bond Payments

The annual payments which have to be made on a $100,000, 8 percent, twenty year bond can be written out as:

(16) $PV = 100 = 8/(1.08)^1 + 8/(1.08)^2 + ... + 8/(1.08)^{19} + (8 + 100)/(1.08)^{20}$

where figures in the numerator are in thousands of dollars. The 8 percent interest of $8,000 is paid at the end of each and every one of the 20 years. But only on the last day of the term of the bond, at the end of twenty years, is the principal repaid.

That this sum of discounted payments equals 100 can be calculated in four different ways: (1) The calculation can be done by brute force. Take each numerator and divide by 1.08 raised to the appropriate power. Then add up the twenty figures and the total should be 100. (2) Another way is to use interest rate tables. In the table for 8 percent annual payments can be found the present value of twenty annual $1 payments $(P/A_{i,n})$. It is 9.8182. Multiplying this by 8 yields 78.560, or $78,560, the present value of the twenty $8,000 payments. You can also find the present value of a dollar received twenty years in the future, $(P/F_{i,n})$. which is 0.2142. Multiply this by the $100,000 repayment of face value, and you have $21,460. When the two present values are added together they come to $100,020—slightly off the mark because of rounding. (3) Recognize that all the terms with 1.08 in the denominator comprise a geometric series. The sum of this geometric series is:

(17) $S = PV_{8\%,20yrs} = a\,R\,(1\text{-}R^n) / (1\text{-}R)$

where, $a = 8$; R, the ratio of successive terms, is $1/1.08$; and $n = 20$. That sum should be 78.5456. Add to it $100/1.08^{20}$ and the third approach is complete. (4) Use a computer program. The spreadsheet on my Macintosh computer claims it can do the job.

Mortgages and Mortgage Payments

The mortgage approach has the repayment of the loan made by equal annual payments, A.

(18) $PV = 100 = A/(1.08) + A/(1.08)^2 + ... + A/(1.08)^{20}$

The simplest way to calculate the magnitude of A is through the use of interest tables, if they are readily accessible. There it will be found a column with the heading $A/P_{i,n}$. It is the annual payment, A, for a present value, P, of one $1 at an interest rate of i, with n annual payments. For an interest rate of 8 percent and twenty annual payments, the figure is 0.1019. If the mortgage is for $100,000, multiplication by that number yields annual mortgage payments of $10,190 per year. (This has the same present value of $100,000 as does the payment to bondholders of $8,000 per year plus $100,000 at the end of the twenty years.)

Table 14.2.   **The Effects of a Change in the Interest Rate on $1 Million Loans of Different Durations**

Duration	Annual Payments		
	8%/yr	10%/yr	% Difference
5 years	250,500	263,800	5.31
30 years	88,800	106,100	19.48

Correcting Mistakes in Inflationary Expectations

At the time a loan is consummated the interest rate can be viewed as the sum of a real rate of interest plus the expected inflation rate, $E\{p^*\}$:

(19) $i = Ri + E\{p^*\}$

If the inflation rate turns out to be less than expected, lenders will be receiving higher real interest than anticipated. In addition, with a lower rate of inflation, interest rates tend to decrease and this increases the value of all outstanding loans. On the other side of the transaction, those who borrowed in the previous period are paying a higher interest rate than the new norm. But there are usually ways which allow borrowers some avoidance of their paying higher interest rates than those which arise during the term of a loan. Bonds have "call provisions" which allow the borrowers to redeem the bond at a number of specified dates prior to the due or redemption date of the bond. The sums required to pay off the higher-interest bonds can be obtained by floating a bond issue at the now lower interest rate. And mortgages frequently have provisions for early repayment of the remaining principal—a sum frequently obtained through a new mortgage at a lower interest rate. But what if the original interest rate turns out to be lower than the rates which evolve? The disadvantaged lender has no alternative but to suffer. If the bonds and mortgages are kept, lower than current interest is received; if sold a capital loss will be experienced with its market and present value of the security based on discounting future payments by the now higher interest rate.

The Effects of an Interest Rate Change on the Cost of Capital Goods

Investment spending is generally modeled as decreasing as the interest rate increases. But does a given change in the interest rate yield the same change in present value for capital goods of the same price but different durabilities, different expected economic lifespans? This question is addressed by an example in which (1) there are two different capital goods, (2) the price of each is $1 million, and (3) both involve loans in the amount of their cost, loans to be repaid in equal annual payments, the first in five, the second in thirty years.

What are the annual payments at 8 and 10 percent interest rates? By what percentage do the payments increase in going from 8 to 10 percent per year loan? The results are shown in Table 14.2. (The calculations are based on the assumption that payments are made at the end of each year.) The increase in the interest rate from 8 to 10 percent, increases the annual cost of a five-year loan by 5.31 percent and the thirty-year loan by 19.48 percent. Thus, the cost of structures is more sensitive to changes in the interest than is the cost of equipment.

A New Issue of Stocks and Retained Earnings

Funds can be raised by issuing additional shares in a corporation. The advantage is that this poses no repayment obligation, whereas bonds do. The disadvantage is that additional shares water down the value of the shares of the existing owners. In effect, existing shareholders provide funds to the corporation by the reduction in the value of their shares.

Please recognize the difference between new issues of stock and that sold in stock markets. New issues are sold outside of stock markets. Stock markets are *secondary markets*. They handle subsequent sales of the new shares, usually undifferentiated from older shares. This, of course, assumes that shares of a corporation are traded on an exchange.

The buying and selling of shares on an exchange then involves the transfer of shares of ownership between buyer and seller. The corporation whose shares are being bought and sold receives no proceeds whatever from these transactions. Transactions in secondary issues is a form of gambling in which the seller is betting that there are more profitable uses of the value of the shares sold while the buyers is betting that the purchase involves the most profitable use of his money.

Retained earnings arise from corporations paying dividends which are less than the corporation's earnings. The earnings retained, when used for investment purposes, represents involuntary funding by shareholders.

Investment Spending and Its Volatility

John Maynard Keynes considered investment spending to be volatile and the major source of the business cycle, particularly that of the Great Depression. In 1929 gross private domestic investment was $139.2 billion and in 1933 it was $22.7 billion, both in 1982 dollars. The former was 19.6 percent, the latter 4.6 percent of real gross national product. At that time Keynes model seemed supported by the facts. Real gross private domestic investment includes spending on non-residential structures, producers' durable equipment, and residential structures. Among the important aspects of investment spending bear examination of three are briefly considered: (1) Has investment spending been volatile in the post–World War II era? (2) How sensitive is it to changes in the interest rate? (3) Do changes in investment spending lead to changes in overall spending?

An issue of concern is the alleged volatility of investment spending. During the 1947–1990 period real gross private investment spending averaged 16.06 percent of real gross domestic product or spending; The high for the period was 17.68 percent, the low 14.60 percent. If unemployment is used as a measure of economic depression, the two worst unemployment rates during the period took place in 1982 (9.7 percent) and 1983 (9.6 percent). In those years investment was 14.9 and 15.6 percent of gross domestic product—less than the average but not by very much. Is relative investment spending volatile? One way of measuring this is by means of the standard deviation which amounted to 0.91 percent. This means that in almost two-thirds of the years, in the 1947–1990 interval, gross private domestic investment fell between 15.15 and 16.97 percent.

Another way of measuring the variability of a distribution is through use of the coefficient of variation:

> *The coefficient of variation* of a distribution is the ratio of its standard deviation to the mean of the distribution.

The standard deviation of gross private domestic investment is 0.91 percent, and the mean of the distribution, as mentioned above, is 16.06 percent. The coefficient of variation is accordingly 5.7 percent (*0.91/16.06*): Investment in almost two-thirds of the years fell within 5.7 percent of the mean.

Based on the data described, I would say that investment spending as a percentage of overall spending has been reasonably stable since the end of World War II. But this may be the wrong way to look at the relationship between investment spending and the gross domestic product. It is possible, however, that a drop in investment spending is followed by a roughly proportionate drop in gross domestic product. This would leave investment spending as roughly the same percent of gross domestic product as it had been previously.

Do Changes in Investment Lead Changes in Gross Domestic Product?

With the relationship between investment and overall spending reasonably constant, it might be more illuminating to work with changes in these variables There are two reasons for this: (1) Although the ratio of the variables may tend to be reasonably constant, their changes or first differences can be quite different. Consider the series 100, 101, and 103. The last point is only 3 percent greater than the first. But the first differences are 1, and 2, a 100 percent difference. If our concern is actually with changes in the gross national product, first differences of that variable and investment spending can yield a finer grained view of the relationship. (2) And, a better model may be that *changes* in investment lead

Figure 14.6. **Annual Changes in Gross National Product and Gross Private Domestic Investment in Current Dollars, 1947–1990**

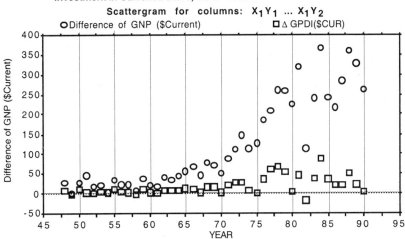

to *changes* in gross domestic product or overall spending.

In Figure 14.6 can be found plots of annual changes in gross domestic product, the squares, and annual changes in gross private domestic investment, the circles. As can be seen the increases and decreases in changes tend to be simultaneous. With annual data it appears that changes in investment spending do not lead changes in gross domestic product.

Investment Spending Models

It takes no genius to create a substantial number of models of investment, and that will be done presently. In these models the form of investment will not be specified. Each could either be gross investment, gross non-residential or gross residential investment. Nor is the form of the variables specified. They can be either real or nominal. I can then claim that each model stands for six models. The models follow:

> 1. The most obvious relationship we know is that investment, I, is an increasing function of gross domestic product, Y: $I = f(Y)$.

> 2. Recall that a high percentage of structures and equipment are replacements of other structures and equipment and a small percentage is for economic growth. This raises the issue of the *accelerator model*.

Assume that the economy is experiencing no growth, that the capital stock is 100, and that the required replacement is ten per year. If economic activity is constant ten units of capital are produced each year. Then the economy grows by ten percent and 110 units of capital are required. The production of new capital accelerates from ten to twenty units a year, a 100 percent increase: Ten are to replace capital consumed; ten are to increase the stock of capital by 10 percent. After a while the annual capital requirement will level off at eleven units per year, 10 percent of the 110 units of the capital stock required. The accelerator model, simplified, has investment spending as a function of the gross domestic product plus the change in the gross domestic product: $I = f(Y, \Delta Y)$.

3. And we cannot forget that investment spending should vary inversely with the interest rate, i. Our model then becomes: $I = f(Y, \Delta Y, i)$.

4. We have left out a truly crucial variable, the expected rate of return. How to model *expected* anything is difficult. Of course the higher profits are, the higher is the rate of return. We then have investment as an increasing function of gross domestic product, the change in gross domestic product, and profits; and a decreasing function of the interest rate: $I = f(Y, \Delta Y, i, \pi)$.

Of particular concern is the role of the interest rate. When it increases, it increases the cost of capital and should lower investment spending, and the opposite when the interest rate decreases. This would help to validate basic price theory and the view of monetary policy in which economic activity is controlled by varying the interest rate. The estimates obtained from the four models can be seen in Table 14.5

The data used were: for I, Y, and ΔY billions of current dollars per year; for i, Moody's' Baa corporate bond rate in percent per year; and, for π after tax profit per dollar of sales in cents. The investment variable used is gross private domestic investment. All data are from issues of the *Economic Report of the President*.

The first model has investment as an increasing function of gross domestic product. The fit as expected was excellent explaining 98.5 percent of the variance in investment.

The second model adds to the first model, the change in gross domestic product. This captures the *accelerator* and, at the same time, adds what is to some extent a lagged variable. It has, for example, investment in 1948 as a function of the gross domestic product of 1948 and the difference between the gross domestic product of 1947 and 1948. Slightly more of the variance of investment spending is explained in this model.

The third model adds the interest rate. Unhappily, the regression equation contends that when the interest rate increases investment spending increases and that makes no sense. Drop model 3.

Table 14.3.   **Gross Private Domestic Investment Models, 1947–1990**

Model						
	Estimates of Coefficients (t values)					
Constant	GDP	ΔGDP	i	π	adjR^2	DW
1. 3.456	0.1518				0.9854	1.03
	(53.8)					
2. −1.268	0.1229	0.4303			0.9921	1.23
	(24.4)	(6.1)				
3. −12.248	0.1214	0.3800	2.5105		0.9924	1.24
	(24.2)	(5.0)	(1.6)			
4. −43.947	0.1134	0.3056	3.6835	12.5774	0.9938	1.70
	(21.7)	(4.2)	(2.6)	(3.1)		

The fourth model adds profits per dollar of sales, and it shows that when profits increase, investment spending increases. And again the coefficient of the interest rate is positive and wrong. It is possible that the inclusion of one or more other variable in a model distorted the role of the interest rate in determining the amount of investment spending. To examine this, regressions of two other models were made. In the first the investment to gross domestic product ratio was regressed on the interest rate alone. The interest rate coefficient was again wrongly positive. The second model had the investment to gross domestic product ratio as a function of the real interest rate. The coefficient of the interest rate was also wrongly positive, although terribly small. Its "t-value" of 0.0165 indicated that the coefficient was not significantly different from zero.

Finally, I dropped the interest variable from model (4). As a result, I tested a model in which investment spending is a function of gross domestic product, the change in gross domestic product, and profits (per dollar of sales). Alas, the sign of the coefficient of the profit variable became wrongly negative and not significantly different from zero. The best model is then the second in which investment is an increasing function of gross domestic product and the change in gross domestic product.

Did I omit the price of capital goods in what is essentially a set of conventional capital demand models? Well, not exactly. Investment spending, as spending in general, is the price times the quantity purchased. All four models could have been written at the start as $I = PQ$, where I is investment spending, P is the price of investment or capital goods, and Q the quantity of capital goods purchased. The $I = PQ$ formulation arbitrarily implies that the price elasticity of demand for capital goods is unity. This is because for any given amount of spending, here per year, were the price 1 percent higher, the quantity would have to be 1 percent lower—the definition of a unitary elasticity demand function. I think that not terribly unreasonable since in many firms investment spending is a fixed budgeted amount and that implies a unitary elasticity of demand.

More Sophisticated Models

Robert S. Chirinko's article, "Business Fixed Investment Spending: A Survey of Modeling Strategies, Empirical Results, and Policy Implications" (1993) is an excellent presentation of a variety of models of investment spending. A number of matters of interest deserve mentioning:

> 1. The dependent variables are sometimes investment spending and sometimes the ratio of investment spending to the dollar value of the stock of capital.

> 2. The price of capital is explicit. It is sometimes the rental cost of capital and at other times the "shadow price" of capital, the discounted sum of capital's expected marginal revenue products over its expected life.

> 3. Tobin's q theory is of interest to experts in the field. The model has investment spending as an increasing function of q which is the ratio of the value of the firm to the replacement cost of its capital stock.

> 4. In his summary and conclusion Chirinko wrote:

> It appears to this author that, on balance, the response of investment to price variables tends to be small and unimportant relative to quantity variables (1993, p. 1906).

Once again the quantity system is found to be of greater importance than the price system.

Summary

The market for capital goods is one of the most important in the economy. It covers the plant and equipment and residential housing. The former goods are productivity enhancing and, some believe, the locus of the business cycle. The latter enhances the ambience in which we spend much of our lives, the home.

Business investment is the inflow into the stock of productive capital. Investment goods exist in three forms: structures, equipment, and inventories. A new structure may have an important role in providing a better ambience for workers and machines. It may also allow the introduction of equipment and processes which enhance productivity. Beyond that, it is generally passive with respect to production.

New equipment, replacement and additional, is the most common source of advancing productivity. Inventory includes goods waiting to be used in production, goods-in-process, replacement parts, and finished goods yet to be sold. The capital stock at a given date is that of a previous date plus the intervening inflow of investment minus the outflow of capital consumption. Important measures of the capital stock beyond its magnitude are the capital stock per worker and its vintage. Most of the gross investment inflow is to replace consumed capital. Net investment, the addition to the supply of capital, tends to be about 20 percent of gross investment.

The criterion for profit maximization for a risk-free investment is that the expected rate of return equals the interest rate. Risk and uncertainty add to the rate of return required to justify an investment. Risk implies that there exists a risk distribution function obtained from experience with the same or similar past investments. The expected risk on a new project is drawn from that distribution. There is no record exploitable to estimate the magnitude of uncertainty, and decision-making in the face of uncertainty is frequently characterized as the entrepreneurial function. Successful entrepreneurs are able to estimate the uncertainty of various new products and in so doing pick those destined to yield substantial profits. Uncertainty can be thought of as the expected value of an investment drawn from a subjective uncertainty distribution function.

One institution and two markets are cited as the setters of the interest rate. The FED sets the federal funds rate which underlies the interest rate banks charge for short-term loans. Then there is the market for money. The demand for money is based on the transactions, precautionary, and speculative motives. The higher the interest rate, the higher the opportunity cost of holding money, so less is held or demanded. The supply is set by the FED. The other market is that for loanable funds. It is the market of in which many groups of borrowers demand loans and many groups of lenders supply them.

The real interest rate is the nominal interest rate discounted by the rate of inflation. It normally exists in a narrow band of roughly zero to 4 percent. But sometimes it is substantially more and at other times substantially less. A higher real interest rate indicates that expected inflation was greater than that which actually occurred. A lower real interest rate is related to expected inflation lower than that realized. Borrowers compensate for the problem of finding that they are paying higher interest rates than those currently available by calling their bonds and refinancing their mortgages. In addition the longer the expected life of a capital good, the less is the interest in the real interest rate of a single year.

Investment tends to be portrayed as volatile but gross investment is actually a fairly stable portion of gross domestic product. It is also portrayed as leading gross domestic product so that when it increases or decreases, some time later gross domestic product increases and decreases. It does not appear to lead gross domestic product.

Empirical work on investment spending indicates that it is an increasing function of gross domestic product and the change in gross domestic product. But despite the clarity of the logic, it does not appear to vary negatively with the interest rate. This calls into question how the FED and monetary policy function. Another surprise is that investment spending did not appear to be an increasing function of profits, at least when represented by profit per dollar of sales.

Finally, in Chirinko's survey of empirical investment models, he found that the effect of price variables on investment spending was small as compared to quantity variables.

Questions on Chapter 14

1. What are the categories of capital goods? Why are they all investments?

2. Assume that the structure in which work is performed is more than adequate. The temperature, air flow, illumination are all satisfactory. Then in what ways, if any, could a change in the structure help to increase productivity.

3. Why are goods in process a form of capital? Why is it that if the price of goods in process increased, less of it might be demanded? (Vague hint: Do not lose sight of the fact that the demand for goods in process, as other factors, is a derived demand.)

4. Explain why an increase in the federal funds rate dictated by the FED tends to increase the interest rates which banks charge on short-term loans.

5. In both the market for money and the market for loanable funds, the demand is seemingly for money. In actuality the demand is very different. Explain.

6. Use a simple example or set of examples to show why the interest rate which brings present value to zero is the rate of return.

7. Investment spending seems to be largely a function of the size of the economy and not sensitive to interest rate variations. What reasons can you think of which would have firms investing the same amount at low and high interest rates?

8. Assume that: (1) There are two capital goods used to manufacture two different products. (2) You have the distributions of their rates of return during the past twenty years. (3) Both have the same average rate of return, but the standard deviation of A's distribution is twice that of B. Why is it riskier to invest in A? How, if at all, does time affect your answer?

CHAPTER FIFTEEN

Market Failures

People, institutions, societies, and economies all have their imperfections. So it is unexceptional that what is called a market economy has its share of failures. But the fact that perfection is non-existent in no way diminishes the disutility of market failures. They can be depressing and deadly to people, families, and societies. They cry for solutions.

Unemployment and Underemployment

Unemployment is an economic failure because it is a manifestation of the failure of a market to equilibrate as viewed along the quantity axis. Underemployment, as that of adjuncts, is a failure of a market to equilibrate along the price axis.

Unemployment

Why does the labor market fail to equilibrate quantities supplied and demanded? It cannot equilibrate for two reasons: (1) The demand for labor is highly inelastic. As a result about a 6 percent reduction in the real wage is required to increase employment by 1 percent. The drop in real earnings of about 5 percent decreases consumer demand more or less counteracting the positive effect on employment of the real wage cut. (2) Wage changes lead to price changes. Were the wage reduced by 6 percent prices would fall by about 4 percent. As a result, very large reductions in the money wage are required to yield small decreases in the real wage. Such large wage reductions are far beyond social norms and quite impractical. There is no way to change the wage elasticity of demand for wages nor the relationship of wages and prices. Thus, the market surplus cannot move the market to equilibrium. With wage flexibility incapable of equilibrating the labor market, aggregate demand increases seem to be required.

It should be noted that consumer sovereignty means little without job sovereignty which sometimes requires the assistance of the sovereign government.

Underemployment

I am taking a very narrow view of underemployment—one in which workers have the skills to perform the work available. They are actually performing the work, but they receive less compensation and have far less job security than others. With less compensation for these underemployed, the disequilibrium found is with respect to price.

The two groups of workers considered here are: part-time workers who want full-time employment, and contract workers doing full-time work who desire regular employment. In both cases the work is available; underemployed workers are performing it.

Part-Time Workers Desiring Full-Time Employment

Part-time workers generally receive lower hourly compensation than full-time workers performing the same or comparable work. They are paid less per hour, and they receive few, if any, fringe benefits other than those required by the law. In addition, they have less job security than full-time employees.

Many of us are in daily contact with such workers, qualified people who are employed as part-time instructors, "adjuncts." Adjuncts are much cheaper per course, and they can be easily laid-off or not hired. They frequently have to work at two or even three institutions to support themselves. There are some departments and even whole schools which are staffed by a relatively small number of faculty members and a large contingent of adjuncts.

A growing group of part-time workers who are discriminated against with respect to pay are welfare recipients assigned to municipal workfare activities. They tend to receive pay which is a fraction of that which they would receive were they regular employees.

Contract Workers Desiring Regular Employment

By contract work I mean full-time work performed for a firm by non-employees with the work the same or very similar to that performed by regular employees. The difference between the contract and regular employees tends to be that contract workers do not receive the fringe benefits of regular employees and they lack the job security of regular employees.

The past decade has seen workers traditionally immune to layoffs subject to them—under the name of downsizing. Frequently, the firm effecting the layoffs is both profitable and overstaffed. But just where they are overstaffed cannot be determined without a margin of error. The number of different tasks performed in a modern corporation are legion and laying off just the right number in just the right areas of work is not possible. Isolated areas of understaffing sometimes

Table 15.1.   **Shares of Money Income and Adjusted Family Income, 1966**

Families	Percent of Income Received	
	Unadjusted	Adjusted
	(percent of total income)	
Lowest fifth	4.3	3.7
Second fifth	11.3	9.9
Middle fifth	17.3	16.1
Fourth fifth	24.5	22.6
Highest fifth	42.6	47.9
Top 5 percent	16.0	22.1
Top 1 percent	4.8	10.5

Source: Pechman and Okner (1974), Table 4–2, p. 46.

sometimes leads to the offer of contract work to laid-off workers rather than re-employment. This is another form of discrimination.

But perhaps my branding of part-time and contract work as market failures is wrong. These workers are less costly than full-time workers. Is the market failure the norm of employing full-time workers? Breaking such a norm would in part reverse the triumph of the firm over the market as the allocator of scarce resources, and adversely change the character of work and employment in our society.

The Distribution of Income with Adjustments of Pechman and Okner

Much can be favorably said for the economy which arguably yields the highest per capita standard of living in the world. But that praise must be diminished if the distribution of income is a manifestation of the rich getting relatively richer and the poor getting relatively poorer. This is particularly true if there is no credible evidence indicating that the rich have been increasing their productivity relative to the poor. Thus, the applause granted the economy may be manifest by one hand clapping.

Realize, in addition, that the distribution of income has always been more disparate than government statistics indicate. This was shown in the wonderful study by Joseph A. Pechman and Benjamin A. Okner, *Who Bears the Tax Burden?* (1974). To answer the question, the authors revise, along economic lines, the government's distribution of income statistics. This allows them to then determine the incidence of taxes on the various income groups. In Table 15.1 can be found the official income distribution and the adjusted distribution of Pechman and Okner. The adjustments, which are discussed in the next section, are for non-reporting and underreporting of income.

Table 15.2.   **The Share of Aggregate Income Received by Each Fifth and Top 5 Percent of Families, 1966, 1980, and 1995**

Year	Lowest	Second	Third	Fourth	Highest	Top 5 Percent
1966	4.3	11.3	17.3	24.5	42.6	16.0
1980	5.3	11.6	17.6	24.4	41.1	14.6
1995	4.4	10.1	15.8	23..2	45.8	20.0

Sources: The 1966 data are from Table 15.1. All other data are from the *Statistical Abstract of the United States*, 1997, Table 725, p. 470.

Consider the magnitude of the changes arising from adjustments wrought by Pechman and Okner. In the unadjusted distribution, the top 1 percent of income recipients had incomes 12 percent more than the lowest 20 percent of income recipients. In the adjusted distribution, the top 1 percent of income recipients had incomes 238 percent more than the lowest 20 percent group. In addition, Table 15.1 shows that after adjustments 80 percent of families had a lower share of income than had previously been thought.

Table 15.2 is intended to indicate the trends in the distribution in the 1966–1995 period. From 1966 to 1980 the 60 percent of families with relatively low income gained a slightly higher share of aggregate income. But in the 1980–1995 period the tables were turned as the top 5 percent of families increased their share of income by 37 percent or by 25 percent as compared to their 1966 share.

The adjustments of Pechman and Okner consist of subtractions from and additions to income. The subtractions are "receipts from private pensions and annuities and government retirement benefits ... that are not financed through payroll taxes"(p. 14). These sums had been counted as family income in the year in which the contribution was made. (Unadjusted statistics include as family income social security and welfare benefits in the year in which payments are received.)

An addition to the government income data is dollar value of the fringe benefits covering health and other welfare benefits. And "the major forms of nonmoney income that are included in income are unrealized capital gains and net imputed rent on owner-occupied dwellings" (p. 15).

The capital gains adjustment was not based on the annual increases of share prices as registered on stock exchanges but, more conservatively, on corporate retained earnings in a given year.

The sense of including the rental value of owner-occupied homes may require a bit of explanation. Assume there are twin brothers living side by side identical in all respects. They rent homes which are adjacent. Both have $200,000 in 7 percent bonds from which they receive interest income of $14,000 per year.

Then one of the twins buys the house he rented with the $200,000 in bonds. Official income statistics will now have the renting twin with $14,000 more in income than his homeowner brother. But the rental value of the home purchased, its imputed value, is $14,000. Pechman and Okner adjusted official income figures to reflect this as is done by a number of European countries.

The above adjustments have resulted in the major differences between the income statistics normally published and those of Pechman and Okner.

Surplus Capacity

The surplus of resources goes far beyond the unemployment of labor. Capital structures and equipments are idle most of the time, and there are often huge amounts of unused commercial space. Recognition of the international character of surplus capacity shows the problem to be even more serious than we tend to recognize. Louis Uchitelle described the dilemma this way:

> The Asian financial turmoil may be the first stage of a developing world-wide crisis driven mainly by ... overcapacity, the tendency of the unfettered global market to produce more cars, toys, shoes, airplanes, steel, paper, appliances, film, clothing, and electronic devices than people will buy at high enough prices (1997, p. 3).

Surplus capacity represents a waste of resources and disequilibrium of troublesome proportions.

Inflation

Inflation is a zero-sum game in which the magnitude of the dollars lost by some equals the magnitude of the dollars won by others. Were the price of hot dogs increased from $1 to $2, the sale of each one would have buyers losing $1 and sellers gaining $1 per hot dog—a zero-sum game. Nonetheless, inflation does cause problems. Before going into them, however, data on the 1947–1990 inflation rates are provided in Figure 15.1. It is a plot of the overall price index, the gross domestic product deflator.

The inflation peaks and growth are related to important historic occasions. The 1947 peak came after the World War II wage and price controls were brought to an end. The next peak came after the start of the Korean War in June of 1950. The increasing inflationary trend of the 1960s is related to our increasing involvement in the war in Vietnam. The increasing 1972–1975 inflation rate is related to the embargo of exports of petroleum to the United States in 1993 by the Oil Producing Export Countries (OPEC). The subsequent increase is related to OPEC's tripling the price of crude oil in 1979. The subsequent decline in inflation largely reflects the commitment of the FED and the Reagan administration to cut the rate of inflation.

Figure 15.1.   **The Inflation Rate : The GNP Deflator, 1947–1991**

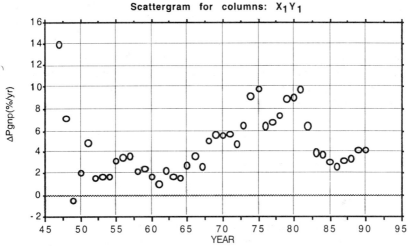

Among the problems caused by inflation are arbitrary changes in the distribution of income, a loss of purchasing power for those with relatively fixed incomes, lenders paid with dollars of less value than anticipated, the non-legislated increase in non-indexed income taxes, the enduring character of the inflation process, and the unemployment created to attenuate it.

Arbitrary Changes in the Distribution of Income

Two groups are examined here. The first consists of borrowers and lenders. The second those on fixed or semi-fixed incomes.

Borrowers and Lenders

There are winners and losers in the zero-sum game of inflation. For unanticipated inflation borrowers tend to be winners, lenders to be losers. Those who benefit include homeowners with outstanding mortgages, the federal government, and corporations—particularly those with mid- and long-term debt obligations. All can pay off their debts with less valuable dollars than those anticipated. Recall that the real interest rate increased substantially after the two OPEC-ignited inflations of the 1970s was tamed. One of the causes may have been that lenders who were burned twice were reluctant to purchase bonds and other debt instruments at what had been traditional yields.

With respect to the unanticipated end of inflation, lenders tend to be the winners and borrowers the losers—limited by the extent to which borrowers can replace an existing loan with one at a lower interest rate.

The Market Value of Bonds and Unanticipated Inflation

Recall the claim that lenders lose if unanticipated inflation arises. Allow an example to give some idea of the magnitude of that loss. Assume that the face value of a bond is $10,000, that it pays 6 percent or $600 per year, that it will be redeemed at the end of five years, and the market rate of interest for comparable bonds is 6 percent so that *(1+i)*, the discount factor, is 1.06. The present value, *PV*, of the bond is:

(1) $PV = 600/(1.06) + 600/(1.06)^2 + ... + (600 + 10,000)/(1.06)^5$

Solving for the present or market value of the bond yields:

(2) $PV = 10,000$

The value of the bond equals its face or nominal value.

Now, assume all the above conditions remain in place except that the interest rate unexpectedly jumps to 12 percent per year. The discount factor is then 1.12 and present value of the bond becomes:

(3) $PV = 600/(1.12) + 600/(1.12)^2 + ... + (600+10,000)/(1.12)^5$

The present value of the bond drops to:

(4) $PV = 7,837$

The loss in market value caused by the increase in the market interest is 21.63 percent. The fewer the years to the due date of the bond, the less is the effect on the market value. But the greater the number of years to the redemption of the bond, the greater the loss in market value. Had the due date been thirty years away, the jump in the interest rate from 6 to 12 percent, would have decreased the present and market value of the bond from $10,000 to $5,167—a loss of almost half of the original value of the bond. The unreality of the example is eased by the fact that a thirty-year 6 percent bond may very well run into a 12 percent condition along the way to its maturity—but then there are fewer years to maturity and a lower effect on the value of the bond.

Thus, you can see that an increase in the inflation and interest rates can hurt 'enders. And the extent to which lenders are hurt borrowers are benefited.

Fixed and Semi-Fixed Income Recipients

There are some people who live on fixed incomes. Others have part of their income, such as social security retirement income, indexed to the rate of inflation. Both are hurt by the force of inflation.

Assume that the inflation rate has been running in the 2.5 to 3.5 percent per annum range for a number of years. Many of us would be quite pleased with such modest and normal rates. But the response of "no problem" does not really mean that there are no problems. There are two groups which find themselves in trouble: (1) All workers whose pay increases by less than the inflation rate find themselves going backward with respect to the purchasing power of their earnings. Workers earning the minimum wage, during a period in which it is constant, would be among those disadvantaged. Modest inflation might also hurt workers in industries facing strong foreign competition, workers in industries recently deregulated, and those faced with decreasing demand because of the baby bust and other factors. (2) Private pension plans frequently pay a fixed amount of dollars irrespective of the inflation rate. The more the price level inflates, the lower is the purchasing power of such a pension. Even modest rates of inflation can badly diminish the value of such pensions over the course of time. At a 3 percent inflation rate, for example, the purchasing power of a fixed income is halved in twenty-four years—not much more than the life expectancy of the average 65-year-old college instructor.

Arbitrary Tax Increases

Until 1985 taxpayers suffered from "bracket creep" with inflation-fueled increases in nominal incomes putting them into higher tax brackets. This was advantageous to the government and very helpful in making the World War II–related gross federal deficit lower, as a percent of national income—lower virtually every year until the tax cuts of the Reagan administration. But since 1985, the income brackets are geared to the consumer price index, so the inflationary component of income increases no longer places taxpayers in higher tax brackets.
  But not all tax-related matters are indexed to rid the tax of inflation-oriented increases. An allowable cost to business is the depreciation of its capital stock. Assume that $1 million in equipment is depreciated over a five-year period. With $200,000 per year exempt from tax, the business should be able to amass the $1 million required to replace the subject equipment. But, if after five years inflation-driven prices increase the replacement cost of the equipment to $1.2 million, the depreciation allowance is inadequate. This problem has been responded to, not by indexing, but by accelerating depreciation rates.

Anti-Inflation Unemployment and the Inflation Cycle

Price inflation may be a monetary phenomenon in the long run but in the short run it is largely a function of wage inflation. This is because labor costs represent almost three-quarters of the cost of products. Break wage inflation and the price inflation is broken. That is done by increasing unemployment—the Phillips curve relationship discussed below.

That high inflation rates are broken with increasing unemployment is not intended to imply that the inflationary impulses come from the labor market. To the contrary, the high inflation periods of the 1970s and 1980s came from inflation in product markets, particularly the markets for crude oil and petroleum products. But product market inflation causes us to want and, at that time, to get higher pay. This leads to a cycle of more price increases which lead to more wage increases, to more price increases, and so on.

Lowering aggregate demand does little directly to lower prices in an economy of cost-based prices. But increased unemployment does cut wage inflation and then price inflation. Thus, unemployment is used to turn the inflation cycle downward. That the unemployed suffer to lower the inflation rate is conveniently overlooked by those of us who gain from this practice.

The Exaggerated Fear of Accelerating Inflation

Many neoclassical economists believe that unemployment rates lower than a certain level will cause the rate of inflation to accelerate, to increase to infinity in the long run. The critical unemployment rate is described by this mouthful: the non-accelerating inflation rate of unemployment. It is frequently abbreviated to its acronym, *NAIRU*. The process of ever-increasing inflation can be explained with the help of the accelerationist form of the Phillips Curve:

(5) $$P^*_t = -a + b \cdot 1/U_t + E\{P^*_t\}$$

where a and b are constants; P^*_t is the rate of inflation in year t; and U is the unemployment rate. The function thus far, $P = -a + b \cdot 1/U$, is the Phillips curve relationship between inflation and unemployment. The accelerationist Phillips curve adds on to it $E\{P^*_t\}$, the expected rate of inflation in year t.

The expected rate of inflation is a shift variable driving the Phillips curve to positive infinity at rates of unemployment less than the NAIRU rate *and negative infinity at higher unemployment rates.* The latter basic matter is rarely, if ever, mentioned by proponents of the accelerationist model even though the unemployment rate has frequently been greater than what is held to be the NAIRU.

Substituting numbers for the parameters a and b, and the expected rate of inflation should be of assistance in understanding the acceleration process. The magnitudes for a and b chosen, -4 and 24, imply a 6 percent non-accelerating rate of inflation. The inflation rate of the previous year is the usual proxy for the expected rate of inflation. Thus:

(6) $$P^*_t = -4 + 24 \cdot 1/U + P^*_{t-1}$$

Assume that the unemployment rate is and remains at 8 percent. Equation (6) then becomes:

(7) $$P^*_t = -4 + 3 + P^*_{t-1} = -1 + P^*_{t-1}$$

Thus, for the magnitudes of the parameters chosen, the 8 percent unemployment rate will cause the inflation rate to be lowered by 1 percent a year. If at the start the inflation was 4 percent, it would be 3 then next year, then 2, 1, 0, –1, –2, –3, –4, –5, approaching minus infinity, in the limit.

Assume alternatively that the unemployment rate is held at 4 percent. Again, start inflation at 4 percent per year. Equation (6) then becomes:

(8) $$P^*_t = 2 + P^*_{t-1}$$

According to equation (8), the rate of inflation will increase by 2 percentage points each year. If the inflation rate is initially 4 percent, in subsequent years it would increase to 6, 8, 10, 12 percent and so forth, approaching infinity in the limit.

Assume that the coefficient of the lagged inflation term to is 0.8. What will the long-run or equilibrium rate of inflation be? Equation (6) now becomes:

(9) $$P^*_t = -1.0 + 0.8 \, P^*_{t-1}$$

In long-run equilibrium the inflation rate of year t equals that of year $t-1$. Thus, in the long run: 0.2 P* equals –1 or P* equals –5 percent per year. After many many years of 8 percent unemployment, instead of the inflation rate rate approaching minus infinite percent per year, it approaches minus 5 percent per year—not exactly the same.

If the unemployment rate is kept at 4 percent, we have from equation (6):

(10) $$P^*_t = 2 + 0.8P^*_{t-1}$$

The long-term result is an inflation rate approaching 10 percent per year, again very much less than infinite percent per year. And if the coefficient of the lagged inflation term is 0.9, the long-run rate of inflation approaches 20 percent per year—again, far from infinite percent per year.

The coefficients of the lagged inflation variable in the regressions I ran tended to be close to 0.85. Nonetheless, there is some probability that the magnitude of the actual parameter is equal to or greater than 1—but there is the same probability that it is equal to or less than 0.7. Thus, my bias is to stick with the 0.85 result.

Table 15.3. **Consecutive Years with Less than 4 Percent Unemployment and the Rate of Inflation, 1950s and 1960s**

	(1)	(2)	(3)
Year	Unemployment	Inflation (GNP)	Acceleration
	(%)	(%/yr)	(Yes/No)
1951	3.3	5.02	
1952	3.0	1.59	No
1953	2.9	1.57	No
1966	3.8	3.55	
1967	3.8	2.57	No
1968	3.6	5.01	Yes
1969	3.5	5.57	Yes

Sources: Column (1) EROP 1991, Table B–39, p. 330. Column (2) EROP, 1991 Table B3, p. 290. My calculation of percentages.

Given: (1) $P^*_t = -4 + 24 \cdot 1/U + 0.85P^*_{t-1}$; (2) $U = 4$ percent, (3) and, $P^*_{t-1} = 3$ percent/year.

Find: P^* in P^*_t, P^*_{t+1}, P_{t+2} and in the long run.

$P^*_t = 2 + 0.85 \cdot 3 = 4.55$ percent/year; $P_{t+1} = 2 + 0.85 \cdot 4.55 = 5.7$;
$P_{t+2} = 2 + 0.85 \cdot 5.7 = 6.845$
In the long run the rate of inflation is in equilibrium, $P^*_t = P^*_{t-1}$. Then,

$P^* - 0.85P^* = -4 + 6$; or $0.15P^* = 2$; or $P^* = 13.33$ percent/year.

A rate of inflation of 13.3 percent per year is hardly desirable, but it is far more desirable and realistic than is one approaching infinite percent per year.

It is one thing to play games with models and parameters; it is another to look at the record to get some idea of the magnitude of acceleration. Changes in the inflation rate were either unusually low or unusually high for more than one year.

I like low unemployment and as can be seen in Table 15.3 there were three consecutive years with less than 4 percent unemployment in the 1950s and four in the 1960s. This gives us five cases to examine. In three the rate of inflation decreased in subsequent years; in two it accelerated. An important problem with the data is that the low unemployment years were wartime years—the Korean War in the early 1950s, the Vietnam War in the 1960s. Wartime conditions may have stifled wage and price increases, but these were periods in which the labor movement was stronger than it has been in more recent decades and that implies more power to obtain wage increases than is currently the case.

It is interesting that virtually the same economists who claim there is no such thing as involuntary unemployment also claim that low unemployment is undesirable because of its terrible inflationary implications. My point is not that low unemployment is not associated with inflation but that concern for the empirical facts should predominate over sophisticated models which badly exaggerate the prospects of inflation and deflation.

Externalities

Perhaps the most important failure of free market economics is its inability to deal with externalities. Being free of government constraint, means being free to pollute. Some externalities may prove to be trivial in social significance. Others may threaten the existence of many inhabitants of planet earth. Cut down a stand of old redwoods and the spotted owl is extinguished; allow carbon monoxide exhausts to create a greenhouse effect, and we are in danger of accelerating the melting of the polar ice-caps and flooding the low-lying areas of the world. Problems such as these involve externalities:

> *Externalities* are the effects of production and consumption on people and property not engaged in the subject production or consumption

External costs or benefits arise in production and consumption. The *transaction* is not the locus of the externality, it is the locus of the failure to set an efficient price—one which covers marginal cost plus the cost of negative externalities, minus the value of positive externalities.

The logical array of externalities involve (1) consumers affecting other consumers, (2) producers affecting other producers, (3) consumers affecting producers, and (4) producers affecting consumers. In all cases the externality can be positive or negative.

Examples of the array of externalities follow: (1) A positive externality occurs when more people attend a fifty-year reunion and a better time is had by all. A negative externality occurs when a consumer drives a car which pollutes the air breathed by other consumers. (2) The training of apprentices by builder A is a positive externality when the trained workers are hired by builder B. The dirty exhaust fumes of factory A are a negative externality to the white facade of B's office building downwind from A. (3) The bees in the garden of consumer X help propagate the crop of farmer Y—a positive externality. The exhaust fumes of cars on the highway destroys some of Y's crop—a negative externality. (4) The scrap wood of a producer is used by a consumer for shelving books—a positive externality. Factory effluents pollute the river precluding fishing and swimming in it—a negative externality.

The most important externalities are those of production and consumption negatively affecting consumers. It is exemplified by the air pollution coming from the production and use of cars. This pollution damages the ability to breathe and shortens the lifespan. Even more troublesome, from a long-term perspective, is the possibility that our air pollution is causing a greenhouse effect which warms the earth, melts polar ice caps, and some day floods coastal areas throughout the world.

Those who have spent time in downtown Mexico City or Santiago, Chile, know how cars, trucks, and buses can make the air unbreathable to some and unhealthy to all. Industrial runoffs have wreaked havoc on bodies of water. Some years ago Lake Erie was called a dead sea. The "beautiful blue Danube" became dirty brown with industrial wastes. The Mississippi, in the St. Louis area, at times looks like a floating junkyard. Ocean, lakes, and rivers are important to consumers, the ecology, future generations, and industries. The imperfect state of our ambience is a matter of concern to many.

Much of consumption involves negative externalities. Cars and recreational vehicles pollute our air and kill other consumers. Scrapped cars and their tires and batteries pollute the land. The toxic chemicals of batteries—ubiquitous in cars, toys, cameras, clocks, flashlights, and tools—have the same negative effect. Much of the packaging of consumer goods is not biodegradable and increasingly pollutes the land. Special negative reference is made of the material of the century, plastics of all sorts and kinds. They are essentially non-biodegradable, forever marring the planet. And we know production to be, in many ways, a more dangerous source of pollution. We have used nuclear power for more than half a century and have yet to find a satisfactory way to store its wastes.

Correcting Negative Externalities

There are a number of different ways to correct in whole or part the costs of externalities: (1) The costs can be internalized. (2) Those harmed by an externality can negotiate a resolution with its producer. (3) The government can impose regulations to curtail the externality, tax individual polluters, or create a bubble—a pollution reduction standard for a group of polluters in the same area.

Internalizing Costs

Internalizing the external costs of a good is an appealing way to respond to the problem of externalities. By internalizing the costs which escaped the process of exchange, the actual and higher social cost and price is attained. This altered higher price is the one appropriate to the efficient allocation of resources.

Internalizing external costs assumes that the magnitude of external costs can be quantified. This is generally reasonable for costs imposed on non-human resources. Calculations can be made regarding the clean-up costs of an oil spill or the cleaning of the facade of a building. But sometimes the correction is disputed. Over the years General Electric dumped toxic waste materials into New York State's Hudson River. The Environmental Pollution Commission has ordered them to dredge the area of the Hudson which contains these wastes. But General

Figure 15.2.   **The Effect of Internalizing the External Costs of Auto Production and Use**

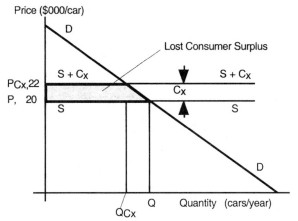

Electric claims that this will stir up the polluting materials, while the pollution will subside if they are just left alone. Although it is in General Electric's self-interest to do nothing, the issue they raise should nonetheless be confronted. Determining the cost assigned to a polluter can be a complex problem.

 The problem of determining the cost of an externality is deepened when human illness or death from pollution is the issue. What dollar value should be assigned to work time lost and pain and suffering experienced from a pollution-related illness? Even more problematic: What is the cost to be assigned for each year of life lost as a result of pollution? Should it be based on the loss of an individual's income or are there more general factors to consider? How can it be proved that an individual's death was caused by pollution? Is the value of a year of life lost for a person earning $100,000 ten times that for a person earning $10,000. What if the former is a loathsome loner and the latter the loving husband and father of a large family? Human factors complicate determining the dollar value and cost which should be internalized by the polluter.

 In addition, who bears the burden of the price increase arising from the internalization of external costs? The answer can be seen in Figure 15.2. The analysis is the same as that used to determine the burden of a tax increase. The internalized cost has to be put in the form of dollars per unit of production, C_X. In this case the figure is arbitrarily $2,000 per car. This is the magnitude of the upward shift in supply, a shift representing a decrease in supply. At the lower supply of $S + C_X$, fewer cars are sold. The lost consumer surplus is shown. As shown, the entire burden of internalization falls on the consumer. If the supply function were positive sloped or if producers decide to absorb some of the external cost, there would be some sharing of the burden.

 Actually, in the case of automobiles the response to pollution control has been

Figure 15.3.   **The Total Cost and Benefit of Pollution Control**

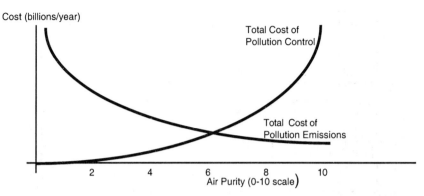

through regulation rather than the internalizing of external costs. The regulation has been the requirement that cars be equipped with pollution reduction devices—first pollution control valves and, more recently, catalytic converters. These increase the price of a car to the extent of their cost per car. There are also miles per gallon regulations which reduce the consumption of gasoline and pollution. This has led to smaller, lighter cars with more efficient engines which are not truly comparable with their more polluting forebears.

Minimizing Social Cost

The minimization of social cost approach tends to recognize that, from an economic perspective, it is not desirable to completely eliminate pollution. To require that effluents do *absolutely no damage to the environment* would make many products so expensive that few could afford them and the social benefit would be slight. This is illustrated in Figure 15.3 which shows that the cost of pollution control, TC_{pc}, skyrockets as totally pure air is approached. In addition, the damage done to people and property, the total cost of pollution effects, TC_{pe}, by slightly impure air is so low that little benefit is incurred in going from slightly impure to perfectly pure air. The goal economists propose is the minimization of social cost, SC, the sum of the total cost of pollution effects and total cost of pollution control.

The two cost functions have been added and the result appears in Figure 15.4. Note that the social cost is high when the air purity is very low, as sickness and death occur, as well as when it is very high, which requires very, very expensive complex pollution control devices.

The Marginal Condition. Consider the minimization of social cost, SC, from a mathematical perspective:

(11) $SC = TC_{pe} + TC_{pc}$

Figure 15.4.   **The Social Cost of Pollution**

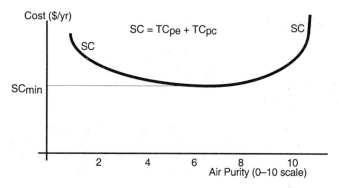

Social cost equals the total cost of the damage to people and property, *Tpe*, plus the total cost of pollution control devices, TC_{pc}. At social cost minimum the slope and derivative of the social cost function with respect to air purity, *AP*, equals zero.

(12) $dSC/dAP = MC_{pe} + MC_{pc} = 0$

At social cost minimization the marginal cost of the effects of pollution on people and property plus the marginal cost of the pollution control devices equals zero. The absolute magnitude of the slopes of the total cost function are equal at social cost minimization.

Maximizing Net Social Benefit

The negative of the total cost of pollution emissions is the total benefit of pollution emissions. Were the total cost of pollution emissions very high, the total benefit would be very negative. And if the pollution is very low, its total cost of pollution effects would be very low and total benefit of the same low magnitude but negative. If the total cost of pollution emissions is $1 million, the total benefit is minus $1 million. Do not expect the benefit of air pollution to be positive. Net social benefit, *NSB*, is the difference between the total benefit of pollution emissions, TB_{pc}, and the total cost of pollution control:

(13) $NSB = TBpe - TCpc$

The maximization of social benefit occurs at the level of air purity at which the slope and derivative equals zero. The maximization condition is accordingly the equality of marginal benefit of air purification devices and the marginal cost of the devices required to bring it about.

And that occurs at the same air purity level as does social cost minimization.

Private Negotiations and the Coase Theorem

The idea that private negotiations may be better than governmental actions in resolving externality problems is that of Ronald Coase as presented in his 1960 article, "The Problem of Social Cost." His thinking on this is summarized by what is frequently called Coase's Theorem:

> Once the costs of carrying out market transactions are taken into account ... a rearrangement of [property] rights would only be undertaken when the increase in the value of production consequent upon the rearrangement is greater than the costs which would be involved in bringing it about (1968, pp. 343–345).

Assume that straying cows destroy $100 worth of wheat and the dairy farmer is obligated to pay his wheat-growing neighbor $100. Nobel Laureate Coase argues that this seemingly efficient approach is in fact inefficient. He contends that the problem arises just as much from the growing of wheat as from the stray cows. Why curtail the production of milk, as a consequence of the increased cost of production, when a higher value of production might be obtained by curtailing the production of wheat?

For an example of the Coase theorem assume the following: (1) that the field accessible to the cows is expected to grow $100 worth of wheat a year, (2) that the incursion of the cows will make this wheat worthless, (3) that the expected profits from the sale of the wheat are $12, and (4) that the expected profits from the milk of the offending cows is $100. It would then be profitable for the wheat farmer to stop cultivating this field for any annual payment greater than $12. The dairy farmer would be better off as long as the annual payment to his neighbor was less than $100. Assuming that there are no other alternatives, any negotiated settlement must be in the range of $12 to $100. It would be socially advantageous in terms of the value of production and the amount of profits for the parties to reach a settlement within the above range as an alternative to the payment of $100 for the wheat destroyed by errant cows.

Coase recognizes that transaction costs may make it impossible for the parties to reach an agreement. The dairy farmer would not agree to a settlement if the settlement amount plus transaction costs exceeded $100; the wheat farmer would not accept an offer which left him with less than $12 after the subtraction of his transaction costs. The initial bargaining range is $88. If the sum of the transaction costs equals $88, there can only be one settlement amount, namely one which yields the wheat grower a net benefit of $12 at a cost of $100 to the dairy farmer, inclusive of transaction costs. If transaction costs exceed $88 no settlement is possible.

There are other obvious alternative courses of action, such as the dairy farmer erecting a fence, but they are overlooked here in order to maintain a focus on Coase's insight predicated on the rearrangement of property rights.

The limitations of private negotiations to solve externality problems should be recognized. The most common pollution is that of air and water. Air is a public good, and our waterways are almost all publicly owned. In addition, a single air or water polluter may negatively affect many—not just the farmer next door. The unbelievable diesel exhaust fumes of some of our local buses pollutes the air inhaled by many. And the polluting of a lake or river by a producer can destroy its use by commercial fishermen and thousands who otherwise fish and swim in it for fun. Finally, many are unable or unwilling to work out differences with others—as civil court case loads show. All of this means that unless the government takes action, little of the problem of externalities will be resolved.

Alternative Governmental Actions

The government uses several techniques to handle the problem of negative externalities: (1) It enacts regulations which specify performance standards and pollution control devices. (2) It sets effluent and related standards and levies fines on those who fail to meet them. (3) It sets effluent standards and subsidizes firms to help them meet the standards. (4) It sets effluent standards for an industrial area and for the individual plants in it. Plants which exceed the standards are allowed to sell their excess to others in the "bubble."

Pollution Control Devices. America's love affair with the car spanned the years from early in the twentieth century to today. But the car and its relatives, trucks and buses, have turned out to be not only an instrument of pleasure but of pain in the form of pollution. Substantial pollution arises from the production of motor vehicles—from the production of raw materials to that of the finished product. And their use and disposal are polluting. As the number of motor vehicles multiplied and air quality worsened, the car became and is an important target for those concerned with air pollution. That trucks and buses have been exempt from pollution standards is an unfortunate reflection of the power of their producers and users.

The pollution of the air by cars represents a bad and sometimes tragic market failure. Bad air sickens and kills. The task of addressing the problem has escaped the market mechanism and is, therefore, that of the government. How should the government handle or ameliorate that part of the pollution problem related to cars? It could set effluent standards for producers and a system of penalties, fines against producers who fail to meet the standards. Alternatively, it could specify one or more anti-pollution devices—devices which should limit the pollution to an unstated amount known to government regulators and others.

The choice of device should be in accord with cost-benefit analysis.

Government sometimes grants firms substantial subsidies to purchase the anti-pollution devices required to meet regulations—particularly if the firm's position is that the cost will cause a plant shutdown. These subsidies indicate the community demand for jobs. Some cities bar some or all vehicles from their central business district to reduce congestion and pollution. In an interesting case, the King of Norway was denied a permit to drive in downtown Oslo on the grounds that he indicated no compelling need to do so.

Effluent Standards. Effluent standards tend to be more desirable to economists than government determination of the pollution control devices which must be used. They allow companies, inventors, and entrepreneurs to display their genius in resolving an effluent problem. But sometimes, as in the automobile industry, manufacturers have been able to pressure politicians into delaying and relaxing the standards.

Performance standards are especially appropriate if they go no further than the leading edge of the state of the art, provided that the anticipated incremental costs are such that a commensurate incremental benefit is expected. Then requests for delay can be countered with: "Have you considered applying X device or Y system to meeting our standards?"

The other side of effluent standards consists of effluent fines or taxes. The more the firm exceeds the standard, the more tax it pays. Fines should equal the marginal cost of the effects of the pollution on people and property. Environmentalists tend to oppose such fines characterizing them as licenses to kill.

Bubbles. The Germans have a number of areas in which there is much heavy industry production and pollution. Their pioneering effort was to set effluent standards for each plant in the region and to recognize that meeting those standards would be relatively cheap for some plants and relatively expensive for others. As a result they placed plants in an area under a conceptual bubble. Producers in the bubble who reduced pollution more than was required were allowed to sell their excess to other producers in the bubble. This reduced the pollution to the extent required by the government and gave the plants the flexibility of working out the most efficient way to do it. Our limited exploitation of this approach seems successful in curtailing pollution.

The bubble approach implies that, at the required purity levels, for some firms the marginal cost of the pollution control exceeds the marginal benefit obtained, and for other firms the marginal cost of pollution control is less than the marginal benefit. It makes sense to economists that the latter creates greater purity than required and sells it to the former.

The Politics of Pollution. Politics are too often a factor in the determination of aspects of regulation. Auto manufacturers frequently sought the delay of mile-per-gallon standards through the good offices of appropriate members of Congress. Power plants which burn high-sulfur fuel were required to attach scrubbers to their smoke stacks to reduce noxious emissions. But this would have disadvantaged producers and users of high-sulfur coal so the regulation was unnecessarily extended to users of low-sulfur coal. Another example of political influence is that involving General Electric and its pollution of the Hudson River: As stated in a *New York Times* article,"Under pressure from the General Electric Company and a powerful upstate Congressman, the United States Environmental Protection Agency has decided to slow down completion of an important study of PCV contamination in the Hudson River" (1998). But even with the political dimension of the problem, it is hard to envisage progress being made to attain purer air and water without government intervention.

Misinformation and the Lack of Information

For buyers and sellers to rationally pursue their interests, information about the price and quality of products is required. But misinformation has often been supplied as exemplified by misleading interest rate claims on consumer loans and mileage decreases on the odometers of used cars.

Before Congress passed the Truth-in-Lending Act, financial institutions frequently claimed they were charging substantially lower interest rates on consumer installment loans than was true in fact. At a 12 percent annual interest rate, the equivalent of a 1 percent per month rate, a $1,200 loan would be repaid with 12 monthly payments of $106.62. The interest rate lending institutions liked to quote for the 12 percent loan was 6.62 percent. (In testifying before a congressional committee chaired by Senator Paul H. Douglas on what became The Truth in Lending Act, I dubbed the practice "half-truth in lending." To set the record straight, although not a fan of his production function, Douglas is a heroic figure to me. He was a distinguished economist, a World War II hero, and a top-flight member of the United States Senate.)

A fairly common practice of private sellers and used-car dealers was to set odometers back to indicate that the car had less than its actual use. The practice is now illegal, which has helped to reduce misinformation in this area. Area newspapers occasionally check the listed weight on meat and poultry packages and generally find errors beneficial to the supermarket. It is less than rare to find a lower octane of gasoline sold at a higher octane price. If you are charged for more gasoline than your tank holds, exhibit a bit of skepticism. And next time you consider buying a jar of cranberry juice— juice not "cocktail"—read the label. The odds are high that grape is the principal juice. The information failures mentioned are indicative of the value of the warning of the Middle Ages, caveat emptor—let the buyer beware.

Until relatively recent times many were unaware of the extent of the negative effects of cigarettes—effects which until 1997 were known to and stoutly denied by cigarette manufacturers. And there was no information on the cholesterol, fat, and sodium content of packaged foods until the government required information on "nutrition facts" and "ingredients" to be provided on most food containers. One could theorize that some private firms would provide such information about its products to obtain a competitive edge on their rivals or that some consumer research organization would publish and sell such information. Why did that not happen? The freedom not to provide important product information to buyers had to be abrogated by the coercive power of the federal government.

The Inability of Private Enterprise to Provide an Infrastructure

Had we a completely free (of government) economy our history would have been one of colossal failure since it would have been unable to provide an infrastructure for the economy—even of the crudest form. Without a coordinated infrastructure, our economy could not have proceeded beyond a relatively primitive state.

The Power of Eminent Domain

Why is it that government can provide the infrastructure while private markets and marketeers cannot? It is to a substantial extent because of the power of sovereign governmental agencies from the federal to the municipal level. Particularly important is the power of *eminent domain*—the power of the sovereign state to appropriate property for public use. In the United States this power has the responsibility to grant due process to affected property owners which allows them to receive a "fair price" for the property taken. Without this historic power it would be difficult to imagine the existence of our systems of streets, roads, and highways, as well as bridges, tunnels, canals, railroads, pipelines, and cables. The power of eminent domain has allowed us to build an advanced national economy. Without it, the economy would consist of a set of primitive local economies.

Ground Transportation

People and goods have been transported above, on, and under the ground and on water—on lakes, rivers, and canals—by horse-drawn vehicles, barges, cars, trucks, trains; pipelines, and ships. Ground and underground transportation require coherent land rights. By coherent I mean that the land controlled allows the transportation path to approach a straight line except for variations which respond to relevant characteristics of the terrain and other important uses of the land. Why would the market economy tend to fail at this? It is because of the great difficulty of amassing the required land at market-level prices. Speculators with inside information that a railroad was going to be built from A to B or a bridge from *C* to *D* would buy the parcels of land required and would be unwilling to sell that land except at a price commensurate with a king's ransom. And some people with required land might refuse to sell it at any price. The task is far, far easier for a sovereign government to accomplish using its power of eminent domain.

This is not to say that no unjust gains have been made in the course of using eminent domain. Democrat party boss William Marcy Tweed played a dubious role in the construction of the Brooklyn Bridge, a wonderful massive, useful sculpture, which links the New York City boroughs of Manhattan and Brooklyn. In more recent times some politicians knew in advance that a bridge was to be built linking Brooklyn and Staten Island. They bought up some of the land required for the bridge and were well rewarded when they were paid its "fair market value."

Airplane and Ship Transportation

Were air and waterways privately owned, the task of developing coherent routes would be the same as that of amassing the land required to build coherent roads and highways. In addition, airplanes need airports and ships need docks with both posing the problem of amassing the required land—a requirement far more efficiently handled by the government than by free market transactions.

Communications

The postal system was started during our colonial period. Intercity postal service required "post roads" with the first being the Boston Post Road between New York City and Boston. It served as the beginning of a communications-transportation system linking the economy and its citizenry. The postal system remains an important means of communications even with the competition of the telephone, private carriers such as the United Parcel Service, and e-mail. Local phone services, cellular phones aside, require hard wiring from a phone company station to the local resident or business. These lines are strung on poles above ground and in cables below ground. The cables are usually placed on public property and sometimes on privately owned property. In both cases government is involved. Cellular phones currently require a system of transmitters —usually placed on public property at negotiated prices.

Much modern long-distance communications involve the transmission of information through the use of electromagnetic waves of various frequencies. Users of the spectrum include radio and television stations; airplanes, airlines, and flight controllers; users of wireless and cellular telephones; long-distance telephone, e-mail/ethernet providers; cable TV companies; and public agencies such as police and fire departments, and the Defense and State Departments. The range of usable frequencies is limited and this curtails the number of channels of information which can be accommodated. In a metropolitan area you can easily count, for example, the number of AM radio stations on the dial. Were more authorized, the signals of one would interfere with those of another. At the outset, particularly the start of radio broadcasting, the demand for channels or stations was modest. Nowadays the demand for electromagnetic channels is far greater than the supply.

The existence of this scarce resource, the electromagnetic spectrum, raises two issues: Who own the spectrum? How should its use be allocated? Just as the public owns the air, it owns the electromagnetic spectrum with its control vested in government. By and large, as with other resources, its private use should be allocated by price—an approach that has just been started for new stations. But the major broadcasting systems are not measurably charged for the use of the scarce resource they exploit. The value of this congressional magnanimity has been estimated as more than $10 billion. Congress could hardly provide more welfare to a small number of networks, their well-heeled owners and executives.

Public Education

Were all education produced and sold by private institutions many Americans, particularly the poor, would not be able attend school. According to Horace Mann and others who led the free education movement, illiterates could not be the informed citizens required to make democracy work. Citizens without education would also be unsuited for much of the work of an advanced industrial economy. There could be no pretense of a "level playing field" were equal educational opportunities not available to all. Moreover, since business requires workers with adequate skills and the ability to learn new skills, they are not opposed to the existence of government-supported schools. If it is agreed that all who are capable of literacy should have the opportunity to be literate, the private market would fail to meet this goal.

It is generally agreed that the lower the level of education, the more justified is its provision by government. But subsidization of higher levels of education has been questioned by some economists. This is because our public universities tend to be populated by children of the middle class, but the poor help pay for these universities in taxes more than is justified by their enrollments. One might then, arguably judge tax-supported higher education as somewhat of a misallocation of resources.

Banking Chaos

The twenty-year charter of the first Bank of the United States expired in 1811. The War of 1812 followed, and with it, T. Harry Williams, Richard N. Current, and Frank Freidel report, arose chaos in banking:

> After the first Bank's charter expired, a large number of state banks sprung up. These issued vast quantities of banknotes ... and often did not keep a large enough reserve of gold or silver to redeem the notes on demand.... The variety of issues was so confusing as to make honest business difficult and counterfeiting easy (1967, p. 302).

Bank failures have been a major cause of economic crises and up to recent times. Bank failures were involved in the financial panic of 1907 which led to the creation of the Federal Reserve System in 1913. Bank failures greatly worsened the tragic dimensions of the Great Depression of the 1930s. After the Great Depression, the Federal Reserve System was given the power to serve the banks as "the lender of last resort," and forty years of banking system stability ensued.

Recently, from January 1982 to May 1990, 1,075 banks failed. A great majority of them were savings and loan associations and just over half of them were in the oil states of Texas, Oklahoma, and Louisiana. During this period 389 banks failed in Texas, 106 in Oklahoma, and 56 in Louisiana. Were federal government assistance unavailable, the people and economies of these states would have been badly hurt and the contagion may have spread throughout the whole country.

Why were the banks of the oil-producing states in such a perilous condition in the second half of the 1980s? Crude oil prices doubled from 1971 to 1973 and again from 1973 to 1974. This helped to create a boom and expansion in the enriched oil-producing states. But between the end of 1985 and mid-1986 oil prices fell by about one-half and the boom was badly depressed. This hurt important borrowers such as those developing residential housing and shopping malls. Bankrupt developers defaulted on their loans, and many lending institutions, bereft of the required liquidity, failed as well. In addition, interest rates soared to double digits in the late 1970s through the mid-1980s. Banks which paid depositors lower rates found them withdrawing funds, and with the need to retain these funds, to retain their liquidity, banks had to substantially increase the interest rates paid depositors. This was a deadly situation because they had to pay high interest rates to depositors while they were receiving relatively low rates from their portfolio of loans—loans mainly made during a period of relatively low interest rates.

The bail-out involved massive help from federal government deposit insurance funds augmented by about $200 billion from the general treasury. The history of bank failures is the history of market failure. Had the federal government, with our money, not helped the many troubled banks, the economy would have been badly upset.

There is a certain irony to the government coming to the rescue of banks, their shareholders, and depositors. One might judge it to represent the socialization of risk and the privatization of profit.

Public Goods

Public goods and services have two distinctive elements which make it impossible for them to be profitably produced:

> *Public goods and services* have two special characteristics: Consumption of the good is *not* mutually exclusive. And it not possible to exclude consumption of the good or service.

Consider the example of national defense as a public good. First of all, my consumption of national defense services does not preclude your consumption of it. Consumption is not mutually exclusive. Secondly, it is not possible to exclude the consumption of the service. If the armed services protect you from an enemy they must protect me as well. If I cannot be excluded from receiving the benefit why should I pay for it? More broadly, why should anyone pay for defense services when no one can be excluded from consuming it? The result is that national defense cannot be profitably provided by a private profit-making firm. It is a public good which must be provided by government if it is to be provided at all. The sovereign government has the power to make each of us pay for national defense—whether we like it or not. The market would fail badly in such a venture.

This is not to say that all or even most government-provided services are public goods. Education, for example, is not a public good. Nor is welfare to the poor, farmers,and others. These can be meritorious services which only the government can adequately provide.

The total demand for a *private good* is the horizontal sum of the individual demand functions. If you and I, at $1 per hot dog, demand one a week, the horizontal sum is two per week at that price. But the total demand for a *public* good is the *vertical sum of the individual demand functions.* That is shown in Figure 15.5. The result is that at a price of $0.32 billion per unit, the quantity of defense/war services demanded is 100.

The Anti-Government Position: The Libertarian View

The above discussion portrays the government as the institution which provides the infrastructure of the economy and saves us, or attempts to save us, from market failure and potential market failure. The Libertarians, economic anarchists in an earlier age, are opposed to any government involvement in the economic system. The are the true believers in laissez-faire capitalism—in the ability to make economic decisions free of government restraint or involvement. They believe that everything should be privately owned—including all volumes of air, land, ocean, sea and so forth. All schools, libraries, parks, and playgrounds should be privately owned and run with no government involvement whatever. There would be no FED. The medium of exchange would be gold.

Figure 15.5.   **Demand for a Public Good: The Vertical Addition of Individual Demand Functions**

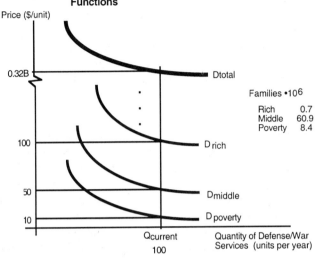

Price ($/unit)

0.32B — Dtotal

Families •10⁶

Rich	0.7
Middle	60.9
Poverty	8.4

100 — D rich

50 — Dmiddle

10 — D poverty

Qcurrent
100

Quantity of Defense/War
Services (units per year)

There would be no inflation unless a major gold strike took place. Pollution would be taken care of by the private owners of land, air, and water. If you pollute the air I own, either you pay me an agreed-to sum or I will sue you. There would have to be a system of courts protecting property rights.

I have made much of the government's essential role in creating the economic infrastructure. But with that infrastructure in place, according to the Libertarian view, all that need be done is to sell it to private parties.

Milton Friedman, who is not a Libertarian, is also very concerned with personal freedom. He feels that we should all be free to practice medicine or surgery or anything else our heart desires. And we should be allowed to do these things whether or not we have any schooling in or knowledge of the field. So if you have trouble finding a job as a biology teacher, hang up a shingle stating that you are a surgeon. To protect those of us who need the services of a physician or surgeon, all that need be done is to look up your rating in a publication such as *Consumer Reports.* I suspect that this position is also that of Libertarians.

Note that in a sense Friedman's proposal represents a return to the past. Barbers were the surgeons of the past, and their knowledge of the field was often less than perfect. It should also be noted that Friedman is a proponent of governmental activities at the most local level possible. But that is a level at which we historically have the most regulation. Local governmental agencies license barbers and beauticians, plumbers and electricians—as well as physicians and surgeons. And they have wonderfully detailed building codes and zoning regulations, regulations which sometimes disallow the dumping of garbage in the community that creates it. "Not in my backyard" is a very old local point of view. Were that the position of all locales, a garbage fairy would be require to bring it to a netherland.

Libertarians, by the way, do not take kindly to the concept of externalities which did not infringe on property rights. My late friend, colleague and distinguished Libertarian, Murray N. Rothbard, said, for example, that it would require males to pay attractive young females for their dress in miniskirts.

Finally, historically, the United States has moved from being a near libertarian economy to one with a significant government presence. Why is that?

Discrimination

Discrimination is a market failure to the extent that it causes one group to be treated differently than another with respect to education, pay, employment, promotional possibilities, access to public and private facilities, and housing. Discrimination is an integral part of the history of all nations in dealing with heterogeneity—people who are different from those who dominate because of their gender, religion, nationality, skin color, language, or political creed.

Shortly after the Preamble to our Constitution states that our mission is "building a more perfect union" and providing for "the general welfare" the following words can be found:

> Representatives ... shall be apportioned among the several States ... according to their respective Numbers, which shall be determined by adding to the whole Number of free Persons ... three-fifths of all other Persons (Article 1, Section 2).

The "other Persons" were largely Black, brought to the land of the free and the home of the brave as slaves.

Mill and Veblen on Discrimination Against Women

In 1848, John Stuart Mill posed the problem of discrimination against women this way: "It deserves consideration, why the wages of women are generally lower, and very much lower, than that of men" (1961, p. 400). His analysis follows:

> When the efficiency is equal and the pay unequal, the only explanation that can be given is custom; grounded either in prejudice or the present constitution of society, which, making almost every woman, socially speaking, the appendage of some male (p. 400).

Just short of a half-century later Thorstein Veblen presented a broader and deeper analysis. In *The Theory of the Leisure Class* (1899), Veblen contends that discrimination against women played a powerful role in economic history: The work assigned to tribal women was the precursor to the work assigned to the industrial occupations. In all barbarian communities, the work of men was interesting, challenging, and of high status. The work of women was boring, repetitive, and unworthy of commendation. The practice of seizing women from the enemy as trophies gave rise to a form of ownership-marriage. Finally, Veblen claims that the ownership of women led to the ownership of private property, a fundamental requirement of capitalism. Veblen's sweep of analysis is at times breathtaking.

More Contemporary Models

Two more contemporary models of discrimination are presented. In the first those discriminated against are segregated from the dominant class which performs the discrimination. The two groups trade with each other as if they were separate nation states. In the second model the two groups are integrated but those discriminated against are perceived to be either less productive or more costly than they actually are. In both models discrimination in pay and employment is resolved or ameliorated by the quest of capitalists for maximum profits.

Segregation and Intergroup Trade

The assumptions are: (1) The segregated group has a substantially lower capital to labor ratio than the dominant group. (2) Dominant-group capitalists are profit maximizers, and this makes them anxious to sell capital to the segregated group up to the point at which they maximize profits. (3) Some of the capital sold is that used by dominant-group workers. (4) The price charged for the capital is its marginal product in the discriminated-against society.

The results of dominant-group capitalists selling capital to the segregated group are the following: (1) Dominant-group capitalists increase their profits. (2) Segregated-group capitalists increase their profits. (3) At equilibrium in the trading of capital, the marginal productivities of labor and capital are equal in both social groups. (4) As a result, segregated labor increases its pay to equal that of the dominant-group workers. (5) But the pay of dominant-group workers decreases since they have less capital at their disposal.

Thus, free trade should end discrimination in pay per hour and profit per unit of capital. This desired outcome has not occurred because of the opposition of dominant-group workers whose earnings would drop.

The model has two elements of basic unreality. The first is that some of the capital sold by dominant-group capitalists consists of capital instruments currently used by dominant-group labor. In reality, what would be sold are newly produced capital goods which labor would be glad to help produce since it yields them more work and greater earnings. Second, labor, almost without exception, favors increased exports since, as just stated, it increases their employment and earnings. It is imports which labor opposes with some regularity. This is because of the fear that low-paid foreign labor will, in effect, take their jobs from them.

Although labor and capital both favor exports such intergroup trade appears to have had no measurable influence on the problems of segregation and discrimination. As a result, the value of the free trade model is subject to question.

Employment and Pay Discrimination

Employer perceptions are that those discriminated against are less productive than they are in reality or that they cost more than they do in reality.

Employers tend to practice the discrimination norms of the society. But by refusing to employ those perceived to be less productive or more costly they limit the available supply and drive up the pay they must award their dominant-group employees. Thus, discrimination has a cost. But the cost can be avoided by profit maximizers employing those discriminated against.

The supply available to employers who do not discriminate is augmented by those who have been discriminated against. This drives down the wage that non-discriminating employers have to pay their employees. Firms with these lower labor costs tend to have lower prices, and they should tend to drive the discriminators out of business or out of their discriminatory practices.

Despite the free market model theoretically destroying discrimination, in reality much discrimination remained, resulting in governmental policies intended to bring it to an end.

An Alternative View on Discrimination

The basis of the neoclassical discrimination models is that it costs employers to discriminate. But if discrimination is costless, as I believe it is, the basis of the models is destroyed.

The supply of labor is an abstraction of limited interest to an employer. The supplies of interest are those which cover the skills required or demanded by the employer—the demand for a certain number of computer scientists, programmers, accountants, clerks, skilled machinists, electricians, skilled and unskilled assemblers, porters, washroom attendants, dishwashers, for people adept at marketing, and so forth. Categorize these jobs into two groups: superior and inferior. For inferior jobs the pay is relatively low; there are no promotional ladders; and they involve the kinds of work that dominant class workers avoid. If there are enough dominant-group workers available to fill the superior jobs, there is no cost associated with assigning discriminated-against workers to the inferior ones. And this is the norm throughout the world.

High-wage monopolistic firms which employ few Blacks were frequently glad to have them as porters, janitors, toilet attendants, foundry workers, and the like. With dominant-group workers elsewhere employed, the supply of labor available to firms in low-wage sweatshop industries tends to be limited to the supply of those discriminated against by others—frequently members of new immigrant groups.

But employing people essentially branded as inferiors in inferior jobs is a world-wide phenomenon. The Germans employ "guest workers" to perform inferior work; the Israelis employ Palestinians; the Indians assign it to the Untouchables. We have Mexicans picking crops and living in abysmal circumstances, work and living conditions which dominant-group workers avoid. There is no monetary cost to such practices and, therefore, no economic force against discrimination.

Monopolization

Business is the dominant institution in the economy and society, and in that group big business is most powerful—particularly in the sphere of politics. They, in effect, make a mockery of the ideal of one person, one vote. They have power on all governmental levels, particularly on the local level. Every time a firm of substance threatens to leave a locale, they are granted tax abatements. The mayor of New York City, who has trouble finding funds to improve the physical condition of ghetto schools, is quick to suggest a half-billion dollar program to keep the Yankee baseball team within the city limits. And substantial benefits have been recently granted to the New York Stock Exchange in response to their assertion that they might otherwise move their operations to New Jersey. Like it or not, big business distorts the operation of the body politic and, in when tax favors are received, the allocation of resources.

We tend to accept, without question, favored tax treatment to firms that may otherwise leave a locale. They do us a favor by their provision of jobs. Yale professor Charles Lindblom suggests the matter should be considered just the other way. We give business special rights, including those of limited liability and the freedoms granted individuals under the Constitution. For this they have the responsibility of providing the society with jobs. Were this the prevailing ethos, the role of big business in our society might be quite different.

By the way, the subsidization of bank X or brokerage firm Y discriminates against all other banks and brokerage houses in the community. It also poses an incentive for others to develop plans to leave a community so that they may obtain similar tax abatements, thereby enlarging the extent of discrimination.

What about the economic conduct of big and somewhat smaller business? The bigger business is, the less is the opportunity for outside entrepreneurs to enter the industry. Bill Gates's Microsoft has taken any number of steps to expand its operating system control and to advance and control other computer-related areas. The 1999 anti-trust case against Microsoft has exposed a host of activities intended to stifle competitors from obtaining or maintaining a toehold in the industry. The defense is that this is the way all major firms in the industry act. This may be largely true—but it nevertheless involves acts of monopolization which have harmed other entrepreneurs and firms.

Are buyers charged higher prices by those with significant monopoly power than otherwise would be the case? The cold cereal and pharmaceutical industries frequently charge substantially more than would be the case were the industries more competitive. Private brand cereals and generic drugs tend to be far cheaper than brand-named rivals. Some drugs made in the United States are sold in Canada at a fraction of the price we pay here in the United States. Unregulated cable television monopolists seem to be testing how high they can price without political intervention. Monopolization is costly to consumers in a number of product areas.

What is the argument more sympathetic to the existence of monopolies. It is the argument of those who believe in laissez-faire, of the non-involvement of government in the economy and has three main strands. First of all there is the Darwinian view that large firms must have attained their position through their excellence. The second aspect is that technological progress in the hands of potential competitors will do in the monopolizer. After the better part of a century, microwave transmission did end the long-distance monopoly of AT&T, and the development of the personal computer cut IBM and its mainframe-based power down to size. The final element in the laissez-faire argument is that this economy has provided the highest standing of living in the world with the monopolization some decry. It must, therefore, be a good thing.

The late 1990s have seen a large number of mergers and acquisitions of large firms making the same or similar products. The telephone industry broken up by the courts seems to be reconstituting itself. Microsoft appears intent on monopolizing an increasing number of important areas of the computer and related industries. The number of military aircraft and armament producers has been greatly decreased by a significant number of mergers. International mergers of auto manufacturers have decreased the number of firms making this product. Major banks and brokerage houses have joined forces and become more dominant in their industries. All of this appears to be attenuating the not overly strong competition which existed prior to the buildup of bigger firms in some of our major industries. My biased opinion is that this trend is undesirable both to the economy and the body politic.

Government Regulation and Deregulation

The transportation industries, more than others, illustrate *the* problem of regulation: the capturing of the regulatory agency by the industry being regulated and the use of regulation to protect the industry from competition. The classic case is that of the railroads. In 1887 the Interstate Commerce Commission was established, largely to protect farmers shipping their produce to markets from the local railroad monopoly. But, as was immediately seen, regulators of the railroads had to know something about railroading. Thus, members of the commission and their aides frequently had ties to and sympathy for the problems of the railroad industry. Controllers of the industry became protectors of the industry. In that role, they sought to protect the industry from the trucking industry which was duly regulated. The airlines became the next competitive threat, and they were also placed under regulation.

With deregulation, interstate trucking, the railroads, and airlines have lost their areas of protection. Deregulation of the airline industry is particularly interesting.

Deregulation of the airline industry is a product of the Carter Administration. President Carter appointed Cornell Professor Alfred Kahn to perform the task. How successful has it been? On an overall basis airline transportation has become relatively cheaper and the quality of the service has declined. The price drops have been largely in long-distance travel where there are a number of competing airlines. Little positive effect has been experienced on short-distance flights since they generally are serviced by a single airline.

Another consequence of deregulation is the replacement of the government-approved single price by a multiplicity of prices for the same service. My wife and I recently traveled to South America to visit one of our sons. The *New York Times* lists the standard and cheapest fare for that and other flights. They were roughly in a two to one ratio. The fare we obtained from a "consolidator" was roughly half of the "cheapest fare." (The law of many prices also exists in telephone communication. Substantial differences in price can be obtained from the same long-distance carrier. And the same is true in the area of cell phones.) Discriminatory pricing seems to be a common manifestation of deregulation.

Congress may soon consider a "Passengers' Bill of Rights" under which passengers would be informed of the various prices for a given flight. I suspect that this would quickly end price discrimination allowing all of us to pay the maximum price.

Summary

To many the most painful and depressing market failure is unemployment. Another failure involves people doing much the same work as others but with diminished compensation and security. This is a growth area as full-time workers are replaced by adjuncts, contract workers, and those on workfare. These are obviously discriminatory forms of employment. To a modest extent this can be related to the change in the distribution of income under which in recent decades the poor have become relatively poorer and the rich have become relatively richer. My charge of market failure is based on the belief that the relative advance of the rich, particularly top executives, is not based on their relative increase in productivity but on their power to obtain larger rental earnings. Moreover, the boom in the financial packages of chief executives has come about during a period of diminished productivity growth. What is there that justifies this situation?

In addition to surplus workers there is surplus capital. Surplus capacity represents a major failure of domestic and world markets to equilibrate and represents a horrendous waste of resources.

Inflation is another important market failure. It is particularly detrimental to those whose incomes fail to keep up with inflation, lenders who did not anticipate prices rising as much as they did, and workers thrown into unemployment in order to break the price-wage inflation cycle. Hidden in the above are many retirees whose private pensions are badly diminished in value over the years, even by modest annual rates of inflation.

Low levels of unemployment have moved from being a responsibility of the economy to being a threat to the economy under the dubious accelerationist model of the Phillips curve. The big scare is that at rates of unemployment lower than the non-accelerating rate of unemployment, the inflation rate will start a march toward infinity. Accelerationists do not talk much about unemployment rates above the "natural rate," which are the norm and should, with the same reasoning, drive the inflation rate down toward *minus* infinity. Neither side of the model seems well correlated with the facts and the fear of too much employment, of equilibrium in the labor market, is largely invalid.

The more we produce the more we tend to pollute. This is the other side of the most successful economy coin. From a long-run perspective, this is probably the most detrimental of market failures. There are a number of ways economists pose to reduce the amount of pollution. One is to internalize external costs, a clear measure of market failure. Coase suggests another, that individual bargaining can resolve the problem if transaction costs are not too high. But they almost always are very high. Many millions are affected by pollution of the air, water, and land. And with the mobility of air and many sources of water, pollution has detrimental effects on people far removed from its source.

The analysis we now tend to forward is to control effluents to the extent that the marginal cost of the pollution control devices equals either the (negative of the) marginal costs of the effects of pollution on people and property or the marginal benefit to people and property from the use of the marginal pollution control devices. Pollution is arguably the greatest threat to humankind. It is the bitter fruit of production in market, mixed, and command economies.

Markets fail when misinformation or inadequate information is provided to the parties of a transaction. Until recently it was common to misquote the interest rate on consumer loans, and it was not surprising to find that used-car sellers sometimes set back the mileage on odometers. An important lack of information has been in the area of the nutritional content of products. Progress on all these informational fronts has come as a result of government regulation.

Government has played a crucial role in the development of the infrastructure, the building blocks essential to the growth of the economy. That infrastructure could not have been created by free market activities. And the provision of public goods and services is beyond the capability of private enterprise.

Those most opposed to the intervention of government in the market are the

Libertarians. How a libertarian economy would work can be understood by looking backward. The economy of the nineteenth century was largely a free market economy with a government-provided or -subsidized infrastructure. The problems experienced led to the mixed economy of the twentieth century.

Discrimination is an important historical market failure. Neoclassical models claim that discrimination is costly to employers and that the lure of profits should bring it to an end. But it did not. With the market failure of discrimination, government actions have more or less filled the vacuum.

Business is our dominant institution. Its power to set price is the power to set it outrageously high, and on occasion that is just what monopolistic firms and industries have done. Moreover, powerful monopolistic firms sometimes deny entrepreneurs the opportunity of entering their markets. Finally, we have never come to grips with the distortions of the democratic ideal arising from the political activities of our dominant institution.

Questions on Chapter 15

1. How would you define a market failure in a static sense? In a dynamic sense?

2. Is unemployment a market failure if it is being used to lower inflation?

3. Why is it a market failure if the world capacity to produces cars is greater than the world demand for cars?

4. Assume the hypothesis that the poor are hurt more by inflation than are others. What data would you look at to determine if the facts supported the hypothesis?

5. Assume that the supply of labor is positive-sloped and that the demand for labor is negative-sloped, and that the market is in equilibrium. Then the demand for labor increases.
   a. What should happen to the wage?
   b. What should happen to the wage according to the Phillips curve?
   c. What should happen were the accelerationist Phillips curve in accord with reality? (Note: Over time, the three models yield very different results.)

6. Draw a graph of the total cost of the effects of pollution, TC_ϱ, as a function of air purity.
   a. Explain why it is negative sloping.
   b. Explain why the negative of the total cost of the effects of pollution is the total benefit of air purity.

7. Draw a positive-sloped marginal cost of pollution control function and a negative-sloped marginal benefits of air purity function.
   a. Explain why the slope of the marginal cost function is positive.
   b. Explain why the slope of the marginal benefit function is negative.

8. Monopolization is frowned upon in the neoclassical paradigm because it yields higher prices and lower quantities than the competitive market.
   How does this fit with an after-tax profit of 5 cents per dollar of sales in manufacturing?

9. Is the political power of business a problem? Discuss

Basics of Differential Calculus

Why do economists use mathematics and particularly differential calculus? Mathematics offers a very compact way of presenting information and determining the relationships between economic variables thought to be related.
 Consider, for example, the *demand* for **a** firm's product:

(1) $P = f(Q) = 8 - 2Q$

Much useful information can be derived from that function by mathematical manipulation. We can determine the **total revenue** attained at each price and related quantity on the demand function,

(2) $TR = PQ = f(Q){\cdot}Q = (8 - 2Q){\cdot}Q = 8Q - 2Q^2$

It will be shown shortly that the *marginal revenue function,* the slope of the total revenue function, is: $MR = 8 - 4Q$. All of this appears in Figure A1.1.

The slope of a function, here the total revenue function, *is its first derivative.* Thus, we all now know what the first derivative of a function is. All we need learn are the formulas of the first derivative or derivative of a particular kind of function. There are tables which give the first derivatives of a whole host of functions—but people exposed to calculus usually remember the formulas for very common functions. And one of them we might already know. If, for example, the firm sets the price of its product at a price of $4, we have the supply function $P = 4$. It is a horizontal line, its slope is zero, and its derivative is zero.

The Derivation of the Derivative of a Function

The derivation of the derivative of two functions is shown. The first is a linear-function, $y = 6x$. The second has a constant exponent, $y = 6x^2$.

Figure A1.1   **Demand, Total Revenue, and Marginal Revenue**

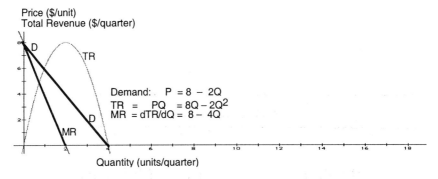

Price ($/unit)
Total Revenue ($/quarter)

Demand: P = 8 − 2Q
TR =   PQ = 8Q − 2Q^2
MR = dTR/dQ = 8 − 4Q

Quantity (units/quarter)

Derivation of the Derivative of a Linear Function

Assume that we have a smooth, continuous function: $y = f(x)$., here $y = 6x$. There are four steps involved in deriving its derivative, dy/dx:

<u>Step 1</u>: Convert all xs in the original function to $x+\Delta x$ and solve for $y+\Delta y$.

$$y + \Delta y = 6 (x + \Delta x) = 6x + 6\Delta x$$

<u>Step 2</u>: Solve for Δy by subtracting the initial function from that obtained in step 1.

$$y + \Delta y = 6x + 6\Delta x$$
$$\underline{-(y \qquad = 6x \quad)}$$
$$\Delta y = \qquad 6\Delta x$$

<u>Step 3</u>: Find $\Delta y/\Delta x$ by dividing the Δy obtained in step 2 by Δx.

$$\Delta y/\Delta x = 6 \quad \text{which is the slope of the function } y = 6x$$

<u>Step 4</u>: Obtain dy/dx by taking the solution of step 3 and allowing Δx approach zero in the limit. $dy/dx = 6$

Now try an example.

<u>Given</u>: $y = 50x$;   <u>Find</u>: dy/dx.
Step 1. $y + \Delta y = 50 (x + \Delta x) = 50x + 50\,\Delta x$
Step 2. $y + \Delta y = 50x + 50\,\Delta x$
$\underline{\quad -(y \qquad = 50x \quad)}$
$\Delta y = 50\,\Delta x$
Step 3. $\Delta y/\Delta x = 50$
Step 4. $dy/dx = 50$ which is the slope of the function $y = 50x$.

In general for a linear function:

If $y = mx + b$, then $dy/dx = m$, where m is the slope of the line.

Differentiation of a Function with a Constant Exponent

Given: $y = -6x^2$ where 2 is the constant exponent.
Find: dy/dx
Step 1. $y + \Delta y = -6(x + \Delta x)^2$
$= -6[x^2 + 2x\,\Delta x + (\Delta x)^2]$
$= -6x^2 - 12x\,\Delta x - 6\Delta x)^2$
Step 2. $y + \Delta y = -6x^2 - 12x\Delta x - 6(\Delta x)^2$
$-(y \qquad = -6x^2)$

$$\begin{aligned} \Delta y &= -12x\,\Delta x - 6(\Delta x)^2 \\ \text{Step 3.} \quad \Delta y/\Delta x &= -12x - 6\Delta x \end{aligned}$$

Step 4. As Δx approaches zero,
$dy/dx = -12x$

In general for a function with a constant exponent, $y = kx^n$, where k and n are constants; $dy/dx = nkx^{n-1}$.
Try putting together the two cases derived—the derivative of a linear function and one with a constant exponent.

Given: $TR = 8Q - 2Q^2$ Find: MR, the slope of TR
Note that the first term on the right side of the equation is linear and the second term a function with a constant exponent.

Then, $MR = dTR/dQ = 8 - 4Q$

Differentiation of the Product of Two Functions

In general if $y = f(u,v)$, $d(uv)/dx = u\,dv/dx + v\,du/dx$, where u and v are functions of x.

In other words, the derivative of the product of two variables equals the first variable held constant times the derivative of the second plus the second held constant times the derivative of the first. An example of this involves deriving marginal revenue from the total revenue function,

Given: Total revenue as $TR = PQ$, the product of two variables with both functions of Q. (P is a function of Q in the demand function. And Q is a function of Q in he equation $Q = Q$.)
Find: Marginal revenue, $MR = dTR/dQ$

$$MR = dTR/dQ = d(PQ)/dQ$$

$$MR = P\,dQ/dQ + Q\,dP/dQ = P + [Q\,dP/dQ]$$

Now apply this finding to the case above in which the demand is: $P = 8 - 2Q$

(3) $MR = d(PQ)/dQ = P + Q\, dP/dQ$

(4) $= 8 - 2Q + Q\ [-2] = 8 - 4Q$

The marginal revenue function has the same price intercept as the linear demand function and comes down at double the slope. Allow another example.

Given: The definitions: (1) $AC=TC/Q$; (2) $MC = dTC/dQ$.
Prove: Average cost at its minimum equals marginal cost: $AC_{min}=dTC/dQ$
    (It should help if you recall the geometry implicit in the problem: AC is
    the slope of a vector from the origin to the total cost curve.)

What we have to do is to get the slope (derivative) of the average cost function and set it equal to zero.

$$dAC/dQ = d\,(TC/Q)/dQ$$

I'll move Q from the denominator to the numerator because I know how to get the derivative of the product of two variables.

$$= d\,(TC{\cdot}Q^{-1})/dQ$$

$$= TC\,(-1)Q^{-2} + Q^{-1}\,dTC/dQ$$

At its minimum the slope of a U shaped average cost function is zero. Thus,

$$0 = -TC/Q^2 + dTC/dQ)/Q$$

Multiply both sides by Q and solve for TC/Q:

$$TC/Q = dTC/dQ \quad \text{or} \quad AC = MC \text{ at } AC_{min}.$$

The Derivative of the Natural Logarithm

In general: If $y = \ln x$, the derivative of $dy/dx = 1/x$. The differential of the function is $dy = d\ln x = dx/x$. The differential of the logarithm of x equals the percentage change in x at a particular point on the function $y = \ln x$.

Consider the price elasticity of demand,

(5) $E = dQ/Q \div dP/P$

The numerator equals $d\ln Q$ and the denominator $d\ln P$ so that,

(6) $E = d\ln Q / d\ln P$

Going one step further, we could model demand as linear in the logarithms of the variables Q and P:

(7) $\ln Q = a + b \ln P$

The derivative of the logarithm of Q with respect to the logarithm of P, $d\ln Q/d\ln P$, is the elasticity of demand and equal to b. An estimate of b is also an estimate of the price elasticity of demand.

Determining Whether an Extremum is a Maximum or a Minimum

I said that where the slope of the average cost function was zero, average cost was at its minimum—but it could have been a maximum. Let us see then how we can tell a maximum from a minimum mathematically and do it for the case of profits. (We would not want to tell the Big Boss he should do X to maximize profits if it's actually the way to minimize them.) The geometry of what is being done mathematically is shown in Figures A1.2, A1.3, A1.4, and A1.5

In A1.2 can be found a total revenue and a total cost function. Profit equals the (vertical) difference between total revenue and total cost, TR and TC.

The profit curve is shown in Figure A.1.3. Note that the slope of the function equals zero at two different quantities. Thus we see that when we say maximum profit occurs when the slope of the profit function is zero. that criterion holds for maximum loss, as well.

Then the derivative of the profit function appears in Figure A1.4. Note that the derivative of profit is the derivative of the difference between total revenue and total cost, $dTR/dQ - dTC/dQ$. These slopes are marginal revenue and marginal cost. Thus, $d\pi/dQ = MR - MC$. The equality of marginal revenue and marginal cost is seen to take place at two rates of output–the first corresponding to maximum loss, the second to maximum profit.

Look at Figure A1.4. What is the difference geometrically between the output rate at which loss is maximized and that at which profit is maximized? At the former output the slope of $d\pi/dQ$ is positive, at the latter negative.

In Figure A1.5 can be found the slope of the $d\pi/dQ$ function: $d^2\pi/dQ^2$, the second derivative of profit with respect to quantity. As expeced, at loss maximization it is positive; at profit maximization it is negative. Moreover, with the slope of the profit curve equal to the difference between marginal revenue and marginal cost, the second derivative is the difference between the slope of the marginal revenue and the marginal cost curve: $dMR/dQ - dMC/dQ$.

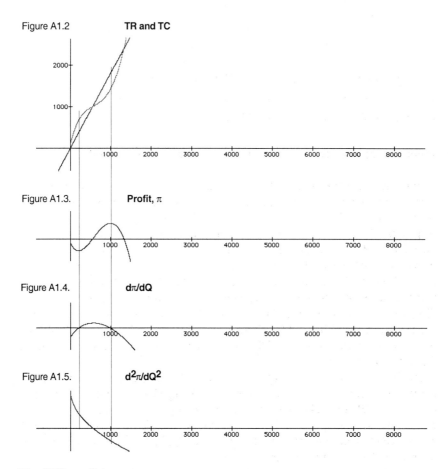

Figure A1.2   **TR and TC**

Figure A1.3.   **Profit, π**

Figure A1.4.   **dπ/dQ**

Figure A1.5.   **d²π/dQ²**

The Differential

The differential, *dy*, of a function, *y* = *f(x)*, is its derivative multiplied by the differential of the independent variable:

(8)   dy = (dy/dx) • dx

As indicated in the text, we frequently talk about marginal matters when in fact we are describing the differential. One could, for example, incorrectly speak of marginal profit, *dπ/dQ*, as an increase in profit when the actual increase is the differential profit: *dπ* = *dπ/dQ* • *dQ*.

Some Words on Integration

Differentiation was viewed as the process of determining the slope of a function. Integration can be viewed as the process of determining the area under a function and reversing the process of integration.

Take the case of the linear total variable cost function

(9) $TVC = 6Q$

The derivative or slope of the function, marginal cost is:

(10) $dTVC/dQ = MC = 6$

Now I want to take the integral of $dTVC/dQ$. That is written this way:

(11) $\int (dTVC/dQ)\, dQ = \int 6\, dQ = 6Q$

were the symbol, $\int$, is the integral sign. Integration turned marginal cost, the derivative of total variable cost back to total variable cost.

In Figure A1.5, marginal cost is constant and equal to 6 and the integral of the function is the area under the function, namely, $6Q$. If the function is marginal cost, the area under the function is total variable cost. Since marginal cost is the derivative of the total variable cost function, integration reverses the process of differentiation. And if $Q=4$, total variable cost is 24.

Note the large number of small rectangles which comprise the area under the curve. Each of them is the product $MC \cdot dQ$ or $(dTVC/dQ) \cdot dQ$. Cancel out the differentials of quantity and you see that each skinny rectangle is a differential of total variable cost. What integration does is to add up, to sum, all of these differentials.

The Constant of Integration

Assume that the total cost function which goes with the above total variable cost function is:

(12) $TC = 10 + 6Q$

Both total function have the same slope, derivative, and marginal cost—all one and the same, $MC = 6$. Thus, there is the same curve and area under it. But that area with Q equal to 4 is 24 but total cost is actually 34. The problem is resolved be adding to the area specified, the value of the integral at $Q=0$—*the constant of integration.* It just happened to be zero in the case of total variable cost so no addition was required. But total cost has a value of 10 at the start.

Figure A1.6.   **Total Variable Cost as the Area Under the Marginal Cost Curve**

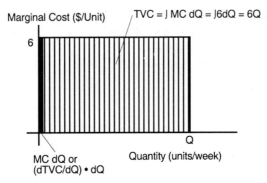

Add that *boundary condition* to *6Q,* the area under the marginal cost function, and the integration of marginal cost to yield total cost is accomplished.

Descriptive Statistics and Regression Analysis Basics

Regression analysis is the most common statistical technique used by economists to estimate the empirical relationship between a dependent and one or more independent variables. Courses in econometric methods tend to be largely concerned with regression analysis. What is intended here is to inform students about regression analysis so they have a clear understanding of the rudimentary use of the approach in this text. To do this advantage is taken of the statistical measures widely know about distributions, such as the distribution of grades in a class. The basic statistical measures in regression analysis are shown to be the same in character.

Distribution of Class Grades

Assume that there are 2 classes; each with 10 students and the distribution of their grades on the same exam are those given in tables 1 and 2.

The Central Tendency: The Arithmetic Mean, X_m

It is not uncommon for students, upon receipt of graded exam papers, to ask What was the class average? This average or arithmetic mean, is a measure of the central tendency of a distribution. And the method of calculating it is commonly known: Add up all the grades to arrive at a total. Divide the total by the number of grades.

In mathematical symbols, the grades or observations are Xs and since there are 10 of them, they are $X_1, X_2, ... X_9, X_{10}$. To save space the observations of the distribution or sample can be specified as: X_i where i is in the range of 1 to 10. Do not lose site of the fact that this refers to the 10 grades in distributions 1 and 2 of table A2.1. The sum of a distribution can be written as $\sum X_i$. For both distributions 1 and 2 the sum or total is 750:

Table A2.1.   **Two Distributions of Grades**

	Distribution 1	Distribution 2
	(grades in percent)	
1	82	95
2	81	94
3	79	86
4	78	80
5	76	78
6	74	75
7	72	72
8	71	65
9	69	55
10	68	50
Total	750	750

The mean of the distribution, X_m, is the sum of the observations divided by the number of observations, n. The sum of both distribution 1 and 2 is 750 and the number of observations in both is 10.

(1) $X_m = 1/n \sum X_i = 750/10 = 75$

The mean of the distributions is its central tendency. It tells us the grade which students tend to get. This is the norm. Higher grades are above the norm of the class; lower grades below the norm.

Were you to select an observation at random from a sample, its expected value, $E\{X\}$, would be the arithmetic mean X_m.

The Arithmetic Mean Minimizes the Sum of the Squares of the Deviations from the Mean.

The deviations from the mean, x, is the magnitude of an observation minus the magnitude of the mean, $x = X - X_m$. If the mean of the distribution is 75 and your grade is 78, the deviation is +3. And if your friend Jan's grade is 72, the deviation is –3. In both cases the square of the deviation is 9. For distributions 1 and 2 the deviations, squares of the deviations, and totals can be found in table A2.2.

To show that the mean minimizes the sum of the squares the following problem must be solved:

Given: A distribution of observations, X_i and K which is a smooth, continuous variable, and the summation $\sum (X_i - K)^2$, the sum of of the squares of the deviation from K.

Find: The value of K which minimizes the given summation.

Table A2.2.   **Two Distributions with Deviations from the Means and its Square**

	Distribution 1			Distribution 2	
X	x	x^2	X	x	x^2
82	7	49	95	20	400
81	6	36	94	19	361
79	4	16	86	11	121
78	3	9	80	5	25
76	1	1	78	3	9
74	–1	1	75	0	0
72	–3	9	72	–3	9
71	–4	16	65	–10	100
69	–6	36	55	–20	400
68	–7	49	50	–25	625
$\Sigma =$ 750	0	222	750	0	2050

The minimum (or maximum) of a function occurs at the point at which the slope or derivative of the function equals zero. So our task is to obtain the derivative of the function $\Sigma(X-K)^2$ with respect to K, set it equal to zero, and solve for K. Since there are two independent variables in the function, the derivative with respect to K is a "partial derivative" of the function. To indicate that a partial derivative is being taken, the symbol ∂ is used instead of d.

(2) $\partial/\partial K \left(\Sigma (X-K)^2 \right) = 2 \left[\Sigma(X-K) \right] (-1) = -2 \left[\Sigma(X - K) \right] = 0$

(3) $\Sigma(X - K) = \Sigma X - \Sigma K = 0$ or,

(4) $\Sigma X = \Sigma K$

(5) $\Sigma K = nK$

(6) $nK = \Sigma X$

(7) $K = (1/n)\Sigma X = X_m$

The value of K which minimizes the sum of the squares of the deviations from K is the arithmetic mean.

Measures of Dispersion of the Distribution: The Variance, Standard Deviation, and the Coefficient of Variation

While distributions 1 and 2 have the same central tendency, the dispersion of the data in the first is less than that of the second. The range of grades in the first is from 82 to 68, that in the second from 95 to 50. There are three related measures of the dispersion of a distribution: the variance, the standard deviation (the square root of the variance), and the coefficient of variation (the standard deviation divided by the mean of the distribution).

Distributions 1 and 2 are repeated in Table A1.2 with the addition of the deviation from the mean, $x = X - X_m$. and its square, x^2. Note that the sum of the deviation from the mean equals zero for both distributions, $\sum x = 0$.
This makes its expected value, $E\{x\}$, the arithmetic mean of the x distribution, equal to zero. It also makes the deviation from the mean an unsuitable measure of dispersion.

The Variance, s^2, is: $s^2 = \sum x^2 / (n-1)$.

Were the division by n, instead of $n-1$, the variance would be the average squared deviation from the mean. Statisticians subtract one from the number of observation because one degree of freedom, one observation, has been used up in calculating the mean—from which our deviations are measured. For the data in distribution 1, the variance equals 24.67 *(222÷9)*. For that of distribution 2 the variance is almost ten times as large, 227.77 *(2050÷9)*,

The Standard Deviation, s, is: $s = (s^2)^{0.5}$.

The standard deviation is the square root of the variance. It is a measure of dispersion in the same units as the data of the distribution. For distribution 1 with a variance of a bit under 25, the standard deviation is ±4.97, slightly less than 5. For distribution 2 which has a variance of 222.77, the standard deviation is ±15.09.

Were the distribution "normal," the range of plus or minus one standard deviation would cover 68.26 percent of the distribution. In both of the distributions given 60 percent of the grades fall within one standard deviation from the mean.

The Coefficient of Variation, CV, is: $CV = s/X_m$

The coefficient of variation is the ratio of the standard deviation of a distribution to its mean. It is a unitless, relative measure of dispersion which allows the comparison of the dispersion of any and all all distributions. The *CV* for our first distribution is 6.62 percent (4.97/75) while that for the second is 20.12 percent of the mean (15.09/75).

Consider two example of the usefulness of the coefficient of variation. It could be used to compare the dispersion of a class with conventional grades based on a maximum of 100 with their dispersion of grades on an SAT exam which has a maximum of 800. Another use would be to compare the dispersion of wages at one time with that of another. The coefficient of variation has been increasing and this indicates that wages of higher paid workers have increased relative to those of lower paid workers.

Least Squares Regression Analysis

Assume that we have a model which contends that Y is an increasing linear function of X, we have data on pairs of these variables, X_1Y_1, X_2Y_2 ... X_nY_n. These data are considered to be a sample of the data found in a very large population. The challenge is to estimate the relationship between Y and X in the best possible way.

The Central Tendency: The Regression Line

Consider some important characteristics of the regression line to illustrate its close relationship to the characteristics of the arithmetic mean. Then, some of the related mathematics are shown. The estimated relationship between Y and X is manifest in a regression line or estimating equation. That line and equation represents the central tendency of the relationship between the variables. It forms the base for various measures of dispersion.

1. The model is the hypothesized relationship between Y and X:

(8) $$Y = A + BX + \mu$$

where, A is the Y intercept, B is the slope of the line, and μ is a stochastic disturbance term. It contains all the independent variables omitted from the model. It is assumed to have an expected value of zero and that its successive values are uncorrelated.

2. The estimates of A and B are a and b making the calculated value of Y, Y_c:

(9) $$Y_c = a + bX$$

This estimating equation is the *central tendency* of the relationship between Y and X.

3. The estimates of A and B are usually made by the *least squares method*. This method involves minimizing the sum of the square of the errors from the regression line where an error, e, is the difference between the actual and calculated value of Y:

(10) $$e = Y - Y_c$$

4. The value of Y_c is the expected value of Y given a specific magnitude of X:

(11) $Y_c = E\{Y|X\}$

Derivation of the Least Squares Estimators of the Intercept and Slope

The error e is the difference between the actual value of Y and its estimated value, Y_c:

(12) $e = Y - Y_c$

(13) $e = Y - (a + bX)$

Take the square of e for all es and add them up:

(14) $\sum e^2 = \sum (Y - (a + bX))^2 = f$

The above expression can be minimized by taking the partial derivative of the function with respect to a, and setting it equal to zero.

(15) $\partial f / \partial a = 2\ [\sum (Y - (a + bX))]\ (-1) = 0$

Note that the for the derivative to equal zero, the expression within brackets must equal zero. Assume that there are n sets of observations of X, Y. With the mean of Y equal to its sum divided by n, $Y_m = (\sum Y) / n$, the sum is n times the mean. The same is true of the sum of X and its mean. As a result the bracketed expression can be rewritten as:

(16) $nY_m - na - bnX_m = 0$

Solving for a yields:

(17) $a = Y_m - bX_m$

We can calculate a if we have the arithmetic mean of both variables and have calculated the value of b.

For the calculation of b, take the derivative of the sum of the errors squared with respect to b:

(18) $\sum e^2 = [\sum (Y - (a + bX))]^2 = f$

(19) $\partial f / \partial b = -2X\ [\sum (Y - (a + bX))]$

Table A2.3.   Data and Calculations for Regression Analysis

Y	X	XY	X^2	Y_c	e	e^2	$X-X_m$	$(X-X_m)^2 = x^2$
17	16	272	256	17.98	−0.98	0.96	−10.1	102.01
19	18	342	324	20.82	−1.82	3.31	−8.1	65.61
22	20	440	400	23.65	−1.65	2.72	−6.1	37.21
27	22	594	484	26.49	0.51	0.26	−4.1	16.81
33	25	825	625	30.74	2.26	5.11	−1.1	1.21
36	27	972	729	33.57	2.43	5.90	0.9	0.81
40	34	1360	1156	43.49	−3.49	12.18	7.9	62.41
41	30	1230	900	37.82	3.18	10.11	3.9	15.21
41	31	1271	961	39.24	1.76	3.10	4.9	24.01
47	38	1786	1444	49.16	−2.16	4.67	11.9	141.61

Σ= 323 261 9092 7279   0.04 48.32   0.0   466.90

Mean 32.3 26.1

(20) $$= -2[\Sigma XY - a\Sigma X - b\Sigma X^2]$$

Again, if the bracketed equals zero, the partial derivative equals zero. Substitute for a: $a = Y_m - bX_m$

(21) $$= [\Sigma XY - (Y_m - bX_m)\, \Sigma X - b\Sigma X^2] = 0$$

Collect terms involving b:

(22) $$= \Sigma XY - Y_m\Sigma X + b\,(\Sigma X^2 - X_m\Sigma X) = 0$$

Solve for b:

(23) $$b = (\Sigma XY - Y_m\Sigma X) \div (\Sigma X^2 - X_m\Sigma X)$$

What we do, or what our user friendly computer with appropriate software does, is to solve for b and insert it, along with the mean of Y and X into the equation which yields a.

An Example.

The model is that investment spending on structures and capital equipment, Y, is and increasing linear function of Gross Domestic Product. The data used are from the 1993 *Economic Report of the President*, table B–1 and cover the years 1975–1984. Calculation is by hand and by computer. I have rounded the data down radically, to ease the burden of hand calculations. The figures for investment, Y, are in tens of billions of dollars per year; the figures for gross domestic product, X, are in hundreds of billions of dollars per year. All other data are my hand calculations and you will see that in effect they are close to but not the same as those of the computer.

The data given are those in the first two columns, those for Y and X. The formula for b requires the following calculations: XY and its sum, the sum of X, the mean of Y and X, and X^2 and its sum. These calculated values are included in the table. Now for the calculation of b:

(24) $$b = (\Sigma XY - Y_m \Sigma X) \div (\Sigma X^2 - X_m \Sigma X)$$

$$= (9092 - 32.3 \cdot 261) \div (7279 - 26.1 \cdot 261) = 1.41722$$

Now we can solve for a:

(25) $$a = Y_m - b \cdot X_m$$

$$= 32.3 - 1.417 \cdot 26.1 = -4.689$$

Thus, the regression equation calculated is:

(26) $$Y_c = -4.869 + 1.417 X$$

Measures of Dispersion: The Variance, s_{yx}^2, and Standard Error, s_{yx}, of the Regression

The variance and standard error are measures of the dispersion of the actual values of the dependent variable, Y_i, from the estimated ones . The errors, $e = Y - Y_c$, are given in table A.2.3.

The Variance of the Regression

The formula for the variance of a simple regression is:

(27) $$s_{yx}^2 = \Sigma e^2 / (n-2)$$

For the problem at hand the sum of the errors squared is 48.32 and that should be divided by 8. Thus,

(28) $$s_{yx}^2 = 48.32 / 8 = 6.04.$$

Were the division done by the number of samples, the variance would be the average value of the error squared. The subtraction of two degrees of freedom, is due to the use of data to calculate the intercept and slope of the regression line.

The Standard Error of the Regression

The standard error of estimate is the square root of the variance:

(29) $\qquad s_{yx} = [\sum e^2 / (n-2)]^{0.5}$

And for the problem with which we are struggling:

(30) $\qquad s_{yx} = (6.04)^{0.5} = \pm 2.46$

The units are the same as those of Y. About two-thirds of the observations should fall within the range of the standard error of estimate—within two lines parallel to the regression line, one 2.46 units higher, the other 2.46 units lower,

The Estimated Slope, b: Its Variance, Standard Error, and t–Statistic

The estimated slope, b, is the central tendency of the distribution of slopes—just as the regression line is the central tendency of the data relating Y to X.

The Variance of the Estimated Slope

The variance of b is given by the following formula:

(31) $\qquad s_b^2 = s_{yx}^2 \div \sum(X - X_m)^2$

It equals the variance of the regression line divided by the sum of the square of the deviation from the mean. In other words, the higher the variance of the the the regression curve, the greater is the variance of its estimated slope; and the greater the observations deviate from the mean of X, the lower the variance of b.

Recall that the variance of the regression line, the sum of the square of the errors divided by $n-2$ was equal to 6.04. In table A.3, above the calculation of the sum of the the deviations from X_m was found to be 466.90. The variance of the slope is accordingly 0.01294 (*6.04/466.9*).

The Standard Error of the Estimated Slope

The standard error of the estimated slope is merely the square root of its variance:

(32) $s_b = (s_b{}^2)^{0.5}$

As a result its magnitude is ±0.11374. in the same units as the slope. Our slope minus its standard error, 1.41772 minus 0.11374, is still quite positive. Why is that of importance? We have hypothesized that Y is an increasing function of X. The greater the standard error of the slope compared to the magnitude of the slope, the greater is the probability that our hypothesis is untrue.

The t-statistic for the Estimated Slope

The t-statistic for b is the ratio of the magnitude of b to its standard error:

(33) $t = b \div s_b$

  The higher the magnitude of b compared to its standard error, the greater is the confidence that the calculated slope is positive. In general, economic empiricists hope for *t-values* which indicate that b, the estimate of B, is significant at the 5 percent level. This means that there is only a 5 percent probability that B equals zero or less; that Y is not an increasing function of X. Tables of *t-values* show that for 8 degrees of freedom, the *t-value* of 1.860 has an 0.05 (i.e., 5 percent) probability. For our problem, with b equal to 1.41722 and s_b equal to 0.11374, t equals 12.46 and that is so high that it is not handled in the tables of the *t-statistic* normally found in textbooks. It indicates that there is practically zero probability that B is zero or negative.

Measures of Goodness of Fit

There are two measures of goodness of fit: the coefficient of determination and the adjusted coefficient of determination. The former is the percentage of the variance of the data explained by the regression equation to the total variance of the data. The latter includes an adjustment for degrees of freedom.

The Coefficient of Determination, R^2

The coefficient of determination, R^2, is the ratio of the explained sum of the squares from the mean to the total sum of the squares from the mean:

(34) $R^2 = \Sigma(Y_c - Y_m)^2 \div \Sigma(Y - Y_m)^2$

  Were all estimated values, Y_c, equal the actual value R^2 would equal 1. And if all estimated values, Y_c, equaled the mean, it would equal zero.
  For our problem involving the relationship between investment spending on facilities and equipment and gross domestic product, $R^2 = 0.951$, the regression explained 95 percent of the total sum of the squares.

The Adjusted Coefficient of Determination, adj R^2

The adjusted coefficient of determination is the coefficient of determination adjusted for the loss of degrees of freedom in calculating the mean of the distribution and the coefficients of the the independent variables. In the equation above R^2 equals the ratio of the sum of the squares of the explained deviation from the mean to the total deviation from the mean. But the explained sum of the squares equals the total minus the unexplained. This allows rewriting the definition of R^2 as:

(35) $R^2 = (\text{total} - \text{unexplained}) \div \text{total}$

(36) $R^2 = 1 - (\text{unexplained} \div \text{total})$

(37) $R^2 = 1 - [\Sigma(Y - Y_c)^2 \div \Sigma(Y - Y_m)^2]$

The adjusted coefficient of determination recognizes that we are essentially using variances in the above formulas and adjusts for the degree of freedom lost.

(38) $\text{adj } R^2 = 1 - [\Sigma(Y - Y_c)^2](n-2) \div [\Sigma(Y - Y_m)^2](n-1)$

Two degrees of freedom are lost in calculating Y_c so the adjustment involves multiplication the numerator by *(n–2)*. And one degree of freedom are lost in calculating the mean of the Y distribution and the denominator is multiplied by *(n–1)*. The adjusted coefficient in our problem is 0.94487.

The Durbin-Watson Statistic, DW

When the model, $Y = A + BX + \mu$ was set up it was pointed out that it was assumed that the expected value of μ was zero and that successive values were not correlated. Our errors are estimates of μ. In table A2.3, it can be seen that the sum of the errors equals 0.04—good enough. But look at the signs of the data. Positive errors tend to be followed by positive erriors and negative by negative. This kind of correlation is common when time series data are used and the Durbin-Watson statistic tests the serial correlation of the residuals. Tables in books on statistics frequently list the low and high levels the Durbin-Watson statistic required to sustain the assumption that the errors are uncorrelated. The tables start with a sample size of 15 but ours is only 10. My extrapolation indicates the statistic should have been in the range of about 1.0 to 1.3 to be 95 percent confident that there was no serial correlation. Ours was well above that figure sadly making our estimates of the parameters of the model a bit suspect.
  The approach shown above is sound; the results are not exactly. A change in the form of the model might help. They are mentioned just in

passing—pursuing them further would draw us too far into the field of econometrics. First differences of the variables could be used: $\Delta Y = A + B\Delta X + \mu$. Lagged variables might help: $Y_t = A + BX_{t-1}$. First differences can be lagged. Lags of different durations can be tried. A warning is that the model you end up with should make sense.

Multiple Regression Analysis

The above model has one dependent variable, Y, and one independent variable, X. The method used to quantify the relationship is called *simple* regression analysis. Frequently, a model has two or more independent variables. Investment spending, Y. might be modeled an an increasing function of the gross domestic product, X, the change in the gross domestic prolduct, ΔX, and the interest rate, Z:

(37) $Y = A + BX + C\Delta X + DZ + \mu$

Estimates of A, B, C, and D are obtained by *multiple* regression analysis. It is conceptually the same as simple regression analysis. The major difference is that the required computations become horrendous and nowadays access to a computer with appropriate statistical software is required.

References

Abraham, Kathryn G. 1983. "Structural/Frictional vs. Deficient Demand Unemployment," *American Economic Review*, vol. 73, no. 4, September, pp. 708–724.

Adams, Walter. 1982. "Public Policy in a Free Enterprise Economy," in *The Structure of American Industry*, 6th ed., edited by Walter Adams, New York: Macmillan, pp. 472–505.

Alchian, Armen, and Harold Demsetz. 1972. "Production, Information Costs, and Economic Organization," *American Economic Review*, vol. 62, no., 5, December; pp. 777–795.

Alfano, Peter. 1989. "Super Bowl Ticket Prices." *New York Times*, January 14, p. 1.

Backman, Jules, ed. 1953. *Price Practices and Price Policies*, New York: Ronald Press.

Baily, Martin N. and Alok K. Chakrabarti. 1988. *Innovation and the Productiv ity Crisis*, Washington: Brookings Institution.

Baumol, William J. 1967. "Macroeconomics of Unbalanced Growth," *American Economic Review*, vol. 57, no 3, June, pp. 415–426.

Becker, Gary S. 1960. "An Economic Model of Fertility," in National Bureau of Economic Research, *Demographic and Economic Change in Developed Countries*, Princeton: Princeton University Press, pp. 209–240.

———.1964. *Human Capital*, New York: Columbia University Press.

———.1971. *Economic Theory*, New York: Knopf.

———.1975. *Human Capital*, 2d ed., New York: Columbia University Press.

Best, Fred. N.d. *Exchanging Earnings for Leisure*, Department of Labor, Employment and Training Administration, R&D Monograph 79, Washington: USGPO.

Blank, David M. and George J. Stigler. 1957. *The Demand and Supply of Scientific Personnel*, Princeton: Princeton University Press.

Blaug, Mark. 1980. *The Methodology of Economics*, New York: Cambridge University Press.

Blinder, Alan S, Elie R. Canetti, David E. Lebow, and Jeremy B. Rudd. 1998. *Asking About Prices: A New Approach to Understanding Price Stickiness*, New York: Russell Sage Foundation.

Bond, Erik W. 1982. "A Direct Test of the 'Lemon Model': The Marker for Used Pickup Trucks." *American Economic Review*, vol. 72, no. 4, September pp. 836–840.

Borges, Jorge Luis. 1970. "Autobiographical Notes," *The New Yorker*, September 19, 1970.

Bound, John and George Johnson. 1992. "Changes in the Structure of Wages in the 1980s," *American Economic Review,* vol. 82, no.3, June, pp. 371–392.

Breech, Ernest R. 1961 [1947]. "The American Method of Pricing," in Jules Backman, ed., *Pricing Policies and Practices,* New York: The Conference Board, pp. 81–82.

Burtless, Gary. 1995. "International Trade and the Rise in Earnings Inequality," *Journal of Economic Literature,* vol. 33, no.2, June, pp. 800–816.

Capen, E.C., R. V. Clapp, and M. Campbell. 1971. "Competitive Bidding in High Risk Situations," *Journal of Petroleum Technology,*vol. 23, June, pp. 641–653.

Chamberlin, Edward H. 1933. *Theory of Monopolistic Competition.* Cambridge: Harvard University Press.

Chandler, Alfred. 1977. *The Visible Hand.* Cambridge: Harvard University Press.

Chirinko, Robert S. 1993. "Business Fixed Investment Spending: Modeling Strategies, Empirical Results, and Policy Implications," *Journal of Economic Literature,* vol. 31, no. 4, December, pp. 1875–1911.

Clark, John Bates. 1965 [1899]. *The Distribution of Wealth,* New York: Kelley.

Coase, Ronald. 1937. "The Nature of the Firm," *Economica,* 4, November, pp. 386–405.

————.1960. "The Problem of Social Cost," *Journal of Law and Economics,* no. 3, October, pp. 1–44.

Cournot, A. A. 1897 [1838]. *Mathematical Principles of the Theory of Wealth,* New York: Macmillan.

Dorfman, Robert and Peter O.Steiner. 1954. "Optimal Advertising and Optimal Quality," *American Economic Review,* vol. 44, no. 5, December, pp. 826–836.

Douglas, Paul H. 1957 [1934]. *Theory of Wages,* New York: Kelley and Millman.

Easterlin, Richard. 1973. "Does Money Buy Happiness? *Public Interest,* no. 30, Winter, pp. 1–10.

Freeman, Richard B. 1976. *The Overeducated American,* New York: Academic Press.

Friedman, Milton. 1953. *Essays in Positive Economics*, Chicago: Chicago University Press.

————.1962. *Price Theory,* Chicago: Aldine.

Gordon, Robert Aaron. 1976. "Rigor and Relevance in a Changing Institutional Setting," *American Economic Review,* vol. 66, no. 1, March, pp. 1–14.

Groshen, Erica L. 1989. "Do Wage Differences Among Employers Last?" Working Paper 8906, Federal Reserve Bank of Cleveland, June.

Hagerty, Michael, James Carmen, and Gary Russell. 1988. "Estimating Elastic ities with PIMS Data," *Journal of Marketing Research,* February, pp. 1–9.

Hall, Robert E. 1986. "Market Structure and Macroeconomic Fluctuations," *Brookings Papers on Economic Activity,* no. 2, pp. 285–322.

Hall, R. J. and C. J. Hitch. 1939. "Price Theory and Business Behavior," *Oxford Economic Papers,* May.

Hamermesh, Daniel S. 1976. "Econometric Studies of Labor Demand and Their Application to Policy Analysis," *Journal of Human Resources,* vol. 11, no. 4, Fall, pp. 507–525.

Heflebower, Richard B. 1955. "Full Cost, Cost Changes, and Prices," in National Bureau of Economic Research, *Business Concentration and Public Policy,* Princeton: Princeton University Press, pp. 361–392.

Hicks, John R. 1963 [1932]. *Theory of Wages,* 2d ed., London: Macmillan.

Hirsh, Fred. 1976. *The Social Limits to Growth,* Cambridge: Harvard University Press.

Houthakker, H. S. and Lester D. Taylor. 1970. *Consumer Demand in the United States,* 2d ed., Cambridge: Harvard University Press.

Jensen, Michael and William Meckling. 1976. "Theory of the Firm: Managerial Behavior, Agency Costs, and Ownership Structure," *Journal of Financial Economics,* no. 3, September, pp. 305–360.

————.1988. "Takeovers: Their Causes and Consequences," *Journal of Economic Perspectives,* vol. 2, no. 1, Winter, pp. 212–48.

Jevons, William S. 1970 [1871]. *The Theory of Political Economy,* Baltimore: Penguin Books.

Johnston, J. 1960. *Statistical Cost Analysis,* New York: McGraw–Hill.

Kahn, Alfred E. 1970. *Economics of Regulation,* New York: John Wiley & Sons.

Knight, Frank. 1965 [1921]. *Risk, Uncertainty and Profit,* New York: Harper & Row.

————.1965 [1933]. *The Economic Organization,* New York: Harper & Row.

Leibenstein, Harvey. 1974. "An Interpretation of the Economic Theory of Fertility," *Journal of Economic Literature,* vol. 12, no. 2, June, pp. 457–488.

Lucas, Robert E., Jr. 1986. "Models of Business Cycles," Yrijo Jahnsson Lecture, Helsinki, Finland.

Machlup, Fritz. 1946. "Marginal Analysis and Empirical Research," *American Economic Review,* vol. 36, no. 4, September, pp. 519–554.

Malthus, Thomas R. 1926 [1798]. *Essay on the Principle of Population,* London: Royal Economic Society.

Marshall, Alfred. 1961 [1890]. *Principles of Economics,* New York:Macmillan.

Marx, Karl and Friedrich Engels. 1957 [1848]. *The Communist Manifesto,* in Max Eastman ed., *Capital and Other Writings by Karl Marx,* New York: Modern Library, pp. 315–355.

Marx, Karl. 1906 [1867]. *Capital: A Critique of Political Economy,* New York: Modern Library.

Mill, John Stuart. 1961 [1848]. *Principles of Political Economy,* New York: Kelley.

Mises, Ludwig von. 1949. *Human Action,* London: William Hodge.

Nelson, Saul and Walter G.Keim. "Methods of Nonprice Competition," in Jules Backman, ed., 1953, pp. 96–115.

Neslin, Scott and Robert W. Shoemaker. 1983. "Using a Natural Experiment to Estimate Price Elasticity," *Journal of Marketing,* vol. 47, no. 1, Winter, pp. 44–57.

Nourse, Edwin G. and Horace B.Drury. 1938. *Industrial Price Policies and Economic Progress,* Washington: Brookings Institution.

Papandreou, Andreas. 1958. *Economics as a Science,* Chicago: Lippincott.

Pechman, Joseph A. and Benjamin A.Okner. 1974. *Who Bears the Tax Burden?,* Washington: Brookings Institution.

Radner, Roy. 1992. "Hierarchy: The Economics of Managing," *Journal of Economic Literature,* vol. 30, no. 3, September, pp. 1382–1415.

Ravenscraft, David J. and F. M.Scherer. 1987. *Mergers, Sell-Offs, & Economic Efficiency,* Washington: Brookings Institution.

Robbins, Lionel. 1935 [1932]. *An Essay on the Nature and Significance of Economic Science,* 2d ed., London: Macmillan.

Robinson, Joan. 1971 [1933]. *The Theory of Imperfect Competition,* London: Macmillan.

Schoemaker, Paul J. H. 1982. "The Expected Utility Model," *Journal of Economic Literature,* vol. 20, no.2, June, pp. 529–563.

Schumpeter, Joseph A. 1954. *History of Economic Analysis,* New York: Oxford University Press.

Siegel, Jeremy. 1997. "Is the U.S. Stock Market Overvalued?" *TIAA–CREF Investment Forum,* no. 1, vol. 1, Spring.

Simon, Herbert A. 1979. "On Parsimonious Explanations of Production Relations," *Scandinavian Journal of Economics,* Carnegie–Mellon University Reprints, pp. 459–474.

———.1986. *"*Interview with Herbert Simon," *Challenge.* Armonk, NY: M.E. Sharpe. November/December, p. 23.

Skinner, Wickham. 1986. "The Productivity Paradox," *Harvard Business Review,* vol. 64, no. 4, July–August, pp. 55–59.

Smith, Adam. 1937 [1776]. *An Inquiry into the Nature and Causes of the Wealth of Nations,* New York: Modern Library.

Stigler, George J. 1961. "The Economics of Information," *Journal of Political Economy,* vol. 69, no. 3, June, 213–235.

Suits, Daniel B. 1982. "Agriculture," in Walter Adams, ed., *Structure of American Industry,* 6th ed., New York: Macmillan.

Taylor, Frederick Winslow. 1915 [1911]. *The Principles of Scientific Management,* New York: Harper & Brothers.

Trend–Lines, Inc. N.d. [1994]. Catalogue.

Tversky, Amos and Kahneman, Daniel. 1986. "Rational Choice and the Framing of Decisions" in Robin M.Hogarth and Melvin W.Reder eds., *Rational Choice: The Contrast between Economics and Psychology,*   Chicago: The University of Chicago Press, pp. 67–94.

Uchitelle, Louis. 1997. "Global Good Times; Meet the Global Glut," *New York Times,* November 16, section 4, p. 3.

Veblen, Thorstein. 1931 [1899]. *The Theory of the Leisure Class.* New York: Modern Library.

Williams, T. Harry, Richard N. Current, and Frank Freidel. 1967. *A History of the United States to 1877,* New York: Knopf.

Wilson, Woodrow. 1961 [1910]. *The New Freedom,* Englewood Cliffs, New Jersey: Prentice–Hall.

Index